PRESENT TENSE

PRESENT TENSE

THE UNITED STATES SINCE 1945

Michael Schaller
University of Arizona

Virginia Scharff
University of New Mexico

Robert D. Schulzinger
University of Colorado, Boulder

Houghton Mifflin Company   Boston   Toronto
Dallas   Geneva, Illinois   Palo Alto   Princeton, New Jersey

Sponsoring Editor: John Weingartner
Senior Project Editor: Susan Piland
Design Coordinator: Martha Drury
Cover and Interior Designer: Catherine Hawkes
Production Coordinator: Frances Sharperson
Manufacturing Coordinator: Holly Schuster
Marketing Manager: Diane Gifford

Cover painting: Wayne Thiebaud, *Urban Freeways*, 1979/1980, oil on canvas.

Text photographs researched by Pembroke Herbert/Picture Research Consultants.

Chapter-opening photo credits

Chapter 1: Franklin D. Roosevelt Library.   *Chapter 2:* Courtesy American Illustrators Gallery/Judy Goffman Fine Art, New York City.   *Chapter 3:* Harry S Truman Presidential Library.   *Chapter 4:* Dwight D. Eisenhower Presidential Library.   *Chapter 5:* Magnum Photos.   *Chapter 6:* John F. Kennedy Library.   *Chapter 7:* Lyndon Baines Johnson Presidential Library.   *Chapter 8:* Magnum Photos.   *Chapter 9:* Wide World Photos.   *Chapter 10:* UPI/Bettmann Newsphotos.   *Chapter 11:* John Locke Studios, Inc.   *Chapter 12:* Jimmy Carter Presidential Library.   *Chapter 13:* UPI/Bettmann Newsphotos.   *Chapter 14:* UPI/Bettmann Newsphotos. *Chapter 15:* UPI/Bettmann Newsphotos.

Credits continue on page I-29.

Printed in the U.S.A.
Library of Congress Catalog Card Number: 91-71961
ISBN: 0-395-51134-8

BCDEFGHIJ-H-95432

We dedicate this book to our children:
Nicholas, Gabriel, and Daniel Schaller
Sam and Annie Swift
Elizabeth Anne Schulzinger

CONTENTS

2

From War to a Troubled Peace: Politics and Society, 1945–1950   *42*

3

A Dangerous New World: From Containment to Korea   *83*

4

The Fifties: Change in the Guise of Stability   *118*

5

The General as President: Foreign Policy in the 1950s *163*

6

Outposts on the New Frontier: Americans at Home and Abroad, 1960–1963   *198*

7

Lyndon Johnson's American Dream *242*

8

The Vietnam Nightmare, 1961–1968 *281*

9

The Politics and Culture of Protest   324

10

The Illusion of Peace: Foreign Policy During the Nixon Administration *363*

11

The Use and Abuse of Power: Domestic Affairs and the Watergate Scandal, 1969–1974   *398*

12

Years of Limits and Malaise, 1974–1980   *439*

13

Happy Days: The Reagan Years at Home   *491*

14

Back in the Saddle: Foreign Policy During the Reagan Years   *533*

15

A Fresh Start for the Nineties *570*

MAPS AND CHARTS

PREFACE

The half-century between the Second World War and the 1990s forms a coherent unit of United States history. As Americans born during this era, all three of us grew up with containment. The Cold War at home and abroad helped define the ways in which we, as most of the post-1945 generation, lived our public and private lives. The end of the Cold War presented an appropriate time to take a fresh look at the events that shaped our experiences.

Also, as teachers, we felt impelled to write a text that emphasized the topics, questions, and dilemmas raised by our students. And as scholars of political and social history, we hoped to write a book that interpreted the broad issues that have dominated the recent past.

We have attempted to provide a balanced account of domestic politics, foreign affairs, and social and cultural change. *Present Tense* develops several interrelated themes that run through the postwar years. Specifically, it explores the legacy of the New Deal and the rise of a large, active federal government; the domestic and international impact of the Cold War; the role of the military at home and abroad; the ongoing struggle by women and people of color for equality; and the impact of mass media, especially television, and popular culture in shaping American ideas and values. Special attention is given to the role of the federal courts as engines of social and legal change; the pivotal role of immigration—particularly Asian and Hispanic—in shaping contemporary society; and the ways in which migration to the Sunbelt have affected economics and politics.

When we began teaching this course, it covered a bit more than twenty-five years of history; we now must explain how topics have evolved over the span of half a century. We try in *Present Tense* to devote equal attention to all periods of the post-1945 era. Hence, eight chapters cover developments before 1969, and seven discuss events since then. The book is organized into chronological chapters, with chapters on domestic events balanced with parallel chapters on foreign affairs. For instance, Chapter 4, "The Fifties: Change in the Guise of Stability," is followed by Chapter 5, "The General as President: Foreign Policy in the 1950s." Two exceptions to this chronological framework are Chapter 8, "The Vietnam Nightmare, 1961–1968," and Chapter 9, "The Politics and Culture of Protest," both of which highlight topics that we believe deserve extended discussion.

Each chapter includes an introduction, a conclusion, and suggestions for further reading. The text is enhanced with maps and photographs to enrich students' appreciation of the content. Each chapter also includes a "Biographical Profile," a special feature focusing on a representative figure from politics or popular culture, beginning with Eleanor Roosevelt and including, among others, Jackie Robinson, Rachel Carson, Malcolm X, and Donald Trump. We also provide an Instructor's Resource Manual that includes learning objectives, chapter synopses, multiple-choice test items, and essay questions.

Many friends and colleagues have helped us develop this work. Our students at the University of Arizona, the University of New Mexico, and the University of Colorado have heard this book take form in our lectures, read draft chapters, and made many useful suggestions. We also thank Karen and Kent Anderson for useful comments on the manuscript, Charles Pennachio for research assistance and the staffs of the history departments at Arizona, New Mexico, and Colorado for their patient help.

Our editors at Houghton Mifflin—Jean Woy, John Weingartner, and Susan Piland—and our freelance development editor, Doug Gordon, were especially encouraging and helpful at every stage. Their keen eyes for detail and language have made this a clearer and, we hope, a better book. We also thank the reviewers who commented on drafts of each of the chapters:

Stephen E. Berk, California State University, Long Beach

David A. Bernstein, California State University, Long Beach

George M. Blackburn, Central Michigan University

Gerald Carpenter, Niagara University

David E. Hamilton, University of Kentucky

Glen S. Jeansonne, University of Wisconsin, Milwaukee

Laura Kalman, University of California, Santa Barbara

Steven F. Lawson, University of South Florida

James I. Matray, New Mexico State University

Julian M. Pleasants, University of Florida

Bruce Schulman, University of California, Los Angeles

Jordan A. Schwarz, Northern Illinois University

Sharon Hartman Strom, University of Rhode Island

Robert B. Westbrook, University of Rochester

Thomas Zoumaras, Northeast Missouri State College

The challenge of reconciling their diverse viewpoints added rigor and richness to our interpretation of the last half-century.

Our deepest thank-you must go to Leonard Dinnerstein, friend, mentor, and colleague. He encouraged this project from its inception—bringing the three of us together—generously shared his deep knowledge of American society, and, in so many ways, helped us to understand what makes a successful textbook.

M.S., V.S., R.D.S.

1

New Deal and World War: Foundations of the Modern Era

As the Second World War reached its fiery conclusion in 1945, Americans began to express their visions of the era that lay ahead. Henry Luce, the influential publisher of *Time* and *Life* magazines, celebrated the emergence of a new "international moral order" and the "first great American Century." Former Vice President Henry Wallace believed the world stood on the threshold of a "Century of the Common Man," a time when the human values of America's New Deal could transform the war-ravaged world.

These two men differed greatly in their political and social philosophies. But they shared a sense that the previous decade had fundamentally altered the American nation and its role in the world. To understand the postwar era, we need to trace the basic changes that occurred during the world war and the Great Depression that preceded it.

Politically, those years were dominated by a single figure: Franklin Delano Roosevelt, elected four times as president. As journalist Theodore White remarked in later years, "All contemporary national politics descend from Franklin Roosevelt." But the changes wrought during those years were far more than political. They were social, economic, military, and technological as well.

The vastly powerful federal government, which touches the life of every American in a myriad of ways, evolved during the Roosevelt presidency. Government's direct intervention in the economy, its provision of extensive social services, its involvement in science and industry—these were products of the depression and world war. For women and African-Americans, the Roosevelt years brought important expansions of opportunity, along with rising hopes and frustrations that had a great effect on postwar society. Most dramatically, the United States assumed a new, all-important position in international relations. By the end of the Roosevelt era, the United States had become a superpower—a difficult, uneasy role that has shaped the nation's history ever since.

THE ROOSEVELT REVOLUTION

Franklin D. Roosevelt's inauguration as president in March 1933 occurred in the midst of the Great Depression, with the American economy perched on the threshold of collapse. Following the dramatic stock market crash on October 24, 1929, over 13 million workers—one-fourth of the labor force—had lost their jobs, industrial production and national income had fallen by half, and foreign trade had fallen by two-thirds. The collapse of five thousand banks wiped out 9 million savings accounts. The ensuing panic created a run on solvent banks as well. Hundreds of thousands of homeowners and farmers faced foreclosure as financial institutions called in loans. On one day in 1932, one-fourth of the land in the state of Mississippi was sold at auction. Millions of homeless throughout the United States slept in makeshift camps derisively called "Hoovervilles," after the incumbent president, Herbert C. Hoover. The title of a popular song asked plaintively, "Brother, Can You Spare a Dime?"

Accepting the Democratic presidential nomination in 1932, Roosevelt promised a "new deal" for the American people, and in his inaugural address the next March he sought to break the mood of despair that gripped the nation. "The only thing we have to fear," he proclaimed, "is fear itself." The "nation asks for action, and action now." This, he made clear, he intended to deliver. Should Congress fail to respond to the challenge, he would seek "broad Executive power to wage a war against the emergency, as great as the power that would be given to me if we were in fact invaded by a foreign foe."

As Roosevelt's words hinted, his New Deal required a federal government that took a direct and prominent role in the economy and society. This was a new phenomenon in American history—a virtual revolution. Within a few years, Roosevelt's administration enlarged the federal government's size and scope so that it touched more people in more ways than ever before.

Until 1933, the only routine interaction between the federal government and most citizens was in the form of mail delivery by the post office. Policies set in Washington rarely affected the everyday lives of ordinary people. There existed no old age pension system, federal unemployment compensation, aid to dependent children programs, federal housing support, stock market and banking regulation, farm subsidies, withholding taxes, or minimum wage—to name only a few policies now taken for granted.

Traditionally, "good government" had meant "minimal government." The United States had no tradition of government commitment to solving social and economic problems. Yet minimal government had failed to stem the ravages of the depression. In Roosevelt's view, the time had come when government had to save capitalism from its own folly by ensuring every American the "right to make a comfortable living." He predicted that a violent revolution of the Right or Left "could hardly be avoided if another president failed as Hoover has failed." His apprehensions may have been exaggerated. American citizens, in the words of one contemporary observer, appeared more in the grip of "fathomless pessimism" than of revolutionary fervor. Still, it seemed likely that disillusion with democracy and capitalism would spread rapidly if government failed to stem the depression.

Roosevelt's New Deal had roots in the turn-of-the-century Progressive movement that had criticized the concentration of private economic power and the consequent loss of individual freedom brought on by industrialization. The Progressives had insisted that government should regulate private business in the public interest. Drawing on this political philosophy, Roosevelt favored an *active* federal government that would mediate between the public welfare and a vibrant free enterprise system. Throughout the 1930s he sought to rescue capitalism by curbing its excesses through reform and regulation.

The New Deal also reflected Roosevelt's complex personal background. Born as the only child into a socially prominent Anglo-Dutch family in upstate New York, Roosevelt never had to struggle for dignity, money, status, or security. Like many young men of patrician background, he viewed self-made millionaires and industrialists as unscrupulous. Roosevelt had an easy self-assurance that disarmed almost all those he met. Although not a deep thinker, he relished those with fiery intellect and recruited them as advisers. His broad but undisciplined mind sought practical solutions rather than detailed theoretical answers to vexing social problems. Supreme Court Justice Oliver Wendell Holmes succinctly described Roosevelt as a "second class intellect, but a first class temperament."

After serving Woodrow Wilson as assistant secretary of the navy and running unsuccessfully as the Democratic nominee for vice president in 1920, Roosevelt suffered a crippling attack of polio. Several years of therapy, beginning in 1921, failed to restore the use of his legs, but the ravages of the disease had two positive outcomes for his political career. Sidelined from active politicking during his prolonged recovery, Roosevelt avoided the bitter party factionalism that divided the Democrats through most of the Republican-dominated 1920s. Also, his struggle with polio "humanized" Roosevelt. Previously considered something of an upper-class dandy who dabbled in politics as a hobby, Roosevelt now suffered through the kind of tragedy that afflicted ordinary people. When he re-entered politics to run for governor of New York in 1928, he related to people in an intimate way. His emotional vigor so overshadowed his physical handicap (he could stand only with the aid of braces, and generally sat in a wheelchair) that the handicap never emerged as a serious liability in an age when such disabilities often ended public careers.

Mobilizing the Government

During the so-called First Hundred Days following his inauguration—a unit of time by which all subsequent administrations have been judged—Roosevelt mobilized the federal government. Working with an eclectic group of university professors and socially conscious lawyers and social workers known as his "Brains Trust," Roosevelt drafted legislation and began staffing new agencies. Although not anticapitalist, most members of the Brains Trust believed that in a complex economy dominated by industrial giants, government must force big business to share its authority with government and, in Roosevelt's words, "distribute wealth more equitably."

Within a short time the New Deal produced a score of recovery programs to boost prices and employment while shoring up banking and financial institutions. The National Industrial Recovery Act (NIRA) encouraged businesses to form associations to raise prices and profits in the hope that this would create new jobs. The Agricultural Adjustment Act sought to raise farm prices by limiting crop production in return for cash subsidies. A new Federal Deposit Insurance Corporation (FDIC) was given the power to regulate and stabilize private banking through tighter supervision and federal insurance of individual deposits. The Securities Act of 1933 and the creation of the Securities and Exchange Commission (SEC) in 1934 put Wall Street under government supervision. The Home Owners Loan Corporation provided funds for refinancing mortgages to tens of thousands of home owners, while the Federal Housing Administration insured private loans for construction. To preserve basically sound industries that faced ruin, the Reconstruction Finance Corporation (started by Hoover) loaned some $10 billion to the private sector. This influx of capital saved millions of jobs and kept factories operating. The Tennessee Valley Authority (TVA)—an ambitious and unique new agency—undertook vast flood control and electrical-power generating projects in the Upper South.

With the passage of the National Labor Relations Act, also known as the Wagner Act, in 1935, the federal government recognized the right of workers to organize into unions and to bargain collectively with employers as a means of improving wages and working conditions. Even so, a series of strikes and other militant actions occurred before the new Congress of Industrial Organizations (CIO) successfully organized such basic industries as steel, coal, and automobile manufacturing. Gradually, the CIO unions abandoned their early anticapitalist stance and became pillars of support for the Democratic party.

In perhaps its most dramatic innovation, the New Deal replaced reliance on private charity for the needy with a system of social rights. The Social Security Act of 1935 created the first national system of old age pensions, unemployment insurance, aid for the blind and handicapped, and aid to dependent children. Initially these programs, some financed by a payroll tax, paid meager amounts that varied widely from state to state. But for the first time, government had sought to alleviate the impact of modern industrial society on the individual.

The federal government also broke new ground by adopting programs to assist the unemployed. A host of agencies, such as the Federal Emergency Relief Administration (FERA), the Civil Works Administration (CWA), the Public Works Administration (PWA), the Works Progress Administration (WPA), the Civilian Conservation Corps (CCC), and the National Youth Administration, provided grants to states for welfare benefits or directly employed the poor in federal work projects. These programs, many inspired by Interior Secretary Harold Ickes and social worker Harry Hopkins, provided work for the unemployed in a variety of fields. Skilled laborers built highways, municipal buildings, schools, seaports, airports, zoos, parks, and dams throughout the United States. The Federal Theater Project hired 12,500 actors who performed nationally. Artists were commissioned to paint murals in public buildings, writers to write travel guides. In New York City alone, the WPA employed more people than the entire American army. At its peak, the WPA had a national work force of 3 million.

Many in Roosevelt's inner circle found a justification for vigorous government action in the ideas of an iconoclastic British economist, John Maynard Keynes. Keynes believed that active state intervention was fundamental to the success of mature capitalism. The depression of the 1930s had so shaken business confidence that recovery without government intervention was unlikely. Investors and entrepreneurs, it was thought, would not risk their reserves until consumer demand reappeared. To increase consumer demand, public money had to be pumped into the economy.

Money might enter the economy in a number of ways. By hiring unemployed workers to build bridges or roads, for example, government could generate a demand for raw materials and machinery. Workers receiving government paychecks would be able to pay for rent, food, and clothing, creating a market for consumer goods. This "pump priming" would create sufficient consumer purchasing power to restore the confidence of the private sector. As the system returned to normal, the government could withdraw its hand from the marketplace. Through this form of "countercyclical" or "stimulative" deficit spending, the government could increase consumer demand in slack times by injecting money into the economy and recoup its losses through higher tax collections when the economy improved.

Orthodox economists and political conservatives bristled at the idea of active public involvement in the private economy, and they considered deficit spending a heresy. Even Roosevelt accepted Keynes's ideas only half-heartedly. He hesitated to support the massive federal spending and central planning that Keynes and his fol-

African-American schoolchildren in an art class sponsored by the WPA in Florida. *Franklin D. Roosevelt Library.*

lowers believed necessary to overcome the depression. Roosevelt also feared making citizens too dependent on the government as an employer of last resort. Nevertheless, his pragmatic approach to the crisis brought profound changes to the American system of governance.

Many of the New Deal programs and agencies expired by the end of the Second World War. A number of them, however—including the SEC, FDIC, TVA, and the Social Security system—survive today. Most important, the New Deal established the principle that the federal government could and would intervene in the country's economic and social life on behalf of its citizens.

Along with the revolution in the size and scope of government came a change in the profile of federal appointees. Previously most federal officials had been white, Anglo-Saxon men from the business community. The New Deal reached out to Catholics, Jews, African-Americans, and women with professional experience in social work, labor unions, and universities. These appointees brought diverse views to policy deliberations and acted as spokespersons in Washington for working, minority, and ethnic Americans. Some of Roosevelt's closest advisers, such as Thomas Corcoran, James Farley, Ben Cohen, Sam Roserman, Henry Morgenthau, Jr., and Felix Frankfurter, came from Irish or Jewish backgrounds. In contrast to his predecessors,

Eleanor Roosevelt

Between 1933 and 1945 Eleanor Roosevelt transformed the role of First Lady. Not content to be a mere hostess and model housewife, she crusaded for human rights and social justice, becoming a national symbol of reform and an inspiration to many women and minorities.

Little in Eleanor's early life foreshadowed her later rise to prominence. Born into an elite family, raised by a stern grandmother after her parents' death, she lived a shy and emotionally insecure childhood. When she married her distant cousin, Franklin Roosevelt, his mother objected to the match and made life difficult for her daughter-in-law. The couple had six children, one of whom died in infancy. Although Eleanor and Franklin always admired each other, as early as 1918 his extramarital affairs created an emotional distance between them.

Roosevelt worked closely with Jews, leading some critics to refer to his administration as the "Jew Deal." Labor Secretary Frances Perkins, the first woman in a presidential cabinet, played a critical role in promoting new social legislation. Harry Hopkins, the first professional social worker to serve a president, became a frequent and influential adviser on both domestic and foreign affairs. First Lady Eleanor Roosevelt, a political activist who sprang from a tradition of feminist progressive women, also influenced Roosevelt's thought on social issues. This multiplicity of voices enriched Roosevelt's presidency and brought the concerns of diverse groups and classes to national attention.

After polio crippled Franklin in 1920, Eleanor became politically active, often serving as his surrogate in Democratic party affairs. She played a role in Al Smith's 1928 presidential candidacy and in her husband's administration as New York governor from 1929 to 1933. During these years she worked closely with social workers, unions, and women's reform groups.

As First Lady, Eleanor Roosevelt vigorously promoted the New Deal agenda and, unfettered by the political restrictions that bound her husband, pushed a variety of more radical measures. Trade unionists, sharecroppers, and women's groups considered her their pipeline into government. She also emerged as the administration's leading advocate for the rights of African-Americans. At a segregated meeting in Alabama, she insisted on sitting in the "coloreds only" section. When the Daughters of the American Revolution refused to rent a concert hall to African-American singer Marian Anderson, Eleanor Roosevelt offered the White House grounds for the performance. She always maintained that she acted first as a citizen and only afterward as a First Lady. Beginning in 1937, she wrote a popular newspaper column, "My Day," that appeared in hundreds of papers.

Even after 1945, Eleanor Roosevelt continued to speak and write on great issues of the day. Her achievements and her support for unpopular causes inspired hope among many of her contemporaries and established her as a model for younger generations of social activists. ■

Achievements and Failures of the New Deal

To a large degree, Roosevelt relied on his appeal to the "forgotten man" to stimulate widespread interest in New Deal programs. Part of his effectiveness stemmed from his ability to speak to the American people en masse. Few national leaders used the radio (or, later, television) as effectively to bond with the public. Roosevelt initiated "fireside chats," live radio broadcasts through which he addressed millions of listeners in their living rooms. His audience considered the president a guest in their homes and planned evening activities around his broadcast chats.

Roosevelt's relations with the other media were no less impressive. He cultivated the White House press corps, holding nearly one thousand formal or impromptu news conferences—far more than his successors—and engaging reporters in lively give-and-take. Print journalists so admired Roosevelt that conservative publishers had a difficult time expunging favorable commentary from their newspapers. In the weekly newsreels shown in every movie theater in this pretelevision age, Roosevelt was constantly seen in action, whether cutting a ribbon to open a new bridge or kissing a baby. In fact, Roosevelt was the first president to appear on television, then only an experimental medium, when he opened the New York World's Fair in April 1939.

Roosevelt's appeal stretched broadly across traditional factions and spoke particularly to the disenfranchised. The New Deal coalition included the traditional Democratic party machines, labor unions, and voters from virtually every ethnic and minority group. The children of immigrants and minorities, helped by New Deal social programs, developed a greater sense of belonging and self-worth. These supporters contributed to Roosevelt's landslide presidential victory of 1936 and his re-election in 1940 and 1944.

Millions of Americans experienced real, tangible benefits from New Deal programs. Some people were put to work, others received farm support payments or were able to refinance mortgages. Rural residents could recall the day on which electric power, funded by the federal government, first came to their homes. Roosevelt's programs and personality restored hope to vast numbers of Americans and countered the lure of fascism and communism.

Yet there were signs, even in the heady early days of the New Deal, that it would not be an unqualified success. Although the unemployment rate fell dramatically from its high of 25 percent in 1933, it still hovered at 16.9 percent in 1936—as compared to just 3.2 percent before the stock market crash in 1929. Unemployment continued at an unacceptably high level throughout the 1930s. Moreover, many people fell through the gaps in the New Deal assistance programs. Some of the starkest images came from the "Dust Bowl" states of Oklahoma, Arkansas, and the Great Plains, where drought, wind, and plagues of grasshoppers forced the mass migration of small farmers. In the same years, in industrial cities of the North and Midwest, waves of strikes often led to violence and bloodshed.

Despite Roosevelt's landslide re-election victory in 1936 and the establishment of large Democratic majorities in Congress, the New Deal's struggles increased in the president's second term. Roosevelt caused a number of political problems himself with a bungled attempt to pack the Supreme Court. Through 1937, a group of conservative justices (Willis Van Devanter, James C. McReynolds, George Sutherland, and Pierce Butler) dominated the Supreme Court. Dubbed by critics the "Four Horsemen," they and Chief Justice Charles Evans Hughes and Justice Owen Roberts formed a majority that struck down such key New Deal legislation as the National Industrial Recovery Act and the Agricultural Adjustment Act. The conservatives insisted that the sanctity of private contracts remained the supreme constitutional priority, and that not even a national economic emergency justified government interference in private economic matters such as the setting of wages. Nor did the federal government's constitutional right to regulate interstate commerce confer authority to regulate prices, standards, and working conditions. As a result, between 1934 and 1936, the high court voided more pieces of major federal legislation than in any other comparable period in American history.

Roosevelt insisted that the Constitution provided authority to meet "extraordinary needs by changes in emphasis and arrangements without loss of essential forms." Fearing further judicial assaults on New Deal programs, he asked Congress in 1937 for authority to appoint up to six additional Supreme Court justices. Most Republican and many Democratic members of Congress opposed this effort to pack the court and rebuffed the president.

In mid-1937, however, one justice who usually voted with the conservatives switched sides, and another announced plans to retire. (This "switch in time," one Washington wag commented, "saved nine.") Although the effort to add additional justices failed, an emerging liberal majority on the court upheld the pro-labor Wagner Act, a minimum wage law, and key provisions of the Social Security Act. The court had turned a decisive corner. From 1937 on, the federal government exercised broad economic regulatory power over private contracts and commerce without fear of judicial intervention.

Just as the Supreme Court affirmed the right of the government to intervene deeply in the economy, a severe recession in 1937 and 1938 shook popular confidence in Roosevelt's leadership. Cuts in government spending and the initiation of the Social Security tax, which withdrew several billion dollars from circulation, probably brought on the downturn. The unemployment rate rose again, reaching 20 percent in 1938. After waffling, Roosevelt recommitted himself to a higher level of public spending and management of the economy. But his influence with Congress had waned, and he barely managed to shepherd the landmark Fair Labor Standards Act through Congress in mid-1938. The act banned child labor, established a federal minimum wage, and limited the regular workweek to forty hours for many occupations. Yet the law did not cover agricultural and household domestic positions, jobs held largely by women, African-Americans, and Hispanics.

In the 1938 congressional elections, Republicans picked up eighty-one House and eight Senate seats. These Republicans joined with conservative Democrats in blocking further New Deal innovations. They demanded balanced budgets, curbs on labor unions, and, under the banner of defending states' rights, no federal help for racial minorities.

This conservative bloc created the House Committee on Un-American Activities, later to achieve notoriety in the postwar years. The committee charged that Roosevelt's "left wing followers in the government are the fountainhead of subversive activities." Under attack from politicians whose support he needed to deal with growing threats from Germany and Japan, and hoping to repair his tattered relations with business leaders, Roosevelt backed away from reform.

Soon the outbreak of war pushed social progress even further into the background. Eventually Roosevelt would say to a close aide, "Tommy [Corcoran], cut all this New Deal stuff. It's tough to win a war."

AMERICA AND THE WORLD CRISIS

Until the late 1930s, the focus on the Great Depression limited public concern with foreign affairs. Roosevelt barely mentioned world events in his 1933 inaugural address. He did promise that America would act as a "good neighbor," especially in dealing with Latin America, and this policy resulted in the removal of occupation troops from Haiti, the lowering of tariffs, and the extension of trade credits to countries in Latin America.

Early in his first term, Roosevelt extended diplomatic recognition to the Soviet Union. Ever since the Russian Revolution in 1917, the United States had refused to recognize the Soviet government. Public school teachers had often been urged not to mention the name "Soviet Union," and many maps showed the country as a blank spot. Recognition, the president hoped, might boost trade with the newly industrializing country and ally the Soviets with the Western democracies in opposing Nazi Germany and Imperial Japan. However, lingering suspicion of communism, disputes over payment of Czarist debts, and revulsion toward Josef Stalin's brutal collectivization of agriculture and political purges prevented much cooperation before 1941.

By the mid-1930s a spirit of isolationism was widespread. Many Americans, including a substantial number in Congress, believed that the nation should have little to do with conflicts between foreign countries. For example, congressional hearings of the mid-1930s focused on charges that British and French propagandists and American arms makers, so-called merchants of death, had hoodwinked the United States into entering the First World War. These charges increased the public's distaste for foreign affairs and led Congress to pass Neutrality Acts between 1935 and 1937 that restricted the president and private Americans from giving economic assistance to foreign nations at war.

These laws, which did not distinguish between aggressor and victim, coincided with a burst of aggression by Germany, Japan, and Italy. All three countries were ruled by fascist or ultranationalist regimes that claimed special rights, frequently on the basis of race, to conquer their neighbors. The Italian invasion of Ethiopia in 1935, Italian and German support of the Fascist revolt in Spain in 1936, German remilitarization and annexation of Austria in 1936 to 1938, and Japan's invasion of China in 1937 evoked little more than tongue-clucking from the American government.

In September 1938, when the German dictator Adolf Hitler demanded the partition of Czechoslovakia, Roosevelt supported the decision of the British and French governments to "appease" Hitler's appetite, delay war, and, possibly, turn the German dictator's wrath toward the Soviet Union. After the fateful meeting in Munich, where the British and French sealed the fate of the Czechs by agreeing to Hitler's demands, Roosevelt cabled British Prime Minister Neville Chamberlain two words: "Good man." Only later, when Hitler turned his fury on the West, did the Munich agreement and the term *appeasement* take on the aura of cowardly capitulation.

Like most Americans (and many Europeans), Roosevelt hoped to preserve the world balance of power while taking as few risks as possible. American leaders recognized the dangers of German domination of Europe and Japanese control of Asia, but hoped other nations would take responsibility for containing the aggressor nations' advances. Only after Hitler violated the Munich agreement by seizing all of Czechoslovakia, and then followed his aggression with a demand for Polish territory, did the British and French abandon their policy of appeasement. By then it was nearly too late for them, or the United States, to act.

In September 1939, after signing a neutrality pact with the Soviet Union, Hitler invaded Poland. Britain and France responded by declaring war on Germany. With its two major European friends facing the might of Nazi Germany, Roosevelt pressed Congress to permit England and France to purchase American arms, so long as they used their own money and ships to transport the weapons. This "cash-and-carry" policy helped the Allies, but at little cost or risk to the United States. Until mid-1940, Roosevelt hoped that indirect American assistance would suffice to resist Germany and Japan.

Just weeks after the outbreak of war in Europe, the President received a stark indication of the growing German threat. Nuclear physicist Albert Einstein, himself a Jewish refugee from the Nazis, sent Roosevelt a letter warning that German scientists had taken the first steps in harnessing atomic power for military use. If German scientists developed an atomic bomb, Einstein predicted, Hitler would win the war.

Roosevelt authorized a group of high-level officials to begin an atomic weapons program, code-named the Manhattan Project. By 1945, some 150,000 people were working on some phase of the $2 billion project to construct the ultimate weapon. As many of the participants realized, the bomb would have a profound effect on the world ever after. The massive development project also marked a marriage of government, science, and industry that became a hallmark of post-1945 national security policy.

By June 1940, Germany's mechanized *Blitzkrieg* ("lightning war") victories in Western Europe had left only Britain resisting Nazi power. (Russia remained neutral until attacked by Germany in June 1941.) Japan, which by then occupied large portions of China, joined Germany and Italy in the Axis Alliance and began threatening European and American colonies in Asia.

As Germany stepped up its air and submarine attacks against Britain, Roosevelt stretched his constitutional powers to the limit. He transferred war ships to the British and ordered the American navy to prevent German submarines from entering a large portion of the Atlantic. The American army, then comparable in budget ($500 million) and size (185,000 men) to the Bulgarian army, desperately needed to expand. When Roosevelt prodded Congress to pass the nation's first peacetime draft in 1940, his opponents labeled him a warmonger. One senator charged that Roosevelt's policies would "plow under every fourth American boy." When the law expired in 1941, Congress authorized the draft's extension by a single vote.

Polls in the summer of 1940 revealed that while 75 percent of Americans supported aid to England and China, the public opposed direct participation in the war. Roosevelt, who had decided to seek an unprecedented third term in 1940, felt obliged to pledge that the nation's youth would not be sent into any foreign wars. (If attacked, he later explained, the United States would of course respond.) Only after his re-election in November did Roosevelt publicly state his support of the British and Chinese war efforts.

If England or China surrendered, Roosevelt declared, Americans would be "living at the point of a gun." To prevent this, he proposed a massive aid program called Lend-Lease, which would make America the "arsenal of democracy." In a vivid fireside chat, the president compared the aid to lending to one's neighbor a fire hose to keep the sparks from spreading. In March 1941, Congress, by a lopsided vote, passed legislation providing $7 billion in military aid for nations resisting Germany and Japan. Secretary of War Henry Stimson referred to the Lend-Lease bill as a "declaration of economic war" against Berlin and Tokyo.

Roosevelt sent American troops to occupy Greenland and Iceland and ordered navy ships in the Atlantic to hunt down German U-boats. By the autumn of 1941, the German and American navies were engaged in an undeclared war that led to the sinking of an American destroyer vessel. When Nazi armies invaded Russia in June, Roosevelt quickly approved Lend-Lease aid to the Soviets.

With American attention turned to the crisis in Europe, Japan took the opportunity to seize southern French Indochina, demand special access to oil from the Dutch East Indies, and insist that Washington stop military aid to China. In response, Roosevelt shifted naval units to the Pacific and imposed a trade embargo on Japan, leaving Tokyo with only a few months' reserve of petroleum. Most observers expected Japan to attack Southeast Asia in search of oil if the United States continued the embargo.

Roosevelt insisted that Japan had to quit the Axis Alliance, withdraw forces from China and Indochina, and make a nonaggression pledge before he would lift the oil embargo. Japan, under the *de facto* leadership of General Tojo Hideki, demanded immediate resumption of oil sales and a cutoff of aid to China before considering any pullback.

When discussions broke off on November 26, 1941, American officials expected a Japanese attack in Southeast Asia or the Philippines and sent warnings to commanders there and in Hawaii. But American intelligence gave no hint that Japan's leaders had designated the Pacific fleet, based at Pearl Harbor in Hawaii, as the first target.

The Grand Alliance

On December 7, 1941—a date, Roosevelt said, that would "live in infamy"—Japan mounted a surprise air attack on Pearl Harbor. More than 2,400 people were killed; eight American battleships were damaged or sunk. Like it or not, the United States was now caught up in the world war. At Roosevelt's request, Congress immediately declared war on Japan. On December 10, Germany and Italy then declared war on the United States. As Japanese forces rolled to a string of easy victories in Southeast Asia, the shock and humiliation shook an American citizenry that had felt immune from war in Europe and Asia. But Germany and Japan, by engaging America's vast military potential, had assured their own doom.

The attack on Pearl Harbor ended dissent over participation in the war. On New Year's Day in 1942, the United States, Great Britain, the

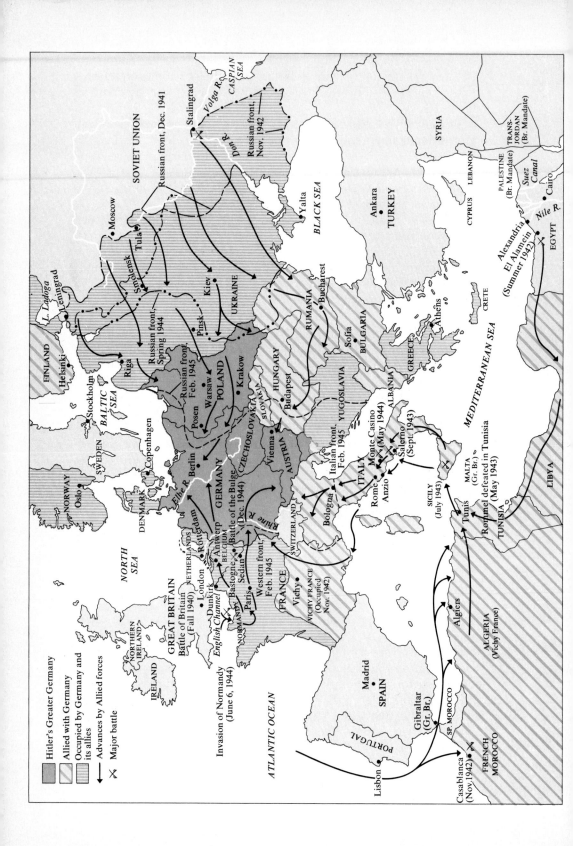

Hitler's Greater Germany

Allied with Germany

Occupied by Germany and
its allies

Advances by Allied forces

Major battle

SOVIET UNION

CASPIAN SEA

Volga R.

Stalingrad

Russian front, Dec. 1941

Russian front, Nov. 1942

Don R.

Russian front, Dec. 1941

Moscow

Tula

Smolensk

Leningrad

L. Ladoga

Helsinki

FINLAND

Stockholm

SWEDEN

Oslo

NORWAY

Copenhagen

DENMARK

BALTIC SEA

Riga

Russian front, Spring 1944

Russian front, Feb. 1945

Posen

Berlin

Elbe R.

GERMANY

Rotterdam

NETHERLANDS

Antwerp

BELGIUM

Battle of the Bulge (Dec. 1944)

Bastogne

Sedan

NORMANDY

English Channel

London

Dunkirk

Battle of Britain (Fall 1940)

GREAT BRITAIN

NORTHERN IRELAND

IRELAND

NORTH SEA

ATLANTIC OCEAN

Paris

Western front, Feb. 1945

FRANCE

Vichy

VICHY FRANCE (Occupied Nov. 1942)

SWITZERLAND

Rhine R.

Invasion of Normandy (June 6, 1944)

Pinsk

Kiev

UKRAINE

Krakow

Warsaw

POLAND

SLOVAKIA

CZECHOSLOVAKIA

Vienna

AUSTRIA

HUNGARY

Budapest

RUMANIA

Bucharest

BULGARIA

Sofia

YUGOSLAVIA

Italian front, Feb. 1945

ALBANIA

GREECE

Athens

Yalta

BLACK SEA

Ankara

TURKEY

CYPRUS

SYRIA

LEBANON

PALESTINE (Br. Mandate)

TRANS. JORDAN (Br. Mandate)

Suez Canal

Cairo

Nile R.

EGYPT

Alexandria

El Alamein (Summer 1942)

CRETE

MEDITERRANEAN SEA

LIBYA

Monte Casino (May 1944)

Rome

Anzio

Bologna

ITALY

Salerno (Sept. 1943)

SICILY (July 1943)

MALTA (Gr. Br.)

Tunis

Rommel defeated in Tunisia (May 1943)

TUNISIA

ALGERIA (Vichy France)

Algiers

SP. MOROCCO

FRENCH MOROCCO

Casablanca (Nov. 1942)

Gibraltar (Gr. Br.)

Madrid

SPAIN

PORTUGAL

Lisbon

Soviet Union, and twenty-three partners issued a "Declaration of the United Nations," a pledge to fight for victory against the Axis. Roosevelt and his military advisers resolved that the United States would provide Lend-Lease aid to Britain, Russia, and China, helping them carry the bulk of the fighting against Germany and Japan. As soon as possible, Anglo-American armies would open a second front by invading Western Europe to relieve the pressure on the Soviets, who, until 1944, faced about two-thirds of all German forces. Roosevelt anticipated that the Allies would crush Germany and the Soviets would then join in the final assault on Japan.

The proposed American military strategy encountered numerous obstacles. British Prime Minister Winston Churchill, who guided Britain through the war, feared high casualties in an early assault on Western Europe and preferred to wear down the Germans in North Africa and Italy. American commanders believed that failure to attack German forces in Western Europe would prolong the war, increase total casualties, and risk the collapse of the Soviet war effort. Roosevelt knew that Stalin would interpret any delay in opening a second front as encouraging Germany's devastation of the Soviet Union. Because the Russian armies were taking the brunt of the fighting, Roosevelt promised Stalin a second front in 1942.

Supply problems, British stalling, the competing demands of the Pacific war, and other factors delayed the Allied entry into France until June 6, 1944 (see map). By then the Soviets had, at a cost of nearly 20 million civilian and military dead, pushed German forces out of Russia and into Poland. The delay in establishing a second front aroused Stalin's suspicion that the Allies would fight Germany to the last Russian, then move to control Europe themselves.

The behavior of Russian leaders tended to arouse similar fears in London and Washington. For example, beginning in 1942 the Soviets demanded that Roosevelt and Churchill approve the transfer of parts of prewar Poland and southeastern Europe to the Soviet Union. Although Western leaders regarded these concessions as violations of the rights of the Poles and the other nationalities involved, they also recognized that the Soviets had a justified interest in creating a security zone in Eastern Europe, the route of two German invasions since 1914. Churchill and Roosevelt eventually accepted Soviet demands in return for Stalin's promise to respect the political independence of the rest of Eastern Europe.

Despite a basic affinity between Roosevelt and Churchill, the two men argued frequently over American demands for the dissolution of the British and other European empires, over Washington's insis-

◀ **The Allies on the Offensive in Europe, 1942–1945**

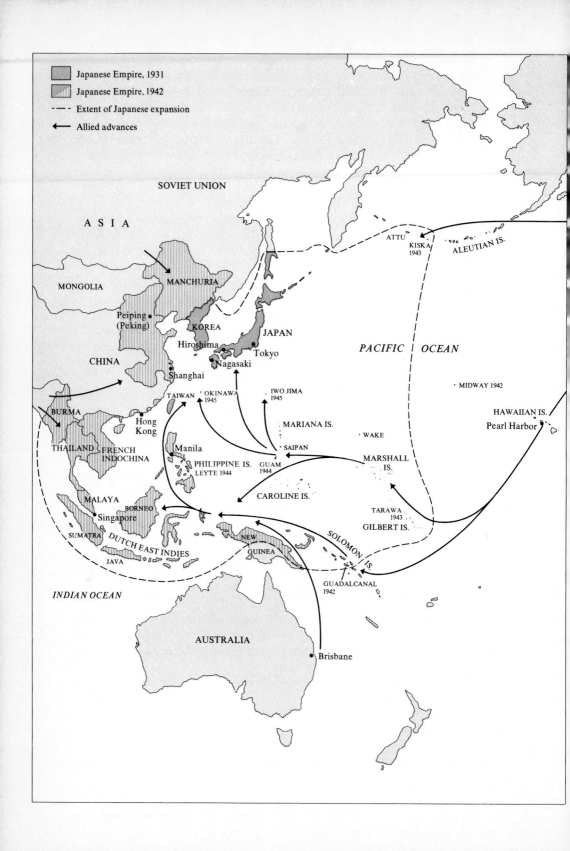

Japanese Empire, 1931
Japanese Empire, 1942
Extent of Japanese expansion
Allied advances

SOVIET UNION

ASIA

ATTU
KISKA
1943
ALEUTIAN IS.

MONGOLIA

MANCHURIA

Peiping
(Peking)

KOREA

JAPAN

Hiroshima

Tokyo

PACIFIC OCEAN

Nagasaki

CHINA

Shanghai

· MIDWAY 1942

TAIWAN

OKINAWA
1945

IWO JIMA
1945

HAWAIIAN IS.
Pearl Harbor

BURMA

Hong
Kong

MARIANA IS.

· WAKE

THAILAND

FRENCH
INDOCHINA

Manila

· SAIPAN

MARSHALL
IS.

PHILIPPINE IS.
LEYTE 1944

GUAM
1944

MALAYA

BORNEO

CAROLINE IS.

Singapore

TARAWA
1943

SUMATRA

DUTCH EAST INDIES

NEW

GILBERT IS.

JAVA

GUINEA

SOLOMON IS.

INDIAN OCEAN

GUADALCANAL
1942

AUSTRALIA

· Brisbane

tence that Britain lower trade barriers in the postwar period, and over the proper conduct and goals of the war. At times Churchill seemed more interested in safeguarding British interests in the Mediterranean than in defeating Hitler. Like the Soviet Union, Britain also worried about America's power in the postwar world.

Shaping the Postwar World

At the Bretton Woods Conference in 1944, the United States unveiled plans for the International Bank for Reconstruction and Development (World Bank) and the International Monetary Fund (IMF). The former would make loans for postwar reconstruction; the latter would stabilize currencies, reduce trade barriers, and promote commerce. The dollar, backed by gold, would become the standard international currency. Treasury Secretary Morgenthau boasted to his staff that by the war's end, the power of the dollar would be so great that Roosevelt alone "would write the peace treaty."

Roosevelt also hoped that wartime trust and cooperation would create support for a new world political order. At a series of summit meetings held between 1941 and 1945 in Washington, Teheran, Casablanca, Cairo, Malta, and Yalta, the president sketched plans for a postwar international organization, the United Nations, dominated by what he sometimes called the "Four Policemen"—the United States, the Soviet Union, Great Britain, and China. Each nation would be predominant in a security zone, or sphere of interest, most important to it. At the same time, each would work toward open world trade, the gradual decolonization of empires, and the rehabilitation of a democratic Germany and Japan. Roosevelt first pressed these points in August 1941, before the United States formally entered the war, when he and a skeptical Churchill issued a proclamation called the Atlantic Charter.

Although the diplomatic and strategic logic of the war often seemed confused, by 1945 a pattern had emerged. As Stalin remarked, "whoever occupies a territory also imposes on it his own social system." Thus, the British and Americans, joined by Charles de Gaulle's Free French, eventually established pro-Western, anti-Communist regimes in North Africa, Italy, Greece, France, western Germany, Japan, and southern Korea. As American forces advanced across the Pacific (see map), Washington took possession of hundreds of islands formerly in the possession of Japan, declaring them "strategic trusteeships." The British, French, and Dutch rushed to recolonize Southeast Asia as Japan retreated. As Russian forces pushed

◄ The Pacific War

the Nazis toward Berlin, Stalin similarly imposed pro-Soviet regimes in most of Eastern Europe.

Allied leaders made several efforts to rationalize this division of spoils. For example, in October 1944 Churchill tried to make a deal with Stalin that would give Russia the preeminent role in the political reorganization of Rumania and Bulgaria, and a partial influence in Hungary and Yugoslavia, in return for British control of Greece. With a wink, Churchill told Stalin that their agreement should be recorded in "diplomatic terms and not . . . use the phrase 'dividing the spheres' because the Americans might be shocked." Stalin did not seem amused.

Roosevelt, hardly naive, preferred delaying most bargaining until the war's end, when he thought the American position would be stronger. Nor did he favor any action jeopardizing wartime cooperation. Although several of his advisers urged confronting Moscow, perhaps even cutting off Lend-Lease aid once German troops had been pushed out of Russian territory, Roosevelt refused to risk a break in the alliance and declared that everything would be negotiable after victory.

But by February 1945, as the imminent collapse of the Axis Alliance became apparent, the Allies could no longer defer discussing postwar issues. Roosevelt and Churchill joined Stalin for a crucial meeting at Yalta, a Soviet city on the Black Sea. Critics of the Yalta agreements later charged that Roosevelt had acceded to Stalin's demands out of naivety, deteriorating health, or perhaps even Communist sympathies. Why else would an American leader sanction a dominant Soviet role in Poland or grant concessions to Russia in Manchuria? "Yalta" became shorthand, especially among Republicans, for softness on communism.

In fact, the Yalta agreements did little more than recognize that Soviet forces already occupied the Baltic states of Estonia, Latvia, and Lithuania, Poland, and parts of Rumania and Bulgaria; were poised to invade Germany; and would soon be able to attack Japan. At Yalta, the "Big Three"—Great Britain, the United States, and the Soviet Union—also agreed to participate in the new United Nations organization, exact industrial reparations from Germany, and endorse a Soviet declaration of war against Japan three months after Hitler's defeat.

Stalin demanded special economic privileges in Manchuria (northeastern China) but in return promised not to assist the Chinese Communist struggle against the American-backed Chinese Nationalist government. Roosevelt and Churchill received Stalin's promise to reorganize along more democratic lines the Soviet-installed regime in Poland. A "Declaration of Liberated Europe," signed by the three leaders, pledged cooperation in restoring democratic government in liberated territories.

Roosevelt's aide, Admiral William Leahy, complained that the agreement was "so elastic that the Russians can stretch it all the way from Yalta to Washington without technically breaking it." Roosevelt agreed, but added it was the best he could do under the circumstances. Without continued Soviet cooperation, Roosevelt knew, the Western allies would face a far bloodier road to Berlin and Tokyo. Soviet influence in Eastern Europe and northeast Asia—which Stalin could take with or without permission—seemed a reasonable price for saving American lives and shortening the war. Even American hardliners did not seriously recommend fighting the Soviets to move them out of Poland. Most Americans rejoiced, in fact, when the Russians captured Berlin and when Germany surrendered on May 8, 1945. On the basis of earlier agreements, the Soviet Union turned over part of the German capital and other territories to its allies.

In the next chapter we will examine the United States use of the atomic bomb against Japan to end the war in Asia. Here it is important to recognize that the war ended with the United States and its Western allies dominating most of the industrial world, including North America, Great Britain, Western Europe, and Japan. The Soviets occupied much of Eastern Europe and a fourth of Germany, but their spoils did little to enhance their industrial or economic power. This fact, more than any other, ensured American supremacy after 1945.

Among the warring powers, the United States had made the smallest human sacrifice—about 400,000 dead, compared to a total for all countries approaching 50 million—and had gained the most. Russian civilian deaths during the three-year siege of Leningrad exceeded the total number of military deaths sustained by the United States. America emerged from the war with the world's strongest economy and armed forces, as well as a monopoly on atomic power. When the killing stopped, the United States, with only 6 percent of the world's population, produced half of the world's goods. This relative level of power and economic well-being was not surpassed in the subsequent half-century. As one contemporary noted, "while the rest of the world came out bruised and scarred and nearly destroyed, we came out with the most unbelievable machinery, trade, manpower and money."

WAR ON THE HOME FRONT

The war years had brought to a halt most New Deal social engineering. When Roosevelt announced in 1943 that "Dr. Win-the-War" had replaced "Dr. New Deal," conservative *Time* publisher Henry Luce ran a mock obituary:

Death Revealed: The New Deal, 10, after long illness; of malnutrition and desuetude. Child of the 1932 election campaign, the New Deal had four healthy years, began to suffer from spots before the eyes in 1937, and never recovered from the shock of war. Last week, its father, Franklin Roosevelt, pronounced it dead.

But even if the New Deal was gone, the war itself acted as a catalyst for far-reaching social and economic change. In 1941 the United States still had many characteristics of a rural and small-town society. Of 132 million Americans, only about 74 million, or 56 percent, lived in cities with more than 10,000 inhabitants. About one-third of dwelling units lacked indoor water or plumbing, and two-thirds lacked central heating. Moreover, only 40 percent of adults had an eighth grade education. One-fourth had graduated from high school; one-tenth had attended college, but only 5 percent had completed a college degree. Almost 90 percent of white men (the most affluent group) made less than $2,500 per year. Over half of all wage-earning men and three-fourths of wage-earning women earned $1,000 per year or less.

The economy was still depressed in January 1941. Around 9 million workers, or 15 percent of the labor force, had no jobs. Private investment stood 18 percent *below* the 1929 level. The gross national product (GNP) barely surpassed the 1929 figure.

All of this would change dramatically during the war years. As the war progressed, unemployment virtually disappeared, and ordinary Americans felt the shadow of the Great Depression finally lift from their lives. Private investment quickly surpassed the 1929 level and then continued to soar. The GNP swelled from a prewar level of $90 billion per year to over $212 billion in 1945. Universities and private industries vastly expanded their research facilities. Mass population shifts occurred as millions of Americans moved to the cities. By the war's end, the United States had taken a giant leap from its lingering small-town past toward the urbanized, high-tech present.

Economic Effects of the War

The most obvious economic effect of the war was the surge in federal spending. Defense appropriations rose sharply with the passage of Lend-Lease in 1941. The initial Lend-Lease appropriation of $7 billion ballooned to $50 billion for the war years—an enormous sum compared to the total federal budget of $9 billion for 1939. By the end of the war the figure for the total annual federal budget rose to more than $95 billion (see figure). Correspondingly, the size of the federal

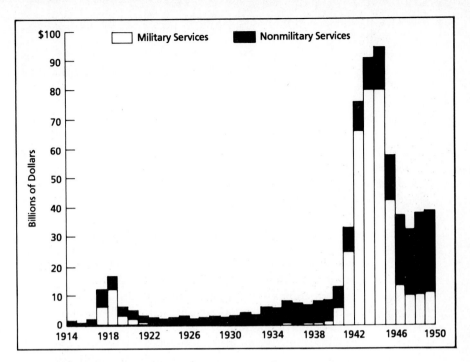

Federal Spending, 1914–1950

bureaucracy more than tripled, reaching 3.4 million workers in 1945–
a number still not surpassed as of 1991.

Another portentous change was the rapid rise in the national debt.
Although Treasury Secretary Henry Morgenthau, Jr., hoped to pay
half of the war's costs by raising taxes, the other half had to be financed by the sale of bonds to individuals and banks. Until the war
the United States had maintained a relatively small debt. Now, with
the help of popular film and radio stars, the government promoted
Treasury bonds so successfully that the bond drives raised $135 bil-
lion. Small purchasers accounted for a third of the total sales, financial institutions for the rest.

In addition to raising money, the government had to mobilize
American industry for the strenuous war effort. For this task Roosevelt turned for help to the business executives he had once denounced as selfish plutocrats. Thousands of corporate executives
signed on to guide the national economy; they were called "dollar-a-
year men" because they kept their business salaries and received only
a token payment from the government. These "war lords of Washington," as one critic called them, exercised unprecedented control

over the national economy by deciding what should be built, where, and by whom.

In May 1943, Roosevelt further centralized planning by asking his recently appointed Supreme Court justice, James F. Byrnes, to head the Office of War Mobilization (OWM). By relying more on incentives than on penalties, Byrnes and his business advisers proved remarkably successful in mobilizing the private sector to produce war goods.

Corporations were initially reluctant to invest the huge amounts of money needed to convert from civilian to military production. For example, it would cost General Motors a fortune to retool plants to produce tanks and jeeps in place of cars. Who would pay for conversion (or reconversion, when the war ended), and how could profits be guaranteed? Should private businesses invest in costly, experimental technology that might have no consumer application? To encourage industrial production, the Justice Department relaxed antitrust enforcement. Washington offered manufacturers the innovative "cost plus a fixed fee" contract whereby the federal government paid research and production costs and purchased items at a guaranteed markup. Largely as a result, corporate after-tax profits swelled from $6.4 billion in 1940 to $10.8 billion in 1944.

Defense mobilization led to other innovations. Before 1941, the federal government spent little money on scientific research. By 1945, not counting the $2 billion spent on atomic bomb research and billions more used to construct synthetic rubber, steel, aluminum, and aircraft plants, Washington funnelled $1.5 billion annually into science research and development. Radar, electronic computers, jet engines, synthetic fibers, wonder drugs like sulfa and penicillin, nuclear weapons, and ballistic missiles all came out of wartime research.

The military's need to process large amounts of data provided a special impetus to the development of computers. Binary digits, the basis of computer logic, had been developed before the war. During the 1930s, the International Business Machines Corporation (IBM) had worked with the Social Security Administration to handle large amounts of information. After 1941, IBM developed code-breaking machines for the war effort, and in 1944 the company built a precursor of the modern computer. By 1946 it had perfected ENIAC, the first large digital computer. (The behemoth filled a large room with hundreds of miles of wire and 18,000 vacuum tubes, and used 140,000 watts of power, but had less computing power than today's laptop models.)

The War Department's Office of Scientific Research and Development (OSRD), headed by Vannevar Bush of the Massachusetts Institute of Technology, poured $2 billion into the vast, highly secret, atomic bomb project. In three new "atomic cities"—Oak Ridge, Tennessee; Hanford, Washington; and Los Alamos, New Mexico—nearly

150,000 people conducted research, refined uranium, and produced weapons. The facilities rivaled in size the entire automobile industry. Additional government funds helped universities build modern scientific laboratories. Universities derived further support by enrolling several hundred thousand officers in army and navy programs for accelerated college degrees.

Research facilities mushroomed not only in universities but also in private industry. By the end of the war, almost 2,500 private industrial research laboratories were employing 133,000 people, twice the prewar number. In an influential study called *Science: The Endless Frontier*, published in 1945, Vannevar Bush proposed creation of a permanent government agency to fund basic research. Congress finally approved the idea in 1950 when it created the National Science Foundation.

Overall, the administration's policies spurred military production that was little short of miraculous. Aircraft plants, which produced barely 2,000 planes a year before the war, turned out nearly 50,000 in 1942 and 100,000 during 1944. By 1945, American industry had produced over 100,000 tanks, 87,000 ships of all types, 2.5 million trucks, 5 million tons of bombs, and 44 billion rounds of ammunition. As a result, Allied soldiers had a three-to-one advantage in arms over their Axis enemies. A story was told of a ship christening at which a woman at dockside was handed a bottle of champagne to do the honors. "But where is the ship?" she asked. "Just start swinging, lady," a worker remarked. "We'll have the ship there in time."

During the war, total productivity increased a startling 25 percent annually. By comparison, the average annual increase in the previous half-century was 2 percent. No one understood the significance of this achievement better than Josef Stalin, who, at the 1943 Teheran Conference with Roosevelt and Churchill, offered a toast to "American production, without which this war would have been lost."

On the negative side, war production gave birth to what later critics, including President Eisenhower, would call the "military-industrial complex." In 1940 the hundred largest American companies produced only 30 percent of goods manufactured in the United States. But wartime spending for high technology benefited large firms more than small ones. By 1945 the "Big 100" American companies produced a whopping 70 percent of the country's defense output, and the ten largest corporations accounted for nearly one-third of war production. The close relationship between the military and large defense contractors would continue after the war.

As big business prospered during the war years, so did its traditional antagonists, the labor unions. For both patriotic and practical reasons, most labor leaders worked closely with government and business leaders. Buoyed by rising wages, major unions took a no-

Launching a "Liberty Ship," one of thousands of vessels mass-produced during the Second World War. *Franklin D. Roosevelt Library.*

strike pledge during the war, and this willingness to cooperate enhanced their emerging role as part of the economic and political establishment. (The one major exception was the United Mine Workers, led by John L. Lewis. Strikes in the coal mines caused major disruptions in 1943.) Among factory workers, union membership increased dramatically, from 10.5 million in 1941 to 15 million in 1945, a third of the non-farm work force. This represented the all-time peak of union membership.

To help pay for the war, the expanding government revised the tax structure and introduced withholding taxes on paychecks. Before 1941, most lower- and middle-income Americans paid little or no federal income tax. During the war the government sought to spread the costs equitably among wage-earning Americans. Taxes therefore rose, but not disproportionately. Before 1941, a married man without dependents earning $2,000 annually paid no federal taxes. In 1945, he paid just over $200. For individuals earning more, the tax bite increased at a progressive rate. As a result, tax revenues swelled from $5 billion to $49 billion by 1945.

At first, the combination of defense spending, full employment, and shortages of civilian goods fueled inflation. Agencies like the National War Labor Board and the Office of Price Administration then imposed a variety of wage and price controls, along with rationing. Consumers needed ration coupons to buy items like gasoline, meat, and sugar. Children were encouraged to collect old cans, tires, and fat, which could be recycled into war goods. City dwellers cultivated millions of tiny "victory gardens" to supplement diets.

But even while ordinary people conserved sugar and saved cans, a remarkable process was occurring. The war years brought about the most dramatic redistribution of income for working Americans in the century. With adjustment for inflation, real factory wages rose from $24 to nearly $37 per week during the war. The share of national wealth held by the richest 5 percent of Americans declined from 23.7 percent to 16.8 percent. The number of families with an annual income below $2,000 fell by half, while the number with annual incomes over $5,000 increased fourfold.

Because of the high employment rate and the shortage of consumer goods, personal savings jumped from $2.9 billion annually in 1939 to over $29 billion annually in 1945. Purchases of "expendables" (jewelry, cosmetics, books, movie tickets) also grew, from $66 billion in 1939 to just over $100 billion in 1944. Record numbers of people attended movies, nightclubs, and racetracks. Though wartime shortages continued, people found ways to enjoy their relative prosperity. Because of the war's stimulus to the economy, the Great Depression at last was history.

Population Shifts

In addition to its economic impact, the war had a dramatic effect on where Americans lived and worked, setting patterns that affected demography for the next half-century. Most obviously, 16 million men and 250,000 women entered military service between 1941 and 1945. Almost all eligible men between the ages of eighteen and thirty-five years served in the armed forces. All told, over 12 percent of the total American population spent time in uniform. Many GIs were sent to parts of the country they had never seen before, and often they liked what they saw. In this way, time spent in the service helped to break down regional barriers.

An upheaval among civilians also took place. Six million rural Americans headed for war work in cities, while as many urban residents moved to jobs in new cities. Many of the migrants were African-Americans who left the states of the old Confederacy to seek jobs in the North and West. With shipbuilding, aircraft manufacturing, and other war industries concentrated on the East and West coasts and in the upper Midwestern states, these areas grew rapidly. Not surprisingly, Washington, D.C., the seat of the expanding federal government, doubled in population.

The Sunbelt—the warm states of the South and Southwest—began its rise during the war years. Even as African-Americans left the old South, cities like Miami and Houston grew. Population also made a major shift westward. Along the West Coast the shipyards, aircraft plants, and staging areas for the Pacific front employed thousands of locals and hundreds of thousands of migrants. Not only war workers, but tens of thousands of military personnel migrated to San Diego, Portland, Seattle, Los Angeles, and San Francisco—or returned from overseas to these cities and decided to remain as permanent residents. California's population grew by over a third during the war, as 2 million people came from the South and from rural areas to work in the aircraft and shipbuilding industries. The population of Los Angeles alone increased by half a million. All told, the West grew 40 percent in population between 1940 and 1950, with much of that explosive growth a direct result of the war.

Women in Wartime

Women's roles changed dramatically during the war, even though gender-based inequality remained deeply ingrained. In 1940, before the United States entered the war, about 27 percent of all women worked outside the home, but only 15 percent of married women did so. Moreover, most women in the labor force held low-paying jobs in light manufacturing, service, and clerical areas.

With the wartime labor shortage came a shift in public policy and private attitudes toward women in the labor force. Women were encouraged to work and to take jobs traditionally held by men—for the time being. A War Department pamphlet put it succinctly: "A woman is a substitute—like plastic instead of metal. She has special characteristics that lend themselves to new and sometimes to superior uses." The Office of War Information (OWI), an agency that produced radio plays, films, and posters in an attempt to mold public attitudes, chipped in with encouragements for women to join the work force. Such appeals swayed public opinion. Before the war, 80 percent of surveyed Americans opposed wives working outside the home; in 1942, 80 percent approved.

By 1945, over 6 million additional women, including 4 million who had been housewives before the war, had entered the industrial work force, accounting for a third of the total. They worked as riveters, welders, assembly line workers, aircraft fabricators, and in numerous other positions previously held only by men. Steelyards, shipyards, and aircraft plants employed virtually no women before 1942, but three years later women made up as much as 40 percent of the work force in key defense plants. African-American women contributed to the trend, entering manufacturing and clerical work in significant numbers for the first time.

Riveting was the most familiar new female job in the defense industry. Women worked in teams, riveting and "bucking" metal plates together in the Lockheed, North American Aviation, Boeing, and Kaiser plants that had sprung up on the West Coast. In Los Angeles, at the peak of the war, 10 percent of all women residents worked in aviation factories. The fictional "Rosie the Riveter," a can-do, muscular woman in bulging overalls, was a familiar figure, celebrated in songs and on posters and magazine covers. Women also ran heavy equipment, drove trucks and trains, and took jobs as "cowgirls" and "lumberjills." Even professional opportunities improved, as newspapers, orchestras, radio stations, and financial institutions recruited women.

Despite the wartime labor shortage, however, women still were often assigned to sex-segregated tasks, received lower wages than men for the same work, and found few support services such as day care for children. Social workers frequently discovered babies sleeping in cars outside defense plants because their working mothers had nowhere else to leave them. Business and political leaders offered various rationalizations for denying women equal pay and access to day care. Women were encouraged to think of factory work as a temporary expedient, to keep their sights on the home, and to be prepared to resume the roles of housewife and mother when their husbands returned from the war.

As men entered military service, women's responsibilities increased in many ways beyond that of wage earner. Women became the center of family life as never before. They also assumed responsibility for critical unpaid work. They served as Red Cross nurses, canteen volunteers, and actresses on tours sponsored by the United Service Organizations (USO). These contributions were celebrated in films like *Stage Door Canteen*, the tale of three pretty USO hostesses who struck up romances with soldiers on leave. Max Lerner, a popular columnist, voiced a common male complaint that war work had created a "new Amazon" who could "outdrink, outswear, and outswagger the men." Surveys by the Labor Department found that although many women resented unequal pay and sexual harassment on the job, they found the new opportunities and responsibilities exciting. Women enjoyed spending and saving their higher earnings, valued the independence and self-confidence that came with earning an income, and liked acquiring new skills. Most employed women hoped to continue working when peace returned—but they did so, as we will see, under changed rules.

African-Americans

Before the Second World War, over three-fourths of all African-Americans lived in the South, working mainly as tenant farmers or domestic help. In the North, they held the lowest rung of industrial jobs. The Great Depression hurt these workers more severely than any other group. Reflecting political realities, New Deal programs never directly challenged segregation; after all, most African-Americans could not vote, and southern Democrats chaired key committees in Congress. Although Roosevelt sympathized with racial minorities, he declined to antagonize the southern Democrats.

Organizations like the National Association for the Advancement of Colored People (NAACP), the National Urban League, and the National Negro Congress protested the denial of work relief benefits to African-Americans. They lobbied politicians and mobilized African-American voters in the North to demand changes. They found important supporters among leftwing political groups, the CIO, and white liberals.

Gradually the New Deal civil rights record improved. Top federal work relief administrators like Harry Hopkins and Harold Ickes hired growing numbers of minorities. Although officials in the South resisted these moves, and segregation in federal programs remained common, African-Americans appreciated these efforts. As one leading black newspaper commented, "what administration within the memory of man . . . had done a better job . . . considering the imperfect human material with which it had to work? The answer, of course, is none."

In the 1932 presidential election, over two-thirds of African-American voters (nearly all of whom lived in the North) had supported the Republican candidate, Herbert Hoover. In 1940, over two-thirds of them voted for the Democratic ticket, a number that grew in later decades. Some critics have charged that Roosevelt deluded African-Americans with rhetoric, or that desperation made them appreciate any crumbs they could gather from New Deal programs. Yet, compared to what preceded it, the New Deal took important steps toward racial justice.

African-American employment at all levels in the federal government tripled between 1933 and 1945, with most of the gains made during the war. Roosevelt's new federal agencies caused a sensation by abolishing segregated cafeterias and offices in their Washington headquarters. An informal "Black Cabinet" of prominent citizens consulted regularly with agency heads and, on occasion, with the president. Eleanor Roosevelt championed the efforts of racial minorities. She met regularly with African-American leaders like Mary McLeod Bethune, an official of the National Youth Administration, invited them to the White House, and legitimized their concerns. She supported civil rights legislation and federal laws against lynching and the poll tax.

Roosevelt's judicial appointments also had a lasting impact on civil rights. With the exception of James F. Byrnes, Roosevelt's eight appointees to the Supreme Court, and especially Justices Felix Frank-furter, Wiley Rutledge, Frank Murphy, Hugo Black, and William O. Douglas, sympathized with efforts to dismantle legal discrimination. By the late 1940s they had struck down state laws excluding minori-ties from juries, established the right to picket against discrimination in employment, outlawed racially restrictive covenants in housing, challenged inequality in interstate transportation, forebade peonage of farm workers, overturned laws mandating lower pay for African-American teachers, and outlawed the white primary system that barred nonwhites from voting in the all-important southern Demo-cratic primaries. These Supreme Court rulings provided momentum for further legal challenges to segregation and for the civil rights movement of the late 1940s through 1960s.

The war, however, brought new dissatisfaction with the pace of change. The United States was fighting enemies who proclaimed the right to enslave or exterminate "inferior" races. Presumably, Ameri-can citizens were united in detesting such distorted ideologies. Yet American minorities at home and in the armed forces still faced dis-crimination and abuse. Law and tradition segregated African-Amer-icans in school, at the workplace, and in numerous aspects of social life.

In 1941, as defense orders poured in to factories, African-American leaders expressed outrage that employment on military production lines remained largely segregated. A. Philip Randolph, head of the Brotherhood of Sleeping Car Porters, a union mostly of African-Americans, challenged racial economic discrimination directly. That spring he announced plans for a mass March on Washington in de-mand of equal employment rights.

To avert the protest march, Roosevelt issued executive order No. 8802, which created a presidential Fair Employment Practices Com-mittee (FEPC) to investigate complaints of discrimination in the de-fense industry. In exchange, the March on Washington was called off. Even though the FEPC lacked enforcement power, it pressed for-merly segregated industries to hire about 600,000 additional African-American workers by 1945. The lure of these new jobs contributed to the migration of about 2 million African-Americans from the former Confederate states to the North and West during the 1940s.

African-American leaders supported the war effort while seeking what they called a "double victory"—a victory over Nazi racism abroad and discrimination at home. The NAACP urged its members to "persuade, embarrass, compel, and shame" the federal govern-ment into acting against racism. Nevertheless, segregation and rac-ism remained the norm both in the military and in civilian life.

Ironically, the shared experience of war helped to remove old eth-nic barriers between white groups. On the battlefields and in the can-teens, white Americans from varied ethnic and religious backgrounds mingled and got to know one another. But the black-white barrier was much harder to crack. When the military drafted a million African-Americans, it placed most of them in menial positions such as cook, driver, or construction worker. The Red Cross maintained segregated blood banks. African-American troops were often commanded by southern white officers, who treated them harshly. Still, African-American soldiers pressed ceaselessly for greater responsibilities and often challenged the status quo. For example, during the war, a young lieutenant named Jackie Robinson—who would later become the first black player in major-league baseball—refused to sit in the segregated portion of a bus. Court-martialed, he defended himself successfully.

After touring units in the Pacific in 1945, NAACP official Walter White commented that most African-American GIs did not see the defeat of Germany and Japan as a full victory because they had to return to a rigidly segregated America: "[They] believe their fight for democracy will begin when they reach San Francisco on the way home."

African-American anxieties were confirmed by several violent wartime race riots, most notably in Detroit in 1942 and in Harlem in 1943. In Detroit, a black-white fight at a park sparked the riot; in Harlem the violence started with the shooting of a black soldier by a policeman. White resentment of blacks seeking homes in segregated neighborhoods and applying for factory jobs previously reserved for whites contributed to the intensity of these conflicts.

In spite of such outbreaks of racial hatred, the war years generally aided the struggle for equality and civil rights. Military service, even in a segregated system, brought a certain sense of empowerment. New employment opportunities, exposure to a world outside the rural South, northward migration, and growing membership in civil rights organizations also gave a tremendous boost to African-Americans. The wartime generation was unwilling to suffer silently; its militancy and expectations were both on the rise. These people and their children would play a critical role in the postwar challenge to segregation.

Mexican-Americans

Mexican migrants and Mexican-Americans also experienced hardship during the war. Since the early twentieth century Mexicans had migrated in large numbers to the United States. During the depression, state and local authorities had pressured 400,000 Mexicans residing in America to return to their native country. But after 1941, as large numbers of agricultural workers entered the armed services or sought more lucrative defense work, farm managers experienced severe labor shortages. Therefore, in 1942 the federal government negotiated a contract labor program with Mexican authorities that continued, in various forms, until 1964.

Under this so-called *bracero* ("laborer") program, the American government promised to supervise the recruitment, transportation, and working conditions of large groups of Mexican farm workers. During the war, this agreement brought in about 1,750,000 farm and railroad laborers. However, the promised supervision of working conditions was so lax that *braceros* were paid as little as 35 cents per day, and many lived in converted chicken coops.

The nearly 2.7 million Mexican-Americans—or Chicanos, as many preferred to call themselves—faced additional problems. Living mostly in the Southwest, they were confronted with segregation in schools, housing, and employment. New social tensions flared in communities like Los Angeles, where rapid growth inflamed traditional racism. Mexican-American youth gangs, whose members were called *pachucos* and dressed in flamboyant clothes called "zoot suits," were frequently harassed by the police and by white servicemen.

In August 1942 a Mexican-American youth attending a party died of unknown causes in the Sleepy Lagoon neighborhood of Los Angeles. Police arrested members of a street gang reported to have fought earlier with the dead youth's friends. Despite the lack of evidence linking the accused to the victim, prosecutors charged twenty-two Mexican-Americans with murder. After a trial, all were found guilty. In 1944, a citizens committee convinced a federal court that the defendants' constitutional rights had been violated, and eventually all the convictions were reversed.

Ethnic relations in Los Angeles were worsened by the actions of sailors and marines on shore leave, who frequently cruised the *barrios* in search of Mexican-Americans wearing zoot suits, whom they attacked and humiliated by stripping. Police often charged the zoot-suiters instead of the marines with disturbing the peace. Among Mexican-American males, the flamboyant clothing represented an assertion of distinct identity and a flouting of white cultural values.

The tensions exploded in June 1943, when hundreds of sailors and marines went on a several-day rampage, attacking Mexican-Americans, African-Americans, and Filipinos in the East Los Angeles *barrio*. Because local police often participated in the attacks, military police were needed to quell the riot. The *Los Angeles Times* reported the incidents with headlines such as "Zoot Suiters Learn Lesson in Fight with Servicemen." When Eleanor Roosevelt suggested that long-standing discrimination against Mexican-Americans might have provoked the riots, the paper accused her of promoting racial discord.

But for Mexican-Americans, as for African-Americans, the war years brought some advances. Service in the military gave young

Mexican-Americans a feeling of personal worth and power. After the war, military veterans took a prominent part in organizing civil rights groups that campaigned against postwar discrimination in the Southwest.

Wartime Anti-Semitism

In November 1938, after the German government had stripped German Jews of most civil and economic rights, Nazi mobs sets upon Jewish businesses, synagogues, and homes, smashing and looting in an orgy that quickly became known as *Kristallnacht*, or "Night of the Broken Glass." Shortly after that incident, German police sent twenty thousand Jews to concentration camps, which later became the sites of mass extermination. Roosevelt remarked that he could "scarcely believe that such things could occur in a twentieth century civilization." As the Nazis conquered eastern Europe, the violence escalated.

European Jews who attempted to flee confronted legal barriers everywhere. Since 1924, the United States' National Origins Act had restricted nearly all immigration from eastern and southern Europe. Even Jews who qualified under the unfilled German quota faced a maze of bureaucratic red tape that made it nearly impossible to obtain entry visas.

In addition to fear of competition for scarce jobs, anti-Semitism within the United States created little sympathy for, and much agitation against, the immigration of even token numbers of Jewish refugees. Roosevelt, who worked closely with many Jewish advisers, was already the target of anti-Semitic remarks. Taking a low profile, he allowed the State Department bureaucracy to place impediments in the path of would-be immigrants seeking sanctuary.

Evidence surfaced in 1942 and 1943 that the Nazis planned to exterminate 10 million Jews with poison gas. Ultimately the Nazis would succeed in killing 6 million Jews. Yet even after the plans became known, British and American strategists rejected the idea of bombing the rail lines and facilities at the death camps. Such diversions from more important missions, Allied leaders argued, would delay victory. Congress rebuffed efforts to allow Jewish children into the United States. American officials even opposed granting temporary refuge to the few thousand European Jews who had slipped away from Nazi control.

In 1944 Roosevelt finally created a War Refugee Board to establish camps in neutral countries or American-occupied territory overseas. Eventually these centers helped save the lives of a few hundred thousand refugees. Only one thousand refugees were admitted directly into the United States. As one scholar has written, "Franklin Roosevelt's indifference to so momentous an historical event as the system-

General Dwight Eisenhower witnessing the tragedy of the Holocaust during a visit to the Bergen-Belsen concentration camp in 1945. *YIVO Institute for Jewish Research, Inc.*

atic annihilation of European Jewry emerges as the worst failure of his presidency."

Roosevelt's failure to champion the cause of Jewish refugees must be seen in the light of the strong American sentiment favoring less, not more, support for Jews. Anti-Semitism flourished in the United States during the 1920s and 1930s. An opinion poll taken in 1942 found most Americans believing that Jews posed nearly as great a threat to national security as Germany and Japan. Leaders of the American Jewish community anguished over the horrors of Nazi persecution, but feared a backlash among Gentile Americans if they spoke out forcefully. As a result, most Jewish organizations refrained from pressing politicians to rescue Holocaust victims. Instead, they called for creating a Jewish homeland in Palestine for those lucky enough to survive.

The Internment of Japanese-Americans

The Japanese-American community was singled out for special persecution during the war on the basis of race and ethnicity. Not only was Japan a wartime enemy, but the United States had a century-long tradition of anti-Asian agitation and hysteria. The surprise attack on

Pearl Harbor, followed by Japan's initial victories in the Pacific, intensified the racial distrust and spurred an exaggerated fear that Japanese-Americans would conspire to aid the enemy.

About 120,000 people of Japanese ancestry lived in the United States in 1941, 94,000 of them in California and most of the remainder elsewhere on the West Coast. The 47,000 who had arrived in the United States before Asian immigration was banned in 1924 were barred from citizenship, but their 70,000 children born in the United States automatically held citizenship. Although virtually no members of this community committed sabotage or illegal acts, their mere existence aroused public hysteria.

Journalists such as Westbrook Pegler demanded that every Japanese man, woman, and child be placed under armed guard. Congressman Leland Ford of California insisted that any "patriotic native born Japanese, if he wants to make his contribution, will submit himself to a concentration camp." General John DeWitt, head of the Western Defense Command, declared that Japanese of any citizenship were enemies. A popular song chortled, "We're Gonna Find a Feller Who Is Yeller and Beat Him Red, White and Blue."

In February 1942 President Roosevelt issued Executive Order No. 9066, followed by congressional legislation, declaring parts of the country "military areas" from which any or all persons could be barred. Nearly every politician in the West applauded the move. Although the regulations also targeted German and Italian aliens (most Italians were later exempted), *all* persons of Japanese ancestry, regardless of citizenship, were affected. In May, the War Relocation Authority ordered that 112,000 Japanese leave the West Coast in a matter of days. Ironically, in Hawaii, where residents of Japanese descent made up a large portion of the population and were vital to the economy, only a few individuals were interned.

Nearly all those affected by the forced relocation orders complied without protest, abandoning homes, farmland, and personal property to speculators. Bleak internment camps were hastily established in several western states. While not equivalent to incarceration in a Nazi death camp, this mass imprisonment marked the greatest violation of civil liberties in wartime America. Families lived in rudimentary dwellings and were compelled to do menial work under armed guard.

Federal courts rebuffed challenges to the government's policies. In 1942, police arrested Gordon Hirabayashi, a college student and native-born American of Japanese descent, for refusing to report to a control center and for violating a curfew. The next year the Supreme Court ruled in *Hirabayashi* v. *United States* that the government could impose curfew on racial grounds for military reasons.

In 1944, the high court addressed the policy of forced relocation in

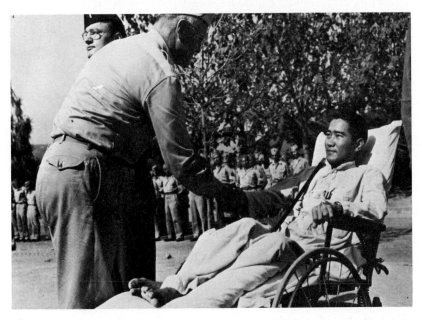

Two aspects of the Japanese-American experience during the Second World War: *top*, a sign at the entrance to the Manzanar relocation center, where many Japanese-American families from the Los Angeles area were forced to relocate; *bottom*, Howard Y. Miyake, a Japanese-American, receives a medal for his bravery during military service in the European theater. *Library of Congress/National Archives.*

deciding a case against Fred Korematsu, a citizen who had refused to leave a designated war zone on the West Coast. *Korematsu* v. *United States* affirmed government power to exclude individuals from any designated area on the basis of military necessity. The court majority claimed that race was irrelevant, because the government could, if it chose, exclude groups besides those of Japanese ancestry. In a powerful dissent, Justice Frank Murphy denounced the *Korematsu* verdict as a "legalization of racism" based on prejudice and unproven fears.

Despite the restrictive relocation orders and the degradation of life in the internment camps, Japanese-Americans contributed significantly to the American war effort. Many male internees volunteered for military duty and served in Europe, achieving recognition for bravery in action. Others worked in the Pacific theater as translators, interpreters, or intelligence officers. As the war progressed, some internees were permitted to leave relocation camps if they agreed to settle in eastern states. By the summer of 1945 all could leave. A fortunate few found that friends had protected their homes or businesses; the rest lost the work of a lifetime.

Despite growing recognition that internment had been a grave error, Congress and the courts hesitated to make formal redress. Congress offered a token payment in 1948, but it was not until the 1980s that several Japanese-Americans convicted of wartime offenses successfully reopened their cases. Files from the Justice Department and Federal Bureau of Investigation revealed that prosecutors had withheld evidence showing that no danger existed to justify relocation. Congress then made a formal apology and offered compensation of about $20,000 per surviving internee.

WARTIME POLITICS

As the wartime economic boom gradually erased memories of the Great Depression, many Americans felt that the reform programs of the New Deal no longer mattered. The 1942 congressional elections, in which 22 million fewer people voted than in 1940, proved disastrous for the Democrats. The Republicans gained nine Senate seats (for a total of forty-three out of ninety-six and forty-four House seats, giving them 209 votes, as compared to the Democrats' 222. Nearly half the remaining Democrats came from the party's conservative southern wing. The new Congress proceeded to kill a number of New Deal agencies, including the Work Projects Administration (successor to the Works Progress Administration) and the Civilian Conservation Corps.

The president's chief of mobilization, James F. Byrnes, gloated that the war had helped elbow the "radical boys out of the way [and] more will go." His prediction proved accurate as nervous Democratic party leaders blamed electoral losses on the left-leaning vice president, Henry A. Wallace. Unlike his more cautious superior, Wallace had actively promoted civil rights and called for postwar economic intervention by the government. Witnessing Roosevelt's obvious physical decline, the party bosses feared that Wallace might assume the presidency at Roosevelt's death or retirement.

Bowing to their complaints, and anxious to keep more conservative Democrats off the ticket, in mid-1944 Roosevelt agreed to replace Wallace with Senator Harry S Truman, a political moderate from Missouri. Truman had gained fame for heading an investigation of profiteering by defense contractors. Committed New Dealers, like the librarian of Congress, Archibald MacLeish, bemoaned the "collapse of liberal leadership."

The Republicans in 1944 nominated New York Governor Thomas E. Dewey for president and Governor John Bricker of Ohio as his running mate. Despite Dewey's charge that the Democrats were "soft on communism" and prisoners of organized labor, he confounded conservatives by accepting many of Roosevelt's innovations and his war aims.

Roosevelt remained the people's choice, aided in part by Dewey's ineffective campaign style and in part by a big push from organized labor, which created the first political action committee, or PAC, to raise campaign funds. Roosevelt easily won a fourth term, though by his smallest majority (53.4 percent). The party lines in Congress remained largely unchanged.

Despite the political challenges and his own concentration on winning the war, Roosevelt made some effort in his last years to impart a vision of postwar reform. In his 1944 State of the Union address he called for drafting a "second Bill of Rights under which a new basis of security and prosperity can be established for all." He described a government commitment to provide jobs, housing, education, and health and retirement insurance for all Americans. The original Bill of Rights had secured liberties by limiting the power of government. A new bill of rights, according to Roosevelt, would expand government power to pursue social and economic justice.

In a draft speech dictated on April 11, 1945, as victory in Europe loomed, Roosevelt appealed to the American people to "conquer the fears, the ignorance and the greed" that made the horror of world war possible. "The only limit to our realization of tomorrow," he declared, "will be our doubts of today. Let us move forward with strong and active faith." But the next day, April 12, the president died of a cerebral hemorrhage. Roosevelt's passing, as much as the imminent victory over the Axis forces, marked the threshold of the postwar era.

CONCLUSION

The Roosevelt years, stretching from the Great Depression to the last months of the Second World War, brought vast changes to the nation and to its role in the world arena. Those years molded the postwar world in fundamental ways that continue to affect us today.

Both the depression and the war prompted rapid growth in the federal government's size and scope of action. For the first time in the nation's history, the U.S. government had a direct and frequent effect on the daily lives of ordinary citizens. The government managed the economy to an unprecedented degree; it began to provide relief to the needy and the elderly; it funded scientific research that changed the face of American industry and made possible the high-tech society we now inhabit.

The Roosevelt years put Americans on the move, literally as well as figuratively. During the war, millions of rural or small-town Americans packed their bags and headed to the major industrial cities. African-Americans left the rural South in huge numbers, and many of them made their new homes in the North and West. The *bracero* program contributed to a substantial influx of Mexican farm and railroad workers. The Sunbelt and the West Coast began their rise to prominence.

For women, the war meant a chance to take jobs traditionally reserved for men—a first step toward the revolution in women's lives that is still occurring. For ethnic minorities, on the other hand, the depression and the war years were times of mingled hope, fear, and disappointment. The wartime internment of Japanese-Americans left a blot on the nation's record that no later compensation could remove. The government's failure to help European Jews escape the Holocaust would seem almost incomprehensible to later generations. Yet the Roosevelt era also brought a rising concern for the rights of minorities and new hopes that protest could lead to improvement—crucial ingredients for the civil rights movement of the postwar years.

Finally, as a direct consequence of the war, the United States emerged in 1945 as the world's leading military and economic power. Europe was devastated. The Soviet Union, though a mighty wartime ally and future competitor, had suffered terrible losses. In the postwar world, America's history would be shaped by its demanding new role as a superpower and by the conflicting ideas of how that role should be played. ■

FURTHER READING

On the depression and New Deal, see: Michael A. Bernstein, *The Great Depression: Delayed Recovery and Economic Change in America, 1929–39* (1988); Paul K. Conkin, *The New Deal*, 2nd ed. (1975); William E. Leuchtenburg, *Franklin D. Roosevelt and the New Deal* (1963); Kenneth S. Davis, *FDR: The New Deal Years, 1933–37* (1986); Alan Brinkley, *Voices of Protest: Huey Long, Father Coughlin, and the Great Depression* (1982); Harvard Sitkoff, *A New Deal for Blacks* (1978); Susan Ware, *Holding Their Own: American Women in the 1930s* (1982); Steven Fraser, *Labor Will Rule: Sidney Hillman and the Rise of American Labor* (1991). On American society during the Second World War, see: John Blum, *V Was for Victory: Politics and American Culture During World War II* (1976); Karen Anderson, *Wartime Women* (1981); Susan Hartman, *The Homefront and Beyond* (1980); Peter Irons, *Justice at War: The Story of the Japanese-American Internment Cases* (1982). On foreign policy, see: Robert Dallek, *Franklin D. Roosevelt and American Foreign Policy* (1979); David Wyman, *The Abandonment of the Jews: America and the Holocaust, 1941–45* (1984); John Dower, *War Without Mercy: Race and Power in the Pacific War* (1986); Martin J. Sherwin, *A World Destroyed: The Atomic Bomb and the Grand Alliance* (1975); William Leuchtenburg, *In the Shadow of FDR: From Harry Truman to Ronald Reagan* (1983).

2

From War to a Troubled Peace: Politics and Society, 1945–1950

On April 12, 1945, Harry S Truman sat with several congressional friends in the office of House Speaker Sam Rayburn. After chairing a boring Senate debate on a water treaty, the vice president savored a stiff bourbon. A phone call from presidential press secretary Steve Early abruptly summoned him to the White House. There, Eleanor Roosevelt delivered the somber news: "Harry, the president is dead." Truman asked if there was anything he could do for her. "Is there anything we can do for you?" she replied; "you are the one in trouble now."

A former haberdasher, regarded by many as a political nobody, the new president was suddenly in charge of concluding the world war and shaping a peace. "Trouble" was indeed an apt word—perhaps too mild a word—for what faced him. Although Germany was on the verge of surrender, Truman faced the thorny problem of relations with the Soviet Union, a wartime ally that was fast becoming a threatening competitor. Within a few months, Truman also had to decide whether to use the atomic bomb on Japan. Heading the most powerful nation in the postwar world, Truman found his every choice greatly magnified in importance. Ever since, historians have debated whether the Cold War and the atomic age would have been different if Roosevelt rather than Truman had made the crucial decisions.

In domestic matters, Truman presided over an economy and society that rushed headlong into the new era. After brief postwar stumbles, including some bitter strikes, the economy continued its expansion, making the Great Depression a receding memory. Meanwhile, the postwar consumer society was born, with brand-new suburban homes, more cars on the road, more appliances, and the beginning of a national love affair with television.

At the same time, however, an anti-Communist hysteria erupted onto the national scene. Fueled by legitimate worries about the Soviet Union as well as by political opportunism, the Red Scare distorted national politics from the end of the world war well into the 1950s. It helped to frustrate attempts by progressives—including, to some degree, Truman himself—to expand the social reforms of the New Deal. Minorities did make progress in establishing their civil rights, but only by enduring a good deal of hostility and violence.

Truman is often remembered as a feisty and irreverent folk hero, the president who posted the famous sign on his desk, "The Buck Stops Here." This image obscures the fact that Truman was not a popular president. In the years of transition from world war to peace, the country's political and social divisions ran deep.

TRUMAN TAKES CHARGE

Harry S Truman came from a modest farming family near Independence, Missouri. As a young man he worked beside his father in the fields and as a bank clerk. When the United States entered the First World War in 1917, Truman, then thirty-three, enlisted in the National Guard and commanded an artillery battery in Europe. At the end of his service he returned to Missouri, married Bess Wallace, and opened a clothing store in Kansas City. When the business failed, he turned to politics.

In the 1920s and early 1930s, Truman served as an elected judge in Jackson County, on the fringe of the area controlled by "Boss" Tom Pendergast's Kansas City political machine. Working in the shadow of corruption, Truman nevertheless earned a reputation as an honest and efficient administrator. In 1934, aided by Roosevelt's popularity as president, he won election to the U.S. Senate as a Democrat.

Truman's early social outlook reflected the racism prevalent in the midwestern border region. "I think one man is just as good as another," the twenty-seven-year-old wrote his future wife, "so long as he's honest and decent and not a nigger or a Chinaman." He also complained that liberal immigration laws had allowed "Japs," "bohunks," and "Rooshans" to contaminate the white man's country. As he matured, Truman expressed greater toleration for ethnic minorities. After taking up his Senate seat in Washington, he worked to convince more liberal Democrats that he supported civil rights and liberties.

Although the freshman senator described himself as an enthusiastic supporter of Roosevelt, the president ignored Truman during the 1930s. After waiting months for his first meeting with Roosevelt, Truman was ushered in and out in less than seven minutes. Roosevelt's staff considered Truman a toady of the Pendergast machine. By 1940, Truman was complaining that the president treated him like an office boy and provided little federal patronage for Missouri. Relations were so strained that the senator spoke against a third term for Roosevelt, who in turn tried to ease Truman out of the Senate by offering him an appointment to the Interstate Commerce Commission. When Truman surmounted the pressure to leave his Senate post and won re-election, partly through the support of urban blacks, his relations with the White House worsened.

During the Second World War, Truman won praise for chairing a Senate committee that exposed price gouging in defense programs. By the 1944 Democratic nominating convention, he emerged as a leading vice-presidential candidate. Roosevelt's deteriorating health worried the competing factions among the Democratic party leadership. Conservative party barons opposed renominating as Roosevelt's running mate the very liberal incumbent, Henry A. Wallace, favoring instead James F. Byrnes. The third alternative, Truman, represented the centrist elements of the Democratic party. After much debate, the power brokers settled on Truman in a deal dubbed the "Missouri compromise."

During the three months in which they served together as president and vice president in 1945, Roosevelt and Truman had little contact. Outside of cabinet meetings, Roosevelt spoke only twice with Truman and told him little about military, diplomatic, or political developments. Truman knew nothing of what transpired in Roosevelt's meetings with Churchill and Stalin. He was, one scholar surmised, "too insignificant a subaltern to be trusted with secrets of state." When Truman became president, Secretary of War Henry Stimson took him aside after the first cabinet meeting to brief him on the Manhattan Project. The new president had known nothing about the development of the atomic bomb, now close to the testing stage, and Stimson seemed reluctant to say more for several weeks.

Truman quickly understood that as vice president he had been kept in the dark on matters vital to national security, and as president he was surrounded by better-informed men chary with their information. In consequence, he grew distrustful of most of the Roosevelt cabinet he had inherited. There was not a "man on the list who would talk frankly," he later recalled. "The honest ones were afraid and the others wanted to fool me."

Within the first four months of his administration Truman established his own chain of command, firing or easing out nearly all the cabinet members who had been close to Roosevelt. The profile of his appointees differed considerably from that of Roosevelt's advisers. In his first two years in office, Truman appointed forty-nine bankers, financiers, and industrialists, thirty-one career military men, and seventeen business lawyers to fill the top one hundred twenty-five federal job vacancies. Journalist Howard K. Smith wrote that power in the United States had shifted from Washington to "some place equidistant between Wall Street and West Point." Among those fired was Henry Wallace, dismissed as secretary of commerce after a public dispute with Truman about how to deal with the Soviet Union.

With the departure of Roosevelt's New Dealers, the liberal and progressive elements in Washington complained that dedicated reformers were being tossed out in favor of small-minded boosters of private interest. Journalist I. F. Stone summed up the opinion of many Democratic progressives when he lamented the replacement of New Dealers by the "kind of men one was accustomed to meet in county courthouses . . . big-bellied, good-natured guys who knew a lot of dirty jokes, spent as little time in their offices as possible, saw Washington as a chance to make useful 'contacts,' and were anxious to get what they could for themselves out of the experience."

Even though Truman proposed extensions of New Deal reforms, progressives considered him a lukewarm liberal and never gave him the support that Roosevelt had enjoyed. Nor was he accepted by the political right, which wanted to eliminate surviving New Deal programs. Politically he wobbled on a tightrope between the right and left, and often it seemed that both sides were shaking the rope to make him tumble.

Rising Soviet-American Conflict

As British, American, and Soviet armies closed in on Berlin in April 1945, President Truman had to respond almost instantaneously to problems he knew little about. Determined to appear a forceful leader, he tended to make snap judgments. Hours after taking office, he boasted that, unlike his predecessor, he would "stand up to the Russians," implying that Roosevelt had been too easy on Josef Stalin, the Soviet dictator.

The president's suspicion of Soviet goals was fueled by talks with the American ambassador to the Soviet Union, Averell Harriman, as well as with Secretary of the Navy James Forrestal, Chief of Staff Admiral William Leahy, and Undersecretary of State Joseph Grew. All had urged Roosevelt to demand a larger role for non-Communists in the government the Soviets had installed in Poland. Their advice appealed to Truman, partly because the positions they recommended gave him an opportunity to distinguish himself from his predecessor.

Ambassador Harriman flew to Washington from Moscow to explain his fear that Stalin was breaking the agreements made at Yalta. He described Soviet actions as a "barbarian invasion of Europe" and claimed that, had Roosevelt lived, he would have become tougher with Stalin. Communism, he told Truman, confronted America with "ideological warfare just as vigorous and dangerous as Fascism or Nazism." Truman, who knew little about the wartime deals, believed Harriman's claim that Stalin considered compromise a sign of weakness. After all, had not appeasement encouraged Hitler?

On April 23, 1945, the President used "words of one syllable" to accuse visiting Soviet Foreign Minister V. M. Molotov of violating promises made at Yalta regarding free elections in Poland. When Molotov disputed this interpretation and complained about Truman's harsh language, the president allegedly retorted, "Carry out your agreements and you won't get talked to like that." Truman boasted of giving Molotov the "straight one-two to the jaw," but in private wondered aloud if he had done right.

In fact, Truman's tough words had little effect on Soviet policy in Poland or elsewhere. Responding to the president's charges of treaty violations, Stalin offered a blunt interpretation of the Yalta accords: "Poland borders with the Soviet Union [which] cannot be said of Great Britain or the United States." Moscow claimed no right to interfere in Belgium or Greece, where the Western allies had imposed governments of their choosing. Stalin made it clear that maintaining a security zone in Eastern Europe was more important than maintaining good relations with his wartime allies.

When Churchill conveyed to Stalin in mid-1945 his fears of an "iron fence" dividing Europe, Stalin angrily dismissed the notion as a fairy tale. But Truman and Churchill were not fooled. Soviet forces had installed puppet regimes in Poland, Rumania, and Bulgaria. Later they used local Communists to take control of Hungary, in 1947, and Czechoslovakia, in 1948.

Stalin's fear of a revived Germany and capitalist encirclement encouraged his ironclad domination of Eastern Europe. Because of longstanding Eastern European distrust of Russia, probably nothing less than total Soviet control could have kept the region in Moscow's sphere. The harsh imposition of Communist control and the large number of Soviet troops maintained in Eastern Europe appalled and frightened Western leaders. Ironically, Stalin's brutal exercise of power aroused the very hostility he feared from the capitalist West.

By the time of Germany's formal surrender on May 8, 1945, Soviet troops occupied Berlin. The victorious Allies had agreed to partition Germany into occupation zones but had not addressed the mechanisms of interzonal cooperation or the manner of extracting reparations from Germany. The Polish-German border problem sparked additional dissent. The Soviets decided to annex a swath of Polish territory along the Russian border and to compensate Poland by grafting onto it part of eastern Germany. The swap displaced millions of ethnic Germans and moved Soviet power closer to central Europe, a chilling prospect to British and American leaders.

Potsdam: The Last Allied Summit

As the disputes over postwar arrangements in Europe raged on, the war continued against Japan. Although American air and naval forces pounded Japan almost at will—the fire bombing of Tokyo in March 1945 killed nearly 100,000 civilians—the marines and army troops suffered tens of thousands of casualties as they assaulted island outposts such as Iwo Jima and Okinawa. Suicide (*kamikaze*) plane attacks proved especially damaging to American forces. Uncertain whether the Soviets would enter the war, and not knowing if the still experimental atomic bomb would work, Truman approved a plan to invade Japan on November 1, 1945.

Truman, Churchill, and Stalin held a summit conference in mid-July in Potsdam, a once opulent suburb of bombed-out Berlin. Amid the rubble of the Thousand Year Reich, the Big Three spent most of their time arguing over German boundaries and reparations, the makeup of the Polish and Rumanian regimes, and the timing of Russia's entry into the Pacific war.

The Allied leaders agreed on little. Although Churchill and Truman accepted the Polish-German boundary changes already made by Stalin, they refused to allow the Soviets access to industrial resources in the British and American occupation zones in western Germany. Stalin charged that this refusal to share resources violated earlier promises and wondered if American and British officials intended to rebuild western Germany as an anti-Soviet state.

Stalin indicated that the Soviet Union would join the campaign against Japan by August 15. Although American military planners still believed that Soviet assistance would help reduce American casualties, Truman worried about the cost of letting Moscow become involved in the Pacific war. Specifically, he feared Soviet support for the Chinese Communists and Stalin's demand for an occupation zone in Japan.

The Decision to Use the Atomic Bomb

On July 16, 1945, in the course of the inconclusive discussions at Potsdam, Truman received a coded message that an atomic bomb had been tested successfully in New Mexico. The president's aides described him as excited and cheered by the prospect of having a weapon that might make Soviet help unnecessary in the war against Japan. Like Roosevelt before him, Truman maintained the policy of not telling Stalin about the atomic bomb. Instead, he casually mentioned the discovery of a new weapon of great power. Stalin, who knew of the Manhattan Project through espionage and had already ordered Soviet scientists to construct a similar weapon, did not press for details, leaving Truman incorrectly thinking that he had "fooled Mr. Russia." At the end of the conference, without inviting the Soviets to join in, the British and American governments issued the Potsdam Declaration, an ultimatum warning Japan to surrender at once or face utter destruction.

Truman ordered that the two available atomic bombs, code-named Fat Man and Little Boy, be used as soon as possible. On August 6 a B-29 bomber named *Enola Gay*, for the pilot's mother, flying from the island of Tinian, dropped the first bomb on Hiroshima, Japan. Two days later, as promised, the Soviets declared war and attacked the

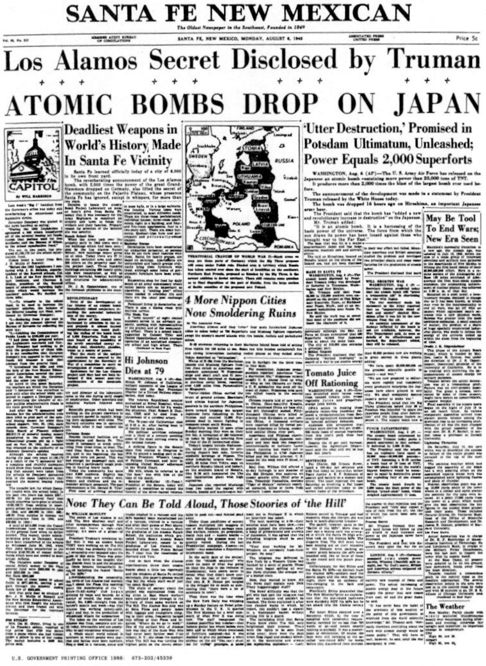

SANTA FE NEW MEXICAN

The Oldest Newspaper in the Southwest, Founded in 1849

SANTA FE, NEW MEXICO, MONDAY, AUGUST 6, 1945 — Price 5c

Los Alamos Secret Disclosed by Truman

ATOMIC BOMBS DROP ON JAPAN

Deadliest Weapons in World's History Made In Santa Fe Vicinity

'Utter Destruction,' Promised in Potsdam Ultimatum, Unleashed; Power Equals 2,000 Superforts

WASHINGTON, Aug. 6 (AP)—The U. S. Army Air Force has released on the Japanese an atomic bomb containing more power than 20,000 tons of TNT.

It produces more than 2,000 times the blast of the largest bomb ever used before.

The announcement of the development was made in a statement by President Truman released by the White House today.

The bomb was dropped 16 hours ago on Hiroshima, an important Japanese army base.

May Be Tool To End Wars; New Era Seen

4 More Nippon Cities Now Smoldering Ruins

Hi Johnson Dies at 79

Tomato Juice Off Rationing

Now They Can Be Told Aloud, Those Stoories of 'the Hill'

The Weather

U.S. GOVERNMENT PRINTING OFFICE 1986: 673-202/45339

The atomic era begins with a war headline. *Los Alamos National Laboratory.*

Japanese in Manchuria. On August 9 a second bomb obliterated the city of Nagasaki. Nearly 200,000 Japanese civilians died in the two attacks, with radiation sickness later claiming additional lives. On August 10, Tokyo sued for unconditional peace, asking only that Hirohito be allowed to continue as nominal emperor. On August 14 Truman agreed, placing Japan and its emperor under the rule of occupation commander General Douglas MacArthur.

Peace brought an outpouring of joy in both capitals. Fujiyama Aiichiro, a business executive and a postwar foreign minister, recalled that once it was learned that the occupying force would be the United States, not the Soviet Union, his colleagues broke out bottles of champagne and toasted the coming of a new era of prosperity.

Publicly, Truman never admitted doubts about the decision to use the atomic bomb. He thanked God for giving him a weapon that saved "thousands and thousands of American lives" and "shortened the agony of war." Almost immediately, however, questions arose about Truman's decision. Some scientists thought a demonstration of the bomb's power in unoccupied territory might have convinced the Japanese to surrender. They questioned Truman's prediction that an invasion would have caused half a million American casualties, especially because intelligence estimates had predicted only 50,000. Truman later ridiculed such "crybaby" scientists who wanted to give Japan a clear warning of the bomb's potential before dropping it on Japanese cities.

American use of the bomb against Japan also raised the question of racism. Would American decision makers have used such a weapon against non-Asians? After all, the president had declared in private, "When you have to deal with a beast, you have to treat him like a beast." Some prominent Americans had called for "gutting the heart of Japan with fire" and "sterilizing every damn one of them so that in a generation there would be no more Japs." As racist as these remarks may sound, historians point out that European cities—Dresden, Germany, in particular—also suffered mass civilian casualties during wartime bombing.

Because Japan had already extended peace feelers, some critics thought the real motive for the atomic attack on Japan was to force a change in Soviet behavior in Europe and speed victory in the Pacific so as to keep Russian forces out of China and Japan. Within days of Japan's surrender, Soviet leaders complained that Truman sought to intimidate Moscow through "atomic diplomacy." Remarks by Truman and his staff suggested that they did consider the Soviet Union when deciding to use the bomb. Secretary of State James F. Byrnes felt that a mistake had been made in allowing the Russians to become so powerful. He stressed the importance of using the bombs not simply to defeat Japan, but to do so in a manner that excluded Moscow from sharing in postwar decisions about Japan. Ambassador Harriman commented that Hitler's greatest crime was the legacy of Soviet control of Eastern Europe. The bomb, therefore, was regarded as a master card in dealing with Russia and Japan.

Truman had originally believed that Soviet entry into the Pacific war would be the key to defeating Japan. When Stalin, at the beginning of the Potsdam meeting, promised to enter the war by August 15, Truman told his wife that Soviet help would end the war a year sooner; "think of the kids who won't be killed." But when he learned of the successful atomic test in New Mexico, the president changed his tune. On July 18 he wrote that the "Japs will fold up before Russia comes in; I am sure they will when Manhattan [the atomic bomb] appears over their homeland."

If Truman believed the Russians would enter the war soon and Japan would collapse immediately thereafter, his own logic should have told him that the atomic bomb could shorten the war by only a few days. In that light, the atomic attack seems less crucial to saving American lives than to ending the war before Soviet forces could move far into China or Japan.

But even without his growing suspicion of Stalin, Truman might have made the same decision to use the bomb. The United States had spent several billion dollars constructing the weapon. Military and civilian decision makers had always planned to use it as soon as possible. With the exception of a handful of scientists, few top leaders gave any serious thought to *not* utilizing the bomb. By 1945 the wartime destruction of cities and civilians had become so commonplace that few moral objections were raised.

The Cold War Begins

Victory over Japan confirmed the United States' place as the world's leading economic and military power. With only 6 percent of the world's population, it produced over half of the world's goods and controlled a majority of the world's wealth. Yet it found no easy way to halt the division of Europe by the "iron fence" or to stabilize much of Asia. When British, Soviet, and American foreign ministers met in London in September 1945, they argued bitterly about who threatened whom. When the Western powers demanded relaxation of Soviet control in Eastern Europe, Moscow responded by blasting "capitalist encirclement" and atomic blackmail. The Cold War that followed from these mutual suspicions dominated world politics for two generations thereafter.

The retiring secretary of war, Henry Stimson, mourned the breakup of the Grand Alliance. In September 1945 he reversed his earlier position and cautioned Truman against the temptation to use the United States' sole possession of the bomb as a means of forcing changes in Soviet policy. Flaunting the weapon would only magnify Stalin's suspicion of American motives, he warned.

It is debatable whether the Cold War would have been appreciably mitigated if Truman had followed Stimson's advice to confer with Stalin about controlling the atomic bomb and compromising in Europe. The security policies of Washington and Moscow were already on a collision course in several major areas of contention. Stalin's determination to forge an inviolable security sphere around the Soviet Union led, inevitably, to his policy of dominating Eastern Europe and subjugating neighboring states. American leaders, for their part, insisted on breaking down international trade barriers and rebuilding the defeated Axis nations, policies that terrified the Kremlin. Washington often confused Moscow's habitual rhetoric about spreading communism with Stalin's somewhat justifiably defensive stance. In this atmosphere of distrust, Americans often blamed the Soviet Union for events over which it had only slight control.

Moreover, like many of his compatriots, President Truman shared the self-satisfied vision articulated by Henry Luce, the publisher of

Time and *Life,* in 1945. The "American experience," Luce wrote, "is the key to the future. America must be the elder brother of the nations in the brotherhood of man." The basic idea that the United States had a special mission in the world arena was not a new one. Now, however, the nation held a uniquely powerful position. To the Soviets—and to other critics of United States policy in the postwar years—an attitude of the sort expressed by Luce smacked of dangerous arrogance. In the years to come, America's desire to act as an "elder brother" would often provoke hostility rather than gratitude.

Chapter 3 will trace the foreign-policy dimensions of the Cold War in the Truman years, detailing the steps that led to a new armed conflict in Korea. Even before American troops went to Korea, however, the Cold War had a deep impact on the lives of American citizens. As we will see later in this chapter, the fear of the Soviet Union gave rise to an anti-Communist movement, a "Red Scare," that sent reverberations through all segments of society.

TRANSITION TO PEACE

At first, in the immediate aftermath of the war, Americans were glad to turn their attention to domestic matters. They cared less about the budding conflict with the Soviet Union than about demobilizing the 12 million GIs, finding them jobs and homes. Young people caught up in the war were eager to return to peacetime jobs and raise families. A popular song, 'Gotta Make Up for Lost Time," captured the sentiment. Sharing these concerns, and eager to demonstrate commitment to Roosevelt's legacy, President Truman presented Congress with a twenty-one-point program calling for a higher minimum wage, federal housing support, a permanent Fair Employment Practices Commission, expanded Social Security benefits, new regional development projects modeled on the Tennessee Valley Authority, and action on Roosevelt's Economic Bill of Rights, which championed full employment, educational support, and health insurance. Republicans dismissed these proposals as a "fly-specked dish of New Deal hash," and Congress failed to act on most of them.

With such disagreement prevailing in Washington, the nation's transition to peace inevitably involved many battles over political and economic issues. Overall, however, the transition took place quickly. After an initial period of high unemployment and inflation, the economy continued to grow. With money in their pockets, Americans rushed to new homes in suburbia, started having children in record numbers, and went on a spree of consumer buying, snapping up home appliances, automobiles, and the newfangled electronic gadgets called televisions.

The Postwar Economy

The basics of demobilization—mustering out the GIs—proved relatively easy. Service personnel received points for time served, and those with the most points were discharged first. In less than two years, the number of Americans in uniform fell by 90 percent.

But the demobilized GIs returned to an economy where the booming production of war goods had ceased. Even before the war ended, mass layoffs had begun in aircraft plants and other key wartime industries. Within a few days of Japan's surrender, nearly 2 million more were out of work. With vivid memories of the Great Depression, many Americans feared a return of widespread unemployment.

Nevertheless, returning servicemen had less difficulty in finding jobs than many experts predicted. A significant number of ex-servicemen replaced women workers, for the industrial layoffs included about 3 million women. Labor unions and factory owners followed the suggestion of a southern senator who called on Congress to force "wives and mothers back to the kitchen." Both private employers and the civil service gave veterans preference over other job applicants. Even though 75 percent of women who wished to continue to work eventually found postwar employment, they had to settle for clerical, sales, and light manufacturing work rather than more lucrative skilled factory labor. Typically, wages declined from about $50 to $37 per week for white women, and to half that for black women. Men experienced a far smaller drop. Still, in 1950, nearly one-third of all women held paying jobs, up from 27 percent before the war.

The huge savings pool of nearly $140 billion that had accumulated since 1941 cushioned the transition to a peacetime economy but raised inflationary pressures. Consumers rushed to buy the cars, appliances, clothes, food, and housing that had been unavailable since 1942. Few people favored rationing or talk of deferring their wants for patriotic reasons.

The long postwar upswing in consumerism had begun—the transformation of America into what we now call a consumer society. Despite some plans for peacetime reconversion, federal agencies had not counted on this intensity of market pressure. For example, consumers thronged to buy the small number of new cars, even though these were built from prewar designs.

In general, consumers demanded a relaxation of production limits but the retention of price controls. Manufacturers, on the other hand, wanted to produce more automobiles and other consumer goods—

and expected the government to sell off war plants at bargain rates— but argued for the elimination of price ceilings. Workers, who had taken a wartime no-strike pledge and accepted wage controls, now clamored for steep wage hikes to allow them to catch up to inflation and buy consumer goods. In short, each group wanted the government to maximize its own opportunity while regulating everyone else. Truman tried to appease these conflicting demands by alternately lifting and reimposing economic controls.

In 1946 the president and Congress battled over the preservation of the Office of Price Administration (OPA), the wartime agency that regulated prices. In June Congress nominally extended the OPA but stripped it of most of its enforcement power. Charging that Congress had made him responsible for price control but had deprived him of the means to achieve it, Truman vetoed the bill. Therefore OPA lapsed into oblivion on July 1, 1946. That month, the cost of living jumped 6 percent. Over the next year, prices rose an additional 24 percent. Shortages stimulated a thriving black market in which merchants held back goods unless consumers agreed to pay a premium under the table.

Despite these pressures, the American economy performed well during the Truman years. The steep inflation of 1946 to 1947 leveled off, to reappear only briefly early in the Korean War, and the gross national product rose an average of 4 percent annually. Meanwhile, the immediate postwar surge in unemployment proved transitory, and the specter of massive unemployment never materialized. The number of Americans with jobs increased from a wartime high of 53 million to 60 million in 1948 and 64 million by 1952.

With modest success, Truman's more Keynesian economic advisers tried to commit the federal government to a policy of full employment, so that everyone "able to work and seeking work" would find a job. A Full Employment Bill, introduced in Congress in 1945, would have empowered the president to take actions to stimulate the economy in times of recession. However, by the time Congress passed an amended version known as the Employment Act of 1946, the bill had been watered down so that it merely supported the principle of creating jobs. The act did create a Council of Economic Advisers to the president and required that the president make an annual economic report to Congress.

Leon Keyserling, Truman's most influential economic adviser, promoted the concept of "growth Keynesianism." Abandoning more radical ideas about central economic planning, regulation, and wealth redistribution, Keyserling believed that wealth could be distributed best by the private sector through consumer-driven prosperity. Government should create demand—and thus jobs—by pumping more spending power into the economy through tax, welfare, and spending policies. As one leading economist put it, "consumption is the frontier of the future." By 1949 these economists were promoting new defense spending as a key to growth.

Labor Troubles and Party Politics

During 1946 a wave of strikes in the automobile, electrical, coal, and transportation industries suggested that the economy was in more serious trouble than was really the case. At General Motors, for example, seeing huge corporate profits and tiny wage increases, the workers went on strike for three months. They had to settle for about half the wage increase they had demanded, and they lost their bid to gain a measure of control over GM management.

In the coal and railroad industries the government still retained its wartime authority. When the unions refused to accept arbitrated settlements, Truman became enraged. At one point he ordered the temporary seizure of coal mines and spoke of "hanging a few traitors" to make "our own country safe for democracy." The president sought legislation to draft striking rail workers into the armed forces, despite Attorney General Tom Clark's doubt about the constitutional basis for such action. Even without such a law, Truman forced an end to the rail strike, causing labor leaders to denounce him as the foremost strikebreaker in America.

By the fall of 1946, the wave of strikes, along with price inflation, shortages of consumer goods, and the perception of Truman as a man out of his depth, eroded support for the Democratic party. Only 32 percent of survey respondents approved of the president's performance. Fearful of a rout in the congressional elections, Robert Hannegan, head of the Democratic National Committee, urged the president not to campaign on behalf of congressional candidates.

In the November election, the Republican party picked up eleven Senate and fifty-six House seats to hold a majority in both houses of Congress for the first time since 1930. Senator Robert Taft, nicknamed "Mr. Republican," emerged as the informal head of his party in Congress. Long critical of New Deal domestic and foreign programs, Taft denounced the "corrupting idea that we can legislate prosperity, legislate equality, legislate opportunity." In the past, he claimed, opportunity and equality came by way of "free Americans freely working out their destiny. . . . That is the only way they can continue to come in any genuine sense."

Despite their new control of Congress and Taft's clear expression of conservative ideology, the Republicans had only modest success in unraveling the New Deal legacy. They did, however, effect significant changes in labor law. Moves to limit the right to strike and to abolish the closed shop—an arrangement that compelled workers to join unions—had begun during the Second World War. Building on such antilabor sentiment, Senator Taft and New Jersey Republican Congressman Fred A. Hartley introduced a law to curb union power. This Taft-Hartley Act of 1947, which passed over Truman's veto, outlawed the closed shop, barred secondary boycotts, made unions liable for a variety of monetary damages, established procedures for decertification elections, and permitted the president to impose an eighty-day cooling-off period in labor disputes during which unions could not strike. Taft-Hartley also required union officials to sign an anti-Communist affidavit. This requirement stirred up bitter internal feuding within labor ranks and encouraged public fears that left-wing labor activists were disloyal.

The law bolstered conservative labor leaders and discouraged new organizing drives, especially in the largely nonunion South, though it did not destroy existing unions that followed its provisions. The greatest impact of the Taft-Hartley Act was felt in the Sunbelt states of the South and West, where legislatures responded to business lobbying by passing right-to-work laws that barred making union membership a requirement for employment. To get out of union contracts, many labor-intensive industries, such as textiles, began to relocate to the Sunbelt.

The GI Bill and Education

Prodded by President Roosevelt and the American Legion (which counted nearly half the House and Senate, Harry Truman, and twenty-six governors among its members), Congress had agreed in 1944 to establish benefits for returning soldiers. The legislators acted out of mixed motives. Fearing wild behavior among GIs, some proposed creating "demilitarization centers" where the violent instincts fostered by war could be tamed. Rumors circulated that the Marine Corps had set aside remote Pacific islands on which members of "killer battalions" would be held for life. Newspapers railed against dumping trained killers on American society. Fortunately, most politicians acknowledged that the nation owed a debt to its soldiers.

The Servicemen's Readjustment Act of 1944, or the GI Bill, as nearly everyone called it, benefited millions of veterans and their families. Because its provisions applied to all who served during the war (although women did not receive full benefits), the bill had a massive impact. The program provided veterans with temporary unemployment benefits, hiring preferences in civil service jobs, new hospitals and health benefits, low-interest loans to start businesses and purchase homes, and tuition and living stipends for college and vocational education.

Demobilized soldiers who could not find work received $20 per week—more than equivalent to the minimum wage of 40 cents per hour—for up to a year. This program alone paid out nearly $4 billion during the postwar years. Those pursuing a college education received $110 a month, plus an allowance for dependents and payment of tuition, fees, and books.

Presidents of elite private universities expressed grave misgivings about subsidizing veterans. They complained that paying men to attend college would undermine merit selection and produce vocationally oriented students uninterested in pure learning. They declined to mention that before 1945 few people of moderate means could attend college, no matter how much they valued education.

The flow of veterans into both public and private universities created a far more democratic system of higher education—a change with far-reaching social consequences. Over 2 million students, or half of the total male enrollment at institutions of higher learning, attended college on the GI Bill. Nearly half of the veterans were married, which forced colleges to drop their prohibitions against enrollment of married students. Couples were housed in Quonset huts, trailers, and converted fraternity houses. Diapers hung everywhere, replacing the usual college insignia. As the mass demand for higher education grew, state legislatures funded public universities more generously than before the war. Federal and state dollars built new libraries, classrooms, dormitories, and laboratories.

In addition to those attending college, nearly 6 million men went to technical and vocational schools on the GI Bill. By 1947, the total outlay for veterans' education had reached $2.25 billion, and that was just a beginning. When the program ended in 1956, the Veterans Administration (VA) had spent about $14 billion on schooling—compared to nothing before the war. The skills acquired by this generation boosted job mobility and incomes, allowing the government to recoup much of its outlay through higher income taxes.

Because a comparatively small number of women had served in uniform, women received few direct educational benefits. Although more women attended college after the war than before, they were steered away from careers that would place them in competition with men. Active sex discrimination and quotas led to a decline in female enrollment in law, business, and medical schools. Harvard Business School, for example, did not admit women until 1963. The writer Fannie Hurst lamented that in the wake of the war, a "sleeping sickness" had spread among the nation's women: "They are retrogressing into . . . that thing known as The Home."

Suburbia and the Baby Boom

During the Truman years, women and men flocked to homes in suburbia. Americans had begun leaving cities in the nineteenth century, but only after 1945 could the United States begin to be called a sub-

GEOGRAPHIC DISTRIBUTION OF UNITED STATES POPULATION, 1930–1970 (IN PERCENTAGES)

Year	Central Cities	Suburbs	Rural Areas and Small Towns
1930	31.8	18.0	50.2
1940	31.6	19.5	48.9
1950	32.3	23.8	43.9
1960	32.6	30.7	36.7
1970	31.4	37.6	31.0

Source: Adapted from U.S. Bureau of the Census, *Decennial Censuses, 1930–1970* (Washington, D.C.: U.S. Government Printing Office).

urban nation. Between 1940 and 1970, the proportion of suburban dwellers increased from 19.5 to 37.6 percent (see table).

Housing construction had virtually stopped during the depression and Second World War. Because of this fifteen-year lapse, and the rising birth rate during the war, returning GIs, former war workers, and new families faced a severe housing shortage. In 1947, 6 million families shared dwellings with friends and relatives. One-half million lived in temporary shelters. In New York City, one pair of newlyweds set up housekeeping in the display window of a department store to advertise their need for an apartment.

Before 1945, the housing industry had focused on building custom homes or urban multifamily buildings. But housing prices in these units generally exceeded the $50 or so per month that most veterans could afford. After the war, the needs of veterans meshed with a new trend in the construction industry: the increasing dominance of large construction firms, those with over 100 employees that built over 100 houses per year. These companies discovered that they could operate profitably by building a great number of similar homes on large tracts of inexpensive, usually suburban, land.

Meanwhile, the National Association of Home Builders and the National Association of Realtors were lobbying to shape the federal housing policy that emerged during the late 1940s. By tradition, banks and other private lenders had followed restrictive mortgage procedures, often demanding 50 percent of the purchase price as down payment and repayment of the balance within ten years. Following the war, however, the Federal Housing Administration (FHA) began insuring thirty-year bank mortgages with only a 5 to 10 percent down payment. Under the GI Bill, the VA provided additional support, so qualifying veterans could often take title for a token $1 down payment. By guaranteeing loan repayment, the FHA and VA persuaded private lenders to relax mortgage terms.

The result of these developments was a housing boom, particularly in suburbia. Housing starts jumped from 114,000 in 1944 to 1.7 million in 1950. By then, federal agencies insured more than a third of all mortgages—a figure that surpassed 40 percent by 1955. In addition to FHA and VA loan guarantees, the government's tax policy promoted housing growth by allowing a deduction for mortgage interest.

Levittown, named after builder William Levitt, became a generic synonym for suburban development. Levitt, a builder of luxury homes before 1941, had pioneered prefabrication techniques for navy housing during the war. In 1947 he decided to mass-produce private homes that the beneficiaries of federal assistance programs would be able to afford. The first Levittown, a planned community of 10,000 (later 17,000) homes, sprang from a 1,200-acre potato field on Long Island, New York. Larger projects followed in Pennsylvania and New Jersey.

In the words of one observer, Levitt made a "factory of the whole building site," doing for homes what Henry Ford had done for the automobile. Materials were precut and assembled by teams of semi-skilled laborers and moved to lots when needed. Roving crews laid concrete foundations en masse, traveling up one side of a street and down the other. In place of union painters and carpenters, Levitt trained workers to do specific tasks, such as spray painting or using power tools, on an assembly-line basis. The company bought its own forests, milled its own lumber, and bought standard-sized kitchen and bathroom appliances in bulk to equip the new houses. Inexpensive linoleum tiles replaced hardwood floors. At the height of Levittown construction, a house was completed every sixteen minutes. Construction costs were $10 a square foot, 30 percent below the industry standard. With a VA loan, a veteran could move into a new home for $56 per month, which was often less than the cost of renting an apartment. When one subdivision opened in 1949, fourteen hundred units sold in a single day.

The Levittown house, like Ford's Model T, set an affordable standard that made home ownership a reality for the postwar middle class. But Levittown was only the most conspicuous example of a widespread trend. Across the United States, surrounding the cities, new suburbs of similar-looking, middle-class houses began to appear. In a chaotic world, the free-standing, single-family, self-contained, all-electric suburban home was presented as a refuge where the homemaker took charge of housework and childcare. Television and the backyard barbecue became centers of entertainment and social life. An associated phenomenon was the rise in suburban shopping centers or malls; their number increased from eight to four thousand in the first postwar decade.

To an extent, suburbia homogenized society by mixing ethnic, social, and political groups that formerly had lived in separate urban neighborhoods. New institutions such as churches and civic clubs replaced extended families and kinship networks. Even though many architectural critics criticized suburbs—labeling them, for example, "slums of the future"—young families who had doubled up with relatives loved the new homes. Many looked forward to improving them and using them as equity to trade up to fancier dwellings later.

Levittown and its successors were designed especially for these young and growing families. The houses could be expanded easily. Kitchens in the front and living rooms in the rear had large windows from which mothers could watch children in the yard. And there were plenty of children to watch. The birth rate, which had been unusually low during the depression, began a dramatic rise in 1944.

By 1946, the nation was experiencing a baby boom that lasted into the 1960s. The birth rate accelerated as families made up for deprivation and lost time. The new suburban communities earned nicknames like "fertility valley" and "rabbit hutch." The average number of children born to an American family increased from 2.4 to 3.2 between 1945 and 1957, when the boom peaked. Annual births rose from 1.2 million in 1945 to 1.8 million in that period.

Young parents in a more relaxed and affluent environment felt uneasy about following their own parents' child-rearing methods. In previous decades, how-to books had described infants as nasty tyrants who, if indulged, cuddled, or overstimulated, would grow up with grave character disorders. Pediatrician Benjamin Spock challenged these assumptions in his 1946 *Pocket Book of Baby and Child Care*. Spock urged parents to have fun with their kids. He encouraged physical contact and emotional nurturing as keys to healthy development. The book sold over 20 million copies within ten years, and 40 million by 1990. Spock and other such authors have helped to make the years since the Second World War a remarkably child-centered era, a time when American parents have worried about their children's wants and needs as never before.

Even as young parents in suburbia read their Dr. Spock and enjoyed their electric kitchens, the same policies that promoted suburban growth were causing serious problems for cities, the poor, and minorities. The FHA gave preference to subsidizing single-family, detached homes in the $7,000 to $10,000 range. Until the 1960s, the FHA provided few loans to assist buyers or improve existing multifamily housing in racially mixed neighborhoods. These so-called redlining practices concentrated African-Americans and other minorities in older cities and kept them out of the suburbs. In 1950, of 20 million suburban Americans, only 1 million were nonwhite. William Levitt captured the prevailing attitude in remarking, "we can solve a housing problem, or we can try to solve a racial problem. But we cannot combine the two." In fact, Levitt's sales organization used contract language that barred "members of other than the Caucasian race" from buying homes. A decade after the development opened, not one of Long Island Levittown's 82,000 residents was black.

Following the war, major cities like New York experienced a population drop. Increasingly, poor blacks and whites and immigrants from Puerto Rico replaced the mobile white middle class. Public and private discrimination contributed to drawing a "white noose" around the increasingly nonwhite cities. As business firms and white families left cities for the suburbs, they took with them the jobs and income that had contributed to urban tax revenues and employment. Generally speaking, the growth of suburbs resulted in a decline of the economies of nearby central cities.

The rise of the suburbs had other lasting effects as well. One was the increased demand for cars and better roads. Between 1946 and 1950, domestic automobile production jumped from 2 million to 6 million annually. By the 1950s, the highway lobby—an umbrella group of automobile makers, road builders, and trucking firms—began to pressure the federal government for a national highway system. As we will see in Chapter 4, the federal response was to create a vast highway network that transformed the American landscape.

Radio and Television

In 1947, as Levittown was rising from the Long Island fields, radio still reigned as the nation's major source of electronic information and entertainment. Out of some 38 million households, 34 million had at least one radio. Radio broadcasts brought news, music, comedy, melodrama, and soap operas to an immense audience. Housewives and children listened to about fourteen hours of programming each week.

Already, however, a newer electronic medium was poised to upstage radio. Considered an oddity when first invented in the 1920s, television had gestated for twenty years. In the late 1930s the National Broadcasting Company, an offshoot of David Sarnoff's Radio Corporation of America (RCA), began experimental commercial television broadcasts from New York. Only a few thousand people owned the 5-inch receivers, and there was little to watch on them anyway. One broadcast by a mobile unit consisted of hours of planes

the picture
tells the story...

Dramatic evidence of its performance ability is the quality of the picture you see on Motorola TV. No other picture can compare in clarity, sharpness, depth and stability. To produce such visible perfection—and to maintain dependable performance night after night at the same consistent quality—the finest skill of 682 engineers has been concentrated in designing the most advanced and most dependable TV chassis in the world today... with exclusive new features for even greater picture enjoyment.

Outstanding Examples of Leadership Features

Anti-Reflection Glare Guard
Exclusive optically-curved screen and non-reflecting "Absorbellite" TV tube eliminate 96% of all light reflection glare interference.

Exclusive Area Selector Switch
Adjustable multi-power amplifier tube can be switched instantly from normal strength to double reception power for distant "fringe" areas.

ONLY MOTOROLA TV HAS ALL THE FEATURES FOR FINER TV PERFORMANCE

By the late 1940s, television had joined the American family. *Courtesy of Motorola.*

landing at New York's La Guardia Airport. Federal rules at the time limited the sale of commercial advertising, which pays for the bulk of television programming today.

Although most television broadcasting ceased with the attack on Pearl Harbor, the war spurred technological progress in the mass production of high-quality electronics that made it possible to build better and cheaper television equipment. The Federal Communications Commission (FCC) advanced the cause of television in 1945 by resolving a long-running dispute between television and FM radio, which shared part of the waveband. FM was displaced to a less favored spot, facilitating televised broadcasts.

In 1946 the FCC licensed twenty-six new television stations to serve the public. Retooled factories hired many of the thousands of electronics workers trained during the war. Sets remained both scarce and expensive for a time, and only a few programs were televised each night. Taverns bought most of the early postwar receivers, discovering that customers liked to drink, socialize, and watch sporting events.

Soon, however, dramatic and variety shows joined the schedule, and enough television sets were produced so that ordinary families could buy them. By 1949, about a million homes, mostly in large cities, received broadcasts on sixty-nine stations. Ten years later, six hundred stations reached 44 million households with televisions.

Television's influence on American life was soon manifest in ways both large and small. In 1948, both the Democrats and the Republicans held their presidential nominating conventions in Philadelphia because the city possessed a co-axial cable hookup that allowed viewing by an audience of 10 million. In cities with television stations, movie ticket sales plummeted, old-time vaudeville revues died, and attendance at live sporting events fell. The "Milton Berle Show," television's first great hit, attracted such large audiences that water pressure in cities dropped during the show's commercial breaks as viewers rushed to the toilet. Other hit shows starred comedians Jack Benny, Sid Caesar, and Lucille Ball, as well as a puppet named Howdy Doody.

In Chapter 4 we will look at the effect of television on American culture through the 1950s. For the immediate postwar period, the significant point is the eagerness with which Americans latched on to this novel form of entertainment. The children of the burgeoning suburbs would grow up with a new and very complicated force in their lives—the magic, flickering television tube.

Television's emergence also had an influence on radio. As the home audience turned its attention to the newer medium, radio stations became less profitable, and this prompted many of them to change their formats. In some large cities, stations targeted a new audience, African-Americans, a change that involved playing more rhythm-and-blues music. By the mid-1950s, the increased exposure for R&B paved the way for its evolution into rock 'n' roll.

THE RED SCARE

During the first decade following the wartime victory, a mounting anti-Communist movement dominated political debate. Part of the tension came from disputes dating back to the 1930s, pitting left-wing factions in the Democratic party, labor movement, and intellectual circles against centrists and conservatives who abhorred the Soviet Union. Republican politicians who hated the New Deal but failed to win votes on that platform charged that Roosevelt's programs had eroded liberty at home and contributed to the rise of international communism. This mixture of ideological fervor and political opportunism, combined with the rising suspicion of Soviet intentions in the postwar era, fed a Red Scare that began in 1946 to 1947 and soon grew to fever pitch. As we will see in the next chapter, the Republican senator from Wisconsin, Joseph McCarthy, gave his name to the movement, but it was well underway by the time he emerged as a national figure.

Domestic communism was, in fact, a tiny, nonviolent movement. The American Communist party had only twenty thousand members at the end of the war and soon shrank. Although generally a loyal supporter of Soviet policy, the party neither advocated violence nor plotted to overthrow the government. In any case, the Federal Bureau of Investigation (FBI) had infiltrated the party so thoroughly that it could not organize so much as a picnic in secrecy.

Nevertheless, anticommunism seized the popular imagination in the United States. Ever since the Bolshevik Revolution of 1917, Americans had feared the Soviet message of world revolution. There had been a widespread Red Scare in 1919 to 1920. Even after Roosevelt recognized the Soviet regime in 1933, United States leaders remained suspicious of Stalin's motives. The murderous intensity of Stalin's forced collectivization and political purges in the 1930s, when millions of Soviet citizens were killed, gave good cause for Western distrust of the Soviet regime. Although Hitler's attack drove the Soviet Union and United States together, this uneasy alliance shattered when the common threat evaporated. Soviet domination of Eastern Europe and encouragement of anti-Western movements in Asia, Africa, and the Middle East convinced many Americans that Moscow had revived its plans for world conquest and would use local Communist movements as pawns. Truman's own response—his tendency to describe programs like the Marshall Plan (see Chapter 3) in terms of a global struggle against Communist totalitarianism—intensified the public concern.

Other politicians exploited the rising fear and helped to fan it into hysteria. Certain conservatives linked the New Deal, liberalism, and progressive politics to "the Reds," primarily as a way of discrediting them all. For example, racists labeled as Communists those campaigning against segregation. Conservative union leaders found it possible to oust left-wing opponents in the labor movement by calling them stooges of Moscow. Republican politicians, stymied by the continued popularity of New Deal reforms like Social Security, discovered that voters might desert the Democratic party if it could be tarred with charges of softness on communism. Pubic opinion proved volatile and easily swayed by such sensationalist charges.

The Government Crusade Against Subversion

The House Committee on Un-American Activities (HUAC) played a particularly influential role in stirring up the Red Scare. Between 1944 and 1946, Democrats John S. Wood of Georgia and John Rankin of

Mississippi used the committee as a forum to attack liberal causes. Rankin, the most active member of the panel, took pride in extending to the nation's capital a law modeled on those in twenty-two states, which banned interracial marriages. He accused the Red Cross of bowing to Communist pressure in removing labels designating the race of donors from blood bank bottles; this, Rankin charged, was done to "mongrelize this nation." In 1945 he complained of a conspiracy among "alien-minded Communistic enemies of Christianity"—in other words, Jews—to take over the nation's media.

In November 1946, to counter charges of Democratic waffling on subversion, President Truman established a Temporary Commission on Employee Loyalty. Stung by continued Republican attacks and that party's gains in the 1946 election, Truman issued Executive Order No. 9835 the following March, creating a Federal Employee Loyalty Program to verify the loyalty of government employees.

In accordance with this program, Attorney General Tom Clark compiled a list of eighty-two supposedly subversive organizations. Applying looser standards, congressional committees developed a list of over six hundred groups. Membership in any one of these "totalitarian, Fascist, Communist or subversive" organizations could, by itself, constitute reasonable doubt of a federal employee's loyalty and justify dismissal. Clark warned that "[Communists] are everywhere—in factories, offices, butcher shops, on street corners, in private businesses—and each carries with him the germs of death for society."

The loyalty program required current and prospective federal employees, regardless of the sensitivity of their jobs, to undergo an investigation. Hearsay and anonymous accusations, as well as information from wiretaps and mail openings, could be used to discredit someone. Reasonable doubt rather than proof was sufficient to impeach a person's loyalty. Ultimately, the program placed the burden of proving their loyalty on those under scrutiny.

At loyalty board hearings, the accused were typically asked whether they socialized with members of other races, had any homosexual inclination (itself grounds for removal), what they thought of the government's foreign policy, and what political or philosophical beliefs they held. Several diplomats stationed in China during the Second World War were fired for "consorting with known Communists" a result of the fact that they had been assigned to Communist headquarters. By the early 1950s, over 5 million government employees had undergone some form of security check. Several thousand quit under protest. A few hundred were fired for association with groups on the attorney general's list.

Neither the loyalty program nor later congressional witch hunts unearthed many spies. Of course, the Soviet Union, like the United

States, routinely sought inside information on its opponent's nuclear energy capabilities, military plans, and high technology. Typically, Soviet agents recruited disgruntled employees who nursed grievances or needed cash to gather and pass on information. Since few people so recruited had political motives, loyalty probes were virtually useless in uncovering their activities. The Kremlin generally avoided using American Communists as spies because they seldom had access to useful information and were closely scrutinized by the FBI. Still, a few spectacular cases, such as the alleged treason of Alger Hiss (discussed below), created the impression that Communist sympathizers were often spies.

A judicial attack on communism began in July 1948 when a federal grand jury indicted twelve top American Communist party officials, including Eugene Dennis and Gus Hall, for violation of a prewar law, the Smith Act. The 1940 law, originally directed toward Fascists as well as Communists, made it a crime to advocate the overthrow of the government by force or to belong to a group advocating such action. In the postwar climate it was used almost exclusively against the Communist party.

The trial, begun in January 1949, deteriorated into a shouting match among defendants, defense attorneys, the judge, and prosecutors. The government offered writings from Marx and Lenin, as well as testimony from ex–party members, to prove that the Communist movement followed Kremlin orders to overthrow the government. The defendants argued that a capitalist "kangaroo court" that excluded racial minorities and poor people from the jury had no right to try them. In October the jury found the party leaders guilty, and Judge Harold Medina sentenced them to prison. He also sentenced five defense attorneys to prison for failing to control their clients' disruptive courtroom behavior.

In 1951, in *Dennis* v. *United States*, the Supreme Court upheld the conviction of the Communist party leaders. Writing for the majority, Chief Justice Fred Vinson ruled that citizens had no right to violent rebellion where the opportunity for peaceful and orderly change existed. In vain, dissenting justices Hugo Black and William O. Douglas argued that American Communists did not in fact advocate violent opposition to the government.

By the time of that ruling, Democratic and Republican politicians had vied with one another to pass new and more stringent legislation to restrict subversive activities. Republicans Karl Mundt and Richard Nixon, as well as Democrats Pat McCarran and Hubert Humphrey, introduced anti-Communist legislation in 1949 and 1950. A compromise measure, the McCarran or Internal Security Act of 1950, declared the existence of an international Communist conspiracy that posed an immediate threat to the United States. The law ordered all

Communist-affiliated organizations and individuals to register with a Subversive Activities Control Board or face a $10,000 fine and five years in prison. Mail sent by registered groups had to be labeled, "Disseminated by a Communist organization." Real or alleged Communists were denied passports and barred from jobs in government or the defense industry. The law permitted the deportation of naturalized citizens and the detention without trial of alleged subversives during periods of emergency. Even President Truman found it difficult to stomach. When he vetoed the bill in September 1950, he called it the "greatest danger to freedom of speech, press and assembly since the Sedition Act of 1798." Congress promptly overrode the veto, helped by the votes of three future presidents—Representatives John F. Kennedy and Richard M. Nixon and Senator Lyndon B. Johnson.

Hollywood on Trial

With the cooperation of FBI director J. Edgar Hoover, the HUAC stepped up its activities in 1947. J. Parnell Thomas, a New Jersey Republican named to chair HUAC when his party won control of the House, announced the discovery of a Red plot to overthrow the government. It was not the Communist party he was talking about, nor alleged subversives in the federal bureaucracy. The plot's headquarters, Thomas declared, were in the Hollywood film industry.

Even during the wartime alliance with the Soviet Union, Hollywood had never been much of a radical hotbed. The movie industry had released perhaps three films overtly sympathetic to Moscow. It was more noted for aiding Allied propaganda with war films like *God is My Co-pilot* and *Thirty Seconds over Tokyo*. But other factors made Hollywood an enticing target for HUAC. Jewish immigrants headed several of the eight major studios. Most had rejected their ethnic roots, anglicized their names, and made movies celebrating an idealized America. Nevertheless, the anti-Semitic John Rankin found them an irresistible target, and Thomas was eager to generate publicity.

Communism had made inroads among only a small number of screenwriters. Poorly paid and usually at odds with studio heads, the writers had formed a left-leaning union, the Screen Writers Guild. Studio bosses like Jack Warner and Sam Goldwyn hoped that by cooperating with congressional Red hunters, they could punish the guild and convince HUAC of their own true Americanism. Warner, for example, complained to the committee about screenwriters who poked fun at the American political system or attempted to arouse sympathy for the "Indians and the colored folk."

The committee subpoenaed testimony from ten writers and directors whom it considered suspicious, including Dalton Trumbo, Ring Lardner, Jr., and John Howard Lawson. Several of the group were current or past Communist party members. Expecting a sympathetic Supreme Court, dominated by Roosevelt appointees, to overturn any contempt citation from Congress, all of these writers and directors refused to testify, citing the First Amendment's protection of speech and political association. But the deaths of several members of the Roosevelt Court, and Truman's selection of more conservative replacements, changed the odds. The high court affirmed the convictions for contempt of Congress, and the writers and directors went to jail for terms of up to one year. As a small solace, HUAC's chairman, J. Parnell Thomas, was convicted of taking salary kickbacks from his staff and joined writer Ring Lardner, Jr., in a Danbury prison.

Following the Hollywood hearings, studios pledged not to hire Communists. They created a blacklist of screen and television actors, writers, and directors who had either refused to cooperate with congressional investigators or had been named as suspect in someone else's testimony. Soon, publications such as *Red Channels* listed the names of hundreds of artists who found themselves locked out of jobs. Strangely, a cash donation to these self-appointed censors could sometimes remove a name from their rolls.

After 1949, most message films boosted the anti-Communist movement. Movies like *The Iron Curtain* (1948), *The Red Menace* (1949), *I Was a Communist for the FBI* (1951), and *My Son John* (1952) all portrayed Communists as evil conspirators willing to do anything to betray America. Not incidentally, they also affirmed Hollywood's loyalty.

The Widening Hysteria: Chambers and Hiss

As the anti-Communist hysteria mounted, many public schools and universities required teachers to sign loyalty oaths or face summary dismissal. At Berkeley, the University of Michigan, and New York's City College, among others, faculty were fired for refusing to sign oaths or because of alleged Communist sympathies. Labor unions purged their rolls of suspected Communists. The Catholic church, spurred by Francis Cardinal Spellman of New York, called on the faithful to combat the "aggression of enemies within." America would not be safe, the cardinal declared in 1949, "until every Communist cell is removed from within our own government, our own institutions, and not until every democratic country is returned to democratic leadership."

Attacking liberal reform as communistic became common. The American Medical Association labeled Truman's 1949 call for national health insurance a "monstrosity of Bolshevik bureaucracy." Southern conservatives attacked civil rights programs as part of a Communist-inspired conspiracy to undermine American unity. In this climate, it became difficult for progressives to advocate any substantial social reform.

In 1948 HUAC began its most famous campaign against a particular individual. For several years Whittaker Chambers, an editor at *Time,* had been telling various government officials that he had been part of a Soviet espionage ring in the mid-1930s. Chambers claimed that members of the Roosevelt administration fed him material to pass on to Moscow. According to his account, he lost faith in communism after 1937 and became an avid Christian. Anxious to confess past sins, Chambers told his story to Congressman Richard M. Nixon and other members of HUAC. In August 1948 they presented him to the public.

In his initial testimony, Chambers described the espionage ring and mentioned that former State Department official Alger Hiss was a secret Communist, though not among those passing information. When Hiss fought back with a libel suit, Chambers embellished his story by naming Hiss as one of the informants.

In contrast to the disheveled and nervous Chambers, Hiss seemed a paragon of charm, eloquence, and professional accomplishments. He had worked for several New Deal agencies before rising in the State Department hierarchy, had attended the Yalta conference, and had helped organize the founding meeting of the United Nations. He had never been an influential policymaker, however, because his responsibilities lay in administrative and legal matters. After the war he had left the State Department to head the prestigious Carnegie Endowment for International Peace.

When Hiss first responded to the allegations, he denied even knowing Chambers and brought a libel action against his accuser. Following this persuasive rebuttal, some of the HUAC panel thought the committee had been embarrassed. Then Richard Nixon of California, who had won office in the 1946 election by linking his opponent with subversive elements, took up the apparently lost cause. He arranged a face-to-face meeting between Chambers and Hiss, coaxing from the latter an admission that he had known Chambers under a different name—a real possibility, as Chambers had used many aliases. Subsequently it became clear that the two men had met several times during the 1930s.

The Republican party pushed the case with new vigor after November 1948, when, despite predictions, Harry Truman defeated Republican Thomas Dewey for the presidency. Nixon urged Chambers to escalate his charges. HUAC and the FBI provided Chambers with derogatory information on Hiss; Chambers used the information to construct a new accusation that Hiss had passed government secrets to him up to 1937 or 1938. To prove the point, he and Nixon accompanied reporters to Chambers's Maryland farm, where Chambers reached into a hollow pumpkin and extracted several rolls of microfilm. The FBI determined that the films and associated papers (dubbed, collectively, the Pumpkin Papers) were secret documents, many of which had been retyped on a machine owned by the Hiss family. Although the statute of limitations on espionage had lapsed, a federal grand jury indicted Hiss for lying about his Communist affiliations and contacts with Chambers.

Many of the Pumpkin Papers were neither secret nor the type of material likely to have crossed Hiss's desk. No evidence linked Hiss to espionage after 1938. But Hiss's reticence about his relationship with Chambers, and the fact that some documents appeared to have been typed on Hiss's home typewriter, undermined the defense. Hiss never was able to explain how the documents came to be typed on his machine.

The trial jury deadlocked in 1949. The government retried Hiss before a second jury, which convicted him on perjury charges in January 1950. Alger Hiss went to jail maintaining that the FBI had built a typewriter similar to his own and used it to forge the incriminating documents. Chambers went on to write *Witness*, a best-selling account of his troubled life, and fingered several other government officials as alleged spies. Nixon parlayed his fame into a California Senate seat in 1950 and the vice-presidential slot two years later.

The Chambers-Hiss case became a political morality play for liberals and conservatives. Republicans felt they had proved a conspiracy. When Truman initially dismissed HUAC's case against Hiss as a red herring, he drove Republicans wild. They believed that Secretary of State Dean Acheson, a friend of Alger's brother Donald, showed his true colors by vowing not to turn his back on Hiss after the conviction. This led Richard Nixon to complain that for years "traitors in the high councils of our own government have made sure that the deck is stacked on the Soviet side of the diplomatic tables." But Democrats who complained about Republican redbaiting had to account for Truman's own anti-Communist rhetoric and his promotion of the government loyalty program which legitimized the scare.

In the next chapter we will see how the Red Scare continued well into the 1950s, bringing to fame or notoriety such figures as Joseph McCarthy, Klaus Fuchs, and Ethel and Julius Rosenberg. Arguments over this era continue today. Some conservatives, while admitting that the hysteria went too far, insist that domestic radicalism did pose a genuine threat to United States security. Those on the left tend to believe that the internal threat was negligible and that the campaign to stamp out subversives merely trampled Americans' right to dissent.

In 1950 Congressman Richard Nixon took grim satisfaction from learning that a federal jury had convicted Alger Hiss of perjury. *UPI/Bettmann Newsphotos.*

DISPLACED PERSONS AND IMMIGRATION

In an era of fervent anticommunism, immigration was often seen as a threat to the American way of life. Senator Pat McCarran complained that the country already had too many "indigestible blocs." Based on a quota system established in the 1920s, American immigration law remained highly restrictive. However, the world war had created compelling new circumstances, and Congress responded with amendments to the law that permitted several hundred thousand additional people to enter the country.

The War Brides Act of 1946 granted entry over the next several years to about 100,000 spouses and children of American military personnel who had been stationed abroad. The largest number of beneficiaries were Asian wives of servicemen who would otherwise have been barred from immigration because of the 1924 Oriental Exclusion Act.

The tragic problem of European refugees proved more difficult. In 1946 a million displaced persons (DPs) huddled in squalid detention camps in Western Europe. They included ethnic Germans driven from Eastern Europe; anti-Communist Poles and Balts (Latvians, Lithuanians, and Estonians) who had fled from Soviet control; and about 200,000 Jewish survivors of Nazi death camps. The American army assisted these refugees but lacked the facilities and personnel to meet their material and emotional needs. Conditions in DP camps were so awful, according to an American government report, that the army appeared "to be treating the Jews as the Nazis treated them except that we do not exterminate them."

In June 1948 Congress passed the Displaced Persons Act, which opened 200,000 slots for these people. But provisions inserted by anti-Semitic legislators minimized the number of Jews who qualified. Although President Truman signed the act, he criticized it as "flagrantly discriminatory" and instructed immigration officers to implement it in ways that benefited Jews. In 1950, after most of the remaining Jewish refugees had gone to Israel, Congress enacted a more liberal law. About 400,000 refugees—the majority not Jewish—entered America under the two displaced persons acts.

In 1952 Congress revised the overall immigration law by passing the Immigration and Nationality Act, also known as the McCarran-Walter Act. Although this new law replaced the ban on Asians with an annual quota of 100 persons for each Asian-Pacific nation, it retained most of the other restrictions from the 1920s. It also empowered the Justice Department to bar suspected Communists and homosexuals and to deport aliens and even naturalized citizens who were accused of subversive activities. Passed over Truman's veto, the act served as the nation's basic immigration law until 1965.

Despite the focus on displaced persons and potential subversives from Europe or Asia, the largest single source of immigrants continued to be a close neighbor—Mexico. Begun in 1942, the *bracero* program (see page 33) brought in several hundred thousand Mexican farm laborers annually, many of whom became quasi-permanent residents. Additional Mexicans entered illegally. Most of the illegal immigrants, known derogatorily as "wetbacks," took low-paying jobs that American citizens shunned. When Truman recommended imposing sanctions on employers of undocumented aliens, Congress balked. In this case, the agricultural demand for cheap labor prevailed over the distrust of foreigners.

PROGRESS IN CIVIL RIGHTS

Dominated by the Red Scare and by suspicion of influences that seemed foreign or un-American, the postwar years were not good ones for the concept of civil liberties. For example, in upholding the convictions of Communist party leaders in the *Dennis* case, the Supreme Court emphasized national security at the expense of freedom of expression and association. By hesitating to apply the Bill of Rights, the Court gave government wide leeway to suppress radical speech and behavior.

The same years, however, brought progress in the area of civil rights for minorities, especially African-Americans. As we saw in Chapter 1, blacks emerged from the New Deal and the Second World War with higher aspirations and expectations, less willingness to settle for a second-class position in American society. For many, Jackie Robinson became a symbol of the new age when he broke major-league baseball's color barrier. Robinson did more than play the game; with his strong hitting and aggressive baserunning, he became an instant star, Rookie of the Year for 1947.

But one great symbol could not win the struggle. Led in many cases by war veterans, African-Americans began voter-registration drives in the South, where they encountered white hostility and sometimes overt violence. After hearing reports of blacks killed or blinded for daring to assert their voting rights, President Truman acted. Even though he privately rejected social equality among races, in late 1946 he established the President's Committee on Civil Rights to recommend steps for the federal government to take. In October 1947, this panel issued a report titled *To Secure These Rights,* which urged government action to ensure that all Americans enjoyed equal opportunity in securing education, housing, and employment. It called for federal laws against lynching and poll taxes, creation of a permanent Fair Employment Practices Commission, and a strong Civil Rights Division within the Justice Department.

When Congress declined to act, Truman used executive authority to bolster civil rights enforcement by the Justice Department. He also appointed a black federal judge and made several other minority appointments. When labor leader A. Philip Randolph threatened in July 1948 to organize a draft boycott against serving in the segregated armed forces, Truman issued an executive order calling for equality of treatment in the services. Still, the armed services moved so slowly that desegregation took another six years.

As the government inched forward, African-American individuals and groups pursued nonviolent direct action inspired by India's Mahatma Gandhi. Two women, one of whom, Patricia Harris, later became a cabinet secretary in the Carter administration, had staged the first sit-in in Washington, D.C., during the war. In 1947 the Congress of Racial Equality (CORE) organized the first "freedom ride" to test a recent Supreme Court ruling against discrimination in interstate transportation. The group made it as far as Durham, North Carolina, before being arrested and sentenced to thirty days on a chain gang.

During the next two years CORE carried out lunch counter sit-ins in northern cities and organized a swim-in at Palisades Park in New Jersey. Although mobs beat the participants, the amusement park and many lunch counters were desegregated. These small and hard-won victories convinced activists of the importance of direct action

Jack Roosevelt Robinson

Baseball became segregated during the 1890s at the same time that Jim Crow laws separated black schoolchildren from whites. Over the next half-century, African-Americans could play only in the Negro Leagues, many of whose teams were owned by the white major-league clubs. During the Second World War, activists demanded that baseball drop its color bar, but it was not until after the war that Branch Rickey, owner of the Brooklyn Dodgers, resolved to challenge the policy of racial exclusion.

Rickey searched for the perfect African-American to integrate major-league baseball—not only a superior athlete, but also a model citizen with an even temperament, a man who would not be fazed by white harassment. The ballplayer he found was Jack Roosevelt "Jackie" Robinson.

Born in 1919 to a family of Georgia sharecroppers, Robinson was uprooted

for mobilizing their communities and maintaining political pressure on the white establishment.

In the legal realm, too, progress was being made. Despite its limitation of civil liberties in the *Dennis* case, the Supreme Court gradually extended judicial protection for the civil rights of minorities. Even before the Second World War ended, in *Smith* v. *Allwright* (1944), the Court overturned the segregationist whites-only primary system that prevailed in some southern states. Two years later, in *Morgan* v. *Virginia* (1946), the Court held that racial segregation on interstate buses violated federal law. This ruling did not prevent the CORE freedom riders from being jailed in North Carolina, but it did establish an important legal precedent.

Other legal decisions helped to combat segregation in housing and employment. At the turn of the century the Supreme Court had ruled

at an early age when his mother moved herself and her children to southern California. Jackie eventually attended UCLA and excelled in several varsity sports. As one of the small number of African-American officers during the Second World War, he successfully defended himself in a court-martial after challenging an order to move to the back of a military bus. In October 1945 Rickey gave him a contract to play with the Dodgers' top minor-league team in Montreal, where he led the league in batting in 1946.

His debut with the Brooklyn Dodgers—marking the integration of the major leagues—came in April 1947. Throughout his first season, Robinson had to endure racial epithets hurled by angry fans and white players alike. At least one team, the St. Louis Cardinals, threatened to walk off the field if Robinson appeared. Through it all, Robinson's extraordinary talent and personal resolve triumphed. He became so popular that the House Committee on Un-American Activities called on him to refute a claim by Paul Robeson, a famous black singer and actor, that African-Americans would not fight in a war against the Soviet Union. Within two years of Robinson's debut, several more black players received major-league contracts.

Robinson played for the Dodgers through 1956. After retirement, he served as vice president of a food company and became a close friend and political ally of Nelson Rockefeller, the Republican governor of New York. After suffering from diabetes for many years, Jackie Robinson died in 1972. ■

that local laws enforcing residential segregation violated the Fourteenth Amendment. It had undermined that decision, however, by permitting state courts to enforce private agreements in contracts that barred minorities. But in *Shelly* v. *Kraemer* (1948), the justices decided that this ruse gave government sanction to illegal discrimination and ordered that state courts could not enforce restrictive clauses in private contracts. On hearing of the new ruling, a furious Congressman Rankin declared that "there must have been a celebration in Moscow last night."

Nothing symbolized more powerfully the unequal status of African-Americans than school segregation. *Plessy* v. *Ferguson* (1896) had permitted school systems that were "separate but equal." By 1938, Chief Justice Hughes suggested that southern states wishing to continue separate-but-equal education ought to make black-only schools truly equal. In 1948, the Court took up the case of Ada Sipuel, who had graduated with a strong record from the State College for Negroes in Langston, Oklahoma. She was refused admission to the University of Oklahoma Law School (the only one in the state) on racial grounds, but was told that a separate school for blacks with "substantially equal" facilities would soon open. Represented by Thurgood Marshall, chief counsel of the National Association for the Advancement of Colored People (NAACP), she sued for admission to the existing school.

Despite rebuffs in the lower courts, Marshall argued the case before the U.S. Supreme Court in 1948. In *Sipuel* v. *Board of Regents of the University of Oklahoma*, the justices ruled unanimously that Oklahoma must provide Sipuel with a legal education "in conformity with the equal protection clause of the Fourteenth Amendment and . . . provide it as soon as it does for applicants of any other group." The university regents then created a sham law school by roping off a tiny area within the state capitol building and assigning three teachers to Sipuel. Marshall challenged this ruse, but the Court declined further action.

Two years later, the University of Oklahoma admitted, under pressure, a sixty-eight-year-old African-American, George W. McLaurin, to its graduate program in education. The university ordered McLaurin to sit in a doorway outside the classroom, use a special desk in a segregated section of the library, and eat alone in a cafeteria annex. When the NAACP challenged these rules, McLaurin was permitted to sit inside the classroom so long as his seat was encircled by a railing with a sign that read: "Reserved for Colored." A unanimous Supreme Court, in *McLaurin* v. *Oklahoma State Regents* (1950), struck down these rules on the ground that the university had imposed inequality on McLaurin even while allowing him into a school with whites.

That same year, the Court decided in *Sweatt* v. *Painter* (1950) that Texas had not provided a black law student with equal facilities by building a makeshift classroom, without a library or real faculty, at segregated Prairie View University. The Court ordered Herman Marion Sweatt admitted to the University of Texas Law School at Austin. This was the first Supreme Court–ordered admission of a black student to an all-white school on the ground that the state had failed in its duty to provide equal, segregated facilities.

In these various decisions, the U.S. Supreme Court had not outlawed segregation or addressed the separate-but-equal rule dating from 1896. However, the rulings encouraged Marshall and the NAACP to escalate the attack on school segregation, placing the system under constant judicial siege.

As we will see in Chapter 4, the legal challenges to segregated education eventually bore fruit in a landmark case, *Brown* v. *Board of*

Education (1954), that struck down the separate-but-equal doctrine. The registration drives and protests of the late 1940s also swelled, by the mid-1950s, into a full-scale civil rights movement that had a profound and lasting impact.

THE POLITICAL SCENE: TRUMAN AND THE 1948 ELECTION

After the Republicans captured both houses of Congress in 1946, they looked forward confidently to winning the White House in 1948. In a way, the late President Roosevelt helped them, for whatever Truman's merits might have been, he suffered inevitably from comparison with his predecessor. Many on the White House staff admitted that when they first heard of Roosevelt's death, they could not imagine Truman sitting in the Oval Office. Roosevelt had reshaped the nation's very concept of the presidency, making it difficult to think of someone else in the job.

Moreover, Roosevelt had been a master of coalition politics, establishing an alliance of labor, urban ethnic groups, minorities, and farmers that is still known (sometimes wistfully) as the Roosevelt or New Deal coalition. Once the depression and world war were over, Truman found it difficult to maintain that consensus and build support for new initiatives. Like Roosevelt, he favored moderate reform, believed in human progress, and supported an active role for the United States in world affairs. But his humble background, folksy style, and testy personality would never appeal to the public as the patrician Roosevelt had done. By 1948, in fact, one survey found that only 3 percent of the voters listed Truman among the most admired leaders of recent decades.

Nevertheless, Clark Clifford, a young Missouri lawyer whom Truman appointed as his special counsel in 1947, developed a political strategy that proved remarkably successful. In a report drafted in November 1947, Clifford urged Truman to attack Republican efforts to unravel the economic and social reforms of the New Deal while pushing a liberal program of his own. Clifford argued that if former vice president Henry Wallace carried out his threat to run for the presidency as a third-party candidate, Truman should identify him in the public mind with communism.

Following this advice, in 1947 and 1948 Truman vetoed sixty-two Republican-sponsored bills that attacked the New Deal legacy. Often the president's veto messages rang with angry language. Conversely, he proposed programs to increase aid to small farmers, raise the minimum wage, liberalize immigration policies, enhance civil rights, reduce taxes for working people, and increase Social Security benefits. As each measure went down to defeat at the hands of Republicans, Truman's standing rose among elements of the Roosevelt coalition.

Truman then abandoned his antilabor stance and recaptured the support of unions through his stinging veto of the Taft-Hartley Bill, which he denounced as a slave-labor act. When Henry Wallace did challenge Truman by running as a candidate of the Progressive party, the White House and liberal allies undermined his appeal. Truman announced, for example, that he was glad not to have the support of "Henry Wallace and his Communists."

Clifford's strategy also included an appeal to urban minorities, who he predicted would form a crucial voting bloc in the 1948 election. By endorsing the recommendations of his Committee on Civil Rights, Truman solidified his support among African-Americans. At the same time, concerned about alienating moderate whites, he took only modest steps to put those recommendations into practice.

The president also reached out to Jews and Eastern Europeans by supporting a liberalized immigration law (see page 72) and by extending diplomatic recognition to Israel. Secretary of State George C. Marshall and Defense Secretary James F. Forrestal strongly opposed the creation of a separate Jewish state in Palestine, fearing it would antagonize Arabs, endanger the West's oil supplies, and enhance Soviet influence in the Middle East. But political adviser Clifford urged Truman to ignore these diplomatic advisers, knowing that the Jewish vote might prove crucial in such states as New York, Ohio, New Jersey, Illinois, and California. Truman agreed, telling a friend that never in his political experience did he recall an instance of "the Arab vote swinging a close election." On May 14, 1948, just minutes after the new nation proclaimed its existence, the United States recognized Israel.

At the same time that Truman was reaching out to labor and minorities, liberal Democrats moved closer to the center by taking a stand against communism. Labor leaders Walter Reuther and David Dubinsky, Eleanor Roosevelt, and influential journalists created the Americans for Democratic Action (ADA) in 1947. The ADA rejected any "association with Communists or sympathizers with Communism in the United States," attacked Wallace's party as a totalitarian group, and placed advertisements charging that Wallace's major donors belonged to subversive organizations. Endorsing Truman as the true successor to Roosevelt, the ADA prevented major defections to Wallace.

Before the Democratic convention opened in July 1948, Truman considered stepping aside if General Dwight D. Eisenhower, commander of the Allied invasion of Europe in the Second World War, could be persuaded to run as a Democrat. But Eisenhower declined, and Truman plunged into the race. At the convention he tried to appease all factions by supporting an innocuous civil rights platform. However, a revolt by party liberals, including the young mayor of

Minneapolis, Hubert H. Humphrey, forced the adoption of a stronger civil rights agenda. Angry southerners, such as Senator James Eastland of Mississippi, denounced attempts to "mongrelize the nation"; others complained that Truman was "kissing the feet of the minorities."

Some southern Democrats walked out of the convention and organized the States Rights party. The presidential nominee of these "Dixiecrats," Governor Strom Thurmond of South Carolina, declared that his party represented the "deepest emotion of the human fabric—racial pride, respect for white womanhood and superiority of Caucasian blood." Civil rights, he insisted, was another term for the Communist ideology of the "radicals, subversives and Reds" surrounding Truman.

Now that the Democratic party had split three ways, Truman's political fortunes looked extremely dim as he began to campaign against Republican nominee Thomas E. Dewey, the governor of New York, who had run against Roosevelt four years earlier. Congresswoman Clair Boothe Luce gloated, "Truman is a gone goose." The incumbent disagreed, ignoring polling data that gave Dewey a nearly fifteen-point lead during the summer of 1948. Truman crisscrossed the nation by train, delivering hundreds of combative speeches. Virtually ignoring the splinter candidates, Wallace and Thurmond, he concentrated his fire on the Republican-dominated Eightieth Congress, the "gluttons of privilege" who "stuck a pitchfork on the back of the farmers," tried to "enslave totally the workingman," and wanted to do "a real hatchet job on the New Deal." A Republican president would bring back depression, he insisted. Enthusiastic crowds roared "Give 'em hell, Harry."

In fact, Dewey was a moderate and decent man who did not intend to roll back the New Deal. But his personality was stiff, and his campaign suffered a terminal attack of overconfidence. Dewey devoted more energy to planning his inauguration than to campaigning, failing even to rebut Truman's charges.

Gradually, Truman's appeal to labor, farmers, urban ethnic voters, and blacks—the Roosevelt coalition—took hold. Also, Truman proved relatively immune to Republican redbaiting. He had covered his flanks with the loyalty program and, despite the defection of the Dixiecrats, appeared conservative in comparison with the Progressive party. The president's tough responses to Soviet pressure in Europe, notably the Truman Doctrine and Marshall Plan (see Chapter 3), were popular among voters. As campaign strategist Clark Clifford had predicted, "in times of crisis . . . the American citizen tends to back up his president." Many polling organizations, however, had lost interest in the seemingly one-sided race and had stopped taking surveys three weeks before the November election.

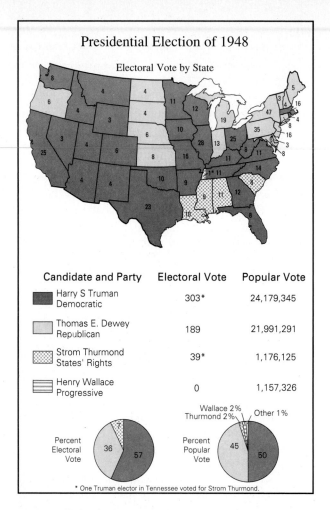

Presidential Election of 1948

Electoral Vote by State

Candidate and Party	Electoral Vote	Popular Vote
Harry S Truman Democratic	303*	24,179,345
Thomas E. Dewey Republican	189	21,991,291
Strom Thurmond States' Rights	39*	1,176,125
Henry Wallace Progressive	0	1,157,326

Percent Electoral Vote: 36, 57

Percent Popular Vote: Wallace 2%, Thurmond 2%, Other 1%, 45, 50

* One Truman elector in Tennessee voted for Strom Thurmond.

Presidential Election of 1948

When the tally came in (see map), Truman beat Dewey by over 2 million votes (24 million to 22 million)—one of the most dramatic upsets in the history of presidential politics. Henry Wallace and Strom Thurmond each received slightly more than 1 million votes, and their parties soon dissolved. Journalist Walter Lippmann, noting Truman's success in making the campaign a referendum on the New Deal, commented wryly, "of all Roosevelt's electoral triumphs, this one in 1948 is the most impressive."

Now president by election rather than simply by the death of his predecessor, Truman tried to emerge from Roosevelt's shadow by proclaiming his own reform program, the Fair Deal. He introduced legislation for national health insurance, public housing, expanded Social Security benefits, a higher minimum wage, greater protection for civil rights, an agricultural support program that favored small farmers, and repeal of the Taft-Hartley Act.

Few of these measures came to a vote in Congress. The enduring coalition of Republicans and southern Democrats tied up most of the Fair Deal package in committee. Congress passed a very modest public housing bill and expanded Social Security, but Democrats could not muster the votes to repeal the Taft-Hartley Act. The outbreak of the Korean War in June 1950, Republican gains in that November's congressional election, and a series of scandals involving Truman cronies largely frustrated reformers.

Thus the Fair Deal remained more promise than reality. Nevertheless, Truman's proposals did set a social agenda for later administrations, and in this sense they were more influential than politicians of the time could guess. Ironically, Truman's own anti-Communist fervor had helped to block reform by inflaming public suspicion of liberal social policies.

CONCLUSION

Overall, the early postwar years were a time of consolidation for the New Deal's social reforms. Neither President Truman nor more radical reformers succeeded in winning large-scale expansions of social services. Nor, in most cases, did conservatives succeed in turning back the clock. The Roosevelt legacy of a large, active federal government was preserved.

Among the most influential postwar domestic programs were those in education and housing. Because of the GI Bill of 1944, which eventually financed education for more than 2 million college students, higher education took on a more democratic character. At the same time, liberal FHA and VA loan-guarantee policies helped to start a postwar building boom, a key element in postwar prosperity.

Important characteristics of postwar America were emerging: higher education for greater numbers; a middle-class population shift from cities to suburbs; a growing concentration of minorities in the central cities; surging interest in consumer products, such as home appliances and televisions; and a baby boom that by the 1950s and 1960s would lead to an increasingly youth-oriented culture.

For women, the heroic wartime days of Rosie the Riveter were gone. Women were turned out of wartime industrial jobs and encouraged to stay home with their families. Although many managed to return to work, they generally had to settle for lower-paying jobs. More attended college than before the war, but they were steered away from fields such as law and business.

For ethnic minorities these years brought similarly mixed results. Although Congress modified the immigration law to admit hundreds of thousands of European refugees, anti-Semitic provisions restricted the number of Jewish Holocaust survivors who could enter. Mexicans continued to flow across the southern border to serve American agriculture, but they earned little respect for their work. In the same years, however, African-Americans made significant progress in establishing civil rights through voter-registration drives and the new tactics of the sit-in and freedom ride. Sometimes the activists encountered bloody resistance, and the legislative and executive branches took only small and slow steps to help. Yet crucial court victories set the scene for the major civil rights challenges of the 1950s.

All of this took place under the shadow of the Cold War and the domestic anti-Communist campaign. Harry Truman, catapulted into the presidency in 1945, had wasted little time in confronting the Soviet Union and ordering the atomic bomb dropped on Japan. At home, by emphasizing the Russian threat and starting a federal employee loyalty program, he helped to stimulate the growing worry about a Red menace. Other politicians capitalized on the situation, and a widespread hysteria ensued. In the next chapter we will see how one man, Joseph McCarthy, came to symbolize the Red Scare in the early 1950s, while the ramifications of the Cold War led the United States into a new armed conflict in Korea. ∎

FURTHER READING

On the Truman presidency, see: Robert J. Donovan, *Conflict and Crisis: The Presidency of Harry S. Truman, 1945–48* (1977), and the same author's *Tumultuous Years: The Presidency of Harry S. Truman, 1949–53* (1982); Alonzo S. Hamby, *Beyond the New Deal: Harry S. Truman and American Liberalism* (1973); Norman D. Markowitz, *The Rise and Fall of the People's Century: Henry A. Wallace and American Liberalism, 1941–48* (1973); Keith W. Olson, *The G.I. Bill, the Veterans, and the Colleges* (1974). On civil rights, see: Nicholas Lemann, *The Promised Land: The Great Black Migration and How It Changed America* (1991); Mark V. Tushnet, *The NAACP's Legal Strategy Against Segregated Education* (1987). On the origins of the Red Scare, see: David Caute, *The Great Fear* (1977); Athan Theoharis, *Seeds of Repression: Harry S. Truman and the Origins of McCarthyism* (1971); William L. O'Neill, *A Better World: Stalinism and American Intellectuals* (1983); Richard M. Freeland, *The Truman Doctrine and the Origins of McCarthyism* (1972). On immigration, see: David Reimers, *Still the Golden Door*, 2nd ed. (1992); Leonard Dinnerstein, *America and the Survivors of the Holocaust* (1982).

3

A Dangerous New World: From Containment to Korea

Although the United States emerged from the Second World War as the world's premier military and economic power, it found global events surprisingly difficult to shape. Neither its atomic monopoly nor the fact that it produced half the world's wealth assured American security. The elimination of German and Japanese power had removed the historic barriers to Russian influence in Europe and northeast Asia. Economic chaos in Europe and Japan and anticolonial rebellions in the Third World also brought opportunities for the Soviets to extend their sway.

The two sides in the developing Cold War held radically different views of the world situation, and one dispute after another compounded the misunderstandings. In this atmosphere of mutual distrust, Washington developed the strategic philosophy known as containment, first articulated by George Kennan. Containment required using long-term, patient strength to prevent the extension of Soviet influence around the globe. The Truman Doctrine and the Marshall Plan, aimed at stabilizing and reconstructing Europe, were outgrowths of this general philosophy.

The failure of the Soviet Union's Berlin blockade in 1948 to 1949 showed that America was achieving its basic goals in Western Europe. But the Cold War continued to intensify. Many of the administration's critics decried the "loss" of China to the Communists. When the French needed help in their struggle against a Communist-led anticolonial movement in Vietnam, the United States began its long, unhappy involvement with Southeast Asia.

As the nuclear arms race, spiced with sensational cases of espionage, raised public fears of mass annihilation, Senator Joseph McCarthy took center stage, claiming to have uncovered Communist agents throughout the government. Even as he drummed the Red Scare to a new frenzy, troops from Communist North Korea invaded South Korea. Although later historians would downplay the Soviet role in this invasion, Truman and his advisers had little doubt whom to blame. Soon the United States found itself in a new war that would claim tens of thousands of American lives and more than a million Koreans and Chinese.

EAST-WEST DISPUTES

Historians who have tried to fathom the causes of the Cold War often emphasize the differences in perception between the two sides. Neither side understood the other very well; each exaggerated the other's aggressiveness and expansionism. In the United States, as we saw in Chapter 2, the political exploitation of the Red Scare tended to discourage rational analysis in favor of emotional outcries.

Nevertheless, each party in the Cold War had some legitimate concerns in the early postwar years. American leaders worried especially about Moscow's creation of Soviet-dominated governments in Eastern Europe. By the end of 1945, Truman had agreed to recognize the puppet regimes in Poland, Bulgaria, and Rumania, but where would Stalin stop?

For its part, the Soviet Union watched with deep suspicion as the United States extended its military power and influence. Well before the collapse of the Grand Alliance, American military planners had decided to establish a global network of naval and air bases. When the war ended, the United States quickly put this idea into practice. For example, hundreds of Pacific islands captured from Japan were annexed as "strategic trusteeships." The Joint Chiefs of Staff saw these bases as vital to protect access to raw materials, to deter foreign aggression, and, if that failed, to intercept and counterattack an aggressor. The advent of long-range bombers and atomic weapons, as well as the rapid demobilization of American ground forces after 1945, made it imperative to establish defensive positions as far as possible from America and as close as feasible to potential enemies. Not surprisingly, the Soviets were less eager to see American military bases all around the globe.

In this section we will look at the differing perceptions of the two sides and then at some of the early postwar disagreements that hardened the mutual suspicions and made it increasingly difficult to keep the Cold War from escalating.

The View from the West

Despite the Red Scare and the widespread mistrust of the Soviet Union, most American leaders did not foresee a sudden Soviet military attack in Western Europe or elsewhere. They did not think Stalin would go to war to expand Communist influence. Rather, most officials guessed, the Soviets would try to take advantage of power vacuums created by economic chaos or anticolonial revolts.

President Truman probably understood that the Soviet Union was more of a long-term and cautious rival than an immediate military threat. Yet early in 1946 he ruminated that he was "tired babying the Soviets." "Unless Russia is faced with an iron fist and strong language," he reasoned, "another war is in the making." To his wife and daughter he remarked that a "totalitarian state is no different whether you call it Nazi, Fascist, [or] Communist." There "really is no difference between the government which [Soviet foreign minister] Molotov represents and the one the Czar represented—or the one Hitler spoke for."

Former British prime minister Winston Churchill, voted out of office in July 1945 but still a hero to many Americans, encouraged anti-Soviet sentiments. At the time, Great Britain faced bankruptcy and required a multi-billion dollar emergency loan from the United States. Like many of his compatriots, Churchill felt that he could raise support from the United States by presenting Britain as a partner in a campaign against Soviet expansionism. Speaking in Fulton, Missouri, on March 5, 1946, to an audience that included President Truman, Churchill declared dramatically that "from Stettin [Poland] in the Baltic to Trieste [Italy] in the Adriatic, an iron curtain has descended" across Europe. He proposed an alliance of all English-speaking people, backed by the atomic bomb that "God has willed to the United States," to tear down the curtain and protect the Middle East.

A year earlier, Churchill had spoken of an "iron fence" dividing Europe, but now he had hit on an even more memorable version of the phrase—one that would be echoed again and again over the next forty years. Although most prominent Americans initially resisted his call for a crusade against the new Soviet empire, the Iron Curtain speech symbolized a critical development in Western perceptions.

The View from the Kremlin

Soviet dictator Josef Stalin had his own doubts about the possibility of peaceful cooperation between East and West. Fearful of superior American economic and military power, he tried to isolate the Soviet heartland and the Eastern European satellite nations from contact with the outside world.

In a widely publicized speech to Soviet citizens delivered in February 1946, the Communist leader warned that it was in the nature of capitalism to prepare for war. He called on the hard-pressed Russian people to make greater sacrifices to develop heavy industry and safeguard their nation. Stalin referred to the threat of "capitalist encirclement" to justify his harsh regime and suppress demands for greater liberty and more consumer goods.

There is little evidence to suggest that the Kremlin either anticipated an American attack or considered using Soviet forces to attack the West. Nevertheless, Supreme Court Justice William O. Douglas, reflecting the view of many prominent Americans, called Stalin's speech a "declaration of World War III." For his part, the Soviet leader reacted angrily to Churchill's Iron Curtain speech that same month. He compared the British statesman's views to those of Hitler. The "racial theory" that those who spoke English should rule the world,

Stalin complained, sounded like an incitement to war with the Soviet Union. In the aftermath of this exchange, the Soviet government rejected the offer to join the American-sponsored World Bank and International Monetary Fund. Washington's formula to reduce world trade barriers, Soviet Foreign Minister V. M. Molotov declared, might "look like a tasty mushroom" but was really a "poisonous toadstool" designed to ensure American economic mastery.

After cutting off the Soviet bloc from Western economies, Stalin ordered a crash "Five-Year Plan" to develop heavy industry without aid from capitalist countries. Although this plan was probably intended as a defensive measure to protect the backward Soviet economy, Stalin's behavior impressed Americans as another effort to disrupt and divide the postwar world.

Changing Alliances

In 1946, Washington formally abandoned the plan, devised during the Second World War, of dismantling German heavy industry and giving Russia reparations—a plan, American officials complained, that had been drafted by economic idiots. Because the Soviets and Western powers seemed likely to retain separate occupation zones in Germany, American officials halted the shipment of reparations to the Soviet Union and instituted a merger of the British, American, and, later, French sectors into a single political unit, which eventually became West Germany. In September 1946, Secretary of State James Byrnes declared as America's goal the reconstruction of the German economy and suggested redrawing the German-Polish-Soviet boundaries to deprive Moscow of territorial gains. This evolution in American policy was bound to antagonize the Soviets, who were extremely sensitive not only to boundary questions but also to any attempt to rebuild Germany, a nation that had invaded Russia in both world wars.

In another decision that moved the United States closer to its wartime enemy and further from its former ally, Washington dropped a prohibition against using the services of former Nazis. The War Department's secret Operation Paperclip brought over 700 German scientists to the United States. Some were physicians who had performed horrible "medical" experiments on concentration camp inmates; others had overseen the death by exhaustion and starvation of slave laborers. Instead of prosecution, they were given new identities, if necessary, and hired as federal employees.

The postwar fortunes of rocket scientist Wernher von Braun exemplified this switch in American policy. As Germany collapsed, von Braun surrendered to American forces, along with several hundred colleagues and truckloads of data. One of the group explained, "We despise the French; we are mortally afraid of the Soviets; we do not believe the British can afford us; so that leaves the Americans." The scientists directed American commandos to a hidden stockpile of one hundred German V-2 rockets, located in the Soviet occupation zone. These weapons were whisked to an arsenal in New Mexico, and the U.S. Army later provided the von Braun team with a new laboratory in Alabama. Stalin fumed over the "revolting and inexcusable" blunder that had permitted America to get the rocket engineers.

Tensions in Iran and Turkey

In 1946 Soviet-American tensions mounted when disputes arose in Iran and Turkey. During the Second World War the Allies had deposed the pro-Nazi shah of Iran and jointly occupied that country. By early 1946, British and American forces had departed, but the Soviets lingered, demanding an oil concession like that held by the British for decades and supporting a separatist regime in northern Iran. Moscow also revived a long-standing demand that Turkey permit joint Soviet control over the Dardenelles, one of the strategic straits linking the Mediterranean with the Black Sea. Some American diplomats feared a Russian sweep across Turkey into the Mediterranean and across Iran to the Indian Ocean.

Declaring that the United States might as well find out now rather than later whether the Russians were bent on world conquest, Truman issued tough warnings to the Soviets and dispatched naval units to the Mediterranean. Stalin might be willing to probe, but he had no desire for a military showdown with the far more powerful United States. He backed down quickly in both Iran and Turkey. These incidents convinced policymakers that only firm resistance could halt what they perceived as the Soviet drive for world domination.

The Soviet Union may well have had expansionist goals. But its motives—a quest for resources, security, and influence—were no different from those of traditional empires. During the Second World War, when discussing Soviet interest in the Turkish straits, Stalin had asked how Churchill and Roosevelt would respond if Egypt closed the Suez Canal or if a South American nation threatened the Panama Canal. But few Americans could see any logic in such comparisons. Just as the Soviets' moves to enhance their security in Eastern Europe had aroused American suspicions, Russian meddling in Iran and Turkey convinced the United States that Stalin had targeted those areas for a takeover.

Atomic Deadlock

Suspicion affected nearly all areas of Soviet-American relations, including efforts to control atomic weapons. Estimates varied as to when the Soviets would build an atomic bomb of their own. Some American physicists thought it could be done within five years. Manhattan Project director General Leslie Groves, who had a low regard for Soviet science and mistakenly believed that Russia lacked high-grade uranium ore, thought the American monopoly secure for twenty years. His expectations were to prove false.

Hope that the atomic monopoly would compel Stalin to accept American demands faded quickly. Whenever the subject of the bomb entered Soviet-American discussions, Russian negotiators toughened their positions. Determined not to allow the Americans to think he feared the weapon, Stalin told his colleagues that atomic bombs were meant to frighten those with weak nerves.

With the goals of preserving at least a modest edge in armaments and, perhaps, avoiding a dangerous arms race, the United States proposed in March 1946 that the Soviets accept a plan for international control of atomic energy. As originally drafted by Dean Acheson and David Lillienthal, the scheme called for placing nuclear research and materials under international supervision. While other nations implemented the program, the United States would retain its atomic monopoly.

The next month, Truman named financier Bernard Baruch to present the plan formally to the United Nations. Baruch took a harsher line toward the Soviets, insisting on an American-dominated, veto-proof control commission with the right to manage all atomic facilities within the Soviet Union. Truman encouraged this approach, telling Baruch that "we should not under any circumstances throw away our gun until we are sure the rest of the world can't arm against us." The Soviets rejected such a humiliating plan. They proposed an immediate ban on existing—that is, American—bombs, but suggested that a compromise might be possible. Baruch balked, insisting that Moscow accept his original formula, which was known by that time as the Baruch Plan.

In the middle of the United Nations debate, the United States conducted a dramatic series of atomic bomb tests at Bikini atoll in the Pacific. Through these tests, some of which were broadcast live over the radio, Truman hoped to sway the Soviets' position by demonstrating that the United States intended to keep its preeminent military power and continue with the development of nuclear weapons. When Stalin refused to blink, the Baruch Plan died and the Soviets accelerated their own nuclear research.

At home, Truman backed pleas by American scientists for legislation placing control of atomic energy in civilian hands. The Atomic Energy Act of 1946 created an Atomic Energy Commission (AEC) staffed by civilian appointees. To prevent, in Truman's words, "some dashing lieutenant colonel [from] deciding when would be the proper time to drop one," the AEC retained possession of atomic weapons until the president authorized their transfer to the military and their use. The Atomic Energy Act virtually barred sharing atomic data with other nations.

The creation of the AEC could not, however, make Americans feel easy about the existence of nuclear weapons. The term "atomic age" had come into use in 1945, and the knowledge that nuclear weapons could destroy the world in a matter of minutes was affecting the national psyche. Some Americans made light of the danger by naming tavern drinks "atomic cocktails" or enjoying hit tunes like the "Atomic Polka" and "Atom Bomb Baby." In 1946 a French fashion designer christened a new type of bathing suit the "bikini," after America's Pacific test site. But the vision of a nuclear holocaust had begun to haunt people's imaginations.

The underlying anxieties were expressed in *Life* magazine's chilling fictional account of the "36-Hour War," published in November 1945. The article presented lurid descriptions of a mushroom cloud rising over Washington, D.C., and missiles hitting other cities. Although *Life* assured its readers that America "won" the fictionalized atomic war, the victory seemed dubious. Drawings showed technicians in protective gear checking for radioactivity in front of the New York Public Library's marble lions—the only things standing amid the city's rubble. In December 1945, when *Time* named Harry Truman its "Man of the Year," a mushroom cloud on the cover dwarfed the picture of Truman.

THE BIRTH OF CONTAINMENT

Curiously, despite the growing international tensions and hostile rhetoric, the Soviet and American governments took steps to reduce their military commitments through 1946 and early 1947. For example, the United States cut its military budget and built few atomic bombs in this period. In fact, the tiny atomic arsenal consisted mostly of component parts requiring complex assembly, and relatively few planes were equipped to carry the weapons. Stalin, too, cut military expenditures, backed off in Turkey and Iran, withdrew troops from northern Norway, pulled his forces out of Manchuria, and supported American mediation efforts in the Chinese civil war.

Nevertheless, by the end of 1947, the United States had begun major programs to resist Communist guerrillas in Greece, expand its nuclear arsenal, and forge a Western military alliance—and all of these steps were justified as responses to Soviet threats. How and why did this change occur? The answer involves a complex of factors, including instability in certain parts of the world, American strategic perceptions, Soviet actions, and domestic American politics.

The "Long Telegram" and the Clifford Report

By early 1947, chaos engulfed so much of the world that it appeared vast new riches might simply fall into the lap of the Soviet Union. A nearly bankrupt Britain prepared to abandon India, Palestine, and Greece. Vietnamese and Indonesians had risen against their colonial masters. In China, civil war raged. Simply preventing starvation in occupied Germany and Japan cost the United States nearly $1 billion per year.

As early as February 1946, George F. Kennan, second in command in the United States embassy in Moscow and the leading State Department expert on Soviet affairs, had analyzed the deteriorating relations between the United States and the Soviet Union in an 8,000-word telegram sent from the Moscow embassy to Washington. In July 1947, the influential journal *Foreign Affairs* published an expanded version, written by Kennan under the pseudonym "Mr. X." In these documents Kennan argued that Stalin provoked tensions with the West as a means of justifying to the Soviet people his harsh dictatorship. Kennan portrayed Soviet policy as a "fluid stream which moves constantly, wherever it is permitted to move," toward a goal of imperial domination. Although Soviet power was "impervious to the logic of reason," it remained "highly sensitive to the logic of force." Instead of accommodating the Kremlin, Kennan believed, Washington should respond with "long-term, patient but firm and vigilant containment." Before long, the term *containment*, or halting the extension of Soviet influence wherever that might occur, became the operating principle of American foreign policy.

The timing of Kennan's "Long Telegram," which immediately followed Stalin's bellicose speech of February 1946 and preceded United States–Soviet confrontations over Iran, Turkey, Germany, and the Baruch Plan, prompted policymakers to view it as a guide for decoding Soviet behavior. American officials liked Kennan's assertion that Soviet leaders felt an ideological compulsion to treat the outside world as hostile. This explanation of international tension held the West blameless, dismissed the importance to Russia of its huge wartime losses, and obscured the reality of Soviet economic weakness.

A few months after Truman received Kennan's telegram he assigned his counsel, Clark Clifford, to use it as the basis for policy recommendations. Clifford's study, presented to Truman on September 24, 1946, further simplified Kennan's already simplified point by asserting that the language of power was the only language Stalin understood. The president was already in favor of a get-tough policy toward the Soviet Union. Four days before receiving Clifford's report, Truman had fired Commerce Secretary Henry A. Wallace for delivering a foreign policy speech in New York City in which he condemned the arms race and the foreign policies of both Moscow and

Washington, calling for a more conciliatory approach on both sides. Denouncing Wallace's speech, the president complained to Clifford that the "Reds, phonies and the parlor pinks are becoming a national danger."

Despite his condemnation of Wallace's remarks, Truman did not publicly release Clifford's inflammatory report. He explained to former vice president John Nance Garner that "there is too much loose talk about the Russian situation." Moreover, as Truman tacitly acknowledged, few direct flashpoints of Soviet-American confrontation existed. The Soviets were far more likely to exploit political and economic problems in Europe and Asia than to seek military confrontation.

The gravest problem in Europe and Japan, as knowledgeable officials in Washington realized, was a huge "dollar gap" of more than $8 billion—the difference between the value of American exports and the amount of dollars foreign customers had available to pay for them. The dollar gap threatened to halt world trade. This imbalance could continue only for as long as the United States government and private lenders provided credit. They would risk doing so only if Europe and Japan showed signs of industrial recovery. Once credits disappeared, foreign nations would cease trading with the United States, perhaps causing the kind of global collapse that fed the Great Depression and Second World War.

Policymakers agreed that successful containment of Soviet influence depended on reconstruction of the European and Japanese economies. As long as the "greatest workshops of Europe and Asia—Germany and Japan"—remained idle, Undersecretary of State Dean Acheson warned, peace and prosperity would never be achieved. Yet most members of Congress rejected this approach because reconstruction of Europe and Japan would require a major increase in foreign economic aid, something never before done in peacetime. Only a simple, dramatic issue might mobilize Congress and the public.

The Truman Doctrine and the Marshall Plan

Since 1944, a brutal civil war had raged between Greek monarchists, supported by Britain, and the leftist coalition known as EAM, from the Greek initials for National Liberation Front. EAM had led the anti-Nazi resistance and now fought the corrupt and repressive regime in Athens. It included both Communists and non-Communists.

On February 21, 1947, the financially hard-pressed British government informed Washington it could no longer afford to support the Greek regime. Although the Truman administration had already provided $200 million in aid to Greece, assuming the full British burden would cost more. The United States ambassador to Athens warned that the Soviets regarded Greece as a ripe plum ready for picking and that the rebels would mount an all-out offensive when Britain withdrew its support.

The new secretary of state, George C. Marshall, who had served as military chief of staff in the Second World War, explained the Greek situation to congressional leaders. Marshall, never a dramatic orator, spoke of humanitarian reasons for assuming Britain's burden. As the politicians yawned, Undersecretary Dean Acheson took charge. He described a battle like the classical struggle between Athens and Sparta. The United States and the Soviet Union were divided by an "unbridgeable ideological chasm." Acheson depicted the contest as one between democracy and liberty, on one side, and dictatorship and absolute conformity, on the other. If the United States walked away, then, "like apples in a barrel infected by one rotten one," the "corruption of Greece would infect Iran and all to the East."

After a stunned silence, Senator Arthur Vandenberg, the Republican chairman of the Senate Foreign Relations Committee, reportedly said that if Truman told this to Congress, it would support an aid program. According to another version of the same meeting, Vandenberg declared that if the Democrats wanted to provide a WPA-style welfare program for Greece, Truman needed to "scare hell out of the American people."

Accordingly, the president told aides not to write him a speech that sounded "too much like an investment prospectus" but one that proclaimed "America's answer to the surge of Communist tyranny." Shunning advice from Kennan that he not make anticommunism the major theme of a foreign aid request, Acheson's draft stressed the "global struggle between freedom and totalitarianism."

When Truman addressed Congress on March 12, 1947, he declared that "it must be the policy of the United States to support free peoples who are resisting attempted subjugation by armed minorities or by outside pressures." Almost immediately, this statement was dubbed the Truman Doctrine. Specifically, Truman called for a $400 million program of aid to Greece and Turkey. Turkey was added to the program in part to defuse the Turks' anger over American aid to their traditional Greek rivals; moreover, by enlarging the area included in the aid program, the administration spurred Congress to take the danger more seriously.

Swayed by Truman's appeal, the Republican-dominated Congress passed the aid bill quickly. In practice, the term "supporting free peoples" meant defending any regime threatened by communism—or, often, non-Communist rebels—even if, as in the case of Greece, the government in power was not democratic. As Senator William Fulbright later wrote, "more than any other factor, the anti-communism of the Truman Doctrine" became the "guiding spirit of American foreign policy" for forty years.

Years later, policymakers would use the Greek experience as a model for American intervention in Vietnam. Greece, however, was a unique case—and the civil war there did not involve direct Soviet influence. It was Yugoslavia, rather than the Soviet Union, that supplied aid to the Greek Communist rebels. Josep Tito, the Yugoslav leader, had visions of annexing Greece to a Balkan federation dominated by Yugoslavia. But Stalin resented such empire building by his subalterns; in mid-1948 he denounced Tito and tried to topple him. Searching for new friends, Tito halted aid to the Greek rebels and forced them out of Yugoslav sanctuaries. This change, along with American aid to the Greek government, brought a defeat of the insurgents by late 1949.

The greatest impact of the Truman Doctrine, however, came not in Greece but in Western Europe. On June 5, 1947, speaking at Harvard University, Secretary of State Marshall revealed the outlines of a European Recovery Plan (ERP), which soon became known as the Marshall Plan. To prevent the Soviets from taking advantage of European economic collapse, the plan offered a multiyear, comprehensive program to assist industrial recovery and trade. Although German industry was considered especially important, the program would include other nations as well. Truman asked Congress to back up these ideas with a $27 billion appropriation. The Truman Doctrine and the Marshall Plan, he explained, were "two halves of the same walnut."

Technically, the Marshall Plan did not bar participation by the Soviet Union or its satellites. However, certain provisions virtually ensured that the Soviets would reject the program. In order to participate, Moscow would have had to open its financial books for American scrutiny and coordinate economic policies with the West. The Soviet foreign minister, V. M. Molotov, attended the first planning conference in Paris and proposed that each European nation present its own wish list to Washington, without establishing any common program. When this tactic failed, Molotov stormed out, to Washington's great relief. Poland, Hungary, and Czechoslovakia also reluctantly withdrew to avoid offending the Soviet Union.

Congressional Approval for the Marshall Plan

While Washington and its European friends worked out the details of an aid program, Truman urged Congress to provide interim assistance. Republican leaders balked until Stalin gave Truman an unintended assist. The Soviet dictator encouraged Communist labor unions in Italy and France to go on strike, creating a scare in the United States. One savvy French politician remarked, "because we have a 'communist danger' the Americans are making a tremendous effort to help us. We must keep up this indispensable communist scare."

A Soviet-inspired coup in Czechoslovakia also helped convince Congress to act on the Marshall Plan. On February 25, 1948, Czech Communists—supported by a massing of Soviet troops on the Czech border—seized power in Prague and brought their nation into the Soviet bloc. The sense of crisis deepened on March 5 when General Lucius Clay, commander of American forces in western Germany, warned of a "subtle change" in Soviet behavior. He felt that war might come with dramatic suddenness.

Neither the Czech coup nor Clay's warning really surprised American officials. State Department and military personnel had anticipated a Soviet move to stifle Czechoslovak independence as a means of sealing off Eastern Europe from the Marshall Plan. Nevertheless, Truman played up these incidents in a speech to Congress on March 17, 1948. Pleading for passage of the Marshall Plan and measures to boost military preparedness, he argued that recent events showed the intent of the Soviet Union to dominate the remaining free nations of Europe.

Congress finally passed a trimmed-down version of the Marshall Plan and also appropriated funds to rebuild the economy of Japan. Over the next several years, the United States provided more than $15 billion in Marshall Plan and Japanese assistance, the equivalent of at least $85 billion in 1990 dollars.

Institutionalizing the Cold War

Along with foreign aid programs, Truman's administration reformed the military and intelligence arms of the government. For years, the navy, army, and Army Air Corps had squabbled over funds, each service seeing the others as a threat to its own survival. At the same time, the nation lacked an independent intelligence agency to collect and assess vital information. Each uniformed service and the State Department collected intelligence separately and interpreted it in ways that benefited its own organization. To add to these burdens, the military draft had lapsed after the war, creating chronic manpower shortages in the uniformed services.

The National Security Act of 1947 addressed many of these problems. It consolidated the separate War and Navy departments into a Department of Defense, led by a civilian defense secretary. However, the three armed services (army, navy, air force) retained their separate identities. The act formally named the military head of each service to the Joint Chiefs of Staff and made all of these leaders military advisers to the president. Congress also revived the peacetime draft.

The new law created a National Security Council to advise the president on foreign policy, as well as a Central Intelligence Agency (CIA) to gather and analyze intelligence. Soon the CIA expanded its role to include covert missions abroad. The CIA's first test came in Italy, where it funded anti-Communist parties and helped secure their victory in elections during 1947 and 1948.

In 1948, Washington began rebuilding American military power. The atomic arsenal grew from 15 to more than 200 bombs by 1950. The United States also encouraged Western European nations to form a mutual defense pact as the first step toward creation of the North Atlantic Treaty Organization a year later.

The Berlin Blockade and Airlift

In response to the Marshall Plan and the changes in American military and intelligence services, Stalin imposed even tighter economic and political control on his Eastern European satellites and purged Communist party members he feared might harbor liberal or independent tendencies. Most dramatically, in June 1948, the Soviets imposed a blockade on land routes into West Berlin, the non-Communist enclave deep inside eastern Germany.

The question of control over and access to the American, French, British, and Soviet occupation zones in Germany was a thorny issue and one ripe for exploitation. Before June 1948, the Western nations had already agreed in principle to unite their occupation zones into a single unit. Seeing that he had failed to prevent the restoration of a potentially powerful West German state, Stalin tried to drive the Western powers out of Berlin, lest that city become an anti-Soviet rallying point. When, as part of the unification process, Washington decreed a currency reform for the Western-occupied zones of Germany and Berlin, Moscow declared it a violation of earlier occupation agreements, and Russian troops were ordered to stop all road and rail transport into the divided city from the West.

Although air corridors over Berlin had been guaranteed, the rules governing land access to Berlin were vague. Occupation commander General Lucius Clay urged Truman to allow him to shoot his way through Soviet barriers. If Berlin fell, he warned, "western Germany will be next." Given Moscow's large advantage in ground forces, Truman opted instead for an airlift to run the blockade. He also bluffed by sending sixty atomic-capable B-29 bombers, without atomic weapons, to England.

As the president had guessed, Stalin did not want to start a war. Soviet planes never challenged the massive American air transport lifeline into the besieged city. In May 1949 the Soviets lifted the blockade. The Berlin airlift had lasted nearly a year, becoming a symbol of American resolve and Soviet brutishness. It hastened the creation of what the Soviets greatly feared, an independent West German state, the Federal Republic of Germany, in May 1949. In rebuttal, the Soviet

A United States transport plane helps to supply Berliners cut off by the Soviet land blockade in 1948. *UPI/Bettmann Newsphotos.*

Union created the East German state, the German Democratic Republic, the following month.

The Berlin airlift had other, less tangible results as well. It modified the feelings many Europeans, recently victims of Nazi aggression, harbored toward Germany. Instead of former enemies, Germans became victims of the Cold War. The airlift also seemed a further illustration of the ability to make the Soviets back down through a show of strength.

The Creation of NATO

When the frustrated Russians lifted their blockade of Berlin, the United States had, by most measures, won the Cold War in Western Europe and Japan. The Marshall Plan nations and Japan were on the road to economic recovery. The state of West Germany, led by Konrad Adenauer, had come into existence. Communism had lost its attraction for most Europeans. Stalin's efforts to keep Japan and Europe weak, divided, and isolated from the United States had failed miserably. George Kennan considered the American position so strong that he urged his superiors to offer Moscow a deal unifying Germany as a militarily neutral nation. He thought this might stabilize Europe while reducing tension, but top American policymakers scoffed at the idea.

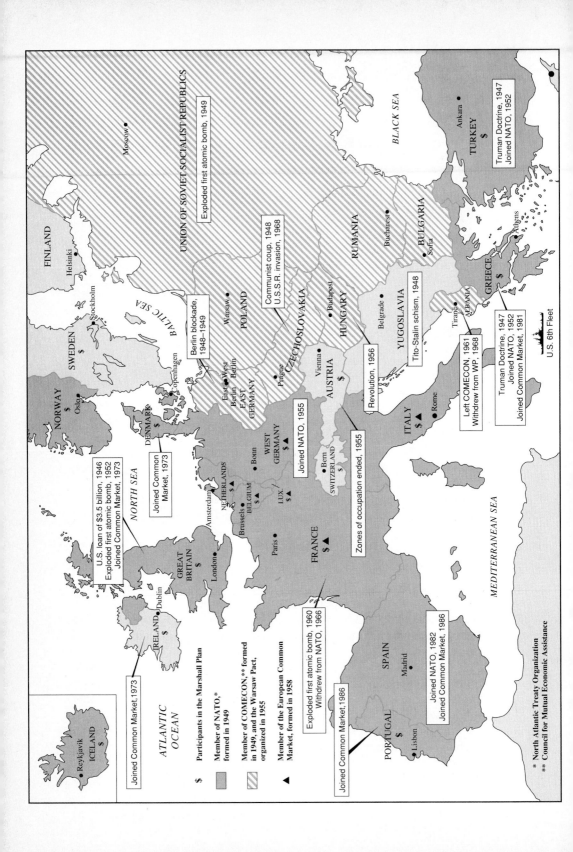

Following Truman's election in November 1948, he appointed Dean Acheson, the former undersecretary of state who had briefly left the State Department, as the new secretary of state, replacing the ailing George Marshall. Acheson favored a military alliance, including West Germany, to resist any potential Soviet threat. In April 1949 he oversaw creation of the North Atlantic Treaty Organization (NATO). The NATO pact pledged the United States, Britain, France, Belgium, the Netherlands, Italy, Portugal, Denmark, Iceland, Norway, and Canada to a common defense; Greece, Turkey, Spain, and West Germany joined later. NATO, Acheson told Congress, would go beyond a "balance of power" to give the West a "preponderance of power" over Moscow. Congress approved the NATO treaty in mid-1949, along with a billion-dollar Mutual Defense Assistance Program (MDAP) to supply weapons and technology to NATO members. This military aid supplemented the Marshall Plan.

For Eastern Europe, the Soviets countered with a Council for Mutual Economic Assistance (known as the CMEA or COMECON) and later with the Warsaw Pact. By formal alliance as well as ideology, Europe was now divided in two (see map).

FURTHER RAMIFICATIONS OF THE COLD WAR

Even as the Marshall Plan and NATO were overcoming any serious threat of Soviet influence in Western Europe, the Cold War brought new concerns. Soviet development of an atomic bomb prompted Washington to reevaluate American security needs. Communist successes in China and Vietnam led to demands for deeper American involvement in those regions. Meanwhile, some sensational espionage cases raised fears that the Soviets could gain dominance simply by stealing American nuclear secrets.

The Nuclear Arms Race and NSC-68

In September 1949, American planes collected air samples indicating that an atomic explosion had occurred inside the Soviet Union, years earlier than expected. One high government official described the Soviet achievement as an insult to the American people. Many feared that the Soviet Union's possession of nuclear weapons would place it on an equal military footing with the United States and encourage it to take direct military action. Public anxiety found expression through

◄ **Divided Europe**

J. Robert Oppenheimer

In the immediate aftermath of the Second World War, J. Robert Oppenheimer acquired the glamour of a movie star. Celebrated as the father of the atomic bomb, he was featured on the cover of *Time.* Yet few people knew much about this shy, vain, and driven man.

"Oppie," as his colleagues called him, had grown up in New York City, attended Harvard, and studied physics in Europe before returning to teach at Berkeley and the California Institute of Technology. Before the war he helped to educate a generation of leading physicists. He also supported many left-wing causes, and his wife, brother, and sister-in-law all supported the Communist party at one time or another.

Despite these associations, Oppenheimer became head of the secret atomic

increasingly frequent sightings of "unidentified flying objects," or flying saucers, a phenomenon that peaked in the early 1950s.

The Soviet bomb triggered a debate in Washington over whether to build a new bomb a thousand times more powerful than the first atomic weapon. This superbomb, or hydrogen bomb, was to use the energy derived from the fusion of hydrogen atoms; the atomic bombs used energy derived from the splitting, or fission, of atoms. Those who opposed development of the superbomb doubted that Soviet atomic weapons would greatly alter the American military advantage because the Russians lacked an effective delivery system. With some modification, American atomic bombs could be made far more powerful than the early prototypes. Thus, the superbomb might not have any advantage in deterring an enemy. Others, who favored a slow approach to the exceedingly costly build-up of nuclear weapons, believed that Washington should first try to negotiate an arms control pact with Moscow. If Stalin stalled or raced ahead with his own hy-

weapons laboratory at Los Alamos, New Mexico, in 1942. In July 1945, while his colleagues celebrated the successful test of the first atomic bomb, Oppenheimer recited to himself an apocalyptic passage from a Hindu religious classic: "I am become death, the shatterer of worlds."

After the war, he resumed his academic career and served as a high-level adviser to the Atomic Energy Commission. As an advocate of the international control of atomic energy, he helped draft the ill-fated Baruch Plan of 1946. But by the early 1950s his outspoken opposition to development of the hydrogen bomb, which he considered a militarily useless terror weapon, earned him the wrath of powerful enemies. His criticism of the bomb was denounced as an effort to aid the Soviet Union; he was even accused of passing secrets to the Soviets. In 1954, at a dramatic review of his security clearance, the FBI played up his past friendships with Communists. Although no evidence linked him to disloyalty, in the tense atmosphere of the Red Scare the accusations proved damning. In May 1954 the AEC stripped him of his security clearance and dismissed him as an adviser on atomic policy.

This verdict ended Oppenheimer's public career. He returned to academics, and in December 1963 President Lyndon Johnson belatedly awarded him a public service medal in recognition of his contributions to American science. Oppenheimer died in 1967. ∎

drogen bomb project, the United States would still have the option of matching him.

The influential physicist and government adviser, J. Robert Oppenheimer, who had directed the original atomic bomb project, raised serious technical and moral objections to the hydrogen bomb. He doubted that a workable hydrogen bomb could be built. Because atomic fission bombs could be made powerful enough to destroy any Soviet military target, he feared that a superbomb would become a weapon of genocide. George Kennan agreed, calling for talks with Moscow to halt a spiraling arms race.

Yet neither Oppenheimer nor Kennan, both of whom were about to be eased out of their positions, persuaded top policymakers. Acheson selected hard-liner Paul Nitze to replace Kennan as head of policy planning in the State Department and as chair of a committee that urged rapid development of the hydrogen bomb. President Truman needed little convincing. America had to make the bomb, he said later, if "only for bargaining purposes with the Russians." After getting the nod to proceed in January 1950, American scientists exploded a prototype hydrogen device in November 1952. But a Soviet test of a hydrogen bomb occurred the next August.

When Truman asked Acheson to undertake a comprehensive study of American security policy, the secretary of state again tapped Nitze for the job. In the resulting top-secret document, issued by the National Security Council and numbered NSC-68, Nitze assumed that the risk of a Soviet attack was considerably greater than ever before. Without specifying why, he claimed that Soviet behavior showed a new boldness that "borders on the reckless." Nitze advocated tripling American defense spending, from $13 billion to $50 billion annually. This increment would be used to fund both conventional forces and a new generation of nuclear weapons and delivery systems. Nitze confided to his staff that such huge sums were unlikely to be appropriated except as a result of a scare campaign to shock the public.

NSC-68, given to the president in April 1950, painted a lurid picture of the Kremlin as motivated by "fanatical faith" to "impose its authority on the rest of the world." It greatly exaggerated Soviet military strength, claiming that by 1954 Moscow would possess the nuclear capacity to destroy the United States. The report called for an immediate and large-scale build-up of nuclear and conventional weapons to meet each new Soviet challenge promptly anywhere in the world.

Acheson, who privately admitted the study's verbal excesses, hoped it would "bludgeon the mass mind of government" into action. Other high officials supported the proposed increase in defense spending for a variety of reasons. For example, members of the president's Council of Economic Advisers argued that large defense expenditures would boost industrial output and employment, strengthening the economy. Yet Truman remained cautious. He endorsed NSC-68 in principle but worried about its high price tag. Before long, however, the outbreak of the Korean War would make the proposal for higher defense expenditures a reality.

The "Loss" of China

In October 1949, a month after the confirmation of a Soviet atomic test, the administration received more bad news when Communist leader Mao Zedong (spelled Mao Tse-tung in the old transliteration) established the People's Republic of China. After four years of civil war, Nationalist party leader Jiang Jieshi (Chiang Kai-shek) had fled to the island province of Taiwan. The Communist victory mobilized administration bashers in Congress and disheartened Americans who considered China their favorite, but now lost, charity.

Jiang Jieshi and Mao Zedong at an American-sponsored peace conference in 1945. Civil war soon followed. *Jack Wilkes/Life Magazine,* © *Time Inc.*

China policy had been in disarray since 1945. The long civil war between the Communists and Kuomintang (Nationalists, or KMT) had resumed as soon as Japan surrendered. Truman tried to help Jiang by giving him over $2 billion in military and economic aid between 1945 and 1949, but Nationalist incompetence and Communist strength mitigated its effect.

During 1946, General George C. Marshall served a year as Truman's mediator in China, trying to arrange a political compromise. Both Nationalists and Communists, however, believed they could win a military showdown and opposed real power sharing. Marshall gave up in January 1947, pronounced a plague on both Chinese factions, and returned to Washington to become secretary of state.

Thereafter the administration pretty much wrote off China, assuming it would either remain in chaos or come under Communist control. Military aid seemed pointless, as the Communists drove well-armed Nationalist troops from positions that American advisers regarded as easily defensible. In private, Truman called Jiang a crook, and many senators agreed that more aid to Jiang was "money down a rat hole."

The prospect of a Communist China did not worry most professional diplomats. Moscow did not play a significant role in the civil war, and China was so poor that any Chinese-Soviet alliance was likely to drain rather than enhance Soviet resources. State Department experts even predicted that the Chinese Communists would soon fall out with the bullying Soviets.

To appease Republican critics, Truman had included in 1948 a small China Aid Act within the Marshall Plan. It hardly mattered, since many of Jiang's generals sold their weapons to the Communists. Jiang himself fled to Taiwan (then called Formosa) before most of the assistance authorized in 1948 reached the mainland.

In August 1949, the State Department issued a massive report known as the *China White Paper* that condemned the Communists for their subservience to Russia but insisted that Jiang, not the United States, had "lost China." Although Truman kept the Chinese Communists at arm's length, he would not use American forces to defend Jiang's precarious regime on Taiwan.

Truman and Secretary of State Dean Acheson tried to calm worried legislators by saying that Washington would wait until the confusion of the Chinese civil war had settled before it would consider recognizing the People's Republic of China. In January 1950 the president terminated military aid to Jiang's government in exile on Taiwan. Acheson, in a speech before the National Press Club in Washington, urged turning away from China and concentrating instead on developing the "Great Crescent," the lands on the rim of China, stretching from Japan through Southeast Asia to India. Southeast Asian resources, he stressed, were vital to both Europe and Japan. In a remark little noticed at the time, he also described South Korea as outside the United States defense perimeter in Asia. Republican critics labeled the White Paper a whitewash and accused Truman and Acheson of coddling Chinese Communists.

Drawing the Line in Vietnam

By 1950 the United States had begun assisting French forces fighting a Communist-led uprising in French Indochina, comprised of Vietnam, Cambodia, and Laos. During the Second World War Vietnamese guerrilla leader Ho Chi Minh had cooperated in the anti-Japanese struggle, and in 1945 he appealed for American support in securing independence. Roosevelt had urged the French to loosen their hold on Vietnam, but Truman seemed less inclined to support anticolonial movements. Few American diplomats knew much about Southeast Asia, and those who sympathized with the independence movements were usually ignored.

In 1947 Dean Acheson, then undersecretary of state, spoke for the administration when he declared that in colonial areas, "all Stalinists masquerade as nationalists." Condemning Ho's Vietminh guerrillas as Soviet dupes, Acheson warned that their victory would expose all of Southeast Asia to Moscow's influence. He was also concerned that loss of the colony could weaken French resolve to resist Soviet expansion in Europe.

Still, Washington's uneasiness over supporting a colonial war led Acheson to insist that France go through the motions of naming a Vietnamese as the colony's nominal ruler, with the promise of eventual independence. To Washington's dismay, France selected Bao Dai, a disreputable playboy descended from Vietnamese royalty, as their puppet emperor. One American diplomat protested that Bao Dai's "entire political following consisted of a pimp and three prostitutes." Nevertheless, in February 1950, after China and the Soviet Union recognized Ho's insurgent government, Washington felt obliged to recognize Bao Dai's puppet regime. That spring, American support for the French effort took physical form as the first American arms and advisers arrived in Saigon.

Drawing the line in Vietnam did not placate a coalition of legislators and citizens, loosely organized into a China lobby, which blamed the administration for losing China and underrating the threat of communism in Asia. Republican senators such as Kenneth Wherry of Nebraska, William Knowland of California, and Pat McCarran of Nevada, along with Minnesota Representative Walter Judd and publishers Henry Luce and Roy Howard, insisted that more aid would have saved Jiang. They accused Dean Acheson and China specialists in the State Department of holding Communist sympathies. A young Democratic congressman from Massachusetts, John F. Kennedy, charged that the administration had deserted China, "whose freedom we once fought to preserve. What our young men had saved, our diplomats and president have frittered away."

Fears of Espionage

In the same month that Washington recognized Bao Dai's regime, British agents arrested Klaus Fuchs, an emigré German scientist, who confessed to being part of a spy ring that had passed secrets to the Soviets from the American nuclear laboratory at Los Alamos, New Mexico. By the summer of 1950 evidence from Fuchs led to the arrest of American Communists Julius and Ethel Rosenberg, who were charged with heading the conspiracy.

At a sensational and highly publicized trial, the Rosenbergs denied committing espionage, even though a relative who had worked at Los Alamos confessed to giving Julius information during the Second World War. After sifting the evidence for years, many historians conclude that Julius Rosenberg probably did pass a variety of industrial secrets to the Soviets, but the atomic data seem to have been relatively unimportant. Whatever the truth may have been, the two Rosenbergs were convicted, and in 1953 they died in the electric chair. Fuchs and others were sentenced to prison.

In retrospect, many scientists now believe that espionage played a minor role in Soviet weapons development. In the heightened atmosphere of the early 1950s, however, with the Red Scare raging and Alger Hiss just convicted of perjury in his own spy case (see page 69), both government officials and ordinary Americans worried that traitors were giving the Kremlin vital data. After Fuchs's arrest, Senator Homer Capehart rose to ask: "How much more are we going to have to take? Fuchs and Acheson and Hiss and hydrogen bombs threatening outside and New Dealism eating away at the vitals of the nation. In the name of Heaven, is this the best America can do?"

THE RISE OF JOSEPH MCCARTHY

Amid worries over international espionage and traitors at home, a hitherto obscure senator, Joseph R. McCarthy of Wisconsin, staked his claim to fame. A relative latecomer to the Red Scare, the senator so dominated the years from 1950 to 1954 with his antics that *McCarthyism* became the catchword for the era.

McCarthy came from a poor farm family and worked his way through high school, college, and law school. He won election to a county judgeship in the early 1940s by describing his opponent as senile. During the war he served as a Marine desk intelligence officer in the Pacific. By flying several routine missions in the tail gunner's seat of an airplane, he established a combat record that he exaggerated in 1946 when he campaigned for the Senate as "tail gunner Joe." A split within Republican ranks secured his nomination. He won election against a weak Democrat in a strong Republican year.

By 1950 McCarthy had earned the label of "worst senator" among journalists. His reputation sank further when he spoke in favor of exonerating Nazi storm troopers convicted of massacring American prisoners of war. In need of a re-election issue, he borrowed reports from his friend, California Congressman Richard Nixon, and on February 9, 1950, told a gathering of Republican women in Wheeling, West Virginia, that America faced defeat because Dean Acheson, "this pompous diplomat in striped pants and a phony British accent," had turned over the formulation of foreign policy to subversives. "I have here in my hand," he declared, "a list of 205 [Communists] whose names were known to the Secretary of State and who nevertheless are still working and shaping the policy of the State Department."

During the next week he repeated the speech several times, frequently changing the number of Communists. McCarthy's crude

As lawyer Joseph Welch (hand on brow) listens, Senator Joseph McCarthy lectures a special Senate committee about the supposed Communist conspiracy in the United States. *UPI/Bettmann Newsphotos.*

arithmetic derived from a list of State Department employees who had been accused of a variety of improprieties, not subversion. McCarthy soon labeled as Communists and traitors the "whole group of twisted-thinking New Dealers who have led America to near ruin at home and abroad."

McCarthy was a cynical opportunist who came to believe his own ravings. Taking advantage of Truman's rhetoric and anti-Communist policies, which seemed to legitimize accusations of political disloyalty, the Wisconsin senator and his supporters simply turned these charges against the Democrats. His conspiracy theory provided simple answers to complex questions. America did not need a Marshall Plan or NATO to win the Cold War, only a purge of Red sympathizers in government.

Democratic senators tried to expose McCarthy as a fraud during the spring of 1950. They established a committee, chaired by Millard Tydings of Maryland, which demanded that McCarthy document the charges of treason he had brought against diplomats. McCarthy's outrageous behavior turned the hearings into a circus. Each time he failed to provide details on one of his alleged card-carrying Communists, the senator popped up with another name, just in time for reporters to insert it in late editions of their newspapers. Senator Robert Taft and other supposedly responsible Republicans encouraged his guerrilla attacks. "If one case fails," Taft told him, "try another." The cascade of accusations and lies became difficult to refute, and the hearings ended in acrimony.

In November 1950, McCarthy took revenge on Tydings by helping his virtually unknown Republican opponent, John M. Butler, win an upset victory. McCarthy's staff prepared a fake photograph purporting to show Tydings and former Communist party leader Earl Browder in friendly conversation. Even though Tydings's campaign was hampered by other factors, such as his segregationist stance, which turned black voters against him, McCarthy took credit for toppling the veteran Democrat. His success convinced many potential critics to avoid speaking out against him.

McCarthy's tactics and manipulation of the mass media presented journalists with ethical and professional problems. Accustomed to verbatim reporting of politicians' statements, news reporters became a vehicle for outright lies and misrepresentations. Journalist George Reedy recalled that covering McCarthy was a shattering experience for honest reporters, who felt obliged to take what McCarthy said at face value and give it coverage because he was a senator. Reedy knew that "Joe couldn't find a Communist in Red Square. He didn't know Karl Marx from Groucho." But, for nearly four years, McCarthy's charges paralyzed the State Department and terrified other government agencies. Diplomats such as John Carter Vincent, O. Edmund Clubb, John S. Service, and John Paton Davies were purged because of absurd charges that they had lost China. McCarthy's influence grew even stronger after the Republicans captured a Senate majority in November 1952.

Meanwhile, in the summer of 1950, the NSC-68 report, which advocated a massive increase in defense spending, languished on the president's desk while Truman pondered how to justify the cost of implementing its proposals. Then, as one of Acheson's aides later remarked, "Korea came along and saved us."

THE KOREAN WAR AND ITS CONSEQUENCES

The North Korean invasion of South Korea on June 25, 1950, transformed the Cold War into a hot one. It also transformed American defense strategy, even though most Americans could not locate Korea on a map. When the fighting stopped in 1953, defense spending surpassed the levels envisioned in NSC-68, and several hundred thousand American troops were on station with NATO. Moreover, the war created a precedent of great significance: by committing the country to an extensive military effort without a congressional declaration of war, Truman set the pattern for Vietnam and other American military involvements in the following decades.

The Beginnings of Conflict

In August 1945, Soviet and American military planners had divided the Korean peninsula, a Japanese colony since 1910, into temporary occupation zones north and south of the 38th parallel. When Moscow and Washington fell out, the division hardened. The Soviets sponsored a Communist regime, the Democratic People's Republic of Korea, led by veteran Korean Communist Kim Il Sung, north of the dividing line. In the south, the United States supported a right-wing government, the Republic of Korea, led by Syngman Rhee, a Korean exile who had lived in the United States for decades. Soviet and American occupation forces departed by 1949, leaving behind rival regimes, each claiming the right to rule an undivided Korea. Violence within and between both states was so common that between 1945 and 1949 an estimated 100,000 Koreans died in political strife.

"From the standpoint of military security," the Joint Chiefs of Staff wrote in 1947, the United States had "little strategic interest in maintaining the present troops and bases in Korea." For political reasons, however, State Department planners worried that abandoning the South Korean government would be interpreted as a betrayal of United States friends and allies in the Far East. Washington's major concern after the departure of American forces was that Syngman Rhee's repressive rule would drive South Koreans to revolt or that he would attack the North to force more American aid. The handful of American military advisers remaining in South Korea after 1949 urged giving Rhee only defensive weapons lest he provoke a war. Although Dean Acheson had refused to pledge in advance that the United States would defend the Republic of Korea against attack, the Truman administration had pushed hard for economic aid, overcoming Republican opposition.

Whatever their misgivings about South Korea, American decision makers reacted to the North Korean invasion as if it were a direct Soviet challenge to Western security, rather than a civil war in a divided country. Although Stalin probably approved Kim Il Sung's invasion plan and provided weapons, Moscow's involvement was limited. Initially, China played even less of a role. Yet American policymakers consistently focused on the perceived Soviet threat in the region and largely dismissed the Korean origins of the war. The relationship between the Soviet Union and North Korea, one official remarked, was "the same as that between Walt Disney and Donald Duck."

Even before he learned any details of the invasion, President Truman exclaimed, "By God, I'm going to let them have it." He saw Korea as the "Greece of the Far East." If the invasion succeeded, Truman believed, Russia and its puppets would be encouraged to "swallow up one piece of Asia after another." Among Truman and his advisers, the only doubt was whether Korea might be a diversion to cover Soviet thrusts into the Middle East or Europe.

The American Offensive

During the crucial days after the North Korean invasion, the Soviet delegate to the United Nations was boycotting meetings in order to protest America's refusal to seat the Chinese Communist delegation. Thus, with no Russian opposition, the United States was able to secure quick United Nations support for military aid to South Korea. On June 27 the Security Council called on United Nations members to furnish assistance to South Korea "to repel the armed attack and to restore international peace and security in the area." The same day, Truman ordered American air and naval forces into Korea, and three days later he sent ground forces as well. He used the draft system, extended by Congress, to build up the army. Congress was not asked to declare war; in fact, Truman referred to the military intervention as a "police action."

When the United Nations gave its imprimatur to a joint force under an American commander, Truman assigned this critical role to General Douglas MacArthur, who headed the occupation forces in Japan. Although a number of countries eventually sent token forces, 90 percent of the United Nations troops were American, and MacArthur received instructions from Washington to keep the United Nations uninvolved in strategy and tactics.

At first, the American and other United Nations troops were expected merely to back up the South Korean army. But the collapse of that army drew the United States into a central combat role. In the early weeks, American troops could do little more than maintain a toehold at the southern port of Pusan. But American planes and ships controlled the air and sea lanes, and from his headquarters in Tokyo General MacArthur assembled a large force to counterattack. On September 15, 1950, MacArthur supervised a daring amphibious assault behind enemy lines on the coastal city of Inchon (see map). Within two weeks American troops had driven the North Koreans out of the South and achieved the original goal of the war.

The deceptively easy victory at Inchon, and the appearance of infallibility it gave to MacArthur, persuaded President Truman to expand American goals. Instead of merely restoring the prewar border, Truman ordered MacArthur to cross north of the 38th parallel and unify the entire country under Rhee's regime. Truman and Secretary of State Acheson hoped this would deter future proxy aggression by Stalin and deflate Republicans who had accused the administration of "appeasement" in Asia.

MacArthur, bored with the administration of occupied Japan, described the Korean War as "Mars' last gift to an old warrior." From the opening round he chafed at talk of limited war, which brought only limited glory, and called for a crusade to crush the Communist regimes in Korea and China. MacArthur confided to an aide his obsession with victory in a wider war and his hope that the Chinese Communists would provide a pretext for the United States to expand the conflict. He would then "deliver such a crushing defeat it would be one of the decisive battles of the world, a disaster so great it would rock Asia and perhaps turn back communism."

Truman several times considered firing the general, whom he had earlier ridiculed as a "stuffed shirt, . . . play actor and bunco man." But as a potential Republican presidential candidate—he had sought the nomination in 1944 and 1948—MacArthur had to be treated with

The Korean War, 1950–1953

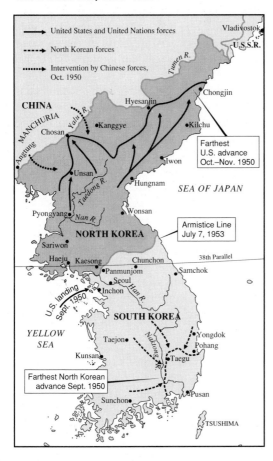

care. He could not be recalled without provoking a tremendous re-action among the many Americans who regarded him as a hero.

Administration officials actually worried more about the war end-ing too quickly, before Congress funded the NSC-68 proposals, than about its escalating out of control. Washington all but ignored warn-ings from the Chinese during October 1950 that American forces should not cross the 38th parallel into North Korea or approach the Yalu River, which separated North Korea from Manchuria, China's industrial heartland. MacArthur, like Truman, dismissed Chinese threats to defend North Korea as bluff. During an October conference on Wake Island, the general assured the president that the war was practically won. If the Chinese dared enter the war, MacArthur pre-dicted, there would be the "greatest slaughter." The prophecy came partly true, but not exactly as the general had supposed.

Chinese Counterattack and Stalemate

In November 1950 Chinese troops stunned MacArthur—and Ameri-cans at home—by crossing into North Korea and driving American forces south to the 38th parallel in a humiliating retreat. Five years earlier the Chinese had fought beside Americans as allies. Now "Red Chinese Hordes," in newspaper parlance, slaughtered GIs in human-wave attacks.

Complaining, falsely, that China had attacked without warning, MacArthur blamed Washington. He told the Joint Chiefs of Staff that he faced an entirely new war that could only be won if he received massive reinforcements, troops from Taiwan, and permission to at-tack China by air and sea.

Most civilian and military officials in Washington disagreed. In their minds the real danger remained a Soviet threat to Europe and Japan. George Marshall, recently appointed as secretary of defense, warned that Russia would be happy to see American and Chinese forces slaughter each other in a strategic backwater. Officials consid-ered, but rejected, using the atomic bomb. Few appropriate military targets existed in North Korea, and ineffective battlefield use of the bomb might undermine its effectiveness as a deterrent threat. Using it against Chinese cities would be immensely destructive and, diplo-mats concluded, would almost certainly bring the Soviets into the war.

Now willing to accept an armistice restoring the prewar boundary, the administration abandoned plans to unify Korea by force. Yet both American and Chinese leaders found it difficult to negotiate a quick peace. Mao Zedong hoped that by pushing American forces out of Korea, he could compel the United States to abandon Taiwan and allow China into the United Nations. Although Truman was willing

American troops head toward the battle front in Korea as peasants flee the fighting. The war killed and wounded millions of Koreans. *UPI/Bettmann News-photos.*

to settle for a divided Korea and, possibly, a deal over Taiwan and Chinese membership in the United Nations, he feared a political backlash should he do so.

Once China entered the war and the front line bogged down, the public showed little sympathy with the limited aims of preserving South Korea and building up NATO and Japanese security. Soldiers complained they did not want to "die for a tie." Senator McCarthy insisted that Democratic sabotage had led to "American boys [lying] dead in the mud [with] their faces shot away by Communist machine guns." Senator Taft accused Truman of violating United States law and the Constitution by sending troops to Korea without formal congressional approval. Hoping to regain popular support, the administration pushed through the United Nations General Assembly a resolution condemning China as the aggressor in Korea. This resolution outraged Beijing and buried the chance for an early armistice. By 1951, nearly two-thirds of the American public expressed dissatisfaction with the administration's handling of the war.

By April 1951 the battle lines in Korea had stabilized; American forces had succeeded in stopping the Chinese army near the 38th parallel without resort to atomic weapons or attacks on China. But when Truman prepared to send Mao a peace feeler in March 1951, MacArthur sabotaged it by publicly ridiculing China as a second-rate power and demanding that its army in Korea surrender to him or face attacks on Chinese cities. The general followed these public statements with a letter to Republican congressman Joseph Martin in which he agreed with the politician's charge that Truman was guilty of the murder of American boys. Calling again for a war against China, MacArthur asserted, "There is no substitute for victory."

Outraged by MacArthur's political grandstanding, Truman decided to recall him. On April 11 the president sacked MacArthur and replaced him with General Matthew Ridgway, the field commander who had blunted the Chinese drive south. Republican politicians were appalled by this rebuff of a popular leader who voiced the anti-Communist sentiments of many. Senator Richard Nixon remarked that the "happiest group in the country are the Communists and their stooges." Senator McCarthy charged that Truman's policy in Korea was a "sinister monster of many heads and many tentacles, a monster conceived in the Kremlin and then given birth to by Acheson."

On April 19, after arriving home to huge parades in his honor, MacArthur told both houses of Congress that Truman's policy of confining the war to Korea condemned all Asia to Communist rule. He brought the audience to tears by closing with the lyrics of an old army song, "Old Soldiers Never Die, They Just Fade Away." But the MacArthur craze passed quickly.

During inconclusive Senate hearings that summer into the general's recall, China agreed to peace talks. Nevertheless, the talking and fighting continued for two more years, until July 1953. In Chapter 5 we will see how the Eisenhower administration used force and compromise to secure an armistice restoring the boundary close to its prewar location. By then, over thirty thousand Americans and more than a million Korean and Chinese soldiers had died.

Consequences of the War

An immediate and obvious consequence of the Korean War was the expansion of the American defense budget. By 1953, defense spending reached $52 billion, up from $17 billion in 1950; the NSC-68 proposals had become reality. The military budget would remain high throughout the 1950s. Moreover, America expanded its international defense network during the war. Besides assuring the military security of Japan and placing several hundred thousand troops on station with NATO, Washington sent extra aid to the French for their struggle in Vietnam. Additional American arms also went to Taiwan and the Philippines. New American military bases opened in such places as Morocco and Spain.

The soaring defense expenditures had a major domestic impact on the Sunbelt states of the South and Southwest, reinforcing the demographic trends that had begun during World War II. The Sunbelt continued to explode in population. California grew fastest, followed by Florida and Texas. With its large concentration of aircraft plants and excellent state university system, California attracted engineers, skilled workers, and Pentagon dollars. About half of all the jobs created in California during these years derived from defense spending.

But the most important consequences of the Korean War lay in the precedents it set for American intervention. It established the idea that the United States could and would engage in direct combat to preserve allied regimes against Communist-led aggression, even in far-flung corners of the world. Although some of Truman's critics charged that national defense should concentrate on regions closer to home, the administration's view prevailed. Further, by asserting his right to commit troops without explicit congressional authorization— and by overcoming the few opponents who challenged this notion— Truman defined a presidential prerogative that later inhabitants of the White House would use with increasing frequency. Politically, however, the war was not a success for Truman, and the frustration over the long military stalemate helped to doom the Democrats in the presidential election of 1952.

TWILIGHT OF THE TRUMAN YEARS

Public resentment over the stalemate in Korea and the recall of MacArthur was not the only trouble Truman faced in 1951 and 1952. A series of petty scandals put his administration on the defensive. Truman appointees in several government agencies were condemned as bribe takers, "five-percenters" who awarded government contracts in exchange for 5 percent kickbacks. White House aide General Harry Vaughn confessed to accepting seven deep freezers as gifts from a contractor. And Senator McCarthy continued to accuse the administration of coddling Communists.

In mid-1950, Senator Estes Kefauver, a Tennessee Democrat, tried to deflect attention from the Red Scare by investigating organized crime. In dramatic televised hearings, he called witnesses who described an international criminal conspiracy nearly as frightening as communism—the Mafia. The public loved the parade of thugs Kefauver hauled before the television cameras. The attempt to divert attention from McCarthy failed, however, when the Korean War broke out. To make matters worse, Kefauver revealed links between mobsters and many Democratic city bosses.

The Democrats were so disunited that in 1951 Republicans secured ratification of the Twenty-second Amendment to the Constitution, limiting future presidents to two terms. The first president to whom it applied, Republican Dwight Eisenhower, condemned it as "an act of retroactive vindictiveness" against Roosevelt rather than the product of "judicious thinking about the institutions of the Republic."

The election of 1952 signaled the end of an era of Democratic-led reform. The urbane, articulate Democratic nominee, Illinois governor Adlai Stevenson, proved no match for his Republican opponent, Second World War hero General Dwight D. Eisenhower, who could have secured either party's nomination. Even though Eisenhower offered few clues about how he would govern, the public rejoiced at his assertion that if elected he would "concentrate on the job of ending the Korean war." Stevenson dismissed this as a "promise without a program," but Americans trusted the general to end the war honorably.

The war issue combined with charges of Democratic corruption and subversion to doom the party of the retiring president. Eisenhower beat Stevenson in a landslide, and Republican legislative candidate rode his coattails into slender control of both houses of Congress.

CONCLUSION

By the time Harry Truman left office, the basic outlines of American Cold War policy were firmly established. To contain the perceived Soviet threat, the United States had expanded its military budget, extended its bases worldwide, and committed itself to an ongoing nuclear arms race. It had begun to rebuild Western Europe and Japan with the Marshall Plan and other aid programs. Through NATO, the CIA, and the National Security Council, it had institutionalized the Cold War. Most important, it had established the principle that America would intervene—with aid, with airplanes, or if necessary with American troops—whenever it appeared that the Soviet Union or a client state was trying to extend Communist influence.

In Greece and Berlin, the American response was quick and successful. In Vietnam, the ultimate cost of American involvement would not be known for many years. In Korea, however, the United States found itself in a long and frustrating war that succeeded only in reestablishing the status quo at the cost of many lives. Yet doubts about the strategic need for a non-Communist Korea were swept away in the anti-Communist crusade.

All of these ramifications of the Cold War had their root in the suspicions and misunderstandings between East and West at the end of the Second World War. As the United States and the Soviet Union struggled to ensure their own security, each denounced the other's alleged aggressive intentions. Stalin and Truman both oversimplified complex problems; they blamed each other for many of the economic and political crises that afflicted postwar Europe and Asia. Historians have debated for years about the extent to which history might have been different if the two sides had understood one another better.

In Western Europe, at least, Truman essentially succeeded in winning the Cold War. But the frustrations of the Korean conflict, along with the fierce anti-Communism that Truman himself had helped to spawn, contributed to the Democrats' fall from power in 1952. In contrast to Truman, the new president, Eisenhower, is remembered as presiding over years of relative tranquility. In the next two chapters we will see whether in fact the Eisenhower era was as stable and secure as its popular image suggests. ■

FURTHER READING

On the Cold War, see: Melvyn Leffler, *A Preponderance of Power* (1991); Gregg Herken, *The Winning Weapon* (1981); Michael Hogan, *The Marshall Plan* (1987); Daniel Yergin, *A Shattered Peace* (1977); John Gaddis, *The United States and the Origins of the Cold War, 1941–47* (1972); Robert M. Blum, *Drawing the Line* (1982); Michael Schaller, *The American Occupation of Japan: The Origins of the Cold War in Asia* (1985). On McCarthyism, see: David M. Oshinsky, *A Conspiracy So Immense: The World of Joe McCarthy* (1983); Thomas C. Reeves, *The Live and Times of Joe McCarthy* (1982); Ellen W. Schrecker, *No Ivory Tower: McCarthyism in the Universities* (1986). On the Korean War, see: John Halliday and Bruce Cumings, *Korea: The Unknown War* (1987); Michael Schaller, *Douglas MacArthur: The Far Eastern General* (1989); Callum A. MacDonald, *Korea* (1987); Burton I. Kauffman, *The Korean War* (1986).

4

The Fifties:
Change in the
Guise of Stability

After twenty-three years of depression, global conflict, cold war, Red Scare, and fighting in Korea, the period beginning in 1953 seemed to most Americans an era of well-deserved stability and prosperity. The "fifties" as a distinct epoch began with the election of President Dwight D. Eisenhower and ended in 1961 when John F. Kennedy entered the White House. Early in this period the Korean War and McCarthyism faded, Soviet dictator Josef Stalin died, and the overwhelmingly popular Eisenhower brought a sense of security to American life.

Many of the era's symbols, including Hula-Hoops, Davy Crockett caps, new forms of popular music, exaggerated automobile tail fins, and Disneyland, suggest the affluence and the cultural complacency of the period. Especially for the white middle class, confidence in material progress and the perfectibility of American society coexisted alongside a fervent anti-Communist ideology and anxiety about nuclear destruction.

Following the turbulence of the last two decades, the home seemed a safe haven. Just as containment of communism characterized foreign policy, a form of domestic containment, stressing traditional gender roles and domesticity, dominated American social life. In the ideal suburban family, the American mother would keep house and raise the children while her husband went off to a white-collar job. The kids would grow up with a strong sense of American values.

Yet the idea of containment presupposes the existence of unsettling forces to be contained. In fact, beneath the surface stability, the 1950s were years of change and upheaval. Not only did continued population movements, the automobile, television, and advanced technology change the face of American life, but critics began to complain that the apparent consensus of American society was a hollow one. Youth developed their own subculture, centered on rock-'n'-roll music, and it alarmed their elders. Meanwhile, the civil rights struggle erupted in the South, demanding that Americans confront issues that had too long been ignored.

EISENHOWER'S RISE TO LEADERSHIP

General Dwight D. Eisenhower, widely known by his nickname "Ike," chose politics as a second career at age sixty-two. Despite this late beginning, he became one of the most popular and successful presidents in the postwar era. During his eight years in the White

House, he averaged an approval rating of 64 percent. The public was reassured by his calming, grandfatherly style and seldom questioned his rather disengaged stewardship of domestic policy. Were it not for the provisions of the Twenty-second Amendment to the Constitution, which barred a third term, he might easily have won re-election in 1960. Veteran journalist Walter Lippmann remarked, "Ike could be elected even if dead. All you would need [to do was] to prop him up in the rear seat of an open car and parade down Broadway."

Born in Denison, Texas, in 1890 into a large, pious, and poor family, Eisenhower grew up in Abilene, Kansas, and attended West Point despite his parents' pacifism. He graduated in 1915 but, because few promotions were available during the interwar period, had risen only to the rank of major by 1939. With the start of the war in Europe, however, Eisenhower ascended quickly to prominence, helped by Army Chief of Staff General George C. Marshall, who considered him among the most promising men in the army. By 1944 Eisenhower was a four-star general and commander of the Allied forces in the European theater. His ability to manage and conciliate the Allied armies sped victory and won him acclaim as a talented and humane leader.

After the war Eisenhower served successively as army chief of staff, president of Columbia University, and, during the Korean War, the first supreme commander of NATO. Ambitious but wary of politics, he rebuffed both Democratic and Republican invitations to seek the presidential nomination in 1948. Four years later he still coveted the White House but disdained the idea of compaigning for office, seeking instead a "draft" that would nominate him by acclamation.

Despite Eisenhower's wartime ties to Roosevelt, he held fairly conservative views on economics and social programs, favoring private enterprise over government intervention as a solution to most problems. He was, however, a confirmed internationalist who supported containment of communism, the Marshall Plan, and the "Europe-first" orientation of the Truman administration. Eisenhower resented and feared the anti-NATO, "Asia-first" ideas of Republican presidential aspirants such as Senators Robert Taft and Joseph McCarthy and General Douglas MacArthur. To ensure that none of these men would become president, early in 1952 Eisenhower made his decision: he resigned his NATO command and entered the Republican primaries, securing enough delegates to defeat his chief rival, Taft, at the party's nominating convention. Eisenhower placated the Republican right by tapping California Senator Richard M. Nixon as his vice-presidential running mate.

Eisenhower's campaign, an observer remarked, was "a masterpiece of evasion." His vagueness calmed fears that a Republican in the White House would roll back the achievements of the New Deal, while his status as war hero seemed an assurance that he could handle foreign threats. When he promised that, if elected, he would "go to Korea," voters interpreted this to mean that the general who had liberated Western Europe had a secret plan to end the Korean stalemate. Eisenhower's genial authority, warm smile, and charm made up for the banality of his campaign speeches.

In contrast, the Democrats entered the campaign in disarray. No clear candidate emerged before the convention, and few wanted to be associated closely with the unpopular incumbent, Harry S. Truman. Governor Adlai Stevenson of Illinois, a man of modest experience and reputation but whose grandfather had served as vice president in the 1890s, received his party's nomination on the third ballot. Considered a liberal northerner, he tried to balance the ticket by choosing Senator John Sparkman of Alabama, a segregationist, as his running mate.

Stevenson, who wrote many of his own speeches, proved an extremely witty and articulate candidate. Neither in 1952 nor during his 1956 rematch, however, did he propose a feasible alternative to the Cold War or stirring solutions to unresolved domestic problems. Nor did Stevenson elicit much support from the large proportion of union members and minorities among the Democratic rank and file. Moreover, many Catholic Democrats objected to his earlier divorce.

Stevenson's eloquence and intellect, as well as his large, bald pate, led journalists to dub him an "egghead." Many voters disliked his uncanny ability to turn easy answers into difficult questions. He stressed that America faced tough choices and uncertain prospects. The Republicans, meanwhile, exploited public frustration with the Korean War and linked the Democrats to subversion and corruption. Vice-presidential candidate Nixon, who had won election to Congress by slandering his opponents as Communists, labeled Stevenson "Adlai the appeaser" and a "Ph.D. graduate of Dean Acheson's Cowardly College of Communist Containment."

The most exciting moment in the campaign occurred when allegations surfaced that Nixon had pocketed $18,000 in campaign contributions. Eisenhower considered dumping his young running mate until Nixon appeared on television with his family to deny any impropriety. In a maudlin but effective performance, Nixon admitted accepting one personal gift, a cocker spaniel named Checkers, on behalf of his daughters. He refused to give up the dog or the alleged personal profits and suggested, in what became known as the Checkers speech, that only Communists opposed him.

In the November election more Americans—over 61 million—voted than ever before. They opted for change, giving Eisenhower 34 million votes to Stevenson's 27 million (see map, page 122). As a result of racial fears among white voters alarmed by the Democrats' connection to civil rights, the Republicans carried four states in the

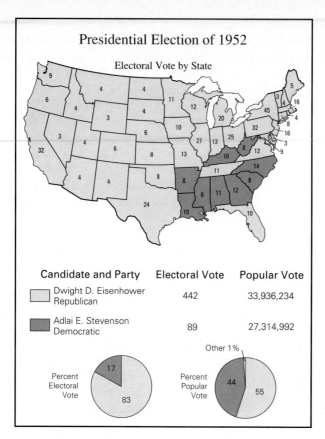

Presidential Election of 1952

Electoral Vote by State

Candidate and Party	Electoral Vote	Popular Vote
Dwight D. Eisenhower Republican	442	33,936,234
Adlai E. Stevenson Democratic	89	27,314,992

Percent Electoral Vote: 17, 83

Percent Popular Vote: 44, 55, Other 1%

Presidential Election of 1952

formerly solid Democratic South. Overall, the Republicans won narrow majorities of nine seats in the House and one seat in the Senate.

THE POLITICS OF MODERATION

Although Eisenhower appeared to be fatherly, detached, and a bit simple—a "national sedative," according to some critics—the reality was more complex. This fatherly figure worked to suppress a violent temper and profane vocabulary. In politics, moreover, he was far from simple-minded.

Personally, he seemed well suited to the conservative branch of his party. Whether on the golf course or at cabinet meetings, Eisenhower felt most comfortable in the presence of white, middle-aged corporate executives. He socialized almost exclusively with such men, and he chose businessmen, financiers, and corporate lawyers for 76 percent of his high government appointments—nearly twice the figure of the Roosevelt and Truman administrations.

Nevertheless, Eisenhower had many disputes with conservative Republicans, including senators Joseph McCarthy, Robert Taft, and William Knowland. For one thing, Eisenhower was not intensely partisan. He did not equate the GOP with patriotism or the Democrats with treason, and he expended little energy campaigning for other Republicans. This stance probably contributed to his public popularity, but it did not endear him to the hard-liners in his party.

Even more important, Eisenhower had no intention of trying to roll back the New Deal legacy—long a cherished plan of conservative Republicans. In his first term, in fact, he approved the extension of Social Security benefits to 10 million additional workers and signed a law raising the minimum wage from 75 cents to $1.00 per hour. He also reluctantly accepted farm subsidies and created a cabinet-level Department of Health, Education and Welfare. Despite his fiscal conservatism and his promise to balance the budget, Eisenhower met his budget goal in only three of his eight years in office. He would not slash services to serve an economic ideal.

On the issue of anticommunism, Eisenhower took a similarly moderate position. He maintained the loyalty program inherited from Truman and approved the firing of many innocent federal employees, but in his public utterances he downplayed the danger of internal subversion. The July 1953 armistice in Korea and the political demise of Senator McCarthy a year later (see Chapter 5) helped to quiet the Red Scare. Eisenhower also attempted to rein in the military budget, which had shot up rapidly during the Korean War.

Other items on his modest agenda were more pleasing to conservatives. He capped or reduced spending in many federal programs, lowered income taxes for the wealthy, eliminated price controls, eased business regulations, and returned some political authority to the states. He pushed through Congress a bill that benefited both the big oil companies and the state governments by turning over to the states the ownership and leasing rights for offshore petroleum deposits. He also backed the Atomic Energy Act of 1954, which licensed private firms to generate nuclear power while limiting their liabilities.

Overall, Eisenhower played midwife to the birth of what historians have called "modern Republicanism." He promoted a moderate conservative movement that recognized a strong role for government in domestic affairs and a permanent global role for America. Beginning in 1955, following the loss of Republican majorities in Congress, Eisenhower often cooperated with such powerful congressional Democrats as Sam Rayburn and Lyndon Johnson. At times, he even considered forming a new centrist political party that might bring Democrats and Republicans together.

After the death of Robert Taft in 1953 and the eclipse of Joseph McCarthy a year later, no nationally powerful Republicans seriously challenged Eisenhower's leadership. A new generation of conservatives was only beginning to emerge. Senator Barry Goldwater of Arizona, elected in the Eisenhower tide in 1952, rejected many tenets of modern Republicanism, but he was not yet an influential figure. William F. Buckley, Jr., gained some attention with his 1951 book *God and Man at Yale*, a critique of liberal ideas and professors at that Ivy League university. In 1955 Buckley founded the *National Review*, a journal critical of both liberal Democrats and moderate Republicans. For the moment, however, the politics of moderation reigned supreme.

A NATION IN FLUX

While Eisenhower exuded an aura of political stability, American life was changing in significant ways. Technology continued the boom begun during the Second World War, and the economy reached new heights of prosperity in spite of three recessions. As population swelled, Americans moved to the suburbs in ever greater numbers. They fell in love with the automobile, inaugurating an age when cars became much more than a means of transportation. Increasingly the home and the family were the center of popular values, reinforced by a widespread religious revival. But critics surveying the social landscape began to insist that important flaws lay beneath the surface prosperity and contentment.

Population, Economy, and Technology

Fueled by the continuing baby boom (see figure), the American population surged by 30 million in the 1950s, reaching 180 million by the end of the decade. When births peaked at 4.3 million in 1957, a third of all Americans were aged 14 or younger. This created exceptional demands for new housing, appliances, toys, and schools. Between 1950 and 1960, total school enrollment in kindergarten through twelfth grade increased from 28 million to 42 million.

Suburban growth, which had begun to accelerate in the late 1940s, transformed living patterns in the fifties. Millions of individuals and families, seeking new jobs or homes or fleeing urban problems, moved from central cities to outlying communities. As noted in Chapter 2 (see pages 57–61), the trend was encouraged by federal credit policies and mass-produced homes. By 1960 the suburban population

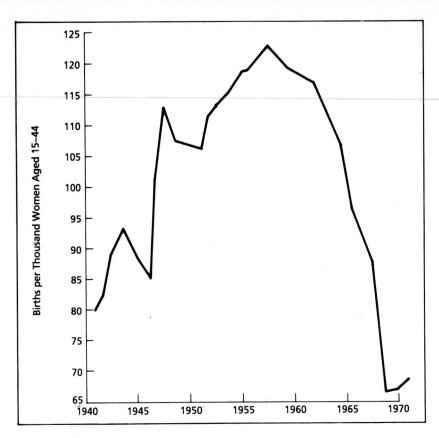

Birthrate, 1940–1970

of 60 million equaled that of all urban areas. Except for the South and West, where rural-to-urban migration continued, most large cities either lost population or barely held even during the 1950s.

Soon employment took the same route as the population. At first, suburbanites usually commuted to jobs in central cities, but by 1960 most worked closer to home. Suburban employment and manufacturing rose dramatically, while employment in the twenty-five largest cities declined about 7 percent during the decade. Downtown commercial districts lost business to suburban shopping centers surrounded by acres of parking lots.

Regionally, the American population continued to shift west, with California growing by 50 percent. Florida and Texas also attracted many newcomers. The gains in urban population in the West and suburban population in the Northeast came partly at the expense of rural America. The number of agricultural workers fell to barely 6 percent of the population, down two-thirds since America entered the Second World War.

Economic growth during the 1950s averaged more than 4 percent annually, despite recessions in 1954, 1958, and 1960. Inflation remained below 2 percent, unemployment levels below 5 percent, and a record high employment of 66.5 million was reached in 1960. The GNP nearly doubled between 1950 and 1960, to $500 billion (see figure). Measured in constant 1954 dollars, this represented a per capita increase of about 25 percent (from $2,096 to $2,536). Median family income grew from about $3,000 to $5,657. Real wages rose by 30 percent.

With high employment and higher incomes, Americans found more ways to spend their wages. Lenient bank lending policies and the advent of the credit card also stimulated consumer spending. The Diners Club and American Express credit cards were both introduced during the 1950s, followed by oil company, hotel chain, and department store credit cards. Sears promoted its cards so aggressively that

Gross National Product, 1946–1970

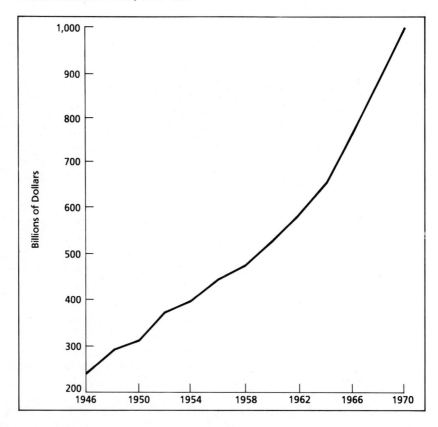

by 1960 over 10 million Americans held them. As a record number of young families furnished homes and clothed children, private debt climbed from $73 billion to $200 billion between 1950 and 1960.

The profile of industry and business also changed. Mergers accelerated, with the result that the two hundred largest corporations controlled over half of all business assets by the end of the decade. Traditional industries such as iron, steel, textiles, and mining shrank, while chemicals, aviation, drugs, plastics, fast food chains, discount retailers (such as Kresge's, later K mart), and electronics expanded. Overall, heavy industry and manufacturing declined, and new job growth clustered in the service, clerical, and managerial sectors. By 1956, white-collar workers outnumbered blue-collar workers for the first time.

Many of the newer industries invested heavily in research and product development. By the middle of the decade, some half-million workers were employed in the research divisions of about three thousand companies. The federal government also increased its science investment, financing over one-half of all research activity by universities and corporate laboratories. The combined federal and private commitment to research and development, which had become significant during the Second World War, intensified in the 1950s.

As a result of this commitment, new technologies produced jet aircraft, new medicines, and consumer electronics. Antibiotics, tranquilizers, and Dr. Jonas Salk's polio vaccine (discovered in 1953 and widely available by 1955) revolutionized medicine. The transistor, developed by Bell Laboratories in 1948, made possible miniaturized radios and other devices. IBM used transistors in its computers, creating a billion-dollar market for mainframe computers by 1960. That same year, a revolution in document copying took place when Xerox introduced its model 914 copier. The Boeing 707, the first regularly scheduled passenger jet, entered commercial service in 1958.

Meanwhile, the labor movement struggled, with only partial success, to hold its own. In 1955 the American Federation of Labor and the Congress of Industrial Organizations overcame their long-time rivalry and merged to form the AFL-CIO. But congressional investigations into union ties to organized crime, along with the federal conviction of Teamsters Union president Dave Beck, tarnished labor's image and led to new legal restrictions on the labor movement. Although the number of union members remained fairly steady, the unionized proportion of the total work force declined with the loss of jobs in heavy industry. The unions that managed to penetrate the newer white-collar sectors, such as the American Federation of State, County and Municipal Employees (AFSCME), accounted for a growing percentage of union membership.

Throughout the decade, business leaders and some economists boasted of creating a "people's capitalism" that ensured the equal distribution of abundance and erased class divisions. In fact, wealth remained highly concentrated, as it had throughout the century. In 1960, 1 percent of the population possessed one-third of the nation's wealth; the top 5 percent of the nation's wealthiest controlled over half of the wealth. Yet half of all families had no savings account, and 40 million Americans, almost one-fourth of the population, lived near or below the poverty line, then figured as an income of $3,000 per year for a family of four. The poverty rate was especially high among the elderly, racial minorities, and rural Americans, the least visible elements of the population.

The New Auto Age

Along with suburbia, the automobile industry boomed during the 1950s. The two went hand in hand. Nine out of ten suburban families owned a car, as compared to only six of ten urban households. Women driving station wagons full of children became emblems of suburban life.

On average, domestic auto manufacturers produced 7 to 8 million cars and trucks annually. By 1960, Americans had nearly 70 million vehicles on the road. Two-thirds of the nation's employees drove to work. In Los Angeles County alone, more cars plied the freeways than in all of Asia or South America.

These cars were not the staid models of the 1940s. Detroit built sleeker, bigger, gaudier, and more expensive machines than ever before. The public adored two- and three-tone models, tail fins, wraparound windshields, power steering, automatic transmissions, and air conditioning. This emphasis on power gadgets and sex appeal helped to spur automania as a cultural force. Auto tourism became a major form of family leisure. Nat King Cole's hit song "Get Your Kicks on Route 66" reflected the increasingly common cross-country family trips to national parks and new amusement complexes like Disneyland. Motel chains proliferated. So did other spinoff industries such as fast-food outlets and drive-in theaters.

Responding to demands from business, local governments, and auto-owning citizens, the federal government decided to upgrade the nation's inadequate highways. By 1956 a bipartisan movement in Congress, supported by organized labor, the construction trades, oil companies, car manufacturers, tire makers, and civil defense advocates who argued that better roads would speed evacuation from cities in time of war, won passage of the National System of Defense Highways. This massive building program authorized construction of forty thousand miles of new highways, with Washington paying 90 percent of the initial $50 billion tab through collection of excise taxes levied on tires and fuel.

Power, style, and consumer appeal made the 1950s the decade of the automobile. *Courtesy of Chevrolet.*

The interstate highway system dwarfed anything built by the New Deal; and although the title of the bill suggested the highways were necessary primarily for defense purposes, the road-building program had important subsidiary effects. By subsidizing the car culture with six thousand miles of city-to-suburb freeways while denying funds for inner-city mass rail or bus transit, government promoted suburban development at the cost of the cities. In Los Angeles, General Motors Corporation allegedly conspired to eliminate the profitable and efficient mass transit system, making car ownership a necessity.

The public's love affair with the automobile allowed manufacturers to ignore their products' poor safety and efficiency records. The mounting traffic death toll (forty thousand in 1959) elicited little concern, although a young Harvard law student, Ralph Nader, worried enough to begin probing auto safety as early as 1957. But the big Detroit automakers either ignored their few critics or dismissed them as deviants.

By the early 1960s, many urban planners and ordinary Americans began to question the wisdom of dividing cities with smog-producing freeways while permitting mass transit to decay. When the full cost of buying and maintaining private automobiles was calculated, cars seemed less of a bargain. But during the fifties nearly everyone celebrated public road subsidies for private automobiles. Gasoline was cheap, highways were "free," and America's future was on the road.

Women, Men, and Sex

"Of all the accomplishments of the American woman," *Life* magazine's editors boasted in a special Christmas 1956 issue on women, "the one she brings off with the most spectacular success is having babies." The editors expressed relief that the new woman acted more feminine than her mother did in the thirties and forties. In Eisenhower's America, a "steelworker's wife and Junior Leaguer alike do their own housework." According to the magazine, the new woman gracefully conceded to men the top jobs in the work place.

During the 1950s, American women reversed a hundred-year trend by marrying younger and having more babies. As divorce rates declined, advice columns, television shows, and schools emphasized "traditional" gender roles, which placed a husband at work and his wife in the home. A fear of sexual chaos brought on by the Cold War emerged as a common theme. Popular literature discussed the dangers posed by "loose women" and "sex perverts" who might be in league with the Soviet Union. Senator Joseph McCarthy, whose close aide Roy Cohn was a secret homosexual, joined Republican party chairman Guy Gabrielson in warning that "sexual perverts [had] infiltrated our government" and were "perhaps as dangerous as real Communists."

The dominant domestic ideology of the period, which Betty Friedan labeled "the Feminine mystique" in her 1963 book of that title, defined women as wives and mothers. In fact, a third of all women worked for wages, and total female employment grew in the 1950s from 16.5 million to 23 million, representing a third of the work force. Nevertheless, the ideology placed women at home, raising children and creating a bulwark of social stability. Sex, though not discouraged, was to be limited to marriage. Masculine men would exercise control over the sexually submissive, competent homemakers at their side.

In 1959 *Life* magazine ran a feature called "Their Sheltered Honeymoon" that fused two of the decade's central themes: family life and nuclear terror. The illustrated story depicted a pair of newlyweds about to spend their honeymoon in an underground fallout shelter stocked with canned goods and appliances. Hinting at the erotic undertones of two weeks of "unbroken togetherness," *Life* asserted that "fallout can be fun." This seemed the ultimate portrayal of the nuclear family in the nuclear age.

Parenthood became an expression of responsible citizenship and motherhood the fulfillment of female sexuality. A book published in 1947 and popular for a decade thereafter, *Modern Women: The Lost Sex*, by Dr. Marynia Farnham and Ferdinand Lundberg, described unmarried, childless women as emotionally disturbed. The authors

A newlywed couple, caught up in the anxiety of the nuclear arms race in 1959, prepare to spend a two-week honeymoon in an underground bomb shelter. *Bill Saunders.*

urged laws barring older single women from teaching since they "cannot be an adequate model of a complete woman."

Despite warnings from self-declared experts that higher education inhibited fertility, a growing number of women attended college. Their careers, however, still had definite constraints. Adlai Stevenson exhorted women at Smith College not to feel frustrated by their distance from the "great issues and stirring debate" for which their education prepared them. A woman could be a good citizen, he claimed, by helping her husband find value in his work and by teaching her children the uniqueness of each individual.

Prodded by such assertions from civic leaders and the media, it is not surprising that the average mother in the 1950s had between three and four children, usually by age thirty. As noted earlier, the birth rate continued to rise until 1957. At the same time, contraception, accepted by all the major faiths except the Roman Catholic church, became common as the method for spacing pregnancies and limiting births.

In spite of the formal sexual orthodoxy of the era, there were portents of a more emancipated future. Notably, sex was more openly discussed and displayed during the 1950s than in most earlier periods. Popular science became a vehicle for sexual openness in 1953 when Dr. Alfred C. Kinsey published *Sexual Behavior in the Human Female,* a sequel to his 1948 work on male sexuality. This second Kinsey report, a bestseller like its predecessor, was a turgid read and a statistically inaccurate compilation of six thousand case histories that revealed a simple truth: women, like men, engaged in a wide variety of sexual acts both before and after marriage. In the climate of the times, many people considered this finding "dirty" and offensive. Criticized for funding Kinsey's research, the Rockefeller Foundation withdrew its support.

But displeasure at the Kinsey report did not prevent artistic representations of sex from becoming more open in the 1950s. In the film industry, for example, the Hollywood Production Code had long barred use of words like "virgin" and "seduction" and restricted the sexual content of films. Even married couples were shown sleeping in separate beds. But by the mid-1950s, partly because of a change in personnel among the censors, the code was relaxed. Movies did not necessarily improve, but sex became far more graphic than before.

During the same years, the Supreme Court overturned several state laws restricting publication of serious erotic literature like D. H. Lawrence's *Lady Chatterley's Lover.* Such books became more widely available, and writers of less renown also offered some steamy reading. The decade's most popular novel, *Peyton Place* (1956), sold almost 10 million copies. The book jacket promised that author Grace Metalious, a young housewife, lifted "the lid off a small New England town," exposing lust, rape, incest, alcoholism, murder, and hypocrisy.

Playboy magazine was surely the most influential erotic innovation of the decade. Its glossy centerfolds brought bare-breasted women into millions of homes, displaying them like one more new consumer product. When Hugh Hefner first published *Playboy* in December 1953, he featured the rising starlet Marilyn Monroe as "Playmate of the Month." Slick, upscale, replete with the hedonistic "Playboy philosophy," selections from serious writers, and airbrushed photographs of busty beauties, *Playboy* represented a quantum leap from the grimy "girlie" magazines of prewar years. By 1956, its circulation had reached one-half million per month.

Besides pressuring women into domestic roles, the massive profamily propaganda of the fifties had stifled many men, who, fleeing commitment, found temporary relief in *Playboy.* Hefner pitched his magazine to college students and young status-conscious men who wanted to date, not marry, the centerfold models. Willing to spend their salaries on the expensive stereos and pricey liquor advertised in *Playboy,* they fantasized about worry-free sex, with no house payments or children to complicate the enjoyment. Critics of the magazine joked that a generation of young men grew up thinking that naked women had a staple through the navel, where the centerfold opened.

Religion in American Life

Even as *Peyton Place* tickled their hedonistic fantasies, Americans experienced a religious revival during the 1950s. By the end of the decade, two-thirds of the population claimed formal church membership and attendance, up from 48 percent before the Second World War. Ninety-seven percent professed a belief in God. Religious popularizers like Billy Graham became media celebrities, appearing in newspapers, on radio and television, and on best-seller lists. Hollywood turned out Biblical epics like *The Robe* and *The Ten Commandments*. A new translation of the Bible sold millions of copies. For those without time to read it, *Reader's Digest* issued an abridgment.

Presbyterian minister Norman Vincent Peale's *The Power of Positive Thinking* (1952) was on the best-seller list for three years. Negative thinking, not external realities, Peale counseled, caused personal problems. In his writing, lecturing, and broadcasting, Peale mixed religion, popular psychology, and a promise that positive thinking was the path to riches and popularity. Imitators published books with titles like *Pray Your Weight Away* and *The Power of Prayer on Plants*. Evangelist Billy Graham and Catholic prelate Fulton J. Sheen also portrayed faith as a balm for everyday problems and gathered large TV audiences. Graham and Peale remained extremely popular for the next forty years, often consulting with presidents.

President Eisenhower encouraged this trend by designating a "float to God" at the head of his inaugural parade in 1953. He later kicked off a "Back to God Campaign" by calling "recognition of a Supreme Being . . . the first, the most basic, expression of Americanism. Without God, there could be no American form of government, nor an American way of life." The president hosted White House prayer breakfasts, and Congress added the words "under God" to the Pledge of Allegiance and put the motto "In God We Trust" on paper money. "Christian faith is back in the center of things," *Time* concluded in 1954.

Christianity, like parenthood and the suburban nuclear family, became a measure of Americanism and a rejection of atheistic communism. Surveys revealed that a large majority of Americans considered atheism a subversive threat. The decade's highest profile atheist, Madeline Murray O'Hare, was frequently assaulted when she tried to speak in public. Like Eisenhower, few people stressed doctrinal differences or weighty theological issues; rather, religion served to unify society. As Will Herberg, a professor of Judaic studies, noted in his incisive 1955 study, *Protestant-Catholic-Jew*, religion, especially in suburbia, tolerated almost any content or none at all. Rather than reorienting life to God, religious observance served a social function in new communities. As uprooted ethnic Americans shed their traditions and left their old urban neighborhoods behind, "religious association became the primary context of self-identification and social location."

Herberg's point seemed affirmed by the ways in which Americans expressed religious sentiment. High schools and colleges held "religious emphasis" weeks, civic and athletic events began with a brief prayer or moment of meditation, telephone companies began dial-a-prayer service, and the Ideal Toy Company introduced a praying Barbie doll. Churches often functioned as suburban social centers, hosting Little League teams, adult education classes, and other community activities.

Critics of Mass Society

During the 1950s, most social commentators agreed that the United States had solved the major material problems afflicting society. The persisting pockets of poverty, such as those among African-Americans, were seen as minor embarrassments rather than as major problems. An influential analysis published by Daniel Bell near the end of the decade, *The End of Ideology,* argued that the passionate ideological crusades of earlier years no longer had relevance. The United States had mastered the production of abundance and now had only to decide how to allocate the wealth.

Nevertheless, some critics began to question the social mores and culture that arose from the decade of calm prosperity. This general theme appeared in such books as David Riesman's *The Lonely Crowd* (1950), Sloan Wilson's *The Man in the Gray Flannel Suit* (1955), William H. Whyte, Jr.'s *The Organization Man* (1955), John Keats's *The Crack in the Picture Window* (1957), and Richard Gordon's *The Split Level Trap* (1960). Riesman and Whyte discussed the eclipse of the "inner-directed" personality. Instead of relying on internal drives and values, they charged, Americans had become "other-directed," little more than sheep who sought approval and rewards from peers. According to Whyte, the bureaucratic structure of big business stifled a healthy competitive spirit. No longer spurred by drive and vision, the organization man looked to "the group as the source of creativity." "Belongingness" became the ultimate need.

Besides the tendency to mindless conformity, critics attacked the all-pervading consumer culture. In a trilogy of best sellers criticizing the advertising industry—*The Hidden Persuaders* (1957), *The Status Seekers* (1959), and *The Waste Makers* (1959)—journalist Vance Packard blamed mass marketing and the concept of "planned obsolescence" for turning citizens into insatiable consumers who pursued the accumulation of appliances and gadgets as life's highest purpose. Other exposés of suburbia portrayed shoddily built subdivisions full of haggard men, tense and anxious women, and demanding kids.

In a widely read critique, *The Affluent Society* (1958), economist John Kenneth Galbraith noted the triumphs of liberal capitalism since 1945. Yet public services were in terrible shape, Galbraith pointed out, and many groups still experienced poverty. Galbraith called for government intervention to ameliorate the public squalor that persisted in the midst of private luxury. His argument was partly undermined by the title of his book, which led some readers to think he believed that poverty no longer existed.

Only a few of the social critics claimed to find basic structural flaws in American society. One of these was sociologist C. Wright Mills, whose book *The Power Elite* (1956) asserted that a small group of military, business, and political leaders controlled the country in such a way as to leave the majority of Americans powerless. Herbert Marcuse, a German émigré philosopher, blended Freudian psychology and Marxism in his *Eros and Civilization* (1956), which argued that a tiny minority manipulated the lives of most people and developed unique forms of psychological repression. In 1960, in *Growing Up Absurd*, Paul Goodman criticized schools and other institutions for stifling creativity and individualism.

Despite the apparent tranquility of the decade, these critics offered evidence that America's problems had not disappeared or been forgotten. In the realm of popular culture, too, as we will see in the following sections, there were some signs of dissatisfaction with American society. All of these rumblings foreshadowed the radical challenges that emerged in the 1960s.

POPULAR CULTURE

Along with its social and economic changes, the decade of the 1950s brought important developments in popular culture. The evolution of television, sports, music, and literature had a lasting impact. In some respects, the developments in popular culture helped to reinforce the decade's family-oriented ideology, but in other areas Americans found that their own culture revealed fundamental clashes in values.

Television: Successful Entertainment or Vast Wasteland?

Newton Minnow, newly appointed chairman of the Federal Communications Commission (FCC), shocked a gathering of broadcast

Walt Disney

Perhaps no other person has had a greater effect on popular culture in twentieth-century America than Walt Disney. But his beginnings were both modest and unusual. As his *New York Times* obituary put it, he founded his empire on a mouse.

In 1923, after producing crude cartoons for movie houses in Kansas City, twenty-two-year-old Walter E. Disney moved to Los Angeles to join his older brother Roy. They collaborated on a series of short cartoons called *Alice in Cartoonland.* After moderate success, Walt conceived a new cartoon starring a mouse called Mortimer—later renamed Mickey. In 1928 Disney released *Steamboat Willie,* a wildly successful short feature that introduced Mickey Mouse to the world and earned the brothers a fortune.

executives in 1961 by describing their industry as a vast wasteland. He charged that television, in its drive to deliver a mass audience to advertisers, pandered to the lowest common denominator and avoided serious programming. This harsh judgment reflected the disappointment many intellectuals felt with the most popular entertainment medium in human history.

The television industry expanded quickly in the early 1950s, as the FCC sped up the licensing procedures. As the size of TV sets increased, quality improved and prices fell to an average of $200. By the time Eisenhower took office, in 1953, half of all American homes had a set. For the rest of the decade sales ranged between 5 and 7 million units annually. By 1960, 90 percent of all homes had at least one receiver. As early as 1956, Americans spent more time watching television than working for wages.

Evening television became the social focus of family life in most

Soon Walt took the creative lead in the partnership. In addition to short cartoons featuring Mickey Mouse and Donald Duck, he oversaw the production of such animated classics as *Snow White and the Seven Dwarfs, Pinocchio, Fantasia,* and *Sleeping Beauty.* By the mid-1950s he was in his heyday, and he turned his attention increasingly to the new medium of television, producing shows that included "Davy Crockett," "Zorro," and "The Mickey Mouse Club."

By that time he had also begun to devote himself to a venture that his brother and many business associates dismissed as "Walt's screwy idea": an amusement park in Anaheim, outside Los Angeles. When Disneyland opened in 1955, it proved a huge commercial success. The so-called Magic Kingdom, with its squeaky-clean atmosphere and upbeat themes, became a beacon for tourists from around the world. By the early 1960s Disney began work on a larger theme park in Florida, Walt Disney World, along with a planned community that he dubbed Epcot, or Experimental Prototype Community of Tomorrow. Although this vast project opened in 1972, Disney did not live to see it.

At the time of his death in 1966, Walt Disney Productions estimated that 240 million people a year watched at least one Disney movie, 100 million saw a Disney television show, and 800 million read a Disney book or comic. Each year nearly 7 million people visited Disneyland. Clearly, Walt Disney had left his mark on many different facets of popular culture. ◼

homes. It also spurred a variety of subsidiary industries. *TV Guide* appeared in 1952, quickly becoming ubiquitous. The TV dinner made its debut two years later, allowing families to stay tuned without breaking for meals. The content of most television shows was neither better nor worse than that of most forms of popular culture in earlier decades. Television provided distraction from the daily routine and brought into the home music, drama, and diversions otherwise inaccessible to many people.

Initially, the comedy, crime, western, variety, quiz, and soap opera shows on television resembled radio programs with the addition of scenery. Some early comedy-variety offerings, like "Your Show of Shows" (1950–1954), provided quality writing and acting. A fair amount of sophisticated live drama aired through the mid-1950s on such shows as "Kraft Television Theater," "Playhouse 90," and "Studio One." But toward the end of the 1950s Hollywood began selling old movies to television and producing low-budget, made-for-TV movies. This effectively removed most original drama from television.

Among the most successful comedy shows of the 1950s was, "I Love Lucy," which ran in several formats from 1951 through 1974, and became a model for many subsequent situation comedies, or sitcoms. Lucille Ball played Lucy Ricardo, the scatterbrained wife of Cuban-born band leader Ricky Ricardo, played by Desi Arnaz, her real-life husband. Each week Lucy and her friend Ethel Mertz schemed to get jobs, impress their husbands, and achieve respect. Their plans usually backfired, forcing Ricky and Fred Mertz to rescue their wives. On the most popular episode of the show, aired on January 19, 1953, Lucy re-enacted the recent birth of her son. Although pregnancy was seldom depicted on television, the scriptwriters had blended fiction and reality by coordinating the season's story development with Lucille Ball's so-called expectation. This episode drew a much larger share of the nation's television viewing audience than President Dwight D. Eisenhower's inaugural speech the next day.

Because of technical limitations with live remote filming, news coverage was not a staple of television until the early 1960s. Still, Edward R. Murrow, a pioneer radio and TV investigative journalist, produced some exceptionally good work for CBS, including an exposé of Senator Joseph McCarthy on "See It Now." But most television news came in a fifteen-minute format. Coverage resembled the "March of Time" newsreels shown in theaters—long on emotional images and the pithy narration of human interest stories, short on news content and analysis. As innovations such as the video camera made it possible to follow breaking stories, the television networks expanded nightly news coverage to one-half hour in 1963, and then they promoted the programs heavily to win audience share.

Television producers generally provided entertainment, not intellectual enlightenment. "Howdy Doody," a light-hearted romp using marionettes and mock Indians, set the tone for children's programming. Westerns like "Hopalong Cassidy" and "The Lone Ranger" also played to young viewers before adult westerns such as "Gunsmoke" and "Cheyenne" came into vogue. Milton Berle's vaudeville show was a huge hit on Tuesday nights in the early 1950s. "Today," NBC's struggling morning variety show, almost went off the air until it featured a chimpanzee named J. Fred Muggs, who became a national celebrity.

Soap operas and quiz shows dominated daytime airwaves. Inexpensive to produce, they appealed to busy housewives, who could break up the household routine with TV viewing. "Queen for a Day," in which bedraggled women told hard-luck stories in return for prizes, merged the soap opera and quiz show formats.

In the evening, family-oriented sitcoms proliferated. The decade's big hits included "The Adventures of Ozzie and Harriet," "The Danny Thomas Show," "The Donna Reed Show," "Leave It to Beaver," "Father Knows Best," and "The Honeymooners." Except for the last in which bus driver Ralph Kramden (Jackie Gleason) and his sewer worker buddy Norton (Art Carney) schemed to get rich—these were middle-class fables in which white suburban families with a homemaker mother and a father who worked in a service job lived idyllic lives. Minorities appeared only as servants. The scripts were often clever, and audiences found the solutions to the characters' problems comforting. But television's need to attract mass audiences to earn advertising revenue ensured that its content would appeal to the greatest possible number and that complex social or economic issues would not be discussed.

A quiz show scandal in 1959 tarnished television's reputation as the purveyor of clean values. In 1955 a few prime-time quiz shows with large cash prizes, such as "The $64,000 Question" and "Twenty-One," captured the public's fancy. In dramatic encounters, one or more contestants, isolated in glass booths, competed for cash prizes. To heighten suspense, the questions were kept in bank vaults and brought to the studio by armed guards. Each week's winner proceeded to a new round, tougher questions, and bigger prizes. These shows attracted huge audiences and earned large profits for both the networks and sponsors. Producers often coached contestants on how to smile, grimace, fidget, and knit their brows while pondering questions. Some contestants secretly received further help, including the answers to questions.

In 1956 Charles Van Doren, a young, articulate English professor at Columbia University, won $129,000 on "Twenty-One"—a great improvement on his $4,400 academic salary. NBC hired him as a consultant for $50,000 annually. Parents and teachers wrote to praise Van Doren as a role model for children. Two years later the bubble burst. In 1958 the man dethroned by Charles Van Doren complained to New York journalists that Van Doren had received answers in advance. Both a grand jury and a congressional subcommittee investigated the scandal. Van Doren first protested his innocence but eventually broke down and gave the investigative committee details of the cheating. The prospect of wealth and fame had corrupted him, Van Doren explained. He had agreed to continue the scam because of the good effect it was having on the national interest in education. In the wake of this scandal, networks canceled most of the quiz shows. Van Doren lost his teaching job and, along with several producers and contestants convicted of perjury, received a suspended sentence.

The scandals paved the way for Newton Minnow and others to question the value of television. Should it be admired as a source of entertainment and information or despised as a form of cultural pabulum? Just as today's social commentators disagree about television's worth, historians have mixed feelings about its contribution to the 1950s.

Sports in the TV Age

After the Second World War, professional and college sports assumed a growing significance in American life, becoming a sort of social sharing through which people affirmed the superiority of their country, their community, and their lives. By the late 1940s, professional leagues in basketball and ice hockey had joined those in baseball and football to provide increasing sports entertainment for an avid public. Sports took on the trappings of a secular religion, in which people gave vast significance to the fortunes of their favorite teams. Winning coaches, such as Oklahoma's football coach Bud Wilkinson, became sought-after speakers whose opinions on any variety of topics were listened to reverently. In the suburbs, Little League baseball and football, modeled on the professional leagues, enrolled millions of children.

Television was part of this change, because it elevated players to unprecedented fame and gave the fans a new and often closer look at their idols. Initially, TV cameras worked best in small arenas or other venues in which a single camera could pan the playing area. Boxing, wrestling, and roller derby fared well on TV, as did baseball. As the technology evolved, multiple and remote cameras improved the coverage of football and basketball, and sports occupied a growing portion of the TV schedule. By the 1960s, sports had become a major part of broadcasting. Television also became the key to sports profits, for TV payments soon exceeded the revenue from ticket sales.

In other ways, however, the economic structure of professional sports often seemed a throwback to feudalism. According to a 1922 Supreme Court ruling, reaffirmed in 1972, baseball clubs were exempt from federal antitrust regulations. Football and basketball teams claimed similar rights. As a result, teams could use reserve and option clauses in players' contracts to prevent them from signing with any other team. Similarly, the annual player drafts gave teams exclusive rights to bargain with the players they drafted. These restrictions bound a professional athlete to his original team unless the team decided to trade or sell him. When players dared to question contract restrictions, some club owners accused them of having Communist sympathies.

Desegregation proceeded slowly in professional and college athletics. After Jackie Robinson broke baseball's color line in 1947, professional teams began to hire black athletes, although the pace varied from one sport to another. Some southern college basketball teams refused to recruit African-Americans or play against teams that did. Because the segregated programs gradually became uncompetitive, their fans' frustration helped force them to recruit blacks as well as whites.

As the nation's population shifted toward the West and the Sunbelt, the owners of professional teams began to move franchises to these areas, often provoking outcries from loyal fans. When baseball owner Walter O'Malley took his Brooklyn Dodgers to Los Angeles in the late 1950s, New Yorkers decried his betrayal and demanded a congressional investigation. But during the next decade many teams relocated. While the old fans protested, fans in the new cities hastened to the stadiums and arenas or watched the games on television.

Rock Around the Clock

In addition to sports, the 1950s brought a revolution in popular music. A dynamic new form, rock 'n' roll, along with improved recording technology and the emergence of a large cohort of teenagers with money to spend, created a vast new market in commercial music.

Before the advent of rock, mainstream fifties music featured pleasant, unchallenging songs like "How Much Is That Doggie in the Window," "Cherry Pink and Apple Blossom White," and "The Ballad of Davy Crockett." In contrast, African-American popular music, often called "race music," vibrated with religious and sexual energy, but white audiences had little exposure to it. To make the distinctive black style more acceptable, some disc jockeys called it rhythm and blues, or R&B. After 1945 R&B influenced southern "hillybilly" and western "cowboy" music, creating the hybrid country-and-western style.

In 1952 Cleveland disc jockey Alan Freed began an R&B radio show called "Moondog's Rock 'n' Roll Party." Like the term *jazz*, "rockin' and rolling'" originally referred to sexual intercourse. To appeal to his white audience, Freed toned down the sexual references, connecting the words *rock 'n' roll* to the style of dancing associated with the music. From then on, the barriers between white and black music began to tumble. Although a direct correlation is hard to establish, it is interesting that white audiences opened their ears to black music at the same time the civil rights movement was challenging the racism of white society. In 1954 Freed moved to New York and cultivated a growing radio following.

That same year Bill Haley, a portly, nearly middle-aged white band leader, recorded "Rock Around the Clock," an exuberant tune that became the theme song of the popular film *Blackboard Jungle* (1955). The movie chronicled the struggle of a young teacher in a run-down inner-city high school who tried to motivate alienated, poor youth. It

Elvis Presley in 1956. His exuberant singing style shocked adults and excited youth. *UPI/ Bettmann Newsphotos.*

touched on problems of race, class, and delinquency—unusual themes in commercial art. The film's message—crime does not pay, and middle-class values are a salvation—is scarcely remembered. But "Rock Around the Clock," critics and audiences agreed, gave *Blackboard Jungle* its "insurrectionary power." The music brought white middle-class youth to their feet. Theater owners reported spontaneous dancing in the aisles.

The record industry was especially eager to appeal to white youth because they represented an enormous market. "Teenagers," a relatively recent term for those who enjoyed a prolonged adolescence before entering the labor force, formed an expanding group during the 1950s. Early in the decade they purchased around 40 percent of all records, radios, and cameras and over half of all movie tickets. Their numbers and economic impact grew steadily, so that by 1959 the teenage market—including money spent by parents on teenagers and by teenagers on themselves—topped $10 billion per year. With so much at stake, record producers hustled to find more white recording artists who employed the black sound in a form acceptable to white teenagers.

The biggest find was a nineteen-year-old part-time truck driver from Tupelo, Mississippi—Elvis Presley. Born poor, he had taught himself the guitar and learned the R&B style. His first record in 1954 earned him appearances on regional radio shows, and within a year he was a star throughout the South. In live performance, he aroused his fans, both female and male, by undulating his body and thrusting his hips in a style he attributed to revivalist preachers. Presley virtually created the image of the hypersexed male rock star, replete with long hair, leather jacket, a sneering expression, and a sultry demeanor.

By 1956, "Elvis the Pelvis" became a national sensation. He released a series of hits, including "Heartbreak Hotel," "Don't Be Cruel," "Love Me Tender," and "I'm All Shook Up," that sold over 14 million records that year. He appeared on Ed Sullivan's popular TV variety show, where the cameras focused above the waist to conceal the young man's suggestive pelvic thrusts. Over 80 percent of all American viewers watched this performance, a number unsurpassed until the Beatles made their television debut in 1964.

Between early 1956 and March 1958, when the army drafted him, Presley released fourteen consecutive million-seller records. By 1966 he had sold 115 million records. Presley's success not only set a standard for other white rock singers, but also spurred white acceptance of African-American artists such as Ray Charles, Chuck Berry, Little Richard, and Fats Domino.

At the same time, technical improvements in the recording industry helped to boost sales. New high-fidelity techniques, as well as the introduction of 45 and 33⅓ rpm discs, brought recorded music far closer to the original sound. The combination of a new musical style, better recordings, and an avid audience sent record sales soaring from under 189 million in 1950 to 277 million in 1955 and about 600 million in 1960. In 1959 a "payola" scandal tarnished the industry's reputation by revealing that many disc jockeys, including the rock pioneer Alan Freed, accepted payoffs from record companies in return for broadcasting their music. Nevertheless, the industry grossed over $500 million annually by the end of the decade, with teenagers buying 70 percent of all the records.

While the young went wild over rock 'n' roll, parents recoiled at its influence. To counter Presley's attraction, many parents encouraged their children to listen to clean-cut artists like Pat Boone, Ricky Nelson, and Frankie Avalon. While these vocalists had some appeal, none rivaled Presley. *Life* magazine contrasted his "bump and grind routine" to the more respectable performances of all-American crooner Frank Sinatra. Sinatra himself called rock 'n' roll the "martial music of every sideburned delinquent on the face of the earth." Some clergy condemned Presley's music as satanic, and many cities refused to permit rock concerts at public facilities. According to a congressional report, "The gangster of tomorrow is the Elvis Presley type of today."

In fact, some rock lyrics made fun of middle-class values. Besides its generally sensual, even sexual emphasis, rock music ridiculed work ("Get a Job"), downplayed school ("Don't Know Much About History"), mixed religion with sex ("Teen Angel"), scoffed at authority ("Charlie Brown, You're a Clown"), and celebrated irresponsibility ("Rock Around the Clock"). Popular music had never before so blatantly defied social mores or so distinguished youth from older generations. Thus, for many adults, rock 'n' roll became a convenient shorthand for explaining the problem with the country's young people.

Fears of Youth in Rebellion

Elvis Presley, the outlaw leather look, and rock 'n' roll's unleashing of teenage emotions fueled popular anxieties about youth. So did films like *The Wild Ones* (1953), *Rebel Without a Cause* (1955), and *Blackboard Jungle* (1955). These three movies featured actors Marlon Brando, James Dean, and Sidney Poitier as young toughs who oozed anger, sexuality, and contempt for their elders. Their fictional characters presented an even stronger challenge to the order of things than did Holden Caufield, the alienated teenage hero of J. D. Salinger's exceedingly popular novel *Catcher in the Rye* (1951). Despite the films' overt messages that violence and immorality were wrong, most teenagers who flocked to see Brando, Dean, and Poitier cheered the unrepentant rebels, not the characters who accepted their elders' advice.

A youth subculture was beginning to emerge, and many parents worried about it. They blamed the popular culture—rock music, movies, books, comics, even the television programs that to later generations would seem so innocent. Some people invoked the Communist specter. Early in the decade, Justice Department officials helped one Hollywood studio produce a film warning that "throughout the United States today, indeed throughout the free world, a deadly war is being waged." The "Communist enemy," the film declared, was trying to subvert American youth by spreading drugs and encouraging obscenity in the mass media.

Fear of an epidemic of juvenile crime grew especially intense in the mid-1950s. Parents, journalists, police, and politicians warned that juvenile delinquency among all classes threatened the foundations of society. Some blamed working mothers for slighting family discipline. Others argued that comic books, television, movies, advertising, and music glamorized crime.

It is unclear whether these fears had a real basis. The FBI assembled local police reports to produce a national crime profile, which did indicate an increase in juvenile crime. However, because each community employed different criteria, the statistics were unreliable. Once delinquency became a hot topic, police tended to report offenses they had previously overlooked as trivial. Increased sensitivity to juvenile crime, rather than a surge in deviance, probably accounted for the statistical rise. Indeed, most youthful lawbreakers committed "status" offenses that, if done by adults, would not be crimes at all. These included curfew violation, consuming alcohol or cigarettes, driving without a license, truancy, running away from home, consorting with immoral persons, and defying parental authority.

A dramatic increase in violent crime and drug use, mostly of heroin, did occur among minorities in the burgeoning urban ghettos. Youth gangs flourished in the ethnic ghettos of New York, Chicago, Los Angeles, and a few other large cities. But the majority of African-American and Hispanic gangs in the low-income housing projects were not violent. Despite scare stories, youth gangs outside these enclaves had only tiny memberships. Complaints about gangs often served as code language for criticism of minorities.

In 1953 the Senate created a subcommittee to investigate juvenile delinquency. Senator Estes Kefauver of Tennessee sat on the panel and, after the Democrats took control of the Senate in 1954, served as chair. As in the 1950 anticrime hearings, Kefauver was motivated at least in part by a desire to attract the kind of attention that the Red Scare had brought Joseph McCarthy. Kefauver argued that juvenile delinquency essentially stemmed from a moral breakdown in the home and community, exacerbated by comic books glorifying crime. Prominent educators and mental health professionals joined the senator's plea for media self-censorship as the best way to protect youth and as an alternative to government controls.

Ironically, once the public furor subsided, juvenile crime began a steep and well-documented increase. The primary reason was the large number of baby-boom children entering their teenage years.

Be There or Be Square: The Beats

A more intellectual form of rebellion was provided by the Beats, a small, loosely defined group of iconoclastic writers who captured public attention in the late 1950s. Their defiance of social and literary convention, as well as their dabbling in drugs, Eastern mysticism, and homosexuality, outraged the middle class and excited many teenagers and young adults. Beatniks, as they became known, shunned Christianity, work, materialism, family life, patriotism, and interest in winning the Cold War.

The Beat writers included poets Allen Ginsberg and Kenneth Rexroth and novelists Jack Kerouac, William Burroughs, and John Chellon Holmes. Most began writing in New York early in the decade and drifted toward San Francisco. Ginsberg gained national attention in 1956 when San Francisco police charged him with obscenity for publishing his poem *Howl*, a highly personal cry against American materialism and mass society. At his trial, prominent writers and critics defended the poem, which discussed madness, drugs, travel, ecstasy, and various forms of sexuality. The Beats achieved further fame in 1957 with the appearance of Kerouac's best seller *On the Road*, a raucous, thinly fictionalized account of the author's cross-country travel with his unconventional friends.

The Beats' defiance of the "square" world struck a chord, but emulation of their behavior was mostly confined to superficial elements of style. Some people gathered in dark cafés to listen to poetry and jazz music and sip espresso. More important, college students, generally the epitome of conformity in the 1950s, began to read the Beats and ponder their challenges to social and sexual conventions. The Beat Generation was an important precursor to the youth rebellion of the 1960s.

SPUTNIK AND THE SCHOOL CRISIS

During episodes of national self-doubt, political leaders, journalists, and parents frequently lambaste the public schools. Deficient schools have been blamed for everything from decline in voter participation to low rates of capital investment and job growth. In the mid-1950s, the juvenile crime scare coincided with complaints that schools were turning out illiterates unable to perform basic tasks or, most important, compete with the Russians.

Many political liberals and professional educators saw the problem as the lack of federal aid to public schools. Without more money for buildings, equipment, and libraries, they argued, teachers could not cope with surging enrollments and the constant accumulation of new information. Only higher salaries, paid for by taxes, would lure talented college graduates into teaching.

Conservatives, on the other hand, blamed the educational establishment itself, including teacher training colleges and unions, for poor student performance. The right wing believed that John Dewey's popular ideas of "progressive education," with their emphasis on social relevance, democratic ideals, and pragmatism, had undermined respect for the acquisition of basic skills, traditional values, and culture. They called for a return to basics, more classroom discipline, and the teaching of religious values.

In 1955, Rudolf Flesch published a diatribe against public education called *Why Johnny Can't Read and What You Can Do About It*. An instant best seller, it spawned a host of imitators. Flesch attributed low reading levels to permissive teachers who failed to assign serious literature or to drill students rigorously. An advocate of German teaching methods, he urged citizens to employ this more demanding model in American public schools.

The debate over education took on a life of its own, with few participants managing to show that educational quality had actually declined. Neither liberal nor conservative critics fully acknowledged that part of the problem lay in the changing nature of mass education. Before the Second World War, relatively few students finished high school and even fewer went to college. Public primary schools sought to instill some basic discipline and rudimentary reading and arithmetic skills. The wealthy attended private schools, and talented students of modest means benefited from special college preparatory courses in public high schools.

Postwar prosperity resulted in many more working-class youth attending high school. As blacks and Hispanics migrated to urban areas, they became a major presence in public schools, increasing the cultural and social diversity in schools as well as the proportion of working-class students. These factors, combined with the baby boom and the rapid expansion of suburbs, put education at all levels under stress. Moreover, a growing number of parents now expected schools to play a more comprehensive role than ever before. Schools were expected to teach job skills, citizenship, and a sophisticated science, math, and literature curriculum to a broader cross section of students than in earlier decades. To complicate the problem, by tradition American schools were locally funded and controlled, making it difficult to promote change at the national level.

The critique reached new heights after October 1957 when the Soviet Union launched the first artificial satellite, *Sputnik I*. (See Chapter 5 for a discussion of the space race.) Anxiety over the Cold War added fuel to the crisis in education. Journalists and politicians described the Soviet Union as the model of successful mass education. Communism, it seemed, had won the space race by winning the science and technology education race. What would Moscow win next?

Life's special 1957 issue on the crisis in education contrasted the "typical" hard-working Soviet sixteen-year-old with his "slovenly" American counterpart. The Soviet youth, dedicated to becoming a nuclear physicist, read Shakespeare, studied calculus, and kept in shape by playing volleyball and avoiding sex. The American youth could barely read comic books and spent his spare time listening to rock music and lusting after girls. "The spartan Soviet system," *Life* concluded, "is producing many students better equipped to compete with the technicalities of the space age." Almost immediately, an enterprising author published a volume titled *Why Johnny Can't Read and Ivan Can*.

In fact, the Soviet successes in education were greatly exaggerated. Nevertheless, *Sputnik* forged a national consensus in favor of federal aid to education. Before the crisis, southern Democrats opposed federal spending because they feared it would erode local control and spur integration. Northern liberal Democrats worried about opening public coffers to parochial schools. Lobbyists for parochial schools feared that higher school taxes would hurt their ability to charge tuition and erode their client base. Most Republicans simply opposed spending money on social programs. But the clamor to catch up with the Russians changed things.

Senator Lyndon B. Johnson of Texas, Democratic majority leader and presidential aspirant, chaired an investigating committee assessing the impact of Moscow's space coup. Long an advocate of federal support for education, he now warned of a widening science and technology gap, with communism the likely victor in the "battle of brainpower." Besides an increase in space and military appropriations, Johnson called for creating a "reservoir of trained and educated minds" through federal aid to schools.

Congress and President Eisenhower cooperated in September 1958 to pass the National Defense Education Act (NDEA), a billion-dollar package, supplemented by state grants, that provided aid to schools and universities. It granted funds for construction, student loans and scholarships, and the teaching of science, mathematics, and foreign languages. In the following two decades, NDEA and successor programs had a huge impact on American education at all levels, from primary grades through graduate and professional schools. As with the GI Bill of a decade earlier, loans and fellowships allowed many more students to pursue advanced degrees. By 1960, the United States granted ten thousand doctorates annually, three times the pre–Second World War number. Foreign students flocked to American universities, making the United States a world center of higher education.

With educational assistance provided through the NDEA, a record number of students enrolled in college during the 1960s. As never before, Americans assumed that a bright student, whatever his or her social background, should and would go to college. However, the large group of confident, intellectually curious students hitting college campuses coincided with growing American military involvement in Vietnam. Not surprisingly, this generation of college students would play a major role in challenging the Vietnam War in the 1960s.

CIVIL RIGHTS AND CIVIL LIBERTIES

The general complacency most white Americans felt during the 1950s contrasted starkly with the African-American experience. More than ever before, blacks challenged the legal and political foundations of the status quo. Their civil rights struggles, assisted by the federal courts, tore down the formal barriers to equality that had been erected in the aftermath of Reconstruction.

Like much of the population, African-Americans were highly mobile after the Second World War, continuing the migration patterns of the war years. In the rural South, the program of federal agricultural subsidies dating from the 1930s helped to limit the production of cotton and other crops and finance farm mechanization. One effect was to push black sharecroppers off the land. Some went to southern cities like Atlanta and Birmingham. More went north and west (see map, page 150). Overall, about one in five African-Americans left the South in the 1950s, reducing the minority population there to 20 percent.

The migrants did not find residential integration in their new communities. Just as the newcomers arrived, white Americans were leaving cities for the suburbs. During the 1950s the nation's twelve largest central cities lost 3.6 million whites while they gained 4.5 million nonwhites. By 1960 over half of all African-Americans lived in the largely poor and mostly black central cities. The new suburban communities remained nearly all white.

Despite the situation in the North, it was in the South that segregation came under sharp attack. Court decisions, boycott movements, and new laws undermined the legal and social pillars of racism.

Struggle in the Courts: The *Brown* Decision

By 1952 the most influential African-American organization, the NAACP, was pressing five suits against public school segregation. In earlier cases brought by the NAACP, the Supreme Court had ordered southern states to admit minority students to all-white graduate schools when no "separate but equal" facilities existed. A majority of justices seemed willing to chip away at segregation by forcing states to honor the "equal" part of the "separate but equal" doctrine of the *Plessy* decision of 1896.

The five new suits before the high court in 1952 were eventually combined under the heading of one key case, which involved Linda Brown of Topeka, Kansas. Each morning she had to walk past a nearby "white only" school to a bus stop where she would be transported to a "colored only" school. NAACP chief attorney Thurgood Marshall abandoned the piecemeal strategy and likened "separate but equal" to the black codes that were established to restrict African-American rights after the Civil War. The doctrine could be sustained, Marshall argued, only if the Supreme Court agreed "that for some

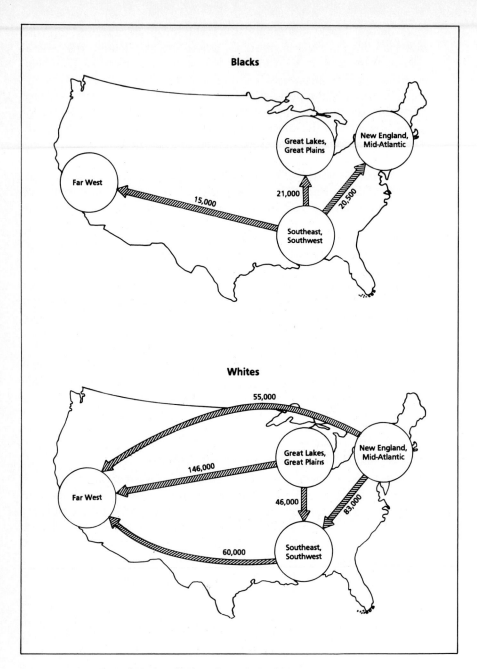

Blacks

Great Lakes, Great Plains

New England, Mid-Atlantic

Far West

15,000

21,000

20,500

Southeast, Southwest

Whites

55,000

Great Lakes, Great Plains

New England, Mid-Atlantic

Far West

146,000

46,000

83,000

60,000

Southeast, Southwest

Average Annual Regional Migration, 1947–1960

reason Negroes are inferior to all other human beings." Insisting that segregation violated the Fourteenth Amendment, Marshall also submitted research by psychologist Kenneth Clark suggesting that African-American children educated in single-race schools suffered lasting emotional and intellectual damage.

The Supreme Court heard arguments in *Brown* v. *Board of Education* late in 1952 but delayed ruling. Chief Justice Fred Vinson, like several associate justices, had misgivings about segregation but agreed with the contention of lawyers defending racial segregation that states had a right to set their own school policy, however discriminatory it might be. In September 1953, in the midst of these deliberations, Vinson died. Associate Justice Felix Frankfurter privately quipped that Vinson's timely demise was "the only proof I've ever seen of the existence of God." A year before, presidential candidate Eisenhower had secured support from Governor Earl Warren of California by promising him the first opening on the Supreme Court. Eisenhower had some qualms about appointing Warren to the most influential seat on the court, but honored his promise.

Neither Eisenhower nor most other Americans imagined how fateful this appointment would become. Warren had scant interest in legal scholarship or precedent; he viewed the Supreme Court as a unique force for protecting the weak, oppressed, and disadvantaged who had little political influence, locally or nationally. His vision and activism brought the Court into the center of national politics and made him the most influential chief justice in over a century.

Warren ordered a rehearing of the *Brown* case in December 1953. Then he persuaded all eight associate justices to join him in a unanimous opinion, issued in May 1954, that struck down segregation in public education. Although some legal scholars noted that segregation had flourished after the Civil War despite passage of the Fourteenth Amendment, Warren simply rejected the *Plessy* decision of 1896 and put forth an essentially new interpretation of the Fourteenth Amendment.

For Warren, the issue was simple justice. To segregate school children

from others of similar age and qualifications solely because of their race generates a feeling of inferiority as to their status in the community that may affect their hearts and minds in a way unlikely ever to be undone. . . . Segregation with the sanction of law, therefore, has a tendency to retard educational and mental development of Negro children.

In education, he declared, "separate but equal has no place. Separate educational facilities are inherently unequal."

Critics charged that the ruling misconstrued the Constitution and relied on dubious social science data. Others accused the Supreme Court of usurping congressional and state power by making, rather than interpreting, the law. Warren's defenders retorted that the *Brown* decision yielded the correct moral, if not legal, verdict. In fact, the Supreme Court had taken action reluctantly to resolve a moral, legal, and political issue that neither Congress nor the president would confront. Civil rights had been stuck in a political gridlock that only the Supreme Court seemed capable of unraveling. Chief Justice Warren therefore believed the Court had an obligation to push the nation toward racial equality.

In practice, the *Brown* decision affected only public schools, not the comprehensive web of segregation laws that prevailed in twenty-four states as well as the District of Columbia. Moreover, the Supreme Court delayed implementing its ruling and called for consultation between local authorities and judges. During 1954 and 1955, the high court heard the NAACP demand "integration now" while southern states requested delays and demagogues called for "segregation forever." During this interim period, the Court's delay and President Eisenhower's uneasiness over the desegregation ruling helped fuel a massive resistance movement.

Warren again spoke for a unanimous Court in May 1955, ruling in a case called *Brown II* that school segregation must be ended everywhere in the nation. However, because local conditions varied, school districts were permitted to make a "prompt and reasonable start towards full compliance" under the oversight of federal district courts. Although desegregation should begin with "all deliberate speed," the court issued no timetable.

Southern officials hoped that federal district judges would wink at delays and, as a Georgia official remarked, define a "reasonable time as one or two hundred years." When district judges insisted on early action, however, segregationists dug in their heels. In several southern states, White Citizens' Councils sprang up to intimidate parents and school boards attempting to integrate the schools. Over one hundred members of Congress signed a "Southern Manifesto" opposing the *Brown* decision. Senator Harry F. Byrd, a Democrat from Virginia, called for massive resistance, and several state legislatures in the South declared they would defy the supposedly unconstitutional Supreme Court rulings.

These states passed laws forbidding officials to carry out any action to mix races in public schools. Several curtailed or abolished public schools, turning over the buildings to all-white private academies. At one point Mississippi and South Carolina actually amended their constitutions to abolish public education, and Virginia closed public schools for several months. Because of resistance and hostility, in 1960 most schools in the South and many in the North remained as segregated as before. Far from being resolved, the issue would become the focus of public debate again and again in later decades.

Eisenhower and Civil Rights

Despite his generally humane impulses, President Eisenhower did little to promote the Supreme Court rulings. His own encounters with minorities had taken place almost exclusively in the ranks of a segregated army, where blacks and Filipinos served him as subordinates. As army chief of staff in 1948 he had defended military segregation, arguing that "if we attempt to force someone to like someone else, we are just going to get into trouble." Of course, equality under law, not the "liking" of minorities, was the real issue. But as president, Eisenhower continued to believe that only changes in white sentiment, not court rulings, could alter segregation. Moreover, as one who preferred to handle national problems in a managerial fashion, he seemed particularly uncomfortable with the heated emotions generated by racial conflict and the struggle for civil rights.

Pressed by the contending factions to endorse or denounce the *Brown* ruling, Eisenhower privately blamed Earl Warren for the crisis and called his appointment of the judge the "biggest damn fool mistake I ever made." Although the president accepted the desegregation decision, he declined to endorse it. He told Booker T. Washington's daughter, "We cannot do it by cold lawmaking, but must make these changes by appealing to reason, by prayer, and by constantly working at it through our own efforts."

Eisenhower's greatest effort on behalf of change came in response to a direct challenge to federal authority in Little Rock, Arkansas. In 1957, the relatively moderate Little Rock school board accepted a court order to allow nine African-American students to enroll in Central High School. But Governor Orval Faubus, an ardent segregationist, called out the National Guard to block them. When a federal court ordered the troops to withdraw, a white mob surrounded the school, taunting and threatening the blacks attempting to enroll. Faced with massive local defiance of a federal court order—and embarrassed by Soviet propaganda publicizing American racism, which found a wide audience in the Third World—Eisenhower felt compelled to send a thousand army troops and ten thousand federalized National Guardsmen to protect the students, maintain safety, and enforce the court order.

The troops stayed a year. In 1958 Governor Faubus closed the Little Rock schools, which reopened as white academies, in an effort to prevent integration. A year later a federal court disallowed this move. The whole episode, including vivid pictures of the howling mob and the frightened but dignified African-American students, became an international embarrassment to the United States.

The administration tried to mollify critics by introducing a civil rights bill to Congress in 1957. Attorney General Herbert Brownell

White students taunt Elizabeth Echford as she braves a hostile crowd to enter Central High School in Little Rock, Arkansas, in 1957. *Wide World Photos.*

pushed the legislation while Eisenhower recuperated from an illness. Brownell had expressed outrage when a Mississippi registrar disqualified an African-American voter for failing to answer the question "How many bubbles are in a bar of soap?" But Brownell also had political motives for pressing a civil rights bill: he hoped that a debate on the question would divide the northern and southern wings of the Democratic party and curb the influence of presidential hopeful Lyndon Johnson.

The ploy failed when Johnson used his persuasive talents to convince a majority of Democrats to support the Civil Rights Act of 1957, an amended version of the bill that declared support for black voting rights but offered no means of enforcement. To make matters worse for the Republicans, when Eisenhower signed the bill he criticized it as going too far, too fast. This helped to solidify the Democratic hold on African-American voters.

Community Action

Shortly before Christmas in 1955, Rosa Parks, a tailor's assistant in Montgomery, Alabama, boarded a bus to ride home. When ordered to vacate a seat and move to the rear so that a white passenger might sit, she felt she had been pushed too far. Parks, a member of the

NAACP, decided to discover "once and for all what rights I had as a human being and a citizen." Besides, she added, "my feet hurt." For her trouble, she was arrested for violating the law requiring separate seating for whites and blacks on public buses.

Rosa Parks was not the first black women to be arrested for breaking this law, but in three recent cases the city of Montgomery had dropped charges to avoid a legal challenge. The Women's Political Council, a group of African-American professional women, knew of Parks's good reputation in the community and her support for civil rights causes, and considered her case an ideal test case. The council conferred with other community leaders, including E. D. Nixon, a local NAACP official, and decided to mobilize grassroots support for a challenge to the law by enlisting the help of Baptist ministers, including Ralph Abernathy and Martin Luther King, Jr., in a black boycott of Montgomery buses.

King, then a twenty-seven-year-old preacher new to the community, came from a prominent family in Atlanta. His father, Martin Luther King, Sr., sometimes known as "Daddy" King, ministered to a large congregation and encouraged his talented son to pursue a broad education, including a doctorate in theology from Boston University. Martin Luther King, Jr., did not initiate the challenge to

The Reverend Martin Luther King, Jr., and his son note where terrorists burned a cross on his front lawn in Atlanta, Georgia. *UPI/Bettmann Newsphotos.*

racism in Montgomery but gradually emerged as a leader because of his talents and passionate oratory. He told local and national audiences that "there comes a time when people get tired . . . tired of being segregated and humiliated; tired of being kicked about by the brutal feet of oppression." The time had come for his people to cease tolerating "anything less than freedom and justice." Influenced by his reading of Thoreau and Gandhi, King applied principles of nonviolent civil disobedience to the boycott. He emerged from the Montgomery ordeal totally committed to the fight against segregation, and by then he had become the most prominent African-American leader since Booker T. Washington.

For a year, some fifty thousand African-Americans walked or rode in car pools rather than ride the segregated buses of Montgomery. Affluent white women aided the boycott by chauffeuring their black maids in their cars. Boycott leaders did not insist on full integration, asking instead that passengers be seated on a first-come, first-served basis, with blacks seating themselves from the rear to the front and whites from the front to the rear. Despite the moderate nature of this request, city officials responded by indicting protest leaders for violating state antiboycott laws and by banning car pools as a public nuisance. Terrorists bombed churches and the homes of activists, including King's. By November 1956 these pressures had nearly broken the movement. But then the Supreme Court overturned Alabama's bus segregation law under which Parks had been arrested. This left the city and bus company no legal recourse and a financial disincentive to resist integration. Thus the combination of grassroots and judicial activism achieved victory.

The Montgomery boycott illustrates the unique role that churches and ministers played in the early civil rights crusade. Because segregation had excluded blacks from most forms of political activity in the South, churches remained the one permissible setting for community organization. They provided a base of support, local leadership, some financial resources, a common language and culture, and a sense of empowerment that could be turned toward political goals. Ministers such as King and Abernathy molded the content of African-American religion into a political weapon by portraying heroes like Moses and Jesus as social revolutionaries. Just as the biblical Jews reached the Promised Land after long tribulation, African-Americans could win freedom, these ministers told their congregations, through faith and a commitment to struggle.

Soon after the Montgomery boycott, local ministers organized the Southern Christian Leadership Conference. Established in 1957, the SCLC brought together community leaders with a mass base of church membership. Ralph Abernathy, Fred Shuttlesworth, Hosea Williams, James Revel, and Andrew Young joined King in the effort.

Though long on vision, the SCLC suffered from many personality disputes among its leaders and constant financial problems.

Other African-Americans independently and collectively challenged segregation by the end of the decade. College students in the South took the boldest initiative. In February 1960, four students from the North Carolina Agricultural and Technical College, after shopping in a Greensboro, North Carolina, Woolworth's store, sat down at the lunch counter to order coffee. When the manager refused to serve them, they stayed there until the store closed and they faced arrest.

Over the next several weeks this tactic spread quickly. Lunch counter sit-ins occurred in over thirty cities in seven states. Many of the protestors were arrested, and some were beaten. Most adopted a strategy of nonviolence in the face of assaults. The effort yielded notable successes, with many national chain stores integrating their lunch counters. Some of the student activists followed Ella Baker into the Student Non-Violent Coordinating Committee (SNCC), which she organized in 1960. Over the next few years, SNCC would play a major role in challenging segregation.

Despite important achievements, at the close of the 1950s most African-Americans still attended predominantly segregated schools and lived in single-race neighborhoods. Few in the South could vote. Many more personal sacrifices by civil rights activists and the intervention of a sympathetic federal government would be necessary to affect real change.

New Policies for Native Americans

During the same period that the federal government and courts began extending new support to African-Americans, the Eisenhower administration and Congress imposed several well-intentioned but ultimately calamitous policies on Native Americans. Reversing New Deal efforts to expand assistance to Indian tribes, the federal government adopted a policy of "termination" that entailed the gradual liquidation of many Indian reservations and social services. The administration and Congress justified these measures as ways to reduce costs and expand states' rights and the rights of individual Native Americans.

Between 1954 and 1960, the federal government withdrew benefits from sixty-one tribes. Many reservations were absorbed as counties into the states in which they were located. The tribes now had to pay state taxes and conform to state regulations. To raise the cash required for taxes, many tribes and individuals had to sell land and mineral rights to outside interests. For example, the Klamaths of Oregon, enticed by offers from lumber companies, sold off most of their ponderosa pine forests. The Menominees of Wisconsin sold much of their reservation land to wealthy Chicagoans who built vacation cabins on it.

The financial gains from these deals proved fleeting. Within a few years the tribes were far worse off than before, with social problems such as unemployment, alcoholism, and suicide taking a growing toll. Thereafter, an increasing number of Indians abandoned the former reservation lands. By the end of the 1960s, half the Native American population had relocated to urban areas.

The Supreme Court and Civil Liberties

Just as the Warren Court promoted civil rights, starting in 1956 the Supreme Court began to unravel the restraints on free speech and political action spun during the Red Scare. Although Eisenhower complained bitterly about Warren's liberal activism, he appointed as associate justice William J. Brennan (1956–1990), who became an even more forceful exponent of civil rights and civil liberties. Three other Eisenhower appointees, John Marshall Harlan (1955–1971), Charles E. Whittaker (1957–1962), and Potter Stewart (1958–1981), were moderates. Hugo Black and William O. Douglas, Roosevelt's appointees, joined Warren and Brennan in a solid four-vote liberal block. On occasion, they won support from Justice Frankfurter or one of the three other Eisenhower appointees. In 1962, President Kennedy's appointment of Arthur Goldberg as associate justice solidified the liberal direction of the Warren Court.

The Court nullified antisubversion statutes in forty-two states through its 1956 *Pennsylvania* v. *Nelson* decision. Speaking for the majority, Chief Justice Warren ruled that only federal, not state, laws could make it a crime to advocate the overthrow of the federal government. In 1957, in *Jencks* v. *United States*, the Court dealt a blow to government witch hunts by insisting that accused persons had the right to examine the evidence gathered against them. That same year, in *Yates* v. *United States*, the Supreme Court overturned the conviction of fourteen midlevel Communist party officials sentenced for violating the Smith Act. The justices ruled that verbal calls for toppling the government did not constitute a crime. To be illegal, an act must involve the attempt to "do something now or in the future."

In subsequent decisions, Warren and Brennan led the Supreme Court to impose severe restrictions on the use of the Smith and McCarran acts. The justices set aside the conviction of Communist party members who had refused to register as foreign agents. The Court also forbade the government to deny passports to accused Communists or to bar them from certain jobs.

EISENHOWER'S SECOND-TERM BLUES

As Eisenhower entered the final year of his first term, the public seemed at ease with his casual style of leadership. The Korean War had ended, Senator McCarthy was a spent force, Stalin's successors called for peaceful coexistence, and the economy was robust. Only Eisenhower's health worried voters. He suffered a serious heart attack in September 1955 and a disabling attack of ileitis, followed by surgery, the next June. His speedy recovery, however, quieted most fears. Eisenhower decided to run again.

Eisenhower harbored doubts about keeping Vice President Richard Nixon on the ticket. He had never liked the brash young man, and now he pondered ways to ease Nixon out. Eisenhower encouraged several cabinet members to seek the nomination while urging Nixon to vacate his job in favor of a cabinet post in a second administration. When Nixon balked, Eisenhower relented rather than provoke the wrath of the Republican right. But his misgivings about Nixon undermined the vice president's stature and hurt his presidential candidacy in 1960.

The Democrats renominated Adlai Stevenson, following a challenge from Senator Estes Kefauver, who then beat out Senator John F. Kennedy for the vice-presidential slot. Stevenson raised serious questions about poverty, the lack of a national health program, and the administration's refusal to fund public schools. A decade later, Lyndon Johnson would revive these ideas in his Great Society programs. Stevenson also appealed for both a more moderate and a more militant foreign policy. As a moderate, he favored ending the draft and halting the open-air testing of atomic weapons; as a militant, he condemned Eisenhower for losing half of Indochina to communism and for not building as many long-range bombers as the Soviets. Nevertheless, Americans overwhelmingly liked Ike and considered Stevenson an articulate loser. As one journalist commented, "The public loves Ike. . . . The less he does the more they love him."

The outbreak of an anti-Soviet uprising in Hungary and the Anglo-French-Israeli invasion of Egypt just days before the election made it seem imperative to return the tried and tested general and statesman to the White House. On election day in November 1956, Eisenhower gathered 58 percent of the popular vote, over 35 million ballots, to Stevenson's 26 million (see map, page 160). The public liked Ike far more than it liked his party, however. The Democrats maintained a four-seat majority in the Senate and a twenty-nine seat majority in the House. The gap was widened further by the congressional elections of 1958, which came in the midst of a recession.

In November 1957, Eisenhower suffered a mild stroke. Although

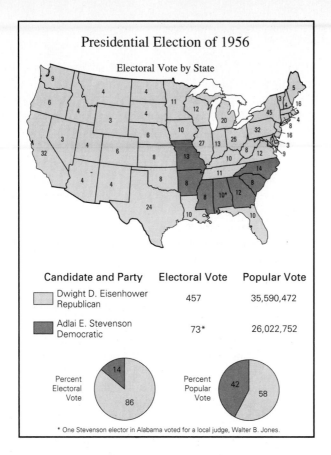

Presidential Election of 1956

Electoral Vote by State

Candidate and Party	Electoral Vote	Popular Vote
Dwight D. Eisenhower Republican	457	35,590,472
Adlai E. Stevenson Democratic	73*	26,022,752

Percent Electoral Vote: 14 / 86

Percent Popular Vote: 42 / 58

* One Stevenson elector in Alabama voted for a local judge, Walter B. Jones.

Presidential Election of 1956

his mental powers were intact, his slurred speech made his public communication even less effective than before. That autumn, several foreign and domestic events called his leadership into question. After his dispatch of troops to Little Rock to protect the black students at Central High School, various critics called his actions either too great or too modest a response. The clamor over *Sputnik* prompted Democrats to ridicule Eisenhower for starving education and spending too little money on space and defense projects. The new Soviet leader, Nikita Khrushchev, began making whirlwind tours of the Third World, offering aid and winning praise for his country's support of emerging nations. In 1958, Eisenhower's powerful chief of staff, Sherman Adams, resigned amid allegations that he had accepted expensive fur coats from a contractor. In Congress, the Democrats took the lead in funding NDEA and space research. To many Americans, Eisenhower began to seem a bit too unengaged.

Life magazine and the *New York Times* ran series on "the national purpose," commenting that the country lacked proper spirit, direction, and leadership. Nelson Rockefeller, a Republican who was elected governor of New York in 1958, joined with the influential Rockefeller Brothers' Fund to sponsor a series of panels that urged increased federal spending to support science and the military and to stimulate economic growth. Democratic presidential hopefuls, including Senators Kennedy, Johnson, and Stuart Symington, echoed these themes in their campaigns.

Under pressure to show more leadership, Eisenhower appointed two study groups, the Gaither Commission and the Commission on National Goals, to report on the national mood and future needs. Their conclusions were so negative that the president kept secret the Gaither Report, which dealt mostly with defense, and delayed release of the National Goals report until after the 1960 election. When *Goals for Americans* finally appeared, it echoed charges by President-elect Kennedy that America's prestige had fallen throughout the world and that more money should be spent to boost defense and promote faster economic growth.

By 1960 political discontent was percolating just beneath the surface. The third economic recession since Eisenhower took office, along with new challenges from Moscow, a Communist revolution in Cuba, and a sense that America needed younger, dynamic leadership, gave the Eisenhower administration a tired, somewhat shabby appearance. Yet Eisenhower remained a hero to most Americans. They credited him with ending the Korean War and delivering peace and prosperity. His bland, comfortable stewardship, like that of the typical father in the era's sitcoms, had reassured most middle-class Americans that they would be allowed to get on with their lives.

CONCLUSION

In retrospect, the fifties seem a curiously contradictory period in American life. While Eisenhower practiced the politics of moderation, churches increased their membership and family values appeared dominant. Middle-class suburban families embraced the trappings of prosperity—the automobile, home appliances, television, sports, jet travel, and other new miracles of consumerism. But young people, inspired by their own emerging subculture, entered a period of ferment. Despite the emphasis on happy families, sex was discussed more openly. Women were going to work in greater numbers, not quite fulfilling their idealized role as housewives and mothers. Intellectual critics challenged the era's conformity and consumerism, and the Beat writers dared to suggest that drugs, sex, and strange religious experiences might be more important than patriotism.

In spite of the overall prosperity, one in four Americans lived near or below the poverty line at the end of the decade, and some economists had begun to pay serious attention to this problem. By then, too, the civil rights revolution was under way; the African-American struggle to end segregation and claim equal rights was in the process of transforming the social landscape. With all of these developments interacting, the fifties were a period of considerable change beneath the guise of security and stability. ∎

FURTHER READING

On Eisenhower and the politics of the 1950s, see: Charles Alexander, *Holding the Line* (1975); Stephen E. Ambrose, *Eisenhower: The President* (1984); Barbara B. Clowse, *Brainpower for the Cold War: The Sputnik Crisis and the National Defense Education Act of 1958* (1981); Fred I. Greenstein, *The Hidden Hand Presidency* (1982). On social change, see: Elaine T. May, *Homeward Bound: American Families in the Cold War Era* (1988); Kenneth Jackson, *Crabgrass Frontier: The Suburbanization of the United States* (1985); Herbert J. Gans, *The Levittowners* (1967); Erik Barnouw, *Tube of Plenty* (1982); Mark H. Rose, *Interstate: Express Highway Politics, 1941–56* (1979). On civil rights, see: Taylor Branch, *Parting the Waters: America in the King Years, 1954–63* (1988); David J. Garrow, *Bearing the Cross: Martin Luther King, Jr., and the Southern Christian Leadership Conference* (1986); Richard Kluger, *Simple Justice* (1975).

5

The General as President:
Foreign Policy
in the 1950s

Shortly after taking office in 1953, President Dwight D. Eisenhower gathered a group of military and diplomatic specialists in the White House sun parlor and asked them to reassess basic Cold War strategy. In a project dubbed Operation Solarium, the experts weighed the policy of containment against more radical proposals to threaten Moscow with nuclear war should it cross a demarcation line or to attempt to push back existing areas of Soviet control through political, psychological, economic, and covert military pressure. Discussion even touched on launching a pre-emptive attack on Russia.

As a candidate, Eisenhower had pledged he would never rest until he had helped liberate the "enslaved nations of the world." Republican spokesman John Foster Dulles, whom Ike appointed secretary of state, had denounced containment as a "treadmill, which at best might keep us in the same place until we drop exhausted." Both men had found Truman's foreign policy unconscionable because it was not designed to win a conclusive victory, and the Republican campaign rhetoric had castigated the Democrats for "abandoning people to Godless terrorism."

With this background, the new president might have been expected to support the more belligerent of the recommendations emerging from Operation Solarium. But Eisenhower quietly named as one of the study's coordinators George F. Kennan, the chief architect of the containment policy, even though Secretary of State Dulles had already removed Kennan from the State Department. Ultimately, the president approved a Solarium report that showed the influence of Kennan's moderate approach.

With the campaign rhetoric behind him, Eisenhower pursued a moderate foreign policy through his two terms in office. His precise approach to foreign affairs was not easy to categorize. Although he declared that America could never rest until the Communist yoke had been lifted from Eastern Europe and China, he resisted calls from the Pentagon and Congress to increase defense spending, fearing that budget deficits would be as destructive as war in the long run. He was willing to threaten other countries with nuclear weapons, but he avoided full-scale conflict and never employed his expanded nuclear arsenal against an enemy. Under Eisenhower's leadership, the United States and the Soviet Union gradually learned how to coexist. Yet the two powers displaced much of their direct competition into an often unsavory contest for influence in the Third World.

EISENHOWER'S APPROACH TO FOREIGN POLICY

Eisenhower's choice for secretary of state, the formidable John Foster Dulles, seemed a marked contrast to the avuncular president. A powerful corporate lawyer active in the Presbyterian church, Dulles had long been touted as the Republicans' chief foreign policy expert. He often wore a sour expression and delivered lectures on Christian virtue and Communist sin. He was so noted for his toughness against communism, in Asia and elsewhere, that Winston Churchill joked he was the only bull who carried around his own "China shop."

During the Eisenhower administration, Dulles and Vice President Richard Nixon frequently made bellicose and controversial statements, creating a widespread impression that they, not Eisenhower, were the real forces behind the administration's foreign policy. In fact, as historians have come to realize, Eisenhower kept both men on a short leash. He used them as front men for floating controversial ideas, warning adversaries, or appeasing Republican hard-liners. In some respects they served as lightning rods to draw criticism away from the president himself, whose own views were less extreme and more difficult to categorize.

The New Look

Operation Solarium, combined with a 1953 strategic plan called NSC 162/3, placed a greater emphasis than before on the use of atomic bombs as weapons and as bargaining chips in the Cold War. In contrast to the previous administration, which had seen atomic bombs as weapons of last resort, Eisenhower's advisers—in theory at least—urged using the bombs as weapons of choice.

For the president, this strategy had economic as well as military benefits. By relying more on nuclear weapons and the air force, the United States could slash the size of its costly ground forces. Unlike military officials who asked for more troops, ships, and conventional munitions to achieve decisive *superiority* over the Soviet Union, Eisenhower favored *sufficiency*—enough striking power to deter or, if necessary, destroy the Soviet Union, but no more than was needed. Attempting to match the Soviets "man for man, gun for gun," he warned, would lead to national bankruptcy. He also pointed out that "every gun that is made, every warship launched, every rocket fired, signified, in a final sense, a theft from those who hunger and are not fed, those who are cold and are not clothed." Following these principles, Eisenhower managed to reduce military expenditures from about $52 billion annually to about $36 billion at the end of his first term. During his second term, however, military spending rose a few billion because of congressional pressure.

The B-52 Bomber

If any mechanical creation deserves a biography, the B-52 bomber is a strong candidate. In 1981, as a prod to Congress to fund the new B-1 and B-2 bombers, President Ronald Reagan complained that the aging B-52 was older than many of the pilots who flew it. Nevertheless, a decade later, B-52 bombers not only remained in the air force arsenal but proved especially effective in the American war against Iraq. Able to carry a larger bomb load than any other plane, the B-52, in the words of an air force general, "cannot be seen or heard until the bombs start falling and then it's like rolling thunder."

Between 1955 and 1963, the air force purchased 744 of these immense eight-engine warplanes. As of 1991, 250 remained on the active roster. The Boeing Company produced the B-52 at

Eisenhower and Dulles christened their strategy the New Look. It depended on what Dulles called the threat of "massive retaliation" against any serious Communist provocation. The administration had inherited a nuclear arsenal of about a thousand bombs. Over the next eight years this stockpile grew to eighteen thousand weapons. An important newcomer to the military's armaments was the huge, eight-engined B-52 bomber, first deployed by the air force in 1955 and so effective an aircraft that it remained in service in the 1990s. Meanwhile, intercontinental ballistic missiles (ICBMs) and submarine-launched missiles were under development. By the time Eisenhower left office, in 1961, the United States had enough air-, sea-, and ground-launched nuclear weapons to destroy Soviet targets many times over—far surpassing Eisenhower's own goal of sufficiency.

Some critics, especially Democratic politicians and career army officers, argued that the New Look and the doctrine of massive retal-

an average price per plane of only $8 million ($35 million in 1990 dollars). The plane carries a crew of six and is three or four times larger than any other combat aircraft flown. With its 60-yard wingspan, its drooping wings appear to flap on takeoff, giving it the appearance of a prehistoric creature bounding down the runway and struggling to fly.

The B-52 had been conceived before the nation possessed long-range missiles. War planners assigned it the mission of carrying nuclear weapons seven thousand miles, from United States bases to the Soviet heartland. But even after the big ICBM build-up of the 1960s, the air force discovered uses for the bomber. In fact, the plane has been used heavily for conventional warfare, especially in Vietnam and the Persian Gulf.

Aircraft designers expected the plane to last only about five thousand flying hours before structural fatigue set in. But the use of new, noncorrosive alloys has extended its useful life to about fifteen thousand hours. With an upgrading of its engines, electronics, and weapons systems, designers now predict the B-52 could be used in combat until the year 2035, eighty years after the first delivery.

During its nearly forty years in service, the B-52 has acquired a mystique. Because of its immense destructive power, one air force commander noted, "it has an ethos, a sense of awesomeness." The B-52 starred in two films about nuclear war, the satiric *Dr. Strangelove* and the somber *Failsafe*. ■

iation locked the United States into an all-or-nothing response to foreign threats. Eisenhower and Dulles responded by introducing three measures to soften the all-or-nothing posture. First, the administration signed anti-Communist military alliances with numerous countries, which promised American material support to local troops fighting in small wars. Second, for situations short of war, the CIA was authorized to carry out covert military operations against unfriendly regimes. Finally, the administration pushed development of tactical atomic weapons for battlefield use even if the superpowers remained at peace. These bombs were meant to deter or punish Soviet surrogates without starting a full-scale nuclear war.

In supporting the development of tactical nuclear weapons, Eisenhower saw no reason why atomic artillery shells should not be used "exactly as you would use a bullet or anything else." Early in his presidency, he approved a policy statement according to which, in the event of hostilities with the Soviet Union, the United States would "consider nuclear weapons to be as available for use as other munitions." Yet, in part because of his military background, Eisenhower was wise enough to fear a nuclear showdown. In 1954, when South Korean strongman Syngman Rhee wanted him to risk war with Russia and China to unify Korea, Eisenhower replied that "if war comes, it will be horrible. Atomic war will destroy civilization."

Defense specialist Paul Nitze related an incident that illustrated Eisenhower's seemingly contradictory beliefs about nuclear weapons. At a meeting attended by Nitze, the president first remarked to the Joint Chiefs of Staff that a nuclear war was too horrible to contemplate. After a short break, he told the military commanders exactly how to go about fighting one.

Ending the Korean War

The policy of relying more heavily on the nuclear threat received its first test in Korea, where fighting continued near the 38th parallel despite two years of peace talks. The major unsettled points included China's demand that the United States observe international law by returning all Chinese prisoners of war (POWs) held in South Korea, including several thousand who had sought asylum. Like Truman before him, Eisenhower feared a domestic anti-Communist backlash if he agreed to repatriate prisoners against their will.

Determined to break the deadlock and end the war, Eisenhower ordered a study to consider the use of tactical atomic weapons in Korea. To his surprise, most military and diplomatic experts were skeptical that atomic weapons would do much good. As the Truman administration had realized, North Korea held few military targets appropriate for an atomic bomb. Furthermore, inconclusive use of the bomb might "depreciate the value of our stockpile," strategists warned. Urban and industrial targets did exist in China, but attacking them would result in large civilian casualties. Moreover, any escalation of the war might endanger South Korea or Japan.

Eisenhower accepted these conclusions but decided to bluff about his willingness to employ atomic weapons. Privately and publicly, American officials spread rumors of imminent plans to use the bomb. When a Korean armistice was achieved in July 1953, Dulles claimed that he had made known to the Chinese the threat they faced and that fear of a nuclear attack had compelled them to accept Washington's plan for voluntary prisoner returns.

In reality, several other factors contributed to the breakthrough. Stalin's sudden death from a stroke in February 1953 brought to power Soviet leaders eager to improve relations with the United States. Moreover, China had grown weary of the costly war and sought better ties with the West. Even as Washington hinted about escalation, Chinese and American negotiators agreed to compromise on the prisoner issue. POWs resisting repatriation would be remanded to a neutral commission to determine their ultimate fate. When South Korean President Syngman Rhee opposed this deal, an enraged Eisenhower threatened to depose him. The diplomatic solution to the POW issue, as much as atomic threats, led to the Korean cease-fire.

The Changing Nature of Communism

Even before the Korean armistice, the Soviet challenge had begun to change. Stalin's death occurred only weeks after Eisenhower took office. During the dictator's final years, he had expanded Soviet military power, behaved increasingly erratically, and initiated new bloody purges. At one point he became obsessed with an imaginary plot by Jewish doctors to poison his inner circle.

Immediately after Stalin's death, power fell into the hands of a triumvirate, Georgi Malenkov, Nikolai Bulganin, and Nikita Khrushchev. Despite some differences, the three new Soviet leaders agreed to do away with Stalin's terror network, promised Soviet citizens a better life, and sought improved relations with non-Communist governments. Malenkov announced that no dispute was so bad, even those with the United States, that it could not be settled peacefully through negotiations.

Moscow also took a more conciliatory line with Communist and nonaligned states. The Soviet Union resumed diplomatic ties with Yugoslavia and Israel, eased strains with China, and began providing economic support to developing nations like Egypt. These measures reversed Stalin's policy of intimidating all other Communist nations while ignoring the nations emerging from the crumbling European colonial empires.

Khrushchev initially seemed the least able member of the triumvirate and the one most committed to the status quo. But by 1955 his skills at inner-party intrigue and alliance building allowed him to oust his colleagues and emerge as the first among ostensible equals. The next year, Khrushchev shocked his country and the world by denouncing crimes of the Stalinist era. Downplaying his own role as a henchman, the new party boss charged that Stalin's "personality cult" had distorted communism and led to the slaughter of several million loyal Bolsheviks and countless Soviet citizens.

Although both Russian and world opinion cheered this break with the past, the changes within the Soviet Union posed a novel challenge for the Eisenhower administration. Should Washington accept at face value Soviet talk of "peaceful coexistence," or should it increase pressure on Moscow now that a less oppressive regime held power? Did Malenkov and, later, Khrushchev really seek cooperation with the West, or were they merely engaged in deception? Some Western leaders, among them Winston Churchill, urged Eisenhower to hold an early summit with the new Kremlin bosses, but, restrained by Dulles, Eisenhower held back for two years.

In public, Eisenhower and Dulles criticized all Communist leaders as slaves of the Kremlin. In private, they admitted that real differences distinguished various regimes. For example, Dulles described China's Mao Zedong as an "outstanding Communist leader in his own right" who was not a Soviet puppet. At the same time, the American leaders were not inclined to extend an open hand toward the Chinese government. Instead of trying to woo Mao with a relaxation of pressure from the United States, Dulles and Eisenhower decided to keep up the pressure as a way of intensifying the strain between Moscow and Beijing.

Eisenhower reacted cautiously to changes in the Communist camp. For whatever reason—fear of a political backlash, a preference to wait passively for the demise of communism, or conflicting advice from his advisers—not until late in his presidency did he begin a serious dialogue with Soviet leaders. Meanwhile, Eisenhower promoted the CIA as one method of holding the line against Communist-inspired change in the Third World.

The New CIA

During his first term Eisenhower appointed General James Doolittle to chair a secret study of the CIA's ability to counter Soviet activities. The study's report warned that America faced an "implacable enemy whose avowed objective is world domination by whatever means and at whatever cost." There were "no rules in such a game," because previously "acceptable norms of human conduct" no longer applied. Americans "must learn to subvert, sabotage and destroy our enemies by more clever and sophisticated and more effective methods than those used against us."

Using the CIA to conduct secret operations had a strong appeal to American leaders. Covert actions provided an opportunity to achieve foreign policy success without the direct costs of war or the scrutiny of public debate. The secrecy of CIA operations also eased the way for activities that few Americans would approve if forced to confront directly.

For example, during the 1950s many scientists thought that mind-altering drugs might be used against troops or as a means to entrap and brainwash individuals. To assess this danger, the CIA undertook a secret project to give doses of LSD—lysergic acid diethylamide—to unsuspecting American citizens. After people were drugged, CIA operatives studied their behavior. Hundreds of Americans—the exact number is unknown—became unwitting guinea pigs in these experiments. Several went insane, and at least one committed suicide. All information about the operation remained secret until the late 1970s.

In foreign affairs, the CIA began to play an important role in America's interventions in the Third World. As a covert arm of government policy, the CIA bolstered friendly governments and sponsored coups against unfriendly regimes the administration felt it could no longer tolerate. During the Eisenhower years the public heard few details of CIA operations; only in later decades were some of these actions brought under public scrutiny.

THE EBBING OF MCCARTHYISM

As Eisenhower developed his approach to communism abroad, Senator Joseph McCarthy continued to attack supposed Reds in American government. Although Eisenhower personally found McCarthy vile, he had done little during the presidential campaign to alert the public to McCarthy's excesses. Even when McCarthy labeled George C. Marshall a traitor who had perpetrated a "conspiracy so immense as to dwarf any previous such venture in the history of man," Eisenhower refused to condemn the senator or defend the accused. Marshall was more than the former chief of staff, secretary of state, secretary of defense, and developer of the Marshall Plan; he was the man who had raised Eisenhower from military obscurity during the Second World War. Yet Eisenhower merely told aides he would not "get into the gutter" with McCarthy.

Early in his first term, Eisenhower made numerous other concessions to the Republican right wing. In 1953 he refused to block the execution of Ethel and Julius Rosenberg, convicted of atomic espionage for Moscow, even though he harbored doubts about the guilt of Ethel. Having promised to clean out the State Department, he allowed Dulles to appoint Scott McLeod, a McCarthy protégé, to purge China specialists who had predicted the Communist victory. Foreign Service officers had to demonstrate "positive loyalty," an indefinable quality, to keep their jobs. Dulles ordered that books by "Communists, fellow travellers, et cetera" be removed from U.S. Information Agency libraries abroad. "Et cetera" proved an especially dangerous category: it included works by such "radicals" as Mark Twain. During Eisenhower's administration, about fifteen hundred federal employees in various agencies were fired as security risks and another six thousand were pressured to resign.

But McCarthyism began to wane after 1954, the year McCarthy himself began to self-destruct. Early in that year, piqued at the army's refusal to give his staff aide David Schine a draft deferment and other special treatment, McCarthy charged the military with coddling Communists. The bizarre allegation focused on an obscure dentist, Irving Peress, who had been drafted, promoted, and honorably discharged despite his admitted Communist sympathies. When high army officials, acting on the president's orders, refused to apologize or open personnel records to the senator, McCarthy charged them with incompetence and treason. Ignoring White House warnings to back off, the Wisconsin Republican declared he did not "intend to treat traitors like gentlemen."

With Eisenhower's quiet encouragement, the army countercharged that McCarthy had tried to blackmail it into giving David Schine special treatment. In April 1954, the Senate launched an inquiry. At the same time, television journalist Edward R. Murrow aired a segment of his show "See It Now" that highlighted some of McCarthy's most unsavory actions. Soon, several members of the Senate began to question their colleague's behavior.

During dramatic televised Senate hearings, which became known as the Army-McCarthy hearings, 20 million viewers had their first close look at McCarthy's vicious attacks on the loyalty of all who resisted him. Army counsel Joseph Welch, the soul of telegenic respectability, parried McCarthy's shrill tirades. After weeks of accusations that failed to prove any conspiracy, a frustrated McCarthy charged that Frederick Fisher, a young lawyer who worked for Welch's Boston firm but who was not a member of the army's legal team, had Communist leanings.

Welch, who had anticipated the accusation, responded to McCarthy's mudslinging with a sad shake of the head and the statement, "I think I never really gauged your cruelty or your recklessness." Unable to stop himself, the senator resumed his attack on Fisher. Finally, Welch declared that McCarthy's forgiveness would "have to come from someone other than me." The lawyer then issued a historic query: "Have you no sense of decency, sir, at long last? Have you left no sense of decency?"

Even though the Army-McCarthy hearings rendered no formal verdict, the senator had failed a critical media test. Opinion polls taken during and after the televised sessions revealed a dramatic slide in McCarthy's approval rating, from nearly 50 percent at the beginning of 1954 to only 30 percent in June. In December 1954, the Senate voted to censure him for "unbecoming conduct."

Eisenhower, who took a bit more credit for the senator's humiliation than was warranted, remarked that "McCarthyism had become

McCarthywasim." The witch hunter himself never recovered from these public defeats. Shunned by old friends, he increased his legendary drinking and died of alcohol-related illness three years later.

AMERICA AND THE CHALLENGES OF THE THIRD WORLD

In the fifteen years following the end of the Second World War, thirty-seven nations emerged from colonialism to independence, eighteen during 1960 alone (see map, page 174). Most of these new states were nonwhite, poor, nonindustrialized, and located in Asia, Africa, or the Middle East. Many had gained independence through armed struggle; in some the violence continued after independence. They had much in common with previously independent but poor nations, especially those in Latin America, where political unrest often became armed rebellion. During the 1950s, at least twenty-eight prolonged guerrilla insurgencies were underway.

All of these emerging nations, loosely called the Third World, existed outside the bloc of the industrialized democracies (First World) and the Communist nations (Second World). Few had democratic governments. Most sought to remain neutral in the Cold War while pursuing economic development and soliciting aid from all sides. Poor nations both envied and resented American power. They often employed the rhetoric of socialism even as they sought the material rewards of capitalism.

Under Stalin, the Soviet Union had ignored or criticized most non-Communist liberation movements. Khrushchev proved more adroit, offering economic and military assistance to emerging nations whether or not they adhered to Moscow's line. This probably represented a Soviet effort to avoid a direct challenge to the United States while still supporting revolutionary goals.

The United States increasingly shared Moscow's concern with the Third World. The emerging nations contained vast raw material wealth and a huge population. Eisenhower and Dulles worried that the Third World's criticism of imperialism and capitalism would provide a wedge for growing Soviet influence. Many Americans also mistrusted any model of national development that deviated from the United States experience.

To halt Communist inroads in the Third World, the Eisenhower administration forged numerous anti-Communist alliances based loosely on NATO. Dulles recruited several Middle East states into a Central Treaty Organization (CENTO), organized Asian nations into the Southeast Asia Treaty Organization (SEATO), and signed bilateral defense agreements with Taiwan, South Korea, Spain, and the Phil-

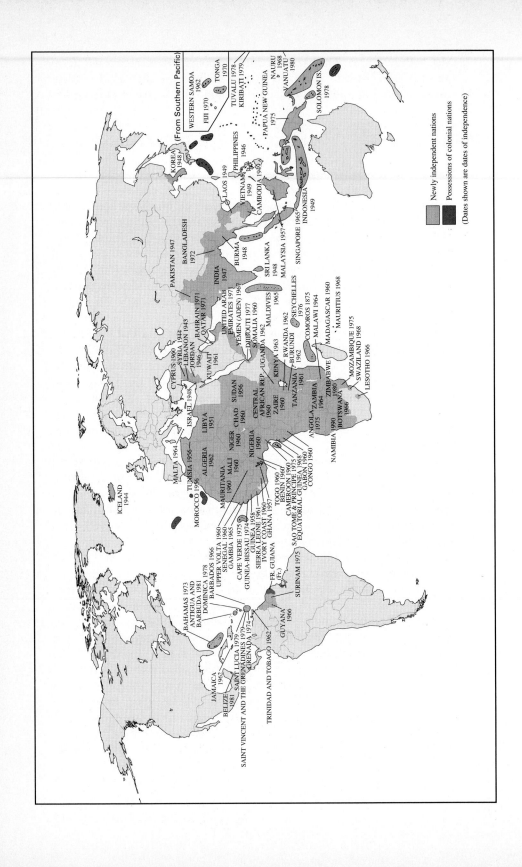

(From Southern Pacific)

WESTERN SAMOA 1962
FIJI 1970
TONGA 1970
TUVALU 1978
KIRIBATI 1979
NAURU 1968
VANUATU 1980
SOLOMON IS. 1978
PAPUA NEW GUINEA 1975

KOREA 1948
PHILIPPINES 1946
LAOS 1949
VIETNAM 1949
CAMBODIA 1949
INDONESIA 1949
SINGAPORE 1965
MALAYSIA 1957
SRI LANKA 1948
MALDIVES 1965
BURMA 1948
BANGLADESH 1972
PAKISTAN 1947
INDIA 1947

SEYCHELLES 1976
COMOROS 1875
MADAGASCAR 1960
MAURITIUS 1968
MALAWI 1964
MOZAMBIQUE 1975
SWAZILAND 1968
LESOTHO 1966
ZIMBABWE 1980
BOTSWANA 1966
NAMIBIA 1990

UNITED ARAB EMIRATES 1971
BAHRAIN 1971
QATAR 1971
YEMEN (ADEN) 1967
DJIBOUTI 1977
SOMALIA 1960
RWANDA 1962
BURUNDI 1962
UGANDA 1962
KENYA 1963
TANZANIA 1961
ZAMBIA 1964

CYPRUS 1960
LEBANON 1943
SYRIA 1944
JORDAN 1946
ISRAEL 1948
KUWAIT 1961
SUDAN 1956
CHAD 1960
CENTRAL AFRICAN REP. 1960
ZAIRE 1960
ANGOLA 1975

MALTA 1964
TUNISIA 1956
MOROCCO 1956
LIBYA 1951
ALGERIA 1962
NIGER 1960
MALI 1960
NIGERIA 1960

MAURITANIA 1960

ICELAND 1944

UPPER VOLTA 1960
SENEGAL 1960
GAMBIA 1965
GUINEA 1958
SIERRA LEONE 1961
CAPE VERDE 1975
GUINEA-BISSAU 1974
IVORY COAST 1960
GHANA 1957
TOGO 1960
BENIN 1960
CAMEROON 1960
SAO TOME & PRINCIPE 1975
EQUATORIAL GUINEA 1968
GABON 1960
CONGO 1960

FR. GUIANA (Fr.)
SURINAM 1975
GUYANA 1966

BAHAMAS 1973
ANTIGUA AND BARBUDA 1981
DOMINICA 1978
BARBADOS 1966
SAINT LUCIA 1979
GRENADA 1974
SAINT VINCENT AND THE GRENADINES 1979
TRINIDAD AND TOBAGO 1962
JAMAICA 1962
BELIZE 1981

Newly independent nations

Possessions of colonial nations

(Dates shown are dates of independence)

ippines. Unlike NATO, most of the new pacts committed Washington only to provide aid and consult with the participants in case of aggression. The pacts had more psychological and political than military values, for when American interests in Asia, the Middle East, or Latin America were at stake, the United States usually acted on its own.

Foreign aid also played a growing role in the administration's effort to influence the Third World. Under Truman, nearly all foreign economic assistance had been sent to Western Europe and Japan. Eisenhower first called for eliminating most aid, offering two-way trade as the best way to help poor countries. But because the poorest nations had little to export and no money with which to buy foreign goods, two-way trade would not substantially help them. Eventually the Eisenhower administration not only increased overall aid levels, but also sent most of its assistance—surplus food, credits to buy American products, military equipment, construction loans—to emerging nations.

Critics pointed to faults in the aid programs for developing nations. For example, providing surplus grain to poor nations under the "Food For Peace" program helped American farmers and fed the hungry, but often delayed sound agricultural development programs in needy countries. Construction loans were frequently squandered on glamorous, expensive projects like sports arenas while basic necessities like irrigation systems and wells went unfunded.

In 1958, writers William J. Lederer and Eugene Burdick highlighted these problems in their best-selling novel, *The Ugly American*. They described a fictional Southeast Asian country, resembling Vietnam, in which ignorant American diplomats knew nothing about their host nation and lived in an isolated "golden ghetto." The fictionalized diplomats contemplated grand development schemes but knew little about the needs of peasant farmers. The hero, a physically unattractive diplomat, defied the stereotype by learning the local language, associating with the people and discovering their real needs, and successfully defending the nation against communism.

Whatever the success of its aid programs, the Eisenhower administration believed that they were not enough to counter the threat of Communist influence in the Third World. By supplying military advisers and authorizing covert actions by the CIA, Eisenhower deepened American involvement with the anti-Communist effort in Vietnam, and soon the United States was intervening in Iran and Guatemala as well.

◀ **The Rise of the Third World: Newly Independent Nations Since 1943**

The Conflict in Vietnam

Eisenhower inherited the war in French Indochina and passed it on to his successors. In 1953 and 1954, as later, policymakers worried that if the Communist Vietminh guerrillas won in Vietnam, first Southeast Asia, then resource-starved Japan, would fall "like dominoes." After this, Eisenhower predicted, the Pacific Ocean would "become a Communist lake."

Since 1950, the United States had spent over $1 billion in Vietnam, providing about 70 percent of the cost of France's war against the Vietminh and its leader, Ho Chi Minh. Yet, as American analysts admitted, French rule was unpopular in Vietnam and unlikely ever to be accepted. Eisenhower and Dulles hoped that if the French granted real power to non-Communist Vietnamese, rather than to the puppet emperor Bao Dai, the war would change from a colonial struggle to a battle against communism. Defending the "freedom" of an independent Vietnam would prove more popular among Americans than saving a colony.

American military experts pressured the French army to try a new strategy designed to lure the Vietminh into a major battle. Then, they predicted, superior power could be used to crush the lightly armed guerrillas. Early in 1954, the French airlifted twelve thousand troops to the valley of Dienbienphu in northern Vietnam, and waited. The resulting battle proved decisive, but not in the way anticipated. With logistic assistance from the Chinese, the Vietminh quickly surrounded the French base and subjected it to nearly ceaseless artillery and ground assault. Cut off from supplies, the garrison faced annihilation. Eisenhower now feared that all of non-Communist Asia might topple.

Washington again urged the French to grant Vietnam independence as a way of building support for expanded American and British military aid. Vice President Richard Nixon went further and recommended sending in American troops. In a message to London, Eisenhower compared the threat in Vietnam to the earlier dangers posed by Hirohito, Mussolini, and Hitler. The French, Eisenhower privately complained, were a "hopeless, helpless mass of protoplasm."

As the battle for Dienbienphu approached a climax late in April, Dulles, Nixon, and the heads of the armed services developed plans for American air strikes against the Vietminh. General Nathan Twining proposed dropping three small atomic bombs around the battle zone to clean out the Communists. Eisenhower replied, "You boys must be crazy. . . . We can't use those awful things against Asians for the second time in ten years." However, Eisenhower did consider a conventional air strike, and he allowed Dulles to threaten atomic retaliation if China sent combat troops to help the Vietminh. But when Britain declined to commit troops to aid the French, and congressional leaders proved unenthusiastic, plans for an air strike evaporated.

Early in May 1954, Dienbienphu fell. The political uproar in Paris resulted in the formation of a new French government, led by Pierre Mendes-France, that pledged to negotiate a quick end to the Indochina war. Talks took place at an international conference in Geneva. Nearly everyone present predicted the Vietminh would soon control all of Vietnam. Eisenhower sent an American observer to the Geneva talks, and Dulles also attended briefly. When asked if he planned to meet with Chinese representative Zhou Enlai, Dulles responded, "only if our cars collide." The United States feared that whatever arrangement emerged from Geneva would merely enhance Communist power and prestige.

Despite this fear, China and the Soviet Union actually played a moderating role at the Geneva talks. Eager to win points with the West, the major Communist states pressed Ho Chi Minh to accept a temporary division of Vietnam rather than immediate control. The Geneva Accords, reached in July, drew an armistice line, intended to be a temporary military division, along the 17th parallel, with French forces moving to the south and Vietminh troops to the north. The key provision called for the departure of all French forces and the holding of national elections in Vietnam by 1956. As the French withdrew from Indochina, they also granted complete independence to Laos and Cambodia.

The Geneva Accords frightened Eisenhower, who anticipated that Ho Chi Minh would probably win the promised election. Dulles warned European leaders that the West must never surrender Southeast Asia, because the stakes were too high. To bolster wobbling dominoes, Dulles flew to Manila in September 1954. There he signed the SEATO alliance, which was essentially a Western pact to police Asia; only two Southeast Asian nations, Thailand and the Philippines, were signatories. Dulles also started to negotiate a defense treaty with Taiwan.

Meanwhile, the United States began providing substantial economic and military assistance, as well as military advisers, directly to non-Communist groups in southern Vietnam. As the French departed, American personnel backed Ngo Dinh Diem, a Vietnamese Catholic (in a largely Buddhist nation) who had lived for several years in Europe and the United States. Attracted by his pro-Western rhetoric, his Christianity, and his anti-Communism, army and CIA officers helped Diem form a government and military force in Saigon.

In 1956 Diem staged rigged elections south of the 17th parallel. He deposed Emperor Bao Dai, who went into exile on the Riviera, and proclaimed himself president of the Republic of Vietnam. Washington recognized this so-called republic, better known as South Vietnam, as an independent nation. The United States dismissed the Democratic Republic of Vietnam (North Vietnam) as a Communist puppet state and rejected its claim to rule an undivided nation. The free, Vietnam-wide elections called for in the Geneva Accords were never held.

In the following years, Eisenhower and Dulles portrayed Diem as a democratic leader and a model for Asian development, ignoring or misunderstanding the many things that made him unpopular in his own land. These included a haughty style, persecution of Buddhists, favoritism toward the Catholic minority, support for landlords against the peasantry, and toleration of widespread corruption. *Life* magazine justified Diem's strong-arm tactics as necessary for a "one-man democracy." Despite an additional $1 billion in American aid, by 1960 a powerful guerrilla movement was challenging Diem and raising once again the specter of a Communist Vietnam.

Oil and Politics in Iran

During the Second World War, American oil companies had begun to displace British, French, and Dutch control of Arab and Persian Gulf petroleum. When Eisenhower took office he inherited a smoldering dispute over control of Iranian oil. In 1951 Iran's nationalistic prime minister, Mohammed Mossadeq, took over the holdings of the Anglo-Iranian Oil Company without paying the compensation demanded by its mostly British owners. Major oil companies organized a boycott, refusing to purchase, transport, or refine Iranian petroleum. American companies supported this action, both to discourage other Middle Eastern expropriations and because it increased the value of their own reserves.

In May 1953, as the Iranian economy deteriorated, the anti-Communist Mossadeq cabled Eisenhower that, unless the boycott ended, he might seek Soviet assistance. Eisenhower rejected Iran's request for support and urged Mossadeq to reach a "reasonable settlement" along the lines demanded by the British.

Shah Mohammed Reza Pahlavi, Iran's nominal monarch, had played little role in the nation's politics since succeeding his father during the Second World War. The young shah resented Mossadeq's influence and saw the crisis as an opportunity to regain real power for the monarchy by playing up the Soviet threat. His interests coincided with those of American diplomats and oil barons, who looked forward to pre-empting Britain's dominant role in the Iranian oil industry. To preclude any Soviet role in Iran and to preserve access to the region's petroleum, Eisenhower authorized a CIA coup to topple Mossadeq and put the shah in control.

Kermit Roosevelt, grandson of Theodore Roosevelt and a veteran spy, played a key role in the coup. Arriving in Teheran in August 1953, he made contact with the shah and with a general in the Iranian army, Fazollah Zahedi. Roosevelt financed violent demonstrations against Mossadeq, enlisting mobs led by circus performers along with army and police personnel. The shah fled briefly to Rome while the army moved to restore order. Zahedi's forces stormed the parliament and arrested Mossadeq, and the general became prime minister. The shah returned to power, and Washington promptly extended $45 million in aid to his government.

An American delegation sent by Eisenhower mediated a deal between Iran and the British oil companies. The settlement allowed Iran to retain control of its oil fields so long as it agreed to market its petroleum at a low price through a consortium in which American companies held a 40 percent stake. The British had hoped to pay less, but discovered too late the cost of calling in the United States to preserve the vestiges of imperial influence.

Intervention in Guatemala

The Eisenhower administration proved especially concerned with blocking Communist influence in Latin America. In Senate testimony in 1953, Dulles spoke of a well-oiled Communist conspiracy in Central and South America. In the past, Dulles explained to his brother Allen, director of the CIA, Washington could afford to ignore turmoil in Latin America. Now, however, the unrest and upheaval would lead to control by Communists.

The small amount of direct American aid to Latin American countries consisted mostly of military assistance. The Defense Department established special training programs in Panama and elsewhere for Latin American military officers. By paying only lip service to democracy, by ignoring social problems, and by aligning itself closely with the region's armed forces, Washington left no doubt that it opposed communism, but not dictatorship or poverty. In 1953, Eisenhower and Dulles identified the major crisis in Latin America as the "Communist infection" in Guatemala, one of the region's poorest nations.

In 1944, a group of reform-minded army officers had overthrown long-time Guatemalan dictator Jorge Ubico. After a relatively fair election in 1945, reformer Juan Jose Arevalo became president. He inherited a desperately poor country whose European-descended elite held nearly feudal control over the large Indian population. Some 2 percent of the population controlled 70 percent of the land. In addition, the American-owned United Fruit Company, a banana grower, held vast tracts of farmland, much of which remained uncultivated.

United Fruit also controlled the railroad, port, and communications infrastructure. Although United Fruit was not the most exploitative employer in Guatemala, its American employees lived in luxury while its peasant workers eked out a living on a dollar a day.

Arevalo abolished forced Indian labor, extended voting rights, imposed a minimum wage law, and began a modest land reform program. These steps were significant but not yet alarming to American interests. In 1951, however, Arevalo's elected successor, President Jacobo Arbenz Guzman, ordered the redistribution to the poor of large uncultivated land holdings and sponsored a variety of new labor and wage reforms. In the Guatemalan context these reforms were revolutionary. Arbenz drafted plans to build new roads and ports that would break United Fruit's monopoly over transportation systems. He also expropriated 400,000 acres of uncultivated company lands, offering $3 per acre compensation, a figure based on the declared tax value of the property.

United Fruit demanded $75 per acre and got the Eisenhower administration to intercede formally on its behalf. The State Department, several of whose leading officials had past business associations with United Fruit, claimed the issue was neither social justice nor land reform but a Communist assault on private property. American officials then cooperated with United Fruit publicists in a propaganda campaign that labeled Arbenz a Communist dupe. By casting the dispute over compensation for banana plantations as a battle between communism and Western-style democracy, the administration and United Fruit created a pretext for intervention. By removing Arbenz, Dulles told the president, Eisenhower would achieve a "Czechoslovakia in reverse." Washington boosted aid to several key Latin American nations, which then joined the United States in sponsoring a resolution before the Organization of American States, a regional organization the United States had helped to found in 1948. The resolution declared that no nation in the Western Hemisphere had a right to a Communist government.

In the summer of 1953, Eisenhower authorized a CIA-sponsored plan to stage a coup in Guatemala. To undermine Arbenz's support within the military, Washington cut off aid to the Guatemalan army and increased assistance to neighboring states. From bases in Honduras and Nicaragua, the CIA organized a small Guatemalan exile force under Carlos Castillo Armas. It also began a massive "disinformation" campaign using pamphlets and radio broadcasts to confuse the Guatemalan people. The broadcasts told of a huge rebel army about to attack. When Arbenz purchased a small arms shipment from Communist Czechoslovakia in May 1954, American officials immediately described this action as part of a "master plan of world communism" that threatened the Panama Canal.

In June, a thousand or so CIA-directed exiles entered Guatemala and set up a base camp. CIA radio stations broadcast reports of a massive invasion backed by the United States. A few small planes dropped anti-Arbenz leaflets in the capital while the pilots threw sticks of dynamite out of their cockpits. In a panic, Arbenz tried to arm a peasant militia. The regular army, frightened of fighting the United States, also feared being supplanted by peasants. Fooled into thinking he faced a large invasion, and deserted by his army, Arbenz resigned on June 27. As the CIA had planned, Castillo Armas and his comrades took over.

Eisenhower considered the Guatemalan coup a model Cold War triumph. At a dinner in their honor, Eisenhower told a gathering of key CIA participants that, thanks to them, America had averted the establishment of a Soviet beachhead in the Western Hemisphere. The new Guatemalan rulers restored United Fruit's lands and rolled back most other reforms. Over the next three decades, a succession of military governments slaughtered an estimated 100,000 Indians, labor organizers, students, and intellectuals who challenged the ruling elite.

Eisenhower later approved CIA operations to overthrow President Sukarno of Indonesia, General Rafael Trujillo of the Dominican Republic, and Premier Patrice Lumumba of the Congo (now Zaire). Although Sukarno survived a botched coup attempt, Trujillo and Lumumba both fell to assassins' bullets. American complicity in their actual killing remains unclear.

Quemoy and Matsu: A New Showdown with China

The Korean armistice did little to improve relations with the People's Republic of China, or Red China, as most Americans called it during the 1950s. Eisenhower gave superficial verbal support to efforts by the Chinese Nationalists on Taiwan (then called Formosa) to reconquer the mainland. Washington also maintained a strict embargo on trade or cultural contact with China.

In 1954 to 1955 and again in 1958, the United States and China came close to war over the fate of several small, Nationalist Chinese–held islands in the Taiwan Strait. The most important of the islands, Quemoy and Matsu, lay only a few miles off the China coast. The Nationalists stationed large military units on these islands and ran commando operations against the Communist regime. In retaliation, and in the hope of destabilizing and eventually taking over Taiwan, the Chinese began shelling Quemoy in September 1954.

Dulles was already negotiating a treaty to defend Taiwan, but not the offshore islands. The Chinese government probably hoped the bombardment would discourage Washington from further assisting

Cartoonist Herblock depicted the anxiety many Americans felt about the Eisenhower-Dulles foreign policy. *From* Herblock's Special for Today *(Simon & Schuster, 1958).*

the Nationalist regime, but in December the administration signed its mutual security pact with Taiwan. Dulles included a secret understanding that the Nationalists would not invade China without American permission. Nor did the guarantee commit the United States to defending all the minor islands the Nationalists held.

In January 1955, Dulles warned the Senate that the United States had to accept the risk of war with China if it wanted to remain a power in the Far East. If that risk was unacceptable, Dulles declared, the United States should leave Asia entirely and establish its defensive perimeter in California. In response, Congress passed the Formosa Strait Resolution, which empowered the president to use force to protect the security of Taiwan and "related positions and territories in that area." Eisenhower and Dulles also issued public warnings about atomic retaliation if Communist forces invaded Quemoy or Taiwan.

Early in 1955, both sides claimed victory in the dispute. China seized a few minor Nationalist-held islands but left alone Quemoy,

Matsu, and Taiwan. Washington then accepted a Chinese proposal to begin ambassadorial-level talks. These talks continued intermittently, in Warsaw and Geneva, for more than fifteen years. They proved useful in resolving some minor problems but did not ease the underlying mistrust between Washington and Beijing.

Tensions flared again in 1958 when China resumed its effort to seize Quemoy. Eisenhower ordered the American navy to resupply the Nationalist garrison. Chinese leader Mao Zedong denounced this intervention but restrained his troops from firing at American ships. In turn, Dulles pressed Taiwan to stop provoking China, and the Communists gradually reduced their artillery barrages to odd-numbered days of the month, eventually substituting propaganda balloons for shells.

During both crises, Mao Zedong feared American atomic power and resented what he considered inadequate Soviet support. Khrushchev, he complained, sought better relations with the United States at the expense of other nations. When Moscow declined to provide Beijing with a promised prototype atomic bomb, China began a crash nuclear development program of its own. By the late 1950s, Mao was accusing the Soviets of "yielding to evil" and "coddling wrong." Khrushchev labeled Mao a renegade and warmonger. Although Eisenhower and Dulles must have been pleased with the Sino-Soviet split their pressure had helped to bring about, they did little to exploit the rift in any positive way.

Suez and Lebanon

Throughout the 1950s and beyond, the Middle East remained in political turmoil. Arabs felt humiliated by Israel's military victory in 1948 and the continued ability of the tiny Jewish state to defeat its far more numerous neighbors. Although at the time Britain and France, rather than the United States, provided most of Israel's weapons, American Jews lavished substantial private economic aid on Israel. Many Arabs considered Israel a colonial vestige and found it a useful scapegoat for their own problems.

Such was the situation when Gamal Abdel Nasser, an Egyptian army officer, toppled the inept and pro-British King Farouk in 1952. Nasser emerged as a popular and ambitious leader who envisioned Egypt as the center of a revived Arab world. He bought arms from the Soviet bloc, but at the same time he sought economic assistance from the West to finance construction of the immense Aswan Dam across the Nile, designed to provide electricity and water for Egyptian farmlands. Dulles initially favored American financing for the project but canceled aid in July 1956, when Nasser extended diplomatic recognition to Communist China. By this time, the Eisenhower administration feared that Nasser's Arab nationalism would destabilize the oil-rich region, opening a path for Soviet influence.

Nasser retaliated for the withdrawal of American support by nationalizing the British-owned Suez Canal, through which much of Europe's oil supply passed. Besides humiliating the West, Egyptian control of the canal and its tolls would help pay for the Aswan Dam. The British and French governments decided to send forces to recover the canal and, they hoped, topple Nasser. They coordinated their plans with Israel, which feared Nasser's influence on other Arabs.

According to the joint plan, on October 29, 1956, the Israeli army crossed the Sinai Desert and camped just east of the canal. Britain and France then announced the dispatch of troops with the stated goal of protecting the Suez Canal from destruction. The European powers demanded that both Egyptian and Israeli armies withdraw from either side of the waterway and leave it in European hands.

These actions by America's allies infuriated Dulles and Eisenhower. They feared that European intervention in the Suez dispute would strengthen Arab nationalism and distract world attention from the crisis in Hungary, where Soviet forces were crushing an uprising. The United States therefore joined the Soviet Union in condemning the Suez attack, and both powers supported a United Nations–mandated cease-fire. With sunken vessels blocking oil shipments through the canal, Dulles pressed Latin American exporters to embargo petroleum sales to Britain and France until the European forces left Egypt. Washington also threatened to block private American aid to Israel. By December 1956, the invaders had left Egypt, Nasser had claimed victory over imperialism, and British Prime Minister Anthony Eden had resigned in disgrace.

Following this fiasco, Britain and France moved to accommodate Arab sentiment by distancing themselves from Israel, and the United States took a more active role in the Middle East. In January 1957, Eisenhower got Congress to approve a resolution empowering him in advance to use force to "block Communist aggression" in the region. Washington hoped to woo conservative Arab rulers in Saudi Arabia, Jordan, and Iraq by posing as their protector against both Soviet influence and Nasser's followers.

The principle Eisenhower proclaimed, the so-called Eisenhower Doctrine, held that the United States could intervene in the Middle East if any nation there requested help to resist a Communist takeover. Initially, however, this seemed a hollow threat. During 1957 a series of plots, coups, and countercoups swept Syria, Jordan, and Iraq. Nasser asserted his influence outside Egypt in mid-1958 when he forged an alliance with Egypt, Syria, and Yemen, creating the United Arab Republic. In July, a pro-Nasser officer, General Abdel Karim Kassim, toppled the pro-Western Iraqi king, Faisal, and considered allying his new government with Nasser.

At this point, Washington feared that Arab radicals would halt Western access to the region's oil, endangering the European and Japanese economies. The Eisenhower administration decided to warn Nasser and his followers against undertaking such action. To do so, Eisenhower took a stand in the tiny country of Lebanon, where for months a political crisis had shaken the government.

Before ending its control of Lebanon during the 1940s, France had imposed a constitution giving greater political power to the Maronite Catholic minority than to the Muslim majority. As the number of Muslims grew, so did their resentment at second-class status. Many began to share Nasser's vision of a unified Arab Middle East. Then, in July 1958, Lebanese President Camille Chamoun, a Maronite, outraged Muslims by suggesting he might stay in office when his term expired a few months later. Radio broadcasts from Egypt called on Muslims to depose the Christian-dominated government in Beirut, and rioting erupted. When Chamoun looked to the United States for assistance, Eisenhower saw an opportunity to intimidate Nasser.

As he told Vice President Nixon, Eisenhower believed that Nasser's true object was to gain control of vital Middle East petroleum supplies in order to destroy the Western world. Similarly, Dulles feared that unless American forces intervened in Lebanon, all governments in the Middle East not affiliated with Nasser would be overthrown. The impact would be felt worldwide, he worried, as people surmised that the United States was "afraid of the Soviet Union."

On July 14, 1958, Eisenhower ordered fourteen thousand marines, with tactical nuclear capability and backed by a large fleet, to suppress what he called a "Communist-inspired" threat to Lebanon. Actually, by the time the marines landed in Beirut, most of the rioting had ended. Sunbathers gaped in awe as landing craft disgorged troops prepared to fight their way ashore.

Nevertheless, the operation achieved its basic aim of safeguarding oil supplies. The Lebanese factions patched together a compromise, and Chamoun surrendered office to another Christian. Iraq dropped plans to ally with Egypt and promised to protect Western-owned oil facilities. Even Nasser backed off after receiving word from Khrushchev that the Soviet Union would not challenge the United States on behalf of Arab dreams. Eisenhower's show of force held the line.

THE HUNGARIAN UPRISING AND REFUGEE POLITICS

Although the Eisenhower administration showed few qualms about intervening in Third World countries when there was any question of Communist influence, little could be done about the regions under direct Soviet control. This fact was emphasized by the 1956 uprising in Hungary. In the autumn of that year, inspired by Khrushchev's

Hungarian freedom fighters rose in revolt against Soviet control in 1956. Here they toppled a statue of Stalin. Shortly thereafter, Soviet forces crushed the revolt. *UPI/Bettmann Newsphotos.*

recent speech denouncing Stalin, citizens in Poland and Hungary revolted against Soviet domination. In Hungary the rising came especially close to success.

A reformist faction among Hungarian Communists gained control of the party and began to dismantle the Stalinist police apparatus. Moscow held back at first, but intervened brutally when reformer Imre Nagy declared that Hungary intended to quit the Warsaw Pact, the military agreement that bound Eastern European states to Moscow. Early in November, in the middle of the Suez crisis, Khrushchev sent Russian tanks into Budapest to crush this heresy.

Although CIA-supported Radio Free Europe had urged Eastern Europeans to revolt, when the Hungarians did revolt, Washington refused to help. Eisenhower feared that American intervention would destroy Hungary rather than free it. "[The] Russians are scared and furious," he noted, and "nothing is more dangerous than a dictatorship in that frame of mind." The president even barred sending to Hungary a group of CIA-trained exiles prepared for guerrilla operations.

Despite Eisenhower's refusal to intervene, the uprising in Hungary created an unanticipated problem for the United States. Some two hundred thousand people, mostly noncombatants, fled the reimposition of Soviet control. Because the 1952 McCarran-Walter Act had set minimal immigration quotas for Eastern Europe, few could enter the United States. As President Truman had predicted, the law became a slap in the face to those "fleeing barbarism."

In 1953, Eisenhower had asked Republican lawmakers to enact an emergency Refugee Relief Act. This act allocated about 200,000 special visas outside the quota system, with half reserved for "escapees" from "Communist-dominated" areas of Europe. A few Chinese also came under its provisions. But in spite of this one-time relaxation, immigration quotas remained in place. Senators William Revercomb and Pat McCarran warned that refugees might be Communist "sleeper agents" sent to subvert America, and many Americans complained that too many foreigners were entering the country. In 1954, Eisenhower responded to an alleged flood of illegal Mexicans by authorizing the deportation of 1 million undocumented migrants during "Operation Wetback."

The mass Hungarian exodus forced Washington to bend its immigration policy. Eisenhower found a loophole in the law that permitted the attorney general to grant refugees "parole," a legal status that allowed them to enter the United States for "emergency reasons or for reasons deemed strongly in the public interest." This provision had been written to accommodate individual hardship cases, not large groups. Nevertheless, Congress approved use of the parole power to admit 38,000 Hungarians and voted special aid for them. Most of the rest settled in Europe.

Lawmakers and the public showed compassion for several reasons. The Hungarians were seen both as victims of Soviet oppression and as an easily assimilable group. The situation repeated itself in 1959 and 1960 when over 125,000 middle- and upper-class Cubans fled Fidel Castro's revolution. Furthermore, by approving use of the special parole provision, Congress avoided prolonged debate over immigration quotas, letting the existing law stand.

The response to the plight of the Hungarians, Cubans, and, later, Indochinese refugees must be understood as a reflection of the Cold War. Policymakers viewed these refugees not merely as victims but as assets in an ideological struggle. Since 1953, over 90 percent of all refugees admitted to the United States had come from Communist nations. Each such entrant represented a failure of communism. Undocumented Mexicans suffered hardships and deprivations as cruel as most Hungarians, yet Mexicans were deported while Hungarians and Cubans were welcomed as symbolic freedom fighters.

THE SPACE RACE AND THE ARMS RACE

In October 1957 the Soviet Union captured world attention by launching an earth-orbiting, basketball-sized satellite, *Sputnik I.* White House Chief of Staff Sherman Adams dismissed the achievement as an "outer space basketball game." A month later, however, the Russians launched the thousand-pound *Sputnik II*, carrying a dog into orbit. Senator Lyndon Johnson of Texas, chair of the Armed Services Committee's Preparedness Subcommittee, expressed astonishment that another nation might achieve technological superiority over the United States. Like millions of Americans, he wondered what it would mean if *Sputnik* carried a nuclear bomb instead of a dog. Senator Henry Jackson of Washington called for a "National Week of Shame and Disgrace." *Life* magazine added to the panic when it described the Soviet satellite as a major defeat for the United States.

The space and missile race had begun during the Second World War with the German V-2 rocket. After 1945, both Moscow and Washington hired German scientists to help develop rocket programs. Because American bombers could be based near the Soviet Union, and because the air force much preferred the glamour of piloted aircraft to impersonal missiles, Wernher von Braun's rocket team in Huntsville, Alabama, received little funding. In contrast, the Soviet Union, which lacked air bases near the United States, saw missiles as a cost-effective way to counter America's geographic advantage.

With the growth of Pentagon budgets after 1950, and with increasing reliance on atomic weapons under Eisenhower's New Look, the pace of rocket research accelerated. Eisenhower was also keen to use rockets to launch reconnaissance satellites capable of providing reliable intelligence on Soviet capabilities. By observing what the Russians really had, the United States could avoid arming too lightly or heavily.

Because spy satellites would take years to develop, Eisenhower approved a stopgap—the U-2 spy plane. A brilliant team of aircraft engineers designed and built the U-2 in eighty-two days at a secret site run by Lockheed Aviation. In 1956 the high-flying spy plane began crisscrossing the Soviet Union at 80,000 feet, photographing rocket test sites and allowing intelligence analysts to keep close tabs on their rivals' progress. Because air force officers tended to interpret intelligence on Soviet power in a way that justified their calls for larger budgets, Eisenhower put the spy plane and its data under the control of the CIA. Although Soviet gunners could not yet shoot down the U-2, it would only be a short time before they could do so.

Because of uncertainty over the legality of space-based reconnaissance, Eisenhower wanted America's first prototype satellite launched on a civilian, rather than military, rocket. This meant building a separate booster, the Vanguard, rather than using the military's Redstone rocket, already near completion. But waiting for Vanguard meant that the Russians would probably win the first lap in the space race. Eisenhower accepted the delay, reasoning that if the Soviets orbited a satellite first, they would establish a legal precedent by overflying America from space. Despite the impression of tardiness, during the late 1950s research and development went forward for nearly all of the American rocket boosters and missile systems deployed through the 1980s.

When *Sputnik I* went aloft, Eisenhower assured his cabinet it posed no threat. He explained his reasons for relying on a nonmilitary rocket and hinted at a closely guarded secret: U-2 pictures revealed that, despite the success with *Sputnik,* the Soviets possessed only a small and unreliable rocket arsenal. The president urged his colleagues to play down *Sputnik,* lest public apprehension bring irresistible pressure to boost America's space budget.

Administration spokespersons therefore belittled the Russian achievement as a gimmick and attributed its development to German scientists, rather than to Communist technological superiority. But this did little to quell public anxiety. Democratic politicians, educators, journalists, and military contractors made common cause in charging through the media that the Russians had humiliated the United States and threatened national security. At the same time, each group sought to use *Sputnik* as leverage to achieve its own agenda: to embarrass the administration, to secure more aid to education, or to force an increase in defense spending. At the Senate committee hearings chaired by Lyndon Johnson, a parade of critics claimed that the Soviets had achieved a scientific Pearl Harbor.

To quiet these critics, Eisenhower advanced the date for launching an American satellite. In December 1957, in the middle of the Senate hearings, a hastily prepared Vanguard rocket exploded on takeoff. Critics promptly dubbed it "Flopnik." Reluctantly, Eisenhower then approved the use of a military rocket, which launched a satellite a few months later.

As the Senate hearings wound down, Johnson warned of widening gaps between the United States and the Soviet Union in aircraft, missiles, submarines, and high technology. Because the United States stood on the verge of losing the "battle of brainpower," he called for increases in space and military appropriations as well as massive federal aid to education. Eisenhower responded by appointing a White House science adviser and increasing funding for the National Science Foundation. He worked with Congress to create the National Aeronautics and Space Administration (NASA), with an initial budget of $340 million. As noted in Chapter 4, he also supported passage of the National Defense Education Act (NDEA), a billion-dollar package providing federal aid for schools and universities.

Shortly after *Sputnik*'s launch a high-level advisory panel, the Gaither Commission, reported to Eisenhower on the expanded Soviet threat. Hoping to force Eisenhower's hand, the authors' leaked their conclusions to journalists. Headlines warned that the United States was about to become a second-class power exposed to immediate threat from a missile-bristling Soviet Union. The Gaither report predicted that the Soviets would soon deploy hundreds of nuclear-tipped ICBMs threatening America's survival. The authors called for accelerating American missile production, increasing military spending by 25 percent, and building a massive system of fallout shelters, at a cost of $30 billion, to protect civilians.

Khrushchev inadvertently contributed to pressures on Eisenhower by boasting that Russian defense plants produced rockets like sausages, snipping them off every hundred feet along the conveyer belt. Democratic presidential hopefuls, among them Senators Stuart Symington, John F. Kennedy, and Lyndon Johnson, warned that the administration ignored a perilous "missile gap." Symington claimed that by the early 1960s the Soviet Union would have three thousand long-range missiles—three times the air force's already inflated estimate.

But to Eisenhower's credit, he expended much of his political capital in holding the line against efforts to raise defense spending dramatically. Unlike the Gaither panel, Eisenhower doubted that civilians could be protected against nuclear bombs. Moreover, U-2 reconnaissance revealed that the Russians had not put their rockets into full production. As with their bombers, they had deployed a few prototype rockets as a bluff—to impress the Third World, refute Chinese criticism, and cover up their comparative weakness. Because Khrushchev knew of the U-2 missions, even if he could do nothing to stop them, it is difficult to guess why he thought boasts would intimidate Eisenhower. By reinforcing the widespread overestimate of Soviet rocket technology, Khrushchev's rhetoric actually helped the cause of Americans who wanted to accelerate the arms race. A military gap did exist, but it favored the United States. Because of American bombers in Europe and Asia, medium-range missiles in Turkey and Italy, and the deployment by 1960 of Polaris nuclear-missile submarines in oceans around the world, the United States had a commanding lead in the arms race.

THE STIRRINGS OF DÉTENTE

Even as the space race joined the arms race to create public anxieties in America and new reasons for disagreement with the Soviets, a countervailing trend began to emerge. Eisenhower and Khrushchev took significant steps toward détente, talking with each other at summit meetings and establishing a temporary moratorium on nuclear tests. Although these efforts produced no lasting agreement, they did set a precedent for future negotiations.

Summitry and the Balance of Terror

The relaxation of tensions stemmed in part from the Soviet possession of a substantial atomic arsenal by 1955. The Cold War rivals had reached a balance of power, or terror; either side could greatly damage or destroy the other. Eisenhower acknowledged that under these circumstances there could be no possibility of victory or defeat in a full-scale war, only varying degrees of mutual devastation. In spite of Dulles's boast that on several occasions his willingness to go "to the brink of war" had forced China and the Soviet Union to back down, Soviet leader Nikita Khrushchev probably hit the mark when he explained that Dulles "knew how far he could push us, and he never pushed us too far."

Moreover, by the mid-1950s growing prosperity in Europe and the changing of the Kremlin guard had taken some of the edge off the Cold War. The creation of an independent West German army and its inclusion in NATO in 1955 formalized the postwar division of Europe. The Soviets responded by creating their own military alliance, the Warsaw Pact, but otherwise accepted Western moves. The Soviets even surprised the United States in 1955 by agreeing, largely on American terms, to a treaty ending the joint occupation of Austria.

Prodded by the NATO allies and his own desire to lessen the nuclear threat, Eisenhower agreed, in July 1955, to meet the Soviet leadership at a summit conference in Geneva. At the summit Eisenhower stunned the Soviets by calling for a policy of "open skies" whereby each side would be free to conduct aerial reconnaissance of the other's military facilities. The United States had little to lose and much to gain from such an arrangement. The Russians dismissed the proposal as a "bald espionage plot," and it went nowhere. Despite the lack of any formal agreement, both sides left the summit praising the "spirit of Geneva," a willingness among opposing blocs to talk.

During Eisenhower's final three years as president, he tried harder to reach some form of accommodation with the Soviet Union. For example, the perennial problem with Berlin re-emerged in 1958. Since the early 1950s, about 300,000 East Germans had fled Communist rule annually, most of them through Berlin. Faced with this population hemorrhage, Khrushchev demanded the withdrawal of Western forces and the creation of a "free," meaning East German–controlled, city. He announced a six-month deadline for the removal of Western troops, prompting members of Congress to demand a sharp increase in American military strength.

Eisenhower responded creatively to both Moscow and Congress. A war over Berlin, he observed, would be a nuclear, not conventional, conflict; therefore it made little sense to expand the size of the army, as some in Congress demanded. To the Soviets, Eisenhower declared that American forces would stay in Berlin; at the same time,

Soviet leader Nikita Khrushchev and his wife Nina visit an Iowa farm family in 1959. Khrushchev wanted to visit Disneyland, but the Secret Service refused, saying it could not guarantee his safety in the Magic Kingdom. *UPI/Bettmann Newsphotos.*

however, he informed Khrushchev that if the deadline for Western withdrawal were set aside, a superpower summit could be arranged. Khrushchev quickly allowed the threat to lapse and accepted an invitation to visit America in the fall of 1959.

In July, before the scheduled visit, Eisenhower sent Vice President Richard Nixon on a good-will trip to the Soviet Union. During an impromptu debate with Khrushchev, held in a model American kitchen at a Moscow trade fair, Nixon proposed shifting the terms of competition with Russia. During what journalists dubbed the "kitchen debate," the vice president boasted that most Americans owned houses stocked with appliances that made life easier for the homemakers. A flustered Khrushchev dismissed these "useless gadgets" but insisted that Soviet housewives had even better washing machines. Confident that America had the edge in the appliance race, Nixon asked, "Would it not be better to compete in the relative merits of washing machines than in the strength of rockets?"

A few months later, the Soviet leader visited the United States and conferred with Eisenhower at Camp David, the presidential retreat in Maryland. The absence of the hard-liner Dulles, who was terminally ill with cancer, raised the chances for conciliation. As in the earlier meeting between Eisenhower and Khrushchev, no formal agreements came from the summit. But the two leaders found it useful to take each other's measure, and both spoke of a "spirit of Camp David," which observers took to mean an informal reduction in tensions. Khrushchev and Eisenhower agreed to meet again in Paris the following spring.

Seeking a Nuclear Test Ban

To Eisenhower, the contacts with Khrushchev offered a chance to reduce the danger of nuclear war and slow the development in America of a garrison state obsessed with security. The president believed that massive defense spending had contributed to America's growing international trade deficit and to the economic recession of 1958. Khrushchev, for his part, felt that a reduction in tension would improve his ability to hold off the hawks in his own camp, including members of the Soviet military establishment who demanded greater missile production. For both Khrushchev and Eisenhower, one of the central issues was an agreement to limit nuclear testing.

Early in his presidency, Eisenhower had broached an "Atoms for Peace" program for international supervision of nuclear materials, but it went nowhere. Between 1951 and 1958 the Atomic Energy Commission (AEC) conducted seven major test series in Nevada and other tests in the Pacific. In some of the Nevada tests, thousands of soldiers were stationed just three miles from ground zero and then marched to the detonation point; the intent was to "train military units to become familiar with new weapons and their characteristics." From a present-day perspective, the ignorance of the effects of radiation is astounding. Many small towns downwind from the test site also received large doses of fallout. In 1954, world attention focused briefly on the crew of a Japanese fishing boat, the *Lucky Dragon*, contaminated by radiation from American detonations in the Pacific.

The AEC downplayed the danger from these tests and from the reactors or factories producing nuclear components. It told the soldiers at the Nevada test site merely to avoid breathing in any dust. The townsfolk nearby were instructed to dust off their clothes and brush off their shoes. The best action, according to the AEC, was "not to be worried about fallout." Workers at the Rocky Flats arsenal and other weapons assembly plants were not even provided with face masks when assigned to sweep up plutonium dust. Throughout the country, schoolchildren were instructed that in case of nuclear war, they would be safe if they crouched beneath their desks.

Many critics thought otherwise. By 1957, vocal opposition to nuclear testing had increased. British author Nevil Shute's best-selling novel *On the Beach* depicted the end of human life caused by fallout from a nuclear war. Nobel Prize–winning chemist Dr. Linus Pauling appeared on Edward R. Murrow's popular television show, "See It Now," to warn of the health effects of fallout. Ten thousand scientists from numerous nations signed a petition in favor of a test ban. At congressional hearings, scientists reported that even small amounts of radioactive strontium deposited in milk increased the dangers of cancer and genetic injury to fetuses. A citizens group, the Committee for a Sane Nuclear Policy (SANE), formed in 1957 and soon boasted twenty-five thousand members in 130 chapters. Its officers included such prominent Americans as writer John Hersey, magazine publisher Norman Cousins, labor leader Walter Reuther, and pediatrician Benjamin Spock. As part of a disarmament program, they called for halting weapons tests.

Eisenhower sympathized with these concerns but would not agree to a test ban unless the Soviets dropped their opposition to on-site inspection. When Moscow hinted that it might relent, American hard-liners panicked. Dr. Edward Teller told Eisenhower that if allowed to conduct tests a while longer, he could build a fallout-free weapon. Because of Teller's claim, which had little validity, Eisenhower temporarily slowed negotiations on a ban. In 1958, however, the president changed tack when his newly appointed science adviser, James Killian, invited to the White House a number of scientists who refuted Teller's views. They also explained that atmospheric testing was unnecessary to maintain a nuclear arsenal, especially if limited underground testing continued.

During 1958 the two superpowers conducted several rounds of large atmospheric nuclear tests. To assuage fears that the Soviet Union might sign a test-ban treaty and then continue testing secretly, American scientists assured Eisenhower that a network of seismic stations could detect most nuclear explosions, even those underground. While their subordinates worked on the terms of a treaty, Khrushchev and Eisenhower agreed to an informal test moratorium effective in October.

Eisenhower proposed a ban on fallout-producing atmospheric explosions but continuation of small underground tests. The smaller tests were difficult to detect and, as American hard-liners noted, would be useful in designing new types of weapons. Khrushchev surprised American negotiators by insisting on a comprehensive ban coupled with limited on-site inspection within the Soviet Union. Although uncertainties remained, agreement at the upcoming Paris summit seemed possible.

However, the May 1960 Paris summit proved a fiasco. On the eve of the conference, an American U-2 spy plane crashed inside the Soviet Union, brought down either by a Soviet missile or by engine failure. Eisenhower had approved this risky mission in the hope of gathering photographic evidence confirming that, despite Khrushchev's bluster, the Soviet Union had not deployed many long-range rockets. Such data would justify greater flexibility in arms control discussions. Sadly, the failed mission proved fatal for this cause.

After American officials released a cover story about a missing weather aircraft, Moscow announced that in fact it had captured a spy plane. When Eisenhower denied this, Khrushchev amazed the world by displaying pilot Francis Gary Powers, who confessed to espionage. The CIA had assured Eisenhower that Powers could not have survived a crash. Eisenhower was so depressed he considered resigning.

When the two world leaders met in Paris, Khrushchev demanded that Eisenhower apologize to the Soviet people for the U-2 mission. Eisenhower refused, and the summit broke up. An important opportunity to limit nuclear testing and slow the arms race had slipped away. The informal moratorium on nuclear testing lasted until the fall of 1961, but both the Soviets and the Americans then resumed their tests.

THE CUBAN REVOLUTION AND EISENHOWER'S FAREWELL

Problems in Latin America added to the foreign policy frustrations of Eisenhower's final years as president. Riots and revolution shattered the administration's confidence in its Latin American policy. When Eisenhower sent Vice President Nixon to Venezuela on a good-will tour, an angry mob stoned his car and nearly killed him. Before this incident, Nixon had praised Latin American military leaders as a "great stabilizing force" against communism.

The Cuban Revolution proved even more frightening. Washington had tolerated Cuba's long-lived military dictator, Fulgencio Batista, because he protected foreign investments and supported the United States in the Cold War. As a reward, Cuban sugar producers enjoyed privileged access to the American market. This profited wealthy landowners, among them many Americans, but few benefits trickled down to plantation workers.

Batista's regime collapsed in January 1959 when Fidel Castro led a guerrilla army into Havana. The son of a well-to-do family who lived for a time in New York, Castro had once dreamed of pitching for an American baseball team. Trained as a lawyer, he led a failed rebellion in the early 1950s, spent time in a Cuban prison, and launched a second revolt in 1956. Initially, Castro called for socialist reform but had no specific Marxist program or links with the Soviet Union.

At first, Washington took a wait-and-see attitude. Castro legalized the small Communist party, made anti-American speeches, ousted moderates from his movement, postponed promised elections, and publicly executed about five hundred of Batista's henchmen. During a visit to Washington in April 1959, Castro insisted he wanted good relations with America. But when he expropriated foreign-owned plantations, paying with bonds at the land's deflated tax value, and signed a trade deal with Russia, Eisenhower decided the Cuban leader was a dangerous pro-Soviet puppet.

Although Castro lost popularity among the Cuban elite, many ordinary Cubans admired his bold challenge to Uncle Sam. Castro's spunk in standing up to the United States also made him something of a hero elsewhere in Latin America. To counter his appeal, Eisenhower approved long-term economic aid to Latin America, a program President John F. Kennedy later redubbed the Alliance for Progress. In mid-1960 Eisenhower decided to eliminate Castro by encouraging Cuban opposition and training an exile army. Mindful of the overthrow of Arbenz, Castro hastened to organize a popular militia armed with Soviet weapons.

After cutting trade and diplomatic ties with Cuba, Eisenhower authorized covert CIA operations. United States intelligence agents tried to undermine Castro's image and his regime while organizing a guerrilla force of Cuban exiles to invade the island. As described in Chapter 6, the CIA plan led to the disastrous Bay of Pigs invasion, for which the next president, John F. Kennedy, took the principal blame.

By the end of his presidency, Eisenhower sensed the limitations of his achievement in foreign policy. Although he had managed various crises in the Third World and preserved peace with the Soviet Union, he had failed to stem the arms race or create a basis for cooperation with the Soviets. Consequently, he worried that American society would face increased regimentation as the nation remained shackled to its huge and growing defense budget.

His reflections on these matters were evident in his remarkable farewell address of January 1961, which has been quoted repeatedly ever since. Eisenhower warned against the temptation to solve domestic problems through "some spectacular and costly action" abroad. The old general deplored the view that a large increase in defense spending would create a miraculous solution to the nation's troubles. The greatest threat to democracy, he observed, came from a new phenomenon, the "conjunction of an immense military establishment and a large arms industry." Americans needed to guard against the unwarranted influence of this "military-industrial complex."

With this turn of phrase, the former military man had sounded a warning that would ring down the decades. It had little immediate effect, however, on the administrations that followed.

CONCLUSION

Any assessment of Eisenhower's foreign policy must take into account the apparent contradictions in his approach. With the hardliner Dulles at his side, Eisenhower began his presidency with a New Look that emphasized the use of nuclear weapons and the doctrine of massive retaliation. Accordingly, he presided over a dramatic build-up of the nuclear stockpile and the development of ICBMs. He also intervened repeatedly in Third World conflicts, often employing the CIA to undermine governments that he considered dangerous. He deepened the American involvement in Vietnam that would have tragic consequences in the 1960s and 1970s.

Nevertheless, most historians see Eisenhower as a president who basically kept the peace. After ending the Korean War, he avoided further direct conflicts with the Soviet Union or China. Although he and Dulles brandished nuclear weapons as the ultimate threat, he never authorized a nuclear attack. In the early years of his administration, he made significant efforts to restrain defense spending, and in his second term he took steps toward détente with the Soviet Union.

Overall, as he tried to deal with the Cold War he had inherited from Harry Truman, Eisenhower built a complex legacy for later administrations. The next chapter will examine how his immediate successor, John F. Kennedy, handled such issues as the space race, missiles, détente, and unrest in the Third World. ■

FURTHER READING

On foreign policy, the arms race, and the Cold War during the 1950s, see: Stephen E. Ambrose, *Ike's Spies* (1981); H. W. Brands, Jr., *The Cold Warriors* (1988); Robert A. Divine, *Eisenhower and the Cold War* (1981); Howard Ball, *Justice Downwind: America's Nuclear Testing Program in the 1950s* (1986); Robert A. Divine, *Blowing in the Wind: The Nuclear Test Ban Debate, 1954–60* (1978); Walter A. McDougall, . . . *The Heavens and the Earth: A Political History of the Space Age* (1985); Stephen G. Rabe, *Eisenhower and Latin America* (1988); George McT. Kahin, *Intervention: How America Became Involved in Vietnam* (1986); John Gaddis, *The Long Peace* (1987); Michael Beschloss, *Mayday* (1986); Garry Wills, *Nixon Agonistes* (1969); Gordon Chang, *Enemies and Friends: The United States, China, and the Soviet Union, 1948–1972* (1989).

6

Outposts on the New Frontier: Americans at Home and Abroad, 1960–1963

By the end of the Eisenhower administration, many Americans were ready for a change. Not only had Eisenhower's grandfatherly style begun to seem unexciting, but social and political attitudes were evolving. Especially among young people, the ideal of a stable, secure, middle-class family in the suburbs was giving way to a desire for more adventurousness, more challenge. In politics, too, the nation's young adults admired high style rather than cautious consensus. Those who embraced this new perspective found a leader to suit their tastes in the glamorous, wealthy, and witty John F. Kennedy.

Often known informally as Jack Kennedy or JFK, he embodied urbane masculinity, combining a dazzling smile and a youthful appearance with what his admirers called toughness—the ability to act decisively without expressing agonizing self-doubts. He exuded curiosity about public affairs and people, read voraciously, absorbed information like a sponge, asked probing questions of subordinates, and spoke beautifully. His press conferences were works of art, and journalists found him a welcome relief from the stolid Eisenhower. He came from a large, rambunctious, and wealthy family that always seemed to be in motion—sailing, playing touch football, goading each other on in constant competition. His wife Jacqueline, slim, sophisticated, and cool, spoke softly and wore her designer clothes effortlessly. They kept company with celebrities from the worlds of art, literature, mass media, and entertainment. His friends winked at his parade of mistresses, and those who knew him from afar adored his personal style and mastery of American politics.

The Kennedy style captivated the mass media, and through them the public. Kennedy's presidency raised expectations that problems could be solved by wit, intelligence, knowledge, energy, and skillful management. Many middle-class Americans felt more optimistic, capable, and encouraged about their country's social, spiritual, and economic prospects during the thousand days of Kennedy's presidency than they did for years thereafter. His murder on November 22, 1963, permanently wounded the American outlook.

In retrospect, however, Kennedy's administration has lost much of its luster. His toughness, knowledge, and energy alone could not meet many of the challenges facing the country. His principal skills were those of technique and style. He was less adept at outlining a compelling vision of the future. Kennedy was a splendid politician, but he was not an advocate of any particular cause. He and his supporters considered it a source of strength and a sign of their maturity that they treated public affairs coolly and dispassionately.

In domestic affairs this detached, pragmatic attitude made Kennedy slow to respond to important emerging issues. Although he courted black voters, he hesitated to commit himself to significant support for civil rights. Only after violent attacks on black and white Freedom Riders and a bloody confrontation over university desegregation in Mississippi did Kennedy announce that he would ask Congress to pass a civil rights bill. On the issue of poverty he responded with some sensitivity but did not manage to develop a program before his death. Many of the initiatives that progressive Americans expected from him remained unrealized until Lyndon Johnson took office.

In foreign policy Kennedy also failed to develop a genuinely new approach, choosing instead to apply his own variant of the policy of containment that had been established more than a decade earlier. His belief in the need for toughness with the Soviet Union encouraged him to risk nuclear war more dramatically than Eisenhower and Dulles had done. Although the American public backed him at the time, historians have taken a more ambivalent view, balancing admiration for his energy and intelligence with disappointment over his obsessive waging of the Cold War.

THE ELECTION OF 1960

The election of 1960 demonstrated how much American politics had changed since the Second World War. Democrats expected that the New Deal coalition of liberals, working class people, Catholics, southerners, and racial minorities would continue to give them an advantage in presidential elections. They believed that the idea of an activist government, promoted by the New Deal, had been accepted by a majority of Americans. They explained away the popularity of Dwight D. Eisenhower as reflecting his personal appeal rather than an endorsement of the Republican party. However, the 1960 election results revealed serious limits in the New Deal coalition and in the public's acceptance of government activism. The Democrats barely won with John F. Kennedy, a moderate candidate from the party's center. Richard Nixon, the Republican candidate, did so well that he remained an important figure in American politics. White southerners continued their flight from the Democratic party, preparing the way for future Republican and conservative triumphs.

Kennedy's Nomination

Only forty-two years old when he announced his candidacy for president in January 1960, John F. Kennedy shook up Democratic party professionals who dismissed him as a brash outsider. Ignoring the advice of older men ("I urge you to be patient," former president

Truman said), Kennedy approached the 1960 election with advantages of which party leaders were unaware. He was already well known to the public: laudatory stories about him and his wife had appeared in many newspapers and magazines; though most of the book had been written by others, he had won the Pulitzer Prize for his 1956 work *Profiles in Courage*; and he had made a memorable impression by nearly winning the Democratic nomination for vice president in 1956. His fresh, youthful vigor stood in sharp contrast to Eisenhower's age and apparent passivity—a difference Kennedy planned to emphasize in his campaign.

Kennedy also forecast that his moderate stance on the controversial issues of the 1950s would distinguish him favorably in voters' minds from members of the party's liberal wing. He astutely concluded that the public mood had become more conservative since the New Deal, and that voters would respond best to a candidate who projected energy and managerial competence, not passionate commitment to causes. The growing influence of television bolstered Kennedy's approach. Impassioned or flowery oratory—a necessary attribute for candidates before the age of television—often irritated TV viewers rather than inspiring them.

Although party professionals and most liberals had their doubts about the young candidate, they could not agree on an alternative. Kennedy dashed the hopes of the older men by winning victories in seven presidential primaries. Senator Hubert Humphrey, a fiery Minnesota liberal, challenged him early, but his campaign died after Kennedy won the West Virginia primary in May. By winning that heavily Protestant state, Kennedy, a Catholic, allayed fears among party professionals that a Catholic candidate could not be elected. By the time the Democratic convention met in July, only Senate Majority Leader Lyndon Johnson of Texas could mount a last ditch campaign against Kennedy. Johnson claimed that Kennedy was too young and inexperienced to grapple with Soviet leader Nikita Khrushchev.

Johnson's bid came so late and Johnson himself had opposed so many liberal initiatives that his bid for the nomination fizzled. Kennedy won on the first ballot. He then astonished his own staff and disturbed party liberals by offering the vice-presidential nomination to Johnson. Kennedy expected that the majority leader would reject the invitation but remain grateful for the gesture. Much to his surprise, Johnson accepted.

Two days later Kennedy addressed fifty thousand Democrats at the Los Angeles Coliseum. In keeping with his belief that the public yearned for firm action but was less interested in specific programs, he announced that "we stand on the edge of a New Frontier—the frontier of the 1960s—a frontier of unknown opportunities and perils—a frontier of unfulfilled hopes and threats." The crowd cheered when he offered not "a set of promises [but] a set of challenges." The New Frontier came with "the promise of more sacrifice instead of more security," and the public was intrigued.

The Fall Campaign

A key element in Kennedy's campaign against Richard Nixon was a series of four face-to-face televised debates. Already television was changing the nature of American campaigns. To achieve an illusion of intimacy with their viewers, candidates had begun to hire media experts to make them appear warm, trustworthy, knowledgeable, energetic, and wise. The first Kennedy-Nixon debate proved crucial, because most voters had never seen Kennedy before, whereas Nixon had been a familiar figure for the last eight years.

Instead of watching an inexperienced youth ridiculed by his opponent, viewers saw Kennedy as a knowledgeable, self-assured, handsome candidate. His crisp, fact-filled delivery made him appear Nixon's equal and erased "experience" as an edge for the incumbent vice president. Nixon, on the other hand, looked terrible. Sweat poured down his face, smearing his make-up. These images affected audience perceptions of which candidate had won the debate. Those who watched on television considered Kennedy the clear winner, whereas those who listened to the debate on the radio thought that Nixon had done a better job.

During the campaign, each candidate tried to convince voters that he would confront the "Communist threat" with more passion than his opponent, and both indicated they would oppose the Soviet Union more vigorously than had the Eisenhower administration. Nixon vowed to defend Quemoy and Matsu, the two small islands off the coast of the People's Republic of China that Eisenhower and Dulles had protected. Kennedy responded with an attack on Eisenhower and Nixon for tolerating a "Communist outpost" in Cuba just ninety miles from Florida. Shortly before the final debate, Kennedy's office released a statement promising "to strengthen the non-Batista Democratic anti-Castro forces." Nixon, aware that the CIA had already developed plans for an invasion of Cuba, feared that Kennedy had deliberately revealed a plot to overthrow Castro. Nixon characterized such a plan as a violation of international law that would rouse anti-American passions throughout the Western Hemisphere.

Beyond using tough anti-Communist rhetoric, Kennedy asserted that Americans were "tired of the drift in our national course" and "weary of the continual decline in our national prestige." He felt the United States was ready for a resolute course of action in world affairs. Although he never mentioned Eisenhower by name—the public retained strong affection for the old war hero—Kennedy subtly contrasted his own youth with the president's age. He implied that Eisenhower's grandfatherly style represented tired disengagement, not the wisdom of a successful general who knew when to act and when to stand pat. He blamed the president for the loss of the U-2 spy plane over the Soviet Union in May 1960. The young Democrat stressed that he represented a new generation of politicians best able to confront the Soviet Union without setting off a nuclear war.

Kennedy deftly turned the issue of his Catholicism to advantage, neutralizing anti-Catholic sentiments and winning the hearts of his fellow Catholics. He gave a brilliant televised performance before the Houston Ministerial Association, a highly skeptical audience of several hundred Southern Baptists, telling them, "I am not the Catholic candidate for President, I am the Democratic candidate, who happens to be Catholic." He promised to resign if he found himself having to choose between violating his conscience and violating the Constitution.

Another gesture helped him secure the votes of blacks. African-Americans had been cool to Kennedy because of his noticeable lack of interest in civil rights legislation during his years in Congress. John and his brother Robert Kennedy melted the animosity with two telephone calls in late October 1960. Civil rights leader Martin Luther King, Jr., had been sent to a rural Georgia jail on a four-month sentence on trumped-up charges stemming from a demonstration for integration of a lunch counter at an Atlanta department store. John Kennedy called the prisoner's wife, Coretta Scott King, expressing his interest in her husband's welfare. His brother Robert, Kennedy's campaign manager, secured King's release by calling the judge to tell him that the harsh sentence made the state of Georgia look bad. The judge relented and ordered King freed. In gratitude, King's father, Martin Luther King, Sr., a Protestant minister, announced that he was dropping his opposition to the Catholic Kennedy. The Kennedy campaign then distributed 2 million copies of a booklet describing the Kennedy brothers' efforts on King's behalf.

In the November election Kennedy won a razor-thin plurality of 118,574 votes out of the total of 68,334,888 votes cast (see map, page 204). Sixty-four percent of Americans voted, the largest proportion since 1920. The religious issue reduced Kennedy's popular-vote margin but actually helped him win electoral votes. Although he lost the backing of about 1 million Protestants who had supported Democrats in earlier elections, these people were concentrated in midwestern farm states that customarily voted Republican in any case. Among Catholics, Kennedy won 80 percent of the vote, up from the approximately 63 percent who had voted for Democratic candidates since Roosevelt, and this gain proved important in the electoral college. African-Americans, too, helped Kennedy win such key northern in-

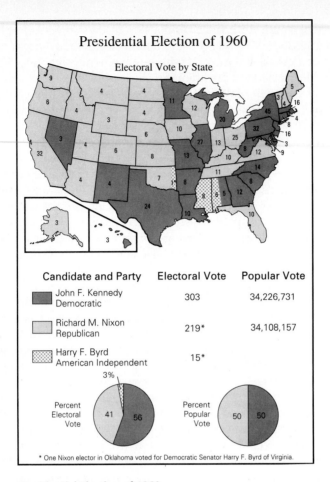

Presidential Election of 1960

Electoral Vote by State

Candidate and Party	Electoral Vote	Popular Vote
John F. Kennedy Democratic	303	34,226,731
Richard M. Nixon Republican	219*	34,108,157
Harry F. Byrd American Independent	15*	

Percent Electoral Vote: 56 / 41 / 3%

Percent Popular Vote: 50 / 50

* One Nixon elector in Oklahoma voted for Democratic Senator Harry F. Byrd of Virginia.

Presidential Election of 1960

dustrial states as New York, Pennsylvania, and Michigan. Although most blacks still could not vote in the South, those who did provided crucial victory margins in North and South Carolina and Texas.

PERSONALITIES AND STYLE ON THE NEW FRONTIER

Kennedy's inauguration took place on January 20, 1961, a bitterly cold day with a blinding sun reflecting from the newly fallen snow. The contrast of the youngest man ever elected president taking the oath while the oldest man ever to hold the office looked on made a powerful impression on most observers. Kennedy heightened the contrast by shedding his coat and hat in the frigid 22-degree weather to deliver one of the most polished speeches of his life, during which he promised to "pay any price, bear any burden, meet any hardship, support any friend, oppose any foe, to assure the survival and success of liberty." Although later historians criticized the alarming rhetoric, at the time Kennedy captured listeners with his stirring phrases, declaring that "the torch has been passed to a new generation of Americans—born in this century, tempered by war, disciplined by a hard and bitter peace." Most of his language challenged the Soviet Union; he insisted, for example, that "only when our arms are sufficient beyond doubt can we be certain beyond doubt that they will never be used." Only once did he hold out an olive branch: "Let us never negotiate out of fear, but let us never fear to negotiate." He continued his calls for sacrifice: "And so my fellow Americans, ask not what your country can do for you—ask what you can do for your country."

Even old rivals considered it a triumphant performance. Senator Barry Goldwater shook his head and told a reporter, "God, I'd like to be able to do what that boy did there." And although a later generation thought that Kennedy had provoked the Soviets, Moscow seemed pleased. The Soviet government newspaper *Izvestia* printed the entire text of the speech.

The brilliant inauguration set the tone of the remaining thousand days of the Kennedy administration. He and his family projected an image of energy, fitness, cultural refinement, and even sexual excitement. Like Eisenhower, Kennedy enjoyed golf, but he kept photographers at bay when he took to the links. Instead, he relished their pictures of his family's rough games of touch football. As the President's Council on Physical Fitness regularly reported on the poor body tone of the nation's elementary and high school students, public schools began requiring their pupils to pass tests of rope climbing, sit-ups, pushups, and chin-ups. The president even encouraged his staff to embark on bone-wearying, organized fifty-mile hikes.

Although he personally disdained classical music and ballet, Kennedy invited cellist Pablo Casals to perform at the White House to show that the nation's political leadership admired high culture. Intellectuals felt valued, in sharp contrast to the harassment they had experienced during the period of McCarthyism. Jacqueline Kennedy touched the same nerve by embarking on a campaign to furnish the White House with authentic antiques, representative of the period of each previous occupant of the White House.

In choosing his advisers and key administrators, Kennedy appointed a group that writer David Halberstam would later call "the best and the brightest." Young, often educated in the Ivy League, many of them boasting fine records in business or academia, these new stars in Washington added to the Kennedy aura. As a group, however, they were not passionately dedicated to causes. Kennedy assembled a cabinet of men who shared his view that managerial competence, not commitment to any particular program, mattered most in the conduct of public affairs. He did not know many of the people he selected to head government agencies, but they had been recommended for their tough hides, intelligence, pragmatism, and skepticism of dogmas. Feeling the need for continued counsel from his closest adviser, he named his thirty-six-year-old brother Robert as attorney general. He included two Republicans in his cabinet: C. Douglas Dillon as treasury secretary, to reassure business leaders, and Robert McNamara, the young president of Ford Motor Company, as secretary of defense. McNamara—ferociously intelligent, impatient with ignorance, focused on numbers and facts—set the tone of the New Frontier. If information could not be summarized in numerical form, McNamara would not use it.

Kennedy also chose another Republican to fill an important post outside the cabinet. McGeorge Bundy, forty-one-year-old dean of the faculty at Harvard and a long-time friend, became national security adviser. Believing that Eisenhower's supposedly disengaged style had hampered the conduct of foreign affairs, Kennedy wanted to elevate the importance of the national security adviser to help make the president the central figure in foreign policy. Under such a system the secretary of state's importance would decline. After a long search for a secretary of state, he settled on Dean Rusk, formerly Truman's assistant secretary of state for Far Eastern affairs.

At the same time that he sought to expand his control of foreign policy, Kennedy limited his options in domestic affairs by retaining J. Edgar Hoover as the director of the Federal Bureau of Investigation. From the beginning Hoover and Robert Kennedy fought bitterly. Hoover refused to acknowledge the existence of the Mafia; Kennedy wanted the FBI to infiltrate it. The attorney general also pressed Hoover to obtain evidence against Jimmy Hoffa, president of the Teamsters Union, but Hoover resisted that idea as well. In Hoover's view, the Teamsters were too powerful and the Mafia too difficult for agents to expose. The FBI director, in turn, forced Kennedy into approving wiretaps on Martin Luther King, Jr., whom Hoover detested and suspected of ties to the American Communist party. In the taps, Hoover received lurid evidence of King's many sexual encounters with women other than his wife. Yet the Kennedys had to keep Hoover in office, because the FBI chief had in his files damaging tape recordings that proved a 1941 sexual liaison between the twenty-three-year-old Lieutenant John F. Kennedy and a woman who worked for Nazi intelligence. Although John Kennedy often seemed to flaunt his extramarital encounters—he brought a stream of mistresses into the White

FBI director J. Edgar Hoover flanked by two men who distrusted and feared him, Attorney General Robert F. Kennedy (*left*) and President John F. Kennedy. *John F. Kennedy Library.*

House and sought new sexual conquests on state visits and vacations—he feared that Hoover's files could destroy him.

The uneasy secret shared with Hoover was only one indication that Kennedy was not the glittering knight he appeared to be. For close observers, a gap soon developed between his dashing media image and the more mundane reality. Even while he remained popular, the public hopes raised by his high style and thrilling oratory were often disappointed.

KENNEDY'S FOREIGN POLICY: THE QUEST FOR VICTORY

Like its predecessors, the Kennedy administration pursued the policy of containing the Soviet Union and opposing revolutionary change in the Third World. Discarding Eisenhower's doctrine of massive retaliation, Kennedy substituted the principle of "flexible response," designed to increase the administration's options for dealing with both the Soviet Union and leftist movements elsewhere. In practice this strategy led to more emphasis on counterinsurgency fighters as well as more ICBMs, and the overall military budget rose. Through 1961 and 1962 the United States confronted the Soviet Union and its Third

World clients as assertively as ever before, hoping for a decisive victory in the Cold War. Particularly in the Cuban missile crisis of October 1962, Kennedy's aggressiveness brought the world to the verge of nuclear disaster.

In the aftermath of the missile crisis, however, ordinary citizens and policy planners paid more attention to the danger of nuclear war with the Soviets. Cold War tensions began to ease in 1963 as authorities in both countries looked for alternatives to their permanent competition. Unfortunately, this early *détente,* or relaxation of tension, did not last.

The Bay of Pigs

The new president worried about Fidel Castro like a man with a toothache: the pain would not get better and Kennedy could not take his mind off it. Defense Secretary Robert McNamara thought that the administration was hysterical about Castro from beginning to end. Fidel Castro's actions in 1960 and early 1961 made Kennedy even more frustrated. Knowing that the United States was arming exiled opponents of his government, Castro began supporting revolutionaries throughout Latin America in response. "That is the reason President Kennedy can't sleep at night," Castro said.

In 1960, under President Eisenhower, the CIA had begun planning an invasion of Cuba by the exiles the agency had armed. By the time Kennedy took office, the operation was nearly ready to go. When the CIA presented plans for the invasion, most of Kennedy's inner circle of advisers approved. CIA chief Allen Dulles informed the president that the prospects for success in the invasion of Cuba were greater than they had been in 1954, when the agency had sponsored an invasion of Guatemala.

Kennedy's main concern was that the White House be able to maintain "plausible deniability" of its involvement. In response, the CIA changed the proposed site of the landing, choosing the swampy Bay of Pigs, and the president banned the American air force from providing cover to the invaders. Later supporters of the anti-Castro invaders claimed that these alterations doomed the operation. In fact, the plan was flawed from the beginning. Castro was popular throughout the island. The CIA's claim that "it is a Cuban tradition to join a winner and [the invaders] will win against whatever Castro has to offer" was sheer fantasy. Castro's large, well-armed army was ready for an attack. Some of Kennedy's own advisers doubted the workability of the plan. Former secretary of state Dean Acheson told the president that "it was not necessary to call in Price Waterhouse [a large accounting firm] to discover that fifteen hundred Cubans [the invaders] weren't as good as twenty-five thousand Cubans [Castro's army]."

The invasion went forward because it seemed easier to continue than to cancel an advanced plan. The president wanted to believe the CIA's optimistic claims. He feared looking weak should word leak out that he had scrapped a plan prepared by the Eisenhower administration. He worried that if the members of the brigade were forced to return to the United States from their bases in Guatemala, they would inform the media of the plan, making it appear that Kennedy's toughness was just a pose developed for the election.

The invasion began at first light on April 17, 1961 (see map, page 210). The brigade hit the beaches after a voice broadcasted through a CIA transmitter in Honduras asked Cubans to rise against their government. That plea had no effect, but Castro's own call to arms for his 200,000-man militia worked perfectly. The Cuban defenders sank many of the invaders' landing craft. Attackers who made it ashore became easy targets for Castro's tanks and fighter planes. By the evening of the first day, Kennedy knew that the operation had failed. Within seventy-two hours the Cuban army had captured 1,189 invaders and killed 114; only about 150 escaped death or capture.

Meanwhile, the Cuban delegate to the United Nations had a field day denouncing the United States for sponsoring illegal aggression. Adlai Stevenson, United States ambassador to the United Nations, had been kept in the dark about the CIA's plans. Unaware of the extent of American involvement in the plan, he told the United Nations Security Council that "no offensive had been launched from Florida or from any other part of the United States." Although this statement was technically correct (the invaders had trained in Florida but had left from Puerto Rico and Nicaragua), the implication—that the United States had nothing to do with the attacks—was clearly false.

In the aftermath of the Bay of Pigs debacle, Kennedy set about restoring the image he had tried to craft of a decisive, successful, and active leader. He embarked on a public relations offensive against Castro, implying that the United States would look for other ways to end Castro's regime. He went before the American Society of Newspaper Editors to blame the victim of the United States attack, explaining that American "restraint" toward Cuba was "not inexhaustible." He pledged never to "abandon . . . the country to communism." The editors loved it, as did the public. A Gallup poll taken the week after Kennedy's speech revealed that 71 percent approved of his overall handling of the presidency and over 80 percent backed his Cuban policy.

Operation Mongoose

Kennedy's obsession with Cuba continued after the failure of the Bay of Pigs invasion. The American government ransomed the approxi-

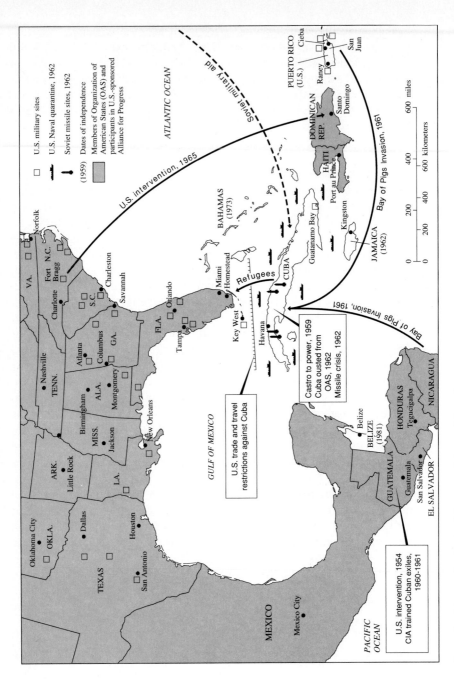

The United States in the Caribbean and Central America

Legend:
- □ U.S. military sites
- ⬧ U.S. Naval quarantine, 1962
- □ Soviet missile sites, 1962
- (1959) Dates of independence
- ▨ Members of Organization of American States (OAS) and participants in U.S.-sponsored Alliance for Progress

U.S. intervention, 1965

Soviet military aid

ATLANTIC OCEAN

PUERTO RICO (U.S.) — Cieba, San Juan, Raney

DOMINICAN REP. — Santo Domingo

HAITI — Port au Prince

Bay of Pigs Invasion, 1961

0 200 400 600 miles
0 200 400 600 kilometers

BAHAMAS (1973)

Guantanamo Bay

JAMAICA (1962) — Kingston

Norfolk — VA.

Fort Bragg — N.C.

Charlotte — Charleston — S.C. — Savannah

Nashville — TENN.

Atlanta — Columbus — GA.

Orlando — FLA. — Miami, Homestead

Tampa

Key West

Refugees

CUBA — Havana

Castro to power, 1959
Cuba ousted from OAS, 1962
Missile crisis, 1962

Bay of Pigs Invasion, 1961

Birmingham — ALA. — Montgomery

MISS. — Jackson

New Orleans — LA.

U.S. trade and travel restrictions against Cuba

Little Rock — ARK.

Oklahoma City — OKLA.

Dallas — TEXAS — San Antonio — Houston

GULF OF MEXICO

Belize — BELIZE (1981)

HONDURAS — Tegucigalpa

GUATEMALA — Guatemala

San Salvador — EL SALVADOR

NICARAGUA

MEXICO — Mexico City

U.S. intervention, 1954
CIA trained Cuban exiles, 1960-1961

PACIFIC OCEAN

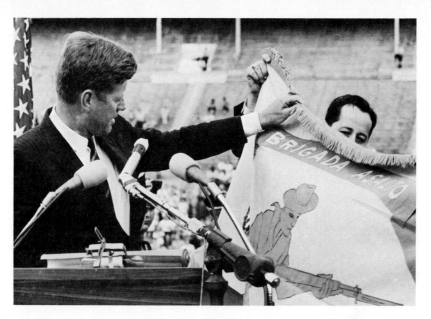

President Kennedy receives the combat flag of the Bay of Pigs invasion brigade at a ceremony in Miami's Orange Bowl. *Wide World Photos.*

mately twelve hundred captured Cubans with $120 million worth of drugs and medical supplies. Veterans of the brigade were given a tumultuous reception in Miami's Orange Bowl. Kennedy accepted one of their battle banners and promised to return the flag "in a free Havana." All the while, his administration proceeded with efforts to discredit, overthrow, or kill Fidel Castro and drafted plans to invade the island once more.

In late 1961 the CIA initiated Operation Mongoose, the code name for the pursuit of various schemes to evict or assassinate the Cuban leader. Kennedy put Colonel Edward Lansdale, a veteran of covert CIA actions in the Philippines and South Vietnam, in charge of the operation. The agency developed a series of almost fantastical schemes. Psychological warfare experts suggested that a full beard represented sexual potency in Cuban culture, so CIA agents tried to discredit Castro in the minds of his people by dropping depilatory powder in his boots. Another scenario involved agents slipping him cigars either laced with LSD to make him incoherent or injected with poison to kill him. At various times would-be assassins tried to poison him, spear him with harpoons as he snorkeled in the Caribbean, or induce him to don a wet suit rigged with explosives. None of these attempts worked.

In frustration, the CIA turned to the Mafia, hoping to make use of its members' experience with murdering their rivals. Mafia chiefs earlier had helped the Eisenhower administration with its efforts to kill Castro, hoping to regain control of their casinos, which had been closed by the bearded revolutionary. Eventually the connection between the administration and the criminals became too hot for top officials, and the matter was dropped. One of the president's several mistresses also shared a bed with the boss of the Chicago Mafia. FBI director Hoover knew of the bizarre triangle and ultimately persuaded Robert Kennedy that exposure of the president's connection with a woman involved with a mobster could embarrass the administration. Kennedy stopped the affair, and the CIA dropped its contract with the mob. By then, however, Castro had learned of the American-sponsored plots on his life and sought help from his patrons in Moscow. Nikita Khrushchev responded with Soviet troops equipped to repel another United States invasion. In mid-1962, the Soviets also agreed to station in Cuba a few dozen intermediate-range ballistic missiles, armed with nuclear bombs.

American Policy Toward the Developing World

Elsewhere in the developing world, the Kennedy administration used a variety of methods—some far gentler than Operation Mongoose, some equally violent—to encourage people and governments to support the United States in its global competition with the Soviet Union. During the election campaign of 1960 Kennedy had accused the Eisenhower administration of indifference to poverty in Latin America and lack of support for independence movements in Africa and Asia. Eisenhower, he said, had ignored the "winds of change" sweeping the Third World and opened the way for the Soviet Union to gain advantages there. Walt W. Rostow, a former professor of economics at the Massachusetts Institute of Technology whom Kennedy had brought to the State Department, explained that the new administration would restore America's prestige among the poor or newly independent states of Latin America, Africa, and Asia by building modern societies there.

Fearing that many Latin American states, racked by poverty, social inequality, and political repression, stood on the verge of social revolutions similar to Cuba's, the Kennedy administration developed a foreign assistance program called the Alliance for Progress. Unveiled in May 1961, the Alliance had roots in Eisenhower's aid program and in the highly successful Marshall Plan that had rebuilt Western Europe from 1948 to 1953. Kennedy obtained from Congress a down payment of $500 million to eradicate illiteracy, hunger, and disease in the Western Hemisphere. Over the next eight years, the United States provided about $10 billion in public assistance; an additional $8 billion came from private agencies. Kennedy also promised to advance political and social reform in Latin America by pressuring the region's political leaders to revise tax and land laws that favored the rich.

The hopes inflated by the Alliance for Progress made disappointment almost inevitable. Creating just and prosperous societies in the Western Hemisphere proved far harder than restoring modern, industrial European countries to the prosperity they had enjoyed before the Second World War. Throughout Latin America, economic growth stalled at an unimpressive average of 1.5 percent per year during the 1960s. Unemployment rose, and the averages for life expectancy, infant mortality, adult illiteracy, and the amount of time children spent in school remained the same.

The Kennedy administration also found it somewhat harder to practice concern for democracy and social justice than to preach it. In the cause of promoting popular, elected governments, Kennedy produced a mixed record. The administration hastened the end of the dictatorship of Rafael Trujillo in the Dominican Republic and supported constitutional regimes in Venezuela, Colombia, and Mexico. On the other hand, it acquiesced in military coups in Argentina, Guatemala, Honduras, and Haiti. The CIA also secretly funded moderate and conservative candidates in Chile to spoil the prospects of Socialist Salvador Allende Gossens in the presidential race of 1964. In most of these episodes, the Latin American governments' attitude toward Castro determined the American response. When the elected regimes opposed Cuba, the United States stood ready to help. When they expressed sympathy for Castro or questioned the right of the United States to sponsor the Bay of Pigs invasion, Washington suspected them of leftist sympathies and stopped sending Alliance for Progress monies.

Another program, not involving covert actions, had perhaps more lasting benefit. The Peace Corps, a project arising from the Kennedy administration's desire to encourage active commitment among American young people, became one of the most popular government programs in recent history. Like other initiatives, the Peace Corps originated from Cold War preoccupations and a sense that Eisenhower had done too little to oppose communism abroad. During the campaign Kennedy proposed that the United States' "inadequate efforts" in confronting the Soviet Union "be supplemented by a Peace Corps." He believed that "our young men and women, dedicated to freedom, are fully capable of overcoming the efforts of Mr. Khrushchev's missionaries who are dedicated to undermining that freedom."

The day after his inauguration Kennedy asked his brother-in-law Sargent Shriver to organize the Peace Corps. By summer 1961 Shriver had laid the foundations, and Congress created the new organization in September. In the remaining twenty-seven months of the Kennedy

A Peace Corps volunteer in the West African nation of Mali helps with the planting. *Courtesy of the Peace Corps.*

administration about seven thousand Peace Corps volunteers, most under the age of twenty-five, went to work in forty-four countries in Asia, Africa, and Latin America. More than half worked in education, fighting adult illiteracy and teaching children. The rest helped in community development, public works, health care, and agricultural programs. The personal impact of their service lasted for generations. Most recipients of the aid admired the earnest young Americans, but, to the surprise of some Corps volunteers, did not choose to transform their culture into one based on the American model. Some Americans learned from the exchange of ideas the Peace Corps promoted. The more sophisticated volunteers returned home with heightened appreciation for cultures other than their own. Many came to question the simplistic anti-Communist assumptions that had created the Peace Corps in the first place. Instead of seeing the problems of poorer lands as reflections of competition between the United States and the Soviet Union, many returning volunteers believed that the United States should try to understand poorer countries in terms of their own culture and history.

The Kennedy administration also created plans for military action in the developing world should the gentler approaches of the Alliance for Progress and the Peace Corps fail in their nation-building role. The administration pressed the Pentagon to elevate experimental counterinsurgency fighters, called Special Forces units but popularly known as Green Berets, into a separate command. Kennedy admired these tough jungle fighters, and he traveled several times to Fort Bragg, North Carolina, to watch the Green Berets train. He saw Special Forces instructors swing from trees and demonstrate how to live off the land by eating snakes, lizards, and berries. The administration dispatched hundreds of these counterinsurgency fighters to Vietnam in 1961 to help the American-sponsored government of Ngo Dinh Diem suppress the growing Communist-nationalist insurgency (see Chapter 8).

In contrast to the Eisenhower administration's indifference toward nationalist movements in Africa, Kennedy took tentative steps toward advancing the aspirations of the newly independent states of Africa. The new assistant secretary of state for African affairs encouraged the black governments of Africa to believe that the Kennedy administration sympathized with their desires for economic development. Hundreds of Peace Corps volunteers served throughout the continent. In spite of these changes, however, Africa remained a relatively low priority in the Kennedy administration. Crises in Latin America, Europe, and Southeast Asia absorbed the bulk of the administration's attention. Moreover, Kennedy feared losing the support of conservatives at home if he openly backed African nationalist or progressive movements.

Where the administration did act decisively in Africa, it assisted conservative elements. In the former Belgian Congo (now called Zaire), for example, a nation that had been independent since mid-1960, the Kennedy administration spent two years trying to install an anti-Communist labor leader as head of the government. In the process, Secretary of State Dean Rusk ordered the CIA to block more radical candidates. The CIA bribed the Congolese legislature into electing Washington's choice, a move Rusk hailed as a "major Soviet defeat." The victory proved ephemeral, however, and the Congo sank into civil war. During this conflict the United Nations tried to arrange cease-fires and create stability, but Washington resented these efforts, fearful that they would interfere with American efforts to promote an anti-Communist faction. Even without American backing, the United Nations eventually suppressed the secession of the richest of the Congo's provinces.

Obsessive anticommunism and preoccupation with events elsewhere also interfered with American efforts to advance independence for Portugal's African colonies of Angola and Mozambique. At first the Kennedy administration backed a United Nations motion condemning Portuguese rule. Later, however, Portugal's dictator threatened to tear up the lease for American military bases on the Azores, islands in the mid-Atlantic that were controlled by Portugal. Portugal's friends in the United States, led by former secretary of state Dean Acheson, argued that the bases were vital outposts in the Cold War. Acheson charged Kennedy with misguided idealism in considering support for African independence movements that might have ties to the Soviet Union. Faced with such opposition, the Kennedy administration gradually dropped its support for self-determination and independence from European rule for the remaining colonies in Africa.

The Berlin Confrontation

In addition to challenging Fidel Castro and attempting to fend off further leftist gains in the Third World, the Kennedy administration also intensified direct American opposition to the Soviet Union. The frigidity in United States–Soviet relations that began with the U-2 incident and the collapse of the Paris summit in May 1960 continued throughout the first year of the new administration. Hoping to demonstrate his mastery of foreign affairs, Kennedy met Soviet Communist Party General Secretary Nikita Khrushchev at a hastily arranged summit conference in Vienna in June 1961. The meeting took place less than two months after the catastrophe at the Bag of Pigs. Although the American public had rallied around their young president after the Cuban debacle, Kennedy's standing abroad had suffered. Earlier reservations among world leaders regarding his youth and lack of experience in foreign affairs seemed to have been borne out by the fiasco in Cuba. Thus Kennedy went to Europe in June to reassure French president Charles de Gaulle that he could recover and also to impress Khrushchev with how tough he could be.

The stop in Paris buoyed the president. As the first lady charmed the aging President de Gaulle, Kennedy's knowledge of issues and his ability to speak clearly and cogently relieved French suspicions. A State Department official watching Jack and Jackie in Paris marveled, "My God, they looked beautiful." But in Vienna, instead of the get-acquainted session he expected to have with Khrushchev, the president found himself caught up in a dangerous crisis involving the future of Berlin.

The former capital of the Third Reich had been occupied by the four victorious allies (the United States, the Soviet Union, Great Britain, and France) since 1945. Emerging Cold War tensions had blocked progress on a formal peace settlement with Germany, leaving the future of Berlin unresolved. The city was divided into eastern and western sectors, and the entire municipality was completely surrounded by the German Democratic Republic (East Germany). Created by German Communists in 1949, East Germany maintained its capital in the part of Berlin controlled by the Soviet Union. The Western powers, however, refused to recognize the sovereignty of the German Democratic Republic or its control over East Berlin. The Federal Republic of Germany (West Germany), also established in 1949, had installed its capital in the quiet Rhine town of Bonn. Since its inception, West Germany had insisted that the two Germanies must eventually be reunited and that East Germany was a puppet of the Soviet Union. Eager for ways to put the Soviet Union on the defensive in Eastern Europe, the Western powers had retained their rights to supervise the affairs of Berlin.

At the Vienna summit, Khrushchev raised the issue of Berlin as a way of bolstering the sagging legitimacy of East Germany and the Communist party there. He had complained about the West's refusal to acknowledge East Germany's sovereignty at the Camp David summit with Eisenhower in September 1959, but the situation had persisted. In the interim, the East German government had pressed the Soviets to do something to boost its prestige. Now, at his meeting with Kennedy in Vienna, the Kremlin leader responded to these pleas by insisting that the victorious Second World War powers finally resolve the German problem by signing a peace treaty recognizing the legitimacy of East Germany and recognizing East Berlin as its capital. If no progress occurred soon, he threatened, he would sign a separate peace treaty with East Germany, ceding to that government control over land and air access to Berlin. Under such a treaty East Germany would be in a position to strangle West Berlin, because that city's economy depended on trade with the rest of West Germany, 120 miles away. The Western powers had been strongly committed to West Berlin's existence ever since they had airlifted supplies to the city in 1948. The loss of West Berlin, many feared, would erode faith in Washington's ability to defend other friendly areas challenged by the Soviet Union.

In addition to his tough stand on Berlin, Khrushchev surprised Kennedy by affirming Soviet support for what he called "wars of national liberation" in Southeast Asia and Latin America. Kennedy responded to Khrushchev's unexpected demands by expressing hopes for friendly relations with the Soviets, but he clearly had been caught off guard. A journalist who accompanied the president's party on the way back from the summit thought that Kennedy looked "tired and a bit used up" after the meeting. Robert Kennedy felt that failure to use American forces to crush Cuba had led Khrushchev to believe Kennedy would not be a strong president.

In the aftermath of the summit the United States came close to war with the Soviet Union over Berlin. Within hours after returning to the United States, Kennedy delivered a somber televised report on his encounter with Khrushchev. He told the public that meeting the Soviet leader was more frightening than reading his speeches. He explained that Khrushchev believed that "the tide of history was moving his way, that the revolution of rising people would eventually be a Communist revolution, and that the so-called wars of national revolution supported by the Kremlin would replace the old method of direct aggression and invasion."

Behind the scenes Kennedy prepared United States military forces for a showdown with the Soviets over Berlin. He recognized that Khrushchev had manufactured the Berlin crisis to demonstrate his own toughness to the Soviet military and his support for the East German government. Nevertheless, the United States behaved as if the crisis could turn into a war. To prevent the Soviets from making good on their threat to limit access to Berlin, Kennedy let them know that Washington no longer felt bound by pledges not to unloose a pre-emptive nuclear strike. He decided that Khrushchev "won't pay attention to words. He has to see you move."

On July 25 Kennedy further defied the Soviets with a bellicose speech. "If we do not meet our commitments to Berlin, where will we later stand?" he asked the American public. He reactivated some reserve units, which were to go immediately to Germany, and increased the armed forces by over 200,000 troops by doubling draft calls and dropping the exemption for married men. The next day he asked Congress for an additional $3.5 billion for military outlays. Included in that figure was $207 million more for civil defense—an amount that prompted morbid speculations among ordinary citizens about the likelihood of nuclear war. Seventy-one percent of those questioned in a Gallup poll agreed that Americans should fight their way into Berlin if access were blocked.

While American anxieties grew, in early August events in Germany changed the course of the crisis. The constant stream of refugees from East to West Germany became a flood in July. That month more than thirty thousand of the best-educated and most skilled East Germans left their dreary police state for the robust economic opportunities of the West.

The East German government responded to the exodus on the night of August 13 by beginning construction of a concrete and barbed-wire fence between East and West Berlin. Within three days the Berlin Wall became an almost impenetrable barrier preventing East Germans from fleeing to West Berlin. The wall would remain in existence for almost three decades, and hundreds of East Germans would be shot trying to escape through it or over it. Yet in 1961, despite the moral outrage in the West, construction of the Berlin Wall actually defused the crisis. It allowed the Soviets and East Germans to stop the flow of refugees without a diplomatic confrontation with the West. Khrushchev spoke no more about a separate peace treaty.

The wall caught the Kennedy administration completely by surprise. The construction of the wall demonstrated that the American military build-up had not intimidated the Communists. Nor had it left the United States the kind of flexible options the Kennedy administration had wanted. On the other hand, many of Kennedy's advisers privately accepted the logic of the solution. Although Kennedy drew cheers from hundreds of thousands when he spoke at the wall in June 1963, declaring "Ich bin ein Berliner" ("I am a Berliner"), it is clear that his Berlin policy did not present the flexible, skeptical approach to world politics that his intellectual supporters expected from him. Instead of more nuance, less reliance on threats of force, and a subtler appreciation of the complexity of world politics, Kennedy stressed simple, direct anti-Communist themes of the Cold War. He confronted the Soviets and Communists everywhere with military force, and then was surprised to discover that the military approach did not yield victory.

The Cuban Missile Crisis

The Kennedy administration adopted a more complex mixture of military threat and diplomatic bargaining during the Cuban missile crisis of October 1962, one of the most pivotal and most dangerous episodes of the Cold War. In the end, the United States forced the Soviet Union to remove missiles and manned bombers from Cuba, but for thirteen days, from October 15 to 28, 1962, the United States and the Soviet Union approached the brink of thermonuclear war.

In the summer of 1962 the Cubans believed that another American-sponsored invasion of their island might be launched at any time. Their fears were realistic: the Defense Department had already drafted plans for a second, larger attack on Cuba. In July, Raul Castro, brother of Cuba's president and the country's minister of defense, visited Moscow and pleaded for Soviet help against the CIA's Operation Mongoose. It was in response to this plea that Khrushchev supplied Cuba with intermediate-range nuclear missiles (IRBMs) and technicians to operate them. The missiles were capable of firing nuclear warheads at targets in the eastern third of the United States. By this time the Soviets had also stationed manned bombers and an estimated 10,000 to 40,000 troops in Cuba. (Khrushchev later claimed that "we stationed our armed forces on Cuban soil for one purpose only: to maintain the independence of the Cuban people and to prevent the invasion by an expeditionary mercenary force which the United States was then preparing to launch.")

Missiles offered little effective protection against the small-scale harassment of Operation Mongoose, but from the Kremlin's perspective the weapons served Soviet interests in several ways. They retaliated against the United States, which had stationed its own IRBMs in Turkey aimed at the Soviet Union. The weapons probably would make Castro feel safer and more grateful than ever for Moscow's help. Most of all, Khrushchev believed that sending the missiles to Cuba had little cost. They really had not increased the threat to the United States, a fact noted at the height of the crisis by Secretary of Defense McNamara. "A missile is a missile," he said during one meeting of the group of high-ranking officials assembled to discuss proper American action. "It makes no difference if you are killed by a missile fired from the Soviet Union or from Cuba." Applying the same reasoning, Khrushchev did not expect that the United States would risk world war to force the missiles out.

Khrushchev did not reckon with America's obsession with Cuba and with the emphasis that would be placed on the Cuba issue as the fall congressional campaigns approached their climax. Even before Kennedy knew the exact nature of the missile build-up, some Republicans, led by Senator Kenneth Keating of New York, repeating information given them by anti-Castro Cubans, claimed that the Soviets had installed IRBMs capable of launching a nuclear attack at any moment. On October 10, Keating declared that the Soviets in Cuba had the "power to hurl rockets into the American heartland." Fearful of a public outcry and of charges that Democrats were "soft," Congress passed a resolution promising "by whatever means may be necessary, including the use of arms . . . to prevent in Cuba the creation or use of an externally supported military capability endangering the security of the United States."

On the night of October 15 the CIA developed photographs taken by a U-2 spy plane that showed construction of a launching site for missiles with a range of about two thousand miles. The site was fifty miles southwest of Havana. The president saw the pictures at 9 o'clock the next morning and exploded that he had been "taken" by the Soviets, who had assured him in September that only defensive antiaircraft missiles would be situated in Cuba. The missiles had to be removed, he said. Otherwise, the United States would be vulnerable to attack, the public would be terrified, and "Ken Keating will probably be the next president of the United States."

An executive committee, made up of the administration's principal foreign and defense policy officials, met secretly over the next twelve days. Their task was to fashion tactics that would force the Soviets to back down and at the same time avoid igniting a world war. Robert

Kennedy chaired most of the meetings. The president attended some of them but usually kept quiet to allow uninhibited deliberations. From the beginning the participants agreed that the missiles presented an unacceptable threat. Moreover, allowing them to stay in Cuba would represent a humiliating setback for an administration committed to waging the Cold War more aggressively than the cautious Eisenhower had.

Although the advisers were united in their refusal to tolerate the missiles, they divided on tactics. One group, led by Secretary of Defense McNamara, favored a blockade, or quarantine, of Cuba to prevent the Soviets from sending in nuclear warheads for the missiles. If the blockade were successful, the analysts reasoned, the Soviets might remove the missiles. Another group, led by Chairman of the Joint Chiefs of Staff Maxwell Taylor and supported by former secretary of state Dean Acheson, thought that an outright air assault on airfields and radar installations supporting the missiles would be less risky than a blockade, which would directly defy Khrushchev, a volatile and unpredictable man. But air strikes carried their own risks. Bombs might kill Soviet technicians as well as Cuban troops, and Khrushchev might then retaliate. As the discussions proceeded, a majority of the executive committee began to endorse the idea of a quarantine of Cuba as a way of forcing the Soviets to remove the missiles. The committee eventually recommended such a blockade.

By Sunday, October 21, the Washington press corps was abuzz with speculation that something was about to happen. On Monday, the blockade began. One hundred eight United States Navy ships patrolled the Atlantic and Caribbean under orders to intercept and inspect the cargo of any vessel bound for Cuba to make certain that it was not carrying more offensive weapons. At 7 P.M. that evening Kennedy went on television to deliver one of the most somber speeches any president had given. He announced the existence of the CIA photographs, which showed that "a series of offensive missile sites is now in preparation on that imprisoned island." He claimed that the Soviet Union had transformed Cuba into a strategic base that threatened the United States and the rest of the Western Hemisphere. He reasoned that the Soviets' actions represented a psychological threat as much as a physical peril. The United States had to force their removal "if our courage and our commitments are ever to be trusted again by either friend or foe." He explained that the quarantine around Cuba would prevent the installation of warheads for the missiles already there.

Americans anxiously waited out the next several days. When the president received news that Soviet ships were steaming toward the navy's blockade line, the tension seemed too much to bear. Robert Kennedy remembered that his brother's face was drawn, his eyes pained. A few hours later, however, navy officials radioed that most of the Soviet vessels had stopped without challenging the blockade. Those that had proceeded through were tankers and passenger ships, which the navy had allowed to pass. As a symbolic gesture, sailors from two United States destroyers boarded a cargo ship chartered by the Soviets. Finding no forbidden weapons, the navy allowed the ship to pass through to Cuba.

The blockade succeeded in preventing movement of further weapons to Cuba because neither the Americans nor the Soviets wanted the situation to deteriorate into war. Quarantine did not, however, settle the matter of the missile sites already under construction. In a series of telegrams to Khrushchev and several secret face-to-face meetings in Washington between United States and Soviet representatives, Kennedy insisted that the Soviet leader demolish the sites and remove the missiles already in Cuba. In one telegram Khrushchev confirmed an offer made by his representative in Washington to remove the missiles and the manned bombers, but he also proposed a swap: he would act only if the United States removed its IRBMs from Turkey. Kennedy ignored the offer of an exchange, and he also did not respond when Khrushchev seemed to reverse himself in a later telegram. Instead, Kennedy repeated that the Soviet missiles had to be eliminated, and he focused on Moscow's initial offer to remove them. Faced with overwhelming American military might and astonished that the young American president would actually risk a nuclear war over a largely symbolic issue, Khrushchev capitulated. He wired Kennedy that he had instructed his officers to "discontinue construction of the . . . facilities, to dismantle them, and to return them to the Soviet Union."

It appeared to relieved Americans that Kennedy had won a great victory. In the aftermath the United States quietly implemented the exchange of missiles in Turkey for those in Cuba. Washington removed its IRBMs from Turkey and promised not to invade Cuba. In return, the Soviets took their manned bombers out of Cuba and pledged never to install offensive weapons on the island.

Fidel Castro felt betrayed by Khrushchev's surrender, and the American suspension of Operation Mongoose, a few days after the crisis subsided, did little to mollify him. He believed that the United States still wished him ill and that now he had no protector. His anxieties had a factual basis. The next spring the State Department created a secret Cuban Coordinating Committee to bring down Castro's government. In October 1963 the committee approved sabotage operations against twenty-two targets on the island.

During the crisis and for generations afterward, Kennedy won high praise for his grace under pressure and the way he sifted conflicting advice and made decisions. By skillful diplomatic initiatives that allowed Khrushchev room to maneuver, he forced the Soviet Union to retreat without a fight. The eventual removal of American missiles from Turkey offered the Soviets a small satisfaction. Yet Kennedy had risked nuclear war to show his toughness toward Khrushchev and Castro. The missiles in Cuba never threatened the security of the United States in the way the president indicated at the time. As his trusted aide Theodore Sorensen later observed, "the United States was already living under the shadow of Soviet missiles which could be launched from Soviet territory or submarines, and, therefore, there was no real change in our situation which required any kind of drastic action."

Détente with the Soviet Union

The extraordinary dangers of the Cuban missile crisis sobered both Americans and Soviets, encouraging officials and ordinary citizens in both countries to look for ways to avoid future confrontations. In the aftermath of the showdown, relations between the superpowers began to improve. In the next six months the two governments agreed to install a direct communications link, a teletype hotline, connecting the Kremlin with the White House. Kennedy abandoned some of his harsh anti-Communist rhetoric and urged other Americans to do the same. Americans and Soviets had a mutual interest in ending the arms race, the president declared. "We all breathe the same air. We all cherish our children's future."

In 1963 the United States and the Soviet Union signed a Limited Test Ban Treaty, ending the above-ground nuclear tests that had resumed in 1961. The treaty banned explosions of atomic devices in the atmosphere, in outer space, or under the ocean. The two sides promised to work on a more comprehensive treaty banning underground nuclear explosions as well.

In another three months, however, Kennedy was dead. Whether he would have made further progress on détente if he had lived is impossible to know.

SPACE EXPLORATION AND TECHNOLOGY

In April 1961, days before the defeat at the Bay of Pigs, a Soviet cosmonaut, Yuri Gagarin, became the first man to orbit the earth. Americans felt ashamed and frightened. The shock of the 1957 *Sputnik* launch was still fresh in everyone's mind. Members of the joint congressional committee on space demanded that the Kennedy administration make good on its campaign pledges to restore the country's flagging prestige. One member told the director of the National Aeronautics and Space Administration (NASA), "tell me how much money you need and this committee will authorize all you need." A newspaper concluded that Soviet successes in space had "cost the nation heavily in prestige" and that "neutral nations may come to believe that the wave of the future is Russian."

In this atmosphere, the Kennedy administration wanted to act quickly. NASA's own reports indicated that the United States led the Soviets in every area of space science; but in the tense aftermath of Gagarin's flight and the Bay of Pigs, Americans wanted definitive victories in the space race. The president told a press conference that he was tired of the United States being second best. He made Vice President Lyndon Johnson chairman of the Space Council and instructed him to look for ways of "beating the Russians." In late May, the president went before Congress to announce a goal of "landing a man on the moon, and returning him safely to earth, . . . before the decade is out."

To fulfill this lunar mission, Congress encouraged NASA to create the Apollo program. Johnson made certain that friends in Texas and nearby states received the lion's share of scientific and construction contracts for Apollo. The Apollo complex followed the contours of the Gulf of Mexico from Texas to Florida, providing jobs, income, and a stake in federal projects to traditionally poor but fast-growing southern states. Johnson called it a "second Reconstruction" for the area. In four years the number of workers employed directly by NASA grew from 6,000 to 60,000. Another 411,000 scientists, engineers, technicians, and clerical staff flocked to the region to work for private firms under contract to NASA.

Even as the Apollo scientists worked feverishly preparing for the moon shot, NASA tried to top Gagarin's orbital flight. In the summer of 1961 two astronauts, Alan Shepard and Virgil Grissom, made space flights lasting about fifteen minutes in capsules launched by Atlas ICBMs. Then, in February 1962, ten months after Gagarin's orbit, Marine Lieutenant Colonel John Glenn was strapped into *Friendship 7* and blasted into orbit. In the next five hours Glenn made three trips around the globe. His success buoyed Americans who had seen too many events that seemed to point to a decline in United States power, influence, and scientific preeminence. Glenn was a guest at the White House and enjoyed a ticker-tape parade down Manhattan's Broadway, the likes of which had not been seen since Charles Lindbergh returned in triumph after his solo flight from New York to Paris in 1927.

While the public's attention was focused on the race between the United States and the Soviet Union for preeminence in manned space flight, more significant competition took place between American and European electronic communications firms. In 1945 science fiction writer Arthur C. Clarke had predicted that global communications could be accomplished much more quickly if signals were beamed to satellites 23,000 miles above the Earth (a height that would perfectly match the satellites' speed to the rotation of the Earth, keeping them stationed over the same spot on the ground), then relayed back to the surface. By the early 1960s, American and European firms had devised the electronics to make such satellites possible; the Soviets had not. And only the United States possessed the booster rockets capable of launching these satellites. In 1962 and 1963 NASA boosters launched communications satellites owned by AT&T, RCA, and Hughes Aircraft. Congress took advantage of this lead by creating a government-chartered monopoly—the Communications Satellite Corporation (Comsat)—owned by private investors and the existing communications companies (AT&T, ITT, RCA, and Western Union). By 1965 most long-distance telephone calls were relayed by satellite. As the decade went on, more and more television pictures, bouncing off satellites, went virtually instantaneously around the globe.

NEW FRONTIERS AT HOME

In domestic affairs the Kennedy administration tried to shake the torpor of the Eisenhower years by promoting an expanding American economy. A policy of increasing income and stimulating the creation of new jobs fit neatly with Kennedy's style of encouraging consensus and downplaying ideological differences. Administration officials resisted endorsing efforts to redistribute wealth, fearing that such programs would provoke antagonism from wealthy and middle-class Americans. Similarly, the Kennedy administration initially paid more attention to the economic and social concerns of the white middle class than to the deprivation of the poor or the hardships endured by racial minorities.

As time went on, however, social pressures encouraged Kennedy to take another look at some of the flaws and inequities in American society. The president's curiosity and his wide reading eventually made him alert to the previously hidden crises of widespread poverty and the degradation of the natural environment. Kennedy and his principal advisers had come of age politically in the late 1940s and 1950s—a time when leaders were expected to stress the positive aspects of American society as the country confronted the Soviet Union in the Cold War. In the early 1960s, Americans looked more critically on their country's shortcomings. Kennedy had spoken eloquently during the 1960 presidential campaign of the need for vigorous action at home and abroad, and although he did not develop many specific details of a domestic program, it was to his credit that he grew intellectually as president. By late 1962 the Kennedy administration had begun to lay the foundations of major domestic reforms that would be undertaken by his successor.

Promoting Economic Growth

When Kennedy promised in 1960 to get the country moving again, to a large extent he was promising to engineer an economic recovery. Economic growth had averaged about 3 percent per year from 1953 to 1960, but the averages masked wild yearly swings, from declines of 2 percent in some years to growth of 5 percent in others. And although prices had increased little during the Eisenhower years, the country had suffered sharp recessions in 1954, 1958, and 1960. Rising unemployment had helped Kennedy win some important industrial states in the Midwest in the presidential election of 1960.

Initial efforts to bolster economic growth proved disappointing. The secretary of the treasury and the chairman of the Federal Reserve Board—both Republicans—resisted efforts to stimulate economic activity through government spending or lower interest rates. Although their conservatism sometimes frustrated Kennedy, his narrow election victory made him wary of direct challenges to the political right. "I need those two Republicans," he said. Rather than stimulate the economy directly, as liberal advisers urged, by creating government programs designed to aid depressed areas, the Kennedy administration decided that a safer course would be to adjust taxes to encourage private investment. In April 1961, Kennedy sent Congress a tax message urging elimination of "preferential treatment of various groups"—the complicated system of tax deductions or "loopholes" that had arisen since 1945. At the same time, he stated that business would invest more if Congress enacted investment tax credits to encourage businesses to modernize their plants and equipment. At first the proposed legislation received little attention because concern over the Bay of Pigs and heightened tensions with the Soviets preoccupied Congress. When Congress resumed work on the tax issue in the summer of 1963, it preserved most of the tax loopholes while giving more preferences to corporations than Kennedy had originally requested. The revised bill finally passed in the early months of the Johnson administration.

In 1962 Kennedy's cultivation of business nearly unraveled as the president engaged in a celebrated feud with Roger Blough, chairman of the board of the United States Steel Corporation. Blough offended Kennedy in April when he appeared to violate an agreement worked out by Secretary of Labor Arthur Goldberg. To forestall demands for a large wage increase, Goldberg had convinced the Steelworkers Union to accept a modest 3 percent wage hike and to agree not to strike. In return, Goldberg and Kennedy expected that a grateful U.S. Steel would hold the line on prices. Instead, Blough announced that his company would charge an additional $6 per ton, approximately 8 percent more than the previous rate. Goldberg, feeling betrayed, threatened to resign.

Faced with the loss of his labor secretary, Kennedy decided to force Blough to rescind the price increase. The Defense Department therefore refused to buy from U.S. Steel, purchasing instead from Inland Steel Company, which had not raised its prices. Within days, U.S. Steel surrendered and rolled back its prices. The price rollbacks and reports that the president had responded to the U.S. Steel situation by repeating one of his father's aphorisms—"all businessmen are sons of bitches"—provoked outrage among many Republicans and business people.

Overall, the economy began to improve in the Kennedy years, though the performance fell short of what had been promised. In contrast to the fluctuations of the 1950s, economic growth held to a steady 3 percent per year. Unemployment began to decline from 6 percent to under 5 percent. In 1961 and 1962, inflation, as measured by the consumer price index, also fell to the nearly negligible rate of 1 percent per year. Business leaders felt reassured by the Kennedy administration's resistance to calls for policies designed to redistribute wealth and income. The steel crisis of 1962 did provoke a sharp drop in the price of shares on the New York Stock Exchange, but this decline was short-lived. The administration's commitment to tax reduction as a means of stimulating economic growth cheered businesses, and the enactment of Kennedy's tax bill early in the Johnson administration helped spark a major economic boom. On the other hand, although the middle class and industrial workers experienced a rise in their standard of living, poor people in isolated rural areas and urban slums did not share in the affluence.

The Waning of the Suburban Ideal

In retrospect, the Eisenhower years represented the height of the post–Second World War love for suburbia. Although the movement of the white middle class to the suburbs continued throughout the 1960s, by the time of Kennedy's inauguration the mood had begun to change. Like the Beat writers and the other critics of 1950s conformity, more Americans became impatient with the ideal of the cozy suburban family home with its shining appliances, its late-model car, its breadwinning father and housewife mother. Not until later in the decade would this shift in attitude become great enough to spawn a full-scale counterculture, but the trend became apparent during Kennedy's administration.

For many men, according to magazines and television programs of the early 1960s, the domesticated crabgrass frontier had become a prison. As early as 1958, *Look* magazine portrayed the middle-class home as a female-dominated place from which men fled. While some men took refuge at the golf course, others followed the advice of *Playboy* publisher Hugh Hefner, avoiding the marriage trap altogether and enjoying, at least for a time, a swinging bachelorhood.

For middle-class white women too, the suburban vision was wearing thin. By this time, new opportunities were opening for women in corporate and service jobs. Although *Ladies' Home Journal* readers said that they still believed in marrying, having children, and dedicating their lives to home and family, more and more young women moved to the city in search of jobs, excitement, and independence. Magazines, newspapers' feature sections, popular novels, and television programs told the story of thousands of young, middle-class, single women who flocked to New York or Los Angeles, sharing apartments, holding down jobs as secretaries, stewardesses, editorial assistants, actresses, and models. Many thousands of young working-class women found employment as receptionists and waitresses.

The parents and older brothers and sisters of these new urbanites had retreated from the horrors of the Great Depression and the Second World War in search of a safe haven. They had married early and pledged themselves to mortgages and families, often in the suburbs. Now the members of a younger generation were ready to put off marriage and take more risks. The age of first marriage rose by about three years for both men and women in the early 1960s. Many young people had absorbed some of the latent rebelliousness in rock-'n'-roll music. They did not want to be safe; they wanted to be suave, swinging, sexy. Life was not a set of commitments but an adventure, full of new things to buy and new thrills to experience.

Technology helped these young adults grow more forthright in their pursuit of sex and fun. For some thirty years birth-control advocates had worked with scientists to develop a contraceptive pill. In May 1960 the effort succeeded when the first oral contraceptive, Enovid 7, was licensed for sale in the United States. More reliable and convenient than the diaphragm, the Pill, as the tablet was soon called, gave women an easy way to control their fertility. Though it originally presented hazards ranging from weight gain and nausea to blood clots and strokes, its enormous and rapid popularity testified to a sexual revolution in progress. Within five years the Pill accounted for 50 percent of contraceptives used in the country. Whether married or single, the millions of women who took the Pill were declaring their intention to pursue sex without procreation.

Hidden Crises: The Natural Environment and Poverty

While they were gradually changing their attitudes about suburban life and marriage, Americans also began to focus on two other concerns that would become increasingly important in later years: the quality of the physical environment and the fate of citizens who had been left out of the post–Second World War prosperity. Although his administration produced few concrete measures in these areas, Kennedy demonstrated some of his greatest adaptability and creativity in responding to the growing public awareness.

In 1962 science writer Rachel Carson published *Silent Spring*, a lengthy indictment of the damage done to the natural environment by the synthetic pesticide industry. Use of synthetic pesticides, a product of technology developed during the Second World War, had increased 400 percent between 1947 and 1962. The United States now sprayed 650 million pounds of deadly chemicals per year over farms, gardens, and homes. As Carson wrote, these poisons did not distinguish among their victims and "should not be called insecticides but biocides." The chemicals remained in the environment, filtering through the soil, entering the ground water, and eventually finding their way into the food chain, where they contaminated animals and humans alike.

Carson's work alarmed the public. Some 200,000 copies of her book were snatched up within a month, and members of Congress and newspapers were deluged with letters demanding federal action. Kennedy met Carson, and he instructed the President's Science Advisory Committee (PSAC) to study the pesticide problem. In May 1963, the PSAC reported that the chemicals had done extensive damage to fish, birds, and other wildlife and that traces of toxic chemicals had been found in humans. The report urged elimination of the use of toxic pesticides. Pesticide manufacturers opposed the recommendations, but seven years later the newly formed Environmental Protection Agency banned the use of DDT, the most harmful pesticide, in the United States.

At the same time that Americans worried about the harm artificial chemicals did to the natural world around them, concern grew about the plight of the fifth of the American population, approximately 25 million people, living in poverty. Largely forgotten since the end of the Second World War, the poorest Americans lived in decaying cities and remote rural areas. Eighty percent of them were white, the remainder ethnic minorities. The poorest of the poor were people over

The Second World War stimulated research and development of new chemicals and synthetic materials generally hailed as miracle products. But miracles do not come free. While other scientists pursued the perfection of plastics, biologist Rachel Carson (1907–1964) spent the war years working for the U.S. Bureau of Fisheries, writing conservation bulletins. In the years following, Rachel Carson would turn her talents to exposing the hazards of new industries spawned by wartime economic mobilization.

Rachel Carson

Unlike most government writers, Carson combined the insights of the scientist with the grace of a poet. As a child growing up in Pennsylvania, she had aspired to a literary career, publishing her first story at the age of ten. But in col-

the age of sixty-five living in rural areas. They had not shared the prosperity of the 1950s, and the Democrats of that decade and the early 1960s, heirs of the New Deal but eager for acceptance from the business community, had mostly ignored their needs. In 1962 Michael Harrington, a former social worker, challenged this indifference in his book *The Other America*. Harrington decried a vicious cycle in which "there are people in the affluent society who are poor because they are poor; and who stay poor because they are poor." He spoke directly to the country's leaders, explaining to them that "the fate of the poor hangs on the decisions of the better off."

Like *Silent Spring*, *The Other America* made a deep impression on intellectuals and opinion makers. Kennedy found *The Other America* a troubling critique of his own timid efforts to revitalize the American economy and make the excitement of the New Frontier reach every-

lege she was inspired to study biology, and she earned a master's in zoology at Johns Hopkins University. During summers in graduate school, she worked at the Marine Biology Laboratory in Woods Hole, Massachusetts, where she developed a lifelong passion for the sea and its environs.

"I have always wanted to write," Carson once told a friend, "but I know I don't have much imagination. Biology has given me something to write about. I will try in my writing to make animals in the woods and the waters where they live as alive and as meaningful to others as they are to me." She lived up to her aspirations.

After writing award-winning nature books, including *The Sea Around Us* (1951) and *The Edge of the Sea* (1955),

Carson wrote the book that would change the way Americans thought about their world. She had long been concerned about the indiscriminate use of one purported miracle product, the insecticide DDT, a substance both lethal and long-lasting. When a friend's private bird sanctuary was sprayed with DDT under a state-mandated mosquito-control program, Carson learned with horror of the mass killing of birds and other insects. In 1962, she published *Silent Spring*, an indictment not only of DDT but of numerous other materials with which humans poisoned the earth, air, and water. Despite vicious attempts by the chemical industry to discredit the book, *Silent Spring* spawned a worldwide outcry and gave birth to the modern environmental movement. ■

one in the country. He asked the chairman of the Council of Economic Advisers to develop plans for a more vigorous assault on poverty. Unfortunately, before a program was ready, Kennedy was murdered.

THE PUSH FOR CIVIL RIGHTS

The movement to end legal discrimination based on race reached its peak in the 1960s. African-Americans had mobilized against segregation for years, and by the 1960s their efforts commanded the attention of most white Americans, provoking a mixture of support and resistance. As public officials gradually realized how important it was to end legally sanctioned segregation, the Kennedy administration began to take steps to aid the effort.

The Stroke of a Pen

In 1961, fully six years after the Supreme Court had ruled that segregation in public schools had to end "with all deliberate speed," separation of the races remained a fact of life across the nation, especially in southern and border regions, including Washington, D.C. Not only were many public schools and universities closed to blacks, so were many public transportation vehicles, bathroom facilities, parks, and privately owned restaurants, motels and hotels, and lunch counters. The National Association for the Advancement of Colored People (NAACP), the most prominent of the black civil rights organizations, had sought to build on the victory in the landmark *Brown* v. *Board of Education* case by persuading the courts to order quicker desegregation and encouraging Congress to pass civil rights legislation protecting black voters. The NAACP desegregated some school districts and saw passage of a civil rights law in the late 1950s, but progress was painfully slow. As noted in Chapter 4, President Eisenhower did not speak out against racial discrimination, and he only belatedly ordered federal troops to Little Rock, Arkansas, in 1957 to ensure the safe admission of black students to that city's Central High School. The modest Civil Rights Act passed that year did not, as blacks had hoped, outlaw discrimination in public or privately owned accommodations. After the sit-in at a Greensboro, North Carolina, lunch counter in 1960, the sit-in movement spread, along with marches, demonstrations, and other protests against legally sanctioned discrimination. Many of these actions involved the newly formed Student Non-Violent Coordinating Committee (SNCC).

As a senator John Kennedy had taken few positions on racial discrimination. During the presidential campaign of 1960 he had become somewhat bolder, but he continued to walk a narrow line on civil rights, hoping to retain the support of traditional white southern Democrats while also winning the votes of blacks. He had refrained from endorsing new civil rights laws, but had condemned Eisenhower for his timidity in not putting the moral authority of the presidency on the side of victims of racial prejudice. The president, Kennedy said, could end discrimination in awarding public housing units "with the stroke of a pen," by signing an executive order. He promised that his protection of minorities would be more vigorous, and blacks believed that the Kennedy brothers' telephone calls on behalf of the jailed Martin Luther King, Jr., signaled sympathy with their cause.

At first, however, Kennedy's administration did little directly to advance civil rights. In particular, during 1961 Kennedy did not sign an executive order ending discrimination in public housing. By the end of the year the Congress on Racial Equality (CORE), a rival of the

NAACP that favored more militant action, sought to shame Kennedy into making good on his promise. CORE organized an "Ink for Jack" campaign, in which supporters of civil rights mailed thousands of ball-point pens to the White House. Kennedy resented the ridicule but eventually, in 1962, signed an executive order that outlawed racial discrimination in public housing.

The Freedom Rides

The "Ink for Jack" campaign represented only a small part of the civil rights effort. Many ordinary citizens believed that much more was required to achieve civil rights and that the government would not act unless pressured from below. By the spring of 1961 blacks and whites joined together in a campaign of civil disobedience to force the federal government to take a more aggressive stand. In early May, two busloads of blacks and whites left Washington, D.C., bound for New Orleans, with interim stops scheduled along the way throughout the South. Calling themselves Freedom Riders, the travelers challenged the state laws prohibiting mixed seating on interstate buses and requiring public accommodations along the way to maintain "whites only" and "colored only" facilities. In practice, such separation meant that nonwhites could not enter most restaurants or relieve themselves in most public rest rooms.

At first the Freedom Riders encountered icy stares from white people and found bus stations mysteriously closed when they arrived. This silent resistance was difficult enough; but when the travelers reached Alabama, their opponents proved much more dangerous. In Anniston, Alabama, a white mob attacked one bus with pipes, slashed the tires, and demanded that the Freedom Riders leave the bus. Although the local police escorted the bus and its passengers out of town, the gang continued its pursuit in cars. After the bus's tires went completely flat, the mob surrounded it, and someone threw a bomb through the window. When the Freedom Riders ran out of the bus, the mob beat them. One white Freedom Rider was punched in the face while others stomped on his chest until he lost consciousness. Even more brutal assaults occurred later in Birmingham. Although police knew that a mob waited for a second bus bearing other Freedom Riders, the officers provided no protection. After the second attack, the governor urged the Freedom Riders to "get out of Alabama as soon as possible."

This inexcusable refusal of local authorities to protect United States citizens goaded Kennedy into action. The violence had been photographed and shown in newspapers and on television, shocking many Americans. Scenes of the howling mob attacking unarmed Freedom Riders also offered a propaganda boost to the Soviet Union on the eve of the Vienna summit. The president, sickened by the sight of violence, ordered United States marshals to Alabama to protect the Freedom Riders, and the Justice Department enjoined racist organizations from further interference with the buses.

At the same time, the reluctance of the administration to take decisive action was evident. No matter how offensive were the attacks on the Freedom Riders, Washington officials remained reluctant to antagonize southern whites. Robert Kennedy asked for a "cooling off period" of a hundred days to let tempers subside. James Farmer, executive director of CORE, acidly replied, "We've been cooling off for 100 years. If we got any cooler we'd be in the deep freeze." Accordingly, CORE ignored advice to stop the demonstrations and continued to arrange Freedom Rides for the rest of the summer of 1961. Federal marshals offered protection against physical assaults on the buses or riders. At the same time Robert Kennedy sought unsuccessfully to persuade the Freedom Ride organizers that voter registration, rather than public demonstrations, would do more for the cause of civil rights.

The Showdown in Mississippi

Like many other white northerners, the Kennedy brothers gradually developed greater concern over racial discrimination as the demonstrations continued. They expressed their greatest commitment to civil rights in September 1962, during a confrontation with Mississippi Governor Ross Barnett over the enrollment of James Meredith, a black man, at the state's university in Oxford. Meredith, an air force veteran, had applied for admission to the University of Mississippi in January 1961. A high school graduate and resident of Mississippi, he was entitled to admission to the state university, but the university refused to enroll him. He appealed its decision in federal court, and on September 13, 1962, Supreme Court Justice Hugo Black, a native of Alabama and former member of the Ku Klux Klan, ordered the university to admit him. Mississippi's state legislature responded by making Governor Barnett a temporary registrar of the university. Playing to strong racist sentiments throughout the state, Barnett vowed not to surrender to "the evil and illegal forces of tyranny." He promised that Meredith would never register.

The president and attorney general spoke several times on the telephone to Barnett. For a while, it appeared that a compromise had been arranged: the governor would save face by resisting the federal marshals who had come to Oxford to escort Meredith into the university, but Meredith would be allowed to register later. That deal fell through, however, as hundreds of whites converged on the college town intent on chasing Meredith away. When Meredith and his escort of federal marshals finally reached the campus, over a thousand white demonstrators blocked their path, screaming "Go to Cuba, nigger lovers, go to Cuba!" They threw rocks and bottles at the line of marshals. Then members of the mob, now numbering over two thousand, opened fire with shotguns and rifles, killing an English reporter and wounding a marshal and a United States border patrolman.

In the midst of the violence, Kennedy addressed the nation. He spent more time calming the fears of white Mississippians than explaining the evils of racial discrimination. He appealed to that state's "great tradition of honor and courage, won on the field of battle." He urged white students, most of whom had not been involved in the demonstrations, to continue to stay on the sidelines, because the "eyes of the nation and the world are upon you and upon all of us." At the same time, Kennedy ordered 23,000 army troops to Oxford to quell the rioting and ensure that Meredith could enroll for classes and study in relative peace. Five hundred troops remained stationed in Oxford until Meredith graduated in June 1963. Martin Luther King, Jr., thought the Kennedy brothers had helped the cause of civil rights but did not fully appreciate how much work remained to be done. Kennedy's effort to compromise with Barnett particularly disturbed King. Such negotiations, he said, "made Negroes feel like pawns in a white man's power game."

The March on Washington

In 1963, Martin Luther King, Jr., sought to increase the momentum of the movement for civil rights. In May he helped organize demonstrations for the end of segregation in Birmingham, Alabama. The protesters found the perfect enemy in Birmingham's police commissioner, Eugene "Bull" Connor, whose beefy features and snarling demeanor made him seem a living caricature of a southern sheriff. Connor's police used clubs, dogs, and fire hoses to chase and arrest the demonstrators. Kennedy watched the police dogs in action on television with the rest of the country and confessed that the brutality made him sick. He later observed that "the civil rights movement should thank God for Bull Connor. He's helped it as much as Abraham Lincoln." The president dispatched the head of the Justice Department's civil rights division to Birmingham to try to work out an arrangement between King's demonstrators and business leaders that would permit desegregation of lunch counters, drinking fountains, and bathrooms. The president made several calls to the business leaders himself, and they finally agreed to his terms.

On June 10, during a national address focusing on civil rights, Kennedy acknowledged that the nation faced a moral crisis. He rejected the notion that the United States could be the land of the free "except for the Negroes." Reversing his earlier reluctance to request civil rights legislation, he announced that he would send Congress a major civil rights bill. The law would guarantee service to all Americans regardless of race in public accommodations—hotels, restaurants, theaters, retail stores, and similar establishments. Moreover, it would grant the federal government greater authority to pursue lawsuits against segregation in public education and increase the Justice Department's powers to protect the voting rights of racial minorities.

African-American leaders found Kennedy's commitment to legislation encouraging, but they wanted assurances that the president would follow through. To maintain pressure on Congress, several civil rights leaders revived the idea, first presented in 1941, of a March on Washington to promote civil rights. The Kennedy administration was not in favor of such a march. Already public opinion polls indicated that a plurality of voters thought the president was pushing integration too fast, and Kennedy worried about the political cost of endorsing the black push for equality.

The March on Washington went forward anyway on August 28, 1963. A crowd of about 300,000 people, mostly black but including all races, filled the mall facing the Lincoln Memorial. Led by folk singer Joan Baez, they sang the spiritual "We Shall Overcome," which had become the unofficial anthem of the civil rights movement. They heard other songs and listened to speeches. John Lewis, a leading Freedom Rider, prepared a militant address that was toned down a bit by march organizers before he delivered it.

The climax came when Martin Luther King, Jr., offered to the watching world an inspiring vision of the future. Although he had invoked these images many times before, much of white America was listening to him for the first time: "I have a dream that one day *all* God's children, black men and white men, Jews and Gentiles, Protestants and Catholics, will be able to join hands and sing in the words of the old Negro spiritual, 'Free at last! Free at last! Thank God Almighty, we are free at last!'" President Kennedy watched on television and told an aide in admiration, "He's damn good." But within three months Kennedy was dead, and the civil rights legislation advocated by the March on Washington needed the support of a new president.

ASSASSINATION

Kennedy's endorsement of civil rights during the fall of 1963 complicated his re-election chances in the South. As in 1960, a key state was Texas, where the Democrats feuded over policies and patronage.

Governor John Connally, leader of the conservative faction, opposed Kennedy's plans for a civil rights bill. The governor was not on speaking terms with the state's liberal senator, Ralph Yarborough, and both Connally and Yarborough distrusted Vice President Lyndon Johnson, whose shifting positions did not satisfy either liberals or conservatives. Seeking to bolster his own standing in his home state, Johnson persuaded several prominent national officeholders, including the president, to visit Texas in the fall.

When United Nations ambassador Adlai Stevenson spoke in Dallas in October, he encountered ugly demonstrations organized by vocal conservatives. Handbills appeared with pictures of Kennedy labeled "Wanted for Treason." The mob swarmed around Stevenson, someone hit him in the face with a sign, and only the protection of a police squad got him out of the hall safely. The attack on Stevenson was only the most recent in a series of violent protests against the administration. The Secret Service had compiled thirty-four credible threats on the president's life from the Dallas area since 1961. Many came from those who espoused extreme right-wing views, but the Secret Service also documented threats from leftists, anti-Castro Cubans, Puerto Rican nationalists, black militants, and several mentally disturbed individuals.

One month after Stevenson's encounter with the mob, Kennedy flew to San Antonio with Jacqueline on November 21 to begin a three-day swing through the Lone Star State. Johnson joined them later that day in Houston and the next day in Fort Worth, where the president addressed businessmen about the importance of Texas defense contractors to the nation's military strength. At 11:20 A.M. Air Force One took off from Fort Worth for the brief flight to Dallas. The presidential jet landed in Dallas at noon, and Governor Connally, his wife Nellie, and President and Mrs. Kennedy entered an open-air limousine for a trip downtown, where Kennedy was scheduled to speak before another business group. The motorcade route had been published days before to ensure the largest crowd possible. Thousands lined the route, and most were smiling, cheering, and waving. Mrs. Connally told the president, "You can't say Dallas doesn't love you." Kennedy replied, "That's obvious." Seconds later, at 12:33 P.M. November 22, three shots rang out. Two bullets hit the president; one passed through his throat and the other exploded through the back of his head. In shock, Mrs. Kennedy rose and climbed onto the rear hood of the car to retrieve part of the president's skull. The Secret Service agent who moved to shield her and guide her back into her seat heard her say, "I have brains in my hand." The motorcade raced to nearby Parkland Hospital, where Kennedy was pronounced dead at 1:00 P.M.

Later that afternoon, police arrested twenty-four-year-old Lee

Harvey Oswald in a movie theater. A Marine Corps veteran and lonely drifter, Oswald had recently returned from a long stay in the Soviet Union. He worked in the Texas Book Depository, the building from which the shots were fired. Oswald had flitted among political causes of the left and right, making it difficult for later investigators to determine his motives. He had contacted the Cuban embassy in Mexico City earlier in 1963, but the Cubans had refused to speak with him, fearing he was a provocateur sent by the CIA. To complicate matters further, Oswald had family ties to a Mafia member who had spoken of his desire to kill Kennedy in order to halt the Justice Department's investigations of organized crime.

The chances of ever discovering Oswald's true allegiances probably disappeared two days after the Kennedy assassination. That Sunday most Americans sat glued to television sets, watching hundreds of thousands of grief-stricken mourners file past a closed casket in the Capitol rotunda. When the networks cut away to the basement of the Dallas police station to show Oswald being escorted to another jail, millions of viewers saw nightclub owner Jack Ruby step out of a crowd and kill Oswald with a bullet to the abdomen.

In December President Johnson appointed a special commission, chaired by Chief Justice Earl Warren, to investigate the assassination. Less than a year later, the Warren Commission filed a report concluding that Oswald, acting alone, had killed Kennedy. The Warren Commission worked hastily, because it believed a speedy report would still rumors of a conspiracy. That did not happen. For years after the murder, many Americans, at times a majority, believed that a conspiracy was behind Kennedy's murder. The list of suspected conspirators was varied and shifting: extreme conservatives, the Mafia, the CIA, Fidel Castro, conservative Vietnamese, even Lyndon Johnson. In 1979 a House committee concluded that more than one person had fired shots at Kennedy's limousine, but FBI scientists rebutted the committee's findings. In the decades after the Warren Report, little tangible evidence came to light demonstrating that its conclusions were flawed.

The persistence of the belief that Kennedy died at the hands of conspirators represented an effort to make sense out of a shocking act that deeply shook many Americans' faith in their institutions. In the years following his death, other prominent figures fell to assassins, and shots were fired at presidents in 1975 and 1981. Within five years of that fateful November afternoon, Americans came to see their society as dangerous, violent, and led by people who lacked Kennedy's ability to inspire the nation. Many traced the beginning of the sense that their public institutions did not work properly to the day Kennedy died.

President Kennedy's casket is borne away from the Capitol en route to burial at Arlington National Cemetery. *John F. Kennedy Library.*

CONCLUSION

After his death, Americans quickly elevated John Kennedy to martyrdom. His optimism, wit, intelligence, and charm—all of which encouraged the feeling that American society could accomplish anything its people wanted—were snuffed out in an instant. He was only forty-six years old. Within six months of his murder, journalist Theodore White bestowed on his administration the name "Camelot." Popularized by the 1962 Broadway musical of that title, the term referred to the mythical kingdom of Arthur and the knights of the Round Table. In this view, Kennedy's 1,037-day administration represented a brief, shining moment during which the nation's political leaders spoke to the finest aspirations of Americans.

The reality was more complicated. Kennedy and his advisers had been formed by the experiences of the postwar world. They represented a new generation, nurtured by the Cold War, an activist government, and the military-industrial complex. Skeptical of ideology and serenely self-confident, officials of the Kennedy administration and their circle of friends believed problems could be mastered and managed. That was their strength, because it encouraged their curiosity about people, trends, and ideas. They learned from setbacks and mistakes, and by 1963 their skepticism even extended to the beliefs expressed in 1960 that the United States could vanquish the Soviet Union through sheer will power. Their self-confidence offered Americans hope.

Yet the style of cool self-reliance favored by Kennedy and his advisers also exposed weaknesses. Their resistance to emotion or passion stunted their ability to empathize with groups that had been excluded from the bounty of American society. In civil rights the Kennedy administration did more than its predecessor, but its principal steps came as a result of intense pressure and dramatic events that could not be ignored. On the questions of poverty and the environment, Kennedy took important first steps; whether his administration would have accomplished significantly more if he had lived longer, historians can only speculate. Overall, his domestic program reflected the politics of consensus, much like his predecessor's.

In foreign affairs he also continued an earlier trend, the reflexive anticommunism of the Cold War, but with a particularly aggressive twist. His propensity for tough confrontation with the Soviets led the world to the brink of nuclear holocaust. Only after the near-disaster of the Cuban missile crisis did he begin to move toward détente.

Advocates of the New Frontier had promised the country a new youth and vigor in the White House, and the Kennedy administration provided these qualities in abundance. It was less successful in offering new substance and new solutions. The burden of acting on many unsolved problems fell on Lyndon Johnson, a very different man who was suddenly elevated to the presidency. ■

F U R T H E R   R E A D I N G

On politics and policies in the Kennedy administration, see: Allan Matusow, *The Unraveling of America: A History of Liberalism in the 1960s* (1984); Herbert Parmet, *JFK: The Presidency of John F. Kennedy* (1983); Thomas C. Reeves, *A Question of Character: A Life of John F. Kennedy* (1991); Theodore Sorensen, *Kennedy* (1965); Arthur M. Schlesinger, Jr., *A Thousand Days* (1966) and *Robert F. Kennedy and His Times* (1978); Theodore H. White, *The Making of the President, 1960* (1961); David Knapp and Kenneth Polk, *Scouting the War on Poverty: Social Reform Politics in the Kennedy Administration* (1971). On space policy, see: Walter A. McDougall, . . . *The Heavens and the Earth: A Political History of the Space Age* (1985). On civil rights, see: Taylor Branch, *Parting the Waters: Amer-*

ica in the King Years, 1954–1963 (1988); David Garrow, Bearing the Cross: Martin Luther King, Jr. and the Southern Christian Leadership Conference (1986). On foreign policy, see: Thomas Paterson, ed., Kennedy's Quest for Victory: American Foreign Policy, 1961–1963 (1989); Michael Beschloss, The Crisis Years: Kennedy and Khrushchev 1960–1963 (1991); Montague Kern, Patricia W. Levering, and Ralph B. Levering, The Kennedy Crises: The Press, the Presidency and Foreign Policy (1983); Richard Walton, Cold War and Counter-revolution (1972); John Lewis Gaddis, Strategies of Containment (1981); Thomas Schoenbaum, Waging Peace and War: Dean Rusk in the Truman, Kennedy and Johnson Years (1988); Trumbull Higgins, The Perfect Failure: Kennedy, Eisenhower and the Bay of Pigs (1987); Richard D. Mahoney, JFK: Ordeal in Africa (1983).

7

Lyndon Johnson's American Dream

Michael Harrington's *The Other America*, his 1962 best-selling critique of economic inequalities in contemporary society, helped spark renewed concern for the problems of poor Americans. By the early 1960s many middle-class Americans believed that the apparent prosperity of the postwar years masked serious flaws in their society. They wanted something better and more uplifting, even if they were uncertain what that might be. As president, Lyndon Johnson acknowledged the widespread desire to distribute the benefits of affluence more evenly to those left behind. He himself had witnessed deprivation firsthand during the Great Depression and was strongly moved to erase it. Addressing Congress in support of the 1965 Voting Rights Act, he recalled the poverty of the rural school in which he had taught in 1928: "My students were poor and they often came to class without breakfast, hungry. They knew even in their youth the pain of injustice. . . . Somehow you never forget what poverty and hatred can do when you see its scars in the hopeful face of a young child." He had not expected to be in a position to do much about the problem, but now that he had the chance, he said, "I mean to use it. . . . I mean to be the president who educated young children . . . who helped to feed the hungry . . . who helped the poor to find their own way."

But Johnson was a man of many contradictions. He came to political maturity in the 1930s as a New Dealer; but as a veteran of rough Texas politics, he learned to fit his opinions to the currents of the times, often shelving his commitment to the poor in order to serve the interests of the richest and most reactionary factions in the Lone Star State. In his thirty years of public life before assuming the presidency, Johnson, a huge man, six feet four inches tall, big-handed, with an enormous face and an overbearing presence, had charmed, flattered, and bullied his way to the top. Rivals and political foes feared, resented, and eventually hated his abusive manner and the twists and turns of his political opinions.

As president, Johnson articulated a vision of a Great Society that included such goals as an end to racial discrimination, equal opportunity for all classes, and the elimination of poverty and inadequate health care. The scale of the undertaking was so vast that disappointments were almost inevitable. By 1966 his carefully cultivated political consensus began to erode under the weight of the war in Vietnam and a white backlash against government efforts on behalf of African-Americans. Unfortunately, the shortcomings of Johnson's character and personality made him an unsuitable leader for such times of political division. Along with Congress, he turned his back on the Great

Society he had eloquently evoked in 1964. He withdrew on occasion into passivity and paranoia. Finally he left Washington in 1969 a nearly broken man, his dream of a Great Society largely unfulfilled.

LYNDON JOHNSON: THE POLITICIAN AND THE PRESIDENT

Johnson told his biographer, Doris Kearns, about a recurring dream from his childhood: "He would see himself sitting absolutely still, in a big, straight chair. In the dream, the chair stood in the middle of the great, open plains. A stampede of cattle was coming toward him. He tried to move, but he could not. He cried out again and again for his mother, but no one came." According to Kearns, Johnson longed for the approval of his refined mother and the world of books, culture, and morality she had brought to his frontier Texas home. However, he had also absorbed his brutal and alcoholic father's contempt for "dreamy thinkers whose idealism led inevitably to ruin and collapse." Thus, throughout Johnson's life, an urge for morality, justice, and culture warred with the bullying side of his nature, learned from his father. The inner conflict created the fear of paralysis evidenced in the dream, along with a corresponding compulsion "to move, keep control, stay in charge."

Johnson's Political Background

Johnson went to Washington in 1931, in the depths of the depression, as an aide to a newly elected Texas congressman who let Johnson run his office and decide how he should vote. Within months, the young aide was congressman in everything but name. When Franklin Roosevelt electrified the country and roused Congress with his First Hundred Days of legislation, Johnson persuaded his boss to drop his natural conservatism and support the New Deal. Two years later, in 1935, Johnson used the contacts he had made among the Texas congressional delegation to win appointment as the Texas director of the newly created National Youth Administration. He worked from 7 A.M. till midnight or later, canvassing the state by car, plane, and phone.

In 1937 Johnson won a special election to Congress as a New Dealer. Billboards showed him shaking hands with President Roosevelt. He took the courageous step for a Texas politician of courting black and Mexican-American voters, telling the black leaders of Austin that, if they supported him, he would someday back voting rights and perhaps a hot lunch program.

Back in Washington he mastered the rules of the House and faithfully voted for Roosevelt's programs. He also became a superlative fundraiser for the Democratic party. By 1948 Johnson wanted to be a senator. In keeping with the Truman administration's ambivalent attitude toward New Deal reforms, he tempered his earlier populism, ran a viciously negative campaign as a moderate against a conservative former governor, stuffed ballot boxes in some key precincts, and won the election by 187 votes. From there he rose fast, becoming the majority leader in the Senate by 1954.

For the remaining six years of the Eisenhower administration Johnson ran the Senate as no one had before him. He perfected the "treatment," a combination of flattery, cajolery, threats, empathy, blackmail, and horse trading to get his way. His relations with the Eisenhower administration were excellent, but liberal Democrats came to distrust him as a Texas wheeler-dealer. His role in managing the civil rights bill of 1957, when he eliminated references to equal treatment in public accommodations, and the Landrum-Griffin Labor Reform Act of 1958, when he sided with business interests against labor unions, offended liberals as the work of a compromiser and closet reactionary.

Johnson toyed with the idea of a presidential run in 1960, but he hesitated. By the time he declared his candidacy, the week before the Democratic convention, it was too late. John Kennedy had virtually assured himself the nomination, and Johnson's attacks on his inexperience did nothing to endear him to Kennedy's intimate advisers. After the convention nominated John Kennedy, Robert Kennedy, the candidate's brother and campaign manager, relayed word to Johnson that Kennedy wanted him as vice president. Johnson dithered and liberals expressed their dismay. But eventually the senator from Texas, reviled by many of Kennedy's most ardent backers as a southwestern political fixer and manipulator, became the Democratic vice-presidential candidate, with the job of carrying Texas and as much of the South as possible.

Johnson defended Kennedy's religion among Texas Protestant voters, who feared a Catholic conspiracy. That won votes. But winning the affection of Kennedy's inner circle proved more difficult. "When am I going to appear with Jack?" Johnson used to ask his staff. One of his aides believed that "some members of the Kennedy staff felt that Johnson wasn't as *refined* as Kennedy, and maybe they shouldn't appear together." Eventually the two shared a stage, but Johnson continued to feel uneasy among Kennedy's advisers.

Johnson helped Kennedy carry Texas by 46,000 votes. His presence on the ticket also contributed to victories in much of the lower South and New Mexico. His service during the campaign temporarily warmed the hearts of Kennedy's inner circle, but for Johnson it proved a curiously joyless victory. One of the supporters who gathered with him to watch returns in an Austin hotel thought he "looked as if he'd lost his last friend on earth. . . . [H]e didn't want to be vice president."

That foreboding was justified. When there were important decisions to make—on Berlin, Cuba, Vietnam, taxes, civil rights—Kennedy and his inner circle made them without consulting Johnson. Instead, the vice president chaired the newly created National Aeronautics and Space Council and a Presidential Committee on Equal Opportunity. In 1961 these seemed remote outposts of the New Frontier. They were, however, important proving grounds for Johnson's own presidency.

Johnson found solace in traveling. When he left Washington for trips to Africa, Europe, and Southeast Asia, he was like a man released from jail. He relished plunging into crowds and making flamboyant gestures, such as calling President Ngo Dinh Diem of South Vietnam the "Winston Churchill of Southeast Asia" and inviting a Pakistani camel driver to visit him in the United States. Photographers and American television crews loved the performances, but State Department officials were concerned about the consequences of Johnson's off-the-cuff utterances and grumbled that he was only a corny, ignorant Texan, unsuitable to represent the United States.

By 1963 even the delights of travel had paled. Kennedy's staff could not stand Johnson, and he knew it. Once the master of the Senate, he withdrew from his old colleagues. The criminal conviction of Bobby Baker, onetime secretary to the Democratic Senate majority and a man Johnson likened to the son he had never had, revived charges that the vice president had illegally made millions while presiding over the Senate. In the summer of 1963 some of Kennedy's aides openly expressed the wish that Johnson—"Uncle Corn Pone," they called him—would voluntarily step down from the Democratic ticket in 1964. In early November 1963 a dispirited Johnson confided to an aide that his future as vice president seemed bleak, and mused about a new career. It came in an unexpected way. On November 22 Kennedy was shot in Dallas, on a trip arranged to stanch the endemic feuding among Texas Democrats.

Johnson Becomes President

Johnson took the oath of office aboard Air Force One with a stricken Mrs. Kennedy looking on, her clothes splattered with the blood of the slain president. As soon as Johnson returned to the Executive Office Building, he asked for two pieces of White House stationery. A shocked Kennedy aide who provided the paper groaned, "The body not cold yet—and he's grabbing for the President's stationery." He did not know that Johnson intended his first letters as president to be handwritten notes to Caroline and John, Jr., the murdered president's children. Thereafter, Kennedy's supporters continued to view Johnson as a usurper, unworthy of the office held by a fallen hero.

Unlike Harry Truman, who became president following the death of Roosevelt in 1945, Johnson asked his predecessor's staff to stay, but it was nearly impossible to forge harmony between Kennedy's circle and the assistants who had served Johnson in the vice presidency. One Johnson aide recalled that the Kennedy staff "snickered and sniped, half performed their tasks, engaged in petty sabotage, busily plotted for the day when a Kennedy and they could take back the White House." For their part, Johnson's aides remembered the slights of the vice-presidential years and vowed to show what they could do. A Johnson staff member from the vice-presidential days remarked that Kennedy started a number of initiatives but could not get the bills passed. "There are those who say he would have done it if he'd had more time, but I don't think so. I don't think he knew or cared very passionately. Johnson did."

Initially Johnson rose above pettiness. He was a whirlwind, putting in a double day: work from 7 A.M. to 2 P.M., followed by lunch and a short nap, then a fresh beginning at 4 P.M. continuing till midnight or 2 A.M. Immediately after Kennedy's funeral he addressed Congress, calling for unity, consensus, and a continuance of Kennedy's vision. He would not permit lawmakers to adjourn for a Christmas break without tackling some important trade legislation, and he even had the White House track down vacationing lawmakers and bring them back to the Capitol. He also asked for early passage of the civil rights bill that Kennedy had supported.

A few weeks later he stood before Congress to deliver his State of the Union message. In it he pledged to continue Kennedy's program, but with a distinctly activist and legislative stamp. Along with civil rights, he emphasized the issue of poverty. "This administration today, here and now, declares unconditional war on poverty in America. . . . It will not be a short or easy struggle, but we shall not rest until that war is won."

The Civil Rights Act of 1964

After his stirring words to Congress, Johnson plunged immediately into the effort to pass the civil rights bill, which had languished in the Senate in the fall. The provisions outlawing segregation in privately owned restaurants, overnight lodgings, and transportation were anathema to southern senators, who complained that they interfered with property rights. Nevertheless, in 1964 the House of Representatives, with the assistance of the Johnson administration, added two additional titles to the bill. One empowered the Justice Department to intervene and file suit where a person's civil rights

Making good on the promises of the Kennedy administration, President Johnson signs the Civil Rights Act on July 2, 1964. *Lyndon Baines Johnson Presidential Library.*

had been violated. The other created a Fair Employment Practices Commission, with the power to outlaw racially based discrimination in hiring and promotion in firms employing more than one hundred people. The House also added provisions in Title VII forbidding discrimination based on sex as well as race; these later had a dramatic impact in reducing discrimination against women. The bill sailed through the House on February 10 by a vote of 290 to 130. Representatives explained their votes as a tribute to John Kennedy.

Things were more difficult in the Senate, however, where southerners and other opponents of the law threatened to defeat it with a filibuster. Johnson went to work with his legendary "treatment" to force senators to vote for cloture (an end to debate) in order to bring the legislation to a vote on the floor. With the aid of Senator Hubert Humphrey, he wooed Everett Dirksen, the Republican minority leader. Dirksen became convinced that the party of Abraham Lincoln could not afford to be responsible for the defeat of civil rights legislation. Finally, two and one-half months after the filibuster began, the Senate passed the law on July 2, 1964, by a vote of 73 to 27. This Civil Rights Act banned discrimination based on race in public accommodations—restaurants, theaters, hotels, motels, and rooming houses. State-supported institutions such as schools, libraries, parks, playgrounds, and swimming pools could no longer be segregated. The Justice Department now had the right to intervene to protect those whose civil rights had been violated. The Fair Employment Practices Commission could bring suit to end discrimination in private employment.

Johnson looked forward to more civil rights legislation after the election of 1964. He told the new attorney general, Nicholas deB. Katzenbach, who took over in the summer of 1964 after Robert Kennedy resigned, "I want you to write me the goddamndest, toughest voting rights act that you can devise."

The Election of 1964

Before submitting a voting rights bill, however, Johnson wanted to be elected president in his own right. He hoped not just to win, but to demolish the Republican nominee. As "president of all the people," he could emerge from the shadow of John Kennedy's legacy. His task appeared to be made easier by recent changes within the Republican party. Ever since the New Deal, Republicans had, during presidential elections, suppressed their most conservative inclinations and nominated nonideological centrist candidates who they hoped could win. Whatever else they believed in, Republican presidential candidates Dewey, Eisenhower, and Nixon all accepted the basic premise of the New Deal: the federal government had a role to play in managing social and economic affairs. Conservatives complained but were regularly outvoted at convention time.

Now conservative Republicans such as Senate Minority Leader Everett Dirksen, House Minority Leader Charles Halleck of Indiana, old supporters of Senator Robert Taft, members of far-right groups like the John Birch Society, and newcomers to the Republican party, among them former president of the Screen Actors Guild Ronald Reagan, had had enough. Enraged by what they considered the arrogance of "the Eastern establishment," they railed against "Wall Street," "international finance," "Madison Avenue," "Harvard," *The New York Herald Tribune*, and "Ivy League prep schools." One advocate of this New Right, Phyllis Schlafly, complained that "a small group of secret king-makers, using hidden persuaders and psychological warfare techniques, manipulated the Republican national convention to nominate candidates who had side-stepped or suppressed the key issues." Never again, vowed conservatives, who promised to nominate one of their own for the presidency.

For their part, eastern Republicans such as Governors Nelson Rockefeller of New York and William Scranton of Pennsylvania were contemptuous of the backwardness and ignorance of people they called "primitives"—midwestern, southern, and western politicians who had never valued the role of government in modern society. Charges flew, and as Theodore White, the chronicler of elections from 1960 to 1980, observed, "by the fall of 1963 this bitterness within the party had reached a condition of morbid intensity." Fighting for the nomination were Governor Rockefeller of New York, a man whose pedigree and career proclaimed "Eastern establishment," and Senator Barry Goldwater of Arizona, standard-bearer for the new conservatives.

Goldwater was a product of the Sunbelt, the fast-growing region of the southern, southwestern, and far western states that had gained wealth, power, and population since the Second World War. He grew up in Phoenix, a city that had swelled from 30,000 inhabitants in his youth to over 800,000 in the metropolitan area by the 1960s. Freed, they hoped, from the crowding, dirt, crime, and zoning regulations of older cities, the new residents of the Sunbelt adopted new political habits. They distrusted government, especially the federal government, which controlled hundreds of thousands of acres of land in western states, and they resented easterners. Few publicly acknowledged that federally funded roads, dams, and electric power grids had made the Sunbelt's growth possible.

Goldwater crystallized these animosities in his 1964 campaign. He sealed his nomination for the presidency with a narrow win over Governor Rockefeller in the California primary in early June. Rockefeller's divorce and subsequent remarriage to a much younger woman, followed by the birth of their child on the eve of the primary, doomed his campaign. For the six weeks before the Republican national convention opened in San Francisco, terrified moderates within the party looked for an alternative to Goldwater. Finding none, they hoped he would tone down his more inflammatory rhetoric.

Goldwater quickly dashed these hopes that he would run as a moderate. His speech accepting the Republican nomination gave no quarter. He decried "bureaucratic make work" programs, "violence in our streets, corruption in our highest offices, aimlessness among our young, anxiety among our elderly." He brushed aside thoughts of compromise: "Those who do not care for our cause, we don't expect to enter our ranks." Finally, he read the moderates out of the Republican party with his famous pronouncement, "Extremism in the defense of liberty is no vice! . . . Moderation in the pursuit of justice is no virtue!"

In Goldwater, Lyndon Johnson found the perfect opponent. Choosing Senator Hubert Humphrey of Minnesota as his running mate, Johnson campaigned as a unifier and a builder of consensus.

In contrast to Goldwater, who seemed sharp, divisive, and ultimately frightening to the public, Johnson looked conciliatory. The Arizona senator alarmed voters with talk of permitting battlefield commanders to have control over nuclear weapons. His proposals to make Social Security private and to sell the Tennessee Valley Authority confirmed suspicions that he was a radical "kook" who wanted to dismantle the most popular programs of the New Deal.

Democrats capitalized on these fears with a series of hard-hitting television advertisements designed to portray Goldwater as untrustworthy. The most famous of the TV spots showed a young girl counting the petals on a daisy. Then the image of the girl faded as a solemn announcer counted backward from 10. The sight of a mushroom cloud arising from an atomic explosion filled the screen, and Johnson was heard in a voiceover: "[T]hese are the stakes. We must learn to love one another, or surely we shall die." Johnson refused to debate Goldwater, letting the TV ads carry the message of his campaign with devastating effect.

Johnson summarized his goals as "to move not only toward the rich society and the powerful society, but upward to the Great Society." He defined the Great Society as "abundance and liberty for all . . . an end to poverty and racial injustice . . . a place where every child can find knowledge to enrich his mind and to enlarge his talents." Johnson drew huge and responsive crowds throughout the country, and a wide consensus of voting blocs supported his campaign: whites and blacks, business and labor, liberals and moderates, Democrats and Republicans.

Johnson's victory on election day represented the greatest presidential landslide since the previous century. He carried forty-four states and 60.7 percent of the popular vote (see map). Nevertheless, there were some ominous signs in the vote distribution. Throughout the South—the base of the Democrats' success in presidential elections since 1932—Johnson received only 51 percent of the white vote, a signal that his party's control of that region had slipped. In fact, this would be the last time that a Democratic presidential candidate would win a majority of the southern white vote. In the Deep South Goldwater's conservative appeal was especially effective. In addition to his native Arizona, Goldwater carried South Carolina, Georgia, Alabama, Mississippi, and Louisiana. White voters there were enraged by the Civil Rights Act, and grave fissures had appeared in the New Deal coalition.

But in the aftermath of Johnson's dramatic victory it was hard to predict any difficulties for the Democrats. In the Johnson landslide the Democratic party added 37 House seats and 2 more seats in the Senate. When the new Congress convened in January 1965, House Democrats outnumbered Republicans by 295 to 140. In the Senate

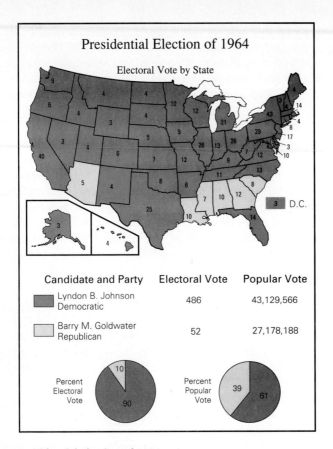

Presidential Election of 1964

Electoral Vote by State

Candidate and Party	Electoral Vote	Popular Vote
Lyndon B. Johnson Democratic	486	43,129,566
Barry M. Goldwater Republican	52	27,178,188

Percent Electoral Vote: 90 / 10

Percent Popular Vote: 61 / 39

Presidential Election of 1964

there were 68 Democrats and only 32 Republicans. Not since Franklin Roosevelt's election of 1936 had either party assembled such massive majorities in Congress. Johnson appeared to have the congressional backing he needed to use the government to revitalize American society.

THE GREAT SOCIETY: SUCCESSES AND DISAPPOINTMENTS

Spurred by Lyndon Johnson, Congress in 1965 and 1966 enacted the most sweeping social reform legislation since the New Deal. Designed to win the War on Poverty and create the Great Society that Johnson had promised, these programs enhanced the role of the federal government in promoting health, economic welfare, education,

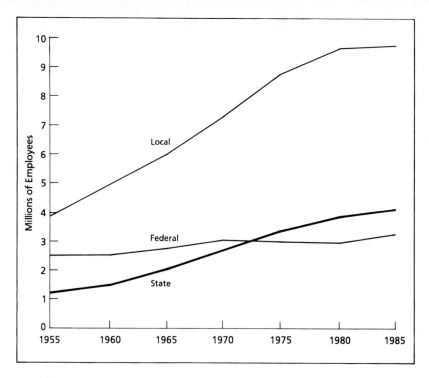

Growth of Government, 1955–1985

urban renewal, and civil rights. Johnson's ambitious new programs not only increased government spending but also required a greater number of bureaucrats to administer them; in contrast to the 1930s and 1940s, however, the greatest need for new government employees was at the state and local levels (see figure). Some of the new programs were very successful, but others left a legacy of disappointment and controversy.

Medical Programs

In 1965, heeding the president's call to improve access to health care for elderly Americans, Congress enacted the ambitious program known as Medicare. Fulfilling a pledge first made by the Truman administration, the legislation created compulsory hospital insurance for Americans over 65 who were covered by Social Security. Congress also included voluntary insurance to cover doctors' fees. A complementary program, known as Medicaid, was enacted in 1966; it allowed participating states to receive matching federal grants to pay the medical bills of welfare recipients or the medically indigent of all ages. After a slow start, all states but Arizona agreed to participate in Medicaid.

Medicare and Medicaid substantially reduced the gap in medical treatment between the poor and the rich. By 1970 the proportion of Americans who had never visited a physician fell from 19 percent to 8 percent. Prenatal visits by pregnant women increased, helping to lower the infant mortality rate by 33 percent. Among African-Americans the change in infant mortality was especially noticeable, declining from 40 deaths per 1,000 births in 1965 to 30.9 in 1970 and 24.2 in 1975.

One problem, however, was the cost of these medical programs, which far outstripped the original estimates. To overcome resistance from the American Medical Association, the administration had agreed that medical services would continue to be provided by private doctors chosen by the patients themselves. Moreover, under the government programs, hospitals and physicians would receive "reasonable and customary" payments for their services. When the inflation rate climbed during the late 1960s, medical charges rose even faster. Partly as a result, the annual cost of the government programs soared from $3.4 billion to $18 billion in ten years.

Antipoverty Legislation

In 1965 Congress passed a spectacular array of measures directly aimed at reducing poverty. For example, it created a food stamp program, providing food assistance to people whose income fell below a level set by the government. The program worked well. Ten years after its enactment, research indicated that government efforts were "almost fully effective in reducing flagrant malnutrition."

Because Johnson considered education a key in the War on Poverty, Congress created the Head Start program to reach preschool children of impoverished families. This too was successful. Later studies revealed that Head Start children gained substantial advantages over poor children who did not enroll. They gained an average of 7 points on IQ tests and were half as likely as nonparticipants to repeat grades in school or be assigned to special education classes. Long-term studies suggested that, as teenagers and young adults, "Head Starters" completed more years of school, worked more steadily, and engaged in less criminal behavior. Congress also provided aid to secondary and higher education through grants to school districts with large numbers of poor children and scholarships and loans to college students.

Another step was the creation of a Job Corps, patterned on the Civilian Conservation Corps of the New Deal. The corps employed

The misery of poverty, largely ignored by middle-class Americans since the Second World War, once more captured the conscience of the nation in the 1960s as Congress and the president vowed to win a War on Poverty. *Wide World Photos.*

100,000 young men and women from poor families. Eight years later, in 1973, Congress expanded the Jobs Corps with the Comprehensive Employment and Training Act (CETA). CETA provided on-the-job training for the chronically unemployed. If they could not find positions with private employers, the government created full-time public service jobs for them. Although costly, this program met its goals. A study conducted in Baltimore concluded that 94 percent of CETA graduates had jobs five years after they participated. Their wages increased too, so that they earned 89 percent of the average wage in their city.

To aid urban renewal, Congress created a Model Cities program, but this was less successful. Originally the planners hoped to concentrate on a few targets, mobilize local leadership, and try a variety of methods to invigorate dying communities. If a few cities could be revitalized, their slums renewed, and their residents provided with useful work, these demonstration projects would act as beacons for other places. As first conceived, Model Cities would work with six communities. By the time it got under way in 1966, however, the number had grown to over a hundred, while the amount of money appropriated remained the same. Powerful members of Congress channeled the lion's share of the benefits to their own districts. As one urban affairs expert put it, "the law provided too little money for too many cities" and so could not even approach the vision of its founders. The program recognized the need to treat urban blight as a complex social as well as physical problem; but the decision to alter it from a demonstration project to a national effort—and at the same time starve its funding—doomed the program from the start.

To oversee the distribution of grants for the Great Society programs, Congress established cabinet departments of housing and urban development and of transportation. The money made a start in reducing the grinding poverty in urban centers, but Congress did not fund the new departments fully in the 1965 to 1967 period. By the time the Johnson administration asked for a new housing act in 1968, much of the enthusiasm for the Great Society had ebbed. The costs of the Vietnam War made Congress reluctant to fund programs designed to replace the dilapidated tenements housing the urban poor. Consequently, the president's proposals to build 6 million low-income dwellings were slashed to less than one-quarter of their original ambitions.

Funding problems also bedeviled the Office of Economic Opportunity (OEO), headed by Sargent Shriver. The OEO was supposed to coordinate the activities of several other agencies: the Job Corps; VISTA (Volunteers in Service to America), a domestic version of the Peace Corps; and the Community Action Programs (CAPs). Despite Shriver's best efforts, OEO had to oversee a vast proliferation of programs with little increase in funds. There were organizational troubles as well. One task of the CAPs was to encourage recipients of government assistance to participate in administering the programs; the goal was defined as "maximum feasible participation." But this goal provoked clashes between traditional local authorities and the neighborhood activists assisted by OEO. In Philadelphia, for example, poor, mostly black residents elected representatives to twelve local boards overseeing the allocation of OEO funds. Major James Tate, a white man who objected to the authority of the local boards, appointed a prominent black supporter, Samuel L. Evans, as the real power in Philadelphia's Antipoverty Action Committee. One OEO inspector lamented that Evans converted Philadelphia community action into "the maximum feasible participation of Sam Evans." Similarly, in Atlanta, the business community ran the poverty program and refused to let poor people sit on the board.

Such conflicts undermined congressional support for funding OEO after 1966. The difficulties of the CAPs typified some larger problems of the Great Society. The Johnson administration was trying to satisfy irreconcilable groups and factions. Johnson truly believed in consensus, a legacy of his congressional career, and thought the way to foster it was to satisfy competing interest groups. But the antipoverty programs, as historian Allen Matusow observed, "sought to appease vested interests that had resisted reform or occasioned the need for it in the first place."

Despite the many flaws of the antipoverty programs and the resistance they elicited, they had some real successes. They helped reduce the number of people living in poverty by about 50 percent in a decade. The standards of medical care improved dramatically. Education reached impoverished rural and urban children in ways that had never before seemed possible. Job training provided a means of breaking out of the cycle of poverty. If the Johnson administration could not vanquish poverty in the United States, it at least gave many Americans an opportunity for a better life.

The Voting Rights Act

On the issue of voting rights, demonstrations in Alabama helped set the stage for congressional action. For six weeks in early 1965, Martin Luther King, Jr., and the Student Non-Violent Coordinating Committee organized demonstrations for the right to vote in Selma. When marching demonstrators were clubbed and tear-gassed by Alabama state troopers, the scenes of violence appeared on national television news. The president sent an emissary to King to arrange a tactical deal that helped to prevent further violence. For the culminating march to Montgomery, thousands of people flew in.

Johnson seized the opportunity to deliver a moving speech before Congress, calling for a voting rights act. If African-Americans did not gain equal voting rights, Johnson declared, "we will have failed as a people and a nation." He asked his fellow citizens to "overcome the crippling legacy of bigotry and injustice"; and, adopting the slogan of the civil rights leaders, he insisted that "we *shall* overcome."

Congress obliged with the Voting Rights Act of 1965, an attempt to ensure the right to the ballot by empowering the Justice Department directly to register voters in localities where discrimination appeared to exist. If fewer than 50 percent of the citizens of a district voted or were registered to vote in 1964, the act assumed that discrimination existed. Literacy tests for voter registration were also outlawed. Over the next three years the law resulted in the registration of an additional 740,000 black voters (see map). The overall rate of African-American registration rose from 31 percent to 57 percent. The law eventually produced an increase in black officeholders as well. The number of blacks in the House of Representatives rose from five

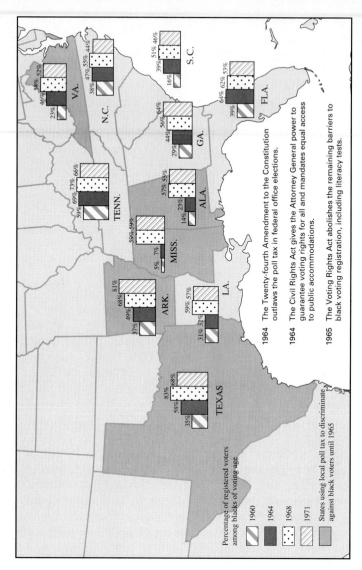

Black Voting Rights, 1960–1971 *Source: Reprinted by permission of Greenwood Publishing Group, Inc., Westport, CT, from Voter Mobilization and the Politics of Race: The South and Universal Suffrage, 1952–1984, by Harold W. Stanley. Copyright © 1987 by Harold W. Stanley and published in 1987 by Praeger Publishers.*

1964   The Twenty-fourth Amendment to the Constitution outlaws the poll tax in federal office elections.

1964   The Civil Rights Act gives the Attorney General power to guarantee voting rights for all and mandates equal access to public accommodations.

1965   The Voting Rights Act abolishes the remaining barriers to black voting registration, including literacy tests.

Percentage of registered voters among blacks of voting age

1960
1964
1968
1971
States using local poll tax to discriminate against black voters until 1965

to seventeen in the next twenty years, and the total number of black public officials increased from 103 to 3,503. In the 1970s and 1980s, African-Americans were elected to the mayor's office in cities ranging from Newark, New Jersey, and Gary, Indiana, to New York, Los Angeles, and Chicago. The change was even more startling in the Deep South: Atlanta, New Orleans, Birmingham, and even Selma selected black mayors.

Benefits for the Middle Classes

Although the Great Society is remembered for its attempt to solve problems resulting from poverty and discrimination, it also sponsored programs that appealed directly to the American middle classes. By funding the arts and humanities, promoting nonprofit television, and helping to clean up the nation's highways, the Johnson administration produced benefits that even the wealthy could appreciate.

To fulfill his promise to "build a richer life of mind and spirit," Johnson sent Congress legislation to create a National Foundation for the Arts and Humanities, a smaller version of the National Science Foundation, which had been in existence since 1950. The new foundation consisted of two divisions: the National Endowment for the Arts (NEA) and the National Endowment for the Humanities (NEH). A Federal Council on the Arts and Humanities was created to supervise the activities of the two endowments. Both directly and through state councils, each endowment offered grants to individuals and to institutions such as universities, museums, ballet companies, and local arts centers.

The NEA and NEH sponsored conferences, produced films, offered fellowships for scholars and creative writers, and funded university courses and new curricula. In the beginning the endowments grew slowly, from a budget of $2.5 million apiece in 1966 to $6.05 million each in 1970. But ten years later each endowment was spending $106 million per year. Together the NEA and NEH had a vast effect on arts and humanities throughout the nation. The proliferation of local theater and dance companies, the development of many young artists and writers, the expansion of scholarly research—all of these were aided by NEA and NEH programs.

Television, too, came under the aegis of the Great Society. To improve programming, Congress in 1967 reserved 242 channels of the TV spectrum for local public, noncommercial TV stations across the country. More significantly, for the first time it provided direct federal subsidies for public programming with the creation of the Corporation for Public Broadcasting (CPB). Governed by a presidentially appointed board, the CPB distributed grants to produce TV shows and helped with the operating budgets of local public TV stations. Programs such as "Sesame Street" for preschoolers and "Nova," a highly regarded series on science, received support from the CPB. Five years later, in 1972, Congress added National Public Radio, a network of noncommercial radio stations. Those stations, and some programs aired on them, received some support from the CPB.

To a certain extent the Great Society also demonstrated a concern for the natural environment. Congress enacted legislation mandating improvement in air and water quality. Moreover, the president's wife, Lady Bird Johnson, took the lead in fostering a more pleasant environment along the nation's roads. Deathly afraid of air travel, she commuted between Texas and Washington on the nation's highway system and was appalled by the junkyards and unsightly billboards lining the roads. She pressed her husband to endorse a Highway Beautification Act, which was passed in 1965. By increasing the federal contribution to interstate highway construction from 85 percent to 90 percent for states that joined the program, the law encouraged states to ban billboards and remove roadside junkyards. Because the law allowed billboard companies wide latitude in devising regulations, it resulted in only minor improvements; nevertheless, this early gesture toward beautification, along with the air and water measures, set the stage for stronger environmental laws in the 1970s.

Immigration Reform

In addition to its efforts to improve the lives of American citizens, Johnson's Great Society had a profound influence on immigration from other countries. In the 1960s the immigration quota system dating from the 1920s was still in effect. In setting limits on entry for many foreign nationals, the quotas reflected deep-rooted racial and ethnic biases. Hoping to erase the stigma of this system, President Kennedy had presented Congress with an immigration-reform package that abolished discrimination against potential immigrants on the basis of national origin.

The bill languished until Kennedy's death, but Johnson resubmitted it to the reform-minded Congress in 1965. When it passed that year, it seemed a moderate modification of America's immigration policy. It phased out the national quota system over the next three years. After 1968 there was a total of 290,000 slots available yearly, divided into 170,000 visas for immigrants from the Eastern Hemisphere and 120,000 for immigrants from the Western Hemisphere. In place of quotas based on national origins, Congress substituted seven categories, or priorities, for immigration. Highest priority was assigned to immigrants in two categories: those holding desirable job skills and those with close relatives (parents and siblings) in the United States. Political refugees were assigned to the seventh category, accounting for the smallest number of visas. This category was largely overlooked at the time but generated controversy later.

Because the law gave first preference to family members, Congress expected that the new mix of immigrants would closely resemble the old mix. Such speculation made sense in the context of the times, but it proved profoundly wrong in predicting the contours of the next wave of immigration to the United States. For a few years after the law came into effect, it worked as planned, with immigrants from southern and eastern Europe coming in large numbers. More than 20,000 Italians entered the United States each year after 1968, and Greek and Portuguese immigration also recorded sizable increases.

By the middle of the 1970s, however, the patterns changed because of worldwide economic trends. Job prospects brightened in Europe and dimmed in the United States, making America less attractive. European immigrants made up 45 percent of the total in 1965 but only 15 percent in the late 1970s. During this period immigration from Asia, the Caribbean countries, and South America shot up. Residents of these lands found the American economy extraordinarily attractive compared with the meager opportunities in their own countries. This was especially true for educated people whose skills qualified them for special preference under the terms of the 1965 law.

Congress did not envision that family reunification provisions would create an immigration chain. For example, a Korean student would come to the United States. After completing college, he had skills qualifying him for immigration preference and, within a short time, could use the family reunification preference to bring over his parents, spouse, and children. As these relatives attained citizenship, they became eligible to sponsor additional relatives. As time passed, an even wider kinship network evolved that created additional opportunities to sponsor the immigration of relatives.

This pattern, which held true for immigrants from nearly every Asian nation except Japan, did not cause an influx of poverty. In fact, many Asian immigrants came from upper-class and highly educated backgrounds. Within a decade of the new law's passage, tens of thousands of Asian physicians and nurses entered the United States. They became the foundation of medical care in many public hospitals. So many professionals emigrated from South Korea, Taiwan, the Philippines, the British colony of Hong Kong, India, and Pakistan that officials in these countries sometimes accused the United States of promoting a "brain drain" of talent needed for progress at home.

By 1979 the seven leading suppliers of immigrants to the United States were all non-European:

Mexico	52,000
Philippines	41,300
China, Taiwan, Hong Kong	30,180
Korea	29,348
Jamaica	19,714
India	19,708
Dominican Republic	17,519

If refugees and undocumented aliens are included, Asia and Latin America provided the overwhelming majority of new Americans.

THE ECONOMY IN THE JOHNSON YEARS

In the early years of his administration, when the Great Society programs were springing into bloom, Johnson's domestic reforms were bolstered by the greatest peacetime economic boom since the end of the Second World War. The effort to apply Keynesian strategies—adjusting government spending to encourage employment and growth and dampen inflation—seemed to work. Unemployment fell to 3.7 percent of the labor force, its lowest level since the Korean War. Economic activity, as measured by changes in the gross national product, grew over 4 percent per year from 1964 to 1966. Government expenditures and receipts were in rough balance for these years.

The boom hastened the rise of the Sunbelt. Spending for the military and for space exploration continued to flow to the states of the South, Southwest, and West. California consolidated its position as the premier defense contracting state, while Texas surpassed New York as the second. By the end of the 1960s federal payrolls accounted for $10 billion per year in the ten states of the Sunbelt, double the amount in all other states combined.

Other businesses grew most rapidly in the Sunbelt. For example, the oil industry, long headquartered in the Northeast, began to relocate to Texas, Oklahoma, and California. Getty, Union, Occidental, and Signal Oil Companies, all based in Los Angeles, grew to prominence. Phillips Petroleum of Bartlesville, Oklahoma, and Tenneco, in Houston, challenged New York–based companies such as Mobil and Texaco.

The sixties also saw an explosion in banking in the Sunbelt. North Carolina National Bank grew the fastest and earned the most money of any bank in the country. San Francisco's Bank of America became the largest in the country, with hundreds of branches serving retail customers. Alert to consumer trends, it promoted its credit card, Bankamericard, among the middle class. In 1965 four big Chicago banks started MasterCard; two years later four California banks created Master Charge. Ads urged participants to use their plastic cards to purchase everyday items—gasoline, clothing, food, television sets, lawn mowers. Card issuers made money three ways: charging interest to purchasers who did not repay their balances within a grace period; collecting a fee from merchants who accepted the cards; and franchising the Bankamericards, MasterCards, and Master Charge cards for other banks to issue throughout the country. Eventually Bank of America sold shares of its credit card business to a consortium of other banks and changed the name of the card to VISA, and Master Charge merged with MasterCard, retaining the latter name.

Sunbelt banks also took the lead in developing bank holding companies, financial concerns that bought small local banks. The new entities, among them the United Bank of Los Angeles, Valley National Bank of Phoenix, and Columbia Savings and Loan of Los Angeles, had assets of over a billion dollars each. They were able to arrange loans for large real estate or industrial development programs that earlier would have had to rely on major Wall Street firms for financing.

Nevertheless, Wall Street was not suffering. The New York stock market enjoyed its greatest growth since the 1920s in the period 1963 to 1966, with prices more than doubling in those years. One effect of this bull market was the development of industrial conglomerates. Audacious deal makers, often from the Sunbelt, arranged for one firm to buy another in an unrelated product area. The parts of the resulting merged enterprise had little to do with one another economically, but the balance sheets showed increased profits. As if to emphasize the company rather than the product, the combined firms took names that had little intrinsic meaning. American Tobacco became American Brands. Ling Temco Vought became LTV. Some of the marriages joined highly unlikely partners. Litton Shipyards, renamed Litton Industries, acquired the Stouffer food company; the renamed LTV, a defense contractor, bought the Wilson meat-packing corporation.

But the tendency to celebrate the economic boom was premature. By 1966 the growing war in Vietnam (see Chapter 8) had unleashed unexpected and uncontrollable inflation. The inflation rate began to fluctuate between 2.5 percent and 4 percent per year. For people accustomed to the many years of price stability since the Korean War, this was a frightening prospect. Keynesians explained the price rise as a result of too much business demand in the wake of the war in

Vietnam. They urged the president to raise taxes in 1966 in order to pay for the war and stem the inflation. Johnson refused, fearing that if he emphasized the need to pay war bills, conservatives would force him to squeeze his Great Society budget. Liberals too would criticize him when they saw how much the war hurt the reform effort. The administration did monitor price and wage increases and establish guideposts for business and labor to follow. Yet it had little success in rolling back those increases it considered excessive.

Interest rates soared in 1966. Banks began paying more than 5.5 percent for passbook accounts, more than savings and loan institutions were legally permitted to offer. Thereafter, owners of savings and loans lobbied Congress to relax the ceilings on what they could pay depositors. Rates on government securities, consistently below 3 percent in previous years, rose to 6 percent. The credit crunch, as it was called, also sent the stock market sprawling in 1966. All of this was supposed to slow the rise in prices, but it did not. In 1966 and 1967 prices rose by more than 4 percent per year; in 1968 inflation hit 6 percent.

Inflation hurt pensioners living on fixed incomes and small savers whose interests rates were kept low by regulation. But in the beginning it helped poor people who had obtained jobs in the boom, because wages for marginal workers rose faster than those of skilled workers. Businesses lost to inflation as higher wages reduced profits, from 10.6 percent of the nation's income in 1966 to 7.2 percent in 1970. Inflation also took its toll internationally. Since 1945, the dollar had been the standard currency of international trade. As prices rose in the United States, European holders of dollars began redeeming their paper currency for gold. The United States Treasury obliged, but by 1968 the $20 billion gold reserves of the United States represented less than one-third of the dollars held by foreigners.

What seemed worst about inflation was its persistence and its tendency to rise over time. A 3 percent rate of inflation might be tolerable if it went no higher. In the last years of the Johnson administration, however, the annual rate of inflation rose steadily, discouraging savings, making long-term investment difficult, and souring the public on further costly programs to aid the poor.

THE SUPREME COURT AND CIVIL LIBERTIES

While Lyndon Johnson promoted his Great Society, the Supreme Court was engaged in other sorts of liberal reform. Still led by Chief Justice Earl Warren, the Court expanded on its work of the 1950s, protecting the rights of individuals, altering criminal law, and regulating national and state voting systems.

Together, Presidents Johnson and Kennedy appointed four justices to the Supreme Court. Byron White, named by Kennedy, became one of the more conservative members. But Arthur Goldberg (1962–1965), Abe Fortas (1965–1969), and Thurgood Marshall (1967–1991) joined with Warren, Hugo Black, William O. Douglas, and William Brennan to consolidate the Court's liberal majority.

Defining the First Amendment

While acknowledging that the freedoms of speech, assembly, press, and religion guaranteed by the First Amendment sometimes had to be balanced against other interests, the Court's liberal majority required the government to show a compelling need to restrict liberty. If it could not, citizens' freedoms could not be abridged.

In *Bond* v. *Floyd* (1966), for example, the Court ruled that the Georgia House of Representatives could not refuse to seat an elected representative of the people, even though he expressed admiration for those who had opposed conscription for the war in Vietnam. A unanimous court held that neither public officials nor private citizens could be punished for opinions that did not violate the law. The Court also offered protection to "symbolic speech." In *Tinker* v. *Des Moines School District* (1969), the Court ruled that students could not be expelled for wearing black arm bands protesting the war in Vietnam. Writing for the majority, Justice Fortas argued that students did not lose their rights when they entered a schoolroom.

In *New York Times* v. *Sullivan* (1964), the Court loosened the restraints on what news media could write or broadcast about well-known figures. The Court ruled that public officials could not win a judgment of libel against a publication merely because a statement was untrue. Only "recklessly false statements" made with "actual malice" were covered by the libel laws. Justice Brennan held that "even a false statement may be deemed to make a valuable contribution to public debate."

Nothing produced more public debate and more confusion on the Court than its efforts to define obscenity. From 1957 to 1968 the Court decided thirteen obscenity cases in fifty-five separate opinions. It never did satisfactorily resolve the question of what was obscene and what latitude the government had in restricting such material. Justice Brennan thought he had found an answer in *Roth* v. *United States* (1957), when he observed that expressions containing "the slightest redeeming social importance" could be protected by the First Amendment. The Court agreed that government could regulate as obscene material that which "the average person, applying contemporary community standards," would regard as appealing "to prurient interests." For the next decade the Court tried to write rules determining what material fit that mold. It failed to do so, acknowledging that the process had to be subjective. Obscenity would remain a controversial issue for subsequent Courts. The Warren Burger Court (1969–1986) changed the definition of obscene material from "utterly without redeeming social value" to "lacking serious literary, artistic, political or social value." This definition permitted more government regulation but was no more successful than the earlier definition in creating a universally accepted standard.

The Warren Court won praise from civil libertarians and stirred opposition from traditionalists with a series of decisions interpreting the First Amendment's ban on the establishment of religion. In *Engel v. Vitale* (1962), the Court banned states and localities from instituting prayers in public schools. Justice Black, writing for the majority, said "it is no part of the business of government to compose official prayers for any group of American people." The decision provoked fury from some southerners. One member of Congress complained that "they put the Negroes in the schools, and now they have driven God out." Over the next several years the Court ruled that schools could not require devotional reading of the Bible. The justices also revived memories of the famous 1925 "Monkey Trial" of John Scopes in Tennessee when they struck down an Arkansas law requiring the teaching of "creation science" as a valid alternative to the theory of evolution. Such a law, the Court decided, was an unconstitutional attempt to establish a state religion.

Conservatives denounced these cases as examples of excessive judicial lawmaking, and to a substantial minority of Christians the Court's rulings were highly offensive. From 1963 through the mid-1980s, opponents of the rulings tried to pass constitutional amendments permitting prayers or Bible reading in public schools. Although these efforts failed, they were a key element in the conservative tide that rose in the 1970s. Many religiously observant men and women who had once voted Democratic became ardent supporters of Ronald Reagan and the Republicans by 1980.

Criminal Procedure

The Court also expanded the meaning of the rights of citizens accused of crimes and set new procedural standards for law enforcement officers. In *Mapp* v. *Ohio* (1961), the Court forced all states to conform to the exclusionary rule, which held that evidence gathered outside the specific terms of a search warrant could not be used against a defendant. In another landmark case, *Gideon* v. *Wainwright* (1963), the Court observed that Clarence Earl Gideon, a man who had spent over half of his adult life in jail or prison, had never had a lawyer to defend him. The decision affirmed that a "fair trial" meant a right to qualified legal counsel. All states that had convicted defendants without lawyers in felony cases had to retry them. If a defendant could not afford an attorney, the state had to provide one.

In a more controversial, 5-to-4 ruling in *Miranda* v. *Arizona* (1966), the Warren Court gave new meaning to the Fifth Amendment's ban against self-incrimination. Ernesto Miranda, when arrested for burglary in Phoenix, had been coerced into confessing by police, who told him that if he remained quiet judges would sentence him harshly. In its opinion on this case, the Warren Court set standards for police to follow when arresting suspects. Accused persons had to be informed in clear language (later called the Miranda warnings) that they had a right to remain silent and that anything they said could be used against them in a court. Police officers had to tell suspects that they had a right to a lawyer and that, if they could not afford to hire one, legal counsel would be provided free by the state.

The Right to Privacy

The right to privacy was also enhanced under the Warren Court. In 1965 the Court struck down an 1879 Connecticut law prohibiting the use of any contraceptive device and penalizing anyone giving advice on birth control. The law had long been ignored, but Planned Parenthood managed to bring a test case. In *Griswold* v. *Connecticut*, Justice Douglas held that the state's ban on contraception violated long-established rights of privacy. Although such a right was not specified in the Constitution, Douglas inferred it from other rights that were specified. Three other justices, Brennan, Goldberg, and Warren, concurred but were troubled by what they saw as Douglas's invention of a new right. Instead, they relied on the rarely used Ninth Amendment, which reserves to the people rights not enumerated elsewhere in the Bill of Rights. They argued that the right of privacy was ancient, older than the Constitution, and that the framers intended to incorporate it through the Ninth Amendment. One of the Court's liberals, Hugo Black, dissented. Black considered himself a strict constructionist, and he could find no specific right of privacy contained in the Constitution. Black's reservations made an impression on some legal scholars, but the popular reaction to the *Griswold* decision was highly favorable, because few people wanted state intrusion into the bedroom.

Voting: One Person, One Vote

The Court also helped set rules for elections, making them more representative and democratic. In *Baker* v. *Carr* (1962), the Court overruled earlier precedents and declared that it and lower courts could decide if the boundaries of state legislative districts were fair. In many states, legislatures had not reapportioned the districts for decades. Rural districts often contained fewer than one-fifth the population of their urban or suburban counterparts. City dwellers complained but were reminded that the U.S. Senate also did not represent voters in proportion to their numbers. After *Baker* v. *Carr*, the underrepresented voters had a wedge with which to sue. They based their appeals on the simple rule of "one person, one vote," and the Court agreed with them. In *Gray* v. *Sanders* (1963), Douglas outlawed a complicated Georgia system of awarding county "units" to candidates for statewide office. The units were based in part on considerations other than population, a practice Douglas said violated the equal protection clause of the Fourteenth Amendment.

The next year the Court decided six apportionment cases involving the state legislatures of Alabama, Colorado, Delaware, New York, Maryland, and Virginia. Chief Justice Warren held that no standard other than "one person, one vote" was acceptable in determining legislative districts. He ordered lower courts to supervise reapportionment to make certain districts were equal in population. He wrote that "the weight of a citizen's vote cannot be made to depend on where he lives."

The End of the Warren Court

By 1968 Earl Warren had been chief justice for fifteen years. He was seventy-seven years old and had presided over some of the most far-reaching decisions in the Court's history. In March of that year Lyndon Johnson announced that he would not seek re-election. Because Warren wanted Johnson to have the opportunity to appoint a chief justice, he told the president that he intended to resign as soon as his successor could be confirmed. A White House aide reported that the chief justice wanted Johnson "to appoint as his successor someone who felt as Justice Warren did." The president needed little prodding, for he had a candidate in mind—Abe Fortas. An associate justice since 1965, Fortas was a long-time friend who had continued to give Johnson political advice after his appointment to the Court in 1965, often violating the tradition of judicial impartiality. During those three years, Fortas had become a stalwart member of Warren's liberal majority.

Fortas's nomination faced immediate difficulties in the Senate. Democrats still had a majority, but Republicans used a number of delaying tactics throughout the summer. They expected Richard Nixon to win the upcoming presidential election and wanted him to appoint the chief justice. Fortas's support for the Vietnam War, as well as his intimate ties to the now-unpopular Johnson, made him unattractive to some Democrats as well. During the confirmation hearings the Senate Judiciary Committee learned that Fortas had received $15,000 for teaching some summer law courses; the money had been raised from men who might have cases before the Court. Faced with charges of cronyism, Fortas asked Johnson to withdraw his nomination in October. Warren remained chief justice until 1969, when President Nixon named Warren Burger, a conservative federal judge from Minneapolis, to replace him. Fortas remained an associate justice until the spring of 1969, when further scandal forced him to resign. While on the Court, he had received $20,000 per year from a foundation underwritten by a man who had been convicted of securities violations. Rather than face impeachment, Fortas stepped down.

The end of the Warren Court marked the conclusion of a sixteen-year epoch of expansion of the rights of individuals and curtailment of arbitrary government power. At the beginning of this period, the Court had outlawed segregation in public schools; by the end it had expanded the First Amendment's coverage in ways affecting the daily lives of most Americans. It had validated the growing pluralism in American life. Yet that endorsement of social changes came at substantial cost to the Court's authority in following years. Traditionalists who bemoaned the very pluralism the Court had affirmed attacked the justices' work. Over the next twenty years, conservatives gained advantages by deriding what they characterized as the social engineering and judicial activism of the Warren Court. While the subsequent Burger and Rehnquist Courts did not reverse most of the decisions of the Warren years, they curtailed many of the applications.

DECLINE OF THE GREAT SOCIETY

Despite the high hopes raised in 1964 and the amazing spate of Great Society legislation in 1965 and 1966, the good feelings lasted barely eighteen months. By late 1966 the impetus behind the Great Society had dwindled. Among the principal reasons for this decline were the war in Vietnam and a white backlash against the extension of civil rights.

Johnson's efforts to secure equality for all races had actually reached their high point in the Voting Rights Act of 1965. With that act, and the Civil Rights Act of 1964, the Johnson administration put the weight of the national government behind efforts to end formal, legal discrimination against racial minorities. Yet most observers realized that ending social and economic inequality between races would require more than removing the legal barriers.

In the summer of 1965, at the graduation exercises of Howard University, a predominantly black institution in the nation's capital, Johnson spoke on the vicious circle of "despair and deprivation" among African-Americans. He explained that the voting rights law was "the beginning of freedom . . . but freedom is not enough." He noted that the unemployment rate for blacks was now double that for whites,

Malcolm X

As the reaction to the 1965 Moynihan report demonstrated, a new spirit of black militancy was on the rise. One of the chief spokesmen was Malcolm X, a man who could never be surprised by the depths of white resistance to the civil rights movement.

His original name was Malcolm Little. Born in Michigan in 1925, he was the son of a Baptist minister who worked as an organizer for Marcus Garvey's Universal Negro Improvement Organization. When Malcolm was only six, his father was killed, probably by agents of a white terrorist group. Soon after, his mother suffered a mental breakdown, and Malcolm and his siblings were sent to foster homes. After the eighth grade Malcolm dropped out of school and headed east, where he fell into criminal activities that ranged from numbers running to procuring prostitutes and selling narcotics.

---

although thirty-five years earlier it had been the same. The unemployment rate for black teenage boys was 23 percent, compared to 13 percent for whites. The poverty rate for whites had fallen 27 percent while that of blacks had diminished by only 3 percent. The reasons for the increasing economic gap between whites and blacks were complex, most deriving from "ancient brutality, past injustice, and present prejudice." But Johnson placed some of the responsibility for black poverty on African-Americans themselves. Drawing on the work of Assistant Secretary of Labor Daniel Patrick Moynihan, he emphasized the dreadful effects of "the breakdown of the Negro family structure." Assuming that a family included an adult male wage earner and a female homemaker, his argument implied a sentimental, idealized view of the family, hardly representative of the reality for either black or white Americans. "When the family collapses," John-

In 1946 he was arrested in Boston for burglary and larceny, and he spent the next six years in prison. There he was converted by the Nation of Islam, the religious group popularly known as the Black Muslims. According to the leader of that faith, Elijah Muhammad, white people were members of a satanic race sent by Allah to punish American blacks, but the day of judgment was near at hand. Abandoning his "slave name" of Little, the young convert began to call himself Malcolm X.

After his release from prison, Malcolm X gradually became the best-known evangelist for the Nation of Islam, so popular that he made his rivals jealous. He took every occasion to denounce not only whites in general, but also blacks who joined the nonviolent civil rights movement, which he called a "mealy-mouth, wait-in, beg-in, plead-in kind of action." A believer in racial separation, he advocated violence as a necessary tool in combating racist evils.

After he referred to John F. Kennedy's assassination as an instance of "chickens coming home to roost," his Muslim opponents had him suspended from the Nation of Islam. Undeterred, he established his own movement, which blended orthodox Islam with African socialism, anticolonialism, and black nationalism. In this period he moved away from the idea that whites must always be the enemies of blacks. But his political evolution came to an abrupt end when he was shot and killed in 1965, evidently in an act of Muslim vengeance. His *Autobiography,* published after his death, established him as a prophet of the rising Black Power movement. ■

son said, "it is the children that are usually damaged," because of the absence of strong father figures. "When it happens on a massive scale," the president explained, "the community itself is crippled."

Johnson's speech, supplemented by Moynihan's fuller exposition of the roots of black poverty in a report called *The Negro Family: The Case for National Action,* was supposed to set the agenda for further government action. That was not to be. A White House conference that met in November with the goal of expanding earlier civil rights legislation broke up in acrimony over the Moynihan report. Some African-Americans, expressing new feelings of racial pride and resentment over what they perceived as meddling by white liberals, denounced Moynihan's conclusions as condescending and racist. A number of critics concluded that the report blamed the victims of discrimination for their plight.

Despite its apparently condescending tone, the Moynihan report represented a serious attempt to address a complex problem. But the early criticism undermined support for it. At the same time, Johnson was being distracted by the growing problem in Vietnam. In July 1965 he committed United States ground forces to the war, and over the next years, as the war consumed ever more of the government's resources and the administration's attention, the problems of poverty and racial inequality received less priority.

Another factor intervened as well. Already, in the summer of 1964, race riots had struck New York City and several other cities in New York and New Jersey. These proved only preludes of what was to come. In August 1965 a major riot erupted in Watts, a predominantly African-American section of Los Angeles. The insurrection sprang from black economic frustrations and rage at the brutality of an all-white police force, but it nevertheless shocked moderate whites, who only five months before had been moved by the nonviolence and moral force of the demonstrators at Selma. White support for racial equality began to erode.

Over the next year, whites resented the efforts of Martin Luther King, Jr., and other civil rights leaders to desegregate housing in northern cities. Suspicion was also aroused by the Supreme Court's affirmation of the rights of people accused of crimes. Moreover, the race riots spread from one city to another after 1965; by 1968, Detroit, Newark, Washington, Cincinnati, and many other cities across the country had witnessed major rioting. Whites were further alienated by the militancy of a newer generation of black leaders (see Chapter 9). By the time of the congressional elections of 1966, white anger at blacks was a key underlying issue.

That year a Gallup poll reported that 52 percent of white respondents believed the administration was pushing too hard on civil rights, a 20-point gain in that opinion in four years. Some Republican candidates denounced "crime in the streets," a euphemism for the African-American uprisings. They opposed the Great Society's plans for open-housing legislation. Democrats, too, fanned white fears of blacks. The unsuccessful Democratic candidate for governor of Maryland ran on a slogan of "Your home is your castle—protect it." One Democratic congressman from Chicago ruefully reported that in "any home, any bar, any barber shop" you will find people "talking about Martin Luther King and how they are moving in on us and what's going to happen to our neighborhoods."

The backlash propelled the Republicans to a gain of 47 seats in the House of Representatives and 3 in the Senate in the 1966 congressional elections. Among the losers in the upper house was Paul Douglas, a long-time Democratic liberal senator from Illinois, who lost in part because white voters in Chicago would not forgive his support of open housing. Backlash had an effect at the state level as well. In California, conservative Republican Ronald Reagan, who condemned the Watts rioters, won the governorship with a margin of nearly 1 million votes. After the election results were in, the defeated Democratic governor, Edmund G. Brown, ruefully concluded that "whether we like it or not, people want separation of the races."

Over the next two years, white distrust of social reform grew. Working-class whites, many descended from eastern or southern European immigrants, came to despise the Johnson administration. As prices rose and the government seemed powerless to stop the inflation, these white ethnics believed that their needs had been overlooked in the efforts to end poverty and forge a Great Society. The urban riots and the Supreme Court's extension of protection to criminal defendants infuriated white ethnic groups. Johnson seemed bereft of ideas to reconstruct his shattered consensus. One day after the United States Army quelled the Detroit riot in July 1967 at a cost of forty-four lives, the president called for a day of prayer for "order and reconciliation among men." He created a presidential commission, headed by former judge Otto Kerner, to study the causes of urban violence. Yet when Kerner submitted his report in 1968 describing the emergence of "two nations, separate but unequal, white and black," Johnson refused to receive it.

Johnson's aides told him that he needed more than prayer to restore his public standing. By the fall of 1967 his public approval rating had slipped below 33 percent, the lowest figure since Truman's dismal standing at the end of the Korean War. Assistants suggested that Johnson might revive his standing in the polls by showing support for police. In an address to the International Association of Chiefs of Police, Johnson drew prolonged applause with an attack on African-American rioters: "We cannot tolerate behavior that destroys what generations of men and women have built here in America—no matter what stimulates that behavior and no matter what is offered to try to justify it."

Thereafter the Great Society ground down. The flood of legislation of 1965 slowed to a trickle after the new Congress assembled in 1967. The only major law passed was a housing bill, submitted in 1968, to replace the dilapidated dwellings of northern cities devastated by riots. This law also banned racial or religious discrimination in the sale or rental of housing. Modified in the Nixon administration, the law ultimately led to the construction of 1.3 million low-income housing units, but the building program benefited rich developers and investors more than poor people.

Other Great Society programs withered at the end of the Johnson administration. Unwilling to fund both the war in Vietnam and the War on Poverty, Congress cut back on the latter. The president lost heart too at the end of his term, as he saw support for the poor become a liability among whites. This reduction of support for the War on Poverty further fueled the backlash over the next decade. Conservative opponents of government assistance to the poor now pointed to the failure of the Great Society to eliminate poverty as proof that such programs could not work. In fact, these programs were underfunded, often mismanaged, and had little input from poor people themselves.

ASPECTS OF JOHNSON'S FOREIGN POLICY

The excitement and controversies created by the Great Society and the dramatic escalation of the war in Vietnam (see Chapter 8) left the Johnson administration with neither the time nor the inclination to think deeply about relations with the rest of the world. Essentially the administration continued the efforts begun earlier in the Cold War to project American power around the globe. Not comfortable with foreign affairs himself, the president relied on advice from the national-security experts he had inherited from Kennedy. Together with men like Secretary of State Dean Rusk, National Security Advisers McGeorge Bundy (1961–1965) and Walt Whitman Rostow (1965–1968), and Secretary of Defense Robert McNamara (1961–1968), Johnson involved the United States in a series of regional disputes in Latin America, the Middle East, and Europe. These controversies produced little success, and they strained relations with long-time friends. By 1968 experts inside and outside of government were calling for a new direction in foreign affairs. At that point the administration attempted to dampen the passions of the Cold War and relax tensions with the Soviet Union. Such efforts at détente stopped short, and it remained for the succeeding Nixon White House to put them into effect.

Intervention and Controversy in the Western Hemisphere

The Johnson administration reversed its predecessor's halting efforts at fostering social reform in the Western Hemisphere. The change was signaled by the new president's appointment of Thomas Mann to direct the Alliance for Progress, the program that provided economic assistance to Latin America. Mann favored the interests of United States businesses, which wanted assurances that their investments were safe and their profits could be brought home, rather than the desires of social reformers who advocated land reform and heavy taxation of multinational corporations in Latin America. In March 1964 Mann announced that the Alliance for Progress should change

President Johnson whispers to Defense Secretary Robert S. McNamara during a news conference at Johnson's ranch in Texas. The president relied heavily on the foreign policy advice of McNamara, one of the holdovers from the Kennedy administration. *UPI/Bettmann Newsphotos.*

its emphasis; instead of focusing on land reform and on reducing the gap between rich and poor, the Alliance should foster economic growth. Henceforth, he said, the United States should be neutral on social reform and should protect its private investments. This so-called Mann Doctrine held further that the United States would not force Latin American governments to adopt democracy if they faced Communist or other revolutionary movements. This policy served as an excuse for relying on Latin American military regimes to protect United States interests.

Besides its suspicion of social reform in Latin America, the Johnson administration also displayed an insensitivity to issues of national pride and identity in the region. Early in 1964, for example, the administration had to confront a host of angry Panamanians. For sixty years Panama had resented North American domination of the isthmian canal and Canal Zone. The 1903 treaty granting the United States the rights to the Zone "as if it were sovereign" continuously irritated Panamanian pride. In 1964 Panamanians became upset when American high school students in the Canal Zone tore down the Panamanian flag and United States authorities refused to raise it again, despite promising to do so. Four days of rioting in Panama left twenty-four Panamanians and four American soldiers dead. Thousands of Panamanians were forced to flee their homes. Johnson took matters into his own hands. Speaking to the Panamanian president personally, he promised to discuss all the important problems. But when talks opened between the two nations, Washington downplayed the issue of the offensive canal treaty. Most Panamanians believed that Washington was stalling.

In 1965, faced with a potential leftist government in the Dominican Republic, the Johnson administration reverted to direct military intervention. Occupying half of the Caribbean island of Hispaniola, the Dominican Republic had long been dominated, directly or indirectly, by the United States. A dictator, Rafael Trujillo, had ruled with American connivance from 1940 to 1961. Toward the end of his regime, however, Washington lost patience with his brutality. In May 1961 he was assassinated, and the Kennedy administration encouraged the democratic election of a successor. In December 1962 the Dominicans elected Juan Bosch president. Bosch, a leftist but non-Communist, soon ran afoul of the Dominican military, which overthrew him in the fall of 1963. The generals sponsored a new government, led by Donald Reid Cabral, but he too proved unpopular.

In April 1965 young army officers sympathetic to Bosch ousted Reid Cabral. Their more conservative seniors panicked and appealed to the American ambassador for help. Shooting broke out on the streets of Santo Domingo, and the United States envoy wired Washington that a Communist revolution was at hand. The embassy passed out a false press release stating that fifty-eight "identified and prominent Communist and Castroite leaders" were directing the pro-Bosch forces. President Johnson decided to send the marines and the army to quell the uprising and install another conservative government. At first the president justified the intervention as necessary to preserve American lives and property. Two days later, on April 30, he explained instead that "people outside the Dominican Republic are seeking to gain control."

The United States forces trounced the leftists and eventually helped put a conservative, Joaquin Balaguer, in power. But the intervention produced a furious reaction. Bosch complained that "this was a democratic revolution, crushed by the leading democracy in the world." At home, liberal opinion was discouraged that the United States had reverted to force, intervening in a way repugnant to most Latin Americans. *The New York Times* chided the president for ignoring the fact that the Dominican people "were fighting and dying for social justice." Robert Kennedy, now a senator from New York, complained that the United States should have consulted its allies in the Organization of American States before acting alone.

Strains in NATO

While intervention in the Dominican Republic helped unravel the domestic consensus over foreign affairs, the war in Vietnam was growing into a major public controversy. At the same time, strains appeared in the NATO alliance, considered the cornerstone of America's overseas commitment since the Second World War. French President Charles de Gaulle attempted to restrain what he considered to be Washington's high-handed direction of the alliance. Europeans had been unhappy during the Cuban missile crisis of 1962, when the United States and the Soviet Union had approached the brink of war without consulting their allies. In the aftermath, France went forward with its own atomic bomb project, and in 1966 the French president announced that his nation's forces would no longer participate in the military arm of NATO. He forced the alliance to move its headquarters from Paris to Brussels. The Johnson administration dismissed de Gaulle as a bitter old man who was trying futilely to restore France's faded glory. Some foreign affairs experts noted, however, that the French leader had correctly criticized the way the United States dealt with its allies. Since 1949 the European allies had grown from dependents to partners, but Washington treated them with condescension. As Henry Kissinger, then a Harvard professor, put it, the United States "tended to confuse periodic briefings and reassurances with consultations."

Conflict in the Middle East

In June 1967 the Six Day War between Israel and the Arab states of Egypt, Syria, and Jordan further strained America's foreign relations and created a bitter legacy. For ten years Egypt had smarted from the military embarrassment it had suffered at the hands of Israel during the October 1956 Suez conflict. Egypt's President Gamal Abdel Nasser had promised social justice in Egypt and unity in the Arab world, but neither had come to pass. Egypt sank further into poverty and despair. Nasser therefore wanted to restore his standing at home by erasing the stain of Suez. With his army resupplied by the Soviet Union, and goaded to action by other Arab states, Nasser looked for ways to threaten Israel in the spring of 1967.

He did so by demanding that the United Nations remove its emergency forces from the Sinai Peninsula, which separated Israel and Egypt. Much to his surprise, the United Nations agreed. Now the Soviet Union urged caution, but Nasser was trapped by his own inflammatory rhetoric. He sent his forces to Sharm el Sheik, at the tip of the Sinai Peninsula, and closed the Strait of Tiran to ships bound for Israel's important southern port of Eilat.

At this point the United States stepped in to head off a war. Johnson feared the unpredictable consequences of a clash between Israel and Egypt. He begged the Israelis not to respond to Nasser until the United States could organize an international flotilla to break the blockade. But Europeans, fearful that the Arab states would cut off their oil supplies, declined to join the effort. Secretary of State Rusk told Israel's foreign minister that only one other nation had agreed to run the blockade.

Faced with what they believed were half-hearted American efforts in their behalf, the Israelis took matters into their own hands on the morning of June 5. In a pre-emptive strike, their air force destroyed Egyptian planes on the ground while their tanks knifed across the Sinai Peninsula. Later that day, Jordan's King Hussein ordered his artillery to shell the Jewish sector of Jerusalem; in response, the Israelis turned on Jordan, and two days later they attacked Syria as well. Within six days Israel had taken the Sinai from Egypt; the West Bank of the Jordan River, including the eastern part of Jerusalem, from Jordan; and the Golan Heights from Syria. After the war, the United Nations called for Israeli withdrawal from the captured territories in return for Arab recognition of Israel's right to exist. The United Nations also asked for a settlement of the problem of Palestinian Arabs, hundreds of thousands of whom had been made homeless by Israel's conquest of the West Bank and Gaza. Neither Israel nor the Arabs implemented these resolutions, and the dispute between Israel, the Arab states, and the Palestinians, who wanted a state of their own, became more bitter than ever.

During the Six Day War Soviet Premier Alexei Kosygin used the hot line, installed after the Cuban missile crisis, to inform Johnson that the Soviet Union would not intervene in the war to help Egypt if the United States did not directly aid Israel. Both sides kept that agreement. In the aftermath of the war, however, a new arms race ensued in the Middle East. The United States became virtually the sole arms supplier for Israel, as Britain and France declared an embargo to protest Israel's attack and to protect their oil supplies. The Soviet Union quickly restored the weapons lost by Egypt and Syria.

Relations with the Soviet Union

Two weeks after the Six Day War ended in 1967, Kosygin visited New York for a special United Nations General Assembly session called to discuss peace in the Middle East. While in New York, Kosygin accepted Johnson's invitation to meet him at Glassboro State College in southern New Jersey to discuss United States–Soviet relations. At this, the first summit meeting of the leaders of the superpowers since the melancholy conversations between John Kennedy and Nikita

Khrushchev in May 1961, the president sought the Soviet leader's help in arranging an end to the war in Vietnam. Kosygin refused, because he wanted to show the North Vietnamese that the Soviet Union could do more for them than could its recent Communist rival, the People's Republic of China.

The two men made more progress in addressing an issue directly affecting the security of each nation—the competition in nuclear arms. Ever since the Limited Test Ban Treaty of 1963, the United States and the Soviet Union had worried about the growth of each other's supply of missiles tipped with thermonuclear warheads. At Glassboro the two leaders promised to begin negotiations to limit the number of bombs each side could aim at the other. Without such an agreement, experts feared, the arms race might deteriorate into an all-out war that nobody wanted. To reduce these risks and to build confidence in one another's intentions, Johnson and Kosygin promised that the Glassboro meeting would be the first in a series of regular summit conferences between leaders of the United States and the Soviet Union.

Steps toward détente went no further in the remaining eighteen months of the Johnson administration. In August 1968, Secretary of State Rusk planned to announce that Johnson would repay Kosygin's visit by traveling to the Soviet Union to begin talks on the limitation of strategic arms. On August 20, however, Soviet tanks rumbled into Prague, Czechoslovakia, to crush the Czechs' experiment with a liberalized socialism. Moscow feared that Czech leader Alexander Dubček secretly wanted to dismantle the one-party state. As *Pravda*, the Soviet Communist party newspaper, explained, Communist states could not stand idly by as one of their number fell "into the process of antisocialist degeneration." Journalists quickly labeled these remarks the Brezhnev Doctrine, after Soviet Party Chairman Leonid Brezhnev. In the climate of hostility evoked by the crushing of Czechoslovakian freedom, Johnson decided he could not afford the political risk of meeting Soviet leaders to discuss arms control. As in previous administrations, genuine détente with the Soviet Union remained only a tantalizing possibility.

CONCLUSION

By the end of 1968 it appeared that Lyndon Johnson's administration could be characterized largely by its failed aspirations. Johnson had done more than any other president since Franklin Roosevelt to spur Americans to reform their society. The Civil Rights Act of 1964 and the Voting Rights Act of 1965 had helped remove the legal barriers facing African-Americans. The War on Poverty reduced hunger and suffering, and Medicare improved access to health care. Meanwhile, Johnson's appointees to the Supreme Court bolstered the liberal group of justices who expanded civil liberties and insisted that electoral districts be apportioned democratically. Yet by the end of Johnson's presidency, most of the early enthusiasm had been lost. The Vietnam War was draining the government's funds and energy. Too many Great Society programs were underfunded or mired in administrative troubles. Race riots had erupted across the country, and a white backlash arose to block further attempts at social reform.

But it was foreign policy, not domestic affairs, that ultimately led to Lyndon Johnson's downfall. As demonstrated by his administration's intervention in the Dominican Republic, Johnson believed in the usefulness of military power for suppressing leftists and Communists in the Third World. In this he was fundamentally no different from his predecessors. Yet, as the next chapter explains, it was Johnson who dramatically raised the stakes in Vietnam and who absorbed most of the blame for the American failure there. ■

FURTHER READING

On the personalities and policies of the Johnson administration, see: Robert Caro, *The Path to Power* (1983) and *Means of Ascent* (1989); Robert Dallek, *Lone Star Rising: Lyndon Johnson, 1908–1960* (1991); Doris Kearns, *Lyndon Johnson and the American Dream* (1977); Merle Miller, *Lyndon: An Oral Biography* (1980); Allan M. Matusow, *The Unraveling of America: A History of Liberalism in the 1960s* (1984); Richard Goodwin, *Remembering America: A Voice from the 1960s* (1988). On Great Society programs, see: James M. Sundquist, *Politics and Policy: The Eisenhower, Kennedy and Johnson Years* (1968); Daniel P. Moynihan, *Maximum Feasible Misunderstanding* (1970); David Reimers, *Still the Golden Door: The Third World Comes to America*, 2d ed. (1992); John E. Schwarz, *America's Hidden Success: A Reassessment of Public Policy from Kennedy to Reagan* (1988); Charles Murray, *Losing Ground: American Social Policy, 1950–1980* (1986); Nicholas Lemann, *The Promised Land: The Great Black Migration and How It Changed America* (1991). On the Supreme Court, see: Melvin Urofsky, *The Continuity of Change: The Supreme Court and Individual Liberties, 1953–1986* (1991); Bernard Schwartz, *Super Chief: Earl Warren and His Supreme Court* (1983); Fred Graham, *The Due Process Revolution: The Warren Court's Impact on Criminal Law* (1977). On foreign affairs, see: Philip Geyelin, *Lyndon B. Johnson and the World* (1968); Thomas Schoenbaum, *Waging Peace and War: Dean Rusk in the Truman, Kennedy and Johnson Years* (1988); Steven J. Spiegel, *The Other Arab-Israeli Conflict: Making America's Middle East Policy from Truman to Reagan* (1985).

8

The Vietnam Nightmare, 1961–1968

In the 1960s American involvement in the war in Vietnam grew from a minor issue of little interest to most people into a frightening nightmare, affecting nearly every aspect of American life. Popular anguish over the seemingly endless war opened deep fissures in many traditional political, social, cultural,and religious institutions. Chapter 9 explores the culture of protest that the Vietnam War helped to foster; this chapter focuses on the war itself and its meaning for American politics and foreign policy.

From the beginning of American involvement in the late 1940s until Lyndon Johnson decided that he could not win re-election in 1968, politicians, diplomats, and military leaders consistently misunderstood the rapidly changing conditions in Vietnam. Their failure to grasp the intensity of revolutionary nationalism in Southeast Asia led to futile attempts to create a non-Communist regime in the southern half of Vietnam. In the devastating war that ensued, American bombs, guns, and money ruined Vietnam physically, economically, and socially. The seemingly endless conflict also took a profound toll on the American GIs who fought it.

As the war dragged on, Americans at home became sick of the brutal and inconclusive fighting. Their revulsion with the war gradually led to a widespread loss of faith in government and authority. On the issues of foreign policy, the public frustration eroded the general consensus developed in earlier decades. Many Americans continued to believe that the United States should oppose communism and revolution abroad, and they became disillusioned with the war because it made little progress against the Communists. Other people, however, decided that the war in Vietnam should not have been fought at all. These misgivings about Vietnam spread into doubts about the overall principle of containment that had governed American foreign policy since the Second World War.

In the 1968 presidential election, Americans voted for change, hoping that a new administration could extricate them from the Vietnamese morass. But more than four years—and another presidential election—would pass before a cease-fire agreement was signed.

THE GROWTH OF AMERICAN COMMITMENT TO VIETNAM, 1945–1964

John Kenneth Galbraith, Harvard economist and the United States ambassador to India, once asked President John F. Kennedy, "Who is the man in your administration who decides what countries are strategic? I would like to have his name and address and ask him what is to so important about this [Vietnamese] real estate in the space age?" The president declined to identify the planner, because it was Kennedy himself who attached importance to Indochina. Like most other high government officials in the years since 1945, Kennedy believed that containment of communism should be the principal goal of American foreign policy. But because involvement in Vietnam represented only a small part of the larger strategy of confronting revolutionary nationalists in the postcolonial world, Americans never thought deeply about events in Vietnam until the United States was deeply involved in the war. From Truman through Kennedy, the successive administrations gradually enlarged the United States commitment to Vietnam, setting the stage for a dramatic escalation under Lyndon Johnson.

The First Indochina War, 1946–1954

Since 1945 the United States had backed alternatives to the Communist Democratic Republic of Vietnam (North Vietnam) established under the leadership of Ho Chi Minh in Hanoi on September 2, 1945, the day the Second World War ended in Asia. The Truman administration refused Ho's pleas for diplomatic recognition. During 1946 war broke out between Ho's Vietminh nationalist-Communist guerrillas and French troops, who were trying to re-establish France's colonial power in Indochina. Despite some uneasiness about supporting colonial rule, the Truman administration backed France and its puppet Vietnamese regime. By the end of 1952 Washington was paying 40 percent of the cost of the war.

During the Eisenhower administration the French required even more American aid. Despite the confident assertion of Secretary of State John Foster Dulles that an additional infusion of $400 million would help France "break the organized body of Communist aggression by the end of the 1955 fighting season," the Vietminh gained strength. By March 1954 the United States was paying 70 percent of the cost of the war, yet the French military position at Dienbienphu became desperate. As noted in Chapter 5, Eisenhower toyed with the idea of an air strike, but ultimately drew back, and the Vietminh overran Dienbienphu on May 7, 1954.

Although Dienbienphu represented a catastrophe for France, Washington almost welcomed the defeat as a chance to demonstrate American anti-Communist resolve. Unlike France, which was tainted as a colonial power, the United States could sponsor a so-called third force comprised of Vietnamese nationalists who opposed both the Communists and the French. This was the approach Eisenhower had in mind when the peace conference convened at Geneva, Switzerland.

Although the United States sent representatives to the conference, it was not a signatory to the Geneva accords, and it soon helped to undermine them.

Nation Building in South Vietnam, 1954–1960

After the Geneva accords partitioned Vietnam along the 17th parallel, the United States became more deeply involved in Southeast Asia than ever. In late 1954 the Eisenhower administration sponsored the creation of the Southeast Asia Treaty Organization (SEATO), a military alliance roughly patterned on NATO. Although the southern part of Vietnam never formally joined SEATO, the United States based its involvement in Vietnamese politics partly on its membership in the alliance. Washington helped to set up Ngo Dinh Diem as prime minister of the southern section, which he proclaimed as the Republic of Vietnam (South Vietnam), and supported Diem when he refused to allow the Vietnam-wide unification elections promised by the Geneva agreements. The United States further assisted Diem in creating an Army of the Republic of Vietnam (ARVN) and a police force.

Eisenhower publicly avowed what came to be known as the domino theory: if Indochina fell to communism, he said, the rest of Southeast Asia would topple like a row of dominoes. General J. Lawton Collins, the special United States representative to Vietnam, recommended in 1955 that Washington withdraw support from the haughty, unpopular Diem, a Catholic in a predominantly Buddhist land; but Secretary of State Dulles declared that "the decision to back Diem has gone to the point of no return."

Vowing to exterminate vestiges of the popular Vietminh in the South, Diem had his army and police arrest twenty thousand former members of the movement and kill over a thousand in a span of three years. These bald actions won praise from American lawmakers who were looking for signs of a legitimate third force. Senator John F. Kennedy, for example, glorified the new South Vietnam as "the cornerstone of the Free World in Southeast Asia, the keystone to the arch, the finger in the dike."

Despite such appraisals, the remnants of the Vietminh, assisted by North Vietnam, managed to mount a campaign of their own. On December 20, 1960, they proclaimed a new National Front for the Liberation of Vietnam (NLF) and began guerrilla attacks against the South. By mid-1961 the NLF forces, referred to as Vietcong by the South Vietnamese, had succeeded in gaining control of 58 percent of the territory of South Vietnam.

The Kennedy Administration and Vietnam, 1961–1963

When he became president, Kennedy decided that the Eisenhower administration had not done enough to help Diem. The new American president saw Vietnam as part of a global struggle with the Soviet Union. After the catastrophic Bay of Pigs invasion and the chilly summit meeting with Nikita Khrushchev, he especially desired some measure of success against Communist movements in the Third World. "How do we get moving?" he asked his staff. They responded with suggestions for using the army's Special Forces, or Green Berets, against the insurrection. Walt Rostow, formerly an economist at the Massachusetts Institute of Technology, now serving on the National Security Council staff, recommended using Vietnam as a showcase of academic theories of development, so that the South could "take off" into modern industrialism.

Kennedy responded to the recommendations of his staff with an additional $42 million beyond the $220 million already being spent per year in aid to South Vietnam. He sent hundreds more troops to advise the ARVN on how to fight, and he ordered 400 Special Forces to lead 9,000 mountain tribesmen in an effort to stop infiltration from North Vietnam. He further directed the CIA to conduct commando raids against North Vietnam. The United States provided heavy weapons to South Vietnamese provincial civil guardsmen (local militias) to use against the Vietcong in rural areas. By late 1961 there were 3,205 American advisers in South Vietnam, and that number rose to 9,000 the next year. The American advisers, who did not limit their activities to advising, helped the ARVN move hundreds of thousands of peasants from their traditional homes to "strategic hamlets" or "agrovilles."

The creation of strategic hamlets made it easier for the South Vietnamese government to hunt for NLF fighters, but the government's harsh tactics also gave the NLF a weapon in its propaganda war against the Saigon authorities. Once the rural people were installed in the relocation centers, which separated them from land their families had tilled for generations, South Vietnamese forces bombed and napalmed the countryside to terrify and exterminate the NLF. Thousands of civilians, including women and children, lost their lives. The NLF used the destruction of the countryside to its own advantage by telling peasants that the Saigon government was bombing and burning its own citizens. Yet General Paul D. Harkins, in charge of the American advisory forces, dismissed complaints that indiscriminate bombing only alienated the population from the Saigon government: napalm "really puts the fear of God into the Vietcong, and that is what counts."

While Harkins kept up a stream of optimistic reports on progress against the insurrection, American field advisers grew disgusted with what they considered the cowardice and corruption of the ARVN and the South Vietnamese government. ARVN officers showed more interest in stealing their subordinates' pay than in engaging the NLF. On January 2, 1963, the NLF scored a huge triumph against the

ARVN at the battle of Ap Bac, twenty miles from Saigon. Colonel John Paul Vann, an American adviser who witnessed the ambush and defeat of a powerful ARVN contingent by an NLF unit, lamented the "miserable damn performance" of the ARVN. Angry at the "failure" and "futility" of the ARVN commanders at Ap Bac, Vann told his superiors that the ARVN leaders were sadly "characteristic of virtually all of the senior officers of the Vietnamese armed forces."

By mid-1963 the Kennedy administration, once so supportive of Ngo Dinh Diem, viewed him and his family as obstacles to success against the NLF. The Vietnamese peasantry disdained the strategic hamlets and hated Diem's connections to the old landlord class. Leaders of the Buddhist sects, who comprised over two-thirds of the population of the South, condemned his pro-Catholic policies and demanded Diem's resignation. Buddhists and students led street demonstrations against the government in June; the police responded with clubs and tear gas. On June 11 a seventy-three-year-old Buddhist monk, Thich Quang Duc, turned the Buddhist uprising from a local affair into an international crisis by immolating himself in the middle of a busy Saigon intersection. His ritual suicide was captured on film and broadcast around the world.

Americans reacted with horror. Senator Frank Church, an Idaho Democrat, told the Senate Foreign Relations Committee that "such grisly scenes have not been witnessed since the Christian martyrs marched hand-in-hand into the Roman arenas." Factually Church was mistaken, because Buddhist monks had practiced self-immolation as a protest against French rule in the nineteenth century, but virtually no Americans knew such details of Vietnamese culture, and their shock ran deep. President Diem's sister-in-law, Madame Ngo Dinh Nhu, provoked further outrage against herself and her family when she scoffed that she would be "happy to provide the mustard for the monks' next barbecues."

By August 1963 the Kennedy administration decided that General Collins had been right eight years before: Diem's family, known as the Ngo family, must either change its ways and broaden its government to include nonfamily members and non-Catholics or be removed from office. In August, to secure Republican support for his policies, the president appointed an old Republican rival, Henry Cabot Lodge, Eisenhower's ambassador to the United Nations and Nixon's vice-presidential candidate in 1960, as the new ambassador to South Vietnam. Soon after his arrival in Saigon, Lodge encouraged a plot by some of the ARVN's top generals to oust the Ngos, but the generals aborted their plans in fear that Diem had discovered the plot. Meanwhile, American officials in Washington kept up the pressure for change in Saigon. In early September, Kennedy granted an exclusive interview to "CBS Evening News with Walter Cronkite." He explained that "I don't think the war can be won unless the people [of South Vietnam] support the effort, and in my opinion, in the last two months, the government [of Diem] has gotten out of touch with the people." When Cronkite asked if the president thought the Saigon government could regain popular trust, Kennedy replied, "I do," adding ominously, "with changes of policy and perhaps with personnel, I think it can."

Diem refused the invitation to go quietly into exile, dug in his heels, and turned on the Americans. His brother Nhu hinted darkly at a deal with North Vietnam that would leave the Ngo family in charge of a neutralized South Vietnam. At this point Ambassador Lodge in Saigon, along with Secretary of Defense Robert McNamara and Assistant Secretary of State for Far Eastern Affairs Roger Hilsman, the officials in Washington most concerned with Vietnam policy, decided to encourage the dissident ARVN generals to reactivate their plans for a coup. On November 1, 1963, the plotters seized control of the presidential palace and captured Diem and Nhu. Informed in advance of the coup, Ambassador Lodge did little to offer the Ngos safe conduct out of the country. Instead, they were murdered by the plotters early on the morning of November 2, and a new government, headed by General Duong Van Minh, took over.

Word of Diem's death shook Kennedy, once one of the Vietnamese president's staunchest backers. When the murder was confirmed, Kennedy turned white and ran from the room. Hilsman, intimately involved in the planning for the coup, seemed much happier. "Revolutions are rough. People get hurt," he nonchalantly told a reporter.

At first, the new government of General Minh seemed to present the opportunity to wage the war against the NLF with renewed vigor. Despite later claims by some of Kennedy's political advisers that he would have reduced the American military commitment after the election of 1964, Kennedy remained dedicated to victory over the Communists up to the date of his assassination, three weeks after Diem's death. In remarks prepared for delivery in Dallas on his ill-fated trip, he said: "We in this country in this generation are—by destiny rather than choice—the watchmen on the walls of freedom. . . . Our assistance to . . . nations can be risky and costly, as is true in Southeast Asia today. But we dare not weary of the task."

Overall, the Kennedy administration bequeathed Lyndon Johnson a terrible burden in South Vietnam. Sixteen thousand United States Army, Navy, and Marine Corps advisers, doing much more than advising the ARVN, now conducted daily operations against the NLF, who continued to increase their control over the countryside. This effort produced diminishing returns. The more fighting the American soldiers did, the less the ARVN fighters and officers seemed willing to do. The government of South Vietnam enjoyed little support except from a coterie of ARVN generals who preferred ease in Saigon to fighting in the field. In the countryside, where over

80 percent of the population resided, the national government had become at best a nuisance and more often an enemy. Despite Kennedy's pleas for Americans not to weary of the war, Vietnamese peasants had lost patience and perhaps hope. The government's strategic hamlets and the widespread use of napalm and other defoliants provided powerful recruiting tools for the NLF. Johnson would have a difficult time pursuing Kennedy's vision of a victorious Republic of Vietnam.

The Gulf of Tonkin Resolution

Soon the new South Vietnamese government of Duong Van Minh proved no more amenable to American advice than had Ngo Dinh Diem and his family. The resistance of the Saigon government to American suggestions for waging the war presented the new Johnson administration with an exquisite dilemma, one it never resolved. The South Vietnamese authorities seemed incapable of winning the war by themselves, so they needed American assistance. Yet the more the Americans helped, the less the South Vietnamese did for themselves, thereby encouraging the Americans to get more deeply involved. The growing United States presence, in turn, helped validate the propaganda claims of the NLF and the North Vietnamese that the South Vietnamese authorities were puppets of the Americans.

On his one trip to the region in 1962, Lyndon Johnson, then vice president, had called Diem "the Winston Churchill of Southeast Asia." When skeptical reporters questioned him about this strange and exaggerated characterization, Johnson responded, "He's the only boy we've got out there." Now new to the presidency and trying to follow Kennedy's policies, Johnson relied on the advice of his predecessor's foreign policy experts. Almost to a man, they believed that the United States needed to increase its presence in South Vietnam, pursue the war more vigorously, and, if necessary, replace General Minh with someone more compliant with Washington's desires. Early in 1964, Walt Rostow, now the head of the State Department's Policy Planning Staff, urged "a direct political-military showdown with Hanoi" before the end of the year. The president, facing an election campaign, favored delay, hoping to keep Vietnam off the front page and the evening news. The president would not turn subordinates away from their militant course, but neither did he want to disrupt the consensus he expected to carry him to victory in the fall.

As Johnson procrastinated, military and diplomatic planners moved to alter the military situation in South Vietnam. In late January 1964 the Pentagon helped engineer another coup in Saigon, one that replaced General Minh with General Nguyen Khanh, who the Americans thought would aggressively fight the war. Johnson ordered Lodge to do what he could to stiffen Khanh's resolve, cabling the ambassador that "nothing is more important than to stop neutralist talk whenever we can by whatever means we can."

In June 1964 some of the president's principal advisers floated the idea of a congressional resolution supporting American air or ground action against North Vietnam. Six weeks later, after the raucous Republican convention had nominated Senator Barry Goldwater for president, two controversial incidents off the coast of North Vietnam justified introduction of such a congressional resolution and provided an excuse for air strikes by United States forces against North Vietnamese naval bases and oil storage facilities. Two United States destroyers, the *Maddox* and the *C. Turner Joy,* had conducted so-called De Soto patrols in support of South Vietnamese naval operations along the North Vietnamese coast bordering the Gulf of Tonkin (see map, page 290). In De Soto patrols, American ships sailing within the twelve-mile territorial limit claimed by North Vietnam conducted surveillance against North Vietnamese coastal radar installations. The surveillance was designed to force the operators to activate the radar devices, which would emit radio signals revealing their location to the electronic equipment on the American vessels. At that point, the *Maddox* and the *C. Turner Joy* would notify the accompanying South Vietnamese patrol boats of the positions of the North Vietnamese installations, and the southern boats would attack.

The De Soto patrols provoked the North Vietnamese navy to attack the *Maddox* on the night of August 2, 1964. Two nights later, in heavy seas, the commander of the *C. Turner Joy* thought his ship was under attack and ordered his crew to return fire. They did so but hit nothing, probably because no North Vietnamese patrol boats were in the area and there had been no hostile fire. As Johnson later acknowledged, "For all I know, our navy may have been shooting at whales out there." The assault on the *Maddox* did occur, although Secretary of Defense McNamara was not telling the truth when he explained that "the *Maddox* was operating in international waters and was carrying out a routine patrol of the type we carry out all over the world at all times."

Despite the falsehoods, McNamara's claims carried the day in Congress, which passed the Gulf of Tonkin Resolution on August 7. The House voted unanimously in favor of this legislation, and in the Senate only two members, Oregon Democrat Wayne Morse and Alaska Democrat Ernest Gruening, voted against it. The resolution authorized the president to "take all necessary measures to repel any armed attack against the forces of the United States and to prevent further aggression." The resolution also permitted "all necessary steps, including the use of armed force, to assist" any member of SEATO that asked for American military aid. Although South Vietnam was not in fact a member of SEATO, the alliance had agreed to extend protection to South Vietnam.

CHINA

Dienbienphu

Black R.

Red R.

BURMA

Hanoi

Haiphong

Harbor mined, 1972

Communist-Pathet Lao victory, 1975

Gulf of Tonkin

NORTH VIETNAM

Maddox
incident, 1964

PLAIN OF JARS

L A O S

Vinh

Mu Gia Pass

U.S. Seventh Fleet
operations during the war

Vientiane

Ca R.

Udon Thani ■   Nakhon Phanom ■

Demilitarized Zone

17°

Quang Tri

Demarcation Line, July, 1954

Khe Sanh

Sépone

Lan Vei

Chau

Hue

■ Khon Kaen

Kham Duc

Da Nang

SOUTH
CHINA SEA

My Lai

T H A I L A N D

Ubon Ratchathani ■

Chu Lai

■ Ta Khli

Quang Ngai

■ Rachasima

Dak To

Kontum

■ Don Muang

Pleiku

An Khe

Qui Nhon

• Bangkok

Duc Co

CENTRAL
HIGHLANDS

Tuy Hoa

K A M P U C H E A

(CAMBODIA)

Mekong R.

Ban Me Thuot

Sattahip

Nha Trang

U.S. invasion, 1970

Dalat

Can Ranh Bay

Bu Dop

SOUTH VIETNAM

Phnom Penh

Vietnamese invasion, 1978

Communist-Khmer Rouge victory, 1975

Bien Hoa

Gulf of Siam

Cholon

Long Binh

Tan Son Nhut

Chau Duc

Saigon

Vung Tau

Vietcong-
North Vietnamese victory
and U.S. withdrawal, 1975

My Tho

Vinh Long

Ben Tre

Can Tho   Mekong Delta

Ho Chi Minh Trail

Ca Mau

Boat-people refugees after 1975

CA MAU PENINSULA

Major battles of the Tet offensive,
January 1968

Major U.S. bases during the war

0   100   200 miles

0   100   200   300 kilometers

The resolution's extraordinarily broad grant of authority to the nation's chief executive had no time limit. Later Johnson would use it to justify the greatly enlarged American participation in the war. Senator Morse predicted that other lawmakers would eventually regret having approved such a blank check for Vietnam. One who did was J. William Fulbright, an Arkansas Democrat and chairman of the Senate Foreign Relations Committee, who had presented the resolution on the Senate floor. Within a year he opposed further United States participation in the war, and he later lamented that his support of the Tonkin Gulf Resolution was "the dumbest thing I've ever done."

The Tonkin Gulf Resolution removed Vietnam from the political debate during the 1964 election campaign. Goldwater, who had earlier berated Johnson for timidity in Vietnam, fully supported the Tonkin resolution and the limited air raid that Johnson ordered against North Vietnam. For his part, Johnson stood serenely in the middle of the road on Vietnam. Most of his listeners believed that he wanted to keep the United States out of a full-scale shooting war while preventing a Communist victory. His major campaign speech on Vietnam sounded moderate but left considerable room for greater American involvement at a later date. He said that "only as a last resort" would he "start dropping bombs around that are likely to involve American boys in a war in Asia with 700 million Chinese." He could not guarantee the future, he said, but "we are not going north and drop bombs at this stage of the game, and we are not going south and run out and leave it for the Communists to take over."

THE AMERICANIZATION OF THE WAR, 1965

The year 1965 marked the point of no return for the United States in Vietnam. By July Johnson had taken a series of fateful decisions that transformed the fighting in Vietnam into an American war. Nevertheless, throughout the period of gradually increasing American military involvement in Vietnam *escalation*, as it was called—the Johnson administration waged a *limited* war. Johnson wanted to break the will of the North Vietnamese without at the same time provoking a military response from the Soviet Union or China. Officials believed that limiting the extent of the war would lessen the impact on the American public, making it easier to sustain political support for the war. It proved nearly impossible, however, to wage a limited war effectively. Every step up the ladder of escalation alarmed potential adversaries abroad and created anxieties at home. Yet efforts to restrict

◀ **Southeast Asia and the Vietnam War**

the scope of the war relieved pressure on North Vietnam and generated opposition from a different group of Americans, those who wanted to defeat North Vietnam quickly with the use of massive military power.

In February 1965, Johnson authorized a sustained bombing campaign against the North, Operation Rolling Thunder. That summer he took the final steps toward a commitment of 100,000 United States ground troops to the war. No longer would the fiction be maintained that American soldiers acted only as advisers to the ARVN; the United States forces conducted widescale operations on their own without accompanying ARVN units. Undersecretary of State George Ball, one of the few high officials skeptical of the importance of Vietnam and doubtful that the United States could prevail, described the United States as mounted "on the tiger's back" in Vietnam. It would prove difficult, he warned, to decide "where to dismount."

The Air War Against North Vietnam

As the South Vietnamese government grew continually weaker, the succession of military regimes nearly drove Johnson apoplectic. News of yet another uprising provoked him to explode, "I don't want to hear any more [about coups]." One of the president's assistants suggested that the coat of arms of the Saigon government display a turnstile.

In this atmosphere, Pentagon planners concluded that bombing the North would help to save the South. General Maxwell Taylor, now ambassador to South Vietnam, told Johnson early in 1965 that air raids would "inject some life into the dejected spirits" in South Vietnam. The president, more prescient than some of his military advisers, worried that "this guerrilla war cannot be won from the air." Taylor reassured him, however, that whereas bombing would not bring about "the physical destruction of the enemy," it would "bring pressure on the will of the chiefs of the DRV [Ho Chi Minh and his advisers]. As practical men, they cannot wish to see the fruits of ten years of labor destroyed by slowly escalating air attacks."

Sustained bombing of North Vietnam began within a month of Johnson's 1965 inauguration. On February 7, 1965, a company of Vietcong soldiers attacked the barracks of the American advisers at Pleiku in the central highlands of South Vietnam, killing eight Americans and wounding 126, and destroying ten planes. Although the assault hardly surprised high American officials, they believed that the cumulative effect of attacks on American forces would further undermine the shaky morale of the South Vietnamese government. Pleiku therefore provided the justification for sustained bombing of the North. Johnson first ordered a single retaliatory mission similar to the one undertaken after the Tonkin incident the previous August, but this did not stop calls for harsher action. Former vice president Richard Nixon urged night and day bombing of the North. On February 13 Johnson authorized sustained bombing of the North in Operation Rolling Thunder. The bombing was extensive. In April, American and South Vietnamese pilots flew 3,600 sorties against targets in the North—fuel depots, railroad yards, bridges, power plants, and munitions factories.

The initial results of the bombing campaign disappointed air war advocates. Despite the expectations of Pentagon planners, the North Vietnamese quickly adapted to round-the-clock bombing. Few industrial targets existed, and the North Vietnamese quickly rebuilt destroyed bridges. The thick jungle provided cover for thousands of North Vietnamese men, women, and children as young as ten years old to carry supplies by hand and bicycle to the South along what became known as the Ho Chi Minh Trail. The North Vietnamese and NLF fighters did not capitulate, and the South Vietnamese government did not become stronger. American military officers believed that even more air attacks were necessary. General Taylor complained that Rolling Thunder should be more than a "few isolated thunder claps." He urged a "mounting crescendo" of air raids against North Vietnam. In response, Johnson relaxed restrictions on targets over the next several months, although retaining final control.

For the remainder of his term Johnson worried about provoking Chinese intervention in the war, with the disastrous consequences the United States had experienced in Korea. To minimize risks of Chinese participation, Johnson avoided bombing close to China's border with Vietnam. For the same reason, he denied repeated military requests to invade North Vietnam with ground troops. Such precautions worked, and China and the Soviet Union did not go beyond supplying North Vietnam with weapons. Yet air war advocates within the United States military believed that Johnson acted too cautiously. They doubted that the Chinese or Soviets intended to enter the war, and they believed the restrictions on bombing targets limited the effectiveness of the air campaign.

The Decision for an American Ground War

As Rolling Thunder offered little more than temporary relief from Vietcong success, the American commander in South Vietnam, General William Westmoreland, called for direct American ground action throughout the South. There is no solution, he wrote the president, "other than to put our own finger in the dike." But Johnson still resisted a full Americanization of the war, and at a speech at Johns Hopkins University in April 1965, he offered "unconditional discussions" with North Vietnam to end the war.

In early May, McNamara, Taylor, and Westmoreland acknowledged that bombing alone would not win the war. At a meeting in Honolulu they agreed that the United States had to fight the war on the ground, in the South, if the Saigon government were to have a chance of surviving. Refusing, however, to endorse Westmoreland's pleas for operations throughout the South, they called for an additional 40,000 United States troops to fight within fifty miles of so-called enclaves, American outposts near the coast.

By June 1965, the enclaves had failed to stem the NLF's advance, and Westmoreland wanted another 150,000 troops deployed to fight the ground war throughout the South. Secretary of Defense McNamara cut Westmoreland's request to 100,000 troops and forwarded it to the president. Throughout July, Johnson consulted with his principal advisers on the future course to take in Vietnam. In these meetings Johnson appeared skeptical of the usefulness of additional American troops, but unwilling to accept the cost of an NLF victory. The only course he could tolerate, therefore, was continued gradual increases in the American commitment—the very policy that had failed over the previous year. He hoped to keep the build-up as quiet as possible to avoid a raucous debate in the press or Congress and to prevent public disillusionment of the sort that had wrecked the Truman administration during the Korean War. He also worried that a congressional debate on Vietnam would ruin his plans for a Great Society.

During the July meetings he asked General Earle Wheeler, chairman of the Joint Chiefs of Staff, "Tell me this. What will happen if we put in 100,000 more men and then two, three years later, you tell me you need 500,000 more? How would you expect me to respond to that? And what makes you think Ho Chi Minh won't put in another 100,000 and match us every bit of the way?" To which Wheeler responded, "This means greater bodies of men from North Vietnam, which will allow us to cream them." Johnson's fear proved prophetic, and Wheeler's reply foretold some of the folly of the commanders' methods in the war.

Undersecretary of State George Ball offered the most spirited dissent, explaining that the United States could not win in Vietnam. He predicted that the struggle would be long and protracted, as in the Korean War, and that once again public opinion would turn against an inconclusive war. The United States would lose more prestige in world opinion when it became obvious that the world's greatest power could not defeat guerrillas. Johnson seemed troubled by Ball's comments. He wondered if Westerners could successfully fight Asians in jungle rice paddies. Still, the thought of a Communist victory appalled him. "But George," he asked, "wouldn't all these countries [in the remainder of Southeast Asia] say that Uncle Sam was a paper tiger, wouldn't we lose credibility breaking the word of three presidents?" Ball's assurances that the United States would gain more by removing itself from an imprudent situation failed to change Johnson's mind.

Eventually all of the president's advisers with the exception of Ball concurred that adding 100,000 Americans to the 90,000 troops already in Vietnam would help stabilize the situation without causing a backlash against the war in Congress or with the public. Most agreed to reject the request from the Joint Chiefs of Staff to call up the reserves, because such a move would dramatically raise the stakes at home and abroad, perhaps necessitating a presidential declaration of a state of emergency and a request for several billion dollars. In that event, Johnson worried, the Great Society would cease, and, worse, "Hanoi would be able to ask the Chinese Communists and the Soviets to increase aid."

At the end of July Johnson decided to inform congressional leaders that he intended to send another 100,000 men by the end of the year, without calling up reserve units. With few exceptions, Republican and Democratic leaders in Congress supported the move. Speaker of the House John McCormack thought there was no alternative. "The lesson of Hitler and Mussolini is clear," he reflected. Senator Russell Long, a conservative Democrat from Louisiana, wondered: "If a nation with 14 million can make Uncle Sam run, what will China think?" Only Senator Mike Mansfield of Montana, Johnson's successor as majority leader, rejected the Americanization of the war. "Whatever pledge we had was to *assist* [South Vietnam] in its own defense. Since then there has been no government of legitimacy. . . . We owe this government nothing."

Johnson was unpersuaded by Mansfield, and at a low-key, midday press conference on July 28, 1965, he announced the additional 100,000 troops. That afternoon Mansfield wrote Johnson that most of the public approved of what he was doing because they trusted him as their president, but "beneath the support there is deep concern and a great deal of confusion which could explode at any time."

FIGHTING THE WAR, 1966–1967

During 1966 and 1967 the number of United States troops in South Vietnam rose from 190,000 to 535,000 (see figure, page 296). Yet this expeditionary force could not prevail against the NLF and even contributed to the further deterioration of the government and armed forces of South Vietnam. The Americans were trying to apply lessons learned in conventional wars (the Second World War and Korea) to a very different kind of struggle against a guerrilla force. The "army

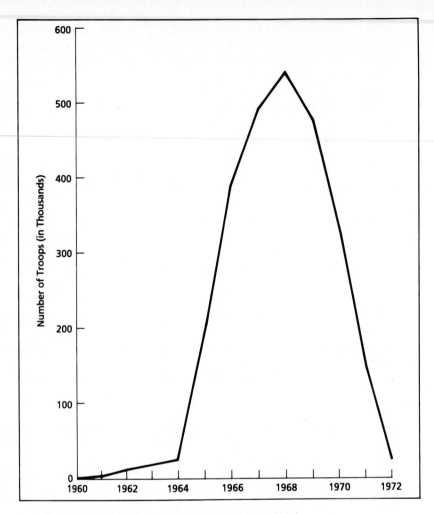

Levels of United States Troops in Vietnam, at Years' End

concept" developed over the past twenty-five years held that wars could be won with advanced materiel and technology—aerial bombardment, tank attacks, artillery, electronic detection fences—rather than with soldiers armed with rifles. These principles seemed to make sense for a productive, industrial society that relied on conscripts. If machines could substitute for soldiers, the casualties would decline and public support would continue. Yet advocates of a high-tech war misunderstood the realities of the war in Vietnam. The army concept removed the American forces from direct contact with the people they ostensibly were helping and ultimately contributed to loss of the war.

The Strategy of Attrition

General Westmoreland tried to perfect a strategy of attrition—that is, a gradual wearing down of the enemy—against the Vietcong and North Vietnamese. He used helicopters to send units of Americans into the countryside on search-and-destroy missions to root out and kill enemy soldiers. Americans would fly out in the morning, pursue the Vietcong in firefights, count the dead, and return to their bases in the evening. The measure of success became the "body count" of enemy soldiers killed, rather than territory captured, the standard in earlier wars. The procedure encouraged abuses. Local commanders, hoping to please their superiors in Saigon, inflated the death figures. Moreover, reliance on the body count offered an incentive to shoot first and ask no questions. On marine remembered that his first night on patrol "about fifty people shot this old guy. Everybody claimed they shot him. He got shot 'cause he started running. It was an old man running to tell his family. . . . Any Vietnamese out at night was the enemy."

Before the United States troops descended from their helicopters, giant B-52 bombers and smaller fighter jets pounded the battlefields. The United States dropped more bombs each month than fell on Europe during the entire Second World War. But the B-52 raids, code-named Arc Light, alerted the Vietcong and North Vietnamese forces that the Americans were on the way, giving them time to withdraw or dive into hundreds of miles of tunnels to protect themselves from the massive firepower. Unexploded bombs and artillery shells also became a weapon used by the Vietcong against the Americans. About 2 percent of the artillery shells and 5 percent of the bombs from B-52s did not explode on initial impact. The enemy developed shrewd booby traps using these unexploded bombs, killing or wounding thousands of inexperienced American troops. In 1966 over 1,000 American soldiers died of wounds caused by booby traps, and in the first six months of 1967, 17 percent of all American casualties resulted from mines or booby traps. The dollar cost of the bombing also mounted quickly to about $2.5 billion per year.

The NLF forces kept gaining strength on the ground with guerrilla tactics developed earlier by the Vietminh. They avoided firefights where they could, forcing the Americans to waste enormous energy and materiel for meager gains. They continued political organization in the countryside even as American bombers flew overhead. One American correspondent, alarmed at the apparent inability of United States commanders to acknowledge the strengths of the NLF, complained to a general, "How do you expect our forces to win the hearts and minds of the people when all they do is take off from one army base and fly overhead at 1,500 feet while Charlie [one of many

Two Vietcong guerrillas carry homemade weapons. The Communists' ingenuity continually bewildered the Americans, who expected that United States technological superiority would easily subdue the enemy. *UPI/Bettmann Newsphotos.*

nicknames for the NLF] is sitting down there and he's got 'em by the testicles jerking, and every time he jerks their hearts and mind follow?"

Despite such complaints, the United States Army continued to rely on search-and-destroy operations. The largest occurred in late 1966 and early 1967. In one such mission, which lasted from September to November 1966, 22,000 United States and ARVN troops, supported by B-52 bombers and massive artillery fire, pursued the NLF northwest of Saigon. In another search-and-destroy operation from February through May 1967, American soldiers followed raids by B-52s that reduced the landscape to the eerie bleakness of the moon, making hundreds of square miles uninhabitable by the Vietnamese peasants whom the Americans were supposedly helping. Americans entering villages to root out the Vietcong sometimes carried out so-called zippo raids, igniting the peasants' thatched huts with tracer bullets, flamethrowers, and cigarette lighters, to deny sanctuary to the enemy.

Such actions not only enraged the peasantry, but also shocked

Americans who saw film footage on the evening news. Yet this enormous firepower failed to eradicate the Vietcong, who simply melted away until the assault stopped. One reporter likened each blow to "a sledgehammer on a floating cork; somehow the cork refused to stay down." An American general later acknowledged that it was physically impossible to keep the enemy from slipping away.

All the while, North Vietnamese commander General Nguyen Vo Giap, the victor at Dienbienphu, thought the Americans were playing into his hands as he waged a protracted guerrilla war. The search-and-destroy operations took Americans away from the heavily populated coastal plain, where the NLF and North gained strength among the population. As the Americans engaged in inconclusive battles in the interior, they paid less attention to "pacification," the effort to bind the peasantry to the Saigon government.

Effects on Vietnamese Society

If anything, the Saigon government lost more of the affections of its people as the American war devastated the countryside. As part of the efforts to deny sanctuary to the enemy, American forces used giant transport planes to spray trees with defoliants. Between 1962 and 1972 the Americans dropped over 1 million pounds of chemicals such as Agent Orange and destroyed more than half of the forests of South Vietnam. Some of the crews jokingly adopted the motto, "Only You Can Prevent Forests," but many crew members later suffered serious health problems that probably derived from the toxins they dropped.

The effects on the crops of the ostensible beneficiaries of the war effort, the South Vietnamese farmers, were immediate and devastating. Deadly defoliants, dropped from planes on a suspected Vietcong area in the afternoon, would soon drift over friendly villages; by the next morning, fruit fell from nearby trees, and leaves on rubber plants turned brown and broke off. Farmers blamed the Americans for loss of their crops, and they feared the defoliants harmed animal and human life as well. The birth of a physically or mentally impaired infant often was blamed on the defoliation campaigns. American forces also used poisons to destroy the rice crop grown in Vietcong areas, expecting the hungry enemy to emerge and fight. The theory overlooked the NLF's practice of buying or taking rice from the peasants, so that the Americans ruined ten pounds of rice grown by friendly farmers for every pound of Vietcong rice they destroyed. South Vietnam, once an exporter of rice, began importing it from neighboring countries and even the United States as the war ground on.

The havoc in the countryside forced hundreds of thousands of peasants to flee their homes. Between 1964 and 1969 more than 4 million South Vietnamese, one-fourth of the population, were refugees at one time or another. Those who remained on their land often did so only because they feared that the Vietcong would redistribute their land if they were gone. Many of those who fled the terror from the skies, the defoliants, the artillery barrages, or the zippo raids swarmed to cities that had neither room nor facilities for them; others languished in squalid refugee camps.

The population of Saigon, under 500,000 in the 1950s, swelled to 1.5 million by the mid-1960s. The capital and other cities near American installations–Danang, Cam Ranh Bay, Hue, to name a few— changed from Asian commercial centers, conducting business in traditional ways, to army boom towns. Seedy bars and brothels sprang up near American bases, with women and girls as young as thirteen prostituting themselves for the GIs. Senator J. William Fulbright complained that the United States had transformed South Vietnam "into a gigantic whorehouse." Over 100,000 Amerasian children were born of liaisons between American soldiers and Vietnamese women. These children of mixed race were scorned by other Vietnamese and, after the Americans departed, suffered terrible privation.

The presence of over 500,000 Americans transformed the Vietnamese economy from the production of food and rubber to a concentration on servicing the newcomers. At first the GIs paid cash in United States dollars. Prices zoomed 170 percent in 1966 and 1967, and many Vietnamese could no longer afford the basic necessities of life. To halt the price rise, the army started paying its soldiers in scrip that could be used only to purchase consumer goods on United States bases. Vietnamese entrepreneurs responded by importing watches, tape recorders, motorcycles, radios, and the like to sell to local people who worked for the Americans and were paid in South Vietnamese currency.

Corruption, already a problem before the Americans arrived en masse, vastly increased in 1966. The government rented space to the Americans at exorbitant prices. South Vietnamese officials took bribes from contractors wishing to do business with United States agencies, including military bases and rural development organizations. Others demanded payment for licenses, permits, visas, and passports. Some Saigon officials traded in opium, and many engaged in the flourishing black market. Everything was for sale—United States government scrip, South Vietnamese piasters, Scotch whiskey, watches, hand grenades, rifles.

Americans often were aware of the corruption that eroded South Vietnamese society, but Westmoreland thought that curing it would alarm the very government the United States wanted to help. General Nguyen Cao Ky, who became prime minister in 1966, acknowledged that most of the generals were corrupt, but thought it did not matter. "Corruption exists everywhere, and people can live with some of it," he explained. "You live with it in Chicago and New York." Some mid-ranking American officials wanted to threaten the government of Saigon with loss of aid if it did not remove corrupt officials. Westmoreland overruled such advice, fearing it would only annoy the government without producing appropriate changes, or perhaps lead to the government's collapse.

By late 1967 the build-up had not won the war. McNamara's prediction of late 1966 that he could "see the light at the end of the tunnel in Vietnam" provoked the rueful rejoinder that what he had glimpsed was the headlight of another train engineered by Ho Chi Minh. Thirteen thousand United States servicemen had been killed. Only the lowest goal—denying a victory to the NLF—had been earned, and that success was not assured. Other American war aims—creating a stable South Vietnamese government, capable of waging the war on its own and winning the affection of its people, and forcing the North to quit—had become more elusive than ever. As American involvement intensified, South Vietnamese society dissolved. People either became dependents of the United States or went underground to join the NLF. The South Vietnamese government, once the object of Washington's confidence-building measures, slipped into dependence or obstructionism.

MILITARY SERVICE AND THE DRAFT

Although the fighting took place far from the United States, the war deeply affected the way Americans lived their lives. Military service became an important, life-changing experience for over 2 million American men. In the typical tour of duty they encountered racial tensions, boredom, drugs, and a widespread brutality against the Vietnamese. Even those Americans who did not fight were changed by the war. Millions of young men spent a substantial part of their late adolescence or young adulthood wondering whether they would be conscripted under the Selective Service system or seeking ways to avoid participation in the fighting. Far more men did not go to Vietnam than went, but the war created deep divisions among people of an entire generation. Those who fought in the war often resented those who did not, and people who did not go to Vietnam sometimes treated those who did with scorn, pity, or condescension.

Selective Service

Unlike the Second World War, when the armed forces needed nearly every able-bodied American man, the military effort in Vietnam required less than half the eligible population. Of the 27 million available men between the ages of nineteen and twenty-six, 16 million never served in the armed forces. Of the 11 million who did, 9 million enlisted more or less voluntarily and 2.2 million were drafted under the terms of the Selective Service Act of 1947. A total of approximately 2.8 million men, along with 6,400 women, actually saw service in Vietnam between 1961 and 1973.

Although the draft took only about 10 percent of the men subject to its call, Selective Service affected the lives of nearly everybody. A major study of the draft conducted after the war concluded that it "cast the entire generation into a contest for survival." Working "as an instrument of Darwinian social policy," the draft, "through an elaborate structure of deferments, exemptions, legal technicalities, and noncombat military alternatives, . . . rewarded those who manipulated the system to their advantage." As the war became more dangerous and American casualties rose to 300 dead per week, many young men wanted to reduce the risk to their personal safety. A number of options were available: deferments for marriage (dropped in 1965), fatherhood, or student status; enlistment in the National Guard or reserves; enlistment in the armed forces with promises to serve in places other than Vietnam; and service in noncombat zones in Vietnam.

The wealthy and educated, those most aware of the intricacies of the system, knew best how to avoid the most dangerous duty. As a result, only 24 percent of eligible men from high-income families entered the military, 9 percent served in Vietnam, and 7 percent saw combat, mostly as officers. Of the eligible men from middle-income families, 30 percent served in the military, 12 percent in Vietnam, and 7 percent in combat. For low-income men, 40 percent entered military service, 19 percent went to Vietnam, and 15 percent saw combat. Such discrepancies produced distressing inequities in the make-up of the forces bearing the brunt of the heaviest fighting.

Draft Resistance

The Selective Service system appeared corrupt and demeaning to those who faced conscription. Kingman Brewster, president of Yale University, perceived "a tarnishing of the national spirit and a cops and robbers view of national obligation" as young men looked for ways to avoid the draft. One young inductee who had the job of filing case histories at the local draft board had his eyes opened as he discovered the ruses others of his generation used to avoid being called up. He telephoned his mother and reported, "The whole set up is corrupt. I don't need to *be* here! I don't need to *be* here! I don't need to *be* here! I simply didn't *need* to be drafted!" Nonetheless, he went to Vietnam and became one of the 58,000 men who died. His feelings that the draft was arbitrary and unfair were common, and a Harris poll concluded that most Americans believed that men who went to Vietnam were "suckers, having risked their lives in the wrong war, in the wrong place, in the wrong time."

Three-quarters of the 16 million men who did not serve in Vietnam admitted that they had changed their life plans to stay away from Vietnam, and a majority (55 percent) said they actively took steps to avoid the draft. Male college enrollments were about 6 to 7 percent higher than they otherwise would have been because of the draft. Twelve percent of men in one survey reported that fear of the draft prevented them from taking time out from their studies, and 5 percent claimed they had changed their course of study to prolong their deferment. Until 1968, graduate students earned deferments, so graduate school applications shot up in 1966 and 1967. The dean of one college of business administration reported that 90 percent of the male applicants to his school had sought admission out of fear of the draft.

Other options remained for those without deferments. Even if drafted, a man had to be physically fit before he could be inducted. Some young men used family doctors to document conditions that would keep them out of the service. One physician commented that "the traditional doctor-patient relationship is one of preserving life. I save lives by keeping people out of the Army." But some doctors resented these young men. One Bloomington, Indiana, physician volunteered to write letters on behalf of his patients to their draft boards. He did so, but his letters noted that the men were fit and urged the boards to induct them as punishment for manipulating the system.

A network of draft counselors, initially sponsored by pacifist churches and organizations, arose to advise young men of their rights under the Selective Service and legal ways to avoid induction. After a 1965 Supreme Court ruling in *United States* v. *Seegar*, conscientious objector status was available to anyone with a "sincerely founded reason" for opposing war. Before that time only members of recognized pacifist sects—for example, Mennonites, Quakers, Jehovah's Witnesses, Brethren—had been entitled to register as conscientious objectors. After *Seegar*, draft counselors advised young men on how to present their antiwar beliefs in a persuasive way: "Sit down and think about why you are against killing people in war. Write down short sentences or ideas (for instance: love . . . brotherhood . . . peace . . . equality . . . personal responsibility)." Counselors advised obtaining testimonials from teachers, scout leaders, or clergy who would vouch for the sincerity of the applicant's beliefs. Not surprisingly, the educated and articulate fared better than the poor and the less well connected at obtaining conscientious objector status. The 172,000 men who did gain such status during the war were expected by their draft boards to perform some sort of alternative service, but almost 50,000 of them were never found by their draft boards.

Some men simply refused induction or tried to evade their draft boards. About 209,000 men were accused of some sort of draft offense, but only 25,000 were indicted, and only 4,000 received prison sentences. Even those who entered the military sometimes refused to accept service in Vietnam. Some 12,000 men went absent without leave (AWOL) to escape an assignment to Vietnam. About 50,000 deserters or accused draft offenders took flight during the war, with 30,000 of them going to Canada. Many of these men quietly came home over the next decade, but 11,000 remained fugitives until 1977, when President Jimmy Carter proclaimed a pardon.

The Tour of Duty

For the men who went to Vietnam, life in the armed forces bore little resemblance to the experiences of their fathers or older brothers in the Second World War and the Korean War—and no likeness at all to the idealized versions of those wars presented in movies and television programs. Vietnam was often a devastating, demoralizing, brutalizing experience. One day a young man would be in the relatively familiar surroundings of his military base at home; the next day, after eighteen hours on an airplane, he would find himself in the alien landscape of Vietnam, in a situation conducive to both frustration and terror. The enemy, often indistinguishable from the local population, could materialize suddenly from the jungle and attack with horrible efficiency. On patrol, a soldier might be blown apart at any moment by a booby trap. Conventional precautions and tactics often seemed irrelevant. It was especially difficult to maintain the troops' morale when they saw more and more lives lost for little or no gain.

The difficulties were compounded by the military's personnel policy. Unlike earlier wars, in which soldiers served for the "duration," soldiers had a one-year tour of duty in Vietnam, spread over thirteen months, with thirty days' leave for "rest and recreation." A mixture of demography, politics, and military management prompted this arrangement. Because the pool of available soldiers far exceeded the number needed, keeping 500,000 men at the front while allowing *all* others to steer free of battle would cause resentment among those who fought and erode public support for the war. Therefore the military limited the time of service and continually rotated the forces.

According to General Westmoreland, fixing the date when a GI would leave Vietnam helped to boost morale and give each soldier a goal. In fact, however, the goal often became self-preservation: men approaching the end of their tours became reluctant to fight. No one wanted to be killed or wounded, but risking death or injury a few weeks before mustering out appeared especially pointless. One commander called the twelve-month tour "the worst personnel policy in history." To make matters worse, units did not stay together throughout their tours, increasing the sense of isolation of soldiers and officers. Napoleon once observed that "soldiers have to eat soup together for a long time before they are ready to fight," but Americans discarded that lesson in Vietnam. Troops killed or wounded were replaced by newcomers, whose tour of duty expired later than those of other men in the unit.

Officers too never remained with units throughout their terms, because the armed forces rotated commanders, down to the level of platoon lieutenants, every six months. Disgruntled commanders complained that the same war was fought over again every six months. The policy arose because it allowed officers to experience a variety of commands, a sure way of gaining promotion in the professional force developed after the Second World War. Such résumé enhancement—"ticket punching," as it came to be known—eliminated the possibility of strong bonds forming between officers and men. In many cases, the young lieutenants who served as platoon commanders never even learned the basic combat skills that would inspire confidence in the soldiers under their command.

The lack of rapport between commanders and soldiers made personal hostilities difficult to control. The murder of officers by enlisted men—often with a fragmentation grenade or other anonymous weapon—became frequent enough to earn its own slang name, "fragging." Moreover, the armed forces reflected the racial tensions of American society. Many black soldiers had no white friends in the ostensibly integrated units. Inevitably, some of the violence among GIs took on a racial tone.

Even worse were the atrocities against the Vietnamese, whom the GIs often referred to as "gooks." In an unsuccessful war against an enemy that could strike without warning and then instantly melt away, soldiers came to disregard the so-called Rules of Engagement that supposedly regulated behavior toward the enemy. Once the body count became the principal means of measuring success in the war, some soldiers adopted the grisly habit of chopping off the ears of dead Vietnamese for trophies. They would "take the dog-tag chain and fill that up with ears," one infantryman recalled. "If we were movin' through the jungle, they'd just put the bloody ear on the chain and stick the ear in their pocket and keep on going. Wouldn't take time to dry it off. Then when we got back, they would nail 'em up on the walls of our hootch, you know, as a trophy." In many cases, the GIs gave up the nearly impossible task of distinguishing the Vietcong from uninvolved civilians; besides burning peasants' houses, they shot any Vietnamese they saw. "If it moves, it's VC [Vietcong]" became a common slogan for American soldiers. The most dramatic atrocity of the war occurred in March 1968, when American soldiers massacred more than two hundred unarmed Vietnamese villagers, mostly women and children, at the hamlet of My Lai; the military managed to keep the incident secret until the next year, but it eventually became a symbol of the war's brutality.

To escape the fear and absurdity of a war without front lines, leadership, or clear goals, many soldiers turned to drugs. Marijuana, opium, and heroin were freely available and inexpensive in the cities, because officials of the South Vietnamese government engaged in the drug trade. So did the CIA, which used profits from drugs to finance a secret counterinsurgency program in the highlands and along the Laotian border. Because soldiers conducting search-and-destroy patrols returned often to bases near the cities, they could obtain drugs for use while fighting. One infantryman who served from mid-1967 to mid-1968 remembered that "in the field most of the guys stayed high. Lots of them couldn't face it. In a sense, if you was high it seemed like a game you was in. You didn't take it serious. It stopped a lot of nervous breakdowns."

As the war dragged on without success, many soldiers despaired. They grew bitter at lectures from well-meaning officers or civilians about the political importance of fighting communism, yet they were equally angry at those who said the war was unwinnable. "You had to have been there" became a refrain of disheartened veterans. Many began to feel used and victimized, and their outlook scarcely improved when they returned home. Back in the United States, the returning GIs received few thanks for their efforts, and in many cases they felt despised as symbols of the unpopular war. After all they had been through, hundreds of thousands of Vietnam veterans suffered from post-traumatic stress disorder and other long-lasting psychological and emotional disabilities.

THE RISE OF DISSENT AND COLLAPSE OF THE COLD WAR CONSENSUS

In addition to the soldiers in Vietnam, at least one man in Washington approached nervous exhaustion as the war expanded: President Johnson. Richard Goodwin, a speechwriter co-opted from the Kennedy camp, believed that Johnson actually became clinically paranoid. Goodwin kept a diary, noting the president's intense reactions to criticism of escalation of the war: "I can't trust anybody anymore. . . . I'm going to get rid of anybody who doesn't agree with my policies. I'm not going in the liberal direction. There's no future with them. They're just out to get me, always have been." Goodwin brought transcripts of tirades like these to a psychiatrist, who told him he was witnessing "a textbook case of paranoid disintegration, the eruption of long-suppressed irrationalities."

Johnson's personal crisis was deepened by mounting criticism of the war from former supporters. Arkansas Senator J. William Fulbright, chairman of the Senate Foreign Relations Committee and an old friend from Johnson's days as majority leader, was among the first moderate public figures to dissent from the build-up in Vietnam. In September 1965 Fulbright told the Senate that "U.S. policy in the Dominican crisis [the previous April] has been characterized by a lack of candor." The same problem plagued Johnson's explanations for his actions in Vietnam, the senator said.

Over the next few months Fulbright undertook a crash course on American policy toward Indochina, and the following February his committee opened televised hearings on Vietnam policy. Numerous creators of American foreign policy since the Cold War told the committee that the administration had headed down the wrong road in Vietnam. George F. Kennan, one of the architects of containment, worried that the "unbalanced concentration of resources and attention" in Vietnam diverted Washington from what he considered to be the true focus of its foreign policy—Europe. General James Gavin, a Second World War airborne hero, urged that the United States stop the bombing, send no more troops, retreat to enclaves in Vietnam, and look for a negotiated settlement. Fulbright expressed disbelief at Secretary of State Dean Rusk's repeated assertions that "this is a clear case of international Communist aggression." The chairman thought that most of the world viewed the conflict in Vietnam as "a civil war in which outside parties have become involved." Two months later Fulbright observed that the war had damaged the Great Society and hurt the nation's relations with the Soviet Union and Europe. He lamented "the arrogance of power," which he defined as a "psychological need that nations seem to have to prove that they are bigger, stronger, better than other nations." Johnson dismissed his old friend's complaints as the bitter recriminations of "a frustrated old woman" who was angry at not having been appointed secretary of state.

While Fulbright and about a dozen other senators dissented from escalation in 1966, more potent opposition to the war arose outside the government in the form of a citizens' peace movement. Opposition to the war in Vietnam joined distinct groups—peace liberals, nonviolent pacifists, and social revolutionaries and radical pacifists. Beginning in 1965, they organized "teach-ins" in which opponents of the war lectured college audiences on the evils of the war. The peace movement also sponsored demonstrations against the administration, a 1967 "Vietnam Summer" of protests against the war, and, in

1968, an effort to "dump Johnson" as president and replace him with someone who would extricate the United States from the endless war.

Some members of the movement agreed with Kennan that Vietnam was diverting American attention from more serious issues. Long-time Socialist party leader Norman Thomas acknowledged that more pressing problems were clamoring for attention, "but it is a practical and emotional absurdity to think that the government or people can or will deal with these and other pressing questions until it stops the war in Vietnam." By 1967 even the least radical participants in the peace movement believed, as Seymour Melman of the Committee for a Sane Nuclear Policy (SANE) put it, "policy change now requires institutional change as well." When the Students for a Democratic Society, a New Left group (see Chapter 9), organized the Vietnam Summer in 1967, one Detroit organizer reported, "I find that I am not really working here to 'end the war in Vietnam'. . . . I am working here to make people *feel* Vietnam, to make them realize that it is part of a pattern which oppresses them, as well as Vietnamese peasants." Along with opposition to the war, a generalized dissatisfaction with American government began to spread.

Public antiwar activism surged in the spring of 1967. Martin Luther King, Jr., who previously had expressed quiet misgivings about the war, openly broke with the Johnson administration. He called for de-escalation, helped organize a new group, Negotiation Now!, and endorsed the Vietnam Summer. On April 15, crowds of 100,000 in New York and 50,000 in San Francisco heard speakers from both the antiwar and civil rights movements call for an end to the war and a recommitment to the goal of racial equality at home. Johnson grew alarmed that King and pediatrician Benjamin Spock, now an antiwar activist, might run for president and vice president, respectively, in 1968. The White House worried so much that Press Secretary George Christian leaked to columnists friendly to the administration FBI files purporting to show King's connections to members of the Communist party.

Federal agencies constantly observed, infiltrated, and harassed dissident and antiwar groups. The FBI compared Senator Fulbright's position during his 1966 Vietnam hearing to those taken by the Communist party. The CIA infiltrated such antiwar groups as Women Strike for Peace, the Washington Peace Center, SANE, the Congress on Racial Equality (CORE), the War Resisters League, and the National Mobilization Committee Against the War. In August 1967 the CIA initiated Operation Chaos, designed to disrupt and confuse the antiwar movement. Agents sent phony letters to editors of publications defaming antiwar leaders; other agents infiltrated antiwar groups who called for bombings or violent confrontation with police.

Eventually the CIA opened files on over 7,000 Americans—in violation of its charter, which stipulated it would not operate inside the United States. The Internal Revenue Service honored a CIA request to examine *Ramparts* magazine's taxes after the gadfly publication revealed that the CIA had secretly funded the National Student Association for over a decade.

The president became frantic as plans developed for a massive march on Washington in October 1967 to demand a halt to the bombing and immediate negotiations to end the war. In order to discredit the movement, Johnson asked his attorney general, Ramsey Clark, to leak information about the left-wing and Communist affiliations of some of the leaders. Nevertheless, on October 21, a crowd estimated at 100,000 assembled on the Mall in front of the Lincoln Memorial to hear speeches opposing the war. Later, a group of about 50,000 marched to the Pentagon, where scores crossed police lines and were arrested.

As important in changing public attitudes as large demonstrations were the nightly televised newscasts showing the fighting and the devastation of Vietnamese society. Satellite technology made possible instantaneous transmission of film shot in Vietnam that day. In a war without front lines, reporters and camera crews traveled with platoons from their bases to the helicopter landing zones and into firefights in Vietnamese villages. They captured on film the flames of the zippo raids, the moans of wounded soldiers, the terror in the eyes of children left homeless during the fighting. What they could not show, because it did not happen, was the sort of scene in which GIs liberated a village to the cheers of grateful residents. For a public brought up on the heroic newsreels of the Second World War, where such pictures had brought tears of pride to the home front, the sharp contrast between the "good war" of 1941 to 1945 and the quagmire of Vietnam proved disillusioning.

As this "living room war" ground on without progress, Americans at home, like the soldiers in the field, had trouble distinguishing friendly Vietnamese from the enemy, and wanted no part of either. The fighting appeared pointless, and the public longed for relief from a war it had not anticipated. Distrust of the government rose sharply in 1967 as observers noted a yawning "credibility gap" between the optimism of the president and his advisers and the continuing violence shown on TV every evening.

Antiwar activities, the failure to achieve victory, and press coverage of the horrors of the fighting altered the way the public viewed the war. Throughout the country there was a sharp division between "hawks" who supported the American war effort and "doves" who opposed it. In the beginning of 1967 most Americans were still hawks, willing to escalate the war if only it could be won decisively.

Army paratroopers use a helicopter to evacuate a wounded soldier during a battle with regular North Vietnamese army forces. Helicopters provided exceptional mobility for the American troops, but such advantages were not enough to win the war—or to quiet the mounting criticism at home. *Wide World Photos.*

Fewer than a third of the public told a Gallup poll that they believed the war had been a mistake. By July that figure had risen to 41 percent, and by the time of the Washington march in October, 46 percent thought the United States should never have entered the war. Yet the number calling for an immediate American withdrawal from Vietnam remained low. A mere 6 percent wanted withdrawal in February, and by December that proportion had risen only to 10 percent. Nevertheless, in the fall, only 28 percent of the public approved of President Johnson's handling of the war. Most Americans found themselves neither hawks nor doves on Vietnam; they simply wanted relief. As the American war entered its third year in 1968, Senator Mansfield's 1965 warning about the shallowness of public support had proved prophetic.

Although no agreement existed about what to do next, the general consensus on foreign policy had shattered. A significant number of people began to question the very basis of American foreign policy. Did the principle of containment mean that the United States should take part in any Third World conflict in which one side identified with socialism or communism? In such places as Vietnam, were the Communists any worse than the regimes the United States chose to support? Would a triumph by the Communists truly weaken the United States' position with respect to its principal Cold War opponent, the Soviet Union? Did it make sense, in any event, for the United States to fight a so-called limited war with much chance of embarrassment and little chance of victory? Although relatively few Americans had clear answers to such questions in 1967 and 1968, the war led many people to think about them.

Looking for a Way Out

By the end of 1967 doubts over further escalation of the war assailed even some of its sponsors. The president wondered about the usefulness of bombing North Vietnam. Secretary of Defense McNamara also became morose at the lack of progress. The effort to secure the countryside had, "if anything, gone backward," he admitted. At one point he recommended an unconditional halt to the bombing to get serious negotiations started, but Johnson refused after learning that the Joint Chiefs of Staff had threatened to resign, jointly, if the bombing was stopped. As he began to despair of winning the war through advanced technology, McNamara wanted out. In the fall of 1967 Johnson accepted McNamara's resignation from the Defense Department, replacing him with long-time Democratic party adviser Clark Clifford in March 1968.

Johnson tried to open negotiations with the North Vietnamese in the fall of 1967. Harvard professor Henry Kissinger secretly relayed to Hanoi through French intermediaries an administration promise to stop the bombing, with the understanding that the pause would lead to prompt discussions with the North. The United States would not demand that the North remove its troops from the South but would assume that Hanoi would not take advantage of the end of the bombing by raising its troop levels. Kissinger's message also indicated that the United States remained firmly committed to the South Vietnamese government, now headed by President Nguyen Van Thieu. Although Washington would permit Vietcong participation in the Saigon administration, the NLF would have to drop its revolutionary program. Washington offered no guarantee that it would reduce its troop commitments or halt the ground war while talks went forward. As Kissinger secretly presented these conditions, the bombing continued, suggesting that the military did not know what the Johnson administration hoped to accomplish. Suffering from the bombing, the Hanoi government rejected these overtures and called once more for the United States to quit what it described as an "illegal" intervention in Vietnam's civil war.

With this rebuff, Johnson sank further into gloom, wary of escalation but incapable of devising a satisfactory negotiating formula. After McNamara announced his resignation, the president's advisers became more hawkish. William Bundy, Clark Clifford, Dean Rusk, Walt Rostow, and Maxwell Taylor told Johnson that he could not satisfy his domestic critics with a bombing halt. Doves had "insatiable appetites," Bundy explained, and they would only demand more concessions. North Vietnam too would view a pause in the bombing as a sign of weakness, and "to stop the bombing now would give the Communists something for nothing."

The president hoped that an optimistic assessment of the war from the battlefield commander might buy time with the restless public. In November General Westmoreland returned to Washington and explained to reporters that he was "very, very encouraged" because "we are making real progress." He told Congress that the North Vietnamese and Vietcong could not hold out much longer. He thought that the United States forces had reached a point where the end of the war was in view.

Westmoreland's rosy scenario made headlines, but Johnson's civilian advisers worried about the effect of the war on domestic tranquility and the position of the United States in the rest of the world. Johnson then assembled a group of so-called Wise Men, foreign policy officials who had served various administrations since 1940, to chart a future path in Vietnam. They supported Johnson's course to date but warned that "endless inconclusive fighting" had become "the most serious cause of domestic disquiet." At the end of 1967 Johnson agreed to review the ground war to find a way to reduce American casualties and turn over more of the fighting to the ARVN.

The Tet Offensive and the Decision to De-escalate

January 1968 brought a military embarrassment elsewhere in Asia, when the U.S.S. *Pueblo*, a navy intelligence ship, was captured by North Koreans near the coast of their country. The *Pueblo* crew would remain captive almost a year, until negotiations finally produced their release in December. But this incident was a minor one compared to what the North Vietnamese and Vietcong had in store.

At 2:45 A.M. on January 30, 1968—on Tet, the Vietnamese New Year—a squad of nineteen Vietcong commandos blasted a hole in the wall protecting the United States embassy in Saigon, ran into the courtyard, and engaged the marine guards for the next six hours. All nineteen commandos were killed, but the damage they had done to Washington's position in Vietnam could not be repaired. The assault on the embassy represented the most dramatic part of a coordinated offensive by the North Vietnamese and NLF forces against the population centers of Vietnam over the Tet holidays. They attacked the Saigon airport, the presidential palace, and the headquarters of the ARVN's general staff. With the benefit of complete surprise, the

A squad of United States marines seek cover in the ruins during the fierce battle to recapture the city of Hue from the Vietcong during the 1968 Tet offensive. *UPI/ Bettmann Newsphotos.*

North Vietnamese and NLF battled with the Americans and ARVN for control of thirty-six of forty-four provincial capitals, five of six major cities, and sixty-four district capitals.

In most areas the Americans and ARVN repulsed the Communists, killing perhaps 40,000 while losing 3,400 of their own. The cost to Vietnamese civilians ran much higher, with 1 million refugees swelling the already teeming camps in two weeks. One of the most grisly scenes occurred in the old imperial capital of Hue, once noted for its serene beauty. The Vietcong succeeded in controlling the city for six weeks. When the battle ended and the Americans and ARVN recaptured Hue, their bombs and artillery had left it, according to one soldier, a "shattered, stinking hulk, its street choked with rubble and rotting bodies." The ARVN uncovered a mass grave containing the bodies of 2,800 South Vietnamese officeholders who had been executed by the Vietcong.

On the American side the principal casualty was the cheery scenario of progress in the war. After Tet, Westmoreland's assurances of the previous fall that an American victory could be achieved within two years sounded hopelessly unrealistic. His claims in the midst of the battle that the United States had defeated the enemy provoked

William C. Westmoreland

William C. Westmoreland grew up wanting to be a soldier. Born in 1914 in a South Carolina cotton-mill town, he thrilled to stories of his ancestors' heroics during the Civil War. After attending West Point, he rose swiftly through the army ranks during the Second World War and Korea, and by age forty-two he was the army's youngest major general. In 1960 he returned to his beloved West Point as superintendent.

Greater responsibility was thrust on Westmoreland in June 1964 when President Johnson named him commander of the American forces in Vietnam. Like most successful officers who had fought in Europe during the Second World War, Westmoreland believed that American military technology could overwhelm any potential adversary; he therefore

derision. CBS News anchor Walter Cronkite, until this point supportive of the Johnson administration, growled, "What the hell is going on? I thought we were winning the war." Cronkite publicly denounced "the optimists who have been wrong in the past." One of the most famous photographs of the war, showing the commander of the Saigon police shooting a Vietcong suspect in the head in the middle of a busy street, outraged opinion at home. So did the comment of a United States Army officer who had helped wrest the village of Ben Tre from the Vietcong: "We had to destroy the town to save it."

In Washington, Johnson, already discouraged by the lack of progress and Robert McNamara's defection, grappled with Westmoreland's request for an additional 206,000 men. Failure to provide them, the general implied, meant losing the war. For Johnson, however, sending that many troops seemed a major escalation; it would risk Chinese or Soviet intervention and shock opinion at home. After Tet,

followed a strategy of attrition, or wearing down the enemy by use of massive firepower. At first the new commander seemed a welcome relief from his ineffectual predecessor, General Paul D. Harkins. Handsome and friendly, Westmoreland got along well with the soldiers, and *Time* magazine named him Man of the Year in 1966.

But Vietnam was not Europe, and Westmoreland never grasped that the United States was engaged in a political struggle more than a military engagement. Over the years his faith in a military solution became less persuasive. After the Tet offensive of early 1968, his optimistic promises to Congress the previous November seemed almost foolish, and President Johnson denied his request for more troops. In June 1968

Westmoreland was recalled from Vietnam to serve as army chief of staff for the next four years.

After his retirement he became bitter about the eventual Communist victory in Vietnam and his own falling reputation at home. By then, military experts had derided his strategy of attrition as ill-informed and unimaginative. From 1982 to 1985 Westmoreland pressed a libel suit against CBS News for claiming that he had deliberately misled Johnson by underestimating the number of enemy soldiers. Finally he dropped the suit, and CBS stated that it had not intended to cast doubt on his truthfulness. This awkward legal resolution only served to emphasize the blight that Vietnam had cast on the general's career. ■

78 percent of the public told a Harris poll that they thought the United States was not making progress in Vietnam, and only 26 percent approved of Johnson's handling of the war. Before he would grant Westmoreland's request, the president asked the new secretary of defense, Clark Clifford, to undertake a complete review of Vietnam policy.

Like McNamara before him, Clifford, once a hawk, now doubted whether more troops promised any progress. "I see more and more fighting with more and more casualties on the U.S. side and no end in sight to the action," he told the president. Civilian experts in the Defense Department revived a 1967 proposal by McNamara to change from a strategy of search and destroy to one of "population security." American forces should protect the bulk of the South's civilian population while encouraging the ARVN to bear more of the burden of the fighting. American casualties probably would decline, reducing public unhappiness at home, but the hope of military victory would

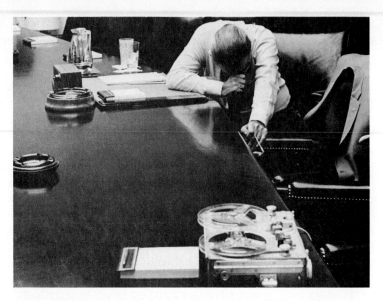

The frustrations of the apparently endless war in Vietnam nearly overwhelmed President Johnson in 1968. *Lyndon Baines Johnson Presidential Library.*

vanish. Clifford therefore pressed for a negotiated settlement. In early March, Johnson rejected Westmoreland's request for another 206,000 men.

Before deciding on future commitments, Johnson held another series of White House debates in mid-March. On one side stood Clifford, who now argued that the public demanded an end to the war, noting the "tremendous erosion of support" among the nation's business and legal elite. These people thought it foolish for the United States to go deeper into the "hopeless bog" of Vietnam. He pointed to European disappointment with the American preoccupation in Vietnam, as proven by the French demands for gold payment for their dollar holdings. On the other side were Secretary of State Rusk and National Security Adviser Walt Rostow. Rusk advocated the public announcement of a partial bombing halt, expecting the North Vietnamese to reject it. Rostow told the president to "hang in there," in the face of a restless and fickle public. As it became clear that North Vietnam and the NLF had not won during Tet, Rostow predicted, the public would renew its support for the war.

Clifford persuaded the president to reconvene the Wise Men, the group of foreign affairs experts who had served earlier administrations. During the last week of March they delivered some shocking opinions to the president. Dean Acheson, secretary of state under

Truman, who had endured his own agony during the Korean War, asserted that the United States could "no longer do the job we set out to do in the time we have left and we must begin to take steps to disengage." Cyrus Vance, former assistant secretary of defense, worried that "unless we do something quick, the mood in this country may lead us to withdraw."

Johnson did not like what he heard but could no longer ignore the mounting pressure to reverse course in Vietnam. Working with a trusted speechwriter, he prepared a nationally broadcast address for the evening of March 31, 1968. In it he promised a partial bombing halt that would limit American attacks to the region immediately north of the Demilitarized Zone at the 17th parallel. He promised to expand this partial bombing halt to a complete one "if our restraint is matched by restraint in Hanoi." He named Averell Harriman, one of the Wise Men, as the head of an American delegation to try to open peace talks with North Vietnam. Then, in a passage he wrote himself and kept secret from everyone but his wife, he withdrew from the 1968 presidential election race. In order to devote himself to the negotiations he had just promised, he pledged that "I shall not seek and I will not accept the nomination of my party for another term as your president."

THE ELECTION OF 1968

Lyndon Johnson had another reason for not seeking the Democratic nomination for president in 1968: he might not have received it. Anguish over the war had turned the Democrats against one another. For several years, many liberals and partisans of the Kennedy family had stifled their misgivings about Johnson because they supported his domestic reform agenda; now, however, they revolted and looked for someone to challenge him for the nomination. Finding a Democratic candidate to run for nomination against a sitting president, even one as unpopular as Johnson, proved difficult. Robert Kennedy, now a senator from New York, refused entreaties to join the battle, fearing defeat and the identification of his campaign as a family vendetta. Senator George McGovern of South Dakota, another Senate dove, also declined. Finally, an obscure Midwestern senator, Eugene McCarthy of Minnesota, allowed himself to be drafted into running in the March 12, 1968, New Hampshire presidential primary.

McCarthy's campaign seemed laughable at first. A retiring, self-deprecating figure, McCarthy shunned the glad-handing customary to politicians. One staff member detected an "inward self-hatred" that made McCarthy doubt whether he actually would be a good president. In the early weeks, McCarthy had few assistants, little money, and virtually no press coverage. Everything changed in February, however, as the public reeled from the shock of the Tet offensive. Thousands of college-age volunteers hurried to New Hampshire to help the campaign. McCarthy made Vietnam the issue, demanding a bombing halt and negotiations. Johnson's supporters took the bait, ran TV ads in which an announcer warned that "the Communists in Vietnam are watching the New Hampshire primary," denounced McCarthy as "a champion of appeasement and surrender," and predicted that he would receive less than a third of the vote. On election day McCarthy received 42.2 percent, coming within a few hundred votes of defeating Johnson in the preference poll; the Minnesota senator also took twenty of twenty-four delegates to the Democratic convention.

McCarthy's showing rattled the President and shook Robert Kennedy, who reconsidered his earlier refusal to enter the race now that it appeared a challenge to Johnson might succeed. After consulting old supporters and trying unsuccessfully to persuade McCarthy to withdraw in his favor, Kennedy announced his candidacy for the Democratic nomination on March 16. Johnson's worst nightmare had come to life. As he explained to a biographer, "the thing I had feared from the first day of my presidency was actually coming true. Robert Kennedy had openly announced his intention to reclaim the throne in the memory of his brother. And the American people, swayed by the magic of the name, were dancing in the streets." Two weeks later, Johnson announced his own withdrawal from the race.

Aftershocks from Johnson's speech still rumbled when, four days later, on April 4, James Earl Ray killed Martin Luther King, Jr., as King stood on the balcony of the Lorraine Motel in Memphis, Tennessee. The assassination ignited another spurt of black rage. Riots erupted in more than a hundred cities; within a week, police, the army, and the National Guard had killed thirty-seven people. Several blocks of downtown Washington were burned and looted. In Chicago, Mayor Richard J. Daley ordered his police to "shoot to kill arsonists, and shoot to maim looters." Spiro T. Agnew, Republican governor of Maryland, elected in 1966 as a moderate on racial matters, summoned the leaders of his state's NAACP and Urban League to Annapolis and warned them that he held them personally responsible for the devastation of Baltimore.

Some white politicians kept their heads. Robert Kennedy heard the news of King's murder shortly before addressing a few hundred supporters on an Indianapolis street corner. He informed them of what had happened and delivered a moving personal appeal for "compassion and love" to "those of you who are black and are tempted to be filled with hatred and distrust at the injustice of such an act." He explained that "what we need in the United States is not division;

what we need in the United States is not hatred; what we need in the United States is not violence or lawlessness, but love and wisdom, and compassion toward one another, and a feeling of justice toward those who still suffer within our country."

Two months later came Robert Kennedy's appointment with an assassin's bullet. Early in the morning on Wednesday, June 6, hours after he had eked out a narrow victory over Eugene McCarthy in the California Democratic primary, Kennedy was shot by Sirhan Sirhan, a Palestinian immigrant angry at the New York senator's support for Israel. Once more the country suffered through a funeral for one of the Kennedy brothers: a Requiem Mass in New York's St. Patrick's Cathedral, followed by a sad train ride south to Washington. Hundreds of thousands of mourners lined the tracks under a blazing sun. One senator on the train recalled that as he looked into their faces, "I saw sorrow, bewilderment. I saw fury and I saw fright." Robert Kennedy was buried next to his brother John in Arlington National Cemetery.

With Kennedy dead, McCarthy continued as the standard-bearer for some of the antiwar Democrats, who hoped to deny the nomination to Vice President Hubert Humphrey, who was supported by the prowar faction. Nevertheless, Humphrey gained the nomination at a tumultuous Chicago convention in August. Inside the hall the McCarthy and Kennedy forces, now backing George McGovern, lost a narrow vote on a "peace plank" in the platform repudiating the Johnson administration's handling of the Vietnam War. Humphrey won nomination by a two-to-one margin; on that same sultry night, the Chicago police force went mad, clubbing and tear-gassing a crowd of ten thousand demonstrators who had come to the city to protest the war in Vietnam. The police chased demonstrators into McCarthy's suite in a downtown hotel, beating several bloody and unconscious. Television cameras caught it all, including the protesters' chant, "The whole world is watching."

After such chaos, the Democratic nomination appeared worthless for Humphrey. Polls put him 16 percentage points behind the Republican nominee, Richard Nixon, the former vice president. After losing a 1962 race for governor of California, Nixon had resurrected his political career by traveling the country, supporting local Republican candidates. A third candidate also ran, Alabama Governor George Wallace, who had broken with the Democrats over civil rights. Some polls showed Wallace gaining 20 percent of the vote, much of it from formerly Democratic, working-class whites, largely but not exclusively in the South.

Both Nixon and Wallace fed public disgust with Vietnam. The Republican nominee, a hawk when escalation had begun in 1965, condemned the present stalemate. While presenting no specific way to end the war, Nixon promised an early "peace with honor" and hinted at a plan to reduce United States participation. Nixon also pursued a "southern strategy" of seeking the votes of white Democrats who were enraged at blacks. Promising to restore respect for law and order, he decried the riots that Johnson and Humphrey had not stopped. His vice-presidential nominee, Spiro Agnew, helped this cause by recalling the angry lecture he had delivered to African-American leaders after the April riots in Baltimore and on Maryland's Eastern Shore. Wallace, for his part, intimated that he could end the war faster than Humphrey. He named retired Air Force General Curtis LeMay, an undisguised hawk, as his running mate, hoping to capitalize on nationalistic feelings. Yet LeMay's inflammatory remarks that he would "bomb North Vietnam into the Stone Age" alarmed voters, and Wallace's campaign began to fade in late September.

Humphrey's campaign languished for six weeks after the Democratic convention. Liberals wanted nothing to do with him even as he ran against Nixon, their old adversary. Johnson refused to release Humphrey from the obligation of supporting the administration's Vietnam policy. Desperate for a way to distance himself from the stalemate in Vietnam, Humphrey announced on September 30 that he favored a total halt to the bombing "as an acceptable risk for peace, because I believe that it could lead to a success in negotiations and a shorter war." Suddenly Humphrey began to close the gap with Nixon, as many antiwar Democrats decided they preferred him to a man they despised.

Talks in Paris between the United States, North Vietnam, South Vietnam, and the NLF began in the summer but stalled over the issue of who could participate. The delegations wrangled for months over the shape of the negotiating table and who could sit where, and the futile discussions came to symbolize the public frustration with the war. The North Vietnamese refused to grant the Saigon government a separate place at the table, and the United States denied recognition to the NLF. The conversations finally progressed in the days before the November election, since the Communist side preferred a Humphrey victory to a win by the more hawkish Nixon. The Nixon camp worried that a breakthrough in the Paris talks might give the election to Humphrey. Henry Kissinger then informed the Nixon campaign that Johnson was preparing an "October surprise" to move the negotiations forward, thereby boosting Humphrey's chances. Working for Nixon, Anna Chennault, a conservative supporter of President Thieu, encouraged him to resist agreement until after the voting, in the hope of electing Nixon. Nonetheless, the weekend before the election, Johnson announced a total bombing halt along the lines Humphrey had promised. The parties scheduled serious discussions on ending the war to begin immediately after election day, November 5.

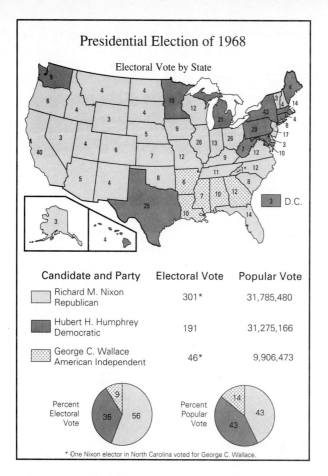

Presidential Election of 1968

Presidential Election of 1968

Electoral Vote by State

Candidate and Party	Electoral Vote	Popular Vote
Richard M. Nixon Republican	301*	31,785,480
Hubert H. Humphrey Democratic	191	31,275,166
George C. Wallace American Independent	46*	9,906,473

Percent Electoral Vote: 9, 35, 56

Percent Popular Vote: 14, 43, 43

D.C. 3

* One Nixon elector in North Carolina voted for George C. Wallace.

Nixon won by a scant 510,000 votes, taking only 43.6 percent of the total vote (see map). Humphrey drew 42.9 percent, Wallace 13.5 percent. Humphrey's supporters believed that given another four days he would have won, because he made up 7 percentage points in the Gallup poll in the five days before the voting. That may have been wishful thinking: the drop in the Democratic portion of the vote from 1964, when Johnson took nearly 61 percent, represented a striking decline. Nearly all of the 57 percent of the public who voted for Nixon or Wallace disagreed with Johnson's handling of the war in Vietnam, as did many of those who backed Humphrey.

The story of events in Vietnam resumes in Chapter 10. Although Nixon took office with an apparent mandate for change, American troops continued to fight in Vietnam for another four years.

CONCLUSION

By the time of the 1968 election, most Americans wanted to end the Vietnam War, though they still disagreed about the means for doing so. The American involvement that had begun quietly under President Truman had been gradually increased by Presidents Eisenhower and Kennedy until Lyndon Johnson took the fateful step of committing the United States to a massive air and ground war. Yet the more the United States contributed to the war effort, the more the corrupt government of South Vietnam grew dependent on American support. The result was a cycle of continual frustration.

The war devastated Vietnam—the land, the people, the society. It also proved tragic for many of the Americans who fought there. By the end of 1968, the war had already cost about 37,000 American lives, a number that would rise to over 58,000 by the time the United States withdrew its forces in 1973. A significant number of American troops who returned physically unscathed suffered long-term psychological and emotional disabilities.

At home, disagreement over the war shattered the general consensus about the proper goals of American foreign policy. Opposition became widespread and bitter, ruining Johnson's chance for re-election in 1968 and throwing the Democratic party into turmoil. Because the war raised doubts about the power of American technology and weapons to mold events around the world, some Americans even began to question the basic assumptions of containment that had guided United States foreign policy since the late 1940s.

By dividing the American public, the Vietnam War also helped to open the deep chasms in American society that were a principal legacy of the 1960s. As the next chapter illustrates, opposition to the war merged with other political and social movements to form a full-scale culture of protest. Many people grew radically disillusioned with American government and society. They distrusted the politicians in Washington and all other forms of authority, and their rebellion stimulated an equally strong conservative backlash. ■

FURTHER READING

For overviews of the Vietnam war, see: George C. Herring, *America's Longest War: The United States and Vietnam, 1950–1975,* 2d ed. (1986); Stanley Karnow, *Vietnam: A History* (1983); Robert J. MacMahon, ed., *Major Problems in the History of the Vietnam War* (1990); Kim McQuaid, *The Anxious Years: America in the*

Vietnam and Watergate Era (1989); Marilyn B. Young, *The Vietnam Wars* (1990). On the politics and diplomacy of the war, see: George McT. Kahin, *Intervention: How America Became Involved in Vietnam* (1986); Larry Berman, *Planning a Tragedy* (1983) and *Lyndon Johnson's War* (1989); Leslie Gelb with Richard C. Betts, *The Irony of Vietnam* (1979); Clark Clifford, *Counsel to the President* (1991). On fighting the war, see: Mark Clodfelter, *The Limits of Air Power* (1989); Neil Sheehan, *A Bright Shining Lie: John Paul Vann and America in Vietnam* (1988); Wallace Berry, *Bloods: An Oral History of the War by Black Veterans* (1984); Mark Baker, *Nam* (1982); Don Oberdorfer, *Tet* (1979). On the home front during the war, see: Lawrence Baskir and William Strauss, *Chance and Circumstance: The War, the Draft and the Vietnam Generation* (1978); Myra MacPherson, *Long Time Passing: Vietnam and the Haunted Generation* (1984); Charles DeBenedetti with Charles Chatfield, *An American Ordeal: The Antiwar Movement of the Vietnam Era* (1990); Nancy Zaroulis and Gerald Sullivan, *Who Spoke Up? American Protest Against the War in Vietnam, 1963–1975* (1984). On the political upheavals of 1968, in addition to the discussion in Chapter 9 of this book, see: Lewis Chester, Godfrey Hodgson, and Bruce Paige, *An American Melodrama* (1970); James Miller, *"Democracy Is in the Streets"* (1987); Todd Gitlin, *The Sixties* (1987); David Farber, *Chicago '68* (1988); David Caute, *The Year of the Barricades* (1988).

9

The Politics and Culture of Protest

Pandora's Box, a purple-painted music palace, was a Hollywood institution in 1965. The hip youth of Los Angeles flocked to the Sunset Strip nightclub to hear their favorite rock-'n'-roll bands, party madly, see and be seen. When civic authorities decided that the club had to be torn down to make way for a wider road and a three-way turn signal, Pandora's patrons held a sit-in in the middle of the Sunset Strip. "I felt like I *belonged*," wrote one teenage protester, "united with a thousand other kids, protesting what THEY were doing to US." Pop singers Sonny and Cher, clad in matching polka dot bell-bottom pants and fake-fur vests, wrapped their arms around each other. Some of the demonstrators held hands and beamed at one another in the moonlight. Others overturned a bus. The Los Angeles Police Department arrived with clubs swinging and sirens blaring. The next morning, the riot on Sunset Strip was front-page news. Songwriter-guitarist Stephen Stills, a member of the popular rock band Buffalo Springfield, found the whole scene deeply puzzling, and recommended caution. "Something happenin' here," he wrote. "What it is ain't exactly clear. . . . We got to stop, children / What's that sound / Everybody look, what's goin' down?"

The Sunset Strip riot embodied the volatile political and cultural energies of the 1960s and early 1970s, a period that is often loosely referred to as "the sixties." The spirit of protest had, by 1965, spread from young blacks unwilling to tolerate the slow pace of racial progress to young whites angry at government policies and sick of the bland pleasures middle-class life offered. Some in the baby-boom generation—those born during the surge in the national birth rate that began in 1944—moved from the civil rights and peace crusades of the early 1960s into more radical movements for Black Power and against the Vietnam War, a few concluding that only violent revolution could bring necessary changes. Others sought to extend the boundaries of acceptable everyday behavior, sampling the psychological challenges, sensual pleasures, and physical risks of the emerging "counterculture." Their political activism was sometimes enhanced, sometimes enfeebled by the cultural forms they created, as they glorified in sexual expressiveness, musical innovation, and pharmaceutical experimentation.

What the sixties would call the "generation gap"—the alienation of the young from the strategies and aspirations of their elders—had been brewing for some time. The pop culture antiheroes of the 1950s, from the brooding, doomed James Dean of *Rebel Without a Cause* to the lip-curling Marlon Brando of *The Wild Ones*, had shown adult

America the face of restless youth. "I mean how do you know what you're going to do till you *do* it?" asked Holden Caulfield, the touching adolescent protagonist of *The Catcher in the Rye*, J. D. Salinger's 1951 anthem for the newborn generation. "The answer is, you don't." Middle-class American parents in the fifties had planned ahead. They knew the price of affluence and were willing to sacrifice and save. Their children took material comfort for granted, yet often found that affluence was not enough. Relieved of the burden of financial worry by the growing American economy of the 1960s, the baby-boomers turned to politics, spirituality, and the quest for an ever better good time.

By the mid-1960s, psychologists and sociologists had documented the growing alienation among America's young. Paul Goodman's *Growing Up Absurd*, Kenneth Keniston's *The Uncommitted*, and Philip Slater's *The Pursuit of Loneliness* depicted a generation at loose ends, disconnected from meaningful relations with other people, lacking a sense of social purpose. Social critics and therapists alike wondered where this vast, free-floating constituency might end up, and whether it would drag society down with its lethargy, lose itself in narcissism, or find something meaningful to do.

If even the children of privilege felt distant from the American dream of riches and stability, others had more reason to feel disaffected and to raise their voices in increasingly angry protest. African-American writer Richard Wright had sounded the note of black rage against racism as early as 1940, with the novel *Native Son*, and in the 1960s black writers from Black Panther leader Eldridge Cleaver to poet June Jordan took up Wright's legacy. From rock singer Janis Joplin to the feminist activists of the women's liberation movement, women too began to find words to defy the restrictions that society placed on them. From these very diverse threads the sixties wove a new politics and culture of protest.

FROM CIVIL RIGHTS TO BLACK POWER

For some fifty years, the National Association for the Advancement of Colored People (NAACP) and the Urban League, under the leadership of careful men like Roy Wilkins and Whitney Young, had led the campaign for African-American civil rights. Civil rights activists believed that their cause was consistent with democratic and Christian principles, and they saw their movement as instrumental in realizing the promise of American life. They used a variety of methods. The NAACP and the Urban League directed their efforts toward legal and judicial reforms. Others, particularly A. Philip Randolph of the Brotherhood of Sleeping Car Porters, developed tactics for public demonstrations against segregation. By the early 1960s, sit-ins, boycotts, and protest marches had become widespread, but the decade would soon see the emergence of more radical approaches.

Coming of Age in Mississippi

By 1964, the civil rights movement had begun to focus on community organization and voter registration as primary tactics in the fight against racism. These methods were used primarily in the South, in states like Mississippi, where racial hierarchy and hatred were particularly open and entrenched. Rank-and-file civil rights workers in organizations like the Congress of Racial Equality (CORE), founded in 1942, the Southern Christian Leadership Conference (SCLC), begun in 1957, and the Student Non-Violent Coordinating Committee (SNCC), founded at an SCLC conference in 1960, faced potential and actual white violence on a daily basis.

Black Mississippian Anne Moody joined first the NAACP, then SNCC, knowing that doing so entailed grave risks to herself and her loved ones. One friend had been shot in the back because white townspeople suspected him of belonging to the NAACP; a local clergyman and his family had been run out of town because he had mentioned the NAACP in a sermon. While organizing blacks in the small towns of Mississippi, Moody learned to live with fear of reprisals. Her uncle and three others were murdered in Woodville, Mississippi, in a campaign of what SNCC leader Robert Moses called "terror killings." Those who dared to speak out against the murders became targets themselves; when they asked federal authorities for protection, they were told, "We can't protect every individual Negro in Mississippi." Again and again, FBI and Justice Department officials stood by while demonstrators were beaten and illegally jailed. "I guess mostly the SNCC workers were just lucky," Moody wrote in her autobiography, *Coming of Age in Mississippi*. "Most of them had missed a bullet by an inch or so on many occasions. Threats didn't stop them. They just kept going all the time."

While Congress debated the Civil Rights Act of 1964, the SCLC's Martin Luther King, Jr., courted a national television audience, combining restraint and eloquence with the use of such nonviolent direct actions as boycotts, sit-ins, and demonstrations. A "conservative militant," King was a pivotal figure in the civil rights movement, retaining the support of white liberals, who provided much of the movement's financial backing, while trying to maintain ties with increasingly frustrated younger African-Americans who staffed the front-line positions in the battle. Confronting white violence with dignity, leading peaceful protest marches, King had dazzled the nation with his "I Have a Dream" speech at the massive 1963 March on

The March on Washington in August 1963 was a highlight of the nonviolent civil rights movement. Among those leading the march were A. Philip Randolph (*front row, far right*), Roy Wilkins (*second from right*), and Martin Luther King, Jr. (*seventh from right*). *UPI/Bettmann Newsphotos.*

Washington. Rank-and-file organizers, however, found King aloof and abstract, and referred to him sarcastically as "De Lawd."

During the summer of 1964, many black and white students spent their college vacations in Mississippi, where white resistance to integration was deep and militant. The Mississippi Freedom Summer Project, operated through the SNCC-affiliated Council of Federated Organizations, attracted more than a thousand students from the North, mostly white, to join veteran black and white southern workers in a campaign to register African-American voters. Volunteers also walked picket lines, attended innumerable meetings, and organized Freedom Schools and community centers to teach remedial reading, government, humanities, and other academic and vocational subjects.

The Mississippi state legislature reacted to the challenge by doubling the state police force, authorizing local authorities to pool personnel and equipment for purposes of riot control, and introducing an anti-invasion bill intended to keep civil rights workers out of the state. White vigilante groups mounted a campaign of intimidation ranging from harassment to bombings and killings. In June, civil rights workers Andrew Goodman, Michael Schwerner, and James Chaney—two northern whites and a southern black—were murdered. Yet the volunteers kept coming, sleeping in shifts on bare mattresses, living on peanut butter, cranking mimeograph machines, and tramping hot streets. Sustained by idealism, SNCC workers wanted not only to end segregation and political repression of African-Americans, but also to oppose the fury of white hatred by living out their own vision of a racially integrated "beloved community" based on respect, affection, and a shared commitment to social justice. To one young white SNCC volunteer, African-American women leaders like Fanny Lou Hamer, Ella Baker, and Ruby Doris Smith Robinson and men like the soft-spoken Bob Moses seemed "wise, caring, courageous, honest, and full of love." Blacks who could not escape the burden of racism inspired younger white college students from the North with their bravery and their tirelessness.

The beloved community was, however, riddled with tension. Living in fear of "nightriders" who fired shots through their windows and telephoned bomb threats, civil rights workers also had to cope with racial friction within their own ranks. Long-time black workers worried that whites were trying to take over the movement without facing the risks blacks encountered daily because of race. Interracial sexual relations caused conflict between black and white women and between women and men.

SNCC succeeded in mobilizing enough voters to form the Mississippi Freedom Democratic Party (MFDP), which mounted a challenge to the whites-only delegation the regular state party sent to the 1964 Democratic national convention in Atlantic City in August. MFDP delegation leader Fanny Lou Hamer testified to the party Credentials Committee that she had been denied the right to vote, jailed, and beaten. "We are askin' the American people," she said, "is *this* the land of the free and the home of the brave?" The MFDP demanded that its delegation be seated in place of the official state delegation. White liberals like Senator Hubert Humphrey of Minnesota and southern conservatives in the party leadership worked out what they termed a compromise: the white delegation was seated, after promising not to bolt the Democratic party later on; and two MFDP representatives received delegate-at-large status. To those who had put their bodies on the line all summer, the compromise seemed a betrayal, the triumph of the politics of expediency over moral right. Two disillusioned African-American spokesmen, Stokely Carmichael and Charles Hamilton, wrote that the lesson of Atlantic City was clear: "Black people . . . could not rely on their so-called allies."

Toward Militance and Separatism

By the time of the Atlantic City convention, African-Americans throughout the country were revealing their frustration at the limited success of nonviolent tactics. Martin Luther King, Jr., framed his endorsement of civil disobedience in the language and spirit of Christian forbearance: "One who breaks an unjust law must do so openly, lovingly, and with a willingness to accept the penalty." However, the black Christian churches King represented, which for a decade had emphasized the necessity of taking the moral high ground, were losing influence with their constituents. After a church bombing killed a group of Sunday school children, Anne Moody told her God,

You know, I used to go to Sunday school when I was a little girl. . . . We were taught how merciful and forgiving you are. I bet those girls in Sunday school were being taught the same as I was when I was their age. Is that teaching wrong? Are you going to forgive their killers? . . . Nonviolence is out. I have a good idea Martin Luther King is talking to you, too. If he is, tell him that nonviolence has served its purpose.

Black civil rights workers had learned through experience that white lawlessness seldom brought penalties. Even King was aware that activists' patience was wearing thin. If nonviolent civil disobedience failed to gain justice, King warned, "millions of Negroes will, out of frustration and despair, seek solace and security in black nationalist ideologies."

King's expectations were fulfilled. Many blacks began to reject Christian forbearance altogether. Some sought new meaning in a black separatist Islamic faith. Malcolm X, the nation's most prominent and eloquent Black Muslim (see pages 270–271), spoke out for black nationalism, explicitly rejected integration, and advocated meeting violence with violence. On the secular front, rioting broke out in Harlem in the summer of 1964.

After the Atlantic City Democratic convention, the ranks of SNCC split. One faction, which included black and white southerners and middle-class white college students, believed in participatory democracy and decision-making by consensus. The other group, dominated by long-time field organizers like James Forman and Ruby Doris Smith Robinson, wanted to move away from a focus on moral and procedural issues to questions of power. Bitterly disillusioned with the fickleness of white allies, they argued that SNCC should be black-led and black-dominated.

By the early months of 1965, the concept of "black and white together" in the civil rights movement was being eclipsed. Malcolm X had begun to tone down his antiwhite message and to seek some new solution to the problem of racism, but he was gunned down in February, allegedly murdered by less conciliatory followers of Black Muslim leader Elijah Muhammad. His death paradoxically convinced some African-American activists that power came only from the barrel of a gun. Other civil rights leaders persisted in trying to channel movement energies into integrated, nonviolent action, but their protests seemed inadequate in the face of white brutality. In March, a national television audience watched as Selma, Alabama, sheriff Jim Clark ordered his men to meet civil rights marchers with clubs and tear gas. Martin Luther King, Jr., and Ralph Bunche led a group of 3,200 people on a fifty-mile march from Selma to the heavily fortified state capitol at Montgomery, where they were joined by 25,000 supporters. In the course of the Selma campaign, three activists were killed. Their deaths underscored for many Americans the violence of the Selma police and the peaceful nature of the march, but the costs of peaceful tactics were becoming unbearable to movement veterans.

Around the nation, African-Americans responded to the slow pace of change with increasing fury. In August 1965, five days of looting and rioting broke out in Watts, Los Angeles's black ghetto. Residents of Watts had reason to be frustrated: although Los Angeles as a whole was booming, blacks in the area were worse off than before. Median income in the area had dropped 8 percent between 1959 and 1965. Many complained that white-controlled local businesses jacked up prices and paid low wages to black employees. Thirty percent of adult men in Watts were unemployed, and of those who did hold jobs, many lacked the cars necessary to navigate the nation's preeminent car-culture city. Los Angeles police, mostly white and sometimes openly racist, did little to win community trust. By the time the riot subsided, thirty-four people had died, four thousand had been arrested, and much of the area had been leveled. The Los Angeles police chief blamed civil rights workers; the city's mayor blamed Communists. From the ashes arose a cry of revolutionary despair that would fuel both the rhetoric of Black Power and the white backlash against African-American rights: Burn, baby, burn.

Black Power

On a march through Mississippi in the summer of 1966, the message crystallized. Those who still supported the goal of integration and the tactics of nonviolence, like Floyd McKissick of CORE and John Lewis, former chairman of SNCC, looked on as Stokely Carmichael, bringing news of the founding of the Black Panther party in Lowndes County, Alabama, announced a new goal, Black Power. To his African-American listeners he declared, "It's time we stand up and take over." To society at large he issued a warning: "Move on over or we'll move on over you."

Within a year, weary veterans of the civil rights movement had been displaced in the public eye by young militants. SNCC became the organizing center of the Black Power movement. Carmichael and the new chairman of the organization, H. Rap Brown, viewed the increasingly common ghetto disturbances as a dress rehearsal for revolution. Meanwhile, the federal government offered only a weak response to urban rioting. President Johnson appointed Illinois governor Otto Kerner to head a commission to study the situation. When the Kerner Commission delivered a report concluding that the United States was shot through with white racism and rapidly becoming two nations, one black and poor, the other white and rich, Johnson did nothing. He was too preoccupied with the Vietnam War to pursue his promised Great Society.

Urging students at black colleges to "fight for liberation by any means necessary," Carmichael declared, "To hell with the laws of the United States." At a Black Power conference in Newark, held on the heels of a riot in which police killed twenty-five African-Americans, a thousand participants approved resolutions affirming the right of black people to revolt and calling for a separate black nation and black militia. In 1968, Carmichael, Brown, and SNCC would be replaced by the Black Panthers as the most visible militant group. Wearing leather jackets and carrying weapons, the Panthers often resembled an elite paramilitary unit, and they aimed a radical rhetoric at the American capitalist system. During the next few years, as the Panthers provoked considerable uneasiness among the white middle class, they became the objects of heavy surveillance by the FBI. They had frequent confrontations with police, including shootouts that left some Panthers dead and others under arrest.

SDS AND THE RISE OF THE NEW LEFT

As African-American groups became more militant, so did other, predominantly white organizations that arose to challenge the structure of American politics and society. Collectively these groups came to be called the New Left, to distinguish them from the Old Left of the 1930s through 1950s.

In the 1950s the Old Left—liberal activists, socialists, and others who advocated fundamental changes in the country—had run aground on the issue of anticommunism. Partly to protect themselves against charges of Communist sympathies, and partly from genuine conviction, liberals in groups like the Americans for Democratic Action had joined reactionaries like Senator Joseph McCarthy in trying to purge the nation of Communists. Most younger activists of the 1960s criticized this obsession with Soviet communism as irrelevant to the task of building progressive politics in the United States.

In contrast to liberals and radicals of the fifties, who lived in the shadow of the Holocaust and the Stalinist terror, those who came of age in the early sixties were beneficiaries of American affluence and the huge expansion of the nation's colleges and universities. Between 1945 and 1965, public spending on higher education rose from $742.1 million to $6.9 billion per year. The booming universities sheltered a small but growing group of students who became serious critics of the wider society. Among their mentors were radical sociologist C. Wright Mills and political theorist Herbert Marcuse. Uneasy in the presence of the world's growing atomic arsenal, ignited by the civil rights movement, they were less wedded to older affiliations than their predecessors in the Old Left, and more optimistic about the prospects for sweeping social change.

Some of these comfortable children coming of age in the early sixties founded the most influential and best-known New Left group, Students for a Democratic Society (SDS). At the 1962 SDS meeting in Port Huron, Michigan, Tom Hayden, one of the early leaders, articulated the organization's concerns and goals in his famous "Port Huron Statement." Beginning by proposing "An Agenda for a Generation," Hayden declared that "We are the people of this generation, bred in at least modest comfort, housed now in universities, looking uncomfortably to the world we inherit." He went on to criticize college students' apathy toward politics and to deplore collegiate complacency. The presence of widespread poverty in the country, and the unchallenged power of what Mills had called the military-industrial complex, threatened the nation's best traditions. Hayden called for a restoration of participatory democracy to make political parties, corporations, and the government more responsive to ordinary people. "America," said Hayden, "should concentrate on its genuine social priorities: abolish squalor, terminate neglect, and establish an environment for people to live in with dignity and creativeness."

Free Speech, Campus Radicalism, and the Free Press

Embracing Hayden's hopeful message, white students flocked into civil rights work in the early 1960s. Some SDS members went south. Others, in 1964, set up the group's Economic Research and Action Project in northern ghettos, attempting to organize an interracial movement of the poor focused on such issues as jobs and community control of social programs.

Soon this involvement in the civil rights movement propelled student activists into taking up other issues in new places. Mario Savio and Jack Weinberg, two veterans of the Mississippi Freedom Summer, returned to the University of California at Berkeley in the fall of 1964 planning to continue recruitment for the movement. When campus authorities forbade their efforts, the Berkeley Free Speech Movement brought radical activity to the campus. Students took over the administration building, declared a strike, and enlisted faculty support for the removal of restrictions on free expression on campus. Free Speech Movement activists expressed both their joy and their anger in four-letter words once thought inadmissible in polite company, and conservative Americans began to see in Berkeley an outpost of lawlessness and libertinism. By 1966, California gubernatorial candidate Ronald Reagan was telling campaign audiences that campus activists indulged in "orgies so vile I cannot describe them to you."

Campus protests quickly spread. By 1965 there were disturbances at Yale, Ohio State, the University of Kansas, Brooklyn College, Michigan State, and St. John's University. Disputes often arose over issues of personal conduct rather than national politics. College students of the fifties had accepted the time-honored doctrine of *in loco parentis*, according to which the institution had the right and the obligation to stand in for parents and regulate students' behavior. But by the mid-1960s the campus regulations—particularly those that attempted to preserve the conservative mating and dating rituals of the fifties—seemed quaint, artificial, and restrictive. Students began to oppose all kinds of limitations on their behavior, from rules governing where they could live, what hours they might be out, and who might visit their rooms to dress codes and smoking regulations. Students at single-sex institutions agitated for coeducation. Returning from a summer spent in loosely structured, sexually volatile communal households while they worked for SNCC or SDS, women and men students alike chafed at campus rules.

Even without the issues of personal lifestyle, national politics provided more than enough cause for dissent, particularly as President Johnson escalated the American war in Vietnam. As nightly television news broadcasts brought American television-watchers pictures of the bloodiness and futility of the nation's policy, government officials' rosy pronouncements seemed patently false. Berkeley's Jack Weinberg admonished his fellow students not to trust anyone over thirty, and enterprising American journalists began to believe that there was no point in trusting *anyone* in power. On campuses, in cities, and on military bases, "underground" newspapers sprang up to offer a more radical alternative to the conventional news sources. These papers penetrated the government's bureaucratic jargon and exposed its attempts to mislead the public. The language of the alternative press was sometimes itself either so obscene or so riddled with Marxist jargon that it presented its own problems in interpretation. Still, radical journalists' seeming paranoia about government surveillance was justified; the underground media were extensively infiltrated by government agent provocateurs, and CIA recruiters joined the National Student Association in big numbers.

Even the mainstream press began to mistrust the information released by "official sources." Investigative reporters like Seymour Hersh of the *New York Times* began to look beyond government press releases to get at the truth of national policy. Jeopardizing his sources in the military, Hersh broke the story of the My Lai massacre in Vietnam. Hersh and other journalists accepted the professional risks of upsetting the previously cozy relationship between news sources and reporters, and they managed to uncover important stories that government officials had attempted to suppress.

Stop the Draft, Stop the War

The Vietnam War soon became the main focus of student protest. Because students—males at least—were directly threatened by the rising draft calls, opposition to the draft mobilized a huge new constituency for the protest effort. When SDS endorsed draft resistance, its membership swelled. Draft-counseling centers sprang up across the country. Women radicals joined the protests in support of their male friends who might be drafted. Some movement members even encouraged women to sleep with draft resisters; according to one slogan that appeared on protest signs, "Girls say yes to guys who say no."

In the spirit of participatory democracy, local SDS chapters and other draft resistance groups pretty much determined their own tactics. Some initiated draft card burnings. Others held sit-ins at Selective Service induction centers, opposed university Reserve Officers' Training Corps (ROTC) programs, protested military recruiters' visits to campus, or demonstrated against corporations involved in defense work. Dow Chemical, the manufacturer of napalm, became a particularly hated target. Between January 1 and June 15, 1968, according to the National Student Association, there were 221 major antiwar demonstrations at 101 colleges and universities involving some 40,000 students.

Although tactics varied widely from campus to campus and from one action to another, there were notable efforts to join student groups with other organizations to orchestrate national protests against the war. In the summer of 1967, 20,000 people participated in the Vietnam Summer, an effort modeled on the Mississippi Freedom Summer and mounted by a coalition of pacifists, liberals, and radicals to mobilize the middle class against the war. Stop the Draft Week, from October 16 to 21, 1967, culminated in a march on the Pentagon in which 50,000 people crossed the Arlington Memorial Bridge, some to picket, some to pray, others to attempt to storm the bastion of the military-industrial complex. Brilliantly if egocentrically recounted in

Norman Mailer's *Armies of the Night,* a prime example of the "New Journalism" developing to probe beneath the surfaces of events, the march on the Pentagon incorporated not only student groups but also many other constituencies ranged against the war. Among those present were Berkeley Free Speech activist Jerry Rubin, childcare expert Dr. Benjamin Spock, linguistics theorist Noam Chomsky, poet Robert Lowell, social philosopher Paul Goodman, and Dagmar Wilson of Women's Strike for Peace. The coalition even had its comic aspects: Ed Sanders, leader of a rock band called the Fugs, proposed a "grope for peace" and with SDS leader Abbie Hoffman coordinated an attempt to levitate the Pentagon.

Student Militance and Campus Uprisings

Sociologist Todd Gitlin, an early president of SDS, noted that as the war became more militant, so also did the antiwar movement. Antiwar demonstrators had often tried to contrast their own peace-loving demeanor with the violence of government policy, carrying signs reading "Make Love, Not War" and putting flowers in the barrels of the guns of police and troops called out to keep order at demonstrations. By 1967, however, antiwar activists were preaching a harder line, and demonstrators adopted a tougher posture. In Oakland, California, protests during Stop the Draft Week turned into bloody confrontations with the police.

SDS, its membership swelling, moved beyond the goals articulated at Port Huron as the organization adopted the slogan "From Protest to Resistance." By 1967, SDS publications began referring to the authorities as "pigs." Insisting that the Vietnamese cause of justice, identified quite simply with the Vietcong and the North Vietnamese, could not get a fair hearing in the United States, some New Leftists declared free speech a sham and shouted down progovernemnt speakers. National Liberation Front flags began to appear at antiwar rallies, alienating many middle-of-the-road Americans. SDS leader Bernardine Dohrn wanted to bring the war home and make the American people feel the torment of Vietnam, but such revolutionary tactics angered most Americans, including many who opposed the war.

Nowhere was campus conflict more spectacular than at Columbia University in New York. Columbia embodied what campus radicals most despised. A bastion of Ivy League privilege in the middle of the ghetto, the university was both a Harlem landlord and a holder of major defense research contracts. On April 23, 1968, the Columbia SDS chapter joined with black militants in taking over university buildings, including Low Library, where students occupied the uni-

Columbia University students occupy a professor's office in April 1968. *UPI/Bettmann Newsphotos.*

versity president's office. Columbia students held the buildings for eight days, after which New York City police moved in with billy clubs and arrested 692 people, three-quarters of them students. Though the siege was over, a student strike forced the university to close early for the year. The stage was set for violent confrontations between students and authorities on campuses across the nation in the next two years.

The American student protests were part of an international drive toward student militance. The Columbia uprising had its counterpart in Paris, where angry protestors erected barricades in the streets and battled police. But not all students—and certainly not all young people—joined the protests. Some opposed only the war and the draft; some sympathized but stayed out of the streets. Many young people—political conservatives, white southerners, working-class youth who did not go to college, graduate students who had invested time and money in pursuit of professional careers—were either unaffected by the protests or opposed to them. Still, campus conflicts not only reflected differences over government or university policies, but also revealed a deep gulf between the "straight" social standards of the older generation and the new beliefs of those who came of age in the sixties.

THE COUNTERCULTURE

At the same time that young people were becoming more radical in political terms, they also began to experiment with new ways of living, inspired in many cases by the Beat writers who had emerged in the 1950s. "The only ones for me," novelist Jack Kerouac wrote in his 1957 epic, *On the Road*, "are the mad ones, the ones who are mad to live, mad to talk, mad to be saved, desirous of everything at the same time, the ones who never yawn or say a commonplace thing, but burn, burn, burn like fabulous yellow roman candles." Along with other writers of the Beat Generation, Kerouac came to symbolize the rejection of bourgeois comfort and the embrace of a life of sensation-seeking, adventure, and personal authenticity. The Beats also represented a male revolt against the middle-class family and the traditional masculine role of breadwinner. Going on drinking sprees and careening around the country, embracing freewheeling sexuality, they distanced themselves from fifties family men in gray flannel suits.

Some of the Beat literati, notably poet Allen Ginsberg, became political dissidents in the sixties. Others, like Kerouac, rejected politics as corrupt. All were involved in a protest against mainstream American culture. "Squares" pursued their American dream in suburban comfort, drinking martinis, breaking the rules of marital monogamy only surreptitiously, confining their aesthetic tastes to the music of television's "Hit Parade." Beats, or Hipsters, had another set of standards for their American dream. They lived in squalid apartments in urban enclaves like New York's Greenwich Village and San Francisco's North Beach, expanded the range of recreational drugs from sweet wine to marijuana and heroin, and listened to the incendiary, experimental jazz of Charlie "Yardbird" Parker, Dizzy Gillespie, and Miles Davis. Aspects of life most African-Americans could not avoid, such as poverty, the Beats adopted by choice. Willing to die early, and, they hoped, leave pretty corpses, young Beat poets celebrated their underground heroes' self-destruction. One need not worry about mundane matters. "If you believe you're a poet," said Gregory Corso, "then you're saved." These were the beginnings of a movement that widened by the later 1960s into the counterculture, a loosely defined phenomenon that involved new types of rock music, drugs, sexual freedom, and various other means of pursuing a liberated lifestyle.

Sex and Rock 'n' Roll

The popular culture the Beats despised was undergoing its own transformation. A revival of folk music, identified with the Old Left during the fifties, meant commercial success in the sixties for protest folk singers like Joan Baez and Bob Dylan. Their folk music helped to harness the energies of political protest and the yearning for social change. But it was rock 'n' roll that served as the primary musical catalyst for the counterculture.

For millions of American girls, the arrival of the Beatles in the United States in 1964 was a watershed. No musicians before or since achieved the mass popularity or cultural influence of these four young Englishmen, John Lennon, Paul McCartney, George Harrison, and Ringo Starr. While "Beatlemaniacs" fantasized about romance with their idols, they also found much to identify with in the Fab Four. Playful, long-haired, wacky, and talented, the Beatles personified both personal independence and a new androgynous sexual ideal. One fan recalled, "I didn't want to grow up and be a wife and it seemed to me that the Beatles had the kind of freedom I wanted: No rules, they could spend two days lying in bed; they ran around on motorbikes, ate from room service. . . . I wanted to be like them. Something larger than life." Another wrote that "I liked their independence and sexuality and wanted those things for myself."

As they had during the Elvis Presley phenomenon of the late 1950s (see Chapter 4), parents began to worry that their children were getting out of control. But the transformation of rock music and the youth culture it represented was only beginning. By the mid-1960s the sentimental love lyrics of the Beatles' early songs gave way to the overt sexual come-ons of other groups, such as the Rolling Stones and the Doors. The Lennon-McCartney request to hold hands became Mick Jagger's invitation to "spend the night together," and this soon attained the urgency of Jim Morrison's plea to "touch me." Many girls accepted the idea. For example, Hollywood clubs and the Sunset Strip attracted thousands of teenage girls, parading in miniskirts, seeking fun and vicarious fame by having sex with members of male rock bands. These "groupies" complied in their own sexual exploitation and subjected themselves to grave health risks, but they also represented a new, open, and defiant insistence on the right to sexual pleasure, for women as well as men.

Though groupies were only a small segment of the youth population, the ideal of sexual freedom was spreading rapidly, galvanized by the rock music that expressed the desires and demands of young people. As the counterculture developed, the music continued to evolve; the performers invented new musical forms and hybrids, pushing folk and rock 'n' roll beyond all the previous limits. Soon a "psychedelic" rock music, often known as acid rock, was celebrating the use of mind-altering drugs. Groups like the Grateful Dead and Jefferson Airplane turned their sets into dizzying, deafening swirls of sound. A young white woman named Janis Joplin sang a steamy,

Janis Joplin

For a middle-class girl growing up in postwar Texas, looks mattered. Janis Joplin, born in 1943, was brainy, talented, and eager to be noticed, but conventional beauty was one thing she did not possess. Instead, she had "problems"—excess weight, severe acne—that made her wretched, rebellious, and outrageous. She began to dress sloppily, to hang out with wild boys, to venture across the Sabine River for nights of drinking and brawling in Louisiana roadhouses. She developed a "reputation." Classmates at Thomas Jefferson High in Port Arthur called her a pig.

Not surprisingly, she left Port Arthur after graduating in 1960, bound for the bohemian shores of Venice, California, but soon she returned to try Texas again. At the state university in Austin, she began to find a place in the spotlight, singing blues and folk and country music in

screeching, tortured, blues-driven rock that gave her almost legendary status as a prodigy of the counterculture.

Like Joplin, most of the avant-garde performers were white. Ironically, at a time when black political leaders were turning from civil rights to Black Power, African-American musicians succeeded in reaching a broad commercial audience by taking a fairly cautious approach. The best-known black recording artists were associated with Motown, the Detroit music company masterminded by black songwriter-entrepreneur Berry Gordy, Jr. Motown singers like Stevie Wonder and groups like the Temptations and Supremes combined musical virtuosity with lush production, precise choreography, glittering costumes, and a bland message. One exception to this trend was James Brown, the godfather of soul music, who marked out the

local coffeehouses. Listeners began to realize that she had a remarkable talent and a unique, unforgettable style. But insecurity stalked her, and some students humiliated her with the title of Ugliest Man on Campus. In 1963 she left Texas once again, heading for San Francisco.

This time, she found her niche in the hip life in California. Within a few years, Janis Joplin became the queen of the San Francisco psychedelic music scene, both a rock-'n'-roll star and a symbol of the counterculture. Bold, swaggering, cursing, she roared through town in beads and bangles, by turns clowning and sinking into despair. She fronted a band called Big Brother and the Holding Company, wringing ecstasy and torment from her amazing voice, reaching national acclaim with a stunning performance at the Monterey Pop Festival in 1967. Even after she paused to establish a new band and redefine her music, she remained a celebrity, and a rock music phenomenon. Still, her personal troubles were never resolved.

"I just made love to 25,000 people," she said after a concert, "and I'm going home alone." Sex was for her an obsession and a puzzle. She was attracted to both men and women, and deeply troubled by her bisexuality. Because none of her many partners could satisfy her for long, she was often lonely. Seeking reassurance and oblivion, she drank a sweet kind of whiskey called Southern Comfort and shot heroin into her veins. Eventually, like all too many other stars of the counterculture, she became a victim of her own self-destructiveness. In 1970 she died of a drug overdose in a seedy Los Angeles motel. ■

frontiers of raw sex appeal. Another black innovator was guitarist Jimi Hendrix, whose incendiary playing helped to develop the psychedelic style.

The Drug Scene

Along with sex and rock 'n' roll, the counterculture featured an abundant use of drugs. The Beatles took lysergic acid diethylamide (LSD), a psychotropic chemical often known simply as "acid," and released their pathbreaking album, *Sergeant Pepper's Lonely Hearts Club Band,* declaring "I'd love to turn you on." "More and more," former SDS president Todd Gitlin observed, "to get access to youth culture, you had to get high." Many in the stoned world stuck to milder forms of intoxication like marijuana, which had a debilitating effect on ambition and short-term memory but was limited in its long-term effects. Some, like rock idols Janis Joplin, Jim Morrison, and Jimi Hendrix, sought in drugs a release from deep-seated pain. They combined addictions to alcohol with substances such as barbiturates, amphetamines, cocaine, and heroin until their dependencies killed them.

The term *psychedelic* referred, in the first instance, to hallucinogenic drugs that distorted perceptions, often in bizarre ways. In the counterculture these drugs were seen as a means of expanding the mind to reach a higher level of experience and understanding. For many, such perception-altering substances as marijuana and LSD became akin to religious sacraments. LSD had first been introduced into the United States as part of a CIA program to develop drugs to use in questioning enemy agents. Harvard professors Timothy Leary and Richard Alpert—the latter soon to embrace Eastern spiritual practices and reincarnate himself as guru Baba Ram Dass—conducted psychological experiments with LSD and, by 1960, were enthusiastic advocates of hallucinogenic drugs. When Harvard fired them for using students as subjects in their research, they became outlaw heroes. Leary founded the League for Spiritual Discovery, established a commune at an estate at Millbrook, New York, and advised the nation's youth to "Turn on, tune in, and drop out."

Still others celebrated the recreational dimension of opening up what British writer Aldous Huxley had called "the doors of perception." Novelist Ken Kesey, who participated in CIA-sponsored drug experiments at Stanford, founded a mobile commune called the Merry Pranksters, which traveled in a wildly painted bus called "Furthur." In cities up and down the West Coast, the Pranksters held "acid tests"—parties incorporating avant-garde rock 'n' roll, multimedia spectacles, and the mass distribution of free LSD. Journalist Tom Wolfe chronicled the Pranksters' activities in *The Electric Kool-Aid Acid Test*, a hyperbolic, typographically psychedelic piece of New Journalism. In San Francisco, the Pranksters joined forces with master businessman Bill Graham to produce the Tripps Festival, an event at the Fillmore Auditorium starring the city's premier acid-rock bands, the Grateful Dead and Big Brother and the Holding Company.

The Growth and Marketing of the Counterculture

Soon new forms of popular behavior and expression grew up around the music and drug scenes. Adopting the Beat Generation's notion that a posture of hipness constituted a form of social protest, counterculture devotees called themselves "hippies." The hippie style, with its flowing hair and bell-bottom jeans, transformed the appearance of American young people. In the name of rejecting Western civilization's uptight materialism, devotees of the psychedelic culture

A hippie wedding in New Mexico. *Lisa Law/Imageworks.*

adopted some of the trappings of Eastern mysticism, sporting bells, beads, flowing robes, and sandals, lighting incense, and festooning their households with Indian print bedspreads. They wove flowers in their hair. They changed their diet, demanding more "natural" foods to enhance spiritual health. They embraced the psychedelic art that appeared on rock posters and T-shirts, a style that used saturated colors, swirling calligraphy, and special photographic effects.

While college students "dropped acid" (swallowed LSD) and laughed hysterically as their friends' faces seemed to melt, the counterculture spread to younger groups as well. Marijuana-smoking high school students discovered that it was more fun to listen to loud music on headphones or blow bubbles in the park than to attend history class. The counterculture became a mass movement, extending beyond California and New York to other urban areas and even to many smaller towns.

As it spread, there were many people ready to capitalize on its economic potential. Bill Graham grew fabulously wealthy promoting rock concerts. Psychedelic artist Peter Max eventually marketed his talents to some fifty companies, including Sears and General Electric. The counterculture spawned new business opportunities for purveyors of dietary and spiritual nostrums, record store operators, and proprietors of head shops, T-shirt stores, health food operations, and hip clothing boutiques.

Jann Wenner, a particularly canny entrepreneur, spotted the marketing opportunity of the decade when he began publishing *Rolling Stone* magazine, a tabloid that began by covering the rock scene and soon expanded into long feature articles and investigative reporting. Wenner made a fortune, meanwhile publishing some of the best of the New Journalism. In *Rolling Stone*'s pages, politics and the counterculture met in such extraordinary forms as Tom Wolfe's history of the space program and Hunter S. Thompson's 1972 series on presidential politics, "Fear and Loathing on the Campaign Trail."

The Summer of Love

By the summer of 1967, there were hippie neighborhoods in most American cities and college towns, often located near campuses. In particular, San Francisco's Haight-Ashbury district had become a magnet for people preaching the virtues of love, dope, music, sex, and "flower power." While radical politicos proclaimed the summer of 1967 as Vietnam Summer, hippies announced a "summer of love." This hedonistic interlude would transform society not by agitating for widescale social change or an end to the war, but by encouraging individuals to drop out of the rat race and sample the pleasures of the flesh. Networks and news magazines predicted the migration of thousands of young people to the Haight that summer, to "crash" in communal pads, "groove" at concerts in Golden Gate Park and at the Fillmore, and shower each other and apprehensive local authorities in peace, love, and flowers. "If you're going to San Francisco," one song's lyrics advised, "be sure to wear some flowers in your hair."

What the Haight got, instead, was a harvest of blight. Most hippies stayed home, but thousands did come. Though many observers of the time believed that the hippie influx into San Francisco represented a revolt against affluence, it was instead a sign that the ideal of the happy American family often papered over serious family conflicts. Class was no distinguishing factor among migrants to San Francisco during the summer of love; the young people came from poor, working-class, middle-class, and wealthy backgrounds. Rather, those who ran off to the Haight were disproportionately children from severely troubled homes. They were as often throwaways as runaways; many were victims of parental abuse or neglect. "The surprising thing about this extraordinary moment in this extraordinary community," wrote journalist Nicholas Von Hoffman, who spent the summer of 1967 observing the scene in the Haight, "is not the number of anxious parents combing the place for their children, nor the number of sad little signs posted on bulletin boards asking dearly loved sons and daughters to return home, but how few there really are compared to the apparently large number of runaway minors."

Few migrants to the Haight had the skills to sustain themselves in a city suddenly flooded with their kind. Thus Haight hippies often turned to panhandling or to the perilous occupations of prostitution and drug-dealing to earn their keep. Drugs traded included marijuana and acid, destructive enough in large doses, and also such addictive substances as amphetamines, cocaine, and heroin, which led to overdoses and outbreaks of hepatitis from dirty needles. The cutthroat drug business kept Haight residents vulnerable to exploitation and physical violence.

Like dope, free love turned out to have a high price. Hippie girls, presumed to be sexually liberated, often found themselves obliged to exchange sex for food and shelter, a practice that led some to conclude that prostitution for cash was a better bargain than sexual barter. The assumption that all "chicks" sought sexual liaisons left Haight women particularly exposed to sexual assault. Sexual promiscuity, whether chosen, forced, or economically necessary, led to epidemic venereal disease. Free medical clinics as well as soup kitchens were overwhelmed by demand.

At its root, the counterculture partook of the social problems and prejudices of American society in general. Crash pads, if hospitable, often re-created conventional household hierarchies. One young woman who went with a girlfriend to the Haight for a weekend reported with some disgust that her friend "moved into the first commune we entered and became a 'housemother,' which means she did all the cooking and cleaning. Very communal." Racial tensions, like gender hierarchy, persisted among the hip as well as the square. Relations between the predominantly white hippies in the Haight and the nearby black community in the Fillmore were terrible.

Rock Festivals: From Woodstock to Altamont

Even as the Haight-Ashbury experience revealed the dark side of the counterculture, the music persisted, helping to keep the spirit of the cultural revolution alive. Promoters had begun to stage large-scale, open-air rock festivals to attract the faithful. These reached a high point with the Woodstock Music Festival of August 1969, a rain- and mud-soaked gathering of 400,000 rock fans in upstate New York. The unexpectedly huge crowd posed many serious problems, particularly in providing sanitation, food, and water. The audience had difficulty actually hearing the music and seeing the stage. Traffic was so bad that state authorities closed down the New York State Thruway. In spite of these troubles, however, many members of the audience would look back on Woodstock as the grandest experience of the sixties. The festival developed an almost mythological aura as the culmination of the counterculture movement.

At the opposite extreme was the festival at Altamont Speedway in California the following winter. In the spirit of dope fellowship, the headlining Rolling Stones made the common counterculture mistake of assuming that anyone who used illegal drugs must have humane values. The Stones had invited the Hell's Angels motorcycle group to provide festival security. The Angels, who resembled flower children only in their taste for dope, stabbed one person to death in front of the stage as Mick Jagger looked on aghast. Before the day was out, four people were dead, and many others had been severely injured. Whereas the promoters at Woodstock had worked hard to ensure that there would be enough medical facilities available to treat injuries and drug freak-outs, medical care at Altamont was sadly inadequate to cope with even run-of-the-mill drug reactions.

Communes

Scenes of mass pathology like those from Haight-Ashbury and Altamont, whether in cities or at what were supposed to be celebrations, led many cultural rebels to conclude that the only salvation for the counterculture lay in cultivating one's own garden. Across the country, disaffected hippies sought spiritual salvation and physical health by getting back to the land. College students moved out of dormitories and into rural farmhouses, bought sacks of brown rice, and planted organic gardens. Most communes were relatively short-lived, falling apart when faced with such issues as how to share expenses, whom to include or exclude, and how to divide up work. Advocates of "doing your own thing" clashed with those who saw a need for organization, and those who took on the task of collecting money for food or rent regularly expected to be turned away with the haughty admonition not to be so uptight and materialistic. The communes that lasted tended to be very hierarchic, such as The Farm in Tennessee, or to be devoted to Eastern religious practices, especially various forms of Buddhism.

Authoritarianism did not guarantee stability. The most infamous of the communes, the murderous Manson Family, left the Haight-Ashbury to settle, finally, in the dry Santa Susana Mountains of southern California. Charles Manson held his mostly female followers so completely spellbound that by December of 1969 they were willing to commit murder at his orders. Even after they had been arrested for multiple homicides, including that of a pregnant actress, Sharon Tate, Manson's disciples continued to express their loyalty to him from their prison cells.

Hippie communes embodied a fundamental tension in American society, the tension between a longing for connectedness and a desire for personal liberty. If most lasted but a short time and seemed more dedicated to escapism than to solving the problems of postindustrial society, they nevertheless represented a desire for a way of life dedicated less to the pursuit of consumer goods than to a vision of a meaningful existence. Often as not, those who experimented with communal living pondered not only human relations, but the complicated connections between people and the natural world. Some who began by raising organic vegetables became pioneers of the environmental movement.

1968: A YEAR OF CATACLYSM AND ITS AFTERMATH

To some extent, the three movements that this chapter has traced—the emergence of Black Power, the rise of the New Left, and the growth of a counterculture—represented separate strands of antiestablishment protest during the sixties. Often they differed from one another in both goals and methods. For instance, the Black Panthers had no intention of wearing flowers in their hair; hippies were frequently indifferent to politics, believing that salvation lay in altering the mind and spirit; and some political radicals of the New Left could not fathom how anyone could lie around smoking marijuana when there was a rally to attend. But the membership of the three movements overlapped, and they shared a basic opposition to mainstream American society and the Vietnam War. As the climate of protest intensified in the late 1960s, there were more and more occasions when the various strands came together. This was particularly true in 1968, a cataclysmic year for American society and politics.

Yippies and McCarthy Kids

On December 31, 1967, some important members of the counterculture and the New Left joined forces. SDS leaders Abbie Hoffman and Jerry Rubin, black activist-comedian Dick Gregory, Beat poet Allen Ginsberg, counterculture writer Paul Krassner of *The Realist*, the nation's oldest underground newspaper, and several others founded the Youth International party, better known as the Yippies. Hoffman was a master at using the media to promote the cause of protest. Employing a combination of militant tactics, freakish pranks, and crazy rhetoric, Yippies would try to make themselves the national media's front-page story. Their particular goals were sometimes hard to determine. They were for freedom, for spontaneity, against the Vietnam War, against racism, against politics as usual. They planned to turn the Democratic national convention at Chicago the following summer into a "Festival of Life" featuring rock music and elaborate practical jokes, a kind of revolutionary dance party.

The Yippies were not the only set of protesters on the political stage, or by any means the most representative of dissident youth. When Senator Eugene McCarthy, a liberal opponent of the Vietnam War, decided to challenge Lyndon Johnson in the 1968 New Hampshire presidential primary, thousands of students turned out for his campaign. Aware that their hippie style would alienate the middle-of-the-road and the middle-aged, they cut their hair, put aside their bell-bottoms, and donned coats and ties or skirts and sweaters, becoming "Clean for Gene." In a paroxysm of political idealism, they took the McCarthy campaign across the nation, converting flower power to grass-roots organizing, their Volkswagen Beetles sprouting the distinctive blue-and-white daisy-shaped McCarthy bumper stickers. When McCarthy nearly defeated Johnson in the New Hampshire presidential primary, they tasted victory and redoubled their envelope-stuffing and precinct-walking. Johnson's announcement on March 31 that he declined to run for re-election was their great moment of triumph.

Assassinations

This well-scrubbed foray into electoral politics fell victim to the national climate of violence and confrontation. The first great shock came on April 4, 1968, when Martin Luther King, Jr., was assassinated by a white supremacist in Memphis, Tennessee. King had gone to the city on behalf of striking sanitation workers, almost all of whom were black, and who represented the abused, overworked, yet politically mobilized people he hoped to reach in his attempts to build an interracial Poor People's Campaign. Seemingly prescient about his doom, King nevertheless maintained hope for the movement. The day before his assassination, he gave a speech in which he explained that "I've looked over and I've seen the Promised Land. I may not get there with you, but I want you to know tonight that we as a people will get to the Promised Land. . . . I'm not fearing any man. Mine eyes have seen the glory of the coming of the Lord."

Despite King's own optimism, many African-Americans could find no way to understand his murder except as proof of the futility of the nonviolent strategy he advocated. "When white America killed Dr. King," said Stokely Carmichael, "she declared war." The riots that broke out in more than a hundred cities lasted more than a week. More than 65,000 federal troops were called out to try to restore order.

Yet, almost miraculously, thousands of activists clung to King's nonviolent vision. Two months after his murder, supporters of the Poor People's Campaign, led now by the SCLC's Reverend Ralph David Abernathy, built a makeshift settlement of tents and plywood shacks in the shadow of the Washington Monument. King's widow,

Coretta Scott King, spoke often during the monthlong existence of Resurrection City, as the protestors called their shantytown, stressing nonviolence but reminding her audience that "starving a child is violence, suppressing a culture is violence, contempt for poverty is violence."

Unfortunately, these words could not stem the tide of violence. After Robert Kennedy announced his candidacy for the Democratic presidential nomination, offering antiwar voters another choice, some of McCarthy's student supporters went over to the Kennedy camp. More significantly, Kennedy became the overwhelming choice of black and Mexican-American voters, who considered him the strongest candidate on civil rights. Minority voters were impressed by Kennedy's support for Cesar Chavez and the United Farm Workers, a predominantly Mexican-American union trying to win rudimentary concessions in wages and working conditions from California grape growers. On the strength of minority support, Kennedy won the California primary on June 5, 1968, getting enough delegates to raise the possibility of a deadlocked Democratic convention. But his shooting by Sirhan Sirhan came only a few hours after the polls closed. When Kennedy died the next morning, many Americans believed that he took with him the sense that electoral politics offered real possibility for change.

The Chicago Convention

For the Democratic convention in August, the city of Chicago became an armed camp as the authorities prepared for strong antiwar protests. Barbed wire enclosed the convention center, 12,000 Chicago police were deployed on twelve-hour shifts, and some 6,000 troops of the Illinois National Guards had been called out, along with about as many army troops. It is unknown how many FBI agents attended. The overwhelming majority of antiwar activists stayed away. On most days during the convention, there were perhaps 4,000 demonstrators, with crowds peaking at possibly 10,000 on August 28. Thus, police generally outnumbered demonstrators by a factor of three or four to one, and federal records suggest that the ranks of the protestors were extensively infiltrated by government agents.

Those who did come to protest were hardly a representative cross section of the antiwar movement. For example, male demonstrators at Chicago outnumbered females by eight or ten to one, imparting a particularly macho flavor to the action. The Yippies came prepared to make a farce out of the convention by bringing along their own candidate, a live pig named Pigasus. "Our concept of revolution," said Abbie Hoffman, "is that it's fun." Paul Krassner terrified city residents by suggesting that demonstrators might attempt to alter people's consciousness by putting LSD into the city's water supply. An infuriated Mayor Daley refused to let demonstrators camp in city parks, a move guaranteeing that there would be plenty of restless people looking for conflict. A small minority of demonstrators representing the extreme left, perhaps as many as three hundred, came to Chicago hoping to provoke violence.

The police obliged, acting without strategy or discipline in a week-long melee observers would come to call a "police riot." Over the course of the convention, they repeatedly cleared Lincoln Park with tear gas and clubs. Police and demonstrators clashed in Grant Park, across from Hubert Humphrey's headquarters in the Hilton, while television cameras recorded the head-bashing and some antiwar convention delegates went into the streets to support the demonstrators. Candidate Humphrey could smell tear gas from his hotel room. Reporters, bystanders, and demonstrators alike were beaten and gassed. A total of 668 people were arrested.

Meanwhile, inside the convention center, Mayor Daley retained control, loading the galleries with supporters waving banners that read, "We Love Mayor Daley." Furthermore, most Americans seemed to believe that the mayor and the police had responded appropriately. Less than 20 percent of those contacted in a national telephone poll thought the police had used too much force in putting down the demonstrations. Hubert Humphrey said the Chicago police had done "nothing wrong." To the strains of "Happy Days Are Here Again," he accepted the presidential nomination, his party in ruins around him.

No matter what Humphrey might do to placate voters who despised hippies and protestors, the Democrats were firmly linked in the public mind with those who had come to demonstrate against the party. Ironically, the protests in Chicago aided the November victory of Republican Candidate Richard Nixon, who had been nominated at a carefully orchestrated meeting in Miami that looked like a love feast compared to the mayhem at Chicago. Nixon seemed a reassuring presence to those he would come to call "the silent majority" of Americans.

Calls to Revolution

While the right gained momentum after Chicago, spurred on by the inflammatory rhetoric of independent presidential candidate George Wallace and Republican vice-presidential contender Spiro Agnew, the left was transformed but not dead. SDS boomed. Some movement leaders, increasingly seduced by the romance of violent revolution, considered the convention a triumph, believing, with Tom Hayden, that "our victory lies in progressively demystifying a false democracy." Hayden and seven others, including Hoffman and Rubin, were indicted for conspiring to incite a riot at the convention. Their trial at the hands of reactionary Judge Julius J. Hoffman became a showcase for the friction between radical dissidents and repressive authorities. When Hoffman ordered one of the defendants, Black Panther leader Bobby Seale, bound and gagged, newspaper sketch artists had a field day depicting the fulfillment of the judge's order. Seale ultimately was tried separately from the other defendants (all white), a judicial move that underlined a persisting racial polarization.

Campus confrontation became the rule of the day. In Berkeley, in May of 1969, police and demonstrators clashed at the battle of People's Park. The park, which belonged to the University of California, had once been a weedy meeting place for dope dealers and their customers, but had been turned into a community garden. The university, claiming it wanted to build a soccer field on the spot, asked police to seal off the area while bulldozers razed the gardens. When marchers moved in to take back the park, the police opened up with birdshot, buckshot, and tear gas. Governor Ronald Reagan sent in 3,000 National Guardsmen, who occupied the park for seventeen days. People's Park became a symbol of radical struggle and of the communal alternative to private property; it also underlined the emerging importance of ecological issues, pitting organic gardeners against bulldozers, tomatoes against tear gas.

Disturbances that spring at Harvard, Stanford, Cornell, and nearly three hundred other campuses included more than a hundred incidents involving arson and attempted or actual bombings. The voices of the counterculture grew more militant. Jefferson Airplane, a San Francisco rock group that had risen to fame by combining powerful vocal and instrumental performance with odes to the mind-expanding power of LSD, turned to celebrating insurrection, crowing "Look what's happenin' out in the streets / Got to Revolution!"

All the while, some antiwar activists worked hard to repair the damaged credibility of the antiwar movement with the public at large. The New Mobilization, a coalition of moderate antiwar advocates, organized massive peace demonstrations in the fall of 1969, calling for a Vietnam War Moratorium. Across the nation, millions of people responded, holding rallies, teach-ins, marches, and meetings. On the day of the Moratorium, October 15, one hundred thousand people gathered on Boston Common; in New York City, a series of mass meetings included one on Wall Street. Nationwide crowd estimates for the October 15 demonstrations ranged from 2 million to 15 million. The following month, more than half a million people gathered in Washington, D.C., for a second Moratorium in the largest demonstration ever held in that city.

This huge, peaceful outcry against the war did have an impact; it attested to the existence of millions of Americans who supported neither the nation's Vietnam policies nor the violent tactics of the extreme left. Yet even moderate antiwar activists were angry and frustrated by their inability to stop the war. The extremists, moreover, made better copy, and police and troops, vastly outnumbering them, met them with ferocity.

On December 4, 1969, Chicago police raided local Black Panther headquarters, killing Panther leaders Fred Hampton and Mark Clark in their beds. SDS splintered, and soon was dominated by a faction calling itself the Weathermen, after a line in a Bob Dylan song, "You don't need a weatherman to know which way the wind blows." Announcing their goal as "the destruction of U.S. imperialism and the achievement of a classless world: world communism," the Weathermen rejected coalition politics of any kind and embraced worldwide revolution. Their heroes, they declared, included Chinese Communist party Chairman Mao Zedong and Central American revolutionary martyr Ché Guevara. Their enemies were "the pigs at home," their vanguard a Revolutionary Youth Movement. "Kids used to try to beat the system from inside the army or from inside the schools," they said; "now they desert from the army and burn down the schools."

A week before the October Moratorium, two or three hundred Weathermen street fighters battled Chicago police in demonstrations that came to be collectively known as the Days of Rage. In the next year, the mixed message of the antiwar movement emerged dramatically. While thousands assembled to light candles and sing "Give Peace a Chance," a relatively few shock troops fantasized about violence, trained for street fighting, and built bombs. Between September 1969 and May 1970, there were at least 250 bombings of draft boards, ROTC buildings, federal offices, and corporate headquarters. In March 1970, three bombers from the Weather Underground, as the Weathermen now called themselves, died when they blew themselves up in a New York townhouse. The following August, a bomb exploded in the University of Wisconsin mathematics building, killing a graduate student who was working on a research project in a facility thought to be empty.

In 1970 there were 9,408 incidents of protest; 731 involved police and arrests, 410 involved damage to property, and 230 involved violence to persons. The confrontations peaked in May, when President Nixon announced that United States troops had invaded neutral Cambodia, a state neighboring Vietnam. The announcement set off a wave of student strikes; at least seventy-five campuses shut down for the rest of the academic year, and students at Northwestern University announced that that institution had seceded from the United States. Some thirty ROTC buildings were burned or bombed in the first week of May, including the one at Kent State University in Kent,

Ohio. Governor James Rhodes called in National Guard troops to restore order on campus, and on May 4 nervous guardsmen opened fire on student demonstrators and passers-by, killing four and wounding nine. Ten days later, police killed two more students and wounded nine at Jackson State, a predominantly black campus in Mississippi. Torn and bloody, the country seemed to be consuming its young—a cannibalism some deplored, some embraced.

As radical and antiwar protest culminated in these violent confrontations, another protest movement was developing—more quietly at first, but perhaps possessing even greater long-run impact. This was the movement for women's liberation, a product of a new feminist consciousness.

THE RISE OF THE NEW FEMINISM

Even in the supposedly quiescent 1950s, there had been some organized and articulate attempts to come to grips with women's issues. In the few cases in which unions had sought to organize service and clerical workers in the immediate postwar period, working-class women had pushed for such goals as equal pay for equal work, and had begun to consider economic and social questions affecting women that would not be fully articulated until the 1980s. Even in its heyday, what writer Betty Friedan would in 1963 call "the feminine mystique"—the idea that women belonged at home because they were nurturing, timid creatures entirely different from competitive, capable men—did not go unquestioned. In the 1950s, magazines including *The Ladies' Home Journal* and *Good Housekeeping* carried articles celebrating the benefits of paid work for women and featured profiles of successful career women.

By 1960, women's issues had begun to receive attention at the level of the federal government. In 1961, President Kennedy established a Commission on the Status of Women (CSW), headed by Eleanor Roosevelt. Something of an anomaly in the masculine atmosphere of the New Frontier, the CSW took tentative positions, such as recommending new programs in adult education so that women might go back to work after raising their children. These pronouncements made it clear that women should not neglect their primary responsibilities in the home.

In the early sixties, Congress began to discuss discrimination against working women. The Equal Pay Act of 1963 made it illegal to pay women less than men for doing the same job. However, the decade's most significant piece of legislation in the area of women's rights became law almost serendipitously. As Congress debated the 1964 Civil Rights Act, a reactionary Virginia congressman, Howard W. Smith, attempted to kill the bill by introducing an amendment that he believed would reduce the whole matter of civil rights to absurdity. Title VII prohibited discrimination on the basis of sex. Encouraged by business and professional women, liberal northerners, led by Representative Martha Griffith of Michigan, pushed the amendment through, and it became law along with the rest of the bill. The Equal Employment Opportunity Commission (EEOC), charged with enforcing the bans on occupational discrimination mandated in the Civil Rights Act, did not at first take sex discrimination complaints seriously, but under pressure it ultimately began to enforce the law.

Meanwhile, as noted in Chapter 6, discontent had been brewing in the tranquil suburbs. Middle-class white women, supposedly fully absorbed in cleaning their houses and raising their children, found domestic life lacking. In 1960, when *Redbook* magazine ran an article titled "Why Young Mothers Feel Trapped" and invited readers to respond, the editors received an astonishing 24,000 replies. In 1963 came the publication of Betty Friedan's *The Feminine Mystique,* which blasted the social waste of isolating educated, talented women in the household, no haven in a heartless world but, in Friedan's memorable phrase, a "comfortable concentration camp." Middle-class American women, Friedan said, felt depressed, useless, and assailed by "the problem that has no name." Speaking for this constituency (and not, for example, for African-American mothers, whose families' survival had long depended on their ability to find paid work of any kind), Friedan believed that the solution lay in giving women meaningful jobs outside the home. In 1966 Friedan was among the founders of the National Organization for Women (NOW), the first national lobby for women's rights since the suffrage era, dedicated to the liberal goals of achieving for women political and economic opportunities equal to those enjoyed by men.

Social Change and Women's Issues

The women's movement gained momentum because it was rooted in widespread, long-lasting social change. Among other factors, more and more women were becoming educated. Between 1950 and 1974, college enrollment for men increased by 234 percent; for women the increase was 456 percent. Even more important, both married and single women were entering the paid work force. During the Second World War, female employment had increased from 27 percent of adult women in 1940 to 36 percent five years later. Female employment dropped off temporarily immediately after the war, but by 1960 37.7 percent of women aged sixteen and over were employed, constituting 33 percent of the total work force. A decade later, 43 percent of women aged sixteen and over, representing 38 percent of the civilian work force, were either working or looking for work. The numbers continued to rise steadily. More and more frequently, the working woman was a married woman: by 1962 married women accounted for 60 percent of the female work force. The working woman was also a mother: as early as 1970, one-third of women with children under six years of age held or sought jobs.

At the same time, women workers had fewer job options than their male counterparts. They generally crowded into female-dominated occupations, including nursing, clerical work, teaching, and domestic work, that paid less than men's jobs. In 1955, the median compensation for women in full-time, year-round employment was 64 percent of men's earnings. In 1960, the figure had dropped to 61 percent, and by 1975 full-time women workers were earning only 58.8 percent of what men earned. Even when they did the same work as men, they were paid less. The EEOC was understaffed and often reluctant to pursue complaints about infringements of the Equal Pay Act. Moreover, employers could skirt the whole issue by writing slightly different job descriptions and giving different titles to men and women employed in substantially the same activities.

Most women who worked reported that they did so out of financial necessity or to improve their families' standard of living, although some said they were seeking personal satisfaction. Still, most Americans assumed that even women who held full-time, paid jobs would continue to do most of the housework. According to figures that changed very little between 1955 and the early 1970s, full-time housewives spent between 52 and 56 hours per week doing housework. Wives who worked full-time outside the home still reported spending about 26 hours per week in housekeeping. And whether or not their wives worked, husbands spent about 1.6 hours per day, or 11.2 hours per week, doing household tasks, including yard work. Men helped at times with shopping, cooking, and laundry, but in general did not do the cleaning or ironing.

Perhaps most important of all, the myth of the happy nuclear family was crumbling. Greater acknowledgment of the tensions within families, signaled by rising divorce rates, concern about women who had been widowed or abandoned, and growing alarm over family violence and abuse, heralded an urgent need to re-evaluate woman's place in American society. If women could no longer count on the family as a protected place, they would have to fashion new ways of making their way in the world.

Emergence of the Women's Liberation Movement

The dramatic changes in women's role in society were bound to have political consequences, particularly as civil rights activists brought racial injustice to the nation's attention, liberal politicians embraced social reform, and radical dissidents questioned the distribution of

A women's liberation protest at the Statue of Liberty. *UPI/Bettmann Newsphotos.*

power in American society. The civil rights effort and the New Left fell short of their explicit political goals, but both proved to be seedbeds for a feminist movement of lasting and immense scope.

In the fall of 1964, SNCC women, including Ruby Doris Smith Robinson, Casey Hayden, Mary King, and Mary Varela, drafted a paper on women's position in SNCC. Robinson recognized that as a woman she shared some common ground with King and Hayden, both white, but as an African-American she also believed that the organization should be black-led and black-dominated. King and Hayden recognized that the turn toward Black Power would leave no place for them in a movement to which they had devoted years of their lives. But if Black Power as a political strategy left them out, as an ideology focusing on difference it enabled them to begin to distinguish the ways in which women's status diverged from men's. A year later, in the fall of 1965, King and Hayden composed anonymously "a kind of memo" to women in the peace and freedom movements, arguing that women and blacks both "seem to be caught up in a common-law caste system . . . which, at its worst, uses and exploits women." When they raised the problem of male dominance among their fellow activists, men generally responded by laughing at them. Several months earlier, at a SNCC meeting where the position of women in the movement had been raised, Stokely Carmichael had quipped, "The position of women in SNCC is prone!" Those who heard the remark, including Mary King, "collapsed with hilarity," but when the laughter faded, the serious question remained.

By June of 1967, women had found a language to express their grievances. They named a problem—sexism (sometimes called "male chauvinism")—and a solution—women's liberation. Liberal NOW activists focused on eliminating discriminatory wage rates and fighting for legal equality for women, pushing hard for an Equal Rights Amendment to the Constitution. The radical feminists, who sometimes began as NOW members but more often came out of the civil rights movement and the New Left, identified a new set of political issues, including childcare, abortion, birth control, sexuality, and the sharing of housework. Soon, meeting in small groups to discuss not only war or racism but also problems that seemed intensely individual and private, they developed a new organizing tool: consciousness raising. By identifying common grievances, they came to the fundamental insight of a new feminist movement, namely, that what appeared to be women's individual problems involved much larger questions of social power, or "sexual politics," in the words of feminist theorist Kate Millett. Feminist writer Robin Morgan turned this insight into the slogan, "The personal is political."

Obstacles to Women's Liberation

From the start, the new feminism, often called "the second wave" to distinguish it from the women's rights movement of the late nineteenth and early twentieth centuries, faced formidable obstacles. All kinds of people felt threatened by the prospect of women's liberation: conservative men, who stood to lose all manner of privileges of sex; middle-class women, especially housewives, who worried that men would simply abandon their breadwinner roles and that women would lose whatever protections remained to them; fundamentalist Christians, who believed that women's traditional role in the family was Biblically ordained; even leftist men, accustomed to treating women as assistant radicals and sex objects. In the late sixties and early seventies, the mainstream press used dismissive language to ridicule the movement. Reporters for *Time* and *Newsweek* who referred to Gloria Steinem and Shulamith Firestone as "women's libbers" never called Eldridge Cleaver or Rap Brown "black libbers."

Moreover, the task of building a movement based on women's common problems, interests, and objectives was deeply complicated by the very diversity of the women the movement hoped to mobilize.

Certainly, race made a difference in women's lives. Even in the early days of SNCC, differences among women had raised tensions; black women had articulated grievances and goals that diverged from those of their white sisters in the "beloved community." Class, age, sexual preference, and occupational status also divided women. Middle-class housewives who had invested their lives in the idea that their husbands would protect them were far less equipped to face the challenges of economic independence than were college-age women battling sex quotas in law school admissions. Lesbian activists saw their interests as diverging in some ways from those of heterosexual women. Mexican-American mothers who made their living as migrant farm workers or domestic servants had different needs from the affluent women who bought the produce they picked or hired them to clean homes.

It soon became clear that women who identified themselves as feminists disagreed sharply on many matters. Some, like Robin Morgan, took a page out of the Yippies' book and sought to shock the public. A week after the 1968 Chicago convention, Morgan and other protesters at the Miss America Pageant in Atlantic City crowned a live sheep "Miss America." Such actions, other feminist activists argued, alienated middle-of-the-road women and harmed the cause of sisterhood.

More fundamentally, because of the enormous diversity of issues affecting women, feminists had different views on both long- and short-term goals for the movement. Some argued that the first order of business was to dismantle a capitalist system that oppressed women in particular. Others believed that the movement should concentrate first on eradicating male domination. Some believed men could be reformed and that women had an obligation to maintain relations with men. Shulamith Firestone declared that "a revolutionary in every bedroom cannot fail to shake up the status quo." Others rejected heterosexuality, some for political reasons, some because women's liberation allowed them to act on a long-hidden lesbian identity. As visions of the women's movement proliferated, so did its tactics, its victories, its failures, its institutions.

By the mid-1970s women had made inroads into male-dominated professions, mounted successful challenges to legal and economic discrimination, founded new enterprises, and claimed new rights. Yet much remained to be done. While the privileges of race and class enabled a few American women to "have it all," many more were highly vulnerable. The wage gap between men and women persisted. If some women made strides in professional circles, many fell deeper into poverty. Chapter 12 describes the social changes of the 1970s that posed new problems for the women's movement.

Although the women's movement has continued, with various shifts in emphasis, to the present day, the other protest movements of the sixties gradually faded or evolved into new, less sensational forms. The New Left never recovered from the cataclysmic spring of 1970, when the killings at Kent State capped a surge of bombings and confrontations. After that, some self-proclaimed revolutionaries went underground. Moderate dissidents seemed dazed by the escalating climate of hatred. Some, declaring themselves burned out, retreated from politics altogether. Many left the movement to pursue other political goals. Eventually, the peace settlement in Vietnam removed the principal issue that had united the many threads of the New Left. But the legacy of 1960s political protest was not forgotten. Most obviously, future administrations knew that an unpopular war abroad might provoke widespread rebellion at home.

The counterculture, once it gained massive publicity in the late 1960s, saw many of its distinctive attributes absorbed by the mainstream culture. Hippie styles in hair and clothing and psychedelic music became popular enough to lose some of their revolutionary impact. More important, society at large became more sexually permissive; indeed, the "sexual revolution" was a primary consequence of the sixties. Recreational drug use spread far beyond the hippie enclaves, winning converts in many segments of American society. As this happened, some of the erstwhile hippies drifted into more conventional lives, or at least their habits no longer seemed extraordinary. Others continued to pursue spiritual fulfillment by way of religious and therapeutic groups that identified themselves as part of a "New Age" of expanded consciousness. Rooting out one's inner demons, whether through meditation, confrontation, long soaks in seaside hot springs, or hard labor in religious communes, occupied some inheritors of the countercultural tradition. Inevitably, also, entrepreneurs began to capitalize on nostalgia for the wild and crazy sixties; a running shoe corporation would peddle a new design with a television commercial soundtrack featuring the Beatles' "Revolution."

Meanwhile, the civil rights movement, transformed by Black Power, had fragmented. Some leaders were in exile; others were dead. Still others began to move into the political mainstream. SCLC workers Andrew Young and Jesse Jackson, who had stood with Martin Luther King, Jr., when he was shot in Memphis, led the next generation of activists and became powers to be reckoned with in the Democratic party. Blacks and women held more and more local and national political offices. Beginning with Carl Stokes of Cleveland, elected in 1967 as the first African-American to become mayor of a major American city, blacks moved into positions of power in the nation's urban centers.

The push for African-American rights also spawned a new, pluralistic politics of difference. By the late 1960s, Native Americans organized to raise public awareness of the history of their oppression, adopting both militant and moderate tactics. Members of the American Indian Movement (AIM) occupied Alcatraz Island and staged a mass protest at Wounded Knee, South Dakota, the site of a notorious massacre of Lakota (Sioux) Indians in 1890. Other Indian advocates would form such organizations as the Native American Rights Fund to pursue legal change. By 1980 Native Americans succeeded in forcing the federal government to return some important tribal lands and provide compensation for other lands that had been confiscated by whites.

Mexican-Americans, galvanized by Cesar Chavez's charismatic leadership and his success in organizing the United Farm Workers, pressed for reform in the treatment of Latinos. Latinos shared a heritage based on Spanish language and culture, but they or their families had come from places as diverse as Mexico, Chile, Nicaragua, Cuba, and Puerto Rico, under enormously divergent circumstances. As they struggled to articulate common goals in organizations like the League of United Latin American Citizens (LULAC) and to come to grips with differences among themselves, they became an increasingly important part of the American political and economic picture, especially in the Sunbelt.

Just as the protest movements of the sixties had mobilized people to seek justice on the basis of race, ethnicity, and gender, they also created the possibility of a civil rights movement based on sexuality. On June 29, 1969, police raided the Stonewall Inn, a gay bar in Greenwich Village. Instead of accepting arrest, patrons fought back with rocks and bottles, a confrontation heralded as the beginning of the gay liberation movement. Gay and lesbian activists moved quickly to redefine homosexuality not as a perversion but as a legitimate sexual identity. If they did not reach a consensus as to whether sexual preference was inborn or chosen, they enabled millions of homosexuals to come out of the closet, redrew the boundaries of sexuality, and organized to claim a share of political power in many American cities. The gay community would face its greatest crisis in the 1980s, when it became the first American group to suffer the devastating epidemic of acquired immune deficiency syndrome (AIDS).

For others who carried on the political legacy of the sixties, the fate of the Earth seemed the most pressing issue. Hippies who had experienced the majesty and endangerment of nature during LSD trips in California redwood groves became advocates of environmentalism. Others took a more political road to the ecology movement;

peace advocates worried about the environmental threat of nuclear weapons, and critics of large corporations focused on those that sold shoddy and dangerous products in the United States and the Third World. In 1970, environmental activists held the first Earth Day, part teach-in, part demonstration, designed to promote awareness of humans' impact on the natural environment. Books like Rachel Carson's indictment of the use of pesticides, *Silent Spring*, Paul Ehrlich's vision of demographic doom, *The Population Bomb*, Barry Commoner's critique of the nuclear industry, *Science and Society*, and Ralph Nader's exposé of the automobile business, *Unsafe at Any Speed*, inspired a new awareness of the connections between technology, politics, personal freedom, and environmental dangers.

A huge and diverse array of organizations would in ensuing years press and expand the environmentalist agenda. Moderate organizations like the Sierra Club and the Audubon Society, working through lobbying and letter writing, mobilized nature lovers on behalf of endangered animals and plants and against development in wilderness areas. More militant groups like Earth First! engaged in what they called "monkey-wrenching," after the title of a novel by environmentalist writer Edward Abbey. Their direct-action tactics included disabling construction equipment and driving metal spikes in trees to destroy the chain saws of logging operations. In time, environmental groups would become a formidable national political force, and Congress would respond to their concerns, establishing a federal Environmental Protection Agency.

CONCLUSION

In the 1960s and early 1970s, the nation's youth launched a frontal assault on conventional behavior, smashing the barriers between public and private life, legitimizing new ideas and forms of behavior. They exposed the depth of racial oppression in the United States, catalyzed the American withdrawal from Vietnam, began a sexual revolution, helped to found a lasting feminist movement and widen opportunities for American women, promoted recognition of the culturally plural nature of American society, and pressed a new concern about the environment.

But these innovations created controversy and carried troubling consequences. Young radicals contributed to the climate of violence that engulfed American society by the 1970s. Moreover, by justifying their sometimes outrageous behavior in the name of personal freedom, they paved the way for what historian Christopher Lasch would call "the culture of narcissism"—the retreat of many Americans into a pursuit of personal pleasure. By 1980 pundits were referring to the 1970s as the "Me Decade," contrasting that era with the more socially involved sixties; but the cultivation of "me" was to some extent a legacy of those radical years, an outgrowth of the Yippies and the hippies, the rock festivals and drugs and summer of love.

Perhaps just as inevitably, there would be a counterrevolution. President Nixon's attorney general, John Mitchell, looked at the turmoil of the late 1960s and predicted that "this country's going to go so far right, you won't believe it." That old enemy of the left, Ronald Reagan, ultimately led the triumphal march as the right seized power in the United States, and even some former hippies and leftists moved to the opposite end of the political spectrum. Jerry Rubin, who had helped to lead the Yippie protest at the 1968 Democratic convention, put on a suit and became a Wall Street wizard; Black Panther Eldridge Cleaver so repudiated revolutionary politics that the 1980s found him running for public office in California as a Republican. Yet the unruly, diverse, sometimes shimmeringly beautiful, sometimes corrosively ugly political and cultural energies unleashed in the sixties could not be suppressed entirely. A multitude of genies had been let out of a plenitude of bottles. ■

F U R T H E R   R E A D I N G

On civil rights and Black Power, see: Clayborn Carson, *In Struggle: SNCC and the Black Awakening of the 1960s* (1981); William H. Chafe, *Civilities and Civil Rights: Greensboro, North Carolina, and the Black Struggle for Freedom* (1980); David J. Garrow, *Bearing the Cross: Martin Luther King, Jr. and the Southern Christian Leadership Conference* (1986); Malcolm X, *The Autobiography of Malcolm X* (1965); Harvard Sitkoff, *The Struggle for Black Equality, 1954–1981*. On the New Left and the antiwar movement, see: Wini Breines, *The Great Refusal: Community and Organization in the New Left* (1983); Todd Gitlin, *The Sixties: Years of Hope, Days of Rage* (1987); James Miller, *"Democracy Is in the Streets": From Port Huron to the Siege of Chicago* (1987); W. J. Rorabaugh, *Berkeley at War* (1989); Kirkpatrick Sale, *SDS* (1973). On the Counterculture, see: Charles Perry, *The Haight-Ashbury* (1984); Charles Reich, *The Greening of America* (1970); Theodore Roszak, *The Making of a Counterculture* (1969); Nicholas Von Hoffman, *We Are the People Our Parents Warned Us Against* (1968); Tom Wolfe, *The Electric Kool-Aid Acid Test* (1968). On women's changing lives and the women's movement, see: William H. Chafe, *The American Woman: Her Changing Social, Economic, and Political Role, 1920–1970* (1972); Alice Echols, *Daring to Be Bad: Radical Feminism in America, 1967–1975* (1989); Barbara Ehrenreich, *Re-making Love: The Feminization of Sex* (1987); Sara Evans, *Personal Politics* (1978); Kate Millett, *Sexual Politics* (1970).

10

The Illusion of Peace:
Foreign Policy During
the Nixon Administration

On July 20, 1969, astronaut Neil Armstrong climbed down the ladder of a lunar probe and became the first person to walk on the moon. When Armstrong radioed to Earth, "That's one small step for man, one giant leap for mankind," the country rejoiced and temporarily set aside the bitter divisions over the war in Vietnam. A few grammarians complained that by dropping the word "a" before "man," Armstrong had contradicted himself, but most observers agreed with Walter Cronkite's enthusiastic comparison of the moon walk with the birth of Christ. For a brief while it seemed that a new age had dawned, and Americans had regained their faith in the future promised earlier in the sixties. The *Apollo 11* mission fulfilled President John F. Kennedy's pledge to "put a man on the moon and return him safely to earth in this decade."

Kennedy had promoted space exploration as part of the global competition between the United States and the Soviet Union. His vice president, Lyndon Johnson, had explained that "failure to master space means being second best in every aspect, in the crucial arena of our Cold War world." But by 1969 the catastrophic war in Vietnam had sapped Americans' optimistic hopes to dominate world politics. Richard Nixon won the presidency in 1968 in part by tapping vast public dismay over the costs of global intervention. He assailed "the policies and mistakes of the past" while focusing attention on the endless fighting in Southeast Asia. He complained that "never has so much military, economic and diplomatic power been used as ineffectively as in Vietnam." Yet his own plans for solving the Vietnam riddle remained murky; his campaign speeches promised only "an honorable end to the war."

Nixon, aware of the war's increasing unpopularity, agreed with many foreign affairs experts who considered Vietnam a drain on American resources and a diversion from the principal focus of United States foreign policy—competition with the Soviet Union. Reducing the attention paid to Vietnam while restoring American freedom of action in the rest of the world became the first foreign policy goal of the new administration.

Within a month of the election, Nixon began what *Time* magazine later called an "improbable partnership" with Henry Kissinger, a forty-five-year-old German-born Harvard professor, whom Nixon selected as his national security adviser. Over the next five and one-half years, Kissinger had more access to Nixon than anyone else in government, briefing him daily on world events, discussing grand strategy in foreign affairs, hammering out positions for negotiations with other countries, gossiping about politicians at home and abroad, and plotting vengeance on rivals everywhere.

From 1969 to 1974, Nixon and Kissinger orchestrated some of the greatest reversals in United States foreign policy since the beginning of the Cold War. Working secretly, contemptuous of the foreign affairs bureaucracy, they produced dramatic meetings with old adversaries, altered the course of the war in Vietnam, reduced tension with the Soviet Union, opened relations with China, and thrust the United States into the Middle East as the principal foreign power. The public cheered them at the time, just as it cheered the success of the astronauts. It seemed that the United States was facing the rest of the world, not to mention outer space, with renewed imagination and purpose. A Gallup poll listed Kissinger as the most admired man in the world in 1972 and 1973. Even long-time political foes came to believe that Nixon had a flair for foreign relations. Yet by the time the president resigned in disgrace over the Watergate scandal in August 1974, détente had soured, and the settlement of the war in Vietnam proved illusory. What Nixon and Kissinger had heavily promoted as the "structure of peace" in 1971 appeared in retrospect more sleight of hand than lasting achievement.

THE IMPROBABLE PARTNERSHIP: NIXON AND KISSINGER

Richard Nixon and Henry Kissinger complemented each other, helping to fulfill one another's ambitions. The president sought intellectual respectability and acceptance from eastern politicians, journalists, and intellectuals. From the time of his virulent campaigns for the House and Senate, throughout his role in the Alger Hiss case and the Red Scare, and even during his service as Eisenhower's vice president, the eastern intelligentsia had reviled Nixon as devious, hypocritical, and unprincipled. Opponents labeled him "Tricky Dick." John Kennedy, who had defeated Nixon in the 1960 presidential election, dismissed him as having "no class." *Washington Post* cartoonist Herblock once pictured him emerging from a sewer. He reminded writer Norman Mailer of "a church usher of the variety who would twist a boy's ear after removing him from church." Even his supporters knew how awkward and unlikable he appeared in an age that admired cool grace. "Let's face it," Roger Ailes, his media adviser, remarked, "a lot of people think Nixon is dull. Think he's a bore, a pain in the ass."

When Kissinger became national security adviser, he brought with him links to prominent and powerful easterners—the sort of people Nixon had alternately envied and scorned throughout his career.

Kissinger had been at Harvard for nearly twenty years, had worked for the Kennedy administration, had advised Governor Nelson Rockefeller in his runs for the presidency, had written extensively for New York's prestigious Council on Foreign Relations, and had already conducted secret negotiations with Vietnam on ending the war. Favorable press reaction to Kissinger's appointment came swiftly. The liberal *New Republic*, pleased with the selection of a professor who did not share Nixon's reflexive anticommunism, expressed relief that Kissinger "brings to his share of responsibility for foreign policy in the nuclear age a sophistication that Mr. Nixon lacks." One former Defense Department official predicted, "We'll all sleep a little better knowing that Henry is down there."

For his part, Kissinger sought access to power, which Nixon could give him. Immediately upon being named national security adviser, Kissinger began concentrating power in the National Security Council (NSC), with himself as the council's only representative to the president. He persuaded Nixon that presidents from Eisenhower onward had been thwarted in their desires to direct foreign affairs themselves—in contrast to Woodrow Wilson and Franklin Roosevelt in the First and Second World Wars, respectively—because the NSC had merely received information from other government agencies without having the power to supervise them. He proposed that the NSC become the "principal forum for [national security] issues requiring interagency coordination," especially when the president had to make decisions affecting the future.

Nixon, who preferred private conversations with trusted aides to formal cabinet meetings where he could not control the agenda, concurred. On the first day of the new administration, the president agreed that the NSC would direct foreign affairs and that he would meet with Kissinger each morning for a review of the world situation. Over the next six months the two men outlined a new course.

One important decision was the so-called Vietnamization of the Southeast Asian war, following a pattern set in the last months of the Johnson administration. Because public opposition rose and fell in response to reports of American casualties, the United States would reduce its military actions on the ground, turning more of them over to the ARVN, the South Vietnamese army. At the same time the air force and navy would step up the bombing of North Vietnam to speed the pace of the Paris negotiations.

Nixon and Kissinger also quietly revived the Johnson administration's tentative steps toward better relations with the Soviet Union. During the first six weeks of the new administration, Kissinger opened a secret "backchannel" line of communication with Soviet Ambassador Anatoly Dobrynin. The national security adviser circumvented Secretary of State William P. Rogers, fearing that the State

Department could not be trusted to follow his blueprint for improving United States–Soviet relations. He tried to enlist Dobrynin's help in pressuring North Vietnam to negotiate a deal on the war. Kissinger also began exploring arms control and trade discussions with the Soviet representative.

Kissinger cultivated the press as assiduously as he briefed the president or communicated with Dobrynin. He leaked hints of the new strategy, and by the fall of 1969 stories began to appear idolizing his "omniscient" or "cosmic" view of foreign affairs. *Newsweek* concluded that "in the blurry milky way of Nixonian Washington, Kissinger's star is one of the few to burn brightly." Nixon's other aides later resented the national security adviser's prominence, but the president seemed pleased that Kissinger offered such access to opinion leaders.

VIETNAM: BACKING OUT WITH GUNS BLAZING

Supportive news stories helped relieve some of the pressure on the new administration to end the war in Vietnam immediately. More important in buying time was the confusion and disarray among opponents of the war following the debacle of the 1968 Democratic convention. Nixon and Kissinger knew, however, that the public would not long stand for a continued stalemate. "I'm not going to end up like [Lyndon Johnson]," Nixon promised. "Holed up in the White House, afraid to show my face on the street. I'm going to stop that war. Fast." Both Nixon and Kissinger wanted a negotiated settlement, one that would preserve American "honor," but they disagreed over what kind of settlement was feasible. Kissinger, according to an aide, did not think that the United States could hope for more than the return of American prisoners of war (POWs) and did not believe that Saigon could ever win the war, whereas Nixon believed that the only way to negotiate an end to the war was by proving to Hanoi that Saigon could win it. Ultimately, the Nixon administration pursued three somewhat conflicting goals at once: reducing public attention to Vietnam, negotiating a face-saving arrangement with Hanoi, and bolstering the military capacity of Saigon.

Vietnamization

In June 1969, Nixon conferred with South Vietnam's president, Nguyen Van Thieu, on Midway Island, explaining Vietnamization, the scheme of turning more of the fighting over to the ARVN. Nixon then publicly announced the withdrawal of 25,000 American troops from the war zone. Fewer American troops meant lower monthly draft calls, which Nixon hoped would reduce young people's anger about the war. In 1969 he also replaced the aging, abrasive General Lewis Hershey as head of the Selective Service System with Curtis Tarr, who promised to make the draft fairer by introducing a lottery in which men were selected randomly on the basis of their birth dates. In 1969 and 1970 the lottery did seem fairer, but in 1971 Nixon created a great lottery "loophole" when he announced the end of all student deferments: through a series of technicalities, that year's entire college freshman class avoided the possibility of ever being drafted. Nevertheless, the administration derived political dividends in 1972 by appealing both to critics of student deferments and to students themselves, 600,000 of whom had escaped through the loophole.

In June 1969 Nixon tried another way of reducing public anxiety about the war in Vietnam when he forswore future use of American troops in Asian wars. In a statement quickly labeled the "Nixon Doctrine" by the press, the president outlined principles to be used after Vietnam. In the future, he said, the United States would provide military and economic assistance but expected "the nation directly threatened to assume the primary responsibility of providing the manpower for its own defense."

At the same time, United States planes expanded the air war to Vietnam's neighboring country, Cambodia, through a series of secret air raids designed to stop the North Vietnamese use of Cambodian trails for infiltrating soldiers and supplies into South Vietnam. Over the next fifteen months B-52s flew more than 3,600 raids, dropping over 100,000 tons of bombs within Cambodian borders. Although the bombing pleased Chairman of the Joint Chiefs of Staff Earle Wheeler, Secretary of Defense Melvin Laird remained skeptical. He ordered an assessment of "the risk of hitting Cambodian personnel." Wheeler responded that "the enemy is suffering human and material losses," but he did not tell Laird whether the bombing fulfilled its purpose of slowing the flow of supplies from North Vietnam to the Communist forces in the south.

Despite efforts to keep the attacks secret, the *New York Times* published reports that the United States had violated Cambodian neutrality with the raids. Nixon railed that he was "being sabotaged by bureaucrats," meaning civilian workers on the NSC staff, whom he suspected of leaking word of the bombing to the *Times*. Kissinger, distraught over the leaks and worried that Nixon might suspect him of disloyalty, arranged for FBI director J. Edgar Hoover to conduct wiretaps on members of the NSC staff—that is, Kissinger's own staff—who were suspected of leaking information. The taps, however, revealed little.

As Kissinger sought to keep suspicious White House aides at bay, Vietnamization went forward. The ARVN strength rose from 850,000 to over 1 million men, and another 100,000 South Vietnamese enrolled in military schools. Meanwhile, the United States encouraged South Vietnam to modernize the promotion and pay system of its armed forces. The Americans turned over huge quantities of weaponry to the ARVN: 1 million rifles, 12,000 machine guns, 40,000 grenade launchers, and 2,000 heavy mortars. Washington also transferred hundreds of planes, ships, helicopters, and trucks to the South Vietnamese.

Whether a better-equipped and better-paid ARVN could prevail over the National Liberation Front (NLF) and the North Vietnamese seemed unlikely in 1969. Despite reforms, many of the earlier problems still plagued the ARVN. About 20 percent of ARVN soldiers listed on rosters were "ghosts," men who had died or deserted but whose names were kept on the rolls so that commanders could pocket their pay. Desertion rates stayed high, and the officers corps remained corrupt and reluctant to fight.

Conditions in the American army in Vietnam deteriorated as Vietnamization proceeded. Formerly, individual soldiers had been reluctant to fight as their tour of duty ended; now whole platoons resisted orders to proceed with the few search-and-destroy operations remaining. No one wanted to be among the last killed or wounded in a war that had now become the responsibility of the Vietnamese. American commanders saw the army disintegrate before their eyes. Drug use rose. In 1970 the command estimated that 65,000 soldiers used narcotics. More frightening were the more than two thousand reports in 1970 of "fragging," as soldiers attacked unpopular officers with fragmentation bombs or rifles. The unpopularity of the war made it difficult to recruit young men to enter American military academies. The modernization of American forces not directly involved in the Vietnam conflict also suffered as the Pentagon continued to spend over $12 billion per year on the war. By the fall of 1969, Secretary of Defense Laird wanted the war ended to prevent further deterioration in the morale of the armed forces he directed.

Intimidating the Antiwar Movement

To retain public support for Vietnamization, the administration tried to neutralize the appeal of opponents of the war, who had regrouped after the climactic events of the 1968 presidential election campaign. The two Vietnam Moratoriums in October and November 1969 (see page 335) attracted millions of people to demonstrations in city squares and on college campuses across the country. During the three days of demonstrations in Washington in November, forty thousand protesters paraded past the White House, calling out the names of the dead Americans killed in the war and depositing slips of paper bearing those names in canisters at the Capitol.

Nixon feigned indifference to the demonstrations, claiming they did not interrupt the football games he watched on television. Despite this show of disdain, he prepared a public relations offensive to turn opinion against the demonstrators. After the first Moratorium, he delivered a nationally televised speech in which he appealed to the "silent majority" of Americans to reject the antiwar movement. "North Vietnam cannot humiliate the United States," he warned. "Only Americans can do that." To make sure of his support, Nixon encouraged Vice President Spiro Agnew to deliver a stinging rebuke to the press. Agnew assailed journalists as "an effete corps of impudent snobs" who sympathized with the antiwar demonstrations. The vice president derided the subtle editorializing of television news commentators who with "a raised eyebrow, an inflection of the voice, a caustic remark dropped in the middle of a broadcast can raise doubts in a million minds about the veracity of a public official or the wisdom of a government policy."

Nixon's "silent majority" speech and Agnew's derision had the desired effects, and the press carried less news of the huge demonstrations in Washington than they had of earlier protests. Moreover, when the *New York Times* in November 1969 broke the story of the My Lai massacre, the incident received relatively limited attention. Lieutenant William Calley, who had led the American platoon that murdered over two hundred innocent Vietnamese civilians in March 1968, was eventually court martialed, as were three of his superior officers. Only Calley was sentenced to prison for his role in the massacre, and sympathy for him as a scapegoat spread widely in the generally hawkish South, where the twenty-three-year-old college dropout had grown up. Nixon capitalized on this sympathy by reducing Calley's life sentence to three years.

The media's muted handling of continued antiwar sentiment pleased Nixon. "We've got those liberal bastards on the run," he crowed, "and we're going to keep them on the run." Attorney General John Mitchell authorized the FBI to tap the telephones of the organizers of the Moratoriums. Six months later Nixon approved a plan to infiltrate, burglarize, wiretap, trick, and provoke into violence a variety of antiwar and liberal groups "who pose a threat to our national security." The scheme was envisioned as a secret White House intelligence operation, beyond the control of the FBI. However, FBI director Hoover, now old and cranky, resented losing control over domestic intelligence to Nixon's aides. When he threatened to leak word of the White House program, the plan died.

The Invasions of Cambodia and Laos

In the spring of 1970 Nixon decided on dramatic military gestures even as he quickened the pace of withdrawal of American forces from the war. In March he announced plans to remove an additional 150,000 troops by the end of the year. At the same time Cambodia's chief of staff, General Lon Nol, overthrew the government of Prince Norodom Sihanouk. Lon Nol, unlike Sihanouk, sided clearly with the Americans and South Vietnamese and wanted them to rid neutral Cambodia of the North Vietnamese, who used Cambodia's border region to support insurgents in South Vietnam. The American generals, worried about the effect on the war of the withdrawal of 150,000 American troops, also pressed Nixon for intervention in Cambodia to show the South Vietnamese that the United States was still willing to help them fight. Nixon himself thought a flamboyant military move could seize the initiative from the Democratic Senate, which that spring had rejected two conservative nominees, Clement Haynsworth and G. Harrold Carswell, for positions on the Supreme Court (see Chapter 11).

In late April Nixon decided to invade Cambodia. On the evening of April 30, he went before the American public to plead for support. "If when the chips are down," he said, "the world's most powerful nation acts like a pitiful, helpless giant, the forces of totalitarianism and anarchy will threaten free nations and free institutions throughout the world." The invasion produced modest military yields, killing two thousand enemy troops and destroying eight thousand bunkers, and it may have bought some time for additional Vietnamization. It failed completely, however, in its larger goal of reversing the military trend toward a victory for the North. The ARVN forces fought poorly, and their incompetence and unwillingness to fight were abundantly evident on evening news programs. The United States and ARVN forces also failed to find the headquarters of the North Vietnamese operations, a supposed "nerve center" located in Cambodia.

Worst of all, from Nixon's point of view, the Cambodian operation provoked some of the most furious antiwar demonstrations of the Vietnam era. As described in Chapter 9 (see page 335), protests against the war, the draft, military-sponsored research, and the Reserve Officers' Training Corps (ROTC) erupted on hundreds of college campuses across the country. After National Guard troops killed four protesters at Kent State University, news of the slaughter further inflamed antiwar passions. Over 100,000 young people spontaneously converged on Washington to petition Congress to end the war. Thousands gathered at the Lincoln Memorial, where one night they were astonished to receive a visit from Richard Nixon, distraught over the outrage his actions had produced. Nixon did little to cool anger by making pointless small talk about college football with young people who wanted the war to end. The president further strained relations with his opponents by publicly describing them as "bums" who were more concerned with burning and looting their campuses than with studying.

A student screams in horror over the body of an antiwar demonstrator slain by the National Guard at Kent State University on May 4, 1970. In the aftermath of the Kent State killings, college students across the country staged protests and strikes. *John Filo/Valley News Dispatch.*

Members of Congress were also infuriated by the Cambodian invasion. Arkansas Senator J. William Fulbright, chairman of the Senate Foreign Relations Committee, thought that Nixon's policies were "undermining the security of our country." Congress responded to the public concern over the Cambodian invasion by repealing the 1964 Gulf of Tonkin Resolution, used by Presidents Johnson and Nixon to justify continued American participation in the fighting. Two Senate doves, Democrat Frank Church of Idaho and Republican John Sherman Cooper of Kentucky, introduced legislation blocking further funding of American operations in Cambodia after June 30. The amendment passed the Senate but failed in the House. In any event, Nixon had already said the troops would leave by that date. The president responded defiantly to lawmakers' efforts to restrict his actions in Vietnam: "If Congress undertakes to restrict me, Congress will have to assume the consequences."

At the same time, Kissinger undertook a further public relations campaign to undermine support for the antiwar movement. When three members of his staff resigned in protest over the Cambodian invasion, he told journalists that their departure marked "the epitome of the cowardice of the Eastern Establishment." He also tried to calm his former colleagues in academia, asking for patience and warning that further protest against the war would provoke a backlash among conservative Americans who favored greater military force in Vietnam.

Neither the counterattacks against the antiwar movement nor the invasion of Cambodia brought the end of the war any closer. The public peace talks in Paris stalled. The North Vietnamese delegation dismissed as a farce American proposals to withdraw troops if the North Vietnamese left the South. Willing to wait for a better proposal, the North Vietnamese threatened to remain in Paris "until the chairs rot." In August 1969, hoping that North Vietnamese diplomat Xuan Thuy would be more forthcoming in private than in public, Kissinger opened secret conversations, but he returned home dispirited. The North insisted that the United States leave Vietnam and cease support for the Thieu regime. Because North Vietnam had not acknowledged the division of Vietnam into separate countries, it would not withdraw its forces from what it considered part of its own territory.

By the middle of 1970, therefore, Nixon's honeymoon with the public over Vietnam had ended. The expansion of the war into Cambodia had revived the domestic turmoil of 1968. Like Johnson before him, Nixon could not appear safely on college campuses across the country. Unlike his Democratic predecessor, however, Nixon appealed to the more hawkish section of the electorate. As long as that portion of the public was satisfied, the administration could progress toward other foreign policy goals. Because antiwar outbursts after the Cambodian invasion had polarized national opinion, hawkish Americans became even more committed to Nixon than before. A few days after national guardsmen killed the Kent State protesters, New York construction workers rampaged through New York's financial district. They beat up antiwar demonstrators, forced officials at City Hall to raise the American flag (lowered in mourning after the Kent State killings), and smashed windows at nearby Pace College. Two weeks later the head of the New York Labor Council led an estimated 60,000 to 100,000 flag-waving union members in a march supporting the invasion of Cambodia and opposing the antiwar demonstrations. Nixon received them warmly at the White House.

The emotional exhaustion following the antiwar Moratoriums and the shock of the Kent State killings, combined with the American withdrawal from Cambodia in June 1970, took their toll on the antiwar movement. As another 150,000 American troops left Vietnam and casualty figures dropped below 100 per week, public concern about Vietnam fell slowly until early 1971. Then anger revived as the ARVN, encouraged by the American command, invaded another neighboring country, Laos, once more looking for the enemy's nonexistent headquarters. Without the large contingent of Americans

Daniel Ellsberg

Until 1967 few people supported the American war effort in Vietnam as ardently as did Daniel Ellsberg, a brilliant former marine officer employed as a civilian analyst for the Defense Department. Yet after 1968 no one opposed the war more strenuously than he did. A man of contrasts and contradictions, he combined deep analytical power with a moral passion for whatever cause he embraced.

Like many other highly educated Americans, Ellsberg had devoted his career to the Cold War. Born in 1931, he graduated *summa cum laude* from Harvard University, then volunteered for three years as a marine officer before returning to Harvard for his Ph.D. In 1965 he joined a Defense Department civilian team that urged reforms on the South Vietnamese government and tried to build support among the peasantry. But

---

who had led them into Cambodia the year before, the ARVN forces stumbled badly as they confronted 36,000 battle-hardened North Vietnamese troops. After six weeks of the bloodiest fighting of the war, in which the South Vietnamese suffered casualties of 50 percent of their forces, the ARVN retreated in disarray from Laos. Administration statements that the ARVN had exercised an "orderly retreat" made no sense to TV viewers who saw film clips of terrified South Vietnamese soldiers clinging to the skids of helicopters, desperately trying to get back to South Vietnam.

The *Pentagon Papers*

On Sunday, June 13, 1971, the *New York Times* began a series of stories on the origins of United States involvement in the war in Vietnam. "My God, there it is!" said former Defense Department official Leslie

the devastation wrought by the United States in Vietnam gradually eroded Ellsberg's faith in the war. Deeply discouraged, he left Vietnam in 1967 and went to work for the Rand Corporation, a Defense Department think tank.

The slaughter during the Tet offensive of 1968 completed Ellsberg's conversion into an opponent of the war. The next year, he concluded that the Nixon administration's policy of Vietnamization was a "bloody, hopeless, uncompelled, hence surely immoral prolongation of U.S. involvement in this war." Burdened with a sense of guilt, he decided to act. He wrote letters to editors demanding American withdrawal from Vietnam, and privately he began to photocopy the 7,000-page secret Defense Department history, the *Pentagon Papers*. In early 1971, with no resolution of the war in sight, Ellsberg delivered copies of the *Papers* to a *New York Times* reporter, hoping their revelation of high-level deceit would shock the public into demanding an end to the war.

The Nixon administration vowed to punish Ellsberg. The Justice Department indicted him for theft, espionage, and conspiracy, and the so-called Plumbers unit broke into his psychiatrist's office to search for damaging information. When the Watergate investigation revealed the extent of the White House campaign to discredit him, the case against Ellsberg was thrown out of court. In later years he continued to speak out against the dangers of war and what he considered the immorality of American intervention in Third World countries. ■

Gelb when he opened his newspaper that morning. "It" was the forty-seven-volume *History of U.S. Decision-making Process on Vietnam, 1945–1967,* popularly known as the *Pentagon Papers,* which Gelb had compiled at Secretary of Defense Robert McNamara's request in1968. Daniel Ellsberg, formerly a Defense Department official who had grown disillusioned with the war, had leaked copies of the *Pentagon Papers* to *Times* reporter Neil Sheehan earlier that spring. The secret history cast a dark shadow over the foreign policy of every administration from Truman through Johnson. The documents revealed that American officials had violated international agreements, manipulated the Saigon government, and deliberately misinformed Congress and the public. The *Pentagon Papers* convinced some people who had previously remained undecided about the war that the government had long known the original commitment to Vietnam was a mistake.

The Nixon administration was divided over whether to suppress further publication of the *Pentagon Papers* or let them see the light of day and use them against its political rivals. Kissinger considered publication of the *Pentagon Papers* "a criminally traitorous act." On the other hand, presidential adviser Charles Colson, a seasoned practitioner of behind-the-scenes tricks on Democrats, said the papers proved that "the bad guys and spies are all left-wing Democrats."

Within forty-eight hours of the first publication, the Nixon administration resolved its disagreements and sought to block further publication, which it feared might upset the delicate negotiations going on with the Soviet Union over arms control and with China over normalization of relations. When the Justice Department sued the *New York Times*, the Supreme Court issued a decision with remarkable speed. On June 30, the Court ruled against the government's demand for "prior restraint" on publication because the government had not met the "heavy burden of showing the justification for the importance of such restraint."

In the aftermath of the Court's rebuff, John Ehrlichman created the so-called Plumbers unit, charged with stopping leaks from government officials, such as Ellsberg's distribution of the *Pentagon Papers.* This unit's operations were more sinister than its playful name. One of the Plumbers, E. Howard Hunt, a former CIA operative, proposed a secret psychological evaluation of Ellsberg to find ways to "destroy his public image and credibility." Later that summer, Hunt led a squad of Plumbers, consisting of several anti-Castro Cuban exiles with ties to the CIA, in a burglary of the office of Daniel Ellsberg's psychiatrist, looking for discrediting information to leak to the press. John Ehrlichman later went to jail for his role in the break-in. The next year Hunt, the Cuban exiles, and G. Gordon Liddy, who had helped plan the burglary, organized the notorious break-in at the Democratic National Committee offices at the Watergate office complex (see Chapter 11).

A Settlement of Sorts: The Paris Peace Agreement

The Paris peace talks stalled in 1971 as neither the United States nor the North Vietnamese would make necessary concessions. For example, Washington would not jettison the Thieu government, and the Communist negotiators refused even to acknowledge that they had troops in the South. For the remainder of the year the United States combined negotiations in Paris with threats to the Saigon government and ferocious bombing. By the beginning of 1972 President Nixon was complaining to Henry Kissinger that he felt terrible pressure to end the war in Vietnam before the November presidential election.

In March 1972, 120,000 North Vietnamese troops launched a full-scale invasion of the South. Only 6,000 of the 95,000 American troops remaining in the South were combat soldiers, and the North Vietnamese met little resistance, approaching to within sixty miles of Saigon. The ARVN threw all its reserves into meeting the assault from the North, allowing Vietcong guerrillas in the South to attack and overrun villages in the heavily populated Mekong Delta, near the capital. In response, Nixon on May 8 ordered the largest escalation of the war since 1968. United States forces mined Haiphong harbor, blockaded other North Vietnamese harbors, and engaged in the most sustained bombing of the North since the war began.

Although some politicians and opinion leaders condemned the escalation, this operation provoked less public opposition than the Cambodian invasion, because the air raids resulted in fewer American casualties. Then, in late summer, the Paris peace talks between Kissinger and a North Vietnamese representative, Le Duc Tho, finally moved forward. The national security adviser pointed to public opinion polls showing Nixon with a 30 percentage point lead over Senator George McGovern, who had been nominated by a divided Democratic party to oppose Nixon in the November presidential election. Nixon would surely win a second term, Kissinger told the North Vietnamese, and therefore they would receive the best possible offer if they reached an agreement *before* the November election. His strategy seemed to work: in October the two sides agreed on the outline of a settlement. The United States would remove its troops within sixty days of a cease-fire agreement and the North would release American POWs. The United States would limit its military aid to the South to replacement of lost weaponry and training of replacement troops. The North could keep its forces in the South but would not raise their numbers after the agreement went into effect. The Thieu government would remain in power but would make a good-faith effort to include other factions, including the NLF. An International Control Commission, similar to the one created by the 1954 Geneva Conference, would supervise the agreements.

Less than two weeks before the presidential election, Kissinger, announcing that "peace is at hand," made public the major features of his agreement with Le Duc Tho. Work remained, he acknowledged, but he expected that the end of the war was near. Although Kissinger's announcement virtually ensured Nixon's re-election, it did not accurately foretell the conclusion of the war. The South Vietnamese government panicked. Fearing abandonment by the United States and realizing that his regime had no more popular support than earlier South Vietnamese governments, President Thieu balked at signing an agreement that permitted any North Vietnamese forces to remain in the South. When no agreement was signed before the

Henry Kissinger and North Vietnamese representative Le Duc Tho (*center*) confer during the Paris peace talks to end the war in Vietnam. *National Archives/Nixon Presidential Materials.*

election, McGovern charged that Kissinger had tricked the public. Few voters responded, and Nixon carried every state but Massachusetts and the District of Columbia.

Safely re-elected, Nixon tried to persuade Saigon to drop its objections to the October agreement. Kissinger's deputy, General Alexander Haig, traveled to Saigon with bribes and threats. If Thieu would agree to the accords, the United States would provide economic and military aid; and hints were dropped that the United States would resume bombing if the North broke the accords. On the other hand, if Thieu continued to reject the Paris agreement, the United States would sign it anyway and leave South Vietnam to fend for itself. Kissinger authorized Haig to tell the South Vietnamese leader that the President had committed himself to ending the war and would "go ahead regardless of anything" Saigon did to stop the deal. Still, Thieu would not sign the accord.

Neither would the North Vietnamese agree to consider significant modifications in the peace agreement to break the impasse. Nixon then tried to bludgeon the North into reopening talks. On December 22 the United States unleashed the heaviest bombing campaign of the war against the North. Over the next twelve days, B-52s dropped 36,000 tons of explosives, more bombs than had exploded in the period from 1969 to 1971. Approximately sixteen hundred civilians were killed in Hanoi and Haiphong. Critics at home and abroad expressed outrage at Nixon's behavior. Several characterized Nixon as a madman. The president's approval rating in public opinion polls dropped to 39 percent. Yet Nixon and Kissinger retained a solid core of support among journalists and foreign affairs experts.

The bombing and Nixon's eagerness to end the war restarted the stalled negotiations. Talks resumed in Paris between Kissinger and Le Duc Tho in early January. They made a few cosmetic changes to the October agreement but kept the major provisions of the earlier draft, and on January 27, 1973, they initialed a cease-fire. The United States promised to withdraw its remaining troops within sixty days in return for release of its POWs. The North promised not to raise the number of its troops in the South. The Thieu government would remain in power, but vague plans for "political reconciliation" would go forward in the South, supervised by an International Control Commission. The Saigon government did not sign the Paris accords, but this time Thieu indicated his approval, provided that the United States promised to protect South Vietnam from future North Vietnamese attacks.

Americans felt great relief at the apparent end of the war and the imminent return of the POWs. The White House press office reported gleefully that "there is great admiration for the president which seems to grow as we move further from Washington." For example, an Alabama paper lauded the "patient, long-suffering efforts of the administration" in bringing about accords that "represent in fact a much better bargain than Sen. George McGovern or other 'dove' critics were willing to settle for."

Yet the peace Nixon had promised in 1968 had been a long time in the making. The four years of the Nixon administration had seen some of the heaviest fighting and worst suffering of the war. Officials estimated that 107,000 South Vietnamese soldiers and approximately half a million North Vietnamese and NLF fighters had lost their lives in the period. Another 20,553 American troops were killed during those four years, bringing the total number of American deaths to over 58,000. The number of civilians killed will never be known; most estimates place it at over 1 million.

There was considerable question whether the cease-fire truly represented "peace with honor," the phrase Nixon had used in the 1968 election campaign to describe his goal. The agreement left the government of South Vietnam in place but did not resolve the fundamental issue of the war: was Vietnam one country or two? The official recognition accorded the NLF and the North's right to keep troops in the South ensured that the struggle would continue. For the Communists, the Paris agreement merely represented another temporary delay in their thirty-year effort to unify the country under their leadership. Certain that history was on their side, they waited for the opportune moment to complete their revolution.

In 1973, however, the Paris agreement appeared to be a major accomplishment. In October 1973 the Nobel Prize Committee announced it had awarded the 1973 Peace Prize to Kissinger and Le Duc Tho for their work on the Paris agreement. Le refused his share, because the political future of the South had not been resolved and fighting could resume at a moment's notice. But in the United States, Kissinger and Le Duc Tho won praise from many editorialists. Harvard economist John Kenneth Galbraith, known for his sharp tongue, put the prize into perspective: "They both worked hard to get the war over and both deserved the money. If they had gotten it over quicker, they would have deserved more money."

In the United States, Kissinger's winning the Nobel Peace Prize marked the high point of enthusiasm over the settlement arranged in Paris. Vietnam faded as an issue for the rest of Nixon's second term as Watergate, a Middle East war, and relations with the Soviet Union took center stage. Yet the fighting in Vietnam had not come to an end. The cease-fire gradually eroded. Each side attacked the other, and the North Vietnamese reinforced their positions in the South. President Thieu refused to bargain in good faith with the NLF leaders to bring them into the government. By the beginning of 1974, five months after Nixon had left the presidency in disgrace, Vietnam stood poised on the verge of climactic battles that would chase Thieu from power and give the final victory to the Communists (see Chapter 12).

DÉTENTE WITH THE SOVIET UNION

Long before the settlement in Vietnam, the Nixon administration had taken major steps in other foreign policy arenas. One of the most significant was an attempt to renew the process of détente with the Soviet Union. Relations between Washington and Moscow had been strained since the August 1968 Soviet invasion of Czechoslovakia. Now, however, Nixon and Kissinger had several reasons for trying to reduce tensions with the Soviets.

First, they believed that improved relations with Moscow might produce a breakthrough in the Vietnam stalemate. Second, Nixon and Kissinger saw that détente with the Eastern bloc would help them maintain control of the NATO alliance. In search of economic markets, Western European governments and businesses were beginning to work out their own pattern of détente. For example, after a new Social Democratic government came to power in West Germany, the Soviets arranged in 1969 to borrow over $1 billion from West German firms and invited scores of them to invest in joint ventures. Soon other Western European businesses joined the rush to sell electronic equipment, build truck factories, construct buildings, and drill for oil and natural gas in the Soviet Union. If the United States maintained hostility toward the Soviets while Western Europe moved toward cooperation, NATO might disintegrate. Moreover, American businesses, wanting their share of the Eastern bloc markets, demanded that Washington lift restrictions on East-West trade.

Finally, Nixon administration officials faced the same basic worry as all other policymakers since the Second World War: the danger of nuclear war with the Soviet Union. An arms control agreement with the Soviets could reduce the likelihood of nuclear war and demonstrate that the two powers could find common ground. In political terms, progress on arms control could help the administration quiet the scientists, editorial writers, and members of Congress who complained that the world faced grave dangers from the development of highly accurate, long-range ballistic missiles.

Arms Control

The Nixon administration conducted three years of highly complicated Strategic Arms Limitation Talks (SALT) with the Soviet Union. At his inauguration Nixon promised "an era of negotiation" with the Soviets, and at his first press conference he advocated replacing nuclear arms "superiority" with "sufficiency" in weapons. Publicly, a SALT negotiating team opened conversations with the Soviets in Helsinki and Vienna, while behind the scenes Kissinger conducted his own conversations with Soviet Ambassador Anatoly Dobrynin.

As the talks went forward, Congress sought to restrict development of an antiballistic missile (ABM) system, first proposed in the last years of the Johnson administration. In August 1969 the Senate came within a single vote of stopping further work on the ABM system. The close call encouraged the administration to work harder on an arrangement with the Soviets. In May 1971 Kissinger's conversations with Dobrynin bore fruit, and the two publicly announced that they had separated the ABM issue from the issue of intercontinental ballistic missiles (ICBMs). They promised to concentrate on working out an agreement to limiting ABM development. Although they proposed only "certain measures" leading toward a SALT treaty restricting development of ICBMs, Nixon was ecstatic at the breakthrough.

Over the next year conversations continued between United States and Soviet diplomats. In November 1971 Commerce Secretary Maurice Stans went to Moscow to sign a series of economic agreements between the two countries. The United States agreed to sell the Soviets $136 million worth of grain and $125 million worth of oil drilling and mining equipment, and to build a $500 million truck factory. Farmers and businesspeople welcomed these transactions; but two years later, when drought raised grain prices at home, consumers complained that wheat sold to the Soviet Union should have remained in the United States to keep prices low.

In March 1972 Kissinger traveled to Moscow to lay the groundwork for a summit meeting between Nixon and Soviet Communist Party Secretary Leonid Brezhnev. Before Kissinger left, Nixon stressed to him the domestic political importance of the upcoming summit. He considered it "vitally important that no final agreements be entered into until we arrive in Moscow." Otherwise there would be no "news value to them." He explained that Democratic congressional critics "will try to make it appear that all of this could have been achieved without any summitry whatever."

Accordingly, when Nixon visited Moscow in May, he conducted a dramatic series of late-night negotiations with Brezhnev, with only Kissinger and an interpreter in attendance. (Secretary of States Rogers was pushed into the background.) These talks at the highest level yielded three significant agreements. An ABM treaty limited each power to only two ABM sites. A SALT-I, or Interim Agreement on Limitations of Strategic Armaments, included a five-year pledge to limit land-based missiles to the number contemplated under the United States arms construction program—a number that reduced Soviet plans by approximately 33 percent. Finally, a document called the "Basic Principles of U.S.-Soviet Relations" contained a promise to base subsequent superpower relations on "the principle of equality." Together the three agreements formed the basis of détente between the two superpowers for the next two years.

Before returning to Washington, Nixon and Kissinger stopped in Iran to cement a strategic connection with Shah Mohammed Reza Pahlavi. "I need you," the president told the Iranian monarch, as a "surrogate" power controlling South Asia under the regional security arrangements envisaged by the Nixon Doctrine. As an inducement to protect Western strategic interests in the oil-rich region of the Persian Gulf, Kissinger offered to sell Iran any weapon in the American arsenal, with the exception of nuclear bombs. Arms sales specialists in the State Department objected that the United States might lose control of its most sophisticated hardware by giving the shah such free access, but Kissinger overrode dissenters with his close relations with the president. Over the next five years Iran bought $8 billion worth of American weapons. Ultimately the American support of the shah backfired when a revolution in Iran made that country an enemy of the United States (see Chapter 12). But that was years in the future.

When Nixon returned to Washington from Moscow and Tehran, he appeared to have engineered a major turning point in United

States–Soviet relations. Old adversaries like Democratic Senators Fulbright, Church, and Claiborne Pell of Rhode Island rushed to support détente. Other lawmakers, however, pointed to flaws in the SALT arrangement. Democratic Senator Henry Jackson of Washington, a candidate for his party's presidential nomination, objected to the concept of nuclear "sufficiency" embedded in the SALT-I agreement, which would allow the Soviets three hundred more land-based ICBMs than the United States. Kissinger argued that the United States retained a technological edge, the most important factor in the nuclear age. The Soviets had accumulated large numbers of nuclear weapons, and those numbers now were constrained by the SALT treaty. The United States, on the other hand, was making major scientific advances in weaponry, an issue for which—on the advice of the Joint Chiefs of Staff—no provision had been made in the SALT agreement.

That fall, Congress approved the ABM treaty and the SALT-I agreement. Yet it also tied Kissinger's hands in negotiating the full SALT treaty promised in the interim accords reached in Moscow. Jackson attached an amendment to the congressional ratification, requiring that the United States demand equal numbers of weapons, as he erroneously claimed had been promised in the "Basic Principles of U.S.–Soviet Relations." Jackson's restrictions proved a straitjacket from which even the artful Kissinger could not escape. The forces of the United States and the Soviet Union were "asymmetrical." The United States relied on a triad of land-based ICBMs, submarine-based missiles, and manned bombers. Moscow's weaponry was concentrated in ICBMs, and therefore the Soviets wanted higher numbers of these to offset the American advantage in other nuclear weapons systems.

The Decline of Détente

Over the next two years Jackson, other politicians, and publicists suspicious of the Soviet Union chipped away at public support for détente. They berated Kissinger and Nixon for failing to criticize the Soviet Union's poor record on human rights. In 1973 Jackson joined with Ohio Democratic congressman Charles Vanik to introduce legislation forbidding the extension of equal trading rights—so-called most favored nation status—to the Soviet Union until that country permitted all citizens who wished to emigrate, most of whom were Jews, to do so. In that year more than thirty thousand Soviet Jews left for the West, more than had ever before been permitted to leave; nevertheless, Jackson saw the immigration issue as one that would fuel his run for president in 1976. The passage of the Jackson-Vanik Amendment in 1974 prevented the Soviets from receiving most favored nation trading status, thereby irritating the Kremlin. The Soviets accused the United States of not treating them as an equal and legitimate power, and détente waned.

Arms control talks made little progress for the remainder of the Nixon administration. As the Watergate scandal grew in 1973 and engulfed the president in 1974 (see Chapter 11), Nixon attempted to regain his public standing with two more summit meetings with Brezhnev. The Soviet leader visited Nixon in Washington in June 1973, and Nixon returned the favor with a trip to Moscow and the Crimea in late June and early July 1974, barely six weeks before his forced resignation. Neither meeting produced major breakthroughs in arms control, although subsidiary pacts were signed to help prevent nuclear war and to limit the power of nuclear test explosions.

THE OPENING TO CHINA

Even more dramatic transformations of United States foreign policy took place with respect to the People's Republic of China. On July 15, 1971, President Nixon announced that National Security Adviser Kissinger had just returned from Beijing, where he had spent two days preparing the way for a presidential visit to China in 1972. Nixon and Kissinger had engineered one of the most dramatic diplomatic turnarounds of the twentieth century in nearly complete secrecy.

Both China and the United States had much to gain by resuming regular diplomatic relations, which had been in abeyance since the beginning of the Korean War. Since 1966 China's leader Mao Zedong had encouraged a "great proletarian Cultural Revolution," during which thousands of young Red Guards had roamed cities and the countryside, terrorizing the population into ideological orthodoxy. Now other Communist officials, led by Zhou Enlai, wanted to end the Cultural Revolution's chaos and open better relations with the rest of the world. China's once close ties to the Soviet Union had deteriorated so greatly that the two fought a bloody border war in 1969 and 1970. Fearful of greater conflict in the future, China wanted ties to the United States to deter Soviet aggression.

Washington, for its part, saw ties to China as a way of reasserting power lost in the Vietnam War. A connection to China would show that the war in Vietnam had not prevented a flexible United States foreign policy, as some critics contended. Beijing might persuade Hanoi to accommodate American peace proposals. Even if China did not help end the war itself, restoration of relations after twenty years could show that the United States had interests other than Vietnam in Asia. Closer relations with China could also put pressure on the Soviet Union in arms control talks or regional disputes. Finally, the

American policy of not recognizing the Communist regime in China was widely regarded as a failure. Most NATO allies had formal relations with the People's Republic of China; the United Nations General Assembly was about to seat Beijing and evict Taiwan.

Kissinger discussed all these issues with Zhou Enlai during his whirlwind forty-nine-hour visit. He found the Chinese leader "one of the two or three most impressive men I have ever met. Urbane, infinitely patient, intelligent, subtle." They agreed that Soviet domination of much of Europe and Asia threatened world stability; they noted that the United States, the world's leading conservative power, could preserve that stability. Although the Chinese promised no help on Vietnam, they indicated that differences over that war should not prevent the United States and China from making progress on other issues. Kissinger in turn observed that American ties to Taiwan should not prevent Washington and Beijing from working together. The two countries agreed to continue talking about their mutual interests over the next seven months as they prepared for Nixon's visit.

The highly favorable reaction to the Chinese breakthrough made the White House jubilant. Some American politicians set aside their traditional animosities toward the administration. Democratic Senator Fulbright told Nixon, "I completely agree with what you are doing." Democratic Majority Leader Mike Mansfield promised understanding for the "delicacy and promise of the situation." Senator Edward M. Kennedy, whose own earlier efforts to travel to China had galvanized the White House initiative, called the visit "historic." Praise also poured in from abroad.

Kissinger arranged the final details of Nixon's visit during the fall of 1971. The United Nations General Assembly's decision to evict Taiwan and seat the People's Republic of China occurred as Kissinger prepared for another visit to Beijing. The national security adviser's disregard for Taiwan caused another rift within the administration and provoked criticism from Democrats. Secretary of State Rogers advised him to postpone the visit to Beijing, but Nixon and Kissinger thought that Taiwan's cause was lost anyway. Senator Kennedy criticized the administration for its haste to visit the Chinese capital before the 1972 presidential election.

In December 1971 war broke out between Pakistan and India over efforts by the residents of East Pakistan, known as Bengalis, to form a new state, Bangladesh. India supported the Bengalis with troops who fought Pakistani soldiers in both the eastern and western parts of the Indian subcontinent. Public opinion in Europe and America backed the Bengalis' desire for independence from western Pakistan, because the more populous but poorer easterners had suffered economically, socially, and politically at the hands of the westerners since the founding of Pakistan in 1947. Washington ignored the abuses committed by the Pakistani government against the Bengalis, however, and tilted toward Pakistan to cement its ties to China. Beijing supported Pakistan, whose leader, Ayub Kahn, had helped arrange Kissinger's July trip. The Soviet Union supported India and Bangladesh, and the Bengali rebellion eventually succeeded.

Complaints that the United States had backed the wrong side in the struggle to create Bangladesh were drowned out by spectacular live television coverage of Nixon's five-day visit to China, which began on February 21, 1972. The president's handshake with Zhou Enlai at the Beijing airport erased the ancient snub by Secretary of State John Foster Dulles, who had refused Zhou's hand at the 1954 Geneva conference on Indochina. Nixon and Kissinger received a well-photographed audience with Chairman Mao Zedong. The president toasted the Chinese in the Great Hall of the People in the heart of Beijing's Forbidden City. He and his wife Pat walked along the Great Wall, and she visited the Beijing Zoo to acknowledge the gift to the United States of two cuddly giant pandas.

While television crews produced miles of film that would be used in ads for the fall presidential election campaign, Kissinger worked on the terms of the new relations between the two powers. The final communiqué issued at Shanghai at the end of the trip, announced that each country would open an "interest section"—an embassy, by another name—in the other's capital. The United States relaxed restrictions on trade with and travel to China. The two powers agreed to disagree over Taiwan, with the United States maintaining its formal embassy there. The communiqué observed that both Communist and Nationalist Chinese believed China to be a single country. While warning the Soviet Union that the United States and China mutually opposed "hegemonism" (Soviet domination), the communiqué promised that their new relationship threatened no one. They did not agree to work to end the Vietnam War, and each country expressed support for its own favorite in that war. Nevertheless, by its existence, the Shanghai communiqué demonstrated that the United States had moved beyond a preoccupation with Vietnam. At Shanghai, Nixon, Kissinger, and Zhou Enlai certified that friendship between Washington and Beijing could go forward regardless of what happened in Indochina.

In the wake of the popular response to the breakthrough in China, political opponents could only grumble that Nixon should have done more. Senator George McGovern, seeking the Democratic nomination in the 1972 presidential race, complained that if Nixon could go to China he should be able to end the war in Vietnam. Another Democratic candidate, Hubert Humphrey, charged that the administration had sold out to Beijing: "Concessions were made by the President

President Nixon and his wife Pat visit the Great Wall during their visit to China in February 1972. *UPI/Bettmann Newsphotos.*

and by Dr. Kissinger, but not . . . by the Chinese." Representative John Ashbrook, a conservative Republican from Ohio, ran in the New Hampshire primary on the Taiwan issue, accusing Nixon of abandoning the island. He received only 7 percent of the vote. According to *Time* magazine, which named Nixon and Kissinger Men of the Year for 1972, détente with the Soviets and the opening of relations with China represented "the most profound rearrangement of the earth's political powers since the beginning of the cold war."

The breakthroughs in relations with Beijing and Moscow, combined with the Vietnam peace agreement of January 1973, established Henry Kissinger's reputation as a masterful negotiator and a brilliant innovator in foreign policy. During the summer of 1973, as Senate hearings on the Watergate scandal put Nixon in deep trouble, the president sought to recoup his flagging political standing by calling attention to his foreign affairs successes. Accordingly, in August he nominated Kissinger to replace the ineffectual and self-effacing William Rogers as secretary of state.

As evidence of what critics labeled his hammerlock on foreign policy, Kissinger retained his position as national security adviser. Yet the critics were few. Public and congressional reaction was overwhelmingly positive, and Kissinger sailed through his confirmation hearings. *Newsweek* magazine called him "the White House genius in residence," and *Time* labeled him a "Super Secretary." State Department officials were excited that their department would no longer be bypassed in major foreign policy decisions. As secretary of state, however, Kissinger continued his penchant for acting alone, using professional advice only when it suited his purposes. This characteristic, along with his domineering manner, eventually alienated many of the foreign affairs specialists.

THE UNITED STATES AND CHILE

Vietnam was not the only Third World country to draw significant attention from the Nixon administration. Like earlier postwar presidents, Nixon wanted to hold the line against radical reform movements in Latin America. By 1970 his administration had become deeply involved in an effort to prevent socialists from controlling Chile.

In August of that year it appeared that Salvador Allende Gossens, a socialist, would receive the highest number of votes in the upcoming Chilean presidential election. If no candidate received a majority, Chile's congress would select the winner. Customarily, however, the congress had bestowed the presidency on the candidate with the highest vote total. Allende's prospects alarmed the Nixon administration, which feared that the election of a socialist might prove a model for other Latin American countries that were resentful of the United States but unwilling to install a Castro-like dictatorship. Kissinger told the Forty Committee, an interagency group supervising covert operations, "I don't see why we have to let a country go Marxist just because its people are irresponsible." The Forty Committee tried bribing the Chilean congress into electing a Christian Democrat as president, but the congress chose Allende. The CIA chief in Santiago then helped arrange the assassination of the chief of staff of Chile's armed forces, General Rene Schneider, and tried to pin the blame on Allende and the socialists. The plot backfired. In Chile, Schneider's murder was widely regarded as the work of the CIA, and Allende took office as president.

Over the next few years, the United States tried, in Nixon's words, "to make the Chilean economy scream." Washington immediately stopped foreign aid to Chile and blocked loans from such government-sponsored agencies as the Export-Import Bank and the Inter-American Bank for Reconstruction and Development. It used its influence with international agencies like the International Monetary Fund, the World Bank, and NATO allies to prevent them from helping Allende's government economically. In these respects Kissinger and Nixon acted against the advice of the American ambassador to Chile. Ambassador Edward Korry acknowledged that Allende's efforts to nationalize American-owned copper mines and telephone companies posed a "conscious challenge to the traditions of the United States defense of its business interests in Latin America." Nevertheless, Korry urged that the United States "cultivate pragmatic relationships with Chile and avoid confrontation."

The administration was divided over how far to push Allende. Kissinger could accept a calm approach because he had little interest in Latin America. (He had once scoffed that Chile represented "a dagger pointed at the heart of Antarctica.") Nixon wanted more active intervention. The nationalization of the Chilean telephone company, owned by the American-based multinational corporation International Telephone and Telegraph (ITT), alarmed Nixon. An ITT lobbyist delivered $250,000 to Nixon's re-election campaign, and the company promised to underwrite a major share of the costs for the 1972 Republican national convention. In return, ITT expected the Justice Department to drop an antitrust suit and help in recovering ITT's nationalized property in Chile.

The CIA also wanted to evict Allende. From 1971 to 1973 the CIA supplied over $20 million to opposition newspapers and political parties, particularly to the Christian Democratic party, which it had funded since 1964. It also paid striking truck drivers who refused to transport food from the countryside to the cities. By June 1973, the Chilean middle class had been squeezed into poverty, and no food was reaching Chile's major cities. The military became angry at the loss of American hardware. Commanders feared the wrath of middle- and upper-class Chileans, whose ranks provided the officers. In August, with the encouragement of the CIA, conservative General Augusto Pinochet began plotting a coup.

On September 11, 1973, a right-wing *junta* of army officers led by Pinochet overthrew the government of Allende. The president was murdered or committed suicide during the coup, and in the next two weeks the new government arrested over twenty thousand socialists and their supporters, killed hundreds, and forced thousands more into exile. Pinochet ruled with an iron fist for the next sixteen years, brutally suppressing political parties, political speech, and union activities. Once he established his power, the United States lifted the restrictions on military and economic aid.

American intervention in Chile revived charges throughout Latin America that the United States opposed movements for economic and social justice even when they came to power peacefully through legitimate elections. In 1975 the U.S. Congress revealed the CIA's role in destabilizing Allende's regime. Many Americans expressed shock and shame that their government had so crudely violated the sovereignty of another state in the Western Hemisphere.

WAR AND DIPLOMACY IN THE MIDDLE EAST

Less than a month after the Chilean coup, war broke out in the Middle East when Egypt and Syria attacked Israel on October 6, 1973. A scholar of American Middle East policy believed that the October war, commonly called the Yom Kippur War, "completed the transformation of the Arab-Israeli dispute from a nuisance into a conflict central to American diplomatic and strategic concerns."

Ever since the 1967 Six Day War, little progress had occurred in bringing Israel and its neighbors to the peace table. The United States had become the principal arms supplier to Israel and Jordan, while the Soviet Union replenished the losses incurred by Egypt and Syria in the Six Day War. The Arab states refused to meet Israel face to face, and the Jewish state vowed not to consider relinquishing territories it had taken in that war—East Jerusalem, the West Bank of the Jordan, the Golan Heights and the Sinai Peninsula—unless its neighbors agreed to make peace. Egypt's President Gamal Abdel Nasser then launched a so-called war of attrition against Israel's forces along the Suez Canal and the eastern Sinai in 1969 and 1970. These events formed the background to the Middle East crisis of 1973.

The Nixon Administration and the Arab-Israeli Conflict

Of all the agencies concerned with foreign policy in the Nixon administration, it was the State Department that paid most attention to the Middle East from 1969 to 1972. Nixon and Kissinger concentrated on Vietnam, détente with the Soviet Union, and the opening of relations with China, leaving the daunting task of resolving the Arab-Israeli dispute to Secretary of State Rogers. Pleased to be out from under the thumb of the imperious national security adviser, Rogers floated an ambitious plan to resolve the conflict in a single stroke. He called on Israel to withdraw from most of the territory captured in 1967 in return for full diplomatic relations and a pledge of peace from its neighbors. But Israel balked at Rogers's plan as a threat to its security. Realizing that Rogers carried less weight with Nixon than Kissinger, Israel's diplomats accurately believed they could ignore his unsolicited proposals without offending the United States. In the summer of 1970, however, Rogers was able to arrange a cease-fire in the war of attrition.

Two months later Nasser died suddenly, leaving Egypt's government in the hands of his little-known vice president, Anwar Sadat. Just as Sadat took power, King Hussein of Jordan evicted guerrilla fighters of the Palestine Liberation Organization from his country in a bloody three-day war. Nixon ordered the United States Mediterranean fleet to send planes and equipment to help Jordan. Thereafter the Middle East receded from public view in Europe and the United States as Sadat consolidated power. An uneasy calm persisted along the Suez Canal, and the guerrilla raids from Jordan into Israel stopped.

By 1973 Sadat found the situation of "no war, no peace" intolerable. He resented the presence of the ten thousand Soviet soldiers Nasser had invited to Egypt, and he feared that the radical government of Syria threatened Cairo's preeminence in the Arab world. Despairing that the United States or the United Nations would ever persuade Israel to withdraw from captured territories, he agreed with Syria to coordinate an attack on Israeli positions in the Sinai Peninsula and the Golan Heights. On October 6, Yom Kippur, the holiest day of the Jewish religious calendar, Egyptian and Syrian forces struck. The attackers achieved more in the first three days of the conflict than Arab armies had gained in three previous wars with Israel. Egyptian troops crossed the Suez Canal and captured hundreds of stunned Israelis. In the north, Syria reclaimed a large portion of the Golan Heights and threatened to slice Israel in two. Within a week, Israel's military position appeared desperate, and Prime Minister Golda Meir begged Washington for a resupply of planes, tanks, and ammunition.

Nixon and Kissinger agreed to the largest airlift of equipment and armaments since the Second World War. Assured of new arms, Israel counterattacked, driving the Syrians off the Golan Heights and threatening Syria's capital, Damascus. In the south, Israel's tanks turned back the advancing Egyptians. A worried President Sadat asked Moscow for aid, a move that Kissinger and Nixon considered a threat to détente. Kissinger traveled to Moscow to cool the crisis. While there, he publicly rejected a Soviet call for a joint United States–Soviet military expedition to impose a cease-fire. It was "inconceivable" for the United States and the Soviet Union to introduce enough troops to stop the fighting. He also warned the Soviets not to move their own military forces into the Middle East in any guise. Before leaving Moscow, he arranged joint sponsorship of a United Nations cease-fire resolution.

Now well supplied by the United States, Israel resisted an immediate end to the fighting. Its tanks crossed the Suez Canal and threatened to destroy Egypt's army and enter Cairo. The Soviets issued a warning to Jerusalem, and Nixon and Kissinger responded by ordering a full military alert of American forces in the Mediterranean and Europe. The alert occurred only days after Nixon had provoked national outrage with his abrupt firing of the special prosecutor investigating White House involvement in the Watergate break-in and cover-up. One newspaper editorial speculated that "this White House may well have felt that it was necessary to display toughness on a worldwide scale to show that President Nixon was fully in command of foreign policy and in no way weakened by domestic events."

The alert passed after nine hours, and a cease-fire was finally cemented. Israeli forces occupied the east bank of the canal, Egyptian troops stood on the west bank, and Israel was in control of more Syrian territory than it had held at the beginning of the fighting. In Washington, Nixon's behavior during the war and the alert worried politicians of both parties. Massachusetts Democratic Representative Thomas P. O'Neill, invited to a White House briefing during the height of the crisis, thought the president was unhinged. He recalled that Nixon "kept interrupting Kissinger. 'We had trouble finding Henry,' he said. 'He was in bed with a broad.' Nobody laughed." Peter Lakeland, an aide to New York's Republican Senator Jacob Javits, informed his boss that "if, as now seems inevitable, Nixon will soon go under in what is likely to be a nasty, squalid, destructive spasm of criminal defiance, Kissinger's own . . . capacity to operate [freely in the diplomatic arena] will be called into doubt."

Shuttle Diplomacy and the Oil Embargo

Lakeland's prophecy about Nixon's future proved accurate, but Kissinger's reputation climbed in the aftermath of the Yom Kippur War. In November 1973 he commenced several rounds of negotiations, quickly labeled "shuttle diplomacy," between the capitals of Israel, Egypt, and Syria. Over the next eighteen months he arranged disengagements of the military forces of the three countries in the Sinai and the Golan Heights. Israel's armies withdrew from the banks of the Suez Canal, permitting the reopening of that waterway. Kissinger also redrew the cease-fire line between Israel and Syria, with the former removing its forces from the old Syrian provincial capital while retaining its control over the most strategic parts of the Golan Heights. Yet no permanent borders were drawn on either front.

The laudatory notices Kissinger had received throughout the Nixon years became even more glowing in the wake of his shuttle diplomacy. The Egyptians called him "the American magician." A Japanese paper referred to him as the "Middle East cyclone." *Time* magazine gushed that "as he whirled through the capitals of the Middle East last week, Henry Kissinger more than ever warranted comparison to Metternich, Talleyrand or other great foreign ministers of the past. . . . No other Secretary of State in U.S. history has ever carried so much power, so much responsibility or so heavy a burden."

The hero worship accorded Kissinger was intensified by the public's desire for a savior from the grim news of the winter of 1973 and 1974. Nixon, re-elected by a landslide in November 1972, now faced impeachment for abuse of power and obstruction of justice. An oil embargo of Europe, Japan, and the United States, proclaimed by the oil-producing Arab countries in protest of Western support of Israel during the October war, doubled the price of gasoline. Nixon encouraged Americans to turn off lights and set thermostats at 65 degrees. Dramatizing the need to conserve fuel, he traveled on an ordinary United Airlines flight to Florida during his Christmas holiday. Although America in 1973 produced 75 percent of the oil it needed, its European allies and Japan depended on the Middle East for over 80 percent of their oil requirements. To prevent their economies from falling into the worst depression since the 1930s, Washington agreed to make up most of their petroleum losses. As a result, the United States, as well as Europe and Japan, made do with approximately 80 percent of its average fuel consumption. In the United States unemployment rose by over two percentage points, to 7 percent, in the six months after the embargo; the stock market fell to its lowest level since 1962; and the economy was in the midst of a sharp, eleven-month recession.

Nixon tried to use Kissinger's soaring reputation as a Middle East miracle worker to arrest the slide in his own standing with Congress, where the House Judiciary Committee had scheduled public hearings on impeachment in July 1974. The president traveled to Egypt and Israel in June, apparently to divert attention from troubles at home. Tumultuous crowds of over 1 million people cheered him on a train ride from Cairo to Alexandria. He encountered a more somber reception in Israel, which had not fully recovered from the setbacks of the early days of the Yom Kippur War. Signs reading "Mr. President, You Can Run, But You Can't Hide" provided grim reminders of what awaited him at home.

Even foreign policy successes—along with their most celebrated agent—appeared tarnished in the final weeks of Nixon's term. The House Judiciary Committee reported that Kissinger had encouraged the FBI to tap his subordinates' telephones. During his Senate confirmation hearings following his nomination as secretary of state in September 1973, Kissinger had acknowledged only the most casual participation in the wiretapping. Now, in a maudlin press conference he arranged to denounce the press for printing these reports, Kissinger exploded. "I do not believe it is possible to conduct the foreign policy of the United States when the character and credibility of the Secretary of State is at issue. And if is not cleared up, I will resign."

His outburst frightened off critics. Lawmakers wanted him to remain in charge while Nixon went down, and fifty-one senators cosponsored a resolution expressing their "complete confidence" in Kissinger, whose "integrity and veracity" they considered "above reproach." Even one of the staff members whose phones had been tapped told reporters, "God, I hope this doesn't bring Henry down. He's the only guy keeping us afloat." The Senate Foreign Relations Committee concluded that even with full knowledge of the wiretaps it would have enthusiastically endorsed Kissinger's nomination as secretary of state.

THE WAR POWERS ACT

As public distrust of the Nixon administration mounted during the Watergate scandal, Congress tried to take back from the president some of its traditional powers in foreign affairs. On November 7, 1973, Congress overrode Nixon's veto and passed the War Powers Act. This law capped efforts, begun with the 1970 repeal of the Gulf of Tonkin Resolution, to reassert congressional influence over foreign affairs and war making.

Although no president had asked for a declaration of war since 1941, the United States had often used military force. Presidents from Truman to Nixon had asserted that events moved so quickly in the nuclear age that no time remained to consult with Congress before deploying American forces abroad. But growing public and congressional unhappiness with President Johnson's and Nixon's handling of the war in Vietnam rendered lawmakers less amenable to appeals from the executive branch for complete freedom of action. Earlier versions of the War Powers Act had passed either the House or Senate; now, as the Watergate scandal undercut Nixon's political standing, the two houses agreed on a single version. By this time, many critics of American policy, both inside and outside the government, had concluded that it was vital to restrict the power of the "imperial presidency"—a phrase coined to describe the chief executive's tendency to act without regard for constitutional, legal, or congressional checks and balances.

The law finally adopted was the work of New York Republican Senator Jacob Javits and Wisconsin Democratic Representative Clement Zablocki, chairman of the House Committee on Foreign Affairs. Both lawmakers were willing to grant the president wide latitude in setting foreign policy, but they also wanted Congress to play a clearly defined role. The 1973 act required that the president consult with Congress "when possible" before sending United States troops into combat or into a zone where hostilities were likely. If the president determined he had to act before telling Congress, the act required him to inform lawmakers within forty-eight hours of the dispatch of

United States troops. Such notification triggered a sixty-day clock, during which time Congress had to formally approve the use of troops and state a time limit for their continued use. If Congress failed to authorize the president's action within sixty days, the president had another thirty days in which to withdraw the American forces from the zone of hostilities.

Some critics of the War Powers Act charged that it did not go far enough to restrict presidents from making war without the approval of the people's representatives. One disgruntled legislative aide predicted, "What you'll have now is a Pentagon file full of contingency plans for 90-day wars." Such objections overlooked what Thomas Franck and Edward Wiesband, two experts on Congress's foreign policy role, called the act's "seminal formula for Executive-Congressional codetermination in one key area of foreign policy." Every president since Nixon has considered the act an unwarranted restriction on the executive's foreign policy prerogatives. Despite subsequent complaints from lawmakers who wanted the law strengthened, and from presidents and their cabinet secretaries who wanted it abolished, the War Powers Act has helped set the boundaries of presidential use of force.

CONCLUSION: AN ASSESSMENT OF FOREIGN POLICY IN THE NIXON YEARS

Immediately after Richard Nixon resigned the presidency in disgrace in 1974, analysts looking for something praiseworthy in his record focused on foreign affairs. The *Christian Science Monitor* believed that he had turned away from the sterile categories of the Cold War, in which Americans saw a Soviet plot behind every world problem. The result has been a more flexible and intelligent foreign policy than would have been expected from a visceral anti-Communist like Nixon. The newspaper wrote that he had "risked alienating many of his longtime cold war supporters, by opening America's door to the Communist world." The authors believed his collaboration with Kissinger re-established White House control over the fractured apparatus of foreign policy. Kissinger's travels to China, the Soviet Union, and the Middle East represented a triumph for United States foreign policy, and his shuttle diplomacy among the capitals of the Arab states and Israel appeared to lay "the groundwork for the difficult and continuing negotiations for peace" that loomed ahead in the Middle East. In the years following Nixon's departure, other analysts recapitulated the view that Nixon conducted foreign policy well, whatever his failings in the Watergate scandal.

Nevertheless, Nixon and Kissinger failed in their central goal of reordering American foreign affairs to create what they proclaimed would be "a generation of peace." They concentrated solely on such problems as the Vietnam War and relations with the Soviet Union, China, and the Middle East—all left over from earlier periods. They failed to adjust to dramatic changes in the international economic and political environment, such as the relative decline in the United States position in international trade and the rise of Third World nationalism. For example, Kissinger and Nixon ignored increasing trade frictions with Japan. They tried briefly to address economic tensions with NATO allies in 1973, but then neglected the question as Middle Eastern issues intervened. Economic and commercial issues bored Kissinger. His economic aide joked that "being economic adviser to Henry Kissinger was like being military adviser to the Pope." Nixon and Kissinger also paid little attention to Central America and Africa, where festering problems of poverty and political repression only worsened. The costs of ignoring relations between rich and poor nations and the fate of individuals oppressed by foreign governments would become more apparent later in the 1970s.

Nixon and Kissinger failed even when measured against what they considered their own greatest achievements. In the late 1970s, journalist Tad Szulc interviewed many dissatisfied government officials in the course of compiling material for a book called *The Illusion of Peace* (1979), a scathing indictment of Nixon's foreign policy. As Szulc noted, many of Nixon's and Kissinger's apparent successes had proved transitory, breaking down by the time of the election of 1976. The peace agreement in Indochina—for which more than twenty thousand additional American lives had been sacrificed after Nixon took office—collapsed in 1975. The much-heralded détente with the Soviet Union, already weakened in 1974, did not survive the Ford administration. The opening to China progressed in the late 1970s, but, curiously, the Carter administration, often criticized for not being alert to the nuances of international relations, actually accomplished more by resuming formal diplomatic relations with China. The high hopes for peace in the Middle East had also diminished by 1974. The Carter administration exceeded Kissinger's efforts by brokering a peace treaty between Israel and Egypt in 1978 and 1979.

Nixon's and Kissinger's methods contributed to both the dazzling promise and the disappointing results of their supposedly innovative foreign policy. By concentrating power in their own hands, they could move quickly, with theatrical flair. Yet the exclusion of foreign affairs professionals and the disregard for congressional opinion came back to haunt them when support and follow-through on various initiatives became necessary. Instead of working with the permanent foreign policy bureaucracy or Congress, Kissinger mocked them. Not surprisingly, they came to resent his high-handedness. As progress toward achieving détente with the Soviet Union, normalizing relations with China, and establishing peace in Southeast Asia slowed toward the end of the Nixon years and during the Ford presidency, Kissinger blamed the difficulties on lawmakers, the bureaucracy, the press, an impatient public, the Democrats—virtually anyone who opposed or questioned him.

When public esteem for Kissinger was at its height, in 1973 and 1974, the press likened him to Metternich, Talleyrand, and Bismarck—all conservative figures from the nineteenth century. Seldom did the admirers of the much-heralded new foreign policy recognize the irony in comparing a modern American secretary of state to figures from Europe's past. For all of its drama and excitement, the diplomacy of the Nixon years represented more the end of an era that began in 1945 than a guide for the future of American foreign relations. ■

FURTHER READING

For general accounts of foreign policy in the Nixon administration, see: Raymond L. Garthoff, *Détente and Confrontation: American-Soviet Relations from Nixon to Reagan* (1985); William G. Hyland, *Mortal Rivals: Superpower Relations from Nixon to Reagan* (1987); Richard Nixon, *RN: The Memoirs of Richard Nixon* (1978) and *In the Arena* (1990); Stephen E. Ambrose, *Nixon: The Triumph of a Politician* (1989); Herbert Parmet, *Richard Nixon and His America* (1990); Henry Kissinger, *White House Years* (1979) and *Years of Upheaval* (1982); Seymour Hersh, *The Price of Power: Kissinger in the Nixon White House* (1983); Robert D. Schulzinger, *Henry Kissinger: Doctor of Diplomacy* (1989); Richard C. Thornton, *The Nixon-Kissinger Years* (1989). On the later years of the Vietnam War, see: George C. Herring, *America's Longest War* (1986); Arnold Isaacs, *Without Honor: Defeat in Vietnam and Cambodia* (1983); Melvin Small, *Johnson, Nixon and the Doves* (1988); Nguyen Tien Hung and Jerrold Schechter, *The Palace File* (1986); Marilyn B. Young, *The Vietnam Wars* (1990). On the Middle East, see: Daniel Yergin, *The Prize* (1991); Steven J. Spiegel, *The Other Arab-Israeli Conflict: Making America's Middle East Policy from Truman to Reagan* (1985); William Quandt, *Decade of Decision* (1977); Alan Dowty, *Middle East Crisis* (1984). On the War Powers Act, see Harold Hyman, *Quiet Past and Stormy Present? War Powers in American History* (1986); Thomas Franck and Edward Wiesband, *Foreign Policy by Congress* (1979).

11

The Use and Abuse of Power: Domestic Affairs and the Watergate Scandal, 1969–1974

Soon after Richard Nixon's 1968 campaign manager, John N. Mitchell, became attorney general in 1969, he tried to calm fears that the new administration intended to demolish the Great Society. "Watch what we do, not what we say," he told reporters, implying that the harsh conservative rhetoric voiced by administration officials was misleading. Nixon and his subordinates might stress such favorite conservative issues as halting street crime, cracking down on campus protests, and ending the busing of schoolchildren to achieve racial balance; but in practice, Mitchell seemed to suggest, they would continue an activist government committed to intervening in most areas of American life. On one level Mitchell proved prophetic: the new administration did preserve many of the government programs of the 1960s, though with important modifications.

Yet Mitchell's comment contained more irony than he realized at the time. Behind the scenes, Nixon administration officials abused their powers and threatened the very foundations of democracy. As Nixon and his subordinates expanded the role of the executive branch, they intimidated critics in the press, on college campuses, and in private research organizations. The administration treated opposition politicians, writers, commentators, and even some actors, athletes, and comedians as personal enemies rather than as political opponents. Nixon's obsession with secrecy, contempt for other officeholders, and disregard of civil liberties culminated in many violations of the law. During the episode known as "Watergate," representatives of Nixon's re-election committee used illegal campaign contributions to finance burglaries and wiretaps against the Democrats. The White House then obstructed investigations of these activities, but dogged reporters, congressional committees, independent prosecutors, and federal judges brought the facts to light. Eventually Watergate became the gravest constitutional scandal of the twentieth century, and it resulted in Nixon's resignation from the presidency in August 1974.

CHANGING THE GREAT SOCIETY

Initially the Nixon administration seemed to adopt the Eisenhower strategy of consolidating rather than repealing the reforms of its predecessors. During the election campaign of 1968, Nixon had endorsed the aims of reducing economic inequality, conquering poverty, and ending racial discrimination, but he complained that the Great Society programs of President Johnson had failed to meet these goals. Nixon claimed that the War on Poverty had been lost because of mismanagement by incompetent bureaucrats. He spoke for the principles of better management and of helping the poor and underprivileged help themselves. But in spite of these goals, the overall tendency of the Nixon administration was to de-emphasize social programs and oppose further progress. The primary social initiatives in the Nixon years came from the other branches of the federal government—Congress and the courts.

A New Approach to Domestic Programs

Following the tenets of many conservative thinkers, Nixon wanted to transfer much of the responsibility for social programs from the swollen federal bureaucracy to states and municipalities. The aim was to increase efficiency, make the programs more responsive to local interests, and reduce federal interference. Conservatives also hoped that programs administered at a local level would be given a more conservative slant.

To accomplish the shift of responsibility, Nixon sponsored *revenue sharing*, a system that lasted for ten years. Revenue sharing sliced funds from federally administered programs in order to make "block grants" available to states and municipalities for use in education, urban development, transportation, job training, rural development, and law enforcement. A block grant was a chunk of money with few federal guidelines governing its allocation; the specific spending decisions were to be made at the state and local levels. The program did help states and cities pay for new buildings, parks, police cars, and jails. However, when times were hard and resources scarce, cities used the revenue sharing funds to meet their daily expenses. Rarely did local governments volunteer to use the federal grants directly to aid the poor. To make certain that some funds were applied to job training, Congress in 1973 passed the Comprehensive Employment and Training Act (CETA), designed to educate poor people for jobs. Over the next ten years some 600,000 CETA graduates found work through the training programs.

At the same time that revenue sharing transferred some responsibilities away from the federal government, Nixon created an Urban Affairs Council, to mirror in domestic affairs the functions of the National Security Council in foreign policy. The Urban Affairs Council would create new programs managed directly by the White House, rather than by agencies over which Nixon had less control. To head this new council, Nixon chose Daniel Patrick Moynihan, who was given the task of directing domestic policy and bending the bureaucracy to his will. Like Henry Kissinger, his counterpart at the National Security Council, Moynihan had been on the Harvard faculty, off and on, for nearly twenty years; he had also held several subcabinet positions since the Kennedy administration. Author of the controversial 1965 study *The Negro Family* (see page 271), Moynihan was convinced that a bleak cycle of poverty kept millions of people permanently in economic bondage. He believed that the only chance of improving conditions for the poorest Americans lay in ending their dependence on welfare payments. This view appealed to Nixon, who believed that a plan that trimmed welfare would both reduce poverty and please a middle class increasingly resentful of the poor.

Attempts at Welfare Reform

Reforming the welfare system presented Nixon with an opportunity to surpass the Great Society while pursuing harsh attacks on "welfare cheats," a theme he had sounded during the 1968 presidential campaign. By the end of the Johnson administration many congressional advocates of the Great Society had become increasingly doubtful that the War on Poverty could be won. Senator Edmund Muskie, the Democrats' popular vice-presidential candidate in 1968, confessed that "the blunt truth is that liberals have achieved virtually no fundamental change in our society since the New Deal." In fact, federal programs designed to lift the poor out of poverty had achieved only limited success because they had not been funded at high enough levels. Under the largest welfare program, known as Aid for Families with Dependent Children (AFDC), individual states established the payment amounts. Eighteen of the poorest states offered less than $31 per month per welfare recipient. In all cases, every dollar earned by a working welfare parent was deducted from the welfare check.

In 1969, Moynihan and the Urban Affairs Council proposed scrapping AFDC and replacing it with a Family Assistance Plan (FAP). Through a "negative income tax," a concept suggested at the end of the Johnson administration according to which poor people would *receive* money instead of paying taxes, the plan would end welfare by offering each poor head of household approximately $1,600 per year. The appeal of the FAP lay in its abolition of the army of welfare workers needed to enforce the strict regulations of AFDC. It would also eliminate the gross discrepancies in payments encountered by poor people in different states. What a person received would depend on income, not the stipulations of legislatures, some of which were generous, most of which were stingy.

A crucial requirement of FAP was that aid recipients would have to hold paying jobs. This provision helped to deflect conservative criticism that the Nixon administration had turned into a supporter of lavish government assistance to the poor. Nixon further appealed to conservatives by distinguishing FAP from a system of guaranteed income: instead of undermining the incentive to work, he said, FAP would increase it. Privately Nixon explained to Moynihan, "I don't care a damn about the work requirement. This is the price of getting the $1,600."

But the work requirement helped undo FAP. It made liberals less enthusiastic for the reform, because it forced welfare mothers to choose between two unacceptable options: caring for their children and forgoing welfare benefits; or leaving their children without proper care while they worked at low-paying jobs. Conservatives, for their part, opposed any kind of guaranteed income and formed an unusual alliance with liberals to defeat the proposed reform in 1970.

The issue of revising the welfare system came to life once more in 1972. Liberals tried to raise the grant money offered under FAP to $2,600 for a family of four, with future cost-of-living increases. Nixon, perceiving political advantages in opposing a Democratic initiative, reversed himself, and welfare reform again failed in Congress. Welfare then became a focal issue in the 1972 presidential election campaign. Senator George McGovern, the eventual Democratic nominee, unveiled a plan to offer a $1,000 grant, taxable at the same rate as other income, to every American. Senator Hubert Humphrey, one of McGovern's challengers for the Democratic nomination, came from far behind and nearly won the crucial California primary by mocking the proposal. The Republicans reaped the political dividends of squabbling among the Democrats. According to one of his aides, Nixon now sensed that "attacking McGovern's plan promised more political advantage than securing passage of a more costly version of FAP."

A few weeks before the presidential election, Congress finally passed a new welfare bill, without a provision for a guaranteed income for poor families with children. It did, however, include a new program, Supplemental Security Income, which provided a guaranteed income for the elderly, many of whom were not poor, and for the blind and disabled of all ages. At the same time, Congress authorized automatic cost-of-living increases, tied to the consumer price index, for all Social Security recipients. Such payments went to rich and poor alike. The attempt to find a substantially better system for helping the poor went no further during the Nixon administration.

Protecting Consumers and the Environment

In the early 1970s Washington began to respond to public demands that the government regular businesses whose activities were deemed destructive of the physical environment, harmful to consumers, or dangerous to worker safety. In April 1970 hundreds of thousands of people rallied across the country on the first "Earth Day," showing their support for environmental causes. Soon after,

Congress created the Environmental Protection Agency (EPA), empowered to investigate and curtail practices destructive of the natural environment.

During the 1970s EPA brought hundreds of suits against industrial polluters of water supplies or the nation's air. For new construction involving federal funds, the agency required environmental impact studies that clearly delineated the effects of such projects on traffic congestion, pollution, housing, wildlife, and a host of other concerns. The EPA set fuel efficiency standards for cars and required manufacturers to reduce carbon monoxide emissions from automobile engines. In studies on the effect of electrical power–generating plants on the atmosphere, the EPA determined that the burning of high-sulfur coal had created "acid rain" in the Northeast and neighboring Canada, harming that region's forests and fisheries. Although such reports altered the public to environmental dangers, they also contributed to a growing sense that some problems exceeded the government's capacity to provide solutions.

Although Nixon signed the act creating EPA, he did not have a deep interest in environmental protection. In 1970, to appropriate about $7 billion to clean up the nation's air and water, Congress had to override the president's veto. Nixon then "impounded"—refused to spend—about $1 billion of the money. By 1973, concerned about excessive federal spending, Nixon had impounded about $15 billion, affecting over a hundred government programs for cleaning up the environment.

Even the usually compliant Justice Department thought the president had gone too far. Assistant Attorney General William Rehnquist wrote that there was no constitutional theory justifying "a refusal by the president to comply with a congressional directive to spend." Democratic Senator Sam Ervin of North Carolina, chairman of the Senate Judiciary Committee's Subcommittee on Separation of Powers, held hearings on impoundment in 1971. The venerable lawmaker declared that the president "has no authority under the Constitution to decide which laws will be executed or to what extent they will be enforced." Legal experts agreed, but various White House officials claimed that such congressional interference would prevent the president from doing his job. Caspar Weinberger, deputy director of the Office of Management and Budget, argued that the president had to look beyond particular statutes to see how his actions would affect the entire body of law and the nation as a whole. The White House believed that the bad economic effects of a budget deficit outweighed the benefits of a cleaner environment, and Nixon continued the process of impoundment.

During the Nixon years, Congress also created a Consumer Products Safety Commission (CPSC) and an Occupational Safety and

Health Administration (OSHA). Both agencies were supposed to make daily life safer and healthier. The CPSC investigated the safety of a wide variety of common household items, from television sets to kitchen appliances. It imposed rules for baby products that were highly popular with parents, but industry objected to the added costs of meeting the new standards. At one point the CPSC ruled that children's pajamas treated with Tris, a highly flammable substance, should be removed from the market. Relieved parents applauded the decision, but the manufacturer, stuck with unsalable merchandise worth millions of dollars, complained that unsympathetic Washington bureaucrats had ruined the company's ability to compete. The pajamas were eventually sold in South America.

OSHA required that work sites be safe for employees and that businesses allow unannounced inspections to ensure that safety codes were being met. Unions and most working people believed that OSHA reduced job-related accidents and even saved lives. Businesses, however, found OSHA's inspectors meddlesome, interfering, and imperious. Many economists and conservative commentators shared this view. Advocates of deregulation, who argued that the economy would function better if government regulations were removed, turned some of their strongest scorn on OSHA.

The environmental and consumer protection agencies created in the early 1970s reflected the public concerns of the time. The Nixon administration went along with these laws, although with less enthusiasm than the laws' sponsors in the Democratic-controlled Congress. Overall, the government did more to address environmental and safety concerns in the early 1970s than at any time in the next twenty years. Nevertheless, the reluctant way in which the administration endorsed environmentalism contributed to the growing atmosphere of suspicion in Washington. Already under fire for his prolongation of the Vietnam War, Nixon drew little sympathy from the liberal and moderate Democrats who dominated Congress. The fights between the president and Congress over impoundment heightened the sense on both sides that the other branch of government could not be trusted.

Civil Rights and Busing

Even as the Nixon administration tried half-heartedly to help the poorest Americans, it energetically opposed further progress on civil rights for the country's black citizens. At first, administration officials were divided in their attitude toward civil rights. Some officials favored further advances for African-Americans, but the Justice Department, charged with protection of the rights of minorities under the 1964 Civil Rights Act, tried to limit the effect of that law. For example, Leon Panetta, head of the Office of Civil Rights in the Justice Department, tried to enforce the law, but he was fired. Before he changed parties and won election to Congress as a Democrat, Panetta complained of "a massive retreat on civil rights" by Nixon.

In fact, the Nixon approach to civil rights came to be governed more and more by the so-called southern strategy—the attempt to woo traditionally Democratic white southern voters. The strategy was formulated by Kevin Phillips in *The Emerging Republic Majority* (1969). Phillips observed that the substantial number of people who had voted for George Wallace in the 1968 presidential election were "in motion between a Democratic past and a Republican future." Attorney General John Mitchell, who continued to be one of Nixon's key political advisers, favored the southern strategy. To appeal to southern white voters, the administration would emphasize such conservative themes as law and order, and it would resist further advances in civil rights.

Already, during the 1968 campaign, Nixon had taken a stand against the busing of schoolchildren to achieve racial integration. In many areas in the northern states, the public schools reflected a *de facto* form of segregation—that is, segregation that resulted not from law, but from the fact that whites and blacks lived in different neighborhoods. As early as 1961, a New York federal district court had ruled that busing of children from one school to another was an appropriate means of achieving racial balance. By the time of Nixon's presidency, federal courts increasingly ordered the use of busing to end *de facto* segregation in northern as well as southern school districts. This led to considerable white protest (see page 409). After contributing to the public outcry against busing, the Nixon administration sponsored a 1974 law demanding that federal courts and government agencies use busing only as a last resort.

The administration also appealed to white conservatives by denouncing the 1968 Supreme Court decision in *Green* v. *Board of Education*. In this case, the Court ruled that the southern use of "freedom of choice" plans—arrangements that allowed parents to select any public school in a district for their children—failed to guarantee racial balance and therefore violated the Court's earlier prohibition of segregated schools in *Brown* v. *Board of Education* (1954). Nixon declared that "the Court was right on *Brown* and wrong on *Green*," and administration officials tried to block implementation of the *Green* decision.

In August 1969, under heavy pressure from the White House, the Department of Health, Education and Welfare (HEW) petitioned the Fifth District Court for a three-month delay in the desegregation of twenty-three Mississippi school districts. This was the first time since 1954 that the federal government had intervened to *slow* the pace of desegregation. HEW's action shocked lawyers in Panetta's Office of

Civil Rights. They refused to defend the administration's position and secretly supplied information to the NAACP's Legal Defense Fund.

The fund appealed to the Supreme Court to reverse the delay, which it did, unanimously, in *Alexander* v. *Holmes County Board of Education* (1969). "The obligation of every school district is to terminate the dual school systems at once," the Supreme Court ordered. The Fifth District Court responded with 166 desegregation orders over the next ten months. Legally mandated segregation ended in the South in the subsequent two years. By 1971, 44 percent of black children in South attended schools where white students constituted a majority. In the North and West, by comparison, only 28 percent of the black school children studied in schools with a majority of white students.

THE BURGER COURT

A major element in Nixon's appeal to southerners, whites, and conservatives during the 1968 campaign lay in his promise to reverse the direction taken by the Supreme Court under Chief Justice Earl Warren by appointing conservative justices to the highest bench. He expected them to revise the Warren Court's decisions expanding civil rights for racial minorities, civil liberties for individuals, and recognition of the rights of criminal defendants. Nixon appointed a new chief justice, Warren Burger, and three new associate justices, Harry Blackmun, Lewis Powell, and William Rehnquist. But together with the holdovers from the Warren era, the new members surprised both supporters and detractors by their rulings. Instead of reversing the Warren Court's emphasis on enlarging the rights of individuals and curtailing the powers of government officials, the Court in the early seventies consolidated the earlier decisions.

Nixon's Appointments to the Court

The expectation that Nixon's victory would allow a Republican president to appoint a new chief justice had motivated Republican senators to block the confirmation of Abe Fortas to that position in the fall of 1968. Shortly after taking office, Nixon nominated Warren Burger of the Court of Appeals for the District of Columbia to serve as chief justice. Burger seemed ordered from a Hollywood casting agency to fill the role. Tall, white-haired, with an imposing deep voice, he was described by the *New York Times*'s James Reston as "experienced, industrious, middle-class, middle-aged, middle-of-the-road, Middle Western, Presbyterian, orderly and handsome." The Senate quickly confirmed him by a vote of 74 to 3.

But controversy engulfed Nixon's next nominees. When Fortas resigned after revelations of financial misconduct, the president tried to implement his southern strategy by selecting southern judges. The nomination of Clement Haynsworth, a South Carolina federal judge, quickly ran into trouble: labor and civil rights groups were angered by a series of decisions he had made as a federal judge that were considered unfavorable to unions and minorities, and moderate Republicans withdrew their initial support of Haynsworth after hearing of his involvement in shady business deals. Despite assertions by liberal justices Brennan and Black that Haynsworth would made a fine justice, the Senate rejected his nomination by 55 to 45 in November 1969.

Angry with the Senate's rejection, and committed to naming a southerner, Nixon in April 1970 submitted the name of a Georgia judge, G. Harrold Carswell of the Fifth Circuit Court. Unlike Haynsworth, Carswell had a poor reputation among judicial scholars. The dean of the Yale Law School told the Senate Judiciary Committee that Carswell had "the most slender credentials" of any twentieth-century nominee. Half the judges on his circuit bench refused to sign a letter endorsing his elevation to the high court. Carswell's fifteen-year-old assertion that "segregation of the races is proper and the only practical and correct way of life in our states" hurt his prospects. He apologized for this remark, but investigators learned that he had recently sought to turn a public golf course into a private, segregated club. Carswell's Senate supporters did him more harm than good by the excuses they offered on his behalf. One remark by a Carswell defender, Republican Senator Roman Hruska of Nebraska, proved especially memorable: "There are a lot of mediocre judges and lawyers, and they are entitled to a little representation, aren't they?" Unmoved by such testimonials, the Senate rejected Carswell 51 to 45.

Nixon sought to turn the twin defeats to his advantage with southerners, complaining that prejudice against southern whites had led to the rejection of qualified nominees. He said he would not appoint another southerner and "let him be subjected to this kind of malicious character assassination." His next nominee for the Fortas seat, therefore, came from the Midwest. Harry Blackmun, an old Minnesota friend of Warren Burger and a sixteen-year veteran of the Eighth Circuit Court, easily won confirmation in 1970. Their long friendship notwithstanding, Blackmun and Chief Justice Burger soon diverged in their opinions, with Blackmun taking the more liberal positions.

Nixon finally appointed a southerner when Hugo Black retired in 1972. He selected Lewis Powell, Jr., of Virginia, former president of the American Bar Association. As chairman of the Richmond School Board and the Virginia State Board of Education, Powell had opposed the popular policy of resistance to school integration. Powell refused to characterize his judicial philosophy as either liberal or conservative, but he did say that as a student at Harvard Law School he had absorbed Felix Frankfurter's views on "judicial restraint."

Nixon chose an outspoken conservative, forty-seven-year-old William Rehnquist, for his next appointment, also in 1972, to replace the retiring John Marshall Harlan. An Arizona attorney, Rehnquist had been an active supporter of Barry Goldwater in 1964. Named an assistant attorney general by John Mitchell, Rehnquist had urged the Justice Department to challenge the Supreme Court's decisions in *Miranda* v. *Arizona* (1966) and *Mapp* v. *Ohio* (1961) that afforded criminal defendants greater protection against arbitrary questioning and searches by police. Despite concerns expressed by civil libertarians, most senators considered Rehnquist highly qualified, and they confirmed him a few days after Powell.

Three of the four justices nominated by Nixon who won confirmation—Burger, Blackmun, and Powell—proved able, moderate-to-conservative figures who retained the thrust of the decisions advanced by the Warren Court. The fourth, Rehnquist, also intelligent and knowledgeable, did want to overrule many of the Warren decisions, but he found himself in the minority for the next decade.

Court Decisions on Civil Rights

The Burger Court's decisions usually consolidated and sometimes expanded the civil rights gains of the Warren years. For example, the Court concluded that discriminatory effects as well as intentions had been outlawed by the Civil Rights Act of 1964. In *Griggs* v. *Duke Power and Light Co.* (1971), Burger spoke for a unanimous court in ruling that the 1964 Civil Rights Act prohibited an employer from requiring high school diplomas or intelligence tests for job applicants if the results would be racially discriminatory. The Court reasoned that the tests and the diploma requirements had no bearing on the job to be performed. Later, in *Washington* v. *Davis* (1976), the Court upheld the legality of a verbal test given to applicants to the District of Columbia's police force because the questions did relate directly to the work performed. A relevant test was permissible, even if it kept most black applicants off the capital's police force.

By far the most controversial civil rights issue to reach the Court during the Nixon years was the use of school busing to achieve racial desegregation. In two important cases, *Swann* v. *Charlotte-Mecklenburg Board of Education* (1971) and *Keyes* v. *Denver School District No. 1* (1973), the Supreme Court elaborated on lower courts' requirements for busing. In the former case, the Court turned its attention from rural southern school districts, in which students of both races lived close to one another, to urban schools, where only busing could achieve integration. In this instance, the Court upheld a desegregation plan that mandated substantial crosstown busing in a southern city. In the *Keyes* case, the justices extended busing to a northern district where legal segregation had never existed but where the board of education had used race as one criterion in drawing school boundaries.

Both the Court and the local officials who implemented busing plans came under heavy abuse from white parents, and in many locations the protest turned violent. In Lamar, South Carolina, an angry white mob attacked school buses carrying black students. Other mobs fire-bombed buses in Denver, Colorado, and Pontiac, Michigan. Irate whites in South Boston cursed and beat blacks who attended classes with whites under court order. Congress responded to the public anger with legislation proclaiming a moratorium on court orders that attempted to achieve "a balance among students with respect to race, sex, religion, or socioeconomic status."

The Supreme Court, however, thought that Congress was playing with words. If Congress had intended to end busing, Justice Lewis Powell ruled in *Drummond* v. *Acree* (1972), "it could have used clear and explicit language appropriate to that end." Generally Congress preferred to straddle the issue rather than confront it directly. Although Congress passed the Nixon administration's 1974 legislation demanding that busing be the last option in desegregating schools, the law acknowledged the courts' authority to enforce the constitutional amendments guaranteeing equal protection to all citizens. In the late 1970s, Congress took a further half-step by forbidding the use of federal funds to buy or maintain buses used for school desegregation.

Overall, the Supreme Court's support for busing helped the cause of school desegregation, but it also contributed to a decline in white middle-class trust in public schools. In urban districts that faced desegregation orders, many parents removed their children from the public school system, either by enrolling them in private or religious schools or by moving to the suburbs. Over the next decade, as this so-called white flight undermined support for public education, most school bond issues brought before voters were defeated. By stimulating white exodus, the busing conflict also hastened the transformation of northern and midwestern urban centers into predominantly poor, black, and Hispanic areas. The less stake the white middle class had in the fate of the cities, the less support it gave to government programs to revitalize urban life. By reinforcing this trend with its decisions on busing, the Supreme Court unintentionally spurred the ongoing crisis in the nation's cities.

Court Decisions on Women's Issues

The most unexpected decisions from the Burger Court prohibited discrimination on the basis of sex, an issue mostly neglected by the generally more liberal Warren Court. A revitalized women's movement (see pages 355–358) had brought women's issues to national prominence. In response, Congress passed the Equal Rights Amendment (ERA) to the Constitution and submitted it to the states in early 1972. The ERA was soon ratified by thirty-five of the thirty-eight states necessary for it to take effect. Though the ERA eventually fell short of adoption, the widespread activism of its supporters helped to focus attention on women's issues.

In this atmosphere of increasing awareness of discrimination against women, the Court invalidated many old laws subordinating women to men. The results pleased advocates of women's rights, but they worried nevertheless about the Court's reasoning. Instead of finding a constitutional right to gender equality, the justices relied on portions of the 1964 Civil Rights Act and the 1973 Equal Pay Act to whittle away at sex-based discrimination. In *Reed* v. *Reed* (1971), for example, the Court invalidated the Idaho practice of giving preference to men over similarly situated women as administrators of estates. The Court held that legislation differentiating between the sexes "must be reasonable, not arbitrary." The same year the Court ruled in *Phillips* v. *Martin Marietta* that Title VII of the Civil Rights Act forbade corporate hiring practices that discriminated against mothers with small children. In *Frontiero* v. *Richardson* (1973) the Court applied Title VII to the military by requiring the armed services to provide the same fringe benefits and pensions to both men and women.

The Court went beyond issues of pay equity and job rights when it overturned all state laws restricting abortions in *Roe* v. *Wade* (1973). Feminists and civil liberties lawyers had challenged a Texas law that made any abortion a felony, with the test case involving a poor, single woman who believed she could not afford to raise a child. Justice Harry Blackmun, writing for a seven-member majority, opened a new era in reproductive law by ruling that the right of privacy established by *Griswold* v. *Connecticut* (1965) was "broad enough to encompass a woman's decision whether or not to terminate her pregnancy." Blackmun sought to balance the state's interest in the fetus's existence with the mother's right to privacy. Therefore the decision provided an absolute right to abortion during the first trimester of a pregnancy, when experts agreed that the fetus was not "viable"—that is, could not live outside the mother's body. During the second trimester, when the viability of the fetus became more of a possibility, states could regulate, but not outlaw, abortions. Only for the last thirteen weeks of pregnancy, according to the *Roe* decision, could state laws prohibit abortion.

Along with the earlier *Griswold* decision, *Roe* reversed a century of government opposition to contraception. The *Roe* decision responded to a widespread public desire to make safe abortions available. Until then, many pregnant women had relied on unsafe "back alley" abortions; others had turned to the so-called abortion undergrounds in most cities and on many college campuses, where women could receive information about abortion and access to safe practitioners. *Roe* changed all this by making abortion readily available, and many women soon took for granted their right to a safe, legal abortion.

However, the *Roe* decision produced more public dissent than any other Court ruling since *Brown* v. *Board of Education* had struck down school segregation in 1954. The justices who wrote the *Roe* opinion and the advocates of women's rights who supported it probably underestimated the anger it would cause. Since 1869 Catholic doctrine had held that life began at the moment of conception, and many Catholics and other traditionalists assailed *Roe* as a judicial sanction for murder. Over the next decade, opposition to *Roe* became even more of a rallying point for conservatives than did the Warren Court's protection of the rights of criminal suspects.

CRIME AND DRUGS

Along with abortion and school busing, crime and drug use became major issues in the Nixon years. The Nixon administration inflamed public fears that the widespread use of drugs, especially heroin, had created a major crime wave. But the administration had no solutions to match its rhetoric.

During the 1968 election, Nixon had blamed the "permissiveness" of Johnson's attorney general, Ramsey Clark, for the rise in street crime. According to one Justice Department official, however, Nixon soon realized that the federal government had few direct law enforcement powers to combat crime in the streets. Faced with a local problem about which the federal government could do little, the Nixon administration tried several principal tactics: it tried to shift the blame for drugs and crime to its opponents; it manipulated statistics to magnify both the original problem and the effect of its own remedies; and, finally, it engaged in drug raids that disregarded the civil liberties of the accused and possibly violated the Constitution as well.

In 1969 and 1970 the administration proposed several highly repressive anticrime statutes that it expected to fail in Congress. "The administration's position in the crime field depends on our ability to shift blame for crime bill inaction to Congress," read one White House political memorandum. Much to the administration's surprise, the Democratic congressional majority, not wishing to appear "soft" on crime, passed anticrime laws in 1970 that increased the sentences for federal crimes, allowed federal marshals to hold suspects longer without bond or charges, and enhanced federal officers' ability to tap telephones.

Although the federal government did not have responsibility for ordinary street crimes, it did have jurisdiction over the illegal sale of narcotics, and the administration played with numbers to make it appear that drug use and crime had recently grown tenfold. In 1971 Nixon announced that the number of heroin addicts in the United States had soared from 69,000 in 1969 to 315,000 in 1970 to 559,000 in 1971. In fact, the number of addicts had not changed particularly in those years; the Bureau of Narcotics and Dangerous Drugs had simply reworked old statistics. The administration also inflated by about twenty-five times the value of property stolen by heroin addicts.

Armed with these inflated statistics about a heroin-induced crime wave, the Nixon administration declared a war on drugs. In early 1972 Nixon created the Office for Drug Abuse and Law Enforcement (ODALE), a secret police force outside the control of the FBI or CIA, ODALE recruited G. Gordon Liddy, a former CIA operative and planner of the break-in at Daniel Ellsberg's psychiatrist's office, to organize raids on suspected drug dealers. Over the next year ODALE agents conducted midnight raids without search warrants. They kicked in doors, grabbed people from their beds, pointed guns at their heads, and threatened death unless people revealed the whereabouts of drugs. When they sometimes determined they had gone to the wrong address, the agents simply said they had made a mistake and left.

Although the drug war undermined civil liberties, it improved Nixon's public image. Several celebrities joined the antidrug effort. Singer Sammy Davis, Jr., who later admitted to his own alcohol and drug abuse, and TV personality Art Linkletter, whose daughter had died while under the influence of LSD, lectured against the danger of heroin. Elvis Presley came to the White House to tell Nixon, "I really believe in what you're doing." The president gave Presley a federal badge for his collection of law enforcement paraphernalia, but because the singer was obviously under the influence of alcohol or narcotics during the visit, Nixon decided to keep the meeting secret.

Although the administration produced additional misleading statistics to indicate that progress had been made, the war on crime and drugs actually had negligible impact on either the use of heroin or the spread of crime. Politically, the crusade enhanced Nixon's position among middle-class Americans most concerned about crime, and it put his Democratic opponents on the defensive. Most significantly, the actions by Liddy and ODALE set the stage for the Watergate scandal by establishing the extent to which the administration would bend or break the law to serve its own purposes.

MANAGING THE ECONOMY

"You can't explain economics to the American people," Richard Nixon once told Undersecretary of the Treasury Paul Volcker. Efforts by his officials to do so seemed to prove the point. Customarily prices remained steady or fell in slow times and rose only in boom periods. But in the Nixon years, in contrast to the expectations of nearly all conventional economists, the United States experienced *both* inflation and slow or nonexistent growth. Nixon confronted this so-called *stagflation* by abandoning his long-held economic positions; in fact, he adopted some policies of political rivals that he had once derided. His change on economic policy was nearly as dramatic as the new foreign policy he crafted with Henry Kissinger. The sudden shifts dismayed supporters who took Nixon for a conventional economic conservative, but they paid political dividends.

During the 1968 campaign Nixon had berated the Johnson administration's efforts to create "guideposts" for businesses to follow in setting prices. These standards were supposed to keep price increases in line with gains in worker productivity, thereby holding inflation down, but they had not worked. Citing his own experience with the Office of Price Administration during the Second World War, Nixon said that governmental price controls "can never be administered equitably and are not compatible with a free economy."

Yet the economy did not behave the way the rules predicted. Inflation, the scourge of the Great Society, stubbornly hovered at around 6 percent. Still worse, unemployment rose steadily from 3.8 percent in 1968 to surpass 6 percent in 1971. Under orthodox economic assumptions, prices should *decline,* or at least not rise, when workers lost their jobs. The Council of Economic Advisers confessed that its most sophisticated analysis "did not generally predict the rate of inflation experienced in 1970." At the time, although experts could describe stagflation, they could not explain it. In later years, economists identified some of the reasons for it: the population bulge of baby-boomers who had reached maturity and begun to spend money on consumer goods; the competition posed by the revived economies of Japan and Germany; and the inflationary effects of the Vietnam War. Even if economists and government officials had seen these problems clearly, they could have done little about them. The causes of stagflation ran so deep, both inside and outside the United States, that government officials were limited in their ability to fine-tune the economy.

Because the experts could not explain why the economy had not followed the conventional prescriptions, the president decided it was time to pay less attention to experts. In December 1970, Nixon shook up the management of economic policy by appointing John Connally, former governor of Texas, as secretary of the treasury. Connally had valuable political connections among conservative Democrats, southerners, and southwesterners, and no background in economic theory. An aide in the Treasury Department charitably observed that Connally "was not the most conceptual person in the world." The new treasury secretary spent the first six months in office avoiding deep analysis of the cure for stagflation and appealing for a partnership between government, big business, and organized labor.

While Connally spoke in generalities, Nixon looked for ways out of the doldrums of stagflation. He acknowledged that government wage and price controls might be necessary. Early in 1971 he told an interviewer, "I am now a Keynesian in economics." Because Keynesianism had been a dirty word during the 1968 presidential election, this was a remarkable turnaround. One reporter likened it to "a Christian crusader saying 'All things considered, I think Mohammed was right.'"

Having acknowledged that it was appropriate to impose wage and price controls, Nixon had to decide when to act. Economic news worsened throughout 1971. Although the United States continued to export more than it imported, foreign expenditures by the government (mostly for the maintenance of hundreds of overseas military bases) and those of private citizens meant that the number of dollars going overseas exceeded the value of foreign currency coming into the United States. Such an economic situation is known as a balance of payments deficit. The problem had worsened during the Vietnam War years, as the central banks of France and West Germany began converting some of their dollars to gold. Experts had been warning since the Kennedy administration that the United States could not forever afford to keep its promise to redeem its currency in gold, and a sudden rejection of dollars by overseas holders could upset the world's trading system. After a further slide in United States exports in mid-1971, international investors began worrying about the dollar's strength, and many bought West German marks instead. In August the Bank of England, previously supportive of United States economic policy, demanded that its holdings in American dollars be redeemed in gold.

Undersecretary of the Treasury Volcker decided that "the jig was definitely up" when he heard the news from London. He telephoned Connally on Friday afternoon, August 13, with the grim warning that "a major crisis [was] developing in the world's monetary exchange system." Over the weekend, economic advisers huddled with the president at Camp David to devise a series of steps to save the dollar and halt inflation. Nixon, the recently converted Keynesian, was also a lifelong political animal: he believed that wage and price controls would stop inflation before the 1972 election. His advisers agreed that wage and price controls, in conjunction with a plan to stop the international flight from the dollar, could work.

On Sunday evening, August 15, 1971, exactly one month after Nixon's startling announcement that Henry Kissinger had just returned from China, the president presented a program called the New Economic Policy. He proclaimed a ninety-day freeze on wages and prices. Thereafter a government wage and price commission would monitor price increases and employee contracts, rescinding excessive increases. This was precisely the Johnson policy Nixon had derided in 1968. Nixon also announced that the United States would no longer convert its currency into gold. On the other hand, American citizens, who had not been able to own the yellow metal since an earlier currency reform during the New Deal, were now free to buy and sell it at the market price. Over the next year the United States and the major trading nations ended the system, created in 1944, of fixed exchange rates among the world's currencies. By 1972 the value of currencies "floated," determined daily in currency exchange markets around the world.

The New Economic Policy tried to slow the escalating trade deficit with a temporary 10 percent surtax on imports. Nixon also cut government social spending by $4.7 billion and reduced business taxes. Coming on the heels of Kissinger's trip to China, the New Economic Policy seemed another example of pragmatic action by an administration willing to break with old orthodoxy. In a Gallup poll taken a week after the speech, 73 percent of respondents approved the new policy.

Although Nixon's policy resulted in some limited economic improvements, nothing could halt inflation after the 1973 Arab-Israeli war and the subsequent oil embargo by Arab oil producers. The price of oil rose 400 percent, and the effects of that increase caused other costs to shoot up throughout the economies of the industrial world. American prices rose by more than 7 percent in 1974 and 1975.

The most far-reaching consequence of the decisions taken in August 1971 involved the disruption of the link between United States currency and gold. The United States gained in the short term, as overseas banks and businesses used their unbacked dollars to invest in U.S. government securities. One expert at the Chase Manhattan Bank later characterized the move as "a well-conceived plan to force foreigners to loan dollars back to the U.S. Treasury to cover our years of deficit spending. In effect these foreign dollar holders had no choice but to loan their money back to us or see the value of their holdings wiped out."

Over the long term, however, the decision to allow the price of currencies to float hastened a serious decline in American industry. Investment in new plants and research in new products slowed in the 1970s and 1980s, because such investments do not pay dividends quickly. Flexible exchange rates made it more difficult for businesses to predict the return on merchandise to be sold overseas in the future; hence investors increasingly shifted their funds to tangible, often nonproductive assets whose value could be realized quickly. By the end of the decade the prices of nonproductive assets like land, commodities, gold, silver, jewels, and art soared. A one-carat investment-grade diamond that cost $1,000 in 1967 shot up to a price of $10,000 in 1973, and by 1979 it was valued at $50,000. The value of some farmland in the United States also increased 500 percent, without a similar change in the value of crops. Banks preferred to lend money for the purchase of tangibles and land rather than invest in the rebuilding of factories or research on new products. Investors shied away from the stock market in the late 1970s, fearing it would not offer profitable returns in the future. This sapped efforts to raise the capital necessary to modernize American manufacturing in the late 1970s. Managers of American manufacturing corporations contributed further to the decline of the country's industrial strength by concentrating on maximizing quarterly profits rather than considering longer-term economic prospects.

The New Economic Policy demonstrated the limits of Nixon's non-ideological, flexible approach to economic management at a time of rapid change. By endorsing Keynesian techniques to reduce inflation and foster growth, Nixon followed the practices of predecessors since the Second World War. Yet fine-tuning the economy proved far more difficult than sponsors hoped. The long-term ineffectiveness of wage and price controls contributed to a growing sense that public institutions could not work.

THE ELECTION OF 1972

With the American economy in some disarray, Democrats originally had high hopes for the 1972 election. Nixon's southern strategy had failed during the 1970 congressional election, with only one southern seat held by a Democrat falling to a Republican candidate. On the eve of election day Edmund Muskie, the vice-presidential candidate in 1968, had persuasively derided Nixon's "politics of fear" in a televised address. In 1971 Muskie had emerged as the favorite for the Democratic presidential nomination. With his rugged good looks and moderate views, Muskie appeared able to unite Democrats, and early 1972 opinion polls showed him tied with Nixon at 42 percent.

Alarmed by Muskie's popularity rating, functionaries of Nixon's Committee to Re-elect the President (CREEP) made plans to discredit him, hoping to arrange the nomination of the *weakest* possible Democratic candidate. During the crucial New Hampshire primary campaign in early 1972, Donald Segretti, a specialist for CREEP, forged a letter that was sent to William Loeb, the vitriolic editor of the *Manchester* (New Hampshire) *Union-Leader*. The letter accused Muskie of laughing at an ethnic slur against French Canadians, a major voting bloc of New Hampshire Democrats. Loeb printed the letter and also blasted Muskie and his wife on the front page. Outraged, the senator stood on a truck in front of the newspaper office and assailed Loeb as a "gutless coward." Muskie appeared to choke back tears as he defended his wife, and immediately the contrast between him, tearful and wounded, and Nixon, the strong world leader, shown on TV that very week at the Great Wall of China, diminished his appeal. Muskie won the primary, but his margin over the runner-up, Senator George McGovern of South Dakota, was smaller than expected. Muskie's moderate, centrist opinions, perfect for the wide appeal of the general election, did not excite primary voters, and he dropped out of the race within weeks.

The McGovern campaign now took off. Unlike Muskie, McGovern had clearly articulated, liberal views. Opposition to the war in Vietnam united an army of fervent volunteers. Activists supporting McGovern opposed the Nixon administration's hostility to civil rights and resistance toward expanding the domestic welfare legislation of the Great Society. Over the next four months McGovern won close to a majority of delegate votes through his primary victories over a crowded field of Democratic opponents.

McGovern's most prominent rivals during this time were George Wallace and Hubert Humphrey. Wallace, in fact, won the Florida primary with white-hot rhetoric. He attacked Nixon as "a double-dealer, a two-timer, and a man who tells folks one thing and does another." Crowds roared when he complained about busing imposed by "anthropologists, zoologists, and sociologists." He did not know which was worst: the "judges who had just about ruined this country"; hypocritical politicians who sent their children to private schools; or the "briefcase-totin' bureaucrats. . . . Yale Ph.D.s who can't tie their shoelaces. . . . Hypocrites [who] if you opened all their briefcases, you'll find nothing in them but a peanut butter sandwich." But Wallace's political momentum ended abruptly in May when a gunman's bullet wounded him, leaving him paralyzed from the waist down.

By June Hubert Humphrey was the sole champion of the "Anybody But McGovern" coalition, an alignment of old-style Democratic officeholders and labor union officials who feared that the South Dakota senator was too liberal, too much the representative of outsiders, to win the general election. Assailing McGovern's liberal positions, Humphrey closed a wide gap to trail by only five percentage points in the June California primary.

By July, when Democrats assembled in Miami for their national convention, McGovern's nomination depended on the interpretation of rules drafted in the aftermath of the chaotic 1968 convention. The new rules had resulted from complaints that Humphrey won the 1968 nomination because political bosses controlled delegate selection in nonprimary states. Reformers wanted various minority groups—students, young antiwar activists, feminists, African-Americans, Hispanics, Native Americans, Asians, and other non-European ethnics—to participate as delegates. McGovern had chaired a commission that urged, but did not require, state delegations to include women, young people, and members of ethnic minorities roughly in proportion to their percentages in each district's population. The rules did require that states selecting their delegations by means other than primaries—through precinct caucuses or conventions, for example—award delegates proportionately on the basis of the candidates' support among participants. States holding primaries could either adopt similar proportional-representation schemes or continue to use a winner-take-all formula.

At the 1972 convention, Democrats decided on a strict interpretation of the new rules. On the first night of the convention, Chicago Mayor Richard J. Daley and fifty-eight of his hand-picked delegates from Cook County were booted off the convention floor for violating the guideline to choose representatives in proportion to the racial, sexual, and ethnic make-up of a district. A reform slate of delegates, which included more women and blacks but fewer old-time politicians, took the Daley delegation's place. On the convention's second night, a majority of delegates guaranteed McGovern's victory by endorsing the winner-take-all formula for California, giving him all of that state's representatives.

The Democrats' endorsement of pluralism brought thousands of representatives of previously excluded groups into the party's decision-making process. The delegates at the 1972 convention were 38 percent female (in comparison to 13 percent in 1968), 23 percent under thirty (2.3 percent in 1968), and 15 percent black (5.5 percent in 1968). If the groups they represented voted in November, McGovern could win through the strength of an electorate that was younger, poorer, and more racially diverse than usual. But if traditionally excluded groups stayed away from the polls, as they had in 1968, he would lose because he had alienated the old base of the Democratic party—the South, labor, Catholics, the white working class, and white ethnics.

McGovern's delegate reforms hurt the men who had run the Democratic party for decades. For instance, only eighteen of the 255 Democratic members of the House of Representatives came to Miami as delegates, whereas customarily more than half attended the convention. Those who were excluded grumbled and threatened. Wayne Hays of Ohio complained that commissions were "trying to reform us [elected officials] out of the party." A Pennsylvania member objected that "you've got quotas for everything—blacks, Chicanos, eighteen years olds. Pretty soon they'll want quotas for draft dodgers." No group seemed more old-fashioned and out of place than leaders of organized labor. AFL-CIO President George Meany had led the Anybody But McGovern campaign to find an alternative to the South Dakota senator. An old cold warrior, Meany found McGovern's opposition to the war in Vietnam absurd. Like most of the working class of his generation, Meany also decried the lifestyles of McGovern's supporters; he blamed the senator for seeming to tolerate the open sexuality and drug experimentation of the young. Meany denied McGovern the endorsement of the AFL-CIO, the first time organized labor had not supported the Democratic presidential nominee.

McGovern's chances declined further when he chose his vice-presidential running mate. Having given little thought to the vice presidency before the convention, McGovern selected Missouri Senator Thomas Eagleton, whose Catholicism and moderate views the candidate hoped would appeal to the traditional Democrats uncomfortable with the antiwar youth backing McGovern. The day after the nomination, news surfaced that Eagleton had been hospitalized three times in the 1960s for depression and exhaustion. Although 10 to 25 percent of all Americans suffer some form of depression in their lives, mental or nervous disorders carried a very serious stigma, especially among older Americans. McGovern decided not to cater to what he considered prejudiced views. He said he was "1,000 percent for Tom Eagleton" and that he did not intend to drop him from the ticket. But Eagleton then admitted he had received electroshock treatment while hospitalized, and that he still took tranquilizers. Pressure from editorialists and his campaign staff convinced McGovern to drop Eagleton. Coming so soon after his 1,000 percent endorsement of Eagleton, McGovern's abrupt reversal made him look unpredictable, weak, and possibly foolish. The process of finding a replacement became a fiasco. After seven prominent Democratic politicians refused to run, McGovern finally selected Sargent Shriver, the Kennedy relative who had formerly directed the Peace Corps and the Office of Economic Opportunity.

In November, Nixon won a massive landslide in which he gained 61 percent of the popular vote and carried 49 states (see map, page 420). Only Massachusetts and the District of Columbia went for McGovern. A number of social and political issues contributed to the size of Nixon's victory. McGovern's support from antiwar activists and political newcomers had alarmed traditional voters. Voter turn-

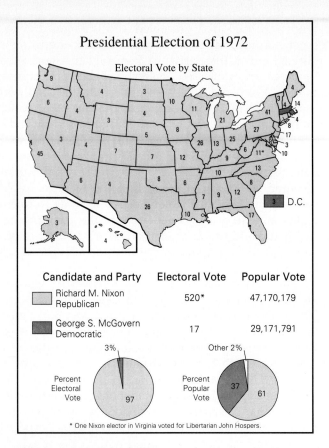

Presidential Election of 1972

Presidential Election of 1972

out declined in 1972, and the election was decided by the same segments of the electorate that typically went to the polls. Eighteen- to twenty-year-olds, allowed to vote for the first time under the terms of the Twenty-sixth Amendment (adopted in 1971), turned out in fewer numbers than any other group, and half of them voted for Nixon after he promised to end the draft in 1973. White working-class Democrats deserted McGovern in droves; 55 percent of blue-collar voters went for Nixon, as opposed to 34 percent in 1968. Fifty-three percent of Catholics voted for Nixon in 1972; 34 percent had voted for him in 1968. The southern strategy finally worked: three-quarters of those who voted for Wallace in 1968 supported Nixon in 1972.

Meanwhile, the New Economic Policy had for the moment tamed inflation, and unemployment had leveled off. Nixon's celebrated visits to Beijing and Moscow gave him and Kissinger the aura of successful statesmen. McGovern's opposition to the war in Vietnam faded as an issue with the public in the last two weeks of the campaign when Kissinger announced, without much basis in fact, that "peace is at hand." Voters ignored McGovern's prescient warning that here was one more trick from an administration that had quietly but steadily escalated the violence in Vietnam for three-and-one-half years while claiming it was preparing to end the war.

THE ABUSE OF POWER

Unknown to nearly everyone but a handful of trusted operatives of CREEP and the White House, an astonishing abuse of governmental power had begun as early as 1969. Ever since he had gone to Washington as a new congressman, in 1947, Nixon had considered himself a victim, never given proper respect by his political adversaries. Even the praise heaped on his foreign policy did not eliminate his feeling that he and his administration were embattled. He believed that Democrats who wished him ill filled most permanent positions in the federal government. He complained bitterly about "sons-of-bitches that kick us in the ass." Feeling isolated and victimized, taking little satisfaction in good news, Nixon lashed out at those he considered his domestic enemies, and he set in motion a series of illegal and unconstitutional abuses of presidential power. The scope of the illegalities was unprecedented, ranging from unfair campaign practices—sometimes trivialized as "dirty tricks"—to using the Internal Revenue Service (IRS) to harass opponents, engaging in domestic espionage, and obstructing investigation of these illegalities by law enforcement agencies.

The Enemies List

During the presidential campaign, George McGovern had tried but failed to arouse public interest in a curious incident: the break-in at Democratic National Committee headquarters at the Watergate office complex in Washington, D.C., on the night of June 17, 1972, by five men employed by CREEP. Throughout the fall, McGovern expressed astonishment at White House Press Secretary Ron Ziegler's assertion that this had been a "third-rate burglary attempt" conducted by overzealous supporters, without direction from higher authorities. McGovern asked voters to consider the possibility that Nixon's men had engaged in "political espionage, political sabotage, and all these dirty tricks that have been played to disrupt the democratic process." Few listened.

In fact, when the Washington police apprehended the five CREEP employees on June 17, they stumbled into a complicated web of abuse of presidential power. The pattern had been set early. For many years Nixon had considered himself undermined by various opponents: Democrats, journalists, intellectuals, academics, and even certain entertainment and sports celebrities. Early in his administration he had proposed a plan to infiltrate opposition groups, had tapped the telephones of rivals and suspected leakers, had ordered the break-in at Daniel Ellsberg's psychiatrist's office, and had otherwise endorsed schemes to make life miserable for his perceived enemies. Nixon saw such enemies everywhere; they included Senator Edward Kennedy, actors Jane Fonda, Gregory Peck, Tony Randall, Julie Andrews, Connie Stevens, and Steve McQueen, the Brookings Institution, columnists James Reston and Rowland Evans, New York Jets quarterback Joe Namath, and comedian Richard M. Dixon, who did silly impersonations of Nixon. The president's lawyer, John Dean, became project coordinator for an "enemies list," with orders to find ways "we can best screw" the more than one hundred people named in it.

The White House commanded the IRS to harass political rivals, some of whom were on the enemies list. In two years the IRS investigated 4,300 such individuals and 1,025 groups and took action against 43 people and 26 organizations. When a newspaper ran a critical series on Nixon's friend Charles "Bebe" Rebozo, Chief of Staff H. R. Haldeman told Dean to have the IRS run a tax check on the editor. Dean also helped the president's supporters who got in trouble with the IRS. Nixon insisted that "tax troubles be turned off" for friends of his. When career officials resisted turning the IRS into the president's private hit squad, Nixon complained. He told Dean that Secretary of the Treasury George Shultz was a "candy ass" for declining to use the IRS to make life miserable for political opponents.

G. Gordon Liddy, the former CIA operative who had helped plan the Ellsberg burglary and run the drug wars, joined the CREEP staff in late 1971. In early 1972 he presented to Attorney General John Mitchell, soon scheduled to leave the Justice Department for the chairmanship of CREEP, a $1 million plan to disrupt the upcoming Democratic convention in Miami by kidnapping Democratic party leaders, putting them in bed with prostitutes, photographing them, and distributing the embarrassing pictures. Intrigued, but unhappy with the price tag, Mitchell told Liddy to come up with a more "realistic" plan. Liddy returned with a $250,000 scheme for eavesdropping on Democratic candidates for the 1972 election. Mitchell approved, and Liddy received $83,000 in hundred-dollar bills from Hugh W. Sloan, Jr., CREEP's treasurer, as the first installment for hiring operatives for the surveillance plan.

Dirty Money

The money delivered to Liddy represented a small part of a cornucopia of secret cash payments. Prominent individuals, corporations, trade groups, and lobbyists curried favor with the Nixon administration by making substantial donations. Since 1969 Herbert Kalmbach, Nixon's personal attorney, had controlled $1 million in cash left over from the 1968 presidential campaign. Kalmbach kept the money in various safe deposit boxes and added to it. During the 1970 congressional campaign, for example, Kalmbach collected another $2.8 million in cash. Donald Kendall, president of Pepsi-Cola, and H. Ross Perot, a Texas oil millionaire, each chipped in $250,000. Unreported by campaign treasurers, the contributions were illegal, and Kalmbach later served six months in jail for this fund-raising.

After the 1970 congressional election Nixon told Kalmbach to concentrate on raising money for 1972. Remembering the 1960 election, when John Kennedy's wealthy father had come up with a fortune to help his son, Nixon wanted never to be outspent again. The indefatigable Kalmbach quickly collected millions. One White House dinner with Nixon, Kalmbach, Mitchell, and five wealthy men yielded $7.5 million in four hours. The desire to buy favors from the government stimulated the flow of a cash bonanza from various businesses. Dairy farmers who depended on government price supports had their lobbying arm, the American Milk Producers, pledge $2 million for CREEP. With the money in hand, Nixon overruled his own economic advisers and raised dairy price supports as the milk lobbyists wanted. In violation of the law, corporations subject to federal regulation also paid Kalmbach.

To hide the illegal sources of the cash, Kalmbach took pains to see that it was properly "laundered," a process by which money is passed through intermediaries' hands to obscure its illegal origin. The problems intensified after April 1972 when a new campaign finance law went into effect, requiring that the source of all contributions be reported. A typical scheme involved $100,000 from Gulf Resources and Chemical Corporation of Houston. The Houston parent company transferred $100,000 to a Mexican subsidiary, which then provided a $100,000 "legal fee" to a Mexico City attorney. He converted the $100,000 into cash and checks payable to himself, then delivered the cash and the endorsed checks to a Texas businessman, who converted everything to cash and negotiable securities, mixed the $100,000 with another $600,000 collected from Houston businesspeople, put it in a suitcase, and flew it by courier to Washington for delivery to Hugh Sloan at CREEP's offices. Most such payments remained secret until 1973, when two investigative reporters for the

Washington Post, Bob Woodward and Carl Bernstein, began to break the story of Watergate.

THE WATERGATE SCANDAL

The harassment of domestic opponents demonstrated the suspicions of the White House; the illegal fund-raising provided the means for additional lawbreaking. The abuses intensified during the 1972 presidential election. After the extent of White House misdeeds became known over the next two years, the president was eventually forced to resign in disgrace.

The Break-in

In April 1972, flush with cash from Kalmbach's fund-raising endeavors, Gordon Liddy hired James McCord and E. Howard Hunt, two ex-CIA operatives who had burglarized offices of Nixon's political opponents, to spy on various offices of the Democratic party in Washington. McCord and Hunt in turn recruited several Cuban exiles from Miami, veterans of the CIA's 1961 Bay of Pigs invasion and the burglary at Daniel Ellsberg's psychiatrist's office, to plant listening devices. In May they botched an effort to bug McGovern headquarters. Eventually they succeeded in planting bugging devices in Democratic Committee Chairman Lawrence O'Brien's office at the Watergate complex. Two weeks later, one of the bugs malfunctioned; the burglars returned to repair it on the night of June 16. At 1:50 A.M. on June 17, a night watchman noticed tape on the door of the Democrats' office and called the District of Columbia police. They arrived and apprehended McCord and four Cubans—Bernard Barker, Frank Sturgis, Virgilio Gonzalez, and Eugenio Martinez. Police were surprised to discover Howard Hunt's White House telephone number in an address book belonging to one of the suspects.

The arrests terrified Liddy, who scurried to destroy evidence linking him, CREEP, and the White House to the burglary. He asked Attorney General Richard Kleindienst to secure the release of the five men, but the request was refused. On the morning of June 17, Liddy went to his office at CREEP to shred files linking him and John Mitchell to plans to bug the opposition.

The Cover-up

Immediately after the arrests the White House began a cover-up. From Washington presidential aide John Ehrlichman called H. R. Haldeman, who was with Nixon in Key Biscayne, Florida. The president's two principal advisers discussed Hunt's and McCord's in-

In the Oval Office of the White House, President Nixon confers with his top aides: (*from left*) National Security Adviser Henry Kissinger, Domestic Policy Adviser John Ehrlichman, and Chief of Staff H. R. "Bob" Haldeman. *National Archives/Nixon Presidential Materials.*

volvement. Because both men had recently been employed by the White House, Ehrlichman and Haldeman feared that further investigation would implicate Nixon. Ehrlichman put John Dean in charge of keeping investigators at bay. White House Press Secretary Ron Ziegler tried to put reporters off the scent by refusing comment on "a third-rate burglary attempt" and asserting that "certain elements may try to stretch this beyond what it is."

Over the next three months Dean, Haldeman, Ehrlichman, Mitchell, and Nixon successfully obstructed the Watergate investigation. On June 20 Nixon told Haldeman to undertake a public relations offensive to squelch public interest in the Watergate break-in. Three days later, Nixon outlined to Haldeman a plan for the CIA to warn the FBI to "stay the hell out of this." Given Hunt's CIA connections, Nixon said, "we think it would be very unfortunate, both for the CIA, and for the country, and for American foreign policy" for the FBI to pursue the origins of the money found on the burglars. Nixon's conversations with Haldeman on June 23 were recorded on tapes and eventually came to light in August 1974, providing proof of the president's efforts to obstruct justice. Later that afternoon, acting FBI director L. Patrick Gray told Dean that the bureau would not interview the Mexican lawyer whose checks had been the source of Liddy's cash.

Like the crime, the cover-up cost money. At the end of June, Dean met Kalmbach in Lafayette Park, across from the White House, and arranged for the master fund-raiser to collect money to purchase the silence of the burglars. Kalmbach quickly gathered about $220,000, which was delivered to lawyers representing the Watergate defendants.

Reporters' efforts to turn public attention to Watergate by following the money trail received little attention at first. Bob Woodward and Carl Bernstein of the *Washington Post* covered the story because they routinely handled relatively insignificant metropolitan news, as the Watergate burglary initially seemed to be. More prominent national affairs reporters, intimidated by earlier administration campaigns against the press and dependent on access to powerful officials, shied away from covering Watergate at first. Woodward and Bernstein wrote several stories linking money laundered in Mexico to the Watergate burglars, but Nixon denied their significance. He told a news conference that "both sides" had made "technical violations" of the new campaign finance law, although he refused to say what the Democrats had done.

In mid-September it appeared that the cover-up had succeeded. A federal grand jury indicted Liddy, Hunt, and the five men arrested at Democratic headquarters. A Justice Department spokesman claimed that "we have absolutely no evidence that anyone else should be charged." Relieved, Nixon called Dean into his office late that afternoon and congratulated him: "The way you handled it [the Watergate cover-up], it seems to me has been very skillful—putting your fingers in the dikes every time that leaks have sprung here and sprung there." Nixon went on to ruminate about his plans for a second administration. He was pleased that Dean had been keeping notes on "a lot of people who are less than our friends." Those people "are asking for it," Nixon said, "and they are going to get it."

The Investigation

Journalists Woodward and Bernstein kept reporting details of Watergate in the months before the November election, but their stories did not have wide impact. They followed the money trail, assisted by an anonymous source who seemed familiar with all the personalities in the White House. They called this informant "Deep Throat," after a currently popular pornographic movie. Deep Throat would meet Woodward late at night in underground parking garages throughout the capital and confirm the journalists' suspicions that secret cash funds had been used for dirty tricks against the Democrats since 1970.

Investigative reporters Bob Woodward (*left*) and Carl Bernstein at work on the Watergate story at the *Washington Post. UPI/Bettmann Newsphotos.*

By late October Woodward and Bernstein believed they had traced the secret funds all the way up to Haldeman. Deep Throat informed them that "from top to bottom, this whole business is a Haldeman operation." On October 25, 1972, the day before Kissinger announced that "peace is at hand," Press Secretary Ziegler attacked the *Post* for "shoddy and shabby" use of confidential sources and issued an unequivocal denial of Haldeman's connection to the secret funds. Two weeks later, Nixon won his landslide re-election.

Watergate faded but did not die in the winter of 1972 and 1973, while public attention was riveted on the savage bombing of North Vietnam and the subsequent Paris peace agreement. Democratic members of Congress kept an eye on news about Watergate, because they worried that CREEP's strong-armed fund-raising tactics threatened to put them out of business. Representative Thomas P. "Tip" O'Neill of Massachusetts, chairman of the Democratic Congressional Campaign Committee, noted that many long-time and reliable donors had not contributed to Democrats' efforts in the 1972 campaigns. The donors explained they had been told by CREEP operatives to give only to the president and other Republicans—or suffer reprisals from federal agencies.

Early in 1973 the Senate decided to create a select seven-member committee (four Democrats and three Republicans), chaired by the conservative constitutional expert Sam Ervin of North Carolina, to investigate the break-in and sabotage against the Democrats in the 1972 campaign. As this Senate Select Committee on Campaign Practices—which soon became known informally as the Senate Watergate Committee—prepared to hold hearings, Nixon's staff planned its strategy to discredit the investigation. They would invoke "executive privilege," the idea that presidential agents could not be compelled to reveal information to Congress, an equal, not superior, branch of the government. Nixon advised his subordinates involved in Watergate or the subsequent obstruction of justice to "stonewall" the committee by banning testimony by White House assistants.

The trial of the Watergate burglars revealed little at first, because they all pleaded guilty and denied White House involvement. The burglars continued to receive payments, and McCord heard from an agent that his wife and family would be taken care of if McCord went to jail for a year. Presiding over the trial, however, was U.S. District Court Judge John J. Sirica, known as "Maximum John" for the tough sentences he handed down. Sirica expressed disbelief at prosecutors' claims that the men charged were the only ones involved in the break-in. He threatened the burglars with long prison terms. On March 19, McCord broke and wrote Sirica that he and other defendants had been under political pressure to plead guilty and remain silent, that others had lied under oath, and that higher-ups were involved in the break-in. On March 23, Sirica revealed the contents of McCord's letter and sentenced Liddy to six years in prison, but delayed sentencing the other defendants in the hope that they would reveal who else had participated.

As Sirica squeezed the burglars for information, Dean found it harder to maintain the cover-up. Hunt wanted another $130,000 of hush money from the White House, threatening he would otherwise reveal the "seamy things" he had done. To Nixon, Dean painted the picture of "a cancer growing on the presidency," because many of the people involved in the Watergate break-in and the burglary of Ellsberg's psychiatrist's office could be indicted. Those exposed included Mitchell, Haldeman, Ehrlichman, and Dean himself. Demands for hush money could go as high as $1 million, Dean said. Nixon replied, "We could get that. . . . And you could get it in cash. I know where it could be gotten." Nixon instructed Dean and other aides called to testify by the Ervin committee or the grand jury investigating Watergate to avoid perjury by saying "I don't remember; I can't recall."

Containment grew harder in April as prosecutors closed in on Dean, offering immunity from prosecution if he divulged what he knew. Dean's possible defection frightened Nixon, who tried unsuccessfully to keep his wavering counsel in line. Fearing that Nixon might make him the fall guy, Dean decided to cooperate with the prosecutors and began telling everything he knew about the cover-up to the Ervin committee's staff. Nixon then tried to discredit Dean as the man who had directed a cover-up without the president's knowledge. He fired Dean on April 30 in a televised speech in which he conceded that "there had been an effort to conceal the facts" about Watergate. He accepted no personal responsibility, implying incorrectly that Dean had acted on his own. As he dismissed Dean, Nixon also decided to jettison Haldeman and Ehrlichman, accepting their resignations but praising them as "two of the finest public servants I have ever known."

Nearly in a panic that the extent of the cover-up would be revealed, Nixon adopted a new tactic of apparently cooperating with investigators. In the opening salvo of the grotesquely named Operation Candor, Ziegler apologized to the *Washington Post* for having questioned the integrity of Woodward and Bernstein. Nixon bowed to public pressure and appointed Harvard law professor Archibald Cox as an independent counsel, or special prosecutor, to continue the Justice Department's investigation of Watergate. Cox, a long-time supporter of the Kennedys, apparently would be allowed to pursue the matter without political interference.

The Senate Watergate Hearings

Nixon's strategy of seeming to accept responsibility for Watergate bought him a little time with the majority of the public, who did not know the extent of Nixon's involvement in the cover-up. However, on May 17 the Senate Watergate Committee began televised hearings that continued throughout the summer of 1973. The committee began with the "footsoldiers" of Watergate—lower-level officials of CREEP, who explained how they handled the money. In the first month of the hearings Sam Ervin, whose folksy appearance and manner could not hide a devastating wit and sharp intellect, became a celebrity. His vice chairman, Tennessee Republican Howard Baker, tried to focus attention on Nixon, repeatedly asking witnesses, "What did the president know, and when did he know it?" At hairdressing salons, muffler shops, bars, and business offices across the country, Americans interrupted their daily routines to stare at TV sets tuned to the Watergate hearings.

In late June, granted immunity from prosecution for what he might reveal, Dean took the stand. For two days he read in a monotone a 245-page statement describing the details of the cover-up. He characterized Watergate as emerging from "a climate of excessive concern over the political impact of demonstrators, excessive concern over leaks, an insatiable appetite for political intelligence." Trying to discredit Dean, Nixon leaked word to the committee that Dean had

Sam J. Ervin, Jr.

One of the most dramatic moments during the Senate Watergate Committee hearings occurred in July 1974, during the testimony of former domestic policy director John D. Ehrlichman. When asked if he believed that ordinary citizens could expect government break-ins and wiretaps in their own homes and offices, Ehrlichman replied that the ancient right to remain free from unlawful searches had been "considerably eroded over the years." That justification for the White House's lawbreaking was too much for Sam Ervin, the North Carolina senator who chaired the committee. His heavy jaws shook as he quoted an eighteenth-century English prime minister: "The poorest man may in his cottage bid defiance to all the forces of the Crown. It may be frail, its roof may shake, the wind may blow through it, the storm may enter, but the King of

helped himself to some of the cash he controlled. A friendly columnist labeled him a "bottom dwelling slug" for betraying his superiors. But he knew so much and had so many details at his fingertips that the slurs had little impact.

The testimony of Nixon's loyalists made matters worse for the president. They stumbled, mumbled, forgot, or fought with the senators. Writer Mary McCarthy described John Mitchell's "small lifeless eyes, like those of a wintering potato," and his "voice, spouting insinuation." John Ehrlichman sounded supercilious as he explained the president's right under national security to order burglaries and surveillances. Haldeman twisted and squirmed in his seat as he refused direct answers to the senators' questions.

The hearings climaxed in mid-July when Alexander Butterfield, in charge of office management at the White House, revealed that Nixon had tape-recorded his own conversations since 1970. Tapes existed

England cannot enter." And yet, Ervin lectured, "we are told here that what the King of England can't do, the President of the United States can."

The exchange with Ehrlichman confirmed Ervin's status as a folk hero. Born in 1896, the venerable senator seemed to represent the common decency of an earlier period. The sordid details of Watergate outraged him. His eye darted, his cheeks quivered. Though this former rural judge claimed that he was "just a country lawyer," he was no simple backwoodsman. His law degree was from Harvard, he read widely—as evidenced by his inexhaustible store of quotations—and he was as shrewd a politician as North Carolina had ever elected to the Senate.

For the liberals in his party he was an unlikely hero, for he had resisted legislation that protected the rights of racial minorities, women, and consumers. Yet, with his colorful personality and moral rectitude, he helped to bring people together at a time when the nation's political fabric was being torn apart. He convinced many conservatives—who might otherwise have seen the Watergate investigation as a liberal vendetta against President Nixon—of the gravity of the charges. He also helped northern liberals understand the common ground they shared with southerners.

The Watergate hearings represented the high point of Sam Ervin's public career. He retired from the Senate in 1975 and spent the next several years practicing law, lecturing on college campuses, and accepting accolades for his role in preserving the Constitution. He died in 1985. ■

that could show whether Dean was telling the truth. Immediately the Ervin committee, Judge Sirica, and Special Prosecutor Cox tried to acquire the tapes. Nixon refused access to them, citing executive privilege. Returning from the hospital where he had gone to recuperate from severe viral pneumonia, the president denied rumors that he was going to resign as "just plain poppycock. Let others wallow in Watergate," he added; "we are going to do our job."

Agnew Resigns

Another scandal hit the White House in late August when the *Wall Street Journal* revealed that federal prosecutors in Baltimore were investigating Vice President Spiro Agnew for bribery, extortion, and tax fraud. Prosecutors determined that Agnew, the former governor of Maryland, had received bribes from builders and engineers in his home state for the past ten years in return for lucrative public works contracts. The payoffs continued even after Agnew left the governor's office: the vice president had accepted brown paper bags of cash in his suite at the Executive Office Building.

Agnew fought against formal indictment with a strategy that made Nixon's position more precarious, because the vice president raised the specter of impeachment. Agnew announced that "the Constitution forbids that the Vice President be indicted in any criminal court," a view denied by most constitutional experts. The proper place to air criminal charges against him, Agnew contended, was in the House of Representatives, empowered to bring impeachment charges against federal officials. Agnew asked House Speaker Carl Albert to begin impeachment proceedings against him, but Albert replied that the House would act after, not before, any criminal indictment.

The vice president's talk of impeachment angered Nixon, who did not want the notion implanted in the minds of members of Congress. The president signaled to Agnew that he should step down to avoid prosecution. Agnew refused the hint and told a cheering throng of Republican women in Los Angeles that he would never resign. But only two weeks later he did. Prosecutors had hard evidence of the bribery, and he realized he could go to jail if he did not strike a deal. He pleaded no contest to one count of income tax evasion, for not reporting or paying taxes on the bribes. Although he subsequently affirmed his innocence, a no contest plea is considered the same as a guilty plea.

Agnew's resignation left a vacancy in the vice presidency and under the terms of the Twenty-fifth Amendment, adopted in the aftermath of John Kennedy's assassination, the president could name a successor, to be confirmed by majority vote of Congress. Nixon selected Republican Minority Leader Gerald R. Ford of Michigan, a Republican stalwart, well liked by his peers. He had little knowledge of or experience with foreign affairs. Democrats thought he was not very bright and enjoyed repeating Lyndon Johnson's taunt that he had "played football without a helmet too many times." He was best known for unswerving loyalty to Nixon through the many dizzying turns of policy, and for his suggestion that Supreme Court Justice William O. Douglas be impeached for expressing sympathy for the constitutional rights of antiwar protesters. If Nixon's own hold on the presidency seemed threatened, critics might think twice about forcing him out in favor of the untested Ford.

The Vote for Impeachment

By October 1973, even the prospect of a Ford presidency could not save Nixon from public wrath as the full dimensions of the cover-up began to emerge. Archibald Cox and the Watergate Committee asked Sirica for subpoenas that would force Nixon to produce the tapes of key conversations with aides on Watergate. The judge ruled against the committee's petition on the ground that the judiciary could not compel the executive branch of the government to comply with requests for the legislative branch. Seeing no other way to gain access to material on the tapes, Ervin accepted a compromise under which Nixon would permit one of his strongest backers in the Senate, John Stennis of Mississippi, who was nearly deaf, to listen to portions of tapes selected by the White House. Stennis would then verify summaries submitted to the committee. Cox, who knew such documents would never stand up in court, declined this unworkable compromise and persisted with efforts to subpoena the tapes.

Nixon, mindful of his conversations with Haldeman and Dean plotting the cover-up, realized that releasing complete tapes to Cox would doom him. On Saturday night, October 20, Nixon asked Attorney General Elliot Richardson to fire Cox. Richardson, who had promised Cox independence, resigned rather than dismiss him. Richardson's deputy, William Ruckelshaus, also quit rather than execute the order. Only Solicitor General Robert Bork, third in command at the Justice Department, was willing to fire Cox. Nixon also abolished the special prosecutor's office and sent FBI agents to prevent Cox's subordinates from gaining access to their files.

A firestorm of protest engulfed Capitol Hill over the next forty-eight hours. Over 1 million telephone calls and telegrams flooded senators' and representatives' offices protesting the "Saturday Night Massacre." People who earlier had given Nixon the benefit of the doubt, believing he would cooperate with investigators, changed their minds and thought he wanted to hide his involvement in lawbreaking. The next week, eight impeachment resolutions were referred to the House Judiciary Committee, chaired by New Jersey's Peter Rodino. The eruption of public anger over Nixon's stonewalling on the tapes forced another White House surrender. The president's lawyer announced willingness to release subpoenaed tapes to Judge Sirica. A new independent prosecutor, Houston lawyer Leon Jaworski, resumed the investigations.

As Jaworski gathered information about the state of the Watergate inquiry, more astonishing revelations fed the public's anger about Nixon's apparent duplicity. White House attorneys cataloguing the tapes discovered that some were missing, and an eighteen-and-one-half-minute gap existed on the tape of a June 20, 1972, conversation with Haldeman. The chief of staff's notes revealed that he and Nixon had discussed Watergate at that meeting and the president had called for a "counterattack," presumably against any investigation of the break-in, during these crucial missing minutes of audio. Soon after Judge Sirica revealed the existence of the gap, Nixon told Associated

Press editors that "people have got a right to know whether or not their President is a crook. Well, I'm not a crook."

While the public struggled to assimilate this outburst, the IRS announced that it would re-examine the president's tax returns for 1970, 1971, and 1972. Nixon had claimed deductions of $576,000 for the gift of his vice-presidential papers to the National Archives. On incomes of over $200,000 he had paid only $700 in taxes one year and a few thousand dollars in taxes the other years. Moreover, his donation to the National Archives had been falsely dated to make it appear to comply with a new law prohibiting excessive valuation of such materials. Eventually, in April 1974, Nixon paid the IRS $264,706 in back taxes and penalties. News of the gap in the tape and of Nixon's tax troubles deeply rattled public opinion, turning many of his erstwhile supporters against him.

As public distrust of Nixon increased in 1974, the staff of the House Judiciary Committee carefully prepared a case for impeachment. Continual requests for tapes and documents produced the typical White House delays and half-compliance. In late April, Nixon appeared on television to explain that he would make edited transcripts of the tapes available to the committee. These documents, he claimed, would show no prior knowledge of the break-in and no participation in or knowledge of the obstruction of justice.

That justification crumbled within days. The House Judiciary Committee voted not to accept edited transcripts and told Nixon that he had failed to comply with the committee's subpoenas for the tapes themselves. The transcripts he did release produced angry denunciations of Nixon, even from friends. Senate Minority Leader Hugh Scott, a Republican, said they revealed a "deplorable, shabby, disgusting and immoral performance" by everyone involved in the conversations. House Republican leader John Rhodes told Nixon to consider resigning, and the *Chicago Tribune* called for quick action on a bill of impeachment.

In late July 1974 the committee had impeachment articles ready. On July 27, in a nationally televised session, six Republicans joined all twenty-one Democrats, forming a majority of 27 to 11, to adopt the first article, which charged Nixon with obstruction of justice for his involvement in the cover-up of the Watergate break-in. On July 29 the Committee voted 28 to 10 on a second, general article, charging abuse of power for Nixon's involvement in the harassment of domestic opponents. The next day, a narrower majority of 21 to 17 indicted the president for unconstitutionally defying its subpoenas. The committee defeated two other articles of impeachment, but the three it had passed were more than enough. If the full House of Representatives adopted these articles, Nixon would become only the second president in United States history to be impeached—the first having been Andrew Johnson in 1868. He would then be brought to trial before the Senate, which would decide whether to remove the president from office.

NIXON'S RESIGNATION

The Supreme Court quickly delivered another blow to Nixon. In *United States* v. *Nixon*, by an 8-to-0 ruling, the Court demanded that he turn over to Sirica tapes of sixty-four conversations deemed essential evidence in the cover-up trials of six former aides. Chief Justice Burger acknowledged that the Constitution protected executive privilege, but he ruled that "when a claim of privilege is based only on the generalized interest in confidentiality, it cannot prevail over the fundamental demands of due process of law in the administration of justice." Nixon's lawyer agreed to turn over the tapes by an August 7 deadline set by Sirica.

On August 5 Nixon released transcripts of his June 23,1972, conversations with Haldeman. In them, the two men had planned how to use the CIA to throw the FBI off the scent of the Watergate investigation. Here was the "smoking gun" his defenders had insisted did not exist, for the conversations showed Nixon's early knowledge of and participation in the cover-up. Nixon conceded in a written statement that the tapes were "at variance with certain of my previous statements" and acknowledged that impeachment by the full House was "virtually a foregone conclusion." Two days later, congressional support for Nixon collapsed with release of these tapes. All the Republican members of the Judiciary Committee who had voted against impeachment said they would now vote for it on the floor. Barry Goldwater told Nixon he would have fewer than ten votes in the Senate when that body had to decide whether to convict him on the House's bill of impeachment.

Nixon's foreign policy advisers worried about his mental stability during these final days. Secretary of Defense James Schlesinger and Chief of Staff Alexander Haig informed military commanders around the world to check directly with them before executing any unusual orders from Nixon. Kissinger and Haig joined with congressional Republicans in attempts to convince Nixon to leave office before the crisis damaged foreign relations.

On the night of August 7, 1974, Nixon called Kissinger to the White House to tell him he planned to resign. Nixon, who seemed to Kissinger to have been drinking, wept openly and clearly felt his fall from grace keenly. He hoped for some later vindication: "Will history treat me more kindly than my contemporaries?" Kissinger tried to assure him that it would. According to one account, not confirmed by Kissinger, Nixon then fell to his knees in prayer, dragging the embarrassed Kissinger down with him to the floor.

Richard Nixon bids farewell to the White House staff after his resignation on August 9, 1974. *National Archives/Nixon Presidential Materials.*

Nixon's impending resignation became public the evening of August 8; in a televised address he told the nation that he intended to leave office at noon the next day. On the morning of the ninth he said farewell to his staff in a tearful, rambling, self-pitying speech in which he recalled his father, his mother, his brothers dying in their mother's arms, Theodore Roosevelt's dead young wife, and an early failure to pass the bar examination. At last Nixon recovered some composure and bade goodbye to his staff and the nation. He climbed into a helicopter on the White House lawn, flew to Andrews Air Force Base, and boarded *Air Force One* for a flight to California, becoming the first American president ever to resign from the nation's highest office. While Nixon was en route to the West Coast, Gerald Ford took the oath of office as the new president. Ford proclaimed that the "long national nightmare" was over.

CONCLUSION: NIXON'S DOMESTIC RECORD AND THE IMPLICATIONS OF WATERGATE

Richard Nixon's defenders tend to focus on his achievements in foreign policy, particularly the steps toward cooperation with the Soviet

Union and China. In some ways, however, his domestic record showed a similar creativity: for example, his early plan for welfare reform and his willingness to scrap his conservative economic approach in favor of wage and price controls. Unfortunately, he was most creative in devising ways to undercut his political opponents. His presidency became dominated by his obsession with his supposed enemies and his determination to get them before they could get him. In the end, most of the substantive changes in domestic affairs came from Congress and the Supreme Court, rather than from the executive branch. While the Court extended its civil rights rulings into the controversial areas of school busing and abortion rights, Congress passed key legislation to protect the environment and promote public health and safety. President Nixon's contributions to these issues did more to divide the nation than to unite it.

Ironically, it was his resignation that unified the country. No other event since John Kennedy's assassination had done more to bring Americans together. A president who had tried to exploit his power in illegal and unethical ways had failed to dominate the government and intimidate his opposition into silence. As his cynical manipulations of people and events became known during the Watergate investigations, Americans asserted their sense of justice and fair play. One of the flood of books on Watergate was entitled simply *How the Good Guys Finally Won.* Besides agreeing that justice had been done, Americans breathed a collective sigh of relief that the country's government had withstood the strain of the Watergate crisis. There was even a certain amount of national pride involved. It seemed that the American federal government, with its system of checks and balances that allowed one branch to curb the excesses of another, was fully capable of resisting the abuse of power.

Some of the national self-congratulation was deserved, and the revulsion felt at Nixon's duplicity was real. Nevertheless, the exposure of the misdeeds of Watergate rested more on strokes of good fortune than on the smooth workings of a system of checks and balances. Many of the White House horrors—the buggings, the dirty tricks, and the break-ins—were known before the election of 1972 and shrugged off as politics as usual. Had not *Washington Post* reporters Bob Woodward and Carl Bernstein kept the story alive in the fall of 1972, the Watergate scandal would have disappeared. Judge Sirica's prickly, skeptical personality also played a major role; a more complacent jurist might well have accepted the prosecution's claim that only seven lower-level CREEP officials were responsible for the break-in. The investigations of the Senate Watergate Committee, along with those of the House Judiciary Committee, helped focus public attention on the affair; but the Senate committee owed its existence as much to Democrats' outrage that CREEP had turned off their party's money supply as it did to concern for the electoral process. Finally, the impeachment process began because of a fight over the tapes. If Nixon had not bugged himself, if he had destroyed the tapes, or if Alexander Butterfield had not revealed their existence, the Watergate story probably would have turned out differently.

Overall, then, the implications of Watergate are difficult to assess. Nixon's abuses of power were finally checked, but perhaps only as a result of fortunate circumstances. Will the system work again if another president tries to subvert the country's laws and institutions?

A 1982 poll of over eight hundred historians identified Nixon as one of only four outright failures in the presidency. But some of the public anger at Nixon's actions dissipated by the late 1980s, when he achieved a sort of rehabilitation, especially with respect to his handling of foreign affairs. More lasting than the fluctuations in Nixon's reputation was a deepening public distrust of politicians, of government in general, and of many other figures of authority in American society. This perhaps was the most fundamental legacy of Richard Nixon and Watergate. ■

FURTHER READING

Politics and domestic policies of the Nixon administration are covered in: Richard Nixon, *RN: The Memoirs of Richard Nixon* (1978) and *In the Arena* (1990); Stephen E. Ambrose, *Nixon*, 3 vols. (1986–1991); Herbert Parmet, *Richard Nixon and his America* (1990); William Safire, *Before the Fall: An Inside Look at the Pre-Watergate White House* (1975); Raymond Price, *With Nixon* (1977); Lewis Chester, Godfrey Hodgson, and Bruce Paige, *An American Melodrama* (1970); A. James Reichley, *Conservatives in an Age of Change* (1981); Timothy Crouse, *The Boys on the Bus* (1976); Kevin B. Phillips, *The Emerging Republican Majority* (1969); Nicholas Lemann, *The Promised Land: The Great Black Migration and How It Changed America* (1991); Daniel Patrick Moynihan, *The Politics of a Guaranteed Income* (1973); Leonard Silk, *Nixonomics* (1972); Melvin Urofsky, *The Continuity of Change: The Supreme Court and Individual Liberties, 1953–1986* (1991). On Watergate, see: Stanley I. Kutler, *The Wars of Watergate* (1990); Jonathan Schell, *The Time of Illusion* (1975); Kim McQuaid, *The Anxious Years: America in the Vietnam and Watergate Era* (1989); J. Anthony Lukas, *Nightmare: The Underside of the Nixon Years* (1976); Theodore H. White, *Breach of Faith: The Fall of Richard Nixon* (1975); Bob Woodward and Carl Bernstein, *All The President's Men* (1974) and *The Final Days* (1976); H. R. Haldeman with Joseph Dimona, *The Ends of Power* (1978); John Ehrlichman, *Witness to Power* (1982); John Dean, *Blind Ambition* (1976).

12

Years of Limits and Malaise, 1974–1980

In January 1975, Edmund G. "Jerry" Brown, Jr., the newly elected governor of California, rode to work in a four-door Plymouth sedan, disdaining the bulletproof Cadillac limousine usually provided the state's chief executive. The unconventional Brown, a former Jesuit seminarian, slept on a mattress on the floor of an unfurnished one-bedroom apartment, refusing to live in the tasteless mansion the previous governor, Ronald Reagan, had had his friends buy for the state. Like many Americans in the aftermath of the Vietnam War and Watergate, Brown expressed profound disillusionment with current institutions. Government agencies did not seem to return valuable services for the taxes they collected, and officials had lost respect among citizens. Brown believed that public officials had to re-evaluate old programs to challenge the assumptions underlying them, and restrain taxation and government spending before popular faith in government would resume.

Brown announced that the nation had entered an "era of limits," when Americans would have to conserve natural resources and watch their spending. His unorthodox views continually astonished people. Brown once left the California Board of Regents speechless by asking for evidence that college students learned more in small classes. The governor also suggested paying janitors as much as judges, because the latter gained worthwhile "psychic income" from their jobs, whereas the former deserved more for their hard physical labor.

For a few years Brown captured perfectly the spirit of the time. He seemed new, different, untainted by Vietnam or Watergate. Impossible to classify as either liberal or conservative, the thirty-nine-year-old governor offered the hope of transcending the searing battles of the sixties and early seventies. At first, Brown symbolized both Americans' hopes for new leadership and their heightened skepticism of traditional politicians. The passions created by the war in Vietnam and the counterculture faded after the Paris agreement of 1973, but the memory of the deceit and lawbreaking of Watergate still burned. "Don't vote; it only encourages them," was a popular bumper sticker in the 1970s, and the 1974 congressional election and 1976 presidential election saw the lowest turnout since the Second World War. In 1975, 69 percent of Americans surveyed in one poll agreed that "over the last ten years, this country's leaders have consistently lied to people."

Americans even distrusted professions they had once admired. The proportion of the public expressing confidence in medical doctors dropped from 73 percent to 42 percent; for corporate executives, the figure fell from 55 percent to 16 percent. Even fewer people had faith in lawyers or members of Congress. As inflation returned and unemployment rose through much of the seventies, Americans also became fearful about their families' future. By 1980, 62 percent of the public believed that the country had entered a period of enduring shortages of resources like petroleum, water, clean air, even food; and a majority agreed that "next year will be worse than this year."

Gerald Ford, the good-natured Midwestern congressman turned vice president who assumed the presidency on August 9, 1974, found himself overwhelmed by a public sense that officials were incompetents or lawbreakers and the programs they administered inefficient or harmful. He tried to heal the wounds of Watergate by asserting, on taking office, that "our long national nightmare is over." Yet a few weeks later his popularity fell sharply when he provided Richard Nixon with a blanket pardon for all crimes he might have committed while president. Ford's standing never recovered, and his plunging fortunes mirrored the public's frustrations. In January 1975, he told Congress that "the state of the union is not good." Twenty months later voters turned him out of office, electing an outsider, former governor of Georgia James Earl "Jimmy" Carter.

Like Jerry Brown, Carter appealed to the yearning for a fresh face with new ideas, unwedded to the past. Liberals initially thought Carter was a liberal, moderates a moderate, conservatives a conservative. A believing Christian who spoke proudly about his religious experiences, Carter declared that a single word, "faith," summarized his campaign for the presidency. A master of symbols, Carter grasped that Americans yearned for control over their institutions and wanted leaders like themselves. In his inaugural parade, instead of riding in the presidential limousine, he strolled arm in arm with his wife down Pennsylvania Avenue. "He's walking; he's walking!" excited spectators screamed. In other ways, too, he appealed directly to the public rather than to Washington insiders. He carried his own overnight bag on and off *Air Force One*. He took his summer vacation on a restored paddle wheeler on the Mississippi River.

By 1980, however, neither Carter's appeals to ordinary people nor the novelty represented by Jerry Brown had revived Americans' faith in themselves, their institutions, or their leaders. The economy, barely recovered from bad times caused by the oil embargo in 1973 and 1974, had fallen into another recession. Foreign competition, inept management, and inflation had devastated basic manufacturing industries. Carter's efforts to restore American standing abroad withered in the face of revolution in Iran and Soviet assertiveness. His outsider status, vital to his election in 1976, made it difficult for him to master the art of governing the large, complicated federal establishment. Moreover, his pollster's diagnosis of a "national malaise"—a deep uneasiness with the state of the country—proved accurate but unhelpful, because the cure remained elusive.

THE FORD PRESIDENCY

From the start of his presidency, Gerald Ford tried to put the memory of Watergate to rest. His homey style contrasted with Nixon's awkward defensiveness. The new president, the adored and adoring father of four happy young adults, seemed at peace with himself, his family, and his country. In contrast to Nixon, who had cheated on his income taxes, Ford paid his fair share. He was often photographed playing golf like a Midwestern small businessman. At first Ford relished his role as a regular guy. "I don't want a honeymoon," he told Congress three days after taking office, "I want a good marriage." He could take a joke, too. He laughed when photographers snapped pictures of his awkward moments—for instance, when his errant golf balls hit surprised spectators or when he stumbled on the gangway and banged his head on the doorway of the White House airliner.

Being ordinary, however, soon made Ford appear unequal to the job of chief executive. On the new NBC-TV series "Saturday Night Live," comedian Chevy Chase began weekly sketches ridiculing the president's apparent clumsiness. When the mostly young, self-consciously sophisticated audience laughed at Ford's missteps, they ventilated wider concerns that their leaders could not manage public affairs. A serious economic recession in 1974 and a Communist victory in Vietnam in 1975 made Americans doubt whether a friendly nature and a happy family life were sufficient qualifications for the post of the nation's chief executive. "Gerald Ford is an awfully nice man who isn't up to the presidency," wrote John Osborne in the *New Republic*.

The Pardon and the Election of 1974

Ford made it harder for his administration to command public esteem by two decisions taken within a month of his inauguration: the appointment of Nelson Rockefeller as vice president and the pardon of Richard Nixon. In some ways Rockefeller seemed a logical choice. An experienced Republican officeholder, he had served fourteen years as governor of New York before resigning in December 1973. He had run for the Republican presidential nomination in 1960 and 1964 and was widely regarded as the leader of the eastern, moderate wing of

President Gerald R. Ford and his daughter Susan visit Independence Hall, Philadelphia, during the Bicentennial celebration, July 4, 1976. *Wide World Photos.*

the Republican party. Therein lay part of the problem: the Republican party had grown increasingly western, southern, and conservative since 1968. The mainstream of the Republican party now consisted of people like those who had booed Rockefeller at the 1964 convention, and these conservatives never forgave Ford for elevating Rockefeller to the vice presidency. Nevertheless, Congress acknowledged that the new president had wide latitude in choosing a vice president, and Rockefeller was confirmed in December. For the first time in history, neither the president nor the vice president of the United States had been elected to their positions by voters, an anomaly that heightened the sense that public institutions did not work well.

Pardoning Nixon did even greater damage to Ford's public standing. Ford believed that a protracted trial of the former president would only rivet the public eye on the misdeeds of Watergate, diverting attention from what Ford was trying to accomplish and hurting Republican chances in the upcoming congressional elections. After returning from church services on Sunday morning, September 8, 1974, Ford announced that he had provided a "full, free, and absolute pardon" to the former president. Nixon formally accepted the pardon, an act equivalent to acknowledging guilt, but he claimed only

"Saturday Night Live"

Some time during the sixties, television lost the youth market. Many people between the ages of eighteen and thirty-four tuned out the broadcast networks and sought their entertainment elsewhere. Advertisers groped toward this audience of millions of consumers but failed to reach them. All that changed suddenly in the fall of 1975. At 11:30 P.M. Eastern Standard Time, on October 11, NBC debuted "Saturday Night Live," an innovative live variety show featuring an iconoclastic comedy troupe, "The Not Ready for Prime Time Players." The troupe was joined by weekly hosts from the worlds of entertainment and politics and by musical guests whose recordings usually stood at the top of the charts.

Producer Lorne Michaels put together a mercurial group of comedy writers and actors who mastered a counterculture humor combining references to sex and drugs, contempt for

to have made "mistakes" in the Watergate affair. The public felt betrayed by Ford and dissatisfied that Nixon would not admit he had broken the law. The new president's approval rating dropped from 72 percent to 49 percent.

As public criticism mounted throughout the fall, anxious Republican members of Congress called on Ford to do something to distance himself, and them, from the memory of Watergate. Some suggested that he make a clean break with the past and fire all cabinet members left over from the Nixon years. Ford refused, not wanting to part with Henry Kissinger's foreign affairs expertise. The president did agree to take the unprecedented step of testifying directly before a House

show business banalities, savage political satire, and suspicion of mainstream consumerism. A headache for the network's censors, "Saturday Night Live" was produced in an atmosphere of bedlam, and its appeal depended on the audience's sensation that anything could happen. In a typical skit, an unsuspecting woman walked into a dry cleaner and found a samurai warrior behind the counter. A killer shark masqueraded as a candygram delivery man. After a series of skits lampooning President Ford, the president's press secretary hosted the show, and even the president made a cameo appearance.

Washington Post television critic Tom Shales described "Saturday Night Live" as "the first network series produced by and for the television generation." One of the show's executives called it "the post-Watergate victory party for the Woodstock generation." With an en-semble initially including Chevy Chase, Dan Ackroyd, Gilda Radner, and John Belushi, the show became a springboard for little-known talent moving into the big time. Cast members found themselves in demand for roles in other television and movie projects, and Chase, Bill Murray, and Eddie Murphy went on to major film careers.

As "Saturday Night Live" aged, its fate mirrored that of the counterculture from which it had sprung. Its humor became more predictable as mainstream America absorbed the countercurrent. The cast members, who had always seemed on the verge of exploding, either self-destructed or took the edge off their art. In its heyday, however, "Saturday Night Live" made the most of the medium's potential for spontaneous communication. ■

subcommittee investigating the pardon. He wanted to "heal the wounds of the past," he explained. Some critics had charged that Nixon had agreed to resign in return for a promise of a pardon. But Ford insisted in his testimony that "there was no deal, period."

Ford's testimony came less than a month before the 1974 elections, in which Democrats overwhelmed Republicans. Despite the low turnout of 38 percent of eligible voters, the Democrats gained forty-six House seats, giving them a majority of 290 to the Republicans' 145 seats—theoretically enough to override a presidential veto without any Republican votes. They picked up an additional four seats in the Senate. They also won almost all governorships in major states. After the election of 1974 there were more Democratic officeholders than ever—more even than after the Democratic landslides of 1958 and 1964.

Anger over Watergate and Nixon's pardon combined with frustration about the sour economy to produce the swing to the Democrats. The country had never recovered from the effects of the Arab oil embargo and the subsequent 400 percent price rise after the 1973 Arab-Israeli war. Unemployment hit 7.1 percent in the fall of 1974, the highest level since the recession of 1958. Prices soared while the gross national product dropped at an annual rate of 9.1 percent in the last quarter of 1974. Ford's response seemed tepid and inept. Committed to voluntary action, he wore a button reading WIN, for "Whip Inflation Now." He reported some of the advice people had written to the White House regarding ways individuals could keep prices down: "clean up your plate before you leave the table"; "guard your health." Had he been more inspiring or had he lived at a time when people wanted to believe their leaders, the results might have been different. For Ford, however, the reaction was ridicule. A Democratic congressman even wrote a song mocking the WIN program. The president's button seemed silly, similar to the childlike drawing of a smiling "happy face" popular at the time.

Troubles in Foreign Policy

Troubles abroad contributed to the gnawing fear that events had slipped out of control, the country's fortunes had plunged, and leaders had lost their sense of direction. The Communists won the war in Vietnam in April 1975, less than nine months after Ford became president. Almost immediately after signing the cease-fire in January 1973, both the Saigon government and the National Liberation Front had broken it. The government of President Nguyen Van Thieu hoped that its offensive against the Communists would encourage Washington to resume direct military support. But Thieu misjudged Americans' disgust with the war and their preoccupation with Watergate and economic difficulties. "I want to get the hell out" of Vietnam, said one conservative Republican congressman who earlier had ardently backed the war. In the fall of 1974 Congress cut in half Kissinger's request for $1.5 billion in additional military aid to South Vietnam.

In early 1975 Hanoi decided that the moment had arrived for a decisive victory. North Vietnamese forces captured an important outpost in the central highlands in March. When Thieu ordered his troops to withdraw, they fled in terror, leaving their weapons behind; the troops fought hundreds of thousands of panicked refugees for space in the clogged roads and on planes leaving for the South. Ford asked Congress for additional military aid, but his heart was not in it, and the aid was refused. Most members of Congress agreed with Wisconsin Democratic Representative Les Aspin who feared that "we would be back in the quagmire" if Congress approved more money.

As the rout of South Vietnam's armed forces quickened in April, Americans fled Vietnam. Television captured the catastrophic end of "Operation Babylift": the crash of a giant transport jet carrying hundreds of Vietnamese orphans destined for homes in the United States. Some considered the death of the children a metaphor for the misplaced idealism and generosity that had led the United States to Vietnam in the first place. Others believed it represented the clash of assumed United States superiority and the reality of a flawed modern technology. The high point of Ford's young presidency came when he announced in mid-April at Tulane University that "the war in Vietnam is over as far as the United States is concerned."

On April 29 the last American helicopters lifted off from the roof of the embassy in Saigon. The next day the remnant of the government of the Republic of Vietnam surrendered, and North Vietnamese and Vietcong troops renamed Saigon Ho Chi Minh City. The Americans evacuated about 150,000 Vietnamese employees and supporters, but they left hundreds of thousands more behind. TV viewers at home were disgusted by images of United States Marines clubbing screaming, terrified Vietnamese to keep them away from the American embassy. Scenes of ARVN soldiers shoving and shooting the weak, the elderly, and women with small children in order to secure a place on the few evacuation planes represented to many the horror, chaos, and futility of the war in Vietnam.

That war had lasted so long that most Americans preferred to forget it, or at least not speak publicly about it. They temporarily followed Secretary of State Kissinger's urging "to put Vietnam behind us." On May 12 Ford took some of the sting out of defeat in Vietnam by ordering marines to attack Cambodian Communist forces that had captured the *S.S. Mayaguez,* a civilian freighter that had strayed into Cambodian waters. The marines destroyed a Cambodian port and lost thirty-eight men before locating the crew of the *Mayaguez,* whom the Cambodians had already released. Nevertheless, the "rescue" operation proved enormously popular at home as a demonstration that the United States could still assert its military power. Members of Congress who had supported the War Powers Act, which required timely presidential notification to Congress of military action, accepted Ford's explanation that he had had to act quickly. "It's good to win one for a change," one Democratic representative told the president.

Détente with the Soviet Union, already strained in the aftermath of the October 1973 Mideast war, declined further in the Ford administration. Kissinger and his Soviet counterparts never fulfilled the promise of the 1972 Interim Agreement on Limitations of Strategic Armaments (SALT-I) to conclude a full-fledged treaty by 1977. In November 1974 Ford met Soviet President Leonid Brezhnev in the Siberian port of Vladivostok, where the two signed a framework for an arms control treaty to be known as SALT-II; but this document never matured into a full-scale treaty. American opponents of détente opposed any arrangement that would permit the Soviets a large advantage in land-based intercontinental ballistic missiles (ICBMs), even though the United States had more bombers and submarine-based missiles. Democratic Senator Henry Jackson of Washington, long suspicious of détente and preparing for a presidential race in 1976, continued to complain that Kissinger had weakened the United States military position and had ignored violations of human rights in the Soviet Union. The Kremlin considered complaints about its human rights record an unjustified interference in its internal affairs, and believed such complaints were a smoke screen for American unwillingness to expand détente. While Kissinger and Ford encountered domestic pressure to demand more of the Soviets, the Soviets began to stiffen their negotiating position.

Calls to push the Soviets on human rights grew louder in 1975. Conservatives complained when Ford would not meet Aleksandr Solzhenitsyn, an exiled Russian novelist who had been stripped of his Soviet citizenship after winning the Nobel Prize for Literature for books describing the Soviet police state. The president's standing slipped further in August 1975 when he attended the Conference on Security and Cooperation in Europe, convened in Helsinki. There, thirty-five European and North American nations recognized the borders created in Europe at the end of the Second World War. The Helsinki Conference produced a declaration of human rights that supported freedom of migration, expression, and religion. Conservatives and cold warriors in the United States ignored that part of the proceedings and criticized American acknowledgment of the legitimacy of Communist rule in Eastern Europe.

Dissent within his cabinet further weakened Ford's position. Secretary of Defense James Schlesinger, who considered détente dangerous, complained that the Soviet Union had accomplished the "largest deployment of improved strategic capabilities in the history of the nuclear competition." By fall 1975 Ford could no longer stand the competition between his secretary of state, who had helped create détente, and his defense secretary, who derided it. On November 1 he fired Schlesinger, along with CIA director William Colby, who had been tarnished by congressional investigations of the CIA's abuses of power. Ford also stripped Kissinger of his position as national security adviser, although Kissinger retained his position as secretary of state.

THE ELECTION OF 1976

In the fall of 1975 Ford continued to appear politically vulnerable, and he barely escaped two attempts on his life. Lynnette "Squeaky" Fromme, a member of the Manson Family—a group of cult murderers who had conducted a homicidal rampage in 1970—shot a pistol at the president in September. A few weeks later, Sara Jane Moore, a minor figure in the melodrama of the kidnapping of newspaper heiress Patty Hearst by revolutionaries calling themselves the Symbionese Liberation Army, also fired at the president. Usually Americans pull together when the chief executive is in danger, but the assaults by two deranged women from society's fringes barely registered with the public. Because Gerald Ford lacked presidential stature, citizens largely ignored the danger to him.

His widely popular wife Betty made more of an impact when she called the Supreme Court's decision legalizing abortion "the best thing in the world, a great, great decision." She told an interviewer that she would not be surprised if her twenty-year-old daughter had an affair; she also expressed the belief that premarital sex probably reduced the divorce rate. Most Americans thought that the first lady's views indicated a refreshing openness to recent social trends. But the reaction from conservative elements of the Republican party could not have been worse for Ford. The highly conservative *Manchester Union-Leader* headlined Mrs. Ford's remarks "A Disgrace to the Nation." Editor William Loeb, the champion of extreme right-wingers, complained that Ford showed "lack of guts" in refusing to disavow his wife's remarks.

Another champion of the conservatives, former governor of California, Ronald Reagan, announced his candidacy for the Republican presidential nomination in November. He complained that "our nation's capital has become the seat of a buddy system that functions for its own benefit." He charged that Ford had become part of the cozy deal making of official Washington and was out of touch with the concerns of ordinary Republicans. Using themes that he had developed over the previous twenty years, Reagan stressed his opposition to a wide variety of institutions and trends: the federal government, Social Security, busing for integration, student radicalism, sexual promiscuity, abortion, the Equal Rights Amendment (ERA), détente with the Soviet Union, and accommodation with the Third World. He advocated lower taxes, prayer in public schools, and an assertive foreign policy designed to erase the stain of the defeat in Vietnam. Reagan defeated Ford in a series of southern and western primaries in which he criticized the Nixon-Ford-Kissinger policy of détente with the Soviet Union. He stood up for fired Defense Secretary Schlesinger, who supported his campaign, and complained that "this nation has become Number Two in military power in a world where it is dangerous—if not fatal—to be second best." Reagan won his greatest support with ardent appeals to retain United States control over the Panama Canal. He opposed the efforts of each administration since Lyndon Johnson's to negotiate treaties that would grant Panama control of the waterway and end United States rule of the Canal Zone.

Ford eked out a narrow victory over Reagan at the Republican convention in Kansas City; his pleas to party regulars not to humiliate a sitting Republican president carried weight. Ford capitulated to the conservatives by dropping Nelson Rockefeller as the nominee for vice president, replacing him with sharp-tongued Kansas Senator Robert Dole. The president toughened the American stand on arms control with the Soviet Union, thereby blocking completion of a SALT-II treaty before the election, and suspended work on the Panama Canal treaty. Ford also accepted a conservative platform that adopted many of Reagan's positions—"less government, less spending, less inflation." The platform called for constitutional amendments prohibiting abortion and permitting prayer in public schools. The party did retain its support for the ERA, a fixture of Republican platforms since 1940.

Democratic primary voters, eliminating several familiar liberal and conservative politicians who had been around for years, chose Jimmy Carter, former governor of Georgia, to oppose Ford in the fall election. A graduate of the Naval Academy at Annapolis, Carter had served in a nuclear submarine before leaving the navy in 1953 to take over his family's peanut warehouse in the southern Georgia town of Plains. He won election to the Georgia state legislature and ran for governor in 1966, but lost to segregationist Lester Maddox. Like many other moderate southern politicians defeated by ardent segregationists in the twenty years after *Brown* v. *Board of Education*, he vowed never to be "out-segged" again; he won the governorship in 1970 in part by accusing his moderate opponent of excessive friendliness to blacks.

Once elected, Carter became a model advocate of the New South, too busy attracting modern industry to the burgeoning Sunbelt to dwell on the sour racial divisions of the past. He declared in his inaugural address that "the time for racial segregation is over," and he ordered a portrait of Martin Luther King, Jr., hung in the state capitol. His governorship drew business to Georgia and healed many racial wounds of the previous decade. He forged an alliance between bankers, realtors, and developers and the black community. Two of his staunchest supporters were Martin Luther King, Sr., and Andrew Young, the first African-American member of Congress from Georgia since Reconstruction. After the catastrophic Democratic defeat in the 1972 presidential election, Carter decided to run for president. As he looked at Massachusetts Senator Edward Kennedy and Alabama Governor George Wallace, the two candidates then believed most likely to run, he realized that each generated strong animosities among large segments of Democratic voters. A gap existed that could be filled by a moderate southerner unbloodied by recent controversies.

A deeply religious man, Carter stressed old Protestant virtues in his campaign for the presidency. He liked to quote a sentence from the neo-orthodox theologian Reinhold Niebuhr: "The sad duty of politics is to establish justice in a sinful world." Virtually unknown at the beginning of 1976, he carefully followed the advice of intelligent political operatives who grasped what the public wanted in the wake of Watergate and Vietnam. Specific programs mattered less than confidence in the rectitude and competence of leaders. At a time when nearly all Washington politicians were under suspicion, Carter effectively used his status as an outsider, untouched by the failures and scandals of the federal government. "I'm not a lawyer, I'm not a member of Congress, and I've never served in Washington," Carter told responsive audiences as he traveled the country in the winter of 1975 and 1976 looking for support in caucuses and primaries. He achieved his first breakthrough at the Iowa precinct caucuses in January 1976 and won the New Hampshire primary in February.

If voters did not know where he stood on specific issues, they admired his honesty. "I'll never lie to you," he promised, and he guaranteed "a government as good as the American people." When forced to take a stand on specifics—abortion, busing, amnesty for draft evaders—Carter tried to occupy the middle ground. He was "personally opposed to abortion" and did not want the government to fund abortions for poor women. Yet he also did not want to overturn the Supreme Court's judgment that abortion was a right. He opposed mandatory busing to achieve racial balance, but he also opposed a constitutional amendment outlawing the practice. He favored a pardon for draft evaders, because acceptance of a pardon meant acknowledgment of wrongdoing; but he opposed giving the draft evaders amnesty, because that would have wiped the slate clean.

By April Carter had emerged as the clear front-runner for the nomination, surpassing George Wallace, Henry Jackson, and two liberals, Senator Birch Bayh of Indiana and Representative Morris Udall of Arizona. Carter's preeminence distressed some Democratic leaders.

Part of the uneasiness about Carter derived from regional or religious snobbery: big-city liberals had little in common with southerners and evangelical Christians. But Carter also raised new doubts among African-Americans when he explained his opposition to low-income housing in mostly white suburbs. He said, "I see nothing wrong with ethnic purity being maintained. I would not force racial integration of a neighborhood by government action." Carter's long-time support for the Vietnam War, his skepticism about many Great Society programs, and his disdain for Washington also seemed a slap in the face to positions taken by Democratic party liberals since the late 1960s. In desperation some party elders encouraged Hubert Humphrey to make another run for the presidency. Suffering from early effects of the cancer that would kill him two years later, the former vice president drew back from another bruising primary fight.

Liberals then looked elsewhere for an alternative to Carter. In May two western Democrats, Idaho Senator Frank Church and California Governor Jerry Brown, defeated Carter in most of the remaining primaries. Brown's campaign drew the most enthusiastic response of the primary season. His mixture of Zen Buddhism and orthodox Catholicism seemed even more exotic than Carter's evangelicalism, but as governor of the nation's largest state he seemed to voters to be more sophisticated than the apparently provincial southerner. Like Carter, Brown doubted the capacity of government officials to solve many social problems. In an era of limits, government programs could not afford to expand, and probably they should shrink. Like Carter, Brown opposed busing for racial balance, adding an environmental twist: he claimed that the buses themselves were part of the problem, burning scarce gasoline and spewing noxious pollution into the atmosphere.

Although Carter won no primaries outside the South after April, he continued to accumulate delegates. He wrapped up the nomination in June. A month later the Democrats met in optimism and harmony, a sharp contrast to their last two gatherings. To appease traditional liberals Carter chose one of them, Minnesota Senator Walter Mondale, as his vice-presidential nominee. Martin Luther King, Sr., who delivered a benediction, declared that "surely the Lord sent Jimmy Carter to come on out and bring America back where she belongs." When the convention adjourned, Carter enjoyed an enormous margin over Ford in public opinion polls, 62 percent to 29 percent.

However, Carter squandered most of that lead. The very qualities that made Carter an attractive nominee—religious earnestness, southern background, unfamiliarity with Washington—troubled urban, suburban, and northern voters as they compared him to familiar, Midwestern Jerry Ford. Americans began to feel better about their country in the summer as they celebrated the Bicentennial of the Declaration of Independence. Americans watched in fascination a series of television spectaculars: a flotilla of "tall ships" in full sail making their way through New York Harbor; a gigantic fireworks display over the Statue of Liberty; the Boston Pops orchestra playing patriotic marches for hundreds of thousands on the banks of the Charles River. Many were surprised at the gentle optimism expressed on the day.

During the fall campaign each candidate reinforced persistent doubts about himself. Arthur Schlesinger, Jr., friend of the Kennedy family and advocate of traditional Democratic liberalism, complained on the eve of the election that voters had to choose between the "weirdness" of Carter and the "dumbness" of Ford. Carter's relatives, who presented stark contrasts to the bland, cheerful Ford family, contributed to the sense of his oddity. In her late sixties Carter's mother, affectionately called "Miz" Lillian, had left her quiet Georgia home for a two-year stint with the Peace Corps in India. The candidate's sister, Ruth Carter Stapleton, was a traveling evangelist and faith healer. His brother Billy became a major embarrassment, guzzling beer in front of his gas station and letting reporters know that he resented his big brother's success. Sophisticated, college-educated suburbanites began to wonder if Carter might not represent a part of America they could not comprehend.

Trying to modernize his priggish image and broaden his appeal to people who felt uncomfortable with excessive moralizing, Carter told *Playboy* that he had "looked on a lot of women with lust" and had "committed adultery in my heart many times." The *Playboy* interview had exactly the opposite effect from what Carter had intended, and it suggested that he had lost some of his early grip on how to appeal to the public. Conservatives and evangelicals wondered why someone whom they considered one of their own was speaking to *Playboy* in the first place. Northerners, city dwellers, suburbanites, and well-educated professionals shook their heads at Carter's apparent naiveté. On a more substantial level, Carter continued his denunciations of Republican foreign policy, claiming it had ignored human rights abuses of other nations and turned the United States into "the arms merchant of the world."

Ford gave Carter an issue in the second of three televised debates when the president mishandled a question on détente with the Soviet Union and United States relations with Poland. He claimed that "there is no Soviet domination of Eastern Europe, and there never will be under a Ford administration." The camera then focused on Carter, whose face broke into a broad grin. "I would like to see Mr. Ford convince the Polish-Americans and the Czech-Americans and the Hungarian-Americans in this country," Carter replied. *Time* magazine labeled Ford's remark "The Blooper Heard Round the World"

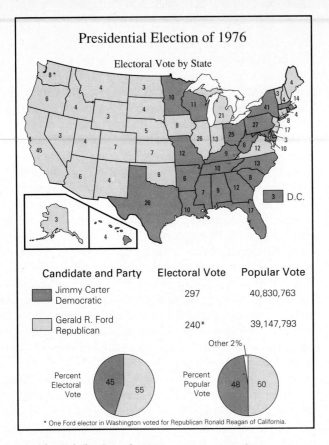

Presidential Election of 1976

Electoral Vote by State

Candidate and Party	Electoral Vote	Popular Vote
Jimmy Carter Democratic	297	40,830,763
Gerald R. Ford Republican	240*	39,147,793

Percent Electoral Vote: 45 / 55

Percent Popular Vote: 48 / 50 / Other 2%

* One Ford elector in Washington voted for Republican Ronald Reagan of California.

Presidential Election of 1976

and questioned his "grasp of foreign policy and even his mere competence."

On election day Carter defeated Ford by taking 50.1 percent of the popular vote, compared to Ford's 48 percent. Carter won 297 electoral votes to Ford's 241. Anger at the Nixon pardon, unhappiness with the sluggish economy, and doubts about Ford's ability to lead persuaded a majority to cast their lot with Carter. His backers admired his sincerity and morality and believed him to be more intelligent than Ford. That was enough to make them suspend doubts about the direction of his policies and concerns that he had gone too far in stressing his lack of ties to official Washington. Could such an outsider follow through on a program even if he had one? Only time would tell.

The narrow victory revealed a divided and troubled electorate.

Ford carried twenty-seven states; Carter won in twenty-three and the District of Columbia (see map). Democrats maintained most of the congressional gains they had made in the landslide of 1974. Ford carried a majority of the white vote. Carter won all states of the old Confederacy with the exception of Virginia. In each of those southern states, black voters turned out in substantial numbers, joining rural whites, who felt pride in one of their own, to put Carter over the top. But many Americans did not bother to vote in a largely issueless fight between two candidates about whom they had substantial doubts. Turnout was only 54.4 percent, which at that point was the lowest percentage in any presidential election since the Second World War. Nonvoters were typically younger, poorer, less well educated, and more likely to be non-Caucasian than people who went to the polls.

Even though his margin was less than he had expected in the summer, Carter won a majority of the votes cast, something Truman, Kennedy, and Nixon had not accomplished in their presidential victories of 1948, 1960, and 1968. The new leader expressed satisfaction that 1976 had been a better year than Americans had experienced in a decade.

JIMMY CARTER AND THE DECLINE OF PRESIDENTIAL AUTHORITY

As president, Jimmy Carter relied on the advice of pollsters and media specialists who had helped him win the White House. They told him to continue emphasizing his outsider status, keep at arm's length the Democrats who dominated Congress, and do things that symbolized his closeness to ordinary people. Carter's decision to follow these prescriptions made him temporarily popular but severely strained his relationship with the professional politicians of the party he ostensibly led.

Deeply divided themselves, the Democrats could not help the president, and often hurt him, when the country encountered hard times. "If this were France," complained Thomas P. "Tip" O'Neill, the new speaker of the House of Representatives, "the Democratic party would be five parties." Competing factions—southerners, blacks, urban ethnics, supporters of organized labor, feminists, former antiwar protesters, consumer advocates, environmentalists, educated professionals, traditional liberals and conservatives—coexisted in an uneasy coalition, broader but less secure than the one assembled by Franklin Roosevelt. The New Deal alignment had made the Democrats a majority party for thirty years, but the war in Vietnam and racial tensions had broken old political ties. The Democratic party of 1977 seemed dominant, but it presented a variety of conflicting programs and approaches to government and society.

Perhaps no politician could have overcome this diversity in a contentious era in which leaders commanded little respect. But in some ways Jimmy Carter was particularly unsuited for the task. His rural, southern background and his moderate to conservative predilections distanced him from may of the other leaders in his party. Moreover, as president, he emphasized skillful management rather than a clearly stated set of principles, and when he did state his principles clearly, he tended to be inconsistent in implementing them. Consequently, the public had little firm idea of what he stood for. When government programs did not work, he also lost his reputation as a manager, and by the end of his term in office he had little authority over the nation that he tried to lead.

The Outsider as President

Bad feelings between Carter and Congress began on inaugural day, January 20, 1977, and the situation never improved. At one of the several inaugural-day balls, Carter offended Speaker O'Neill, an old-fashioned Massachusetts liberal and a force to be reckoned with in the House, by permitting his staff to give O'Neill a bad seat. The speaker never forgave this slight, the first of many at the hands of White House Chief of Staff Hamilton Jordan, a man he began calling "Hannibal Jerkin."

Carter's efforts to follow through on his campaign promises showed how difficult it was to occupy a middle position. On his first day in office he offered a "full, complete and unconditional pardon" for draft resisters. With this generous offer he established a pattern of trying to bridge the chasms separating Americans on divisive issues—and of winning little gratitude for his efforts. The pardon announcement helped retire the lingering controversies over Vietnam, but it diminished the president's sparse political capital. The director of the Veterans of Foreign Wars called the day the saddest one in American history. The Senate came close to passing a resolution of disapproval. At the same time, peace groups claimed that Carter did not go far enough. His pardon had excluded military offenders—deserters and people with less than honorable discharges. The American Civil Liberties Union noted that these people were "more likely to be poor, from minority groups and less educated."

Many of Carter's early policy initiatives and nominations encountered congressional hostility. He offended important Democrats in February 1977 by abruptly canceling nineteen water projects in the southern, Rocky Mountain, and western states. These dams, river diversions, and irrigation systems had dubious economic value in relation to their cost. They also represented tangible evidence of the wastefulness of the despised "Washington buddy system" in which legislators spent years building alliances by agreeing to support one another's pet construction projects. For a president committed to reducing waste and judging each government program on its economic and social merits rather than its popularity with powerful interest groups or prominent politicians, the cancellation seemed logical. Politically, however, the decision angered many Democrats whose local support hinged on their ability to deliver public works to their districts.

The cancellation of water projects hurt Carter and the Democrats most notably in the West, where a complicated alliance of conservatives and environmentalists had gained support for a "Sage Brush Rebellion"—an effort by states to control federal lands within their boundaries. In Nevada, Utah, Arizona, Idaho, Montana, and Colorado, as much as 60 percent of the state's total area was federal land. Several Rocky Mountain state legislatures passed laws demanding that states take charge of federal lands to allow more grazing, logging, mining, petroleum drilling, or recreational development than the federal Bureau of Land Management or the U.S. Forest Service would permit. Earlier generations of westerners had sometimes approved of the federal government as a good steward whose efforts protected local resources in the interest of succeeding generations. But advocates of the Sage Brush Rebellion pictured Washington as the enemy, the home of haughty bureaucrats indifferent to the economic well-being of the West.

Cancellation of another water project by the Supreme Court inflamed feelings that the federal government no longer worked the way people had expected since the days of the New Deal. In *Tennessee Valley Authority* v. *Hill* (1978), the Court ruled that the TVA had to stop work on a Tennessee dam because it threatened the habitat of the snail darter, a tiny fish unique to the region. Environmentalists had brought suit under terms of the Endangered Species Act, which prevented economic development harmful to the existence of threatened species. For southerners used to the cheap electricity and recreational development afforded by the TVA, the Court's ruling brought further estrangement from the government. Initiation of the suit by environmentalists and its hostile reception by beneficiaries of the TVA demonstrated the splintering of the New Deal coalition. The TVA had once symbolized the contributions made by a federal government committed to economic growth, but in the 1970s growth itself became a controversial and divisive goal.

Some of Carter's nominees also ran into trouble with various factions of Democrats. He withdrew the name of Theodore Sorensen, former close adviser to John F. Kennedy, as his choice for director of central intelligence because conservatives objected to Sorensen's pacifism during the Second World War and his support for Daniel Ellsberg in the *Pentagon Papers* case. Later, liberals objected to Carter's nomination of an old Georgia friend, Griffin Bell, as attorney general. Bell belonged to clubs that excluded Jews and blacks, had upheld the Georgia legislature's refusal to seat Julian Bond because of Bond's opposition to the war in Vietnam, and had enthusiastically supported Nixon's controversial nomination of G. Harrold Carswell to the Supreme Court. Liberals did not like the selection of another Georgian, banker Bert Lance, to head the Office of Management and Budget. Venting frustration with Carter's preference for outsiders, veteran Democratic Senator William Proxmire of Wisconsin scoffed that Lance's government experience was "zero, zip, zilch, not one year, not one week, not one day." Lance won confirmation but resigned a few months later in response to charges that he had engaged in improper practices as head of a Georgia bank.

Carter's proposals succeeded with Congress only when it appeared that they did not require higher taxes or add to the federal deficit. For example, pursuing his campaign's distrust of the federal government, he obtained congressional support for plans to end federal price controls over transportation. Deregulation, as it had become known among academic economists in the 1970s, appeared to be a way of reducing costs to businesses by allowing them to operate with fewer government restrictions. In 1978 the Civil Aeronautics Board began the process of deregulating the airline industry, allowing carriers to set their own prices and determine their own routes. The immediate results were dramatically lower fares, more airlines, and a tripling of airline traffic. Airplanes replaced the intercity bus as the standard way to travel, even for the poor. Within a decade, however, the number of air carriers had fallen below the 1976 number, while some bus companies had gone out of business. Airlines also abandoned some cities entirely. The idea of deregulation further divided Democrats; all of them liked lower fares, but many liberals worried that the end of price controls foreshadowed similar efforts to cancel federal regulations that protected the safety and health of workers and consumers.

Divisive Social Issues

Carter's effort to compromise on divisive social issues dissatisfied important groups within his party and left an impression of a confused president who did not know where he wanted to lead the country. For example, he sought a middle ground on abortion where none existed, attempting to bridge the difference between Joseph Califano, head of the Department of Health, Education and Welfare (HEW), who opposed all abortions, and Midge Costanza, the White House liaison to women's groups, who favored a woman's unrestricted right to terminate a pregnancy. When the Supreme Court upheld Congress's amendment to the HEW appropriation, forbidding use of Medicaid funds for abortion except in cases where the life of the mother was threatened, supporters of reproductive choice complained that the decision unfairly penalized poor women. Carter responded that "there are many things in life that are unfair, that wealthy people can afford that poor people can't." His comment revived concerns of some liberals, suburbanites, and people with professional positions that his religious beliefs and regional background made it difficult for him to share the concerns of many contemporary Americans.

The Carter administration also failed to resolve the nation's deep divisions on the question of affirmative action programs. These programs, often mandated by the Equal Employment Opportunity Commission, represented an effort by businesses, universities, and other organizations to compensate the victims of generations of prejudice by giving them preference for jobs or educational opportunities. To guarantee fair representation, many such programs established minimum quotas for minority groups and for women, but this arrangement began to provoke strong resentment among the "majority," those who did not benefit from a quota. Carter supported the Supreme Court's effort to solve the dilemma in *University of California Board of Regents* v. *Bakke* (1978). Allan Bakke, a white man who had been denied admission to the university's medical school, argued that the affirmative action system had produced a reverse form of discrimination, because less qualified black applicants were admitted in his place. Although the Supreme Court decided in Bakke's favor, the ruling was highly ambiguous. A majority of the justices allowed affirmative action programs based on race but invalidated rigid quota systems. Because many Democrats themselves disagreed about affirmative action, the issue threatened to split the president's fragile coalition. The Court's sharply divided ruling failed to still the controversy about the steps that institutions should take to redress previous discrimination.

The Carter administration tried to apply *Bakke* by insisting that recipients of federal grants and contracts adopt affirmative action programs, but not require specific quotas for the protected classes. Neither supporters nor opponents of affirmative action considered Carter's position satisfactory. Disagreements about affirmative action and about "set-aside" programs for certain groups of students, employees, and contractors persisted long after *Bakke*. Many women and members of racial minority groups considered affirmative action meaningless without specific goals for hiring of employees or admission of students. On the other hand, members of traditionally white labor unions feared that affirmative action would threaten their jobs. Similarly, members of European ethnic groups whose forbears had suffered exclusion suspected that the resurrection of quotas might threaten their fragile place in American society.

Economic Problems

In the mid-1970s inflation took a heavy toll on Americans, making many worry about the future. Stagflation—the persistence of slow growth and price rises—remained a serious problem. Prices rose because the growth in American productivity slowed and because the fourfold increase in petroleum prices produced a so-called oil shock that rippled through the economy. Among the hardest hit by stagflation were people whose incomes did not keep pace with price rises. Lenders also suffered, fearing that their loans would be repaid with money worth less than the amount borrowed. Property owners actually gained wealth as the values of their houses appreciated, but their increased net worth on paper did not mitigate the daily distress at the grocery store or the gas pump. The sharp rise in consumer prices became a monotonous ordeal.

After September 1978, as the revolution in Iran sent oil prices soaring, inflation became rampant. The annual rate of increase in the consumer price index climbed steadily from an already high 7 percent in May 1978 to 11.3 percent in July 1979. The cost of goods that people bought and used everyday rose even faster. The pump price of gasoline went up by 52 percent from September 1978 to September 1979. Americans panicked, fearing they could not get gas no matter what they paid. Oil producers, refiners, and service stations took advantage of the fear to gouge consumers. By the summer of 1979, cars were lining up five hundred deep at some service stations. Motorists shouted, shook their fists, and even stabbed one another to get gas. The apparent greed and callousness on the part of the oil companies made people even madder. "It's sort of like sex," said a spokesman for Gulf Oil. "Everybody's going to get all the gasoline they need, but they're damn sure not going to get all they want." States imposed a crude form of rationing by demanding that drivers go to the pump only on alternate days.

Fear of shortages and high prices extended beyond motor fuel. As prices on home heating oil, used mostly in the Northeast and Midwest, shot up during 1979, people in these regions glumly contemplated a cold, expensive winter. Food prices also took off. Consumers felt the pinch every time they went to the supermarket, and TV news broadcasts did not let them forget it when they returned home. One of the most watched segments on the "CBS Evening News" in 1979 became a weekly survey of the cost of a standard market basket of groceries in several cities across the country. Prices climbed everywhere, and soaring fastest were basic staples of the American diet and home—beer, eggs, plastic containers, even toilet paper.

Inflation made it harder for businesses to modernize. Secretary of the Treasury Michael Blumenthal lamented that "you can't figure your rate of return, so you postpone investments." Competitors in Japan and Germany, where inflation remained below 3 percent, spent two to three times more than American firms on upgrading their manufacturing facilities. Economists foresaw a vicious cycle in which prices rose higher in the United States than abroad because businesses would not reinvest profits, but businesses would not invest for the long term until prices steadied.

At the same time, American manufacturing industries experienced a devastating decline because of foreign competition, mismanagement, and aging equipment. Observers called the industrial Midwest the "Rustbelt," a dispiriting characterization of the decline of American technology, engineering, and affluence. Emblematic of the difficulty experienced by American manufacturing was a depression in the automobile industry, once the proud symbol of the country's affluence and its preeminence in engineering. General Motors, Ford Motor Company, and Chrysler Corporation, the three large United States automakers, hardly responded to consumers' preferences for smaller, cheaper cars—which would also be less profitable to the manufacturer—in the wake of the fourfold increase in the price of fuel after 1973. Feeling the pinch at the fuel pump, people paid less attention to Detroit's slick ads and switched to small, less powerful vehicles manufactured in Germany and Japan. By 1979, nearly half the new cars sold in California, the biggest domestic market, came from abroad. Consumers discovered that imports cost less to operate, ran better, and required fewer repairs than cars made in Detroit. American car manufacturers and industry workers suffered terrible losses. United States automakers sold 9.3 million cars in 1978, but only 6.6 million in 1980. Over 200,000 highly paid workers lost their jobs in Michigan, Ohio, and Indiana, the heart of the auto industry. By 1979 Chrysler, the tenth largest company in the United States, was teetering on the brink of bankruptcy. In September 1979 Congress approved a $1.5 billion loan guarantee, or "bailout," for Chrysler. Yet employment in the auto industry continued to shrink, and foreign imports continued to grow.

Throughout the country, other kinds of manufacturing jobs declined as well, especially in large cities. New York City alone lost 234,000 industrial production jobs in the 1970s. The contracting job

At a Jones & Laughlin Steel Company plant in Youngstown, Ohio, a newly unemployed steelworker leaves his job for the last time. Steel was one of the American manufacturing industries that experienced a severe decline in the 1970s and 1980s. *Wide World Photos.*

market for unskilled workers had a severe effect on the urban poor. In earlier decades American cities had proved a magnet for unskilled European immigrants and rural blacks from the South; many of these migrants had found blue-collar work that improved their economic condition. With the loss of industrial employment, however, poverty worsened in many American cities. In northern cities especially— those of the so-called Frostbelt—the deindustrialization, declining tax base, and increased poverty nearly overwhelmed municipal services. New York City came within days of defaulting on its debt before Congress approved loan guarantees—over Gerald Ford's resistance—in November 1975. In the first municipal bankruptcy since the Great Depression, the city of Cleveland actually defaulted on its bonds in 1978.

As manufacturing industries declined, the American economy shifted toward services. The greatest job growth in the 1970s came in such services as information, entertainment, transportation, and retail sales. Local authorities struggled to arrest the decline in manufacturing by offering direct subsidies or tax abatements for service industries to relocate to their areas. New airports were constructed in

Dallas and Atlanta, increasing the growth of these Sunbelt cities. Municipalities in both the Sunbelt and Rustbelt wooed professional sports franchises with construction of new stadiums.

Perhaps ironically, in the midst of the nation's economic woes, professional and large-scale college sports expanded enormously, spurred by billion-dollar contracts from the television networks. ABC, the smallest of the three major networks, was the most aggressive in filling its schedule with sporting events. "Monday Night Football," introduced in 1970, grew in popularity throughout the decade as its unusual camera shots and the hyperbolic commentary of its announcers attracted a wide audience. As the sports franchise owners received multi-million-dollar fees from television for the rights to broadcast their games, players demanded a greater share of the profits. Baseball players struck in 1972 for the right of free agency, or the ability to bargain without restriction with any of the major league clubs. By the middle of the decade the reserve clause, which tied players to one team for as long as the owner desired, had disappeared. The best players bargained as free agents, and salaries soared. By 1979 the average baseball player earned $100,000 for a season. Earnings of professional football and basketball players quickly followed suit. Television revenues were so great that team owners could easily afford the high salaries. The reaction of ordinary citizens, both the followers of sports and people indifferent to them, was mixed. Sports provided entertainment and relief from the turbulence of the day. At the same time, the widely publicized salaries of sports figures made many people feel worse about their own declining economic conditions.

Energy and the Environment

Carter's major legislative initiative promised a national policy for energy. Since the Arab oil boycott in the winter of 1973 and 1974, Americans had spent long hours in gasoline lines, seen oil prices rise four-fold, groaned under the weight of inflation, and worried that half of their oil came from foreign sources. Experts, basing their projections on questionable assumptions that consumption would rise continuously and exploration would yield diminishing returns, predicted that oil reserves in the United States would be exhausted in twenty years and the world would run out of petroleum in fifty years.

In April 1977 Carter unveiled a series of measures to reverse these trends. Like Carter's other programs, his energy policy sought to satisfy a variety of competing and antagonistic regional and economic interests. In the process it offended more people than it pleased. He asked for the creation of a Department of Energy, eventually led by

James Schlesinger, fired as defense secretary in 1975 by President Ford. He called for tax incentives and penalties to encourage consumers to conserve energy and producers to drill more oil and gas wells. As a "last resort" he favored further development of nuclear power.

Carter delivered his first energy speech at the height of his popularity, and he appealed to the morality, goodness, and spirit of cooperation of the American people. "Live thriftily and remember the importance of helping our neighbors," he advised. He warned that "the energy shortage is permanent," encouraged his fellow citizens to begin conservation by turning down their thermostats to 65 degrees, and called his program "the moral equivalent of war." Critics quickly pounced on the contradictory nature of the program. Speaking for the right wing, Ronald Reagan complained that "our problem isn't a shortage of oil, it's a surplus of government." Liberals objected that too much had been offered to oil companies and too little to the poor. The phrase "moral equivalent of war" had the unfortunate acronym of MEOW, which was gleefully seized on by critics as an emblem of Carter's pussyfooting approach.

Congress finally passed a greatly modified version of his energy program in November 1978, about the time oil prices began another sharp rise in response to the revolution in Iran. The final law gave more benefits to both oil companies and their opponents. Appealing to advocates of alternative fuels, many of whom despised the huge multinational oil companies, the law created a Solar Energy Research Institute. On the other hand, Congress authorized investment in a giant Synthetic Fuels Corporation, controlled by Exxon, Occidental Petroleum, and Union Oil of California, to extract petroleum from rocks in Colorado, Utah, and Wyoming. Lawmakers further assisted the major oil producers with plans to spend over $10 billion to fill the "strategic petroleum reserve," first authorized in 1975, in deep Louisiana and Texas caverns.

As Congress struggled to craft an energy policy acceptable to different regions and economic interests, Americans became increasingly skeptical about the ability of technology and engineering to improve their lives. Instead they feared that modern technologies might not be safe. By the early 1970s, for example, residents of the Love Canal area in Niagara Falls, New York, had noticed foul air, blackened trees, a high incidence of cancer, numerous miscarriages, and babies born with birth defects. For several years terrified residents demanded explanations but received no satisfaction. Experts eventually traced the problems to hazardous materials buried thirty years before by the Hooker Chemical Company. The federal government declared an emergency in the area and ordered people to move. None could sell their homes, and few thought the compensation offered was adequate. The Environmental Protection Agency (EPA) warned that the hazardous materials that poisoned the land, polluted the water, and fouled the air of Love Canal might be found in hundreds of locations across the country. "There are time bombs ticking all over," one EPA officer proclaimed. "We just don't know how many potential Love Canals there are."

Fears about the safety of nuclear power, heavily promoted in the 1950s as the cleanest, cheapest form of electricity available, expanded in March 1979 when a reactor at Three Mile Island near Harrisburg, Pennsylvania, badly malfunctioned. A stuck cooling valve over-heated the reactor core, and a meltdown of the deadly nuclear fuel was barely avoided. One hundred thousand residents fled their homes, and many did not believe officials who told them two weeks later it was safe to return. The power plant itself remained perma-nently disabled, its interior deadly for any who entered. President Carter appointed a special commission to investigate what happened. When it met, one member said, "No one knew what was going on at the time, and it scares the hell out of me."

In the wake of the incident at Three Mile Island, television news-man Walter Cronkite reported that the near meltdown had raised the specter of more serious nuclear accidents in the future. As public fears mounted, electric companies responded by canceling over thirty proposed new nuclear power plants. National plans for reducing the use of improper petroleum rested in part on increased use of nuclear power, so cancellation of new nuclear plants made the dilemma of creating an effective energy policy more difficult.

The near catastrophe at Three Mile Island also fed more general fears about degradation of the environment. Washington created a $1.6 billion "superfund," paid for by taxes on polluting industries, to clean up toxic waste sites. The Carter administration also placed over 100 million acres of Alaskan land under federal protection, barring mining or petroleum development. Yet such actions could not reverse concern about the spoiling of the nation's land, air, and water supply. The environmental movement grew, and many environmentalists ex-pressed increasing skepticism about the benefits of unrestrained eco-nomic growth. People paid heed to a highly exaggerated report, from a group of international industrialists and environmentalists called the Club of Rome, which projected that continued economic growth would strain the resources of the planet, eventually creating a night-mare of famine and pollution.

A National Malaise

Overall, the public psychology in the 1970s represented a sharp break from the optimism of the period between 1945 and the 1960s. Just fifteen years earlier, optimistic Americans had expected the future to be better than the past. In the 1970s, in contrast, many feared that society was heading downward and that government leaders could not reverse the trend. By 1979 President Carter's standing had fallen sharply. Many people found themselves in the position of *Newsweek* magazine as it tried to answer the "Eptitude Question—the suspicion abroad in Washington's power factories that Carter and his Georgia irregulars had not yet fully mastered their jobs." Even the sober *New York Times* considered Carter "a sensible president, but not yet a leader or teacher, even for a quiet time."

As politicians squabbled in Washington and the president's popularity fell, backlash against government at all levels grew. In June 1978, Californians overcame the objections of Governor Brown and nearly every other prominent political, education, and business figure in the state by voting by a two-to-one margin to roll back property taxes to the levels of the mid-1960s. The popularity of Proposition 13, as the tax limitation measure was called, derived from several factors. Because of the rapid inflation in home values, taxes on California homes had tripled in the preceding decade. Moreover, voters believed that government did not provide good services for the money it collected in taxes. Anger grew as homeowners contemplated the state's $4 billion surplus. Despite accurate warnings that Proposition 13's restrictions on future tax increases would damage the state's proud public facilities—schools, universities, parks, libraries, highways—voters responded to the plan's sponsor, seventy-five-year-old gadfly Howard Jarvis, when he urged them to "take control of the government again or it will control you."

Passage of Proposition 13 alarmed officials across the country. Governor Brown quickly reversed himself and supported the tax rollback because, he observed, "this is the strongest expression of the democratic process in a decade." Elections in other states confirmed the extent of public anger, but also demonstrated its limits. Measures similar to Proposition 13 passed in four states that had experienced sharp rises in housing prices in the previous decade, but taxation or spending caps were defeated in four others.

Officeholders in both parties lost primaries to conservative insurgents who accused incumbents of supporting taxes. In Massachusetts, liberal Democratic Governor Michael Dukakis, elected first in the post-Watergate Democratic landslide of 1974, lost to a conservative who promised to reduce state taxes. Veteran liberal Republican Senator Clifford Case lost renomination to an advocate of the little-known theories of "supply-side" economists. In the next two years the idea of a substantial cut in income taxes grew from an eccentric theory into the centerpiece of conservative Republicans' program for the 1980s presidential campaign. Ronald Reagan, preparing for another run at the White House, told supporters that opposition to taxes was "a little bit like dumping those cases of tea off the boat in Boston Harbor."

Democrats felt the sting in Washington. Patrick Caddell, Carter's pollster, reflected that "this isn't just a tax revolt, it's a revolution against government." So weak had Carter become that his plan to eliminate loopholes in the federal income tax, which he had called "a disgrace to the human race," went nowhere in Congress. Opposition to new federal spending scuttled plans for national health insurance. Despairing of Carter's timidity and increasing conservatism, Democrats took heart from Senator Edward Kennedy, who at the Democratic miniconvention in December 1978 encouraged support for traditional social welfare programs. "Sometimes," he said, "a party must sail against the wind." Kennedy's powerful speech thrilled Democrats embarrassed by Carter. By the spring of 1979 many Democrats wanted Kennedy to challenge Carter for the 1980 nomination, and the senator seemed ready to make a run. Public opinion polls taken among Democrats showed Kennedy defeating Carter by a two-to-one margin.

By July 1979 President Carter's approval rating in the opinion polls had fallen to a dismal 29 percent, about where Nixon had stood on the eve of resignation. The president knew he had to do something, but what? He rejected the counsel of Vice President Mondale, who argued that the country's problems did not stem from a psychological crisis of confidence; rather, Mondale believed, people were fed up with real economic problems and demanded concrete solutions. Disregarding Mondale's insight, Carter listened to pollster Caddell, who noted a "national malaise" characterized by voters' alienation from traditional institutions. Carter pondered his next move during twelve days of introspection at the presidential retreat at Camp David. The public watched, mystified and apprehensive over his cancellation of a major speech on energy and his consultations with 150 officials and nongovernmental experts. Carter finally returned to Washington on July 15 to apologize for his administration's shortcomings. He acknowledged merit in the complaint that he had "been managing, not leading" the country, and he begged citizens to "have faith in our country—not only in the government, but in our own ability to solve great problems." The next day he fired or accepted the resignation of five cabinet members while retaining his staff of unpopular Georgians. One Democratic representative, appalled at the shakeup, exploded, "Good grief! He's cut down the tall trees and left the monkeys."

As Vice President Mondale had predicted, Carter's reappraisal failed to restore faith in national leadership. During the cabinet shakeup the president appointed Paul Volcker, a twenty-year veteran of the Treasury and the New York Federal Reserve Bank, to chair the Federal Reserve Board. Volcker confronted an economic crisis of high prices, slowed production, and mounting unemployment. As inflation continued throughout the summer of 1979, the stock market fell, and economists predicted an economic slump for the following winter. Volcker responded by driving interest rates above 15 percent to stop inflation, but by the beginning of 1980 prices were still rising, and 8 million Americans were out of work. In April 1980, the economy entered the sharpest recession since 1974. Americans wondered if people could buy a house with mortgage rates at 18 percent. Could they fill up their cars to drive to work? Would there be a job to drive to?

As inflation continued, buyers wanted to own physical assets, not bank accounts whose values declined over time. Americans withdrew $10 billion from savings and loans, where passbook accounts paid no more than 5.5 percent. Trying to stop the outflow, which further limited the amount of money available for home mortgages, Congress increased the cap on federally insured deposits in savings and loans, banks, and credit unions from $40,000 to $100,000. The run on the banks barely stopped. Scores of unscrupulous or uncredentialed financial "consultants" advised people to buy gold, silver, old paintings, or anything scarce that could be resold later. In early 1980 the Hunt brothers of Houston tried to corner the silver market, temporarily driving the price from $5 to $50 an ounce.

President Carter could do little about either the economy or the psychological "malaise" that Patrick Caddell had identified. In the aftermath of the Watergate scandal and the Vietnam War, Congress was less inclined than before to listen to a president, and by deliberately cultivating his outsider status in Washington, Carter had aggravated the problem. Even his own party granted him little authority. The public at large thought him ineffectual and perhaps ridiculous. After one of his attempts to reassure his fellow citizens that the nation's problems could be solved with time and careful planning, a Boston newspaper mocked his speech with the headline, "More Mush from the Wimp."

CHANGING ROLES FOR WOMEN AND MEN

The concerns of ordinary people went beyond their political and economic troubles. In the social sphere as well, there was a sense that old institutions no longer met personal needs. Changes begun earlier in the character of the American family, and in the way people related to one another culturally and sexually, expanded in the late 1970s.

Once considered the ideal arrangement, the nuclear family, headed by a father who worked outside the home to support a mother who cared for the children, became less and less prominent as more people ordered their lives differently. The proportion of women who worked outside the home continued to grow. By 1970 one-third of mothers with children under six years of age held or sought jobs; by 1984 52 percent had joined the work force. In 1975 the Labor Department reported that only 7 percent of American families fit the category of a "typical" four-person household—a married couple living together with their two minor children.

Some people whose lifestyles did not fit this stereotype—divorced men or women, the never married, unmarried couples living together, working women, single mothers, gay men, and lesbian women—had long been targets of anger and degradation. Now they resisted such abuse. Their numbers and self-confidence grew at a time when Americans spoke more openly about emotional issues of sexuality and gender. Yet, in many cases, those whose lifestyles differed from the earlier norms also encountered economic hardship and persistent hostility. At the same time, some traditionalists feared for their cherished values, and they joined a growing conservative movement to reverse threatening social trends.

Divorce and the Feminization of Poverty

Divorce became more commonplace in the 1970s, continuing a trend begun early in the twentieth century. By 1980 experts were predicting that one-half of new marriages would end in divorce. For those marrying for the first time, 44 percent would dissolve their union in divorce; for second or subsequent marriages the proportion of divorces was predicted to reach 60 percent. Couples divorced for many reasons: they no longer cared for one another; one of them found the other physically or mentally abusive; they believed they could make it economically outside marriage; they considered it difficult to repair their deteriorating relationship; or they no longer feared the disapproval of family, friends, religious congregation, or community. Divorce lost the stigma that had once been attached to it. A Gallup poll of young Americans revealed that 67 percent thought separation on the grounds of incompatibility a sensible solution to marital disagreement. "Why on earth," said one sixteen-year-old, "should they struggle on if they just can't make a go of it?"

These changing attitudes coincided with the enactment of "no-fault" divorce laws in every state but South Dakota and Illinois between 1970 and 1980. California led the way with a liberal law permitting either party to divorce when he or she believed that "irreconcilable differences caused the breakdown" of the marriage.

Advocates of the new family relations laws believed they would eliminate the phony testimony of abuse or adultery, the courtroom recriminations, and the skulking inquiries of private investigators that had previously made divorce a nearly unbearable experience. People in unsatisfactory marriages could now find a legal way out and retain their dignity. It was also hoped that the reduced acrimony would make it easier for divorced parents to cooperate in the future rearing of their children. Moreover, no-fault divorce changed the focus for the courts from assessing blame to dividing economic assets. The new laws tried to treat men and women equally, recognize a wife's contribution to a marital partnership, and end old assumptions that women's roles were subordinate to those of men.

No-fault divorce laws achieved many of their goals, but they also brought unintended negative consequences for women and children. On the positive side, the new laws offered hope for those who had previously contemplated years of frustration, emptiness, or abuse in dead or dying marriages. But the divorce revolution hurt at least two classes of women: older women who did not work outside the home and mothers of young children. The laws supposedly treated men and women equally, but they defined equality strictly in dollar terms. Older women who had been homemakers for years found they had few assets and limited job opportunities after divorce. Instead of compensating them for their long periods as mothers and homemakers, the new laws expected them to be as capable of supporting themselves as men were. Alimony, once a staple of divorce settlements, was awarded rarely under the new system.

The economic burden of divorce fell even more heavily on women with young children. In 90 percent of divorces children continued to live with their mothers, but these mother-child units fared poorly compared to the fathers. In the first year after a marital break-up the standard of living of divorced women and their minor children declined by 73 percent; that of divorced men rose 42 percent. Judges divided marital property equally, and in most cases the largest single asset was a family's house, which the court ordered sold. A mother with minor children, possessing only half the proceeds from the sale of a home, found herself looking for new shelter at a time of rising housing costs. Judges ordered child support, but fewer than 10 percent of the awards included provisions for inflation. Moreover, less than half of the fathers paid the full amount of child support assessed by courts; 30 percent of divorced mothers received only partial payments; and 25 percent obtained nothing at all from their former spouses.

Sociologist Diana Pearce coined the term "feminization of poverty" to describe the fastest growing segment of poor people in America.

Of course, the economic problems affected children as well as their mothers. From 1970 to 1982 the proportion of children living in poverty grew from 15 percent to 21 percent. Most of the growth came among children living in female-headed households, and most of these were led by divorced or separated women. Of the 10 million female-headed households with children, 82 percent were headed by divorced or separated women.

At the same time, childbirth among unmarried women and teenagers increased dramatically, placing further burdens on both the mothers and their children. Unskilled, uneducated, and poor young single mothers faced serious hardships. Well-paying jobs were scarce, especially in the depressed cities of the northern Frostbelt. Even when they found work, these mothers often discovered that their paychecks barely covered the cost of childcare. Some of these women, unable to find work or adequate childcare, depended on welfare payments.

The New American Family

Higher divorce rates were only one indication of profound changes in American families. Throughout the 1970s, Americans adopted a variety of alternatives to the traditional nuclear family. The number of adults living alone increased 60 percent in the seventies, so that this group constituted 23 percent of all households by 1980. Some of the increase was accounted for by older, widowed people who were living longer, but most of the rise reflected an increase in the number of single people under the age of thirty-five living alone. Even though living alone was a temporary stage for most of these people, they composed a vast consumer market for vacation clubs, sports equipment, one-person TV dinners, "Soup for One," and tiny appliances. At the same time, the number of unmarried couples living together tripled to 1.6 million, and one-third of them had children. No longer an anomaly, these unmarried, living-together households achieved some acceptance when the Department of Housing and Urban Development agreed to admit them into public housing as long as they exhibited a "stable family relationship."

Yet couples living together encountered the same difficulties over money, sex, and communication that led married people to divorce. Unmarried couples also inhabited a legal gray area, with undefined property rights. In 1977 the California Supreme Court recognized that practices "have indeed changed so rapidly in regard to cohabitation, that we cannot impose a standard based on alleged moral considerations that have apparently been so widely abandoned by many." The Court therefore ruled that actor Lee Marvin owed money—"palimony"—to Michele Triola Marvin, with whom he had lived for years.

Rates of divorce and living together rose, but so did the marriage rate. Whatever changed in practice, Americans wished for an ideal of eternal romantic attachment. Eighty percent of separated or divorced people remarried within three years, but second or third marriages fared worse than first ones. This "serial monogamy," as it soon became known, had especially dramatic effects on children. Sociologists described "blended families" in which children lived with stepparents, stepsiblings, and half-siblings. Experts projected that more than half of all children born in the seventies would spend part of their childhood living in arrangements other than a household headed by their own biological mother and father and with only their biological brothers or sisters. Forty percent would spend time in a single-parent household, almost always headed by a woman. One disadvantage of such situations was a foreboding sense of unpredictability. On the positive side, the best of these blended families offered webs of nurture and affection. When successful, the new living arrangements recreated in different form the warmth of the extended family of grandparents, aunts, uncles, cousins, the old-fashioned group of kin that many thought had been lost.

Child-rearing practices and expectations changed as more women entered the work force. Traditionally mothers had borne the brunt of child care; now non-family members did more of the work. Much of a mother's paycheck went to baby sitters or day-care facilities. Middle-class families improvised a bewildering variety of childcare arrangements. One survey of working mothers reported that their children "may experience three, four or even more kinds of care in a single week, as they spend part of the day in nursery school, another portion with a family day care mother, and are brought to and from these services by a parent, neighbor, or some other person." Single mothers, often poor, frequently left children with grandparents or other relatives. Older children of all classes let themselves into their homes after school. Left alone, these so-called latchkey children had only the companionship of other youngsters or the TV set. Experts said the average child watched 12,000 to 16,000 hours of TV between the ages of two and sixteen.

As mothers assumed a greater wage-earning responsibility, childcare experts encouraged fathers to take a more active role in raising their children. Dr. Benjamin Spock revised his *Baby and Child Care* to show that "the father's responsibility is as great as the mother's." He hoped to "eliminate the sexist biases that help to create and perpetuate discrimination against girls and women." Many men took seriously their roles as caring, involved fathers, as had men in earlier eras, but surveys of the division of labor in the American home consistently indicated that women handled much more of the housework and childcare than men. At their best, the new family arrangements provided a sense that people could control their lives. But the new patterns did not always work at their best, and they sometimes contributed to the increasing sense among parents and children alike that life had grown complicated and frightening.

Many of the changes in families and sexual relationships provoked animosity from traditionalists who considered their own way of life threatened. Opposition to the growing assertiveness of women crystallized in a movement to prevent ratification of the Equal Rights Amendment. Older women, women who did not work outside the home, and women with less than college education joined with conservative men and religious organizations in expressing concern that the ERA would diminish women's standing. In part because of opposition from such diverse groups, the ERA did not become national law. Passed by Congress and sent to the states in 1972, the ERA needed ratification by thirty-eight state legislatures before March 1979 or it would die. After quickly gaining passage in thirty-five states, supporters were stymied in the three more they needed. In July 1978, 65,000 women marched on Washington to pressure Congress to extend the deadline for three more years. It did so, but opponents continued to block passage in state legislatures, and the proposed amendment was never ratified.

Another sign of trouble in the American family came from gruesome reports of physical, sexual, and emotional abuse of children and spouses. No one knew if modern families were more violent than earlier ones, or if behavior once considered acceptable would no longer be tolerated. But the new candor about sexuality and family discord fostered new standards of acceptable conduct toward spouses and children. Most abusive acts went unreported, so that documented cases represented only the tip of the iceberg. Although hard figures were difficult to obtain, experts estimated that between 1.5 and 2.3 million of the 46 million children living with both parents between the ages of three and seventeen had been battered by one or both parents in their lifetime. Between 275,000 and 750,000 youngsters were beaten each year by adults. Similar figures were reported for domestic partners—usually, but not always, women beaten by their mates. Figures for children in single-parent households, where adults often were exhausted by the dual burdens of job and childcare, were probably higher. Sexual abuse of children also seemed to climb, with estimates of 25 percent of girls and 20 percent of boys suffering molestation from parents, stepparents, other relatives, or acquaintances. Greater attention to women's rights also brought to light the growing problem of rape within marriage or living-together relationships. The reported number of rapes and wife beatings soared, and women successfully lobbied to allow prosecution of husbands for raping wives.

The Sexual Revolution and Controversy About Pornography

The sexual revolution of the 1960s had left complicated legacies. Much to the surprise of both advocates and detractors, the idea of sexual freedom was easily absorbed into mainstream culture. Just as surprisingly, however, freedom from traditional restraints did not result in a new code of values. Openness about sex and the erosion of old restrictions freed women. They could say yes and mean it, and say no and mean it too. As more women entered the work force, they helped create sentiment against sexual harassment on the job or in the schools. At the same time, the ending of sexual taboos and the acknowledgment of female erotic desires convinced some men that women were theirs for the taking. Sales of pornographic magazines, books, and movie tickets, mostly to men, reached $4 billion per year. As women asserted their own sexual independence, pornography reaffirmed, in fantasy if not reality, the traditional power of men over women. A prostitute working for the National Task Force on Prostitution wrote, "Pornography is an expression of man's desire to have the effect on women that he knows he does not, in reality, have."

The growth of pornography divided old allies and created unlikely alignments. Advocates of the new freedoms had once resisted all restraints on the dissemination of sexually explicit material. In the 1970s, however, feminists divided over the effects of pornography. In 1976 the organization Women Against Violence in Pornography and Media arose in response to the movie *Snuff*, in which an actress was purportedly killed. Some feminists, believing that pornography incited violence against women and degraded them, joined with religious traditionalists and social conservatives to call for the regulation or banning of pornography. Other feminists joined male advocates of sexual liberation like *Penthouse* editor Bob Guccione to argue that restricting pornography, however repugnant the material, violated the freedom of expression guaranteed by the First Amendment and would eventually foster a backlash against sexual freedom.

Controversy About Homosexuality

Greater openness about sexuality encouraged the approximately 10 percent of the population who were homosexual to seek acceptance from "straight" society and the end of ingrained prejudices and stereotypes. The campaign for gay rights achieved notable gains in the seventies. For instance, the American Psychiatric Association dropped its classification of homosexuality as a "mental disorder" and joined a growing call for the extension of civil rights protection to homosexuals. A major women's conference in Houston affirmed solidarity with lesbians. But by the end of the decade the changing and often uncomfortable relations between people with different sexual orientations provided additional evidence of the fracturing of traditional institutions and the difficulty in creating new ones.

Gay men and lesbian women formed well-defined, separate communities in many large and middle-sized American cities. Although heterosexuals often focused their dislike on the sexual practices of homosexuals, gays and lesbians spoke instead of the love and caring they experienced together. They openly acknowledged their sexual orientation, formed organizations to advance their interests, and published newspapers, newsletters, and magazines addressing their concerns. Gays and lesbians lobbied municipalities, states, and the federal government to eliminate restrictions against homosexuals in employment, in housing, and in various government programs. Some laws changed, but Congress did not act to alter procedures on the national level.

Soon, advocates of conventional morality mounted a counterattack against gays and lesbians. After the Miami City Council banned discrimination against homosexuals, singer Anita Bryant began a campaign to repeal the new law. She complained that the "ordinance condones immorality and discriminates against my children's rights to grow up in a healthy, decent community." In June 1977 Bryant's Save Our Children movement organized a referendum that repealed the law by a two-to-one majority. The size of the vote shook gays and advocates of civil liberties across the country. The National Gay Task Force believed that the vote represented an effort to herd homosexuals back into the closet of denial, where many had shuddered in fear of exposure before the openness of the sixties. According to the task force, the Miami vote suggested that gay people should "pretend we don't exist so that other people can lie to their children." San Francisco Mayor George Moscone, elected with the support of the city's sizable gay community, condemned the repeal as "terribly wrong." Moscone backed a march by five thousand demonstrators against Bryant and other opponents of gay rights. But in November 1978, Moscone and Harvey Milk, the first openly gay member of the San Francisco Board of Supervisors, were gunned down by former supervisor Dan White, who had voted against San Francisco's gay rights law. Although police arrested White with the smoking gun in his hand, he won acquittal on murder charges. The jury accepted White's strange claim that excessive consumption of Twinkies had left him temporarily insane. After the jury announced its verdict, about ten thousand supporters of Milk and Moscone ran through the streets of San Francisco, chanting "He got away with murder."

RELIGIOUS REVIVAL AND A NEW CONSERVATIVE MOVEMENT

Confronting a fragmenting society and challenges to old public and private institutions, Americans expressed renewed interest in religion. In contrast to the earlier revival of the 1950s, when millions had crowded churches and synagogues that avoided dogma and ritual, the most popular sects of the 1970s promised structure, authority, orthodoxy, and a return to lost moral values. The "mainline" Protestant churches—Episcopalian, Presbyterian, Methodist, Congregationalist, and some of the Baptist groups—lost members and influence in the 1970s; so did modern Catholicism and Conservative and Reform Judaism. On the other hand, interest in fundamentalist, Evangelical or Pentecostal Protestant denominations, Mormonism, traditional Catholicism, Orthodox Judaism, and a rich variety of Eastern practices such as Zen, Hinduism, yoga, and Tibetan Buddhism surged. Much of the gain in religious observance came from young people, including members of the sixties counterculture, who looked for meaning and connections in their lives. California Governor Jerry Brown explained that young people yearned to re-establish "neighborhood and community responsibility," and churches promised that. Renewed interest in religion and traditional morality affirmed peoples' sense of their own identity in a changing and often inexplicable world.

Yet the positive contributions of religion were sometimes overshadowed by the unconventional and occasionally self-destructive behavior of some members of new groups. A few dramatic instances suggested that some Americans had become so alienated from ordinary institutions that they had lost their grip on reality. The Reverend Sun Myung Moon, a Korean evangelist with close ties to South Korea's intelligence agency, recruited thousands of mostly young Americans to his Unification Church. Known as Moonies, the church members smiled dreamily, gave their possessions to the church, lived communally, and recruited others on college campuses, in airports, and on public streets. Moon structured every moment in the lives of his followers. At one point he officiated at a mass wedding of thousands of couples who had been paired together by church officials. Conviction on tax evasion charges eventually put Moon in prison.

The most chilling episode in the group-oriented religious ferment came in November 1978, when Jim Jones and the People's Temple became household words. Jones's People's Temple attracted thousands of members, mostly poor and black, in California in the 1970s. Jones promised a racially integrated community in which people of all colors would share everything. He became prominent in San Francisco politics, but growing public opposition persuaded him to lead about a thousand of his entranced followers to the jungles of the South American country of Guyana, where they established a supposedly utopian community, Jonestown. When a congressman visited in November 1978 to investigate claims that members were being held against their will, Jones's followers murdered him. Soon thereafter, Jones and 915 People's Temple members drank cyanide-laced Kool-Aid and died. A tape recorder captured an appalling record of Jones's crazed voice encouraging believers to force poison down their children's throats and commit "revolutionary suicide protesting against the conditions of an inhumane world."

The nation reacted with horror to the news of Jonestown. By this time, some anguished parents whose adult children had joined "cults" were hiring strongmen to seize the young people and "deprogram" them. Cultural observers decried the proliferation of nonrational and antirational approaches to spirituality. For example, historian Christopher Lasch assailed the "hedonism, narcissism and cult of the self" characteristic of several new religious movements.

Writer Tom Wolfe went further, putting a label on the entire culture of the 1970s: the "Me Decade," he called it. Other commentators also criticized Americans' obsession with self-realization and self-fulfillment to the exclusion of deep social or ethical concerns. Many Bible-oriented Christian leaders were particularly distraught at the direction the country was taking. They expressed their frustrations with rapid social change by joining political conservatives in the New Right, which had been growing ever since Barry Goldwater's unsuccessful presidential campaign of 1964.

Committed to overturning liberalism and restoring old values, these religious leaders gave a strong impetus to the conservative movement. Many of them took to the airwaves as television preachers, and a huge "electronic church" developed, with a weekly audience of as many as 100 million viewers. Their popularity further eroded attendance at mainline Protestant churches, which could not offer the same flashy showmanship. The TV preachers of the New Right damned liberalism, feminism, sex education, divorce, the practice of living together without marriage, homosexuality, and the teaching of evolution in the schools. The most successful televangelists, as they were called—including Jerry Falwell, Pat Robertson, Jim and Tammy Bakker, and Oral Roberts—raised millions of dollars in contributions from their viewers. More and more, they connected religion with politics. "We have enough votes to run the country," Robertson declared. In 1979 Falwell formed the Moral Majority, an organization dedicated to "pro-God, pro-family policies in government." He urged other fundamentalist ministers to abandon Jimmy Carter and help raise converts for the Moral Majority and the Republican party.

Another element in the coalition mobilizing against the frustrations of life in modern America was a group of formerly liberal intellectuals, writers, and editors called neoconservatives. Writing for small but influential magazines like *Commentary* and *The Public Interest*, neoconservatives assailed liberals for distorting the original purposes of the welfare state by changing the emphasis from promoting equal opportunity to guaranteeing equal results. They criticized affirmative action programs as "affirmative discrimination." They maintained their earlier support of United States participation in the war in Vietnam, a stance that further alienated them from most liberals, who regretted the war and urged a less assertive American foreign policy. In 1975 neoconservatives formed the Committee on the Present Danger, which spent the next five years lobbying for additional American nuclear weapons to intimidate the Soviet Union. The emerging conservative movement added to the strength of former California governor Ronald Reagan's campaign for the Republican presidential nomination in 1980.

FOREIGN AFFAIRS IN THE CARTER YEARS

Despite Jimmy Carter's troubles on the domestic front, his administration initially succeeded in reversing the direction of American foreign policy, turning away from the Cold War and military confrontation with the Soviet Union toward advocacy of human rights abroad and sensitivity to the needs of poor nations. Early in his term, the president explained that "we are now free of the inordinate fear of communism which once led us to embrace any dictator in that fear." But momentum stopped in 1979, and the last eighteen months of the Carter administration saw a series of foreign policy rebuffs and catastrophes.

The Cold War with the Soviet Union returned with a vengeance as the Soviets became more assertive on their southern borders, in the Middle East, and in Africa. Americans who had opposed détente believed their fears had been vindicated. Distrustful of Soviet moves and fearful of conservatives at home, Carter and his advisers dropped détente, and America became more hostile to Moscow than at any other time since the early 1960s. While this change in policy was occurring, a revolution in Iran culminated in the seizure of the American embassy on November 4, 1979, and the holding captive of fifty-two United States citizens for 444 days. The Iranian hostage crisis virtually paralyzed Carter, undermined public confidence in his foreign policy, and eventually helped cost him re-election.

Triumphs in Panama and the Middle East

The Carter administration began by tackling difficult problems that had defied earlier presidents. In 1976 Gerald Ford had stopped negotiations with Panama on the future of the Panama Canal. Carter resumed negotiations, wanting to "get away permanently from an attitude of paternalism" in dealing with Latin America. In September 1977 the United States and Panama signed two treaties granting ownership of the canal to Panama on December 31, 1999, and giving the United States the right to defend the waterway thereafter. The treaties were popular in Panama and throughout Latin America, where people hoped that the American government seriously wanted to treat its neighbors as equals. Yet the hard lobbying Carter had to do to gain Senate ratification of the treaties exacted a price on his standing in his party. The treaty controversy also helped to rally Republicans behind Ronald Reagan. Reagan complained that "President Carter and his supporters in the Congress seem like Santa Claus. They have given the Panama Canal away."

Carter achieved his greatest triumph in foreign affairs by arranging the first peace treaty between Israel and one of its Arab neighbors, Egypt. As in the case of the canal treaties, the Carter administration went beyond steps taken by its predecessors and initially won praise for its actions, but ultimately provoked a political backlash. Carter believed that Egyptian President Anwar Sadat became a "man who would change history" when he courageously flew to Jerusalem in November 1977 to address Israel's parliament and offer an end to the thirty-year state of war between the Jewish state and its neighbors. Israelis were euphoric in the aftermath of Sadat's trip, while Palestinians and most Arab states other than Egypt damned him as a traitor. The excitement faded in 1978 as Egypt and Israel made little progress in their talks. It was then that President Carter became personally involved as a mediator.

Carter invited Sadat and Israel's Prime Minister Menachem Begin to a series of conversations in Washington, and in September 1978 he arranged a joint meeting with them at Camp David, the presidential retreat in the Maryland mountains. An expected three-day conference extended to thirteen days. Carter dropped all other work to concentrate on bridging the gap between Egypt and Israel. The difficult issues included the details of Israel's withdrawal from the Sinai Peninsula and the future of the 1.5 million Palestinians living under Israeli control in the West Bank and Gaza Strip. Although these issues were not resolved, Carter's determination paid off with the signing of a Framework for Peace in the Middle East that promised a treaty between Egypt and Israel, a five-year transitional authority in the West Bank and Gaza, and negotiations leading to agreement on the final status of the occupied territories.

However, the initial congratulations gave way to suspicions and recrimination. The Israel-Egyptian treaty promised in three months took six months to materialize and another round of personal diplomacy from Carter before it was signed in Washington in March 1979. The other Arab states and the Palestine Liberation Organization (PLO) refused to join the Camp David peace process and ostracized Egypt. Israel did not offer real autonomy to the Palestinians and continued its policy of not dealing with the PLO. American supporters of Israel sensed that Carter admired Sadat but distrusted Begin, and they believed that American financial and political backing for Israel had eroded. Their fears intensified in the summer of 1979 when Andrew Young, the American ambassador to the United Nations, met with the PLO's representative to the world body, in apparent violation of Washington's 1975 pledge not to deal with the PLO. Carter fired Young, but he could not erase the fears of Israel's supporters that his administration had adopted a Mideast policy less favorable to Israel.

Human Rights, Immigrants, and Refugees

Like many other critics of the foreign policy pursued by the Nixon and Ford administrations, Carter believed that the United States had ignored the fate of ordinary people in foreign countries who suffered mistreatment at the hands of their own government. Carter promised to pay far greater attention to the promotion of human rights abroad, hoping thereby to restore the United States's reputation for morality, which had been badly tarnished by the war in Vietnam. The new administration made significant progress in promoting human rights in its first two years. Congress created a new position, that of assistant secretary of state for human rights, and required the State Department to report on the status of individual rights around the globe. Governments that violated basic standards of decency might be shamed into altering their behavior by appearing on a list of abusive authorities. Congress might also reduce foreign aid to nations appearing on such a list.

But the administration soon encountered difficulty in applying standards of human rights strictly and impartially. The State Department criticized some old friends of the United States in Latin America, but political expediency caused the administration to temper its criticism of other long-term partners in important areas of the world. For example, Carter went out of his way to praise the government of the shah of Iran, and the United States continued its strong support for the corrupt regime of Ferdinand Marcos in the Philippines. By 1979 some supporters of human rights had become disillusioned with Carter's apparent inconsistencies. At the same time, Americans who stressed the Soviet threat believed that Carter's human rights policy would undermine certain anti-Communist governments.

Similar inconsistencies arose as the government grappled with the pace of immigration and refugee flight to the United States. The victory of Communist movements in Southeast Asia, combined with poverty and repression in Latin America, propelled millions of people toward the United States. Modifications of the 1965 immigration law led to the planned entry of almost half a million Asian and Hispanic immigrants annually. But this number accounted for only a small part of the total immigration.

The influx of South Vietnamese—some 130,000 in 1975—was hardly noticed at first, because most were educated, skilled, and easily assimilated into American life. From 1976 to 1980, however, a million more Vietnamese, Cambodians, Laotians, and other nationalities fled the harsh life and oppression of postrevolutionary Southeast Asia. They were often called "boat people" because they took to the seas in old, unsafe vessels. About half of them eventually found haven in the United States. The Carter administration funded resettlement programs for these unskilled, rural people, but their new neighbors greeted them coolly.

As Southeast Asians struggled for acceptance, a new wave of Cubans clamored to enter the United States. Unhappy with Fidel Castro's tough rule, many Cubans yearned for the freedom and prosperity they believed existed just a hundred miles north of their deprived island. In March 1980, thousands of Cubans took refuge in foreign embassies in Havana. President Carter believed he could embarrass the Cuban strongman by offering them asylum in the United States, but Castro trumped him by announcing that any Cuban could leave from the port of Mariel. The United States organized a flotilla to transport the *Marielitos,* but a public relations disaster ensued when Castro emptied jails and mental hospitals and ordered the inmates to board the boats for America. These criminals or deranged individuals comprised only a small number of the 130,000 Cubans, but they fanned resentment against all such refugees.

A refugee act passed in 1980 offered asylum in the United States for anyone facing a "well-founded fear" of persecution for religious, political, or ethnic reasons. In practice, people fleeing left-wing or Communist regimes were usually granted protection, but those wanting protection from right-wing authorities found their entry to the United States barred. Some 50,000 Haitian boat people were excluded during the Carter years, and this inconsistency prompted criticism of

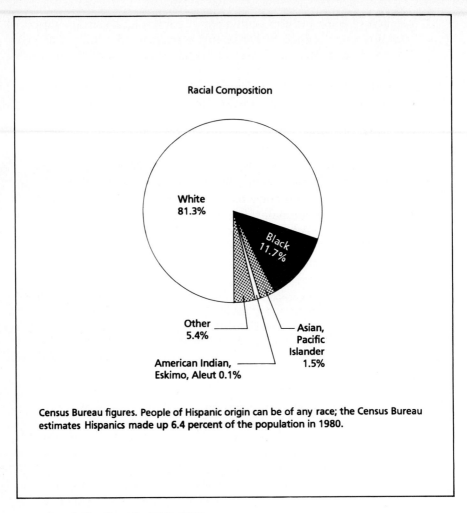

Racial Composition

White
81.3%

Black
11.7%

Other
5.4%

Asian,
Pacific
Islander
1.5%

American Indian,
Eskimo, Aleut 0.1%

Census Bureau figures. People of Hispanic origin can be of any race; the Census Bureau estimates Hispanics made up 6.4 percent of the population in 1980.

Population Growth, 1970–1980

the administration's refugee policy. Moreover, each year during the 1970s several million Mexicans crossed the border without official permission. Some left after a time, but enough stayed to create a pool of between 5 and 15 million undocumented aliens—a further indication of a gap between administration policy and reality.

The influx of millions of non-European immigrants in the 1970s had a significant impact on American population growth, hastening the development of a more multicultural society (see figure). Overall the economy benefited from the new arrivals. Like earlier immigrants, they believed the United States provided greater economic and social opportunities than they could hope for in their homelands.

They worked hard, settling in cities and towns across the country. Koreans opened small fruit and vegetable stands in New York City; Southeast Asians worked in the meat-packing plants of Garden City, Kansas; Cubans became waiters in Miami; and Chinese assembled electronic components in California's Silicon Valley south of San Francisco. The growth of the newer urban areas of the Sunbelt accelerated partly because of the new immigrants from Latin America and Asia. Yet the adjustment of the newcomers to their new land was not easy, and they provoked serious resentment. Coming at a time of economic stagnation, the new immigrants faced the prejudices people of color have often encountered in the United States. Immigrants were beaten up and their businesses and property vandalized in many cities. A movement grew to enact more restrictive immigration laws that would reduce the overall number of immigrants and stem the flow of the undocumented aliens.

The Decline of Détente

The decline of détente between the United States and the Soviet Union, begun in the Ford administration, continued in the Carter years. Nowhere did the president's lack of prior experience in foreign affairs hurt more than in dealing with the Russians. Without firm ideas of his own, Carter tried but failed to weave a coherent policy toward Moscow from the conflicting advice of his two principal foreign policy lieutenants, Secretary of State Cyrus Vance and National Security Adviser Zbigniew Brzezinski. Vance, a former Defense Department official in the Johnson administration, had come to doubt the effectiveness of military force as the Vietnam War wore on. He preferred conciliation of differences and believed that competition with the Soviet Union and communism was less important than the proper management of new international economic and social trends. Brzezinski, a Columbia professor and long-time academic rival of Henry Kissinger, regarded power politics as the key to international relations. He distrusted the Soviets and believed that the competition between them and the Western alliance remained as real as ever.

Carter first followed Vance's advice and tried to reduce tensions with the Soviet Union. The new administration tried to demonstrate that it could conclude a better arms control agreement than the SALT-II treaty, which the Ford administration had abandoned in 1976. In March 1977 Vance took to Moscow proposals to reduce each side's strategic nuclear weapons by 33 percent. Much to his surprise, the Soviets scornfully turned him down, suspecting a trick because Vance went so far beyond what Kissinger had offered. Deeply embarrassed, the Americans resumed bargaining with the Soviets on the basis of the foundations laid previously. Two years later, in June 1979, Carter and Soviet leader Leonid Brezhnev signed the SALT-II treaty limiting each side to 2,400 nuclear launchers.

Had the SALT-II treaty been ready earlier in Carter's term, the Senate might have ratified it. By 1979, however, Carter was a weak president, unpopular even among Democrats. Opponents complained that the treaty gave the Soviets advantages in land-based missiles and criticized Moscow's encouragement of revolutionaries in Africa. National Security Adviser Brzezinski supported the treaty but warned that the Soviets maintained their domineering ambitions. As Carter mobilized support for the treaty, he also tried to demonstrate his concern about threatening Soviet behavior by advocating new, more destructive weapons. In July he approved Defense Department Directive 59, which adopted a "war-fighting" rather than a strictly "deterrent" strategy for United States forces. He accepted West German requests to station midrange Pershing missiles in Europe to counter similar Soviet weapons, and he recommended that all NATO countries increase their defense spending by 3 percent above inflation. Congress and the public found such moves confusing, and in the fall of 1979 the Senate Armed Services Committee voted against ratification of the SALT-II treaty. Facing certain defeat in the full Senate, Carter withdrew the treaty from consideration in January 1980.

Carter justified shelving the treaty on the grounds that the Soviets' invasion of Afghanistan in late December 1979 represented the "gravest threat to peace" since the end of the Second World War. To punish Moscow he refused to send athletes to the upcoming Moscow Olympics, a decision that upset hundreds of would-be American participants; he also embargoed grain shipments, infuriating thousands of American farmers; and he revived registration for the draft, alarming millions of young men. Carter now ignored Vance almost completely and relied on Brzezinski's advice to confront the Soviets. His moderate supporters felt abandoned, whereas neoconservatives and other cold warriors did not trust his newfound toughness.

Bondage in Iran

Americans would have tolerated their troubles in foreign affairs had it not been for the rage and impotent frustration generated by the capture of the United States embassy and its staff in Teheran, Iran, on November 4, 1979. The revolution in Iran had simmered beneath the surface for decades. In 1953 the United States had restored Shah Mohammed Reza Pahlavi to power in a CIA-sponsored coup d'état against a government that had forced the shah into exile. The monarch had then embarked on an expensive effort to modernize his country. Flush with oil revenue, the shah had armed the largest force in the region with billions of dollars in weapons purchased from the

United States since the early 1970s. With the weapons and the development of the oil fields had come fifty thousand American technicians and military advisers. The shah's revolution from above elevated a new class of merchants and technicians who adopted Western mores and techniques. Many of them, however, also resented the monarch's iron-fisted rule. The shah's secret police jailed and tortured thousands of dissenters. Among those most hostile to the rapid social changes were followers of traditional Islam. One of the men most eager to sweep out Western influences, depose the shah, and create a society based on the *Koran* was an elderly ayatollah, or religious leader, Ruholla Khomeini. A long-time opponent of the shah, the exiled Khomeini had fervently encouraged a revolution. By February 1979 Khomeini's followers had triumphed, evicting the shah and greeting the returning ayatollah as a savior.

The Iranian revolution affected American lives directly in the spring of 1979 when the new Islamic government raised the price of oil and indirectly caused gasoline lines in the United States. Throughout the summer of 1979 the United States tried to maintain an acceptable relationship with the new Islamic leadership in Teheran. But when President Carter admitted the deposed shah to New York for medical treatment in October, he infuriated the Iranian revolutionaries. Khomeini told his followers that the admission of the shah represented a plot by "the Great Satan"—the United States—in collaboration with "American-loving rotten brains" in Teheran to restore the shah to power in Iran. Khomeini demanded that the United States deliver the shah to Iran for trial and restore his "stolen wealth" to the Islamic regime. A week later, a mob of chanting revolutionary students seized the American embassy.

The initial reaction in the United States to the capture of about seventy Americans—a group that included diplomats, marines, CIA agents, and a few private citizens doing business at the embassy—temporarily revived Carter's flagging reputation. Showing his dogged energy, he froze Iran's assets in the United States, growled that American "honor" had been besmirched by the militants, and vowed not to travel out of Washington until the hostages came home. His standing picked up among Democrats, who earlier had wanted to replace him on the 1980 presidential ticket with Senator Kennedy. Public opinion polls showed him surging ahead of Kennedy, who had finally entered the race for the nomination. Carter's "Rose Garden strategy" of concentrating on the hostage crisis and ignoring political rivals worked through February 1980, but public patience eventually wore out. After some of the hostages were released, the number in captivity declined to fifty-two, but news broadcasts kept nerves raw by ticking off the number of days they had languished in Teheran since November 4. Relatives and friends of hostages tied yellow rib-

During the 444 days of the Iranian hostage crisis that
began in November 1979, angry mobs in Teheran repeatedly taunted the United States. Jimmy Carter's inability to secure the release of the hostages before the
presidential election of 1980 was a major cause of his
defeat at the hands of Ronald Reagan. *Wide World
Photos.*

bons around trees, mailboxes, and telephone poles to keep the plight
of the captives firmly in the public mind. Senator Kennedy assailed
Carter for "lurching from crisis to crisis," and Ronald Reagan, running for the Republican nomination, implied that "our friend" the
shah would not have lost his throne if the Carter administration had
not betrayed him by criticizing his secret police for torturing political
opponents. Reagan also suggested that Carter's inability to free the
prisoners reflected his general lack of competence.

In April Carter accepted Brzezinski's advice to mount a military
mission to rescue the hostages. Secretary of State Vance objected; he
had promised European allies that the United States would not use
force, and he believed the complicated plan would not work. He told
Carter that he would resign after the operation whether it succeeded

or failed. On April 24 eight helicopters took off from an aircraft carrier in the Persian Gulf, en route to a desert rendezvous with transport planes. One chopper malfunctioned, and the remaining seven flew into a dust storm. Two more were abandoned, and the site commander decided that the five remaining helicopters were not enough to mount a successful rescue operation. He telephoned the White House that he was withdrawing the rest of the force. After receiving orders to leave the desert landing site, another helicopter collided with a refueling plane, killing eight servicemen. The White House announced the failure of the mission, Vance resigned, and some Americans believed the aborted mission was yet another demonstration of the limits of technology.

After the failure of the rescue attempt, public concern about the fate of the hostages diminished slightly. Carter finally left the White House to campaign actively for the presidency. Behind the scenes diplomacy proceeded, and the administration tried to arrange a deal with Iran for the captives' release before election day, November 4, 1980. Unfortunately for Carter's re-election chances, the efforts did not bear fruit until early 1981. One reason the Iranians refused to return the prisoners before the election might have been that they received promises of future favors from the Reagan camp if they kept the hostages until Carter left office. Gary Sick, a staff member on Carter's National Security Council, charged in 1991 that the Reagan campaign promised Iran arms if Teheran retained the prisoners beyond the election. The hostages finally flew to freedom on January 20, half an hour after Ronald Reagan took the oath of office as president.

THE ELECTION OF 1980

The failure to gain the release of the hostages sealed Carter's fate with the electorate. He defeated Kennedy for the Democratic nomination, but the 35 percent of the delegates favoring the challenger sent an ominous sign for the fall. Carter's advisers believed he could overcome Reagan, the Republican candidate, by picturing him as a dangerous reactionary. They feared that a third-party candidate, former Republican congressman John Anderson, presented the greater danger, because he could appeal to middle-of-the-road voters fed up with Carter's apparent incompetence. By Labor Day polls were showing Carter and Reagan running even, with Anderson receiving 15 percent of the vote. Carter refused to participate in a debate with Reagan and Anderson in late September, not wanting to add credibility to the third contender in the race. Anderson's support then dribbled away in October as voters concentrated on the only viable choices—Carter and Reagan.

Finally, Carter and Reagan debated head to head. Carter believed that his greater intelligence and command of the facts would make his conservative challenger appear untrustworthy, but the president badly miscalculated. Carter recalled the limits of the last few years: "We have demanded that the American people sacrifice, and they have done that very well." Reagan, on the other hand, reminded voters how much austerity hurt: "We do not have to go on sharing in sacrifice," he said. Reagan's training as an actor carried the day. Simply by standing next to Carter and not appearing confused or saying something foolish, Reagan became acceptable to people who wanted something, anything, different from what they had experienced in the recent past. In his summary remarks he looked directly at the camera with his cheerful blue eyes and told Americans to "ask yourself, are you better off than you were four years ago?"

Presidential Election of 1980

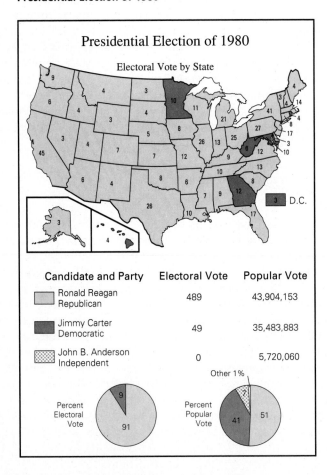

Presidential Election of 1980

Electoral Vote by State

Candidate and Party	Electoral Vote	Popular Vote
Ronald Reagan Republican	489	43,904,153
Jimmy Carter Democratic	49	35,483,883
John B. Anderson Independent	0	5,720,060

Percent Electoral Vote: 91 / 9

Percent Popular Vote: 51 / 41 / Other 1%

A week later, voters answered with a sharp "No!" Opinion surveys showed Carter's support collapsing in the weekend before polling day, as it became clear that the hostages would not yet come home. Voters believed that whatever Reagan did would be an improvement on the hand wringing, the sermons, and the demands for sacrifice of the Carter years. Reagan won 51 percent of the popular vote, Carter 41 percent, and Anderson 7 percent (see map). For the first time since 1954 the Republicans carried the Senate, and they gained 33 seats in the House. "It's a fed-up vote," observed Pat Caddell, Carter's pollster.

CONCLUSION

In the aftermath of Watergate, the Vietnam War, and the upheavals of the 1960s and early 1970s, Americans longed for inspiring leaders and more effective public institutions. Yet the disillusionment and disorientation of the recent past ran so deep that politicians found it virtually impossible to restore public faith in government. Gerald Ford and Jimmy Carter both confronted problems that exceeded their capabilities. Ford, an unelected leader, lacked both a base of popular support and a clearly articulated view of how to restore public confidence. Carter had some advantages over his predecessor, because he could credibly claim to be an outsider who, like most ordinary Americans, was not responsible for the disappointments of the Johnson and Nixon years. By 1980 it became apparent, however, that Carter's good intentions, intelligence, and firmly rooted moral values would not be enough.

The economic and social developments of the times frustrated both the nation's leaders and the public at large. Soaring inflation and a decline in manufacturing industries put the country's economic future in doubt, raising fears that the standard of living would inevitably decline. The oil shock stimulated worries about scarce resources, and at the same time Americans became more aware of the environmental costs of industrial and nuclear development. Although the cultural changes of the 1960s had brought a new sense of freedom to personal relationships, the 1970s also saw a rise in divorce rates, a further decline in the nuclear family, and a confusing growth of alternative living arrangements. Sex was more open but not necessarily happier. Women and gays demanded new respect, but pornography boomed. Many alienated people took refuge from these bewildering trends in new religious sects, some of which were authoritarian or violent. Others turned to a reaffirmation of traditional, Bible-oriented religion, and some were galvanized by televangelists who denounced liberalism, divorce, and all the new social and sexual freedoms.

Crystallizing many of the public frustrations, the television preachers and other conservatives formed political organizations that helped to mobilize support for conservative candidates. When President Carter failed to resolve the Iranian hostage crisis before the 1980 election, the public found a final reason to reject him and turn instead to Ronald Reagan, a conservative champion who promised Americans that their future could still be bright, free from the limitations and the malaise of the 1970s. ∎

F U R T H E R   R E A D I N G

General accounts of society and politics in the 1970s include: Peter N. Carroll, *It Seemed Like Nothing Happened* (1982); Christopher Lasch, *The Culture of Narcissism* (1979); Steve Fraser and Gary Gerstle, eds., *The Rise and Fall of the New Deal Order, 1930–1980* (1989); Michael Barone, *Our Country* (1990); Theodore H. White, *America in Search of Itself, 1956–1980* (1982). On public policy, see: Gerald Ford, *A Time to Heal* (1977); Robert T. Hartmann, *Palace Politics: An Inside Account of the Ford Years* (1980); A. James Reichley, *Conservatives in an Age of Change* (1980); Jimmy Carter, *Keeping Faith: Memoirs of a President* (1981); Mary Berry, *Why the ERA Failed* (1986); Nathan Glazer, *Affirmative Discrimination* (1975); J. Harvey Wilkerson, *From Brown to Bakke* (1979); Melvin Urofsky, *The Continuity of Change: The Supreme Court and Individual Liberties, 1953–1986* (1991); William Julius Wilson, *The Truly Disadvantaged: The Inner City, the Underclass, and Public Policy* (1987).

On women and the family, see: Kristen Luker, *Abortion and the Politics of Motherhood* (1984); Winnifrid D. Wandersee, *On the Move: American Women in the 1970s* (1988); Lenore J. Weitzman, *The Divorce Revolution* (1985). On economic changes, see: Barry Bluestone and Bennett Harrison, *The Deindustrialization of America* (1982); John P. Hoerr, *And the Wolf Finally Came: The Decline of the American Steel Industry* (1988); David Halberstam, *The Reckoning* (1986), about the decline of the auto industry; Lester C. Thurow, *The Zero Sum Society* (1980); William Greider, *Secrets of the Temple: How the Federal Reserve Runs the Country* (1987); Daniel Yergin, *The Prize* (1991), about petroleum policy. On foreign affairs, see: Raymond L. Garthoff, *Détente and Confrontation: American-Soviet Relations from Nixon to Reagan* (1985); William Hyland, *Mortal Rivals: Superpower Relations from Nixon to Reagan* (1987); Gaddis Smith, *Morality, Reason and Power: American Diplomacy in the Carter Years* (1986); Zbigniew Brzezinski, *Power and Principle: Memoirs of the National Security Adviser* (1983); Cyrus Vance, *Hard Choices: Critical Years in American Foreign Policy* (1983); James Bill, *The Eagle and the Lion: The Tragedy of American-Iranian Relations* (1987); Gary Sick, *All Fall Down: America's Tragic Encounter with Iran* (1986); William Quandt, *Camp David* (1987); Walter LaFeber, *The Panama Canal* (1990).

13

Happy Days: The Reagan Years at Home

In 1986 financier Ivan F. Boesky addressed graduating business students at the University of California at Berkeley. Celebrated for his uncanny ability to buy underpriced shares of stock in companies about to be acquired in lucrative mergers, Boesky told his audience that "greed is healthy." Earning and flaunting great wealth, Boesky implied, was the driving force of capitalism, growth, and prosperity. The students sat rapt as this titan of finance explained the canon of the free market. That fall, however, the Justice Department charged Boesky with massive violations of security law. He pleaded guilty to buying inside information from corporate officials, which he then used to manipulate stock prices, acquire companies, and earn, with his associates, a profit estimated in the billions of dollars. Film director Oliver Stone chronicled the rise and fall of a Boesky-like tycoon in the popular movie *Wall Street*, a cautionary tale about the glitter and deceit of the 1980s.

However, the chief emblem of the times was not Wall Street or Ivan Boesky but the reassuring, cheerful president, Ronald Reagan, who presided over the era. Reagan's favorite speechwriter, Peggy Noonan, "had the feeling he came from a sad house and he thought it was his job to cheer everyone up." Catching the spirit of the man and age, Noonan drafted the president's best-received lines for his 1984 re-election triumph. "America is back," she wrote; "it's morning again." College students especially liked such talk of renewal from America's oldest serving president. On campuses where a few years before undergraduates had raged about Lyndon Johnson and Richard Nixon, twenty-year-olds screamed "U.S.A.! U.S.A.!" in response to Reagan's oratory. He tapped a popular yearning to restore a sense of community, real or imagined, that had been lost over the previous two decades. In some ways, Reagan captured the same mood as the television comedy series "Happy Days," which ran on ABC from 1974 through 1984. Expressing a national nostalgia for the 1950s, the show offered funny stories full of the innocence and hope that Americans wanted to believe they still possessed.

At the height of Reagan's popularity in 1986, *Time* magazine described the seventy-five-year-old president as a "Prospero of American memories, a magician who carries a bright, ideal America like a holograph in his mind and projects its image in the air." On the other hand, leading Democrats dismissed Ronald Reagan as an "amiable dunce," and journalists chronicled his many gaffes, such as blaming redwood trees for air pollution. One irate scholar complained that Reagan was the "first modern president whose contempt for the facts is treated as a charming idiosyncrasy." But journalist Bill Moyers hit nearer the mark when he observed, "We didn't elect this guy because he knows how many barrels of oil are in Alaska. We elected him because we want to feel good."

As he exhorted all Americans to believe in their country's greatness, Reagan pursued policies that benefited tycoons like Boesky while neglecting those at the bottom of the economic ladder. During his two terms in office, Reagan reversed many of the liberal programs and values that had dominated national politics since the New Deal. His administration worked to roll back the social welfare network, limit the role of federal courts in promoting civil rights and liberties, reduce government regulation of business and protection of the environment, slash taxes, and foster a conservative social ethic in such areas as abortion rights and the role of religion in public life. Reagan's team insisted that by removing the dead weight of government from the private economy, they could unleash market forces that would create new wealth and foster greater equality. Some commentators said that the long economic expansion of the 1980s proved that the Reagan approach was right. Others pointed to rising homelessness and poverty as a sign that Reagan's happy days were not for everyone. In any case, for most of his presidency, Reagan enjoyed such a high level of public approval that many Americans ignored the substance of his policies and the fact that the results of his administration's actions often contradicted his own beliefs or promises.

THE EMERGENCE OF RONALD REAGAN

Born in Tampico, Illinois, in 1911, Ronald Reagan grew up in a series of small towns along the Mississippi River. He recalled his youth as "one of those rare Huck Finn–Tom Sawyer idylls." Mark Twain's novels actually chronicle hate, superstition, racism, and violence in nineteenth-century America, but Reagan referred to a sanitized version of preindustrial America, his mental world subtly distorted, as one biographer noted, "toward small perfections, like the buildings in Disneyland." In truth, as the younger son of an alcoholic father and a religiously fervent mother, Reagan had a childhood that resembled Twain's novels in ways he preferred not to recall. The family had little money and relocated frequently, often just ahead of the bill collector.

Nevertheless, Reagan's mother encouraged him to participate in amateur theater, and he acted in plays during high school and college. More fortunate than most other children of the depression era, Reagan attended the religiously affiliated Eureka College and after graduation found work as a sports announcer at a small Iowa radio station. He narrated re-creations of baseball games that came into the station via telegraph, describing the games as if they were live. Reagan supplied colorful details and anecdotes so well that many listeners preferred his version to the real thing.

During the harshest years of the depression, Reagan's father Jack sustained the family by working for a New Deal relief agency. Reagan became an avid Roosevelt supporter; he often memorized segments of Roosevelt's speeches and recited them for his friends. Long after Reagan had rejected the New Deal programs, he continued to sprinkle his public statements with lines from Roosevelt. It was Roosevelt, the political optimist and inspirational hero, not the social reformer, who gripped Reagan's imagination.

While covering the Chicago Cubs' spring training in California in 1937, Reagan took a screen test and won a contract with the Warner Brothers film studio. His most memorable prewar films, *King's Row* and *Knute Rockne: All American,* were exceptions to the light, romantic adventures the studio usually cast him in. In 1940 he married actress Jane Wyman. The couple adopted one child and Jane gave birth to a second. Reagan then spent the Second World War in Hollywood, working for an Army Air Corps unit that made morale-boosting films. He probably felt self-conscious about his comfortable assignment, because in later years he concocted elaborate stories about acts of heroism he claimed to have witnessed at the front, and he even implied he had helped to liberate a Nazi concentration camp. In fact, during the war Reagan never left the United States and rarely left Hollywood.

After 1945 Reagan's film career declined, but he became increasingly active in the Screen Actors Guild, serving as union president from 1947 to 1952. Although his marriage to Jane Wyman ended in divorce in 1949, in 1952 he married another actress, Nancy Davis, who soon gave him two more children. During this period, fear of communism transformed his political outlook, as it did for many other Americans. He committed himself to the fight against "the Communist plan . . . to take over the motion picture business" by cooperating with the studio heads and the FBI to blacklist actors, directors, and writers he called "our little Red brothers." Fearing he would become a target of a Red hit squad, Reagan took to carrying a gun for protection.

Reagan's career took a new turn in 1954 when General Electric hired him to host its weekly television series and deliver corporate speeches. Over an eight-year period, Reagan visited GE plants throughout the country, speaking to executives, assembly-line workers, and local chambers of commerce. His after-dinner presentations invariably included an ode to "traditional values," a warning about contemporary threats, and entertaining anecdotes. Year in and year out, Reagan warned of communism abroad and creeping socialism at home. He told audiences that "the individual was, and should be forever, the master of his destiny." Recanting his support for the New Deal—though not relinquishing Roosevelt's best lines—he described business leaders as the dam restraining the socialist tide, despite the burdens of high taxes, government regulation, and Social Security imposed by liberals. Even after he left GE's employment in 1962, Reagan devoted the bulk of his time to delivering the speech he had perfected since 1954. It played particularly well among conservative groups in southern California.

Reagan's Early Political Career

In 1964 Barry Goldwater emerged as the white knight of the conservative movement. Nominated that year for president by the Republican party, he promised to dismantle the New Deal legacy. Yet Goldwater proved a divisive and unpopular candidate, easily caricatured as an extremist itching to unleash a nuclear war and send the elderly and infirm into the poorhouse. Late in the faltering campaign, Reagan offered to make a televised fund-raising speech on Goldwater's behalf.

On paper, the text seemed such a lifeless collection of antigovernment, anti-Communist cliches, with scant mention of the Republican nominee, that Goldwater's staff almost canceled the appearance. But this reading underestimated Reagan's emotional appeal. Brazenly lifting some of the best-known phrases of Franklin Roosevelt, Winston Churchill, and Abraham Lincoln, Reagan declared,

You and I have a rendezvous with destiny. We can preserve for our children this, the last best hope of man on earth, or we can sentence them to take the first step into a thousand years of darkness. If we fail, at least let our children, and our children's children, say of us we justified our brief moment here. We did all that could be done.

Inspired viewers contributed $1 million to the foundering Goldwater campaign. This late infusion of cash did not prevent Goldwater from losing to Lyndon Johnson, but it launched Reagan's political career. Within a few months of Johnson's landslide victory, a group of wealthy Californians organized a "Friends of Ronald Reagan" committee to promote his candidacy for governor of California. At the time, most Republican and Democratic officials dismissed Reagan as a political dilettante, much to their later regret.

Political consultant Stuart Spencer took Reagan under his wing and developed a list of anecdotes, issues, answers, and human interest stories, all arranged on five-by-eight-inch index cards. During the 1966 gubernatorial primary campaign, Reagan spoke for short periods of time, before selected audiences, and avoided questioning by the press. After winning the Republican primary he took aim at the Democratic incumbent, Governor Edmund G. "Pat" Brown.

"I am not a politician," Reagan declared. Instead, he characterized himself as an ordinary citizen opposed to high taxes, government regulation, big spending, waste, and fraud. He promised to reduce the size and scope of state government and to throw out the rascals who had mismanaged the state. In fact, Governor Brown had presided over a period of immense growth in California. Higher education, social services, highways, and water projects had expanded tremendously. But many middle-class citizens resented rising taxes; and the violent Watts riots of 1965, the Berkeley Free Speech Movement, and the student antiwar movement, had left them increasingly hesitant to follow a moderate Democratic governor.

Reagan proved an extremely adept campaigner, especially on television. He focused voter attention on symbolic issues like freedom, personal autonomy, and "traditional values." He linked the moderate Brown to big government, high taxes, welfare cheats, ghetto riots, judges who "coddled criminals," and the "mess" at Berkeley. Despite Brown's efforts to portray Reagan as a dangerous extremist, California voters viewed the challenger as a warm, pleasant man aroused by grievances they shared. In the November election Reagan trounced Brown by a margin of nearly 1 million votes.

Inaugurated in the middle of the night in January 1967—as recommended by Nancy Reagan's astrologer—Governor Reagan took office with no particular agenda. Several months into his first term, he seemed stumped by a reporter's query about his legislative priorities. Turning to an aide he remarked, "I could take some coaching from the sidelines, if anyone can recall my legislative program." Initially he did little more than order across-the-board budget cuts for state agencies, impose a hiring freeze, and ask state employees to work without pay on holidays.

Overall, during his two terms as governor, Reagan combined conservative rhetoric with fairly flexible policies. Several times he sent state police to quell disturbances on the Berkeley campus, and he forced out several liberal administrators. But he never followed through on threats to slash education spending and to investigate "communism and blatant sexual misbehavior" at Berkeley. In 1967 he blamed his predecessor for leaving him a budget deficit, then approved the largest tax increase in state history. Although he boasted of cutting state spending, during his two terms spending doubled, from less than $5 billion per year to $10 billion. When the legislature passed one of the nation's most liberal abortion bills, Reagan signed it, later claiming he was unfamiliar with its provisions.

After finishing his second term as governor in 1975, Reagan returned to the speaker's circuit until, infuriated by President Gerald Ford's selection of liberal Republican Nelson Rockefeller as vice president, Reagan resolved to challenge the incumbent in 1976.

Reagan as a Candidate for President, 1976–1980

Entering the Republican presidential primaries in 1976, Reagan tried to arouse interest in a plan to "save" $90 billion by transferring federally funded social programs to the states. When this issue fell flat, he began attacking President Ford and Secretary of State Henry Kissinger for pursuing arms control and détente with the Soviet Union. Instead of "placating potential adversaries," Reagan called for tougher assertions of American power. He raised particular objections to negotiations to "give away" the Panama Canal.

Ford beat back Reagan's challenge but went on to lose the general election to Jimmy Carter. Reagan then geared up for the 1980 election by resuming his criticism of the Panama Canal treaty negotiations and demanding massive rearmament to counter the growing military power of the Soviet Union. He also supported the tax rebellion evidenced by voter initiatives such as Proposition 13 in California; he called for drastic cuts in federal income tax rates to match events on the state level.

During the 1980 presidential primaries, Reagan continued to emphasize these and similar themes. Economic stagnation, the collapse of détente, and particularly the Iranian hostage crisis made the public receptive to his call for a dramatic change in leadership. Although his chief rival for the Republican nomination, George Bush, referred to his economic ideas as "voodoo economics," Reagan secured the nomination handily and then chose Bush as his running mate. In the general election campaign he avoided stressing his more extreme beliefs, such as his long-time dislike for Social Security; instead, he focused on the themes of renewal, strength, and national pride. "This is the greatest country in the world," he declared. "We have the talent, we have the drive, we have the imagination. Now all we need is the leadership." He ridiculed those who claimed that "the United States has had its day in the sun." Most Americans, he believed, hungered for "a little good news" and for a leader who promised renewed American strength and success. Reagan projected common sense, spoke of grand traditions, and offered simple, reassuring answers to complex questions.

The generalities paid off in his sweeping victory over President Carter in the November election. Only a tenth of those who voted for Reagan told pollsters that they had selected him because he was "a real conservative"; rather, they were disgusted with Carter and attracted to Reagan's vision of a happier, more powerful, less divided America. The election results also showed a notable "gender gap" and "age gap": Reagan drew far less support from women and from the elderly than from young men. Significantly, barely half those eligible cast ballots; many Americans responded to the choice of presidential candidates by choosing no one.

Whether Reagan's victory represented a conservative consensus or not, the conservatives had in fact won considerably more power. Not only did Republicans take control of the Senate and pick up nearly three dozen additional House seats, but several key liberals, such as Senators Frank Church and Birch Bayh, were unseated, often because their opponents had received hefty campaign financing from conservative political action committees. The successful targeting of liberals by conservative groups left Democratic leaders like House Speaker Thomas P. "Tip" O'Neill shell-shocked and in awe of the conservative champion, Ronald Reagan.

THE REAGAN REVOLUTION

In his inaugural address Reagan stressed a few general economic grievances, such as inflation and a burdensome tax system. Playing to the widely held disillusion with public policy, he declared, "In this present crisis, government is not the solution to our problem, government *is* the problem." He pledged to cut inflation, taxes, and wasteful social programs.

In an astute move, Reagan had reached outside his conservative circle to appoint James A. Baker III, a close friend of Vice President George Bush, as White House chief of staff. A veteran of Washington politics, Baker recalled Lyndon Johnson's insight after his landslide victory in 1964: "You've got just one year when Congress treats you right, then they start worrying about themselves." Baker argued that key legislation must be passed during the first few months of the Reagan administration, while the Democrats were in disarray and while Congress offered its traditional deference to a new president. He persuaded Reagan to push for the two things the president wanted most: tax cuts and a defense build-up. "If we can do that," Baker predicted, "the rest will take care of itself." Many conservatives would have liked Reagan to lead a crusade on key social issues—a strong campaign, for example, for constitutional amendments outlawing abortion and legalizing prayer in public schools. But the president showed some of the flexible pragmatism he had displayed as governor of California. Although he often voiced his concern about such issues as abortion and school prayer, he agreed with Baker not to press them very hard with Congress.

The Economic Agenda

Since the 1950s, Reagan had criticized high taxes. A wealthy man, he resented the progressive income tax and told stories indicating that high tax rates discouraged the rich from working harder. He believed that people should be rewarded for achieving wealth, not taxed at higher rates for doing so. On the other hand, he derided "welfare queens" who drove Cadillacs and had their snoots in the public trough. Taken to its extreme, his argument seemed contradictory: the rich would not work harder because they could not keep enough money; the poor did not work harder because they had access to too much money.

However, it was not just an issue of working harder. Like many other conservatives, Reagan believed that a tax cut would promote industrial growth as well as personal wealth. Freed from the burden of excess taxes and given extra capital to work with, the nation's entrepreneurs would unleash the market forces that would spur an economic revival.

Reagan also emphasized the dangers of deficit spending by the government. The Democrats, he said, had "mortgaged our future and our children's future for the temporary convenience of the present." With the national debt approaching a trillion dollars, disaster loomed. The nation would have to stop living beyond its means; in particular, it would have to lower its social expenditures. Besides reducing the deficit, Reagan believed, lower social spending would encourage people to help themselves rather than depend on the government.

Reagan based much of his economic policy on the ideas of Arthur Laffer, a little-known economist. Laffer espoused the irrefutable notion that tax rates set too high or too low would yield insufficient revenues. As rates approached 100 percent, business activity would cease; as rates approached zero, no taxes would be collected. He drew a simple graph (the Laffer curve) representing this concept but neglected to include any numbers. It remained anybody's guess what ideal tax rate would both stimulate economic growth and yield sufficient revenues to reduce the deficit.

Influenced by Laffer's ideas, Republican Congressman Jack Kemp of New York and Senator William Roth of Delaware had propounded a plan in the late 1970s to cut personal and business taxes by 30 percent. Dubbing the concept "supply-side economics," they predicted that lower tax rates would encourage business activity and investments. The Kemp-Roth plan languished during the Carter administration, but when Reagan met Laffer in 1980, the economist's ideas set off what an aide called "a symphony in his ears."

In January 1981, President Reagan unveiled his economic plan before a joint session of Congress. He endorsed a proposal that cut most federal income and business taxes by 25 percent over three years, lowered the top income tax rate from 70 percent to 50 percent, eliminated "bracket creep" (the tendency of inflation to push taxpayers into higher brackets), reduced taxes on capital gains, lowered estate and gift taxes, and allowed faster depreciation on business investments. To reduce federal costs, Reagan also proposed to shift many social programs from the federal government to the states, eliminate numerous welfare programs, trim Social Security benefits, and cut back on parts of the federal bureaucracy that regulated business, the environment, and public health.

Congress enacted most of what the president asked for. The Democratic majority in the House managed to limit some of the social welfare spending cuts proposed by the Reagan administration. On the issue of tax cuts, however, public support proved so overwhelming that the Democrats could not insist on a compromise. Moreover, Reagan convinced many conservative Democrats that a combination of tax and spending reductions would jump-start the economy and lead to a surge in growth that would easily make up for the revenues lost by lowering tax rates. Congress therefore approved the tax cuts as well as many domestic spending reductions during the summer of 1981.

An Economic Seesaw

An economic recession, the worst since the 1930s, began late in 1981 and lasted almost two years. Unemployment rose to over 10 percent, while business failures, farm foreclosures, and homelessness increased dramatically. Critics began to charge that the reduction in taxes and benefits helped the rich and hurt the poor. Reagan's approval rating declined, and the Democrats made substantial gains in the 1982 congressional elections. Nevertheless, Reagan refused to alter his priorities. He blamed the recession and the growing budget deficit on problems inherited from President Carter and predicted that the worst effects would pass before 1984.

Reagan's prediction proved partially correct. The tight-money policy espoused by Federal Reserve Board Chairman Paul Volcker, a Carter appointee, squeezed inflation out of the economy. The rate of inflation fell from about 14 percent in 1980 to below 2 percent in 1983. Interest rates declined from 21 percent to a still high 11 percent. Changes in world markets drove down oil prices, stimulating recovery, at least outside the oil-producing states. Massive defense spending created a boom in high technology and in the aerospace industries of New England, the Southwest, and the West Coast.

By the end of 1983, the worst of the recession had passed. The subsequent economic expansion lasted beyond Reagan's departure in 1989. Supply-siders took credit for creating over 18 million new jobs, spurring economic growth, lowering federal tax rates, and tripling the average price of stocks. Journalists and many Americans agreed that the final six years of Reagan's term marked a period of broad prosperity.

Defense Spending

"Defense is not a budget item," Ronald Reagan told his staff; "you spend what you need." And spend they did. As the new administration took office, Defense Secretary Caspar Weinberger proposed an annual increase amounting to almost 10 percent of the last Carter budget. Over five years, total defense expenditures would reach almost $1.5 trillion. Because of a mathematical mistake discovered belatedly by Budget Director David Stockman, planners had erred in their effort to cap military outlays a few hundred billion dollars below this figure. When Stockman sought to trim the larger-than-intended defense budget, Weinberger complained that even tiny reductions would virtually disarm the Pentagon.

At a White House conference with Reagan, Weinberger displayed impressive charts that showed Soviet nuclear and conventional forces dwarfing those of the free world. Weinberger also held up a poster showing three cartoon soldiers:

One was a pygmy who carried no rifle. He represented the Carter budget. The second was a four-eyed wimp who looked like Woody Allen, carrying a tiny rifle. That was [Stockman's] budget. Finally there was G.I. Joe himself, 190 pounds of fighting man, all decked out in helmet and flak jacket and pointing an M-60 machine gun.

Stockman later said he could hardly believe that a Harvard-educated cabinet officer would bring such a display to the president. "Did he think the White House was on Sesame Street?" But Reagan, committed to keeping the United States preeminent in military strength and determined to challenge the Soviets in foreign policy (see Chapter 14), did not want to deny the armed forces anything they might conceivably need. Even as he cut social programs to reduce the deficit, he accepted Weinberger's proposal for a large increase in defense spending, and Chief of Staff Baker shepherded it through Congress. During Reagan's two terms the defense budgets were the largest in peacetime history.

THE GREAT COMMUNICATOR

Unlike Jimmy Carter, President Reagan had a great deal of success with Congress. Although the Democrats still controlled the House, Reagan managed to have his defense increases, his tax cuts, and many of his social spending cuts enacted. Part of this success stemmed from the abilities of aides such as Baker, but much of it came from Reagan's own personality. He melted the resistance of hard-bitten senators and representatives with anecdotes and grins. He told corny jokes so well that few listeners complained when he repeated them. Even his ideological enemy, Democratic House Speaker Tip O'Neill, admitted that in the evening he liked sitting down to swap Irish stories with the president.

If his charm failed to work with Congress, Reagan appealed directly to the American people. On several occasions, his request that citizens call or write their representatives helped to change close votes. With his experience as a film star and television host, he proved a master of the electronic media, earning the nickname "The Great Communicator." Moreover, his three closest first-term advisers—James Baker, Michael Deaver, and Edwin Meese—understood the role the media played in assuring success. As one observer commented, each presidential action was designed "as a one minute or two minute spot on the evening network news"; every presidential appearance was conceived "in terms of camera angle." For a large portion of the public, television was reality. If Reagan's appeal worked on TV, it did not matter that he depended on cues from a teleprompter. With his uncanny ability to turn clichés into winning phrases, he fostered in his audience a sense of community and a renewed identification with government.

Reagan perfected what some historians have called the "ceremonial presidency." With his ruddy good looks, the richness and tremor in his voice, the twinkle in his eye, he fulfilled the ideal of what a president should be. He loved the trappings of the presidency—the helicopters, parades, and troop reviews. His self-confidence made him appear to be an effective leader, regardless of where he led.

In times of uncertainty, Reagan projected a decisive and reassuring character. When unionized air traffic controllers violated a no-strike law and walked off the job in August 1981, Reagan promptly fired them. Although some people worried about safety in the skies, the public generally considered the controllers' salary demands outrageous and admired Reagan for ordering military personnel to keep commercial planes in operation. Similarly, after the tragic explosion that killed the entire crew of the space shuttle *Challenger* in January 1986, Reagan calmed and soothed millions of grieving Americans. His moving eulogy, written by Peggy Noonan, stressed the theme of renewal. The astronauts had "slipped the surly bonds of earth," but the nation would reach out for new goals and even greater achievements. "That is the way we shall commemorate our seven *Challenger* heroes."

Even in personal suffering, Reagan appeared to advantage. When a crazed gunman, John Hinckley, gravely wounded the president in March 1981, Reagan told his wife in the emergency room, "Honey, I forgot to duck." About to go under the surgeon's knife, he jokingly asked if the doctor were a Republican. "We're all Republicans today" came the reply. Reagan's humor and spunk evoked immense appreciation among Americans who had wondered about the humanity of some of his predecessors.

In some settings, however, Reagan's limitations became apparent, as they had during his governorship of California. News conferences, where questions often confused him, were painful to watch—and were therefore kept to a minimum. He preferred to have every word and action scripted in advance; when a script was lacking, he seemed uniformed about many of his own programs. Once, when a bold reporter asked him to describe his arms control efforts, he drew a blank. Nancy Reagan whispered in her husband's ear: "Tell them we're doing all we can." He dutifully repeated the phrase. Staff members also remarked on his lethargy, his difficulty in learning the names of subordinates or foreign officials, and his tendency to nod off during meetings. In fact, while Reagan supplied the vision and good looks, an inner coterie of advisers ran the country. The president remained detached from the details of governance.

When the media reported his foibles and his slip-ups, the public forgave him. Moreover, such negative reporting was fairly limited, especially in Reagan's first term. Many liberal journalists felt they had to give the benefit of the doubt to a conservative leader selected by a majority of voters. Michael Deaver agreed that for most of Reagan's two terms, he "enjoyed the most generous treatment by the press of any president in the postwar era."

RE-ELECTION AND THE SECOND ADMINISTRATION

By 1984, as the economy climbed out of the recession into its long expansion, Ronald Reagan loomed as a formidable opponent for any Democratic challenger. Most voters enjoyed a few more dollars in their pockets from the tax cut; inflation had practically disappeared; and abstract difficulties such as the growing budget deficit had little impact on the national mood. Reagan's 1983 decision to invade the tiny island of Grenada (see Chapter 14) had been a whopping public success. In 1984 he even managed to share the glory of the American athletes who won a large number of gold medals at the Summer Olympics in Los Angeles.

As it turned out, the Democrats failed to mount an effective challenge in 1984. But in his second administration, like many other presidents before him, Reagan found himself confronted by increasing difficulties and embarrassments.

The Election of 1984

By 1984 the Democratic party was struggling to mobilize an electorate no longer attuned to the New Deal legacy. Civil rights activist Jesse Jackson urged the Democrats to reach out to the poor and disenfranchised of all races in order to win elections. He felt the party had a better chance of electing a president by increasing the voting pool than by trying to wring more votes out of the mere 50 percent of Americans who normally cast ballots. Jackson claimed to represent a racially diverse "Rainbow Coalition," but his strength lay mostly among African-Americans. His association with Black Muslims and his anti-Semitic remarks (such as calling New York "Hymie Town") frightened many whites, Jews, and ethnics of European heritage who had long been part of the Democratic coalition.

Senator Gary Hart of Colorado, another outsider, also urged Democrats to reach beyond their New Deal past. Hart spoke about "new ideas," though he revealed few; he was young, handsome, and telegenic, and he said the future mattered more than ideology. In pursuit of the nomination, he reached out to socially liberal, economically conservative younger voters.

In contrast, former vice president Walter Mondale won endorsements from organized labor, ethnic organizations, women's groups, teachers, environmentalists, and other progressive elements in the party. Critics, however, described Mondale's celebration of the glory days of the Democrats and his search for endorsements as pandering to "special interests." In the end, Mondale accumulated enough support to win the nomination, but Hart and Jackson gave him only grudging endorsements thereafter.

Mondale tried to energize his candidacy by making a public display of considering running mates drawn from a broad list of men, women, northerners, southerners, prolabor Democrats, and ethnic minorities. But his effort to show his concern with diversity appeared to many as simply new evidence that he was beholden to special-interest groups. Mondale finally selected New York Congresswoman Geraldine Ferraro as the vice-presidential candidate. As the first woman nominated for the national ticket by a major party, Ferraro excited millions of Americans. She proved a smart, articulate candidate who easily held her own in debate with Vice President George

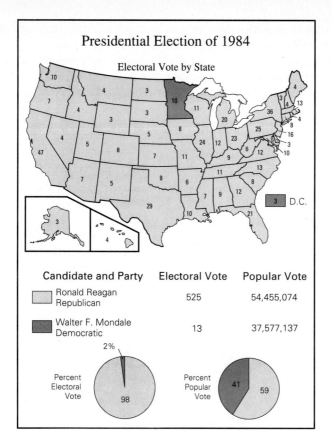

Presidential Election of 1984

Electoral Vote by State

Candidate and Party	Electoral Vote	Popular Vote
Ronald Reagan Republican	525	54,455,074
Walter F. Mondale Democratic	13	37,577,137

Percent Electoral Vote: 2% / 98

Percent Popular Vote: 41 / 59

Presidential Election of 1984

Bush. Questions raised about her husband's financial dealings, however, obscured her critique of the Reagan presidency. Many voters concluded that having served only three terms in Congress, Ferraro was untested. In the end, her presence on the ticket failed to help the Democrats.

Mondale tried valiantly to run a campaign of issues. He bombarded the public with warnings about runaway spending, an out-of-control arms race, environmental disasters, and the unfairness of Reagan's economic policies. His most famous campaign line was: "He'll raise taxes, so will I. He won't tell you, I just did." Commentators briefly praised Mondale's political courage, but within a week decided he was committing political suicide. United Nations Ambassador Jeane Kirkpatrick, a conservative Democrat, dubbed him "bad news Fritz Mondale" and part of the "blame-America-first crowd."

It did not help that Mondale looked and sounded terrible on television, especially in contrast to his opponent. His droopy eyes and droning voice exuded as much pessimism as Reagan generated optimism. His association with the ill-fated Carter also doomed him. Reagan parried Mondale with gibes and one-liners, even turning aside concerns about his advanced age with the remark: "I am not going to exploit, for political purposes, my opponent's youth and inexperience." When a journalist criticized a White House aide about the superficiality of the Republican campaign, the aide retorted: "We are not here to educate America. We are here to re-elect Ronald Reagan."

The president's speeches and commercials emphasized the themes of redemption, patriotism, and family. Mondale complained that while he tried to discuss issues, Reagan patted dogs. In 1980, Reagan had run against government; in 1984, he *was* the government, but it made no difference. His campaign of good feelings carried him to a sweep of forty-nine states (see map, page 505). Democratic candidates nonetheless did much better at the congressional and state levels. The Democrats retained their majority in the House and pecked away at the slim Republican majority in the Senate. In local races where issues such as intervention in Central America and the arms race were discussed, and where Reagan's personality did not come into play, the president's popularity did not rub off on GOP candidates.

Second-Term Complications

During his second administration, several internal staff changes as well as external policy reverses diminished Reagan's luster. The problems began when the highly capable White House chief of staff, James Baker, wanted a change of pace. He and Treasury Secretary Donald Regan, a man not well known to the president, decided to switch jobs, soliciting Reagan's blessing after they had made up their minds. As the new chief of staff, Donald Regan discovered that the president seldom discussed policy with him but seemed endlessly fascinated by the similarity in their names and their mutual penchant for mildly off-color locker-room humor. Many commentators later suggested that Reagan would have had fewer difficulties in his second term if Baker had continued as chief of staff.

Assistant Chief of Staff Michael Deaver and counselor Edwin Meese also left the White House in1985. Deaver was eager to cash in on his access to powerful officials. He opened a public relations firm and fell afoul of influence-peddling laws. Meanwhile, Reagan nominated Meese for attorney general. Soon reports began to circulate that Meese, through a close friend and financial adviser, E. Robert Wallach, had promoted the fortunes of a shady defense contracting firm,

Wedtech. A lengthy investigation by the Senate Ethics Committee and a special prosecutor concluded that Meese had exercised terrible judgment but had not done enough to warrant indictment. Strangely, that seemed enough to justify his confirmation as attorney general. These and other problems of numerous administration officials, which became known as the "sleaze factor," began to dog the administration.

Early in 1985, a minor faux pas escalated into an international embarrassment. Reagan had accepted an invitation from West German Chancellor Helmut Kohl to speak in Germany on the theme of reconciliation while attending a European economic summit. As one of his last assignments, Michael Deaver arranged for Reagan to speak in a military cemetery at Bitburg, where forty-seven Nazi SS troops—Hitler's special thugs—were among those interred. Veterans of all the Allied powers, Jewish groups, and over half the Senate called on Reagan to change the site of his speech. Unaccountably, Reagan downplayed the guilt of the SS troops, suggested that few Germans remembered the war, and observed that the dead storm troopers were themselves victims of Nazism. "Somehow," a White House aide remarked, "we have accomplished the impossible. We have even got the American Legion to criticize Ronald Reagan." In the end, the president made a brief visit to the cemetery, balanced by a quick stop at a concentration camp.

Reagan recovered his poise by the summer of 1986. As the stock market surged to record highs, Congress passed a major tax reform, the economic centerpiece of Reagan's second term. The new tax law, a modification of the flat-rate income tax system proposed by Democrats Bill Bradley and Richard Gephardt, was presented as a way of restoring simplicity and equality to the complex tax code. It closed many tax loopholes and reduced multiple tax brackets to just three, at rates of 15, 28, and 33 percent. The reform eliminated taxes for the poorest Americans, but a quirk in the law allowed the wealthiest Americans to pay a tax rate slightly below that of the upper middle class. Even though most taxpayers ended up paying about the same total as before, Reagan convinced many people that the law had reduced taxes.

The president hosted a Fourth of July celebration at the Statue of Liberty in 1986 that showed him at his best. The extravaganza featured a renovated Statue of Liberty, the biggest fireworks display ever assembled, and Ronald Reagan. As Leslie Stahl, White House reporter for CBS, commented, "Like his leading lady, the Statue of Liberty, the president, after six years in office, has himself become a symbol of pride in America." However, despite the president's broad popularity, he failed to achieve any realignment in national politics. In the congressional elections of November 1986, even as Reagan rode high in the polls, the Democrats regained control of the Senate and increased their majority in the House. The Democratic majority blocked administration proposals to cut social programs further, expand defense spending, or intervene more directly in Central America. Although the president continued to ask Congress to pass constitutional amendments banning abortion and permitting school prayer, these calls were ignored.

By late 1986 the Iran-contra affair—involving a series of weapons-for-hostage deals with Iran, a country Reagan had described as a terrorist state—was becoming public, and during the next year it proved a profound embarrassment to the administration (see Chapter 14). Then, in October 1987, a collapse in stock prices jolted the confident economic mood that had prevailed since 1983. After the Dow Jones Industrial Average hit a record high of 2,700 points in August, it slumped. In mid-October it fell 600 points in a few days, losing almost a fourth of its value and reviving memories of the 1929 stock market crash that had ushered in the Great Depression. Computer-driven stock trading programs and inadequate regulation made the problem worse. Although Wall Street recovered most of its losses within a year, the minicrash created an anxiety about the economy that proved impossible to shake.

The combined impact of the Iran-contra scandal and Wall Street jitters in 1987 might have become Reagan's epitaph. But the president's ability to adjust to circumstances once again surprised Americans. During 1988, relations between the United States and the Soviet Union improved dramatically, creating the possibility for an end to the Cold War. Even though internal Soviet developments were the impetus for most of the changes, the mere fact that they occurred on "Reagan's watch" allowed him to take much of the credit. The public proved quite willing to forget the Iran-contra affair. Reagan left office with an overall 68 percent approval rating, higher than that of any president since Franklin D. Roosevelt, who died in office.

HARD REALITIES OF THE REAGAN ERA

Reagan's high public approval rating, along with his remarkable success at communicating his ideas and faith in America, often gave the impression that the nation's problems were vanishing before the onslaught of a new pride and optimism. In many cases, however, the reality did not match the administration's glowing rhetoric. Some old problems deepened; some disturbing new economic and social trends arose. In the 1990s the nation is still struggling to deal with some of the long-term consequences of the Reagan years.

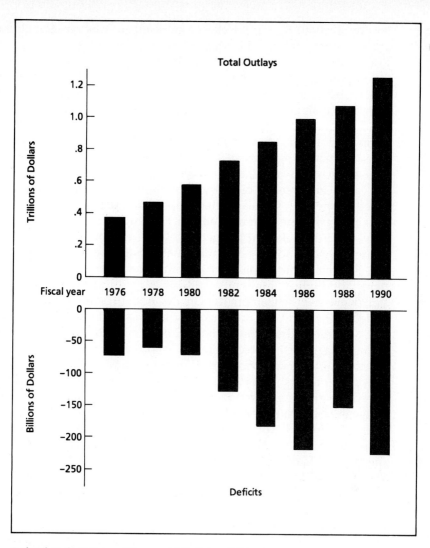

Federal Budget Expenditures and Deficits, 1976–1990

Deficits

Reagan took office bitterly critical of Carter's "runaway deficit of nearly $80 billion" and the cumulative national debt of almost $1 trillion. Yet over the next eight years his administration ran up annual deficits that ranged from $128 billion to well over $200 billion (see figure). The national debt tripled, to almost $3 trillion. The Treasury borrowed about $5,000 for each American, making the $200 billion annual interest tab the third largest item in the budget.

The president denied responsibility for any of this. He blamed runaway spending on what he called an"iron triangle" of Congress, lobbyists, and liberal journalists who coordinated raids of the Treasury. In fact, Reagan never submitted a balanced budget to Congress. New social programs were not to blame, for they were few and far between during the 1980s. Most of the deficit resulted from Reagan's insistence on increasing defense spending at the same time that tax rates were reduced.

Reagan endorsed a constitutional amendment mandating a balanced budget, but stipulated that it apply first to his successors. Congress did pass the Gramm-Rudman-Hollings Act, which mandated steps toward a balanced budget, but Congress then agreed with the White House to adopt accounting methods that virtually gutted the law. Expensive but popular or necessary programs were simply declared "off budget" and not included in figuring the deficit.

The massive Reagan-era deficits did not surprise officials such as Budget Director David Stockman. In 1981 he had told his colleagues that without a "draconian reduction on the expenditure side," staggering budget deficits would result from the administration's policy of reducing taxes and boosting military expenditures. A true believer in leaving nearly everything to private market forces, Stockman hoped the growing deficit would force Congress to agree to a "politically painful shrinkage of the American welfare state." Stockman favored eliminating Social Security, Medicare, support for veterans' hospitals, public housing grants, farm subsidies, public broadcasting, and student loans. Perhaps Reagan shared the hope that these programs would be killed. But when Congress balked at cutting programs that benefited the working and middle classes, the president declined to fight. Reagan and Congress tacitly agreed to cut taxes deeply and cut domestic spending only modestly. Domestic programs were reduced, but not in the extreme way that Stockman believed necessary. This compromise minimized economic pain and maximized deficits.

On average during the 1980s, federal borrowing to cover the deficit absorbed three-fourths of the net savings of all American families and businesses. But even this was not enough; the government also needed large infusions of foreign capital, especially from Japan and Germany. By the late 1980s, foreign investors held between 10 and 20 percent of the national debt. In less than a decade, the United States had slipped from being the world's biggest creditor to the world's biggest debtor.

Because the Treasury had to borrow so much to fund the deficit, fewer dollars were available for investment in research, new plants, and machinery. This ensured that American industry would become less competitive. Although the country began the 1980s with a positive trade balance in manufactured goods, the balance soon turned negative. The foreign trade deficit grew dramatically, surpassing $150 billion per year by the second half of the decade. Every week during the Reagan years American consumers spent on average about $2 billion more on foreign goods than foreigners spent on American products. The cumulative imbalance for the decade approached $1 trillion.

To finance this overspending, more and more American stocks, real estate, and factories were sold to foreign investors who had a surplus of dollars. Some economists saw foreign investment as a healthy sign of confidence in the United States. Foreign investments did provide jobs, at least temporarily, but the profits and decision-making power flowed abroad. Increasingly, American economic security depended on the willingness of Japanese, British, German, Dutch, and Saudi investors to supply capital for American industry as well as for the federal government.

Gaps and Imbalances in the Economic Recovery

The economic expansion of the 1980s was highly selective. Prosperity and wealth tended to flow to both coasts, partly because of defense spending. The Northeast and California boomed. After severe doldrums in the 1970s, Boston and Manhattan blossomed again during the 1980s. In these boom areas, real estate values skyrocketed for both residential and commercial property.

At the same time, much of the Rustbelt in the upper Midwest experienced a further loss of high-paying industrial jobs, continuing the decline begun in the 1970s. In addition, farm states and energy-producing states staggered. Small farmers abandoned the land in accelerating numbers, while cities like Houston, buffeted by falling energy prices, faced economic disaster. As Reagan spoke of "morning in America," the sun set on many traditional industries and small farms, and the Southwest experienced a prolonged recession.

Even in nationwide terms, the long economic expansion of the later Reagan years was less impressive than it looked. Compared to the late 1970s, it was a marked improvement; but if the base of comparison is extended to the entire period from 1945 to 1980, the recovery appears more modest. During most of the 1980s the inflation rate was twice as high as the average for the years from 1947 to 1967. Unemployment also remained higher than in most years between 1947 and 1973. Real wages—that is, wages adjusted for inflation—continued the stagnation begun in the 1970s; in fact, individual salaries declined slightly, although the impact was hidden by an increase in the number of working wives and mothers, whose earnings boosted total family income. Overall, the economy grew about as fast in the 1980s as it had during the 1960s and 1970s.

Meanwhile, federal aid to states fell by almost 13 percent during the 1980s—a casualty of Reagan's budget cuts. The administration also trimmed a few billion dollars from the budget each year by postponing repair of roads and bridges and by ignoring safety problems in nuclear weapons plants. Cities were especially hard-hit by the elimination of federal revenue-sharing funds, which supported programs to help the urban poor and repair infrastructure. Because a growing percentage of poor Americans lived in cities, the impact was severe. The apparent savings realized from these cuts were actually charges passed on to the next generation, which would have to cope with the problems that Reagan's economic policies neglected.

The Culture of Greed

Supply-siders were serious about stopping New Deal–style income redistribution programs. After the accession of substantial American wealth by German and Japanese investors, Reagan-era policies nearly doubled the share of the national income going to the wealthiest 1 percent of Americans, from 8.1 to about 15 percent. The net worth of the four hundred richest Americans nearly tripled. In 1980 a typical corporate chief executive officer (CEO) made about forty times the income of an average factory worker; nine years later the CEO made ninety-three times as much. Lawyers handling business mergers also gained great wealth. More than thirteen hundred partners in major law firms averaged higher pay than the eight hundred top executives in industry.

Correspondingly, the 1980s witnessed a celebration of wealth—critics called it greed—unparalleled in America since the Roaring Twenties. For many people, it seemed that income had become the accepted measure of human value. Professional athletes earned immense sums as teams scrambled to recruit basketball, football, and baseball players from colleges. Congressman Kemp, economist Laffer, and writers Jude Wanniski and George Guilder celebrated financiers and deal makers as secular saints who enriched society. Their heroes—colorful Wall Street operators like Carl Icahn, T. Boone Pickens, Ivan Boesky, and Michael Milken and real estate speculator Donald Trump — earned billions of dollars buying and merging companies and constructing new office towers, apartment complexes, and resorts.

A "merger mania," fueled by the 1981 tax law and a relaxed attitude toward enforcement of antitrust laws in the Reagan Justice Department, gripped Wall Street through 1987. Many of the nation's biggest companies bought out competitors or were themselves swallowed up in leveraged buyouts financed by huge loans bearing high interest rates. Corporate raiders argued that these deals rewarded stockholders and eliminated incompetent management, thus increasing industrial competitiveness.

Because many multi-billion-dollar deals were too risky for banks, insurance companies, or pension funds to finance, Milken and others pioneered the use of junk bonds, high-interest bonds with little security. Financiers attempting to take over large corporations would issue these corporate IOUs to raise money for the acquisition. But repayment of the heavy debt often compelled the purchaser to sell off profitable portions of the newly acquired business. Critics worried that money spent on acquisitions contributed nothing to the economy's productivity because it did not go into research or the development of new products. Still, junk bonds allowed entrepreneurs to raise large amounts of cash quickly, giving both the bought-out owners and the deal makers huge profits.

Following the October 1987 losses on Wall Street, a series of probes revealed evidence of insider trading among some of the most successful financiers. By the end of the decade Boesky, Milken, and many others had pleaded guilty to illegal practices. The junk bond market shrank dramatically, especially as heavily indebted companies began to default on payments and go into bankruptcy.

In addition to the Wall Street wizards, the decade celebrated "yuppies"—a widespread name for young, urban professionals, a group that exulted in its upward mobility during the 1980s. Journalists used the term lavishly in 1983 and 1984, partly to describe Gary Hart's unexpected following among young Americans as he campaigned for the Democratic presidential nomination. Unlike radical protesters or hippies of the 1960s, these young adults were not social rebels. They plunged into the economic mainstream ready to consume. *Newsweek* dubbed 1984 "The Year of the Yuppie" and applauded the group's eagerness to "go for it" as a sign of the "yuppie virtues of imagination, daring and entrepreneurship." Yuppies existed "on a new plane of consciousness, a state of Transcendental Acquisition."

Bona fide yuppies—people born between 1945 and 1959, earning over $40,000 as professionals or managers, and living in a city—totaled about 1.5 million. As candidate Hart learned, they were not a big constituency for Democratic liberals. Even though they rejected restrictive ideas on abortion and enjoyed recreational drugs, most supported Reagan's economic policies. Yuppies aspired to become investment bankers, not social workers. In 1985, one-third of the entire senior class at Yale applied for jobs as financial analysts at First Boston Corporation.

Yuppies spent and overspent on "leisure products" like Porsches and BMWs, designer sneakers, state-of-the-art electronic equipment,

Donald Trump

In an era of megadeals, mergers, and leveraged buyouts, no one grabbed more attention than real estate promoter Donald Trump. Tall, elegantly dressed, given to swaggering with his thumbs hooked inside his belt, and exuding arrogant self-confidence, Trump thrived on publicity. "No one," he boasted, "has done more in New York than me . . . I love to have enemies. . . . I like beating my enemies to the ground."

Trump's empire began the old-fashioned way: he inherited a real estate business from his father. Clever marketing, easy credit, risk taking, and tremendous energy produced a string of impressive accomplishments. He built Trump Tower, a luxury condominium building on Manhattan's Fifth Avenue; Trump's Castle and Trump's Taj Mahal, gambling casinos in Atlantic City; and

and gourmet foods. They also embraced the fitness craze, wore natural fibers, took up jogging, patronized health spas, and ate high-fiber diets. Some commentators suggested that the yuppies included many reformed radicals from the 1960s. Former Black Panther Eldridge Cleaver became a born-again Christian and clothing designer. Fellow Panther Bobby Seale, who had once shouted "Burn, baby, burn," became a chef and made a videotape called "Barbecuing with Bobby." David Horowitz, an SDS activist and one-time editor of *Ramparts* magazine, became a Reagan Republican. Actress Jane Fonda, nicknamed "Hanoi Jane" because of her sympathy for the Communist side during the Vietnam War, made a fortune producing exercise videos. Actually, none of these ex-radicals were bona fide yuppies, but the trend was clear.

By 1988, the overused term *yuppie* had evolved into a slur. Even people who fit the type perfectly did not want to be identified with

he planned to construct a vast apartment house complex called Trump City in Manhattan. Trump's imagination took wings when he bought the Eastern Airlines Shuttle and renamed it, of course, the Trump Shuttle. Among his major possessions Trump counted a $29 million yacht, several private planes, a string of mansions, and a private golf course.

Trump's self-promotion included marketing a ghostwritten book titled *Trump: The Art of the Deal*. It chronicled his profitable victories over gullible competitors. The book became a best seller in part because Trump purchased so many gift copies.

By the end of the Reagan era, Trump had fallen on harder times. Many of his projects, especially the gambling casinos, had been financed through the sale of some $2 billion worth of junk bonds.

When the casino profits proved insufficient to pay both the interest on the bonds and the debts owed to banks, Trump's creditors began moving in. In 1990 he surrendered partial control of his real estate empire and sold part of his holdings in his beloved Trump Shuttle.

Trump's lavish life style also suffered. His creditors put him on a monthly allowance, though one that exceeded the budgets of some small countries. In 1990 his wife Ivana filed for divorce and a large part of his fortune after Donald began courting model Marla Maples. In the New York press, the Trump divorce case overshadowed the collapse of communism in Eastern Europe. Only a tad chastened by these misfortunes, the tycoon published another book in 1990: *Trump: Surviving at the Top.* ■

it. *Newsweek* said that the group was in disgrace, and the *Wall Street Journal* reported that "conspicuous consumption is passé." *New York* magazine, a purveyor to yuppie tastes, ran a cover story boosting altruism and asked: "Had it with pride, covetousness, lust, anger, gluttony, envy and sloth? It's time to start doing good." Few of those with new wealth gave up their stocks, bonds, or BMWs; but it seemed that the outright celebration of greed during the Reagan era was losing its appeal.

The Other Americans

As the media glorified wealth in the 1980s, many Americans at the low end of the economy were growing increasingly desperate. While the average family income of the richest tenth of the population, calculated in constant dollars, rose by more than 27 percent between

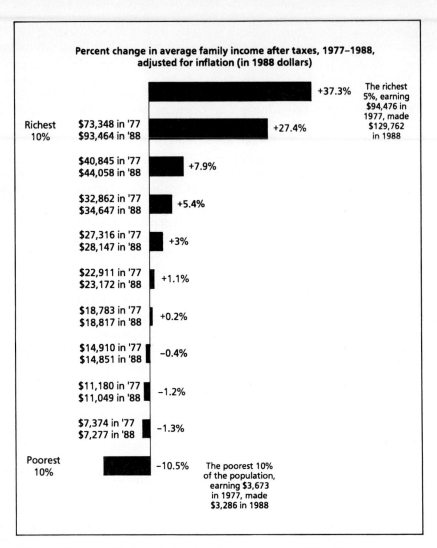

Percent change in average family income after taxes, 1977–1988, adjusted for inflation (in 1988 dollars)

	+37.3%	The richest 5%, earning $94,476 in 1977, made $129,762 in 1988
Richest 10% — $73,348 in '77 / $93,464 in '88	+27.4%	
$40,845 in '77 / $44,058 in '88	+7.9%	
$32,862 in '77 / $34,647 in '88	+5.4%	
$27,316 in '77 / $28,147 in '88	+3%	
$22,911 in '77 / $23,172 in '88	+1.1%	
$18,783 in '77 / $18,817 in '88	+0.2%	
$14,910 in '77 / $14,851 in '88	–0.4%	
$11,180 in '77 / $11,049 in '88	–1.2%	
$7,374 in '77 / $7,277 in '88	–1.3%	
Poorest 10%	–10.5%	The poorest 10% of the population, earning $3,673 in 1977, made $3,286 in 1988

Richer and Poorer: Changes in Average Family Income, 1977–1988

1977 and 1988, the income of the poorest tenth was dropping by more than 10 percent (see figure). The middle segments of the population experienced little net change. The Reagan administration's cuts in the federal income tax rates distinctly favored the wealthy. In fact, for the average American family, the total tax bite—including Social Security, state, and sales taxes—actually *rose* during the 1980s.

As the income gap between the richest and poorest Americans widened to the largest amount since 1945, poverty increasingly became the lot of women and children. The so-called feminization of poverty grew more severe during the 1980s, partly because of the rise in the percentage of unwed mothers. The rate of children living with a never-married mother more than doubled during the 1980s, from 2.9 to 7 percent. By 1989 one of every four births in the United States was to be an unwed mother. African-American and Hispanic women had the highest likelihood of becoming single mothers. Compared to married women, unwed mothers were less likely to receive prenatal care, finish high school, or hold a paying job. The Reagan administration made the situation worse by slashing funds for the Women-Infants-Children (WIC) program, which provided pre- and postnatal care to poor women.

President Reagan justified cutting many programs with the quip that after twenty years of a war on poverty, poverty had won. Superficially, statistics seemed to confirm this view. In the early 1980s, the poverty rate for all Americans stood at about 13 percent, about where it was when Lyndon Johnson left office. However, the nature of poverty had changed over time. In the earlier period, the elderly and disabled had made up a larger share of the poor. Increased spending on Social Security and Medicare had improved their lot dramatically; in other words, contrary to Reagan's implication, government programs *had* helped. For the groups that made up the bulk of the poor in the 1980s—single mothers, young children, and nonelderly men with few job skills—federal welfare spending had not grown significantly; few government programs addressed their needs.

The problems of poverty and the increasing gap between rich and poor were aggravated by changes in the job market. Among the 18 million new jobs created under Reagan—a total only slightly above that achieved during the 1970s—about half paid $20,000 or more annually. Of the remainder, many paid minimum wage and were part-time only. The 11.5 million workers who lost jobs because of plant closings between 1979 and 1984, particularly in the Rustbelt of the upper Midwest, often found replacement jobs paying much less than they had earned previously. With adjustment for inflation, the average hourly worker, who earned $172 per week when Reagan took office, made only $166 when he left.

During the 1980s the growing phenomenon of homelessness and the worsening plight of a seemingly unreachable "underclass" befuddled both conservatives and liberals. The homeless included a variety of people, from women fleeing abusive spouses to the chronically mentally ill. Many lived on urban streets or in subway stations, begging for money and food. In another grim statistic, the decade saw more young African-American men in jail or on parole than attending college. The homicide rate among young black males grew by 66 percent during the 1980s. They were more likely to be killed in their neighborhoods than they had been during tours of duty in the Vietnam War. The plight of the homeless and urban underclass shocked

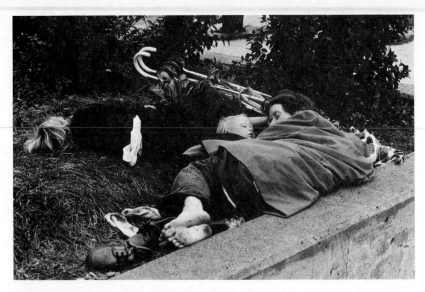

Homeless families became a common sight in many urban areas in the 1980s.
Photo by William Viggiano © 1991.

American sensibilities but did not affect public policy. Although the Reagan administration had promised to maintain a "safety net" for the truly needy, it cut programs designed to help them. Conservatives who saw poverty as the mark of personal failure believed that government efforts to help only deepened the failure. Liberals believed that government had to help, but they had few new ideas to offer.

Effects of Deregulation: The S&L Debacle

As noted in Chapter 12, the Carter administration in the late 1970s had begun eliminating some federal regulations that interfered with competition. Prices declined in the airline and trucking industries after controls were removed. The Reagan administration carried this policy even further, for the president and his advisers saw virtually all government regulations as anticompetitive.

Under Reagan, federal agencies abolished many of their earlier rules, ranging from requirements for stronger car bumpers to environmental restraints on offshore oil drilling. The budgets for agencies such as the Environmental Protection Agency (EPA), the Occupational Health and Safety Administration, and the Securities and Exchange Commission were slashed, ostensibly to save tax dollars. Because of the consequent staff shortages, these agencies were often unable to enforce regulations even if they wanted to. In a number of cases, Reagan appointed agency heads—such as Anne Burford Gorsuch of the EPA and James Watt of the Department of the Interior—who were hostile to the very concept of regulation. Gorsuch and Watt both came under heavy fire from liberals and environmentalists for their weakening of environmental protections.

In the Department of Housing and Urban Development (HUD), deregulation combined with corruption to produce a major scandal. The president appointed an African-American lawyer, "Silent" Sam Pierce, as colleagues called him, to head the housing agency. Pierce earned his nickname by seldom speaking at cabinet meetings—and perhaps because Reagan failed to even recognize him at one ceremonial occasion. Over a period of several years, the administration cut the HUD budget by nearly 75 percent. Pierce and his deputies, with little mandate to engage in government work, used what remained in HUD coffers partly as a private fund to award contracts to friends and political cronies. In 1989 investigators discovered that billions of public dollars intended for low-income housing had been invested instead in luxury apartments, golf courses, swimming pools, and outright scams.

Nevertheless, Pierce's misbehavior paled in comparison with the debacle in the savings and loan industry. During the 1970s, banks and savings and loan institutions (also called S&Ls or "thrifts") had lost large amounts of money and large numbers of depositors because unregulated money market funds paid a higher rate of interest. To make banks and S&Ls more competitive, Congress agreed at the end of the Carter years to raise the federal insurance level to $100,000 on individual accounts and to allow the institutions to pay higher interest rates. In 1982 the Reagan administration prodded Congress to go further and deregulate most thrift operations. Previously, the major activity of S&Ls was to make low-risk, low-profit mortgage loans for single-family homes in the communities where the S&Ls were located. After 1982 they were permitted to invest depositors' funds in undeveloped land, commercial real estate, shopping malls, artwork, junk bonds, and virtually anything else. Any profits from such risky ventures would benefit the S&L owners. But the existence of federal deposit insurance meant that neither the thrift owners nor the depositors risked losing money; if an S&L collapsed, the costs would be borne by the government—in other words, by the nation's taxpayers.

Upon signing the Garn–St. Germain Act of 1982 permitting these new operations, Reagan called it the economic equivalent of a home run. Deregulation would liberate the creative energies of thrift managers and produce greater profits, which would make more money available for home loans. Instead, in many parts of the country, incompetent or corrupt lenders went wild. They invested insured funds in commercial real estate and other high-risk ventures, knowing they would reap any profits that accrued but would have no personal responsibility for losses.

In California, Charles Keating's Lincoln Federal Savings and Loan became a multi-billion-dollar institution virtually overnight by paying high interest rates to attract $100,000 accounts. Most of these funds went into extremely speculative projects. Colorado's Silverado Savings and Loan, whose board of directors included Neil Bush, son of the then vice president, acted similarly. By providing easy commercial mortgage money, the freewheeling S&Ls created a construction boom in certain parts of the country, pumping billions of dollars into the economy. In many of the speculative ventures, the high costs practically ruled out the chance for profit.

In addition to speculation, corruption entered the picture. Lenders found it easy and profitable to collude with builders to drive up the cost of projects, producing bigger fees for all the principals. Some S&L officers made dubious loans to business partners or paid themselves exorbitant salaries, with little fear of exposure. Properties were often "flipped" (sold back and forth) several times in a day for ever higher prices, with thrift managers authorizing the escalating loans in return for kickbacks.

Timely intervention by federal regulators might have limited the cost of the debacle. The collapse of the Penn Square (Oklahoma) bank and the need for a government bailout of Continental Illinois Bank in 1983 and 1984 were clear warning signals. But Reagan's budget cuts had reduced the number of bank examiners. Even when auditors found evidence of malfeasance, political influence could stave off the day of reckoning. Charles Keating of Lincoln Federal Savings and Loan made large contributions to influential senators such as Alan Cranston, Donald Riegle, John Glenn, John McCain, and Dennis DeConcini, who pressed bank examiners to allow Lincoln to stay in business. Because this S&L remained open a year longer than the examiners favored, it accumulated liabilities of some $2.6 billion, all chargeable to the federal agencies that insured the institution's deposits. The cost of the Lincoln failure alone surpassed the cumulative value of all bank robberies in the country over the previous two decades.

By 1989, hundreds of S&Ls had failed, and few of those still in operation remained profitable. The federal government created the Resolution Trust Corporation to take over a huge inventory of vacant buildings and obligations from the failed thrifts. Some economists estimate that the total bailout may cost the American taxpayers $500 billion over several decades. By any measure, this was the biggest bank heist in the nation's history.

CIVIL RIGHTS AND CONSERVATIVE JUSTICE

"Conservatives have waited over thirty years for this day," commented Richard Viguerie, a leading New Right fund-raiser, when President Reagan nominated Judge Robert H. Bork in July 1987 to a vacant seat on the Supreme Court. Viguerie's feelings stemmed from anger about the 1954 desegregation decision and many subsequent rulings by the Warren Court. President Reagan, like many other conservatives, shared these feelings. To him, the Supreme Court and liberal judges throughout the judicial system were responsible for a decline in morals, a rise in premarital sex, and the banishing of God from public school classrooms. In the areas of civil rights and civil liberties, he was particularly concerned to change the direction the country had taken.

Ronald Reagan had long opposed most civil rights laws and supported a constitutional amendment to outlaw school busing. Early in his presidency, trying unsuccessfully to stop Congress from establishing a federal holiday honoring Martin Luther King, Jr., he alluded to rumors about the civil rights martyr's left-wing leanings and steamy sex life. He also outraged civil rights groups by instructing the Justice Department to ask the Supreme Court to restore tax benefits to segregated private schools and colleges; but the Court in 1983 ruled that the IRS had acted properly in denying tax benefits to such institutions. When the 1965 Voting Rights Act came up for renewal, Reagan urged Congress to kill it. Congress renewed the law anyway, but the Justice Department then declined to investigate many allegations of interference with minority voting rights. Instead, Justice officials used some of their resources to investigate voter-registration programs and southern blacks who had been elected to office.

In the field of civil liberties, Reagan believed that the court system had favored the rights of accused criminals to the detriment of government power and victims' rights. A large portion of the American public, fearful of violent crime and increasingly suspicious of courts, shared the president's views. During the 1980s, legislators on both the state and national level responded to public fears with laws that mandated longer, compulsory prison sentences for many crimes. As a result, jail populations practically doubled, and prison construction costs became the fastest-growing category in state budgets. By 1988, about 1 million Americans, nearly one out of every 250 citizens, were imprisoned—a rate of incarceration matched only in South Africa and the Soviet Union. During this period, many states also established the death penalty for heinous crimes.

President Reagan's principal contribution to the campaign for conservative justice lay in his appointments to judgeships. During his

In 1981 Sandra Day O'Connor became the first woman appointed to the Supreme Court. *UPI/Bettmann Newsphotos.*

two terms he was able to appoint about four hundred federal judges—a majority of all those sitting in 1988—as well as a chief justice of the Supreme Court and three associate justices. He had the Justice Department screen candidates carefully to ferret out liberal views on civil rights, civil liberties, school prayer, and abortion. Nearly all Reagan's choices were fairly young, white males of a markedly conservative bent.

The president's first three Supreme Court appointments were confirmed rather easily by the Senate. Sandra Day O'Connor and Antonin Scalia joined the Court as associate justices, and William Rehnquist was promoted to chief justice. But the Senate, which had a Democratic majority after 1986, rejected the 1987 nomination of Robert Bork, the outspoken conservative championed by Richard Viguerie and other members of the New Right. Many senators were offended by Bork's abrasive personality and disturbed by memories of his role in President Nixon's firing of Special Prosecutor Archibald Cox during the Watergate investigation (see page 433). Moreover, Bork's contention that the Constitution offered little protection for privacy, free speech, women, and minorities aroused anger in the Senate. Undeterred by Bork's rejection, Reagan then nominated Anthony Kennedy, who also held conservative legal views but did not antagonize people in the same way as Bork. Kennedy was confirmed in 1988.

Gradually the Reagan appointees changed the tenor of Court rulings. After 1984, the Court whittled away at previous decisions that had made police responsible for alerting suspects to their rights. The Court also approved limitations on bail, affirmed most state death-penalty laws, and allowed the introduction in court of some illegally seized evidence. At first, despite the Justice Department's attacks on affirmative action plans as a "racial spoils system," the Court tended to uphold such plans; but following Kennedy's confirmation, a conservative majority of the Court began to chip away at affirmative action. In a series of cases in 1989—the most important being *City of Richmond* v. *J. A. Croson Company*—the Court disallowed government set-aside programs, which reserved a certain proportion of contracts for minority groups, and made it much harder for women, minorities, the elderly, and the disabled to sue private employers for job discrimination.

These decisions reflected a conservative view of justice that prevailed among the general public. Many Americans agreed with the president that "constitutional loopholes and technicalities" should not limit police and prosecutors. On civil rights issues, the use of school busing and affirmative action plans had created a lingering white backlash.

SOCIETY AND CULTURE IN THE 1980s

In the social and cultural sphere, as in the judicial process, the 1980s were a decade when conservative values re-emerged. President Reagan and many of those who supported him stressed family values, clean living, religion, attention to the basics in education, and cultural unity. At the same time, however, the nation experienced a renewed drug crisis, a decline in the reputation of public education, a series of scandals among right-wing television evangelists, an AIDS epidemic, and such an influx of immigrants that the nation became even more culturally diverse. The many contradictions of the 1980s testified to the bewildering complexity of American society and culture.

Drugs: Just Say No

The 1980s were the decade of the health and fitness craze. Americans began to pay heed to warnings that their health had long suffered because of their often sedentary life, their high-fat diet, and their use of alcohol, tobacco, and caffeine. Exercise became popular, even fashionable. Low-salt, low-fat, and all-natural foods were suddenly in demand. Groups such as Mothers Against Drunk Driving (MADD) campaigned to stiffen state laws against drunk drivers. Antitobacco advocates pressed local governments to mandate smoke-free work places and restaurants.

Meanwhile, however, drug use continued to be commonplace. During the 1980s an estimated 40 million Americans annually consumed an illegal substance. A 1987 survey revealed that half of all citizens under age forty-five had smoked marijuana at least once. In the first part of the decade, public concern about illegal drug use seemed minimal. In 1985 barely 1 percent of Americans surveyed listed drugs as a major national program. But four years later more than half of those surveyed described drug use as the gravest threat to national security.

What had happened to change the public attitude? To a large extent, the change stemmed from the appearance of "crack," an inexpensive cocaine derivative that became widely available by mid-decade. Newspapers, magazines, and television news reports carried frightening stories: robberies inspired by addicts' need for money to buy crack; crack-using parents who ignored or abused their children; preteens who had become dealers; turf wars in which rival dealers shot not only each other but innocent bystanders as well.

Although accurate numbers are hard to come by, many experts believe that drug use among nonminorities and the middle class had peaked in the late 1970s. When cocaine and its derivatives became popular, some of the users came from the middle class, but the greatest concentration of users was found among poor, inner-city, minority youth. For some of these young people, staying high relieved the miseries of daily life. For others, selling drugs provided one of the few avenues of economic and social mobility. The narcotics themselves killed surprisingly few users, about 4,000 to 5,000 in a typical year during this period. In comparison, alcohol-related deaths approached 200,000 annually, and tobacco was responsible for 300,000 American deaths each year. But the violent turf wars and the drug-related crimes killed twice as many people—about 8,000 annually—as the mere use of drugs.

Charging that the nation faced an unprecedented epidemic of drug use, President and Mrs. Reagan urged the public to fight back. "Just say no" was the widely circulated slogan of Nancy Reagan's campaign. Like most other citizens, however, the Reagans seemed more concerned about the escalation of drug-related violence than about the question of why youth used drugs or how to rehabilitate users. The administration focused its antidrug efforts on the dramatic but largely futile campaign to interdict supplies, arrest dealers, and throw users in jail. By 1989 the renewed federal and state war on drugs cost almost $15 billion annually, with most of the money being spent on police and prisons. Much less money and attention went into education or rehabilitation. Meanwhile, among the young and all other sectors of the population, alcohol abuse remained the overwhelming drug problem.

In his enthusiasm to suppress drugs, Reagan urged compulsory urine tests—in effect, chemical loyalty oaths—for millions of workers who showed no evidence of drug abuse. Although advocates of civil liberties objected, courts permitted the tests in many instances. By 1989, federal and state prisons were bursting with drug felons, but cocaine was as available as before. At the end of the decade, when police reported decreasing levels of cocaine use, the authorities claimed success in the drug war. In fact, however, addicts seemed to have switched brands, to heroin and synthetic drugs. The overall problem continued to defy solution.

Education: A Nation at Risk

Since the *Sputnik* scare of 1957, Americans had worried about the quality of the public education system. Concern mounted during the 1980s when stories appeared about high schools turning out illiterates and about Japanese students routinely outperforming Americans on standardized tests. The Department of Education's 1983 study, *A Nation at Risk*, reported that "if an unfriendly foreign power had attempted to impose on America the mediocre educational performance that exists today, we might well have viewed it as an act of war." Ironically, Reagan's own secretary of education, Terrel Bell, issued the report in the hope of generating public opposition to the president's deep cuts in school aid. Most Americans sympathized with the tone of the report, but few agreed on a remedy. Conservatives blamed the faults in the educational system on permissive teachers, sex education, wasteful spending, and a lack of attention to Western cultural traditions and the "three Rs." Liberals complained that public schools were underfunded and hard put to teach both traditional subjects and the high-tech skills needed in a competitive world.

To complicate matters, the affluent middle class, especially in cities, abandoned public schools in growing numbers. Continuing the trend of the 1970s, middle-class parents enrolled their children in private and parochial schools with selective admission policies. With many of the more motivated students gone, the public schools struggled to educate a larger proportion of poor, minority, and non–English-speaking children. Moreover, the flight of middle-class students reduced school districts' ability to raise needed revenues. Parents who opted for private education had little incentive to support new taxes. Working-class parents, many of whom lacked faith in the value of education, often saw school tax increases as just another financial burden. Another trend, the gradual aging of the American population, also contributed to the school crisis, because the elderly—with no young children of their own to educate—tended to oppose additional school expenditures. These problems accentuated the decline of faith in public education.

Religion and Public Life

Jimmy Carter had first linked fundamentalist Christianity with presidential politics, but Ronald Reagan captured the movement. He capitalized on the ability of television-based ministers to mobilize millions of voters on behalf of the Republican cause. Preachers like Jim Bakker, Jimmy Swaggart, Oral Roberts, and Pat Robertson, who represented a variety of Protestant sects and traditions, saw themselves as potential kingmakers. Jerry Falwell, founder of the Moral Majority, admitted that his followers hoped to "bring about a moral and conservative revolution."

As president, Reagan seldom attended church, but he spoke with verve and certainty on religious matters. In 1980 he told a conference of fundamentalist Christian leaders that he considered himself "born again" and that "it was a fact that all the [world's] complex and horrendous [problems] have their answer in that single book—the Bible." He criticized federal courts for not permitting the Bible-based theory of creationism to be taught as a scientific alternative to the theory of evolution, and he urged amending the Constitution to permit the return of prayer to public schools. "You can't endorse me," he told the cheering preachers, "but I endorse you." However, the president's understanding of and commitment to Christianity seemed clouded by later revelations that he and Nancy Reagan frequently consulted astrologers and based some of their decisions on astrological guidance.

By 1985, the combined electronic ministries were raising well over $1 billion annually. Donations from viewers supported a variety of religious, charitable, political, and business causes, often funneled through unregulated funds controlled by such organizations as the Moral Majority, the 700 Club, and the PTL ("Praise the Lord") ministry. Part of the surge in televised fund-raising could be traced to a change in federal regulations. Before the late 1970s, TV stations had donated air time to religious organizations in order to fulfill government requirements for public-service broadcasting. By the 1980s, however, the regulations permitted stations to count religious broadcasts as public service even if the air time was paid for at regular prices. Therefore the stations charged high rates, which only those ministries adept at fund-raising could afford to pay.

The successful televangelists preached two basic kinds of sermons. One fulminated against the threat posed to America by immorality, communism, abortion, and "secular humanism" (the belief that humans, not God, were the basis for morality). The other celebrated a gospel of wealth, a belief that money and nice possessions represented a form of divine grace. The Reverend Jimmy Swaggart epitomized the former style and the Reverend Jim Bakker the latter. Both implied that grace was readily available to those who showed their faith by generous donations.

The televangelists tapped into major trends in the 1980s. Jimmy Swaggart's talk of sin and Satan resembled President Reagan's campaign against godless communism and the Soviet Union's evil empire (see Chapter 14). Jim and Tammy Faye Bakker's PTL show celebrated wealth and conspicuous consumption in much the same way that yuppies admired a BMW automobile. The Bakkers seemed to say that people could not do good unto others unless they felt good about themselves, and feeling good about oneself required a lot of expensive possessions.

Many televangelists were honest and sincere, less inclined to flamboyant exaggeration and flagrant fund-raising than Swaggart and the Bakkers. Moreover, not all viewers accepted the doctrines put forth by the media preachers. Many who watched the shows simply found them entertaining. A large proportion of donors, pollsters found, contributed money out of a sense of obligation to pay for enjoying the spectacle.

Whatever the basis for their appeal, televised ministries suffered a major setback in 1987, when several of the most outrageous televangelists suffered scandal and humiliation. Federal prosecutors indicted Jim Bakker on numerous counts of fraud and conspiracy for bilking followers who had invested $158 million in a combined hotel and religious theme park called Heritage USA. A rival TV preacher revealed that Bakker had forced a female church member to have sex with him and had used donations to pay her hush money. She then posed nude for *Penthouse* magazine. A jury convicted Bakker of cheating investors, and he received a stiff jail term.

Soon other televangelists fell from grace. Oral Roberts became an object of derision when he locked himself in a prayer tower claiming that God would take him away in thirty days unless his flock mailed him $8 million. Jimmy Swaggart admitted that he bought sex from prostitutes. Pat Robertson's crusade for the Republican presidential nomination collapsed amid public ridicule after he announced he would use prayer to divert a hurricane from Virginia to New York.

The personal and financial lapses of certain televangelists had long been rumored. Perhaps the scandals took years to develop because the public hesitated to pin blame on popular religious leaders. But evidence also suggests that the Reagan administration pressured government agencies to overlook charges of lawbreaking in the early 1980s because the electronic churches supported the president.

Sex and Gender

Ronald Reagan and the religious right celebrated the "traditional" family of a breadwinning husband and a wife who served as mother and homemaker. It hardly mattered that the president had been divorced, had married two career women, and had little contact with two of his four children; the image of an old-fashioned, stable family still appealed to many Americans. Yet the so-called traditional household—a married couple and one or more children under age eighteen—continued to decline in the 1980s. In 1970, 40 percent of the nation's households had conformed to that ideal; by 1980 that proportion had dropped to 31 percent, and by 1990, to 26 percent. Moreover, in 1983 the proportion of adult women with jobs surpassed 50 percent for the first time in the country's history.

With women holding a large share of the nation's paying jobs, feminists continued to press for affordable child care, approval of the Equal Rights Amendment to the Constitution, and an end to gender discrimination by employers. But Reagan opposed efforts to develop a national childcare policy, and Republicans in Congress blocked any reconsideration of the Equal Rights Amendment when the deadline for state ratification expired in 1982. After Reagan left office, his appointees to the Supreme Court helped to strike down civil rights legislation that would have facilitated women's ability to sue employers for gender discrimination. Despite Reagan's opposition to most feminist goals, he did win a measure of support for appointing a few women to high-profile posts. During his first term he named Jeane Kirkpatrick as ambassador to the United Nations, Margaret Heckler as the head of the Health and Human Services Department, and Sandra Day O'Connor as the first female justice of the Supreme Court.

The issue of abortion remained controversial. Reagan persuaded Congress to bar Medicare-funded abortions for poor women and to limit funding for other forms of birth control. Instead, he supported "chastity clinics," in which counselors advised teenage girls and unmarried women to avoid pregnancy by avoiding sex. The president also encouraged right-to-life (antiabortion) groups to support politicians opposed to abortion and work against candidates who favored free choice.

Many commentators proclaimed that the 1980s were witnessing the end of the sexual revolution. The announcement was probably premature, but the mysterious outbreak of the AIDS epidemic in the early 1980s brought a health crisis that would indeed make Americans more cautious about sexual relations. A disease apparently originating in Africa, AIDS destroyed the immune system and left people vulnerable to opportunistic infections. The deadly virus was transmitted from one person to another through the exchange of bodily fluids, particularly blood and semen. In the early years of the epi-

The fight against AIDS included a public education campaign to alert people to the danger. *Saatchi & Saatchi.*

demic, sexual transmission was especially prevalent among gay men. Intravenous drug users who shared needles were also at grave risk. Before tests were developed to check the nation's blood banks, many hemophiliacs caught the virus through blood transfusions. By the end of 1990, 100,000 Americans had died from the disease, and medical experts predicted that by the end of 1993 the American death toll would rise to over 200,000. AIDS struck hard in other countries as well, especially in Africa.

Because many of the first people with AIDS were gay men or drug abusers, President Reagan was uncomfortable in even discussing the disease. Along with his conservative backers, he opposed spending much federal money on AIDS research or preventive education during his first term. The president remained silent on the subject while televangelists spoke of God's sending a "gay plague" to punish sinners. Scientists urged public officials to endorse a "safe sex" program promoting the use of condoms in order to reduce transmission of the virus. But many religious authorities and cultural conservatives fought against the idea, believing that the promotion of safe sex merely encouraged promiscuity.

In October 1985 the death from AIDS of Rock Hudson, a popular film star and a personal friend of the Reagans, helped to humanize the disease both for the president and for the public at large. The president appointed a commission that recommended much higher levels of funding for government and private research, education programs, and treatment. The virus had been identified by 1984, and now a search for ways to prevent or cure the disease began in earnest. Reagan urged compassion for people with AIDS but seldom spoke of the subject and refused to endorse his own surgeon general's call for widespread publicity encouraging the use of condoms.

Immigration

Accepting his party's nomination for president in 1980, Ronald Reagan thanked "divine Providence" for making America an "island of freedom" and a haven for refugees fleeing oppression and disaster. Shortly after taking office, he ordered the Coast Guard to tow out to sea any boats of Haitian refugees approaching America. These responses typified the ambivalence many Americans felt about changing immigration patterns.

The shift toward non-European immigration had accelerated since the 1970s. Almost 45 percent of documented immigrants came from Asia and the Middle East, and about as many from Latin America and the Caribbean; just over 10 percent came from Europe. Increased Asian immigration was especially dramatic during the 1980s, as 3.5 million Filipino, Chinese, Korean, and Vietnamese immigrants boosted the number of Asian-Americans in the United States by 100 percent. Although some Asians came as refugee "boat people," most were well educated, and many had family members already living in the United States.

Like the Carter administration, Reagan's immigration officials tended to favor people fleeing from left-wing regimes. Although the 1980 refugee law had offered asylum to people of any nationality who came to the United States because of a "well-founded fear of persecution," the Reagan administration implemented the law selectively. Nearly anyone fleeing Cuba or Nicaragua received political asylum, but most Salvadorans, Haitians, and Guatemalans—whose regimes Washington counted as allies—were classified as "economic" refugees and denied admittance.

Americans concerned with those refused asylum formed a Sanctuary Movement modeled on the Underground Railroad of the pre–Civil War years. Through a network of churches and other institutions, members offered shelter to refugees. Boston and Cambridge declared themselves "sanctuary cities." Immigration officials fought back, winning convictions of several sanctuary workers in federal trials.

Immigration aroused mixed feelings among the general public. African-Americans resented what they saw as favored treatment of the new arrivals. The large number of undocumented Mexicans living in the United States—a number estimated at anywhere between 3 million and 15 million—aroused special concern. Some whites feared the erosion of English as the national language with the proliferation of new cultures and tongues. Voters in California, Arizona, and Florida passed laws declaring English the official state language.

After years of debate about how to control immigration, Congress passed the 1986 Simpson-Rodino Act. It offered legal status to several million undocumented aliens living in the United States but imposed fines on employers who hired new undocumented workers. It remains unclear whether these provisions have affected illegal immigration. As of 1990, the United States permitted about 1 million people to enter per year as immigrants or refugees, historically a very high number.

CONCLUSION

Ronald Reagan relished a particular anecdote that expressed his belief in approaching the future with optimism. He described two boys, a pessimist and an optimist, who received Christmas gifts. The pessimist got a roomful of toys but felt miserable because he was sure there had to be a catch. The optimist got a roomful of horse manure but seemed delighted. He dug around for hours, exclaiming that "with all that manure, there just has to be a pony in there somewhere!"

The story revealed the president's charm as well as his own failure to recognize that in critical areas of public policy, the metaphorical pony might indeed not exist. Reagan's greatest achievement was his restoration of a sense of national pride and optimism among many Americans. He also succeeded in bringing conservative economic and social thought into the political mainstream, and he presided over a long, although modest, economic expansion. Nevertheless, his domestic policies often had painful consequences.

Reagan's insistence on tax cuts combined with massive defense spending swelled the budget deficit and the national debt to staggering levels, creating a severe economic handicap for the nation's future. As he cut social spending on programs that benefited the needy, his economic policies helped to deepen the poverty of many Americans and enlarge the gap between rich and poor. His emphasis on deregulation contributed to the costly S&L debacle. His approaches to drug abuse and education did little to solve ongoing problems, and his early refusal to acknowledge the AIDS crisis delayed the research and treatment efforts. Although his reassuring speeches helped Americans feel a renewed sense of community, the influx of immigrants continued to increase the ethnic and cultural diversity of the United States—an area in which Reagan, with his emphasis on fairly rigid "traditional" values, could offer little guidance.

In sum, the Reagan years left a complicated and often contradictory legacy in many aspects of politics and domestic affairs. As the next chapter illustrates, the same could be said of the Reagan administration's foreign policy. ■

FURTHER READING

On Ronald Reagan, see: Garry Wills, *Reagan's America* (1988); Lou Cannon, *Reagan* (1982) and *President Reagan: The Role of a Lifetime* (1991); Ronald Reagan, *An American Life* (1990); Michael Rogin, *Ronald Reagan: The Movie* (1987); Haynes Johnson, *Sleepwalking Through History* (1991). On the politics and the economic and social policies of the 1980s, see: Donald T. Regan, *For the Record* (1988); David Stockman, *The Triumph of Politics* (1986); Benjamin Friedman, *Day of Reckoning: The Consequences of American Economic Policy Under Reagan and After* (1988); Herman Schwartz, *Packing the Courts* (1988); Bob Schieffer and Gary Paul Gates, *The Acting President* (1989); Kevin Phillips, *The Politics of Rich and Poor* (1990); Randy Shilts, *And the Band Played On: Politics, People, and the AIDS Epidemic* (1987); William Julius Wilson, *The Truly Disadvantaged: The Inner City, the Underclass and Public Policy* (1987); Barbara Ehrenreich, *The Worst Years of Our Lives* (1990); Nicolaus Mills, ed., *Culture in an Age of Money* (1991); Mark Hertsgaard, *On Bended Knee* (1988); Michael Schaller, *Reckoning with Reagan: America and Its President in the 1980s* (1992).

14

Back in the Saddle: Foreign Policy During the Reagan Years

In August 1984, engaging in some banter before delivering a Saturday morning radio commentary, President Ronald Reagan spoke into a microphone he did not know was on. "My fellow Americans," he declared, "I'm pleased to tell you today that I've signed legislation that will outlaw the Soviet Union forever. We begin bombing in five minutes." The president laughed off the remark, as if it were something his friend John Wayne might have said in a Hollywood western. But to critics of his foreign policy, this incident seemed to confirm that Reagan's presidency put America "back in the saddle," all too ready to ride off in pursuit of real or imagined enemies. Soviet leaders considered Reagan's off-the-cuff joke so threatening that they instructed KGB intelligence officers in Washington to report any indications of war preparations such as the stockpiling of food or blood in federal buildings.

As a presidential candidate, Ronald Reagan had insisted that "there *are* simple answers" to complex questions. He complained that America suffered from a "Vietnam syndrome," an inability or unwillingness to use force to resist Soviet pressure and defend American friends and interests abroad. Attributing this weakness to guilt over the Vietnam War, Reagan praised that struggle as a noble cause. His first secretary of state, General Alexander Haig, echoed this sentiment, declaring the time had come for Americans to shed their sackcloth and ashes. The new administration pledged to restore American military superiority, defend allies, and support anti-Communist movements throughout the world. Unlike Dwight Eisenhower, who had made similar remarks but restrained military spending, President Reagan pushed through Congress the largest military budgets that the United States had ever adopted in a time of peace. Between 1981 and 1989, total defense spending ballooned from less than $200 billion to over $300 billion per year.

Beneath the rhetoric, however, the president had largely filled new bottles with old wine. His talk of restraining Moscow's "evil empire" harked back to the Truman Doctrine, the policy of containment, and the birth of NATO. His willingness to intervene in Central America and the Caribbean echoed the policies of Dwight Eisenhower, John Kennedy, and Lyndon Johnson. He even forged ties with many conservative Democrats who had chafed under the Carter administration, appointing them to posts as arms negotiators and diplomats. These new appointees included Jeane Kirkpatrick, Max Kampelman, Paul Nitze, Kenneth Adelman, Richard Perle, and Elliot Abrams. A group of Democratic neoconservative intellectuals, among them writers Midge Decter and Norman Podhoretz, became some of Reagan's most enthusiastic supporters.

Midway through his second term, when the Iran-contra scandal erupted, it appeared that Reagan's primary new contribution to foreign policy had been to assemble a team of staffers who engaged in secret arms deals that violated the law, flouted the authority of Congress, contradicted the president's own publicly announced policies, and ran counter to ordinary common sense. Although Reagan successfully pleaded ignorance of the details of these activities, his reputation was badly tarnished.

Yet by the end of his administration a sudden thawing in relations with the Soviet Union changed Reagan's record dramatically. With Mikhail Gorbachev, the new Soviet leader, Reagan signed a treaty that eliminated an entire category of nuclear missiles. Like their president, most Americans forgot about Reagan's earlier depiction of the Soviet Union as an "evil empire," and opinion polls showed that Americans felt friendlier toward the Soviets than at any other time since the Second World War. Having been elected as a cold warrior, Reagan now took credit for the peace, claiming that his massive defense build-up had forced the Soviets to cooperate. In reality, the reasons for the thaw in relations were much more complex; but by responding to the new conditions, the Reagan administration did achieve a major break in Cold War hostilities.

REAGAN'S FOREIGN POLICY STYLE

As with the president's domestic programs, a yawning gap existed between the rhetoric and the reality of Reagan's foreign policy. Ronald Reagan lived in a world of myths and symbols rather than facts and programs. The Carter presidency, with its emphasis on details and process, had failed to articulate any overarching vision. Reagan stood at the opposite extreme, evoking sunny images of prosperity without stipulating the necessary steps to achieve that goal. He usually dismissed unpleasant events as someone else's responsibility. The public responded enthusiastically to the president's celebration of symbolic victories, such as the invasion of tiny Grenada in 1983, and joined him in quickly forgetting disasters, such as the death of 241 marines in Beirut a few days earlier. Whatever Americans thought about Reagan's foreign policy, they liked the fact that he made them feel good.

Despite Reagan's reputation as an ideological activist, he gave little specific direction to his foreign policy advisers. Until 1983, it is uncertain whether Reagan even thought in terms of a coherent strategy: the accumulation of military hardware and covert paramilitary operations passed for a foreign policy. Nor did he spend much time checking on how well subordinates carried out his orders. During meetings with the National Security Council (NSC) staff, he seldom asked questions and frequently exhibited what aides described as a "glassy look." The president never seemed tempted to utilize the huge military structure created after 1981. Convinced that "negotiating from strength" would yield results by itself, Reagan relied on an arms build-up to wring concessions from Moscow and a rollback of Soviet influence. He may even have hoped that a costly arms race would bankrupt the Soviet Union.

Reagan deferred to his advisers, few of whom could agree on anything. In appointing former Kissinger aide General Alexander Haig as secretary of state, Reagan promised him full authority to make and implement foreign policy. But when Haig submitted his agenda and asked for a response, presidential counselor Edwin Meese informed him the agenda had been "lost." White House aides negated Haig's influence from the moment of his appointment. Haig later described the Reagan policy-making apparatus as a "ghost ship." One heard "the creak of the rigging and the groan of the timbers and sometimes even glimpsed the crew on deck . . . but which of the crew had the helm . . . was impossible to know for sure."

In the absence of central direction, Secretary of State Haig (replaced by George Shultz in 1982), Secretary of Defense Caspar Weinberger, CIA director William Casey, and six successive directors of the NSC—Richard Allen, William Clark, Robert McFarlane, John Poindexter, Frank Carlucci, and Colin Powell—each followed his own tack. For example, Shultz supported negotiations with the Soviets over arms control and a tough military approach toward minor enemies, such as the Sandinistas in Nicaragua, while Weinberger opposed any deals with Moscow that might limit the immense arms build-up. At the same time, Weinberger showed great reluctance to commit conventional forces under almost any circumstances. At one cabinet meeting an exasperated Shultz snapped, "If you are not willing to use force, maybe we should cut your budget." Reagan asked his contentious advisers to compromise—a solution NSC head Robert McFarlane described as "intrinsically unworkable," in light of the secretary of state's and secretary of defense's dislike for one another.

Throughout his first term, Reagan tried to cast the Soviet Union in the role of the devil. The Soviet Union, he remarked, "underlies all the unrest that is going on. If they weren't engaged in this game of dominoes, there wouldn't be any hot spots in the world." This simplistic analysis brushed aside the many social, economic, and political causes of violence in the Middle East, Central America, and Africa. Although Soviet meddling often complicated problems, the absence of Soviet influence would not bring peace to Lebanon, El Salvador, or South Africa.

Restoring the CIA's franchise to conduct paramilitary operations in the Third World emerged as a central feature of Reagan's foreign policy. He appointed his friend and campaign manager, William Casey, to head the intelligence agency. Casey, who had worked in the Office of Strategic Services during the Second World War, made the CIA an active player in the battle against Soviet influence in the Third World. After convincing Congress to abandon Carter-era restraints on covert operations, the CIA funded anti-Communist guerrillas in Angola, Mozambique, Afghanistan, and Central America. The administration boasted that "low-intensity warfare," a term for counterinsurgency operations, was a cheap and fairly safe way to battle Moscow for global influence. Covert warfare minimized the risk of a direct confrontation with the Soviets while giving the administration freedom to act without oversight.

Reagan popularized an idea broached in 1980 by Georgetown University political science professor Jeane Kirkpatrick, whom he later named ambassador to the United Nations. Kirkpatrick had distinguished between "authoritarian" and "totalitarian" governments. The former, like the shah's Iran, might eventually evolve toward greater liberty. In contrast, the totalitarian type of government, exemplified by Communist states, was unlikely to become more democratic. Thus, the United States should support authoritarian rulers against leftist revolutionaries. Reagan employed Kirkpatrick's logic to justify his reluctance to impose sanctions on the racist South African regime or to criticize human rights abuses perpetrated by friendly governments in El Salvador, Guatemala, Chile, Haiti, the Philippines, and Pakistan. Reagan did agree to press dictators Ferdinand Marcos of the Philippines and Jean-Claude ("Baby Doc") Duvalier of Haiti to abandon power, but only when the alternative to their continued rule seemed a left-wing revolution.

An anti-Communist ideological fervor also affected foreign economic assistance programs. The Reagan administration vigorously opposed planned economies and lectured potential aid recipients about the magic of the free marketplace. American officials pressed developing nations to "privatize" their economies by abandoning nationalized industry and central planning. To a degree, the facts justified this argument. Most Communist economies had performed miserably during the previous two decades, while capitalist policies had spurred growth in a number of developing nations, such as those in Southeast Asia. However, the free market failed badly in other instances. For example, Washington spent lavishly to assist procapitalist governments in Jamaica, the Philippines, and El Salvador, with pitiful results.

Continuing a trend begun in the Nixon presidency, most American foreign aid went to a mere handful of countries, and it was generally for military purposes. Israel and Egypt each received several billion dollars, and the Philippines, Turkey, Pakistan, and El Salvador also received large amounts. These six nations absorbed nearly three-fourths of all foreign aid. Overall, however, the United States devoted less than one-third of 1 percent of its gross national product to helping other nations, a lower percentage than that spent by any other industrialized democracy.

Despite blanket hostility toward Communist governments, the administration found it possible to act flexibly. For example, Reagan had criticized Carter's extension of full diplomatic recognition to the People's Republic of China in December 1978. He hinted he might re-establish formal relations with Taiwan, whose government he described as "an American ally," and was determined to sell Taiwan weapons, despite China's opposition. Accordingly, for two years after Reagan took office, Washington and Beijing criticized each other, and China even threatened to downgrade relations with the United States if America sold weapons to Taiwan. But in the end pragmatism prevailed. The United States valued China's anti-Soviet stance and needed Chinese help in supporting anti-Soviet guerrillas in Afghanistan. For its part, China needed Western technology and trade. In August 1982 the two nations agreed that the United States could continue to sell weapons to Taiwan if Washington promised to reduce its sales over time. President Reagan visited China early in 1984. Thereafter he dropped his pro-Taiwan rhetoric and during the remainder of his administration said little, in public or private, about the world's largest Communist nation.

MORE BANG FOR MORE BUCKS: THE NEW ARMS RACE

The pillar of Reagan's foreign policy was his staggering arms build-up. To achieve its announced goal of "peace through strength," the administration developed an ambitious scheme to boost annual defense spending by more than $100 billion. In terms of 1990 dollars, the military budget soared past $300 billion a year (see figure). At full throttle, the Pentagon spent about $34 million per hour, every day.

During the build-up, Washington invested huge sums to procure a variety of advanced weapons, most of which were intended for a nuclear war with the Soviet Union. These weapons included enhanced radiation neutron bombs and artillery designed to irradiate Soviet tanks and troops in central Europe; 100 MX intercontinental missiles, each designed to carry ten nuclear warheads with pinpoint accuracy into Soviet territory; the B-1 intercontinental bomber, intended to replace the fleet of aging B-52s; the "stealth" bomber and fighter, radar-avoiding planes able to penetrate deep inside the Soviet Union; powerful and highly accurate D-5 missiles for mounting on Trident submarines; cruise missiles (slow but accurate pilotless

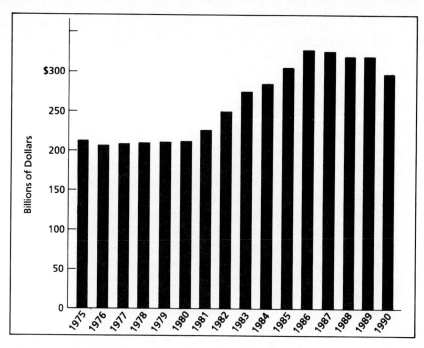

The Military Budget, 1975–1990 (in Constant 1990 Dollars)

drones); and Pershing II missiles that, when launched from Europe, could hit targets inside Russia in a few minutes. In addition to all of this weaponry, the Pentagon developed a modernized, 600-ship navy.

Mounting Anxieties

The new weapons systems were immensely powerful, immensely expensive, and immensely controversial. For example, critics charged that MX missiles were so powerful and accurate that in a crisis the Soviets would be tempted to strike first in order to destroy the missiles before they could be launched; and that American commanders would feel equally pressured to use the weapons in a pre-emptive strike. Thus, instead of enhancing deterrence by preserving a reserve force to retaliate against a Soviet first strike, the new weapons created a situation in which nervous strategists on both sides might feel impelled to be the first to act.

Despite such controversies, Congress appropriated most of the defense funds that Reagan asked for. The Democratic party, which controlled the House but not the Senate during Reagan's first six years, provided little opposition to the administration's arms build-up. The lack of congressional opposition stemmed in part from the fact that two decades of arms limitation talks with the Soviets had borne meager fruit. Moreover, the Democrats were suffering an intense identity crisis because of embarrassment about President Carter's ineffectiveness during the Iranian hostage crisis. Many Democrats appreciated Reagan's tough rhetoric and favored a more assertive foreign policy, even though they feared that the administration might provoke a war.

Although the congressional Democrats failed to provide much opposition to the arms build-up, at the grassroots level many Americans expressed anxiety over the consequences of the new arms race. In 1982 journalist Jonathan Schell, in *The Fate of the Earth*, described the effects of a single hydrogen bomb dropped on New York City; the book was a best seller. Over the next two years the grassroots Nuclear Freeze Movement organized large demonstrations calling on both superpowers to cease building new weapons capable of mass destruction. In 1982 seventeen senators and 128 House members supported a resolution to this effect. The next year, the House of Representatives voted in favor of a nuclear weapons freeze.

Angered by this criticism, Reagan charged that Communist agents were directing the activities of some antinuclear groups. That charge later returned to embarrass him when a large number of Roman Catholic bishops issued a 1983 pastoral letter condemning nuclear weapons as "immoral." The bishops contended that the arms race robbed "the poor and the vulnerable" of government funds and placed "before humankind the indefensible choices of constant terror or surrender." In November of that year, an audience of 100 million television viewers watched *The Day After*, a docudrama portraying the devastation of a nuclear war. Although polls showed that a large segment of the American populace was uncomfortable with the rapid pace of the arms race, Reagan received enough political support to continue to push his weapons programs through Congress.

On the question of arms limitation treaties, the administration adopted a contradictory policy. Reagan denounced Carter's unratified Strategic Arms Limitation Treaty, or SALT II, claiming it locked in a Soviet advantage; he indicated that he would ignore the treaty's restrictions and build whatever long-range nuclear weapons were needed to close the "window of vulnerability" that exposed the United States to potential attack. But the Joint Chiefs of Staff pressed Reagan to stay within the SALT II guidelines, because they restrained the Soviets equally as much as the Americans, if not more. Without admitting it, the Reagan administration honored SALT II, although the president lost no opportunity to criticize it as "fatally flawed."

Although Reagan privately chortled that the Soviets were "squealing like they're sitting on a sharp nail," in public he tried to blunt criticism of his defense policy in mid-1982 by calling for renewed arms control talks with Moscow. But these negotiations—the Strategic Arms Reduction Talks (START) on long-range missiles and the Intermediate Nuclear Forces (INF) talks on medium-range weapons— quickly foundered. In December 1983, the United States began deployment of cruise and Pershing II missiles in Western Europe, in accordance with a decision made at the end of the Carter administration. The Soviet Union denounced the move and canceled further discussions—proving, Reagan said, Moscow's bad faith. When Reagan offered a "zero option"—the removal of all Soviet short-range missiles targeted on Europe in exchange for an agreement not to deploy the cruise and Pershing missiles—the Soviets rejected it as an attempt to guarantee an American advantage.

One Defense Department official, T. K. Jones, tried to calm popular alarm with assurances that most Americans would not only survive but prosper after a nuclear war. Jones suggested that in case of attack, citizens need only "dig a hole, cover it with a couple of doors, and then throw three feet of dirt on top. . . . If there are enough shovels around . . . everybody's going to make it." Despite ridicule from many who heard his pitch, Jones predicted rapid recovery following a global nuclear war.

Star Wars

Beginning in 1983, the president tried to undermine sentiment against nuclear weapons and win public support for his arms build-up through a bold new approach. A Reagan fund-raiser, brewer Joseph Coors, arranged for physicist Edward Teller to visit the White House. Teller, a long-standing advocate of heavy armaments, told the president that secret research indicated that a space-based, nuclear-bomb-powered "X-ray laser" could produce energy beams capable of shooting down Soviet missiles after launch but before they could deploy their nuclear warheads. Mounted on orbiting platforms, the lasers could provide a virtual shield over America.

Reagan, who for years had complained about the lack of a defense against enemy missiles, loved the idea of a high-technology "fix" that would neutralize Soviet weapons. In a March 1983 speech he presented a startling vision of a peaceful future in which a Strategic Defense Initiative (SDI), as he called it, would render nuclear weapons "impotent and obsolete." Reagan proposed a vast research and development project to perfect a space-based antimissile system along the lines suggested by Teller. Critics, who dubbed the concept "Star Wars" after the popular science fiction movie of that name, argued that the project would violate the existing treaty barring Moscow and Washington from deploying antimissile systems.

Even though diplomats and Pentagon officials had almost no advance notice of Reagan's speech, the White House public relations staff had polled focus groups and found solid support for the idea of a "space shield." White House aide Michael Deaver admitted that he and others who were queried had no idea how such a shield would work, but he thought "the concept was a great idea." Most scientists, however, doubted that a system as complicated as Star Wars, which depended on untested technology, would ever work. Even a shield 90-percent effective would allow through enough enemy warheads to obliterate the United States. Some critics judged SDI little more than a mask for large government subsidies that would help American industry compete against Japan. Others speculated that SDI proponents hoped to force the Soviets into a high-technology race that might bankrupt Moscow. For their part, Soviet leaders worried that the mysterious technology might have offensive capabilities.

Whatever the motivations may have been, Reagan convinced Congress to spend about $17 billion on SDI research between 1983 and 1989. The X-ray laser proved a failure, however, and the research focused instead on schemes to protect American missile silos—not the American people—against attack.

International Events and Domestic Criticism

Although the Soviet government denounced Reagan as a warmonger, it mounted no effective response to American initiatives. Old and ailing Leonid Brezhnev, in power since 1964, presided over a lethargic and corrupt administration during his last years in power. His death in 1982 left his colleagues groping for a successor. The Communist oligarchy selected Yuri Andropov, the government's security chief, as party general secretary. Andropov was considered something of a reformer, but he suffered from kidney disease and spent most of his brief term in office on dialysis. Following his death in 1984, party elders tapped as leader a lackluster timeserver, Konstantin Chernenko, ill with emphysema, who lived only a year thereafter. When asked why he did not hold a summit with his Soviet counterpart, Reagan quipped, "They keep dying on me." Only in 1985, when the fifty-four-year-old Mikhail Gorbachev emerged as general secretary of the Communist party, did the Soviet Union have an effective leader.

In the interim, two events gave Reagan opportunities to sharpen his anti-Communist rhetoric. In December 1981, as the Solidarity labor movement in Poland threatened to topple local Communist officials, Moscow pressured the Polish army to impose martial law. Reagan denounced Moscow for unleashing the "forces of tyranny" against its neighbor and urged Americans to light "candles of freedom" in support of the Poles, a symbol that brought a sympathetic response from many Americans. Two years later, in September 1983, a tragic Soviet error disturbed Americans even more. A series of navigational mistakes led Korean Air Lines Flight 007 to stray far off course en route from Alaska to Seoul. After flying for some distance over Soviet territory that included a secret missile test range, the 747 airliner was attacked by a Soviet fighter pilot and all 269 people on board were killed, including a member of Congress.

Reagan immediately branded the event a "crime against humanity" and an "act of barbarism." He insisted that Moscow had knowingly destroyed a civilian aircraft without warning. The facts were far murkier. American electronic intelligence intercepts showed that Soviet air force personnel probably did not realize they were tracking a civilian plane. They thought an American RC-135 spy plane, which had earlier flown nearby, had returned on a spy mission over the missile range. The Soviet pilot later said he recognized the plane as a 747 but believed it was on a spy mission. Thus the shootdown was more a case of mistaken identity than of premeditated murder. Reagan soon learned these facts but refused to amend his words. His version of the incident better justified his anti-Soviet stance and, he admitted, prompted Congress to spend more money on weapons.

The administration's emotional rhetoric, coupled with the inability of Moscow's doddering leadership to explain its actions, buoyed Reagan's public support and assured continued congressional funding for the administration's defense programs. By this time the Pentagon had so much money to spend that defense contractors could not produce enough ships, tanks, planes, and missiles to fill the orders. Therefore, a 50 percent increase in spending did not yield 50 percent more tanks, planes, and ships. The enormous increase did, however, cause costs to soar, quality to decline, and corruption to flourish. Many weapons, rushed into production with inadequate testing, failed to meet specifications.

The fact that so few people, in or out of government, understood the technical aspects of weapons systems inhibited informed debate. Often, the press and the public debated marginal details rather than the overall logic of the buying spree. For example, the B-1 and B-2 bombers cost about $200 million and $700 million respectively per plane, yet neither performed as promised. Ordinary citizens were not in a position to know if the costs were fair or exorbitant, or if the lapses in quality were excusable. Consequently, public anger focused on minutiae—on reports that the Pentagon had paid $500 apiece for the toilet seats and hammers carried on these aircraft. Everyone knew what a toilet seat or hammer cost at a corner hardware store and felt the taxpayers had been bilked. But who felt secure enough to assert how much the air force should pay for a stealth bomber? Congress suffered from similar insecurity and ignorance. Congressional committees held hearings in which irate members denounced contractors for price gouging on small items, but the more serious procurement problems were seldom discussed.

At the end of the Reagan administration, the Justice Department finally indicted several Defense Department officials and contractors for illegal actions. The charges included faking quality-control tests and selling competitors' data to companies that were bidding on contracts. Congress passed new procurement regulations in 1988 and stiffened restrictions on Pentagon officials who took defense-industry jobs immediately after leaving government service. By then, over $2 trillion had gone into Pentagon coffers.

AMERICA AND THE MIDDLE EAST

As it confronted the Soviet Union with its massive arms build-up, the Reagan administration also tried to address some of the thornier problems of the Middle East. Like his predecessors, however, President Reagan found it difficult to impose American solutions. The Arab-Israeli conflict continued to resist peaceful settlement. Prolonged strife in Lebanon and Afghanistan remained unresolved, and a bloody war between Iran and Iraq set the stage for further Persian Gulf problems in the 1990s. Making these issues more urgent was the rise in terrorist attacks around the world, many of them against American targets.

Israel, Lebanon, and the Palestinians

By the early 1980s various armed factions within Lebanon were embroiled in a long civil conflict. At the same time, Israel was bombing sectors controlled by the Palestine Liberation Organization (PLO), a group held responsible for guerrilla and terrorist attacks on Israeli targets. The PLO was the largest of the political organizations that claimed to represent ethnic Palestinians, who had often been displaced or ignored during the repeated Middle East conflicts since 1948.

In June 1982, American Secretary of State Alexander Haig urged Israel to invade Lebanon in order to destroy the PLO's forces. But when Israel acted on this recommendation, Haig's colleague, National Security Adviser William P. Clark, contacted PLO representatives in an effort to negotiate a compromise. Haig, already on bad terms with Reagan's inner circle, quit in a huff. The president then appointed George P. Shultz to head the State Department, and Shultz

The scene after a terrorist bombing leveled part of the American embassy in Beirut, killing sixty-three people in April 1983. *Wide World Photos.*

labored mightily to bring some semblance of order to American policy.

In August, as Israeli forces surrounded Beirut, the United States arranged for the evacuation of the PLO forces it had previously sought to eradicate. Shultz and his aides urged that Israel allow the PLO to establish a homeland on the west bank of the Jordan River in return for guarantees of peace with the Jewish state. To Shultz's dismay, neither Israel nor the Palestinians agreed. Meanwhile, the assassination of Christian Lebanese leader Bashir Gemayel on September 14 sparked Christian massacres of Palestinian refugees. Israeli officials at least passively encouraged these attacks.

As the chaotic Lebanese political scene approached complete anarchy, the United States, France, and Italy sent peacekeeping forces to Beirut, hoping to shore up Christian Lebanese forces and to balance the presence of other military units, which included Shiite Muslim and Druse militias and troops from the Syrian army. Each of these forces dominated parts of the fragile country. But the peacekeeping mission sparked greater animosity, for Lebanese Muslims bitterly resented Western aid to the Christian minority. On April 18, 1983, a suicide squad attacked the American embassy in Beirut, killing 63 people.

Shortly thereafter, American naval ships off Lebanon began shelling Shiite and Druse positions. This retaliation, which was interpreted as further pro-Christian intervention, provoked a desperate act of revenge. On October 23 a Muslim terrorist drove a truck filled with explosives into marine barracks near Beirut's airport, killing 241 marines. French troops were attacked simultaneously.

Although President Reagan offered a moving tribute to the slaughtered young men, he could not explain what they had died for. In his 1984 State of the Union address, he declared that keeping the marines in Lebanon was "central to our credibility on a global scale." But two weeks later, without explanation, the president ordered American troops out of Beirut, and the warring Lebanese factions resumed their communal slaughter.

Like the conflict in Lebanon, the problem of Palestinian refugees and those living under Israeli occupation defied solution. Beginning in late 1987, Palestinians living in territory that Israel had occupied since 1967 began an *intifadah,* or civilian uprising against Israeli authorities. Israeli troops and police responded harshly, killing some seven hundred Palestinians over the next three years.

In 1988, PLO leader Yasir Arafat declared that his organization accepted Israel's right to exist—an important concession that prompted Washington to begin diplomatic contacts with the PLO. However, none of the parties could agree on terms for the establishment of a Palestinian state, the key to any settlement of the Palestinian refugee issue and the Arab-Israeli conflict as a whole. Washington's close ties to Israel complicated negotiations with Arab leaders, who frequently suspected that the United States was less than evenhanded.

Libya and the Question of Terrorism

During the Carter administration the Iranian hostage crisis had focused public attention on the vulnerability of Westerners abroad, especially in the Middle East. Throughout the 1980s, incidents of international hostage-taking and outright terrorism were on the rise, and Americans continued to be among the favorite targets, as in the 1983 attacks on the embassy and marine barracks in Beirut. The risk affected not only diplomats and military personnel but also business people and other civilians.

Terrorism, some observers noted, was the atomic bomb of the weak, and in the 1980s it became the weapon of choice for many frustrated Third World groups, especially those from the Middle East. In reality, the various kidnappings, aircraft and ship hijackings, and bombings were marginal acts in the world arena. On average during the 1980s, more Americans were killed by lightning while playing golf than by terrorist acts. Yet the intense media coverage and the responses of Presidents Carter and Reagan made the issue a major one.

The Reagan administration focused much of its antiterrorist sentiment on Libya's demagogic strongman, Muammar Qaddafi. Flush with cash from the sale of Libyan oil, Qaddafi bought Soviet military hardware and bankrolled a number of terrorist groups operating in the Middle East and Europe. The president and State Department, as well as the mass media, blamed him for causing much of the violence in the Middle East and threatening the lives of Americans abroad. The Libyan leader's flamboyant, aggressive style and his fondness for personally insulting American leaders especially outraged President Reagan.

Eager, as George Shultz phrased it, to put Qaddafi "back in his box," Washington deployed a large naval flotilla in the Gulf of Sidra on Libya's northern coast. Qaddafi, who claimed the gulf as territorial waters, clashed several times with the Americans as he dared them to cross the "line of death." United States and Libyan jets fought air duels over the gulf in 1981 and again in 1988, with the loss of several Libyan planes.

In April 1986, Libyan agents were implicated in the bombing of a Berlin nightclub frequented by American soldiers. Reagan, calling Qaddafi the "mad dog of the Middle East," sent planes to attack Tripoli. One of the targets was Qaddafi's compound. Although the Libyan leader escaped injury in the raid, one of his daughters was killed. Thereafter, Qaddafi remained a bitter critic of the United States but tempered his activities against American allies and interests. The collapse of oil prices after 1986 and continued feuding with his North African neighbors probably had more of a restraining effect on Qaddafi than the threat of another American air raid.

The Persian Gulf

A bloody nine-year-war between Iraq and Iran, fought for regional influence and control of deep-water ports, took the lives of nearly 2 million people between 1980 and 1988. Washington disliked the secular nationalism of Iraqi leader Saddam Hussein as well as the Islamic fundamentalism promoted by Iran's Ayatollah Khomeini. A victory by either, American experts feared, would lead one of the two countries to dominate much of the oil-rich Middle East. To prevent this, Washington played a balancing act, providing secret military aid and intelligence to whichever side appeared to be losing at the time. From 1981 to 1986, this meant helping Iran, but after 1986 Washington assisted Iraq. The United States often coordinated its policy with Israel.

But the Jewish state, most concerned about the nearby threat of Iraq and the safety of several thousand Iranian Jews, more consistently aided Iran.

When Washington abruptly began to aid the Iraqis in 1987, Iran responded by attacking Western oil tankers carrying Iraqi cargo in the Persian Gulf. Reagan ordered the navy to escort ships carrying petroleum, a policy that resulted in several small clashes with the Iranians. The bloodiest incidents involved cases of mistaken identity. In May 1987, an Iraqi pilot, taking the destroyer U.S.S. *Stark* for an Iranian ship, blasted it with a missile, killing thirty-seven sailors. A year later, the captain of the U.S.S. *Vincennes* mistakenly shot down an Iranian passenger plane, killing 290 civilians. This loss may have prompted Iran to sponsor the December 1988 bombing of a Pan Am flight that killed several hundred people.

Finally exhausted by their vast bloodletting, Iran and Iraq signed a cease-fire in August 1988, but without abandoning their conflicting territorial claims. During the conflict, Iraq had developed and used poison gas against Iran and pushed ahead with work on an atomic bomb. Despite these threats, the Reagan administration continued to consider Iraq a useful counterforce to Iran. The expansion of Iraqi power had grave consequences, for it led to Iraq's later invasion of Kuwait and the Persian Gulf war of 1991 (see pages 593–600).

Afghanistan

When Soviet forces invaded Afghanistan in December 1979, they and the puppet government began a brutal struggle against anti-Communist guerrillas, or *mujahidin.* Many of the guerrillas were Islamic fundamentalists who admired the Ayatollah Khomeini's regime in Iran. Despite their beliefs, the Reagan administration supported guerrilla resistance to Soviet domination. The CIA provided military and economic assistance to the *mujahidin,* using neighboring Pakistan as a base of operations. Millions of Afghans fled the country, most of them resettling in Pakistan.

Washington feared that if the Soviets gained control of Afghanistan, they would use it as a steppingstone to dominate the oil-rich Persian Gulf. But the lightly armed guerrillas proved to be formidable opponents of the Soviet invaders. When the CIA made shoulder-fired antiaircraft missiles available, the *mujahidin* neutralized the invaders' air advantage. American officials described the struggle as the Soviets' Vietnam, a strange analogy for this administration to make in light of Reagan's customary reference to that debacle as a "noble cause."

Nearly a decade after the war began, Moscow's new leader, Mikhail Gorbachev, decided to cut his losses. In 1988 he blamed the costly and unpopular invasion on his dead predecessors and ordered Soviet forces out of Afghanistan. Peace, however, remained hard to arrange. The *mujahidin* fell into factional disputes, and the remnants of the Soviet-backed regime in Kabul proved difficult to dislodge. Without a foreign enemy to unify them, Afghan tribes and military factions reverted to their time-honored pattern of civil conflict.

THE NEW BANANA WARS

Throughout the twentieth century, the United States had intervened frequently in the affairs of its neighbors in Central America and the Caribbean. Derisively called "banana republics," these poor nations were often dominated by American corporations and disciplined by American troops when they strayed from the fold. After the Second World War, the CIA usually handled matters without the direct use of American troops, as in the CIA-backed exile invasions of Guatemala in 1954 and Cuba in 1961. President Johnson, however, had sent regular marines and army forces to the Dominican Republic in 1965.

The Reagan administration, obsessed by what it perceived as the Communist threat to the Western Hemisphere and hoping to erase the memory of Vietnam with some old-fashioned muscle-flexing, revived the long-standing tradition of American intervention, including the use of the army and marines. In the Reagan years the United States invaded one country, Grenada; financed civil wars in two, El Salvador and Nicaragua; and used economic pressure in an effort to topple the government in a fourth, Panama.

The Reagan administration's policy toward Central America often seemed a throwback to the early years of the Cold War. State Department officials warned of a "Moscow-Havana" axis, speculating that Cuban agents under the tutelage of the Soviet Union could spread revolution throughout the unstable region. By creating several Cuba-like nations from Panama to Mexico, officials warned, the Soviet Union would gain control of vital sea lanes and pose a military and economic threat to the United States. Reagan also believed that the consequent invasion of refugees from Central America would destabilize American society.

The administration's critics, in the words of Connecticut Democratic Senator Christopher Dodd, thought Reagan and his advisers knew "as much about Central America in 1983 as we knew about Indochina in 1963." A former Peace Corps volunteer in Latin America, Dodd believed that "if Central America were not racked with poverty, there would be no revolution." Nevertheless, the administration tried to win public backing by assembling a commission on Central America headed by Henry Kissinger, former secretary of state. The commission's 1984 report tried, without success, to please all sides. It noted the social and economic roots of the region's problems and admitted that Moscow could not be blamed for everything. Although it endorsed more economic aid, the report stressed the need to fund the military in El Salvador and the anti-Communist guerrillas in Nicaragua.

Neither the president nor his experts convinced Congress or the public that a real danger existed. Few Americans believed that the future of Western civilization depended on what regime held power in Managua or Tegucigalpa. Despite Reagan's continual effort to arouse popular passion for his Central American initiatives, polls taken throughout the 1980s revealed that three-fourths of the public did not know or care what groups the United States favored or opposed in the region. A large majority of respondents opposed sending any troops to Central America, even to stop Communist takeovers.

El Salvador

Unable in most cases to build congressional or popular support for direct intervention, the Reagan administration generally relied on a combination of military aid and covert warfare in Central America. For example, between 1981 and 1988, Washington spent $4 billion to $5 billion in military and economic aid to El Salvador. A terribly poor country in which 2 percent of the people controlled nearly all the wealth, El Salvador had been racked by rebellions since the 1920s. Although the country had nominally been ruled since 1979 by a moderate reformer, Christian Democrat José Napoleon Duarte, El Salvador's right-wing military held the real power.

Even with massive American aid, the Salvadoran military could not rout the leftist rebels from their rural and urban bases. The military squandered much of the money and used the arms to wage a fierce campaign of repression against civilians suspected of sympathizing with the rebels or agitating for social change. Army death squads killed as many as seventy thousand peasants, teachers, union organizers, and church workers. Robert D'Aubuisson, a former army officer and founder of the right-wing ARENA party, was widely judged responsible for this terrorism. Some United States politicians, like North Carolina Republican Senator Jesse Helms, praised D'Aubuisson, even after his assassins killed several American church workers and union organizers.

Most Americans found such behavior distasteful, but Congress had only limited will to defy an otherwise popular president. Congress did limit the number of American military personnel stationed in El Salvador and required that the president periodically certify that "progress" had occurred in the field of human rights. As long as Reagan did so, Congress approved funds for military and economic aid.

After eight years of bloodshed, Duarte's government had neither defeated the guerrillas nor carried out promised reforms. In 1988 Duarte and his followers lost an election to the ultra-right-wing ARENA party. The war, and civilian deaths, continued unabated.

Grenada

In contrast to its prolonged and unresolved intervention in El Salvador's affairs, the Reagan administration achieved a quick victory with one overt military action in Grenada. A tiny Caribbean island and former British colony, Grenada had been ruled by a Marxist, Maurice Bishop, since 1979. Although the Reagan administration had suspended economic aid to Bishop's government in the early 1980s, Grenada seemed too insignificant to bother with before 1983. A few tourists visited the island, but the main American presence consisted of five hundred medical students enrolled in St. George's University School of Medicine. A contingent of armed Cuban construction workers also labored on the island, building an airport that Prime Minister Bishop called a boon to tourism and Washington labeled a potential Cuban or Soviet air base.

On October 12, 1983, a militant faction of the Marxist New Jewel Movement, led by General Hudson Austin, overthrew Bishop, who had recently softened his anti-Yankee rhetoric. Austin murdered his rival, imposed martial law, and announced a strict curfew. Still, the coup did not seem to affect American interests.

The situation changed abruptly on October 23 with an unrelated incident in another part of the world: the terrorist attack on the marine barracks in Beirut, in which 241 Americans lost their lives. Unable to identify the perpetrators or to use the vast American military power to extract revenge, Reagan and his staff felt intense frustration. Seemingly as an afterthought amid the confusion over Beirut, the president's advisers remembered the medical students in Grenada. Although none had been harmed or were known to face danger, administration officials considered their fate sufficiently in doubt to warrant military intervention. Probably they believed that the dramatic rescue of potential American hostages might divert attention from the carnage in Beirut. After consulting with the leaders of a few tiny Caribbean islands whom Washington had otherwise ignored, on October 25 Reagan ordered thousands of marines and army troops to storm ashore and liberate Grenada from what he called a "brutal gang of thugs."

Although the invasion met only limited resistance from Austin's small band of followers and the armed Cuban workers, unexpected

American soldiers search for Communist forces during the 1983 invasion of Grenada. *Wide World Photos.*

logistic problems delayed for several days full control of the island. Despite the administration's massive arms spending, the Pentagon had equipped naval, army, and air force units with incompatible radios. One soldier used a public phone to call Washington; the Pentagon then patched him through to the flotilla bobbing offshore. Lacking accurate maps, invading troops relied on tourist brochures. In the confusion, United States forces accidentally shelled an insane asylum, which accounted for most of the few dozen Grenadian casualties. Only a handful of Americans were hurt. Despite the operation's occasional resemblance to a comic opera, the Pentagon handed out an unprecedented eight thousand medals to the invading force.

Many islanders welcomed the Americans as saviors who might bring peace and prosperity to their tormented island. Free elections soon restored representative government, but Washington rapidly lost interest and failed to fulfill its promises to fund development programs. Grenada returned to its normal poverty and obscurity, searching in vain for a benefactor to complete its airport.

Because of news blackouts, the public learned little about the invasion's snafus. Most citizens expressed joy that the United States had "won one for a change." Television pictures of returning medical students falling to their knees and kissing American soil diverted attention from the school director's insistence that the students had never been in danger. In 1984 President Reagan's campaign staff used footage of the grateful medical students to devastating effect in the campaign against Democratic nominee Walter Mondale, who had initially condemned the invasion as a violation of international law.

THE CULTURE OF JINGOISM AND NATIONAL POLITICS

The celebration of victory in Grenada reflected a wave of jingoism— boisterous nationalism—that Ronald Reagan both stimulated and exploited. Between 1981 and 1987 a host of immensely popular adventure films and novels portrayed new, all-American heroes who refought and won the war in Vietnam, defeated Soviet troops, and crushed Third World upstarts.

In his seemingly endless series of *Rocky* and *Rambo* films, actor-director Sylvester Stallone often beat Russian and North Vietnamese opponents to a bloody pulp. Other films featured similarly simple-minded themes. Kung-fu champion Chuck Norris kick-boxed his way through Vietnam to rescue American prisoners. In the film *Top Gun*, gallant American fliers shot Libyan and Soviet pilots out of the sky. Tom Clancy's best-selling novel, *The Hunt for Red October*, portrayed American victory over Soviet naval forces. In several of the films and novels, the macho hero confronted his superior, demanding to know whether the good guys would be allowed to win this time.

Americans did win big in the 1984 Olympics held in Los Angeles. In some ways, these games were the most overtly political since Hitler hosted the 1936 Olympiad. With the Soviet bloc boycotting the contest, as the United States had four years earlier, American athletes triumphed in a large number of events. Boisterous crowds waved banners proclaiming "We're Number 1" and chanted "U.S.A., U.S.A." American television networks skipped victory ceremonies in which non-Americans took top honors and often declined to broadcast the national anthems of other teams. Riding the wave of patriotism, several television and radio stations changed their call letters to include the sequence USA. The Chrysler Corporation ran car ads that paraphrased the president's 1984 re-election slogan, "America is back."

Ronald Reagan's landslide victory over Walter Mondale in November 1984 prompted House Speaker Tip O'Neill to tell the president, "In my fifty years in public life, I've never seen a man more popular than you with the American people." During the campaign, polling organizations detected some voter anxiety over Reagan's bellicose rhetoric and his push for ever greater defense spending. To allay these fears, the president's aides had him tone down his hard line toward the Soviet Union and Central America. After his victory, Reagan struck a positive note, declaring that in his second term he would push arms control. "I have no more important goal," he stated, than "reducing and ultimately eliminating nuclear weapons." When National Security Adviser Robert McFarlane asked him to select a couple of particular foreign policy goals from a long list that included such complicated issues as arms control, the Arab-Israeli conflict, and proxy wars in the Third World, Reagan beamed, "Lets do them all!"

The president, in fact, paid attention to only a handful of issues. Among these, none engaged him more than the fate of the anti-Communist guerrillas in Nicaragua, known as contras. Reagan accused the Marxist Sandinista party that ruled Nicaragua of arming subversives throughout Central America and of conspiring with Ayatollah Khomeini's Iran. Few Americans suspected that the president actually forging links to Iran was not Sandinista Daniel Ortega, but Ronald Reagan.

THE IRAN-CONTRA AFFAIR

In 1980 presidential candidate Reagan denounced Jimmy Carter for abandoning America's long-term client, Nicaraguan dictator Anastasio Somoza, whose family had ruled that country as a personal fiefdom since the 1920s. Somoza had been overthrown by the Sandinistas in 1979. Beginning in 1981, the new American president accused the Sandinista leadership of turning Nicaragua into a "Soviet alley on the American mainland," a "safehouse and command post for . . . international terror." In one especially vivid speech, Reagan evoked the image of Sandinistas driving a convoy of armed pickup trucks into Harlingen, Texas, a small town on the Mexican border.

The Sandinistas, to be sure, were Marxists; they bitterly criticized America for its long support of the Somoza dictatorship, they solicited Soviet aid, and they socialized parts of the economy. As Reagan charged, they limited dissent and failed to hold fully free elections. But Sandinista human rights abuses paled before the gory record of American allies in El Salvador and Guatemala. Because the entire Nicaraguan population was less than the population of some neighborhoods in Mexico City, Reagan's talk of a grave threat to the hemisphere was clearly exaggerated. Moreover, in 1989, after the United States finally abandoned armed efforts to depose the Sandinistas, they held free elections; when their conservative opponents won, the Sandinistas stepped down from power.

In 1981, Reagan told CIA director William Casey to organize an anti-Sandinista force among Nicaraguan exiles. At first the CIA insulated America from direct involvement by utilizing Argentine military officers to train the guerrillas. But Argentinian support disappeared in 1982, when Great Britain and Argentina fought a brief war over control of the Falkland Islands, a bleak British colony in the South Atlantic claimed by Argentina. Piqued at Washington's support for Britain, the Argentines pulled out of American military actions in Nicaragua and left them wholly to the CIA.

The contras—or, as Reagan called them, the freedom fighters—survived almost entirely on American military and economic aid. By 1985 their ranks had swelled to between ten and twenty thousand men. Some contra political leaders were genuine democrats who had opposed Somoza, but most of the military commanders, who held the real power in the movement, were veterans of the deposed dictator's army.

When members of Congress raised questions about covert operations in Nicaragua, CIA director Casey insisted that the contras were not trying to overthrow the government, but merely helping to block Sandinista military aid to rebels in El Salvador. But Congress grew restive on learning that contra attacks within Nicaragua had killed thousands of civilians. Representative Edward P. Boland, a Democrat from Massachusetts, sponsored a resolution in 1982—the Boland Amendment—that capped CIA aid to the contras at $24 million and required that none of the funds be used to topple the Nicaraguan government.

Reagan, who believed he had complete authority to determine what could be done abroad, described Congress as a meddlesome "committee of 535" and directed his subordinates to circumvent the law. The Pentagon therefore overrode the $24 million cap by donating, at little or no cost, supposedly surplus weapons to the guerrillas. The CIA prepared a booklet on ways to assassinate Sandinista officials and coordinated attacks on Nicaraguan ports and transport facilities. These actions violated both the Boland Amendment and promises made to Congress. Even Barry Goldwater, the conservative chairman of the Senate Intelligence Committee, told William Casey he was angry at CIA deception.

In October 1984, when the initial funds for the contras ran out, Congress decided to bar further direct or indirect assistance by passing a stricter version of the Boland Amendment. It barred the CIA or "any other agency or entity involved in intelligence activities" from aiding the guerrillas. Congressman Boland described the prohibition as "airtight with no exceptions." Speaker Tip O'Neill proclaimed that the contras were "dead."

The obituary proved premature. CIA director Casey, National Security Adviser Robert McFarlane, and Lieutenant Colonel Oliver North, an NSC aide, began raising funds for the contras from abroad. They induced Israel, South Africa, Saudi Arabia, Brunei, South Korea, and Taiwan to make small contributions to the guerrilla force in return for American goodwill or repayment through supposedly unrelated projects. Although Secretary of State George Shultz admonished Reagan that his decision to circumvent Congress might constitute an impeachable offense, his warning went unheeded. Vice President George Bush participated in the discussion but did not quibble with the decision to rescue the contras.

The Rise of Oliver North

Much of the legwork fell to NSC aide Oliver North, a decorated veteran of the Vietnam War. North had joined the NSC staff early in the Reagan administration on the recommendation of his friend, National Security Adviser Robert McFarlane. Speechwriter Peggy Noonan considered North a true believer who "had the sunny, undimmed confidence of a man who lacks insight into his own weaknesses." Although North's devotion impressed many superiors, Reagan aide Michael Deaver worried about his influence on the president and tried "to keep Ollie out of Reagan's office because he was dangerous." Nevertheless, North convinced Reagan that the Boland Amendment did not apply to the White House staff or the NSC, only to the CIA. As he saw it, NSC members could assist the contras and coordinate private fund-raising on their behalf.

While North worked in this vein, the president asked Congress to appropriate $14 million in "humanitarian aid" to the guerrillas. In April 1985 Congress refused. Immediately after the vote, however, Sandinista leader Daniel Ortega inadvertently saved the contras by flying to Moscow to solicit aid. His visit to Soviet leaders angered so many members of Congress that in June they reversed themselves and approved $24 million in nonlethal aid. The amount and its purpose hardly pleased the White House, however. "You can't win a war with blankets and Band-Aids," North complained.

Despite the admitted ban on CIA involvement, CIA director Casey helped North organize a network of private fund-raisers and arms suppliers for the contras. They recruited retired Air Force General Richard Secord and an Iranian-American arms dealer, Albert Hakim, to buy weapons. To supplement the foreign contributions, Republican Party fund-raiser Carl "Spitz" Channel worked with North to raise donations from wealthy, conservative Americans such as Joseph Coors, Nelson Bunker Hunt, and Ellen Clayton Garwood. North narrated a slide show in which potential donors saw pictures of contras in heroic poses and of military hardware with price tags. The colonel would leave the room to avoid technical complicity in illegal fundraising, and Channel would come in to pick up the check. In 1985, this "Project Democracy" raised several million dollars for the contras. North and Casey were so pleased by the response that they discussed using similar methods to finance a more elaborate covert operations program without the trouble of obtaining congressional approval.

The Iranian Connection

In June 1985, Lebanese Shiite terrorists hijacked a TWA flight in Athens, flew it to Lebanon, executed a navy enlisted man on board, and threatened to kill twenty-nine other American passengers unless Israel released seven hundred Lebanese prisoners from its jails. Reagan pledged to resist this extortion but secretly urged the Israelis to comply. They did, winning freedom for the passengers.

Reagan continued to issue vigorous denunciations of terrorism despite this instance of capitulation to it. Shortly after making the TWA deal, Reagan insisted before an assembly of the American Bar Association that America would never make concessions to terrorists. He called Iran and Libya "outlaw states . . . run by the strangest collection of misfits, Looney Tunes, and squalid criminals since the advent of the Third Reich." Soon, however, the president was approving deals directly with the "Looney Tunes."

As his friends knew, Ronald Reagan was easily moved by the plight of Americans taken hostage and by their families' grief. When left to his own instincts, moreover, the president tended to confuse human interest with the national interest. This trait became apparent when the families of seven American citizens held hostage in Lebanon pleaded with him to win their loved ones' release. Unlike the Americans seized in Iran in 1979, these captives were—with the exception of CIA agent William Buckley—private citizens who had continued living in Beirut against government advice. Nevertheless, Reagan wanted everything possible done to win their freedom.

Reagan's ties to Iran may have dated back to 1980, when, some evidence suggests, his aides may have urged the Iranians not to release the American hostages until after the election—an effort to turn voters against Jimmy Carter. Whether this was true or not, administration officials became involved with Iran in July 1985, when an Israeli official introduced Iranian businessman Manucher Ghorbanifar to National Security Adviser Robert McFarlane. Ghorbanifar claimed to represent a "moderate" faction in Iran that sought better relations with Washington. The moderates supposedly favored the release of American hostages held in Beirut by pro-Iranian Lebanese. Ghorbanifar asked that Reagan show his "good faith" by selling a large number of antitank missiles to his Iranian friends for use against Iraq. In return, the moderates would lobby to free at least four American hostages and, when the aging Khomeini died, would work to improve ties with Washington.

Ghorbanifar played several hands at the same time, maintaining links with many factions in the Middle East. Despite a CIA report that dismissed him as a "fabricator and nuisance," McFarlane considered him reliable. In late July or August 1985 President Reagan approved selling Iran 100 TOW antitank missiles, primarily with the goal of freeing hostages. McFarlane quoted Reagan as saying, "Gee, that sounds pretty good." Both men understood that United States law barred arms sales to Iran because the ayatollah's government had been identified as one that supported terrorism. The ban could be overridden if the president signed a waiver and informed Congress. But, disdainful of Congress and fearful of criticism, the president defied the law. He gave a semblance of legality to his actions by not selling the weapons to Iran directly. Instead, in August 1985, Israel sold Iran American missiles from its stockpile, and Washington supplied replacements.

This arms sale, however, did not result in the freeing of any hostages and Ghorbanifar reported to his connections in Washington that the Iranians wanted 400 more missiles in exchange for one hostage. McFarlane demanded the release of William Buckley, who in fact had already been killed by his captors. In his place, Reverend Benjamin Weir was set free in Beirut on September 15, following the delivery of the missiles via Israel the day before. Colonel North wrote the welcome-home statement for the president.

In November 1985, Ghorbanifar promised the release of additional hostages in return for 100 Hawk antiaircraft missiles. McFarlane described this arrangement as a straight "arms-for-hostages deal," and North wrote a memorandum saying "120 Hawks = five American citizens and guarantees that no more will be taken." In November 1985, Reagan approved a direct sale of the arms to Iran. He still declined to notify Congress, although in December he signed a retroactive secret "finding" (destroyed later by an aide to prevent its release) justifying the earlier arms sale. The document called the arrangement an arms-for-hostages trade.

Even though the first three arms deliveries had yielded only a single hostage, North lobbied for more sales. Admiral John Poindexter, who replaced McFarlane as national security adviser at the end of 1985, authorized North to arrange delivery of over 3,000 antitank and 50 antiaircraft missiles in return for six hostages. An irate Secretary of State George Shultz, who opposed the operation, complained that the administration had become hostage to a bunch of "Iranian rug merchants." But the president remained adamant and ordered the arms sales to continue.

North's "Neat Idea"

The first arms sales, via Israel, had yielded a profit of a few hundred thousand dollars, which Oliver North spent on behalf of the contras.

He joked that the ayatollah had made a *"contrabution."* North later explained that he "saw the idea of using the Ayatollah Khomeini's money to support the Nicaraguan freedom fighters as a . . . neat idea." In North's view, the administration could legitimately use arms sales profits to aid the contras because the Boland Amendment applied only to money actually appropriated by Congress. This strange interpretation ignored the fact that North intended to raise funds by selling government property—missiles—at a profit. Federal law required that such profits be returned to the Treasury and also barred the executive branch from spending any funds that Congress had not appropriated. Although President Reagan later could not recall approving the illegal diversion of funds, Admiral Poindexter testified at his trial in 1990 that Reagan encouraged and approved the plan.

In February 1986 North arranged the shipment of 1,000 TOW missiles, which netted a profit of between $6 million and $10 million. The money was turned over to General Secord to buy weapons for the contras. Again, no hostages were released. In fact, two more Americans were kidnapped in Beirut. The Iranians now demanded more and better weapons as well as intelligence data on Iraq.

After several arms shipments, this dubious adventure had freed only a single hostage. But North and Robert McFarlane, who had since retired from the NSC but was still involved in the deal, continued their gambit. In May 1986 they flew to the Iranian capital carrying a gift-wrapped brace of .357 pistols, a Bible, a birthday cake decorated with a brass key, and suicide pills in case they themselves were taken hostage. The Americans promised that if more hostages were released, a plane loaded with weapons would fly from Israel to Teheran. The Iranians demanded that the arms come first and that Washington arrange the release of several Shiite terrorists jailed in Kuwait for murder. Only then might some American hostages be returned. North, anxious to get money for the contras, wanted to consider these terms, but McFarlane broke off negotiations.

In June 1986, Congress bowed to administration pressure and voted to resume aid to the contras. Although this would alleviate some of the pressure to raise private funds, Congress stipulated that the money could not be expended until October. Thus, North still faced a cash-flow problem. On July 26 the Iranians rekindled American interest by securing the release of hostage Father Lawrence Jenco, although several more Americans were kidnapped in Beirut. North then convinced Poindexter and Reagan to approve another arms shipment to Iran in August, earning vital funds for the contras. Once again, no hostages were released.

Just before the November 1986 congressional elections, North pushed for yet another arms sale, hoping that a hostage release might bolster Republican party fortunes. Because Ghorbanifar by this time had lost credibility, Reagan authorized North to meet with a new Iranian middleman and give him a Bible personally inscribed by the president. If Iran helped free more Americans, Reagan hinted, he would pressure Kuwait to release convicted Shiite terrorists. A final arms sale via Israel just before the election resulted in the release of hostage David Jacobsen on November 2. But instead of the hoped-for political boost, the White House faced a crisis.

The Scandal Surfaces

The bizarre scheme began to unravel on October 5, 1986—two weeks before the scheduled release of the contra-aid funds appropriated by Congress—when Sandinista gunners shot down a plane ferrying weapons to the contras. One crew member, Eugene Hasenfus, survived the crash and confessed to being part of a secret American aid program. Although he knew only a few details, Hasenfus provided information that eventually revealed critical parts of the arms supply network.

Three days before Americans went to the polls, *Al Shiraa*, an obscure Lebanese magazine, printed an account of the arms-for-hostages deal. Iranian officials confirmed the story and chortled that the alleged moderates were actually agents of the ayatollah. Although the revelations had not yet become a major scandal, they perhaps helped the Democrats recapture the Senate in the November 4 election.

President Reagan, North, Poindexter, and Casey tried to stem the electoral defeat by lying to Congress and the press about the arms sales and denying any links to Central America. After the election, however, on November 25, Attorney General Edwin Meese announced that evidence in an internal investigation of the matter connected the arms sales to the diversion of between $10 million and $20 million to the contras. In the hours before Meese went public, Poindexter, North, and NSC secretary Fawn Hall held a "shredding party" in which they destroyed some five thousand incriminating documents. When the shredding machine jammed, Hall smuggled sensitive papers out of the building in her boots and underwear. Enough material survived, some of it in back-up files on the main NSC computer, to raise grave concerns about the administration's foreign policy.

As the Iran-contra scandal unfolded late in 1986, President Reagan gamely insisted he knew nothing about any arms-for-hostages deal or the diversion of profits to the contras. By a wide margin, however, the public no longer believed him. Reagan's overall approval rating plummeted to below 50 percent. Anxious to shift responsibility, he tried first to blame the Israelis. When that tactic failed, the president telephoned North, called him a "national hero" whose work would make a great movie someday, and fired him and Poindexter.

The Iran-Contra Hearings

Once Attorney General Meese revealed that the NSC staff had sold arms to the ayatollah and diverted millions of dollars to the contras, the president was forced to name a special three-member review board chaired by a former senator from Texas, John Tower. The Tower Commission report in February 1987 began to flesh out the details, showing how the arms deal had devolved into a ransom scheme designed, in part, to raise illegal funds for the contras. The report portrayed Reagan as remote, disengaged, uninformed, and easily manipulated. The president's acts "ran directly counter" to his promise to deal harshly with terrorism, thereby undermining the nation's prestige and reputation.

In a speech delivered on March 4, 1987, the president sidestepped some of the criticism by humbly accepting the conclusions of the Tower report while denying any real responsibility. The facts might suggest that he had approved ransom payments, he explained, but in his heart he never meant to trade arms for hostages. He also deflected some of the blame by firing Chief of Staff Donald Regan the week the report came out. Even though Regan had played only a small part in the Iran-contra affair, the president appeared to be cleaning house.

Following the appearance of the Tower Commission report, congressional committees began investigating the money trail, trying to discover how the profits were diverted to the contras, who authorized the policy, and who profited from it. Much of the testimony during the summer of 1987 focused on the activities of Oliver North, described by one participant as "the world's most powerful lieutenant colonel."

The telegenic North dominated the hearings through his vigorous defense of his own actions and his president. He chided Congress for ignoring the Sandinista threat and declared that he and Reagan had a moral responsibility to protect national security, even if their actions ran contrary to congressional and legal mandates. Newspapers spoke of "Olliemania," a ground swell of support for the flamboyant officer. His flag-waving narrative obscured the legal and moral squalor of the operation. Former national security adviser John Poindexter also protected Reagan by denying that the president knew of or authorized the diversion of funds. He insisted that "the buck stops with me."

The public inquiry suffered from numerous shortcomings. Congress conducted the hearings at a rapid pace, even though administration stonewalling prevented quick access to crucial documents. North, Poindexter, and other key players lied about their roles, and evidence of their untruthfulness surfaced only later. CIA director Casey died of a brain tumor before his involvement could be probed.

In March 1988 a special prosecutor indicted North, Poindexter,

Ramrod straight, Marine Lieutenant Colonel Oliver North pledges to tell the truth to Senator Daniel Inouye and other members of Congress investigating the Iran-contra scandal in 1987. *Wide World Photos.*

Channel, Secord, Hakim, and others involved in the scandal. Eventually, all were convicted or pleaded guilty, although the Supreme Court later overturned several of the convictions for technical reasons. At his trial in 1990, Poindexter repudiated his testimony before Congress; he declared that the president knew all the details of the Iran-contra operation and had ordered him to break the law and destroy· documents. Reagan's own testimony at Poindexter's trial revealed a painfully confused man with selective memory lapses. He continued to deny any knowledge of his subordinates' misdeeds.

Congress hardly laid a glove on the president during its 1987 investigation. Members of the House and Senate were reluctant to accept evidence linking the president directly to illegal acts. They feared popular retribution if Congress were blamed for bringing down another chief executive. For its part, the public forgave Reagan for ignorance and mismanagement, so long as no proof surfaced to link him directly to lawbreaking. In contrast to Nixon and the Watergate scandal, it seemed plausible that Reagan really did not know or could not remember what was done in his name.

Most Americans cared little about Latin America and did not lose sleep over the diversion of funds to the contras. People did resent the deals with the hated ayatollah, but the congressional hearings did not concentrate on this part of the drama. Moreover, by the summer of 1987, improved relations with the Soviet Union distracted attention from the shabby episode. The Democrats, who now controlled both houses of Congress, favored a relaxation of Cold War tensions. With Reagan more willing to negotiate with the Soviets, they had a strong incentive to mute criticism of his past lapses.

SUMMIT POLITICS

In the wake of the Iran-contra affair, breakthroughs in relations with the Soviet Union helped salvage the Reagan presidency. Unlike all his predecessors since Franklin D. Roosevelt, Ronald Reagan had refused to meet with any Soviet leaders during his first term. After his re-election, however, he spent more time with his Kremlin counterpart than any previous president. Reagan met Mikhail Gorbachev on five separate occasions between November 1985 and December 1988.

Reagan Meets Gorbachev

When Mikhail Gorbachev became general secretary of the Soviet Communist party in March 1985, he was clearly the best educated, most worldly, and least dogmatic man to lead his country since Lenin. He blamed his three predecessors for presiding over a twenty-year period of stagnation. Gorbachev recognized that the Soviet Union had fallen far behind most Western and many Asian nations in economic and technological progress. Apart from the defense sector, Soviet industry produced insufficient and shoddy goods. The old methods of central planning and authoritarian control yielded diminishing returns and were ill suited for international competition in the age of high technology.

Gorbachev proclaimed new policies of *perestroika* (social and economic restructuring) and *glasnost* (openness and democracy). Incrementally, the Soviet leadership moved toward accepting the principles of representative government and market economics. Pulling the Soviet Union out of its torpor, Gorbachev and his colleagues concluded, would require cooperation with the capitalist community. The Soviet leader traveled around the globe, assuring foreign governments that he represented a new type of communism. Britain's conservative prime minister, Margaret Thatcher, called him "charming" and said that he was someone with whom the West could do business.

Reagan came under great pressure to meet the Kremlin leader, partly from his wife, who consulted her astrologer and learned that "Gorbachev's Aquarian planet is in such harmony with Ronnie's . . .

Margaret Thatcher

More quickly than Ronald Reagan, British Prime Minister Margaret Thatcher noticed the changes that Mikhail Gorbachev brought to the Soviet Union. "I like Mr. Gorbachev," she declared after her first meeting with him; "we can do business together." By 1987 Thatcher had helped convince Reagan that Gorbachev's rise to power marked a turning point in East-West relations.

When Conservative members of Parliament selected Thatcher as their party leader in 1975, she seemed an unusual choice. No woman had ever before led a British political party, and she was no daughter of privilege: she came from a modest middle-class background. But with her stern conservative views, she promised to stir things up, and in May 1979 she led her party to electoral triumph, earning herself the office of prime minister.

they'll share a vision." Nevertheless, the first summit, held at Geneva in November 1985, went only moderately well. The two leaders' wives got into a spat. "Who does this dame think she is?" Nancy Reagan complained about Raisa Gorbachev's alleged effort to dominate a photo session. The president and the general secretary also sparred. Reagan condemned Soviet human rights abuses and alleged violations of arms limitation treaties; he repeated his determination to build SDI. In response, Gorbachev denied any treaty violations and complained that Star Wars would violate the existing antimissile treaty.

At dinner, relations between the two couples took a sudden turn for the better when someone brought up Reagan's acting career. The Gorbachevs turned out to be movie buffs and, according to a participant, were "spellbound . . . by every detail" of Reagan's anecdotes

Among the British public, Thatcher provoked intense affection and equally fervent opposition. Known as the Iron Lady or Battling Maggie, she pursued the sort of conservative program that became increasingly popular in many industrialized democracies in the 1980s. She slashed income taxes, sold lethargic state-owned industries to private investors, humbled powerful union leaders, tried to dismantle the welfare state, and led her country to victory in a short, patriotic war against Argentina. In her early foreign policy, she was deeply antagonistic to the Soviet Union.

By cultivating Ronald Reagan, Thatcher revived the special relationship between London and Washington that had lain dormant for some time. The two leaders could not have been more different in personal style. The intense, nearly humorless Thatcher, known for her sharp tongue, worked hard mastering the details of public policy. Reagan, relaxed and good-humored, left the details to others. Yet they were united by their conservative ideology; they met regularly and consulted often by telephone. Hence Thatcher's positive response to the new Soviet leadership had a deep influence on Reagan.

Thatcher remained prime minister until November 1990, serving in that office longer than anyone else in over two hundred years. Eventually her abrasive manner, along with fears that the public had tired of her attacks on the welfare state, led her party to force her to resign. But even as she left office she continued her influence, helping to choose John Major as her successor. ■

from his Hollywood days. Chief of Staff Donald Regan reported that the Gorbachevs "were very pleased to be in the company of somebody who had known Jimmy Stewart, John Wayne and Humphrey Bogart." No one mentioned Reagan's role in driving alleged Communists out of Hollywood.

The leaders met again at Reykjavik, Iceland, in October 1986. Reagan agreed to this summit with almost no advance preparation, fueling speculation that he sought a foreign policy victory on the eve of congressional elections. Gorbachev seized the initiative by proposing 50-percent cuts in long-range missiles and their eventual elimination. In return, the United States would have to abandon plans to deploy Star Wars. Even though an increasing number of American scientists doubted that the missile shield would ever work, the Soviets still feared the offensive potential of the program.

During the unusual meeting, Reagan and Gorbachev began something of a bidding war, each proposing to eliminate large categories of nuclear weapons. The president suggested banning most long-range missiles over a ten-year period, provided the United States could then build a space-based missile defense system to guard against cheating. Gorbachev countered by proposing the total elimination of all nuclear weapons (rather than just missiles) over ten years. Reagan seemed interested, until Gorbachev insisted this be coupled with a ban on Star Wars. Infuriated at continued Soviet opposition to his pet project, Reagan ended the summit.

The president's advisers, startled by what he had proposed, were thankful that the talks broke down before Gorbachev could accept Reagan's terms. In fact, the president had no authority to bargain away British and French weapons. Because Reagan charged that Moscow had a huge conventional military advantage, it seemed bizarre to abandon the West's nuclear deterrent without a cutback of Warsaw Pact forces. National Security Adviser Poindexter told Reagan, "We've got to clear up this business about you agreeing to get rid of all nuclear weapons." Reagan replied, "But John, I did agree to that." "No," Poindexter argued, "you couldn't have." The president persisted: "I was there, and I did." Frustrated by Reagan's behavior, White House Chief of Staff Donald Regan told a reporter, "Some of us are like a shovel brigade that follows a parade down Main Street cleaning up."

Toward the End of the Cold War

During 1987, in the wake of the Iran-contra scandal, Reagan replaced many of his hard-line, anti-Soviet advisers. Former senator Howard Baker took over as White House chief of staff from Donald Regan. The death of William Casey led to the appointment of FBI director William Webster to head the CIA. Poindexter's firing cleared the way for naming Frank Carlucci to head the NSC. Caspar Weinberger's resignation a few months later resulted in Carlucci's promotion to defense secretary. Lieutenant General Colin Powell then succeeded Carlucci as NSC head.

Unlike most of their predecessors, the new men were pragmatic professionals who supported arms control negotiations with the Soviets. Equally important, Nancy Reagan encouraged her husband to pursue an agreement with Gorbachev. A fierce defender of her husband's image, the first lady hoped that an arms control agreement, not the Iran-contra affair, would become the president's legacy.

In the autumn of 1987, Soviet and American arms negotiators agreed on a treaty to remove all INF missiles—that is, intermediate-range nuclear missiles—from Europe. Although these missiles formed only a small portion of the total nuclear arsenal, the agreement to destroy them represented the first time the two superpowers had agreed to abolish an entire category of weapons. Gorbachev even accepted a long-standing American demand for mutual on-site inspection to ensure compliance.

During the negotiations the Soviets made most of the concessions, dropping their demand that an INF treaty be linked to limits on long-range missiles and SDI. Gorbachev had probably decided that because of technical and economic problems, the Star Wars program would never succeed. Reagan, however, claimed that his massive defense build-up had brought the Russians around; he also said that he had known of a Soviet economic crisis since 1986.

In fact, the Soviet economy was in trouble long before 1986. Gorbachev, unlike his predecessors, acknowledged the situation publicly and decided to stop bleeding the civilian economy to support armaments. He recognized that economic modernization required American, European, and Japanese goodwill. Gorbachev also had a far more sophisticated sense of international relations than his predecessors. They had measured Soviet security by the degree to which Moscow dominated or intimidated neighbors and rivals. As the Soviet Union declined economically relative to the rest of the world, Gorbachev made a virtue of necessity. He would seek to enhance Soviet economic and military security through cooperation with neighboring states and other world powers.

Mikhail Gorbachev visited Washington in December 1987 to sign the INF treaty. Undaunted by the Soviet leader's charm, the president quipped, "I don't resent his popularity. Good Lord, I co-starred with Errol Flynn once." This jocularity, apparently so easy and unforced, reaped immense appreciation for Reagan.

Gorbachev revealed a flair for good publicity by hosting a party for American luminaries such as Paul Newman, Yoko Ono, and Henry Kissinger. He charmed members of Congress and the citizens of Washington by bounding out of his limousine and grabbing the hands of pedestrians. "I just want to say hello to you," he gushed. One veteran observer of visiting leaders commented, "The man is a PR genius!" Only Reagan's most conservative backers were critical, disliking the new friendliness with Moscow.

Apart from the signing of the INF treaty, few substantive Soviet-American agreements were reached during the remainder of Reagan's term. Both leaders, however, enjoyed a boost in their domestic ratings from improved superpower relations. In a sense, the waning of the Cold War rescued both Reagan and Gorbachev from a host of domestic problems. The two leaders agreed to meet again in Moscow in June 1988. Simply by appearing in the heart of what he had frequently called "the evil empire," Reagan further blunted the Cold War. Asked if he still considered the Soviets the "focus of evil in the modern world," he answered, "they've changed." The president even embraced his friend Mikhail at Lenin's tomb. The two superpowers still had 30,000 nuclear weapons aimed at each other, but, in the new spirit of the time, few people worried.

During 1988, the Soviets withdrew troops from Afghanistan and supported efforts to end civil conflicts in Africa and Southeast Asia. The dormant United Nations, buoyed by the great-power harmony Franklin Roosevelt had hoped for in 1945, re-emerged as a key forum for mediating these disputes. Reagan met Gorbachev again in December in New York, where the Soviet leader announced plans to reduce conventional forces. Taking a cue from the president's staff, Gorbachev arranged for Reagan and president-elect George Bush to pose for pictures with him in front of the Statue of Liberty. As it became fashionable to predict the end of the Cold War, even the wives of the two leaders made peace. The *New York Times* headlined: "Another obstacle falls: Nancy Reagan and Raisa Gorbachev get chummy."

CONCLUSION

The most vocal anti-Communist president since 1945 seemed to achieve goals that had eluded his predecessors. The United States and the Soviet Union realized fundamental new understandings regarding arms control and cooperation in the Third World. During Reagan's presidency, Mikhail Gorbachev initiated democratic internal reforms in the Soviet Union and laid the groundwork for the end of Soviet domination in Eastern Europe that occurred during 1989. Communism, its own leaders admitted, had failed by every measure. Because these developments took place on Reagan's watch, he and his supporters naturally took credit for them. In a sense, George Kennan's prediction of 1947 proved true: over the long run, containment had forced changes in Soviet behavior.

But explaining the origin of what was already being called the "new world order" requires a broader perspective. Reagan's policy of "peace through strength" probably had less to do with the changes in the Communist world than he believed. The large American arms build-up of the 1980s added to overkill capacity but did not fundamentally change the military balance Reagan had inherited. In fact, the legacy of huge budget deficits partly brought on by the arms race weakened America's economic strength nearly as much as its rival's. Moreover, administration policies toward Central America, the Caribbean, and the Middle East failed to bring any measure of peace or stability to those regions. The Iran-contra affair, in which administration officials engaged in patent illegalities and deceptions, proved the extent to which foreign policy could go wrong under a president who was at best inattentive, at worst disdainful of the law.

Nevertheless, Ronald Reagan deserves credit for responding positively to Soviet initiatives even if he neither caused nor fully understood them. To his successor, George Bush, fell the task of guiding the United States in a vastly different world with abundant possibilities for further change. ■

F U R T H E R   R E A D I N G

On foreign policy during the Reagan era, see: Alexander Haig, *Caveat: Reagan, Realism and Foreign Policy* (1984); Caspar Weinberger, *Fighting for Peace* (1990); Constantine Menges, *Inside the National Security Council* (1988); William Broad, *The Star Warriors* (1985); Strobe Talbott, *Deadly Gambits* (1984); Michael Mandelbaum and Strobe Talbott, *Reagan and Gorbachev* (1987); Kenneth Oye et al., *Eagle Defiant: U.S. Foreign Policy in the 1980s* (1983); John Tower et al., *The Tower Commission Report* (1987); Theodore Draper, *A Very Thin Line: The Iran-Contra Affairs* (1991); Bob Woodward, *Veil* (1987); Jonathan Kwitny, *The Crimes of Patriots: A True Tale of Dope, Dirty Money and the CIA* (1987); Jane Mayer and Doyle McManus, *Landslide: The Unmaking of the President, 1984–88* (1988); Roy Gutman, *Banana Diplomacy* (1988); Michael Schaller, *Reckoning with Reagan: America and Its President in the 1980s* (1992).

15

A Fresh Start
for the Nineties

In December 1989, American musician Leonard Bernstein conducted a joint East-West German orchestra at the base of Berlin's Brandenburg Gate in the playing of Beethoven's "Ode to Joy." On New Year's Eve thousands of American college students joined tens of thousands of jubilant young Germans and other Europeans in dancing atop the Berlin Wall, opened by the Communist authorities to free travel between the two halves of the divided city on November 9. Within a year, Germans were celebrating the dissolution of the Communist regime in East Germany and the reunification of their country.

The Cold War ended in 1989 as democratic governments replaced Communist dictatorships throughout Eastern Europe. Even the Soviet Communist party officially abandoned its seventy-year-old monopoly on political power and proclaimed the virtue of free markets over central planning. President Mikhail Gorbachev, a hero in the West, received the 1990 Nobel Peace Prize for relinquishing his country's rule over Eastern Europe and seeking an accommodation with NATO. The sudden turnaround thrilled most Americans, who believed that the end of the Cold War ushered in a safer, more prosperous, and freer world. People spoke of reaping a "peace dividend" from disarmament; resources spent on arms might be redirected to revitalizing the economy, protecting the environment, and helping the poor.

These dramatic upheavals in world affairs contributed to a sense that the future held a new opportunity to fulfill promises that had gone unrealized since the end of the Second World War. With the virtual surrender of communism, anticommunism no longer played an important part in defining what Americans thought about themselves and the world. The end of the Cold War appeared to herald a bright new age—what President George Bush and others began calling a new world order. As had occurred in the immediate aftermath of the Second World War, however, triumph abroad did not end problems at home or concerns for the future. Hopes for a placid transition to a peaceful, prosperous future were interrupted in the winter of 1990 and 1991 by an economic downturn and a war against Iraq to evict that nation's armed forces from the oil-rich emirate of Kuwait.

Regardless of what happened in foreign affairs, the political, economic, and social trends of the previous twenty years persisted into the 1990s. The United States became a more pluralistic nation than ever. Increasing diversity led to greater sharing of power by different groups; it also made solutions to social problems appear more complex. The difficulty in solving social problems coincided with the reluctance of officeholders to address these issues. Election campaigns grew ever more expensive, forcing politicians to devote more of their energy to fund-raising. Most officials won re-election by avoiding actions that might antagonize influential donors or important voting blocs. Meanwhile, Americans continued to worry that their economic future would not be as bright as their past. Even when the overall economy expanded, the plight of the poor worsened, and middle-class people believed that conditions were not improving for them personally. Public facilities such as roads, bridges, airports, schools, and hospitals deteriorated. At the same time, the divisions of a pluralistic society provoked debate and disagreement over the appropriate meaning of cultural, sexual, and ethnic diversity. As white men increasingly shared power, influence, and social prestige with women, people of color, and new immigrants, the transition to a more diverse society, a "universal nation," produced anxieties and antagonisms of its own.

THE ELECTION OF 1988

After the New York stock market crash of October 1987, many observers believed that one result would be a victory for the Democratic nominee in the 1988 presidential election. Opponents of the Reagan administration noted the possibility of a recession and pointed to uncontrolled federal borrowing and the escalation of the foreign trade deficit as signs that the economic recovery begun in 1982 had not restored prosperity. Democratic candidates for president attempted to turn the 1988 election into a referendum on the competence of Republican political leaders to manage the nation under contemporary conditions. But their hopes proved hollow. Facing a choice between Republican George Bush, the heir of a popular leader, and Democrat Michael Dukakis, a relative unknown, a majority of voters decided that they preferred continuity. The Democrats, who complained that the Reagan years had favored the wealthy and left the country unprepared for the challenges of the future, often seemed to be promoting a return to the pessimism and anxieties of the late 1970s. Rejecting these worries, voters chose leadership that painted an attractive picture of the present.

Democratic Dilemmas

The Democrats' hopes of winning back the White House after Ronald Reagan rested on their ability to resurrect the New Deal coalition, which had splintered during the 1960s. But the Democrats' divisions had never completely healed. Seven of the eight men vying for the party's nomination in 1987 tried to direct the political dialogue away from the contentious issues of race, the distribution of wealth, and foreign policy—issues that had caused severe internal divisions in the party and alienated it from voters. One Democrat, however—Jesse Jackson, a veteran of the 1984 presidential campaign and the first African-American to win a substantial following at the presidential level—proclaimed the glories of the liberal past and lambasted his rivals for "moving their policies to the right like Ronald Reagan."

The other Democratic candidates echoed Gary Hart's unsuccessful 1984 campaign, speaking about the future and the need for competent management of public policy. Hart himself remained the front runner for the nomination in early 1987. Yet he destroyed his own public career in May 1987 in a celebrated sex scandal that pitted a candidate's right to privacy against the public's need to know as much as possible about the character of political leaders. In early May 1987, the *Miami Herald* reported that Hart, a married man, had spent a weekend at his Washington townhouse with Donna Rice, a twenty-nine-year-old model. The *Herald*'s story was quickly followed by pictures in the *National Enquirer* showing Rice sitting on Hart's lap during a yacht trip to the island of Bimini. (The yacht was named, almost incredibly, *The Monkey Business*.) Hart, who had denied rumors about his womanizing, saw his campaign collapse in days.

The controversy surrounding Hart's character set the tone of the remainder of the presidential campaign. It was evident that politicians did not live up to their images, and the media gleefully detailed their shortcomings. The circus of exposure made public life seem coarse. Journalists who exposed the misdeeds of politicians believed that political reporters in earlier eras had failed in their duty to inform the public; but most citizens felt troubled not only by Hart's untruthfulness but also by the way reporters had badgered him. Four months later, another Democratic candidate, Delaware Senator Joseph Biden, also left the race after disclosures that he had appropriated for his own use a speech by a British politician and had distorted his academic background. The public was torn between distrust of politicians and contempt for the "character police" of the press who had caused first Hart and then Biden to leave the race.

By the spring of 1988 only Massachusetts Governor Michael Dukakis and Jesse Jackson remained candidates for the Democratic nomination. The lack of wider competition magnified the prospects of the Massachusetts governor, who consistently defeated Jackson by wide margins in primaries from April to June, making himself seem unbeatable. Dukakis's strength reflected the fact that Jackson could not entirely escape his radical image of 1984. Despite attracting more white voters than he had then, Jackson still aroused racist animosity in many whites, who turned to Dukakis as the only alternative. During the primaries Dukakis avoided the label of "liberal," which had become a political liability. Aware of public resistance to higher taxes, he claimed that he could reduce the nation's large budget deficits by better tax collection rather than by increased tax rates. Without offering a specific agenda, he promised a brighter economic future for the country in which the "Massachusetts miracle"—the rebirth of that state from the ashes of economic decay—would be extended nationwide.

The Triumph of George Bush

In the November election, Dukakis faced Vice President George Bush, the Republican candidate, whom Democrats considered an easy target. "If we can't beat Bush," one Democratic strategist remarked, "we'd better find another country." Hopes that Bush would be a vulnerable opponent seemed validated by the media's presentation of him as an inarticulate, unimaginative weakling. Columnists and cartoonists assailed Bush's patrician background. He came from a prominent Connecticut family; his father had been a United States senator; he had attended an exclusive private prep school and Yale University. Bush's refusal to disagree publicly with Ronald Reagan made some call him a weakling—a "wimp," in the slang of the day, or a "lap dog," in columnist George Will's cruel phrase. Garry Trudeau, creator of the comic strip "Doonesbury," characterized Bush as a mere cheerleader for Reagan, someone who had "left his manhood in a blind trust." Critics like Ann Richards, the keynote speaker of the Democratic convention, belittled "poor George . . . born with a silver foot in his mouth."

These opponents persistently underestimated Bush's initiative, competitiveness, and accomplishments. He had left college to enlist in the armed forces during the Second World War, becoming the youngest fighter pilot in the United States Navy. After Japanese gunners shot down his plane, American sailors rescued him from the Pacific. A navy photographer filmed Bush's safe return to the deck of the carrier. The old movie of the smiling, boyish Bush waving his thanks to his rescuers became one of the most effective TV spots of the 1988 campaign, visually negating charges that the candidate lacked courage. After his graduation from Yale, Bush moved to Texas, where he made a fortune in the oil business. He later entered politics, winning two terms in the U.S. House of Representatives from 1967 to 1971. Defeated in 1970 for a Senate seat, Bush then served in a variety of posts: chairman of the Republican National Committee, United States representative to the People's Republic of China, and director of the Central Intelligence Agency.

During the 1988 primaries Bush defeated several rivals for the Republican nomination by appealing to voters' affection for Ronald Reagan. In one of the most famous statements of the campaign, Bush borrowed a line from movie hero Clint Eastwood, star of numerous cowboy and police films. "Read my lips," he parodied Eastwood: "no new taxes." Critics expected that his repetition of Reagan's themes would ring false, because Bush was an intelligent Washington insider who understood how costly the budget deficit had become to the nation's productive capacity. Once more, however, Bush's detractors failed to understand the depth of middle-class concern that the federal government did not provide good value for money received.

Assured of the Republican nomination in the spring of 1988, Bush had several months in which to plan for a confrontation with Dukakis. Spending hours interviewing small "focus groups" of voters, his consultants identified vulnerabilities in the record of the Massachusetts governor, and the Bush campaign capitalized on them. For example, Dukakis had vetoed a Massachusetts law requiring school teachers to lead their classes in the Pledge of Allegiance to the American flag. Dukakis also had supported a prison furlough program, similar to ones existing in half the states, under which convicts could spend time out of jail. Under Massachusetts' plan, a murderer, Willie Horton, had escaped during his furlough and raped a Maryland woman. Horton was black, a fact soon known across the country. The racism inflamed by Bush's references to Horton reinforced white voters' perception that Dukakis, like several earlier Democratic candidates, did not share the concerns of the middle class.

Bush hammered at Dukakis on the flag and crime issues, assailing him as a "liberal," a word Bush used like a curse. Dukakis's campaign became mired in his ponderous defense of his views on the Pledge of Allegiance and prison furloughs. Bush too seemed to blunder in his surprising selection of forty-one-year-old Indiana Senator Dan Quayle for his vice-presidential running mate. Quayle's undistinguished record made him seem woefully unprepared to take over the presidency if necessary, and his selection horrified many staunch Republicans. News that as a young man Quayle, son of a wealthy Indianapolis newspaper publisher, had used family connections to enter the National Guard, thereby avoiding service in Vietnam, raised the Democrats' hopes. Quayle seemed especially unqualified when compared to the poised Texas Senator Lloyd Bentsen, the Democrats' vice-presidential nominee.

In the November election, however, the misgivings about Quayle were not strong enough to sway many voters. Bush easily won election with 53 percent of the popular vote, carrying forty states (see map, page 576). As had been the case in most presidential elections since 1968, the Republican candidate gained the support of most white people, most men, and the southern states that had once been solidly Democratic.

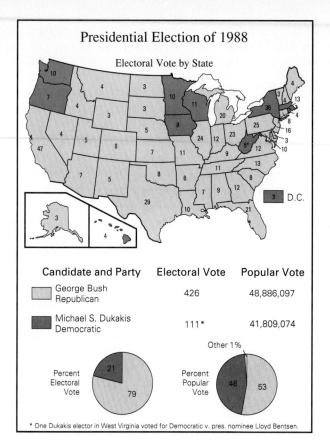

Presidential Election of 1988

Electoral Vote by State

Candidate and Party	Electoral Vote	Popular Vote
George Bush Republican	426	48,886,097
Michael S. Dukakis Democratic	111*	41,809,074

Percent Electoral Vote: 21 / 79

Percent Popular Vote: 46 / 53 / Other 1%

* One Dukakis elector in West Virginia voted for Democratic v. pres. nominee Lloyd Bentsen.

Presidential Election of 1988

The Trivial Pursuit of the Presidency

Nearly all of the major presidential candidates in 1988, in both the primaries and general election, avoided penetrating discussions of sweeping changes in the world's political and economic environment. For example, opposition to the Soviet Union had been a cornerstone of United States foreign policy for forty years, but Mikhail Gorbachev's actions since 1985 had gone far toward ending the Cold War. No candidate presented a clear vision of what the United States would do in a post–Cold War world, and many commentators criticized the candidates for such reluctance to address far-ranging issues. One book describing the campaign was subtitled, *The Trivial Pursuit of the Presidency, 1988.* The authors complained that political technique had replaced the political leadership necessary to make Americans proud of their political institutions.

The charges had merit; the campaign speeches and position statements of the 1988 candidates did lack substance. Yet columnists and academics who despaired of the vulgarity and triviality of the candidates' public offerings left the false impression that politicians of earlier eras had engaged in a more sophisticated discussion of issues. Assertions that the major candidates could and should have provided more serious information also underestimated the dominant role played by television in shaping the way leaders communicated with the public. Because voters increasingly gained their information from television news rather than from printed media, candidates tailored their messages to the TV format. Media consultants—many of whom held both politicians and voters in contempt—helped arrange the candidates' public appearances to produce thirty-second "sound bites" that played well on the evening news. Extended discussions of the issues would not have fit this format. Even the television reporters who analyzed the campaigns preferred to concentrate on the dramatic features of the "race"—as if the candidates were horses in a steeplechase—rather than on the substantive differences between candidates. Changes in party rules, which put more emphasis on primary elections and reduced the influence of professional politicians and officeholders, further magnified the role of television.

THE BUSH PRESIDENCY AT HOME

George Bush's promise to preside over a "kinder, gentler America" than the one existing during the celebrated selfishness of the 1980s seemed to be realized for a time. The president's high popularity in the first twenty months of his administration reflected a general belief that times were good. All major social groups—including women and African-Americans, who had earlier found fault with Reagan—liked George Bush, or at least found little to dislike about him. The endurance of his popularity confounded skeptics as much as had the ease of his victory over Dukakis. Many journalists and Democratic officeholders believed that Bush's negative campaign, devoid of serious discussions of future public policy, would make it difficult for him to establish effective relations with the Democratic-controlled Congress; but these critics proved wrong.

Skepticism about the depth of Bush's popularity overlooked deeper trends. The optimism expressed by middle-class Americans persisted until the economic expansion, begun in 1982, halted in mid-1990. The most important elements in creating general feelings of well-being in 1989 and 1990 were the astonishing changes sweeping the Communist world. Most people agreed that the Cold War had ended. Public problems did not disappear, but for a time they paled in comparison with the end of communism in Eastern Europe, the student demonstrations for democracy in China, and the waning of the threat of nuclear war. Beneath the surface tranquility, millions of people were concerned about a number of issues, such as the continued degradation of the environment, the dangers of crime and drugs, and the right of women to choose abortion. All of these were serious problems for the future. On balance, however, 1989 and the beginning of 1990 represented for large sections of the public one of the most contented periods of the post–Second World War era.

Public Animosity Toward Congress

The high popularity of the president contrasted sharply with the revival of public disdain for Congress. Early in 1989 an unusual coalition of radio talk-show hosts, consumer activist Ralph Nader, and the liberal lobbying group Common Cause fanned rage against a congressional move to raise the salaries of senators and representatives by 50 percent. Shortly thereafter James Wright, the Democratic Speaker of the House of Representatives, was accused of accepting gifts from a wealthy businessman who wanted government favors, using a ruse to accept money from corporations, and intervening with federal regulators to protect Texas savings and loan institutions that had made improper loans in the 1980s. In June, Wright resigned. At the same time, the third-ranking Democrat in the House also relinquished his seat after acknowledging involvement with people tainted by the growing savings and loan scandal. In 1990 further charges of ethical misconduct hit seven senators, a group that included Republicans as well as Democrats. Each was accused of taking money from wealthy contributors who wanted something in return. A number of these senators had skirted the laws requiring disclosure of contributions.

As explained in Chapter 13 (see page 520), five senators in this group were implicated in the widespread savings and loan scandal. Each of the so-called Keating Five had accepted contributions from Charles Keating of Lincoln Federal Savings and Loan, an institution whose ultimate collapse cost the government—and the taxpayers—$2 billion. Keating's efforts to influence Congress and federal regulators represented the most dramatic example of the sorry complex of greed, mismanagement, fraud, theft, and excessive optimism in the thrift industry of the 1980s. Coming on the heels of other congressional scandals, the Keating case further increased the public's disdain for government institutions.

Problems in Education

Ever since the Department of Education had published *A Nation at Risk*, its 1983 study of the poor state of public education, Americans had agonized over the declining level of achievement in schoolrooms across the nation. American students compared unfavorably with students in Europe and Japan, who consistently scored higher on standardized math and science tests. This educational gap, many experts feared, would put the United States at a competitive disadvantage in the world economy. Critics also decried the decline in awareness of public affairs, especially among adults under thirty. Newspaper polls revealed that young adults did not know who occupied high office or what major events had recently transpired in Eastern Europe and China; these young people thought politics pointless and many politicians corrupt. Much of the handwringing over public apathy represented little more than the social elite's longstanding dismay at the low level of sophistication displayed by the masses. Yet the critics' distress also reflected genuine anxiety that a vast segment of the public lacked the knowledge and judgment necessary in a participatory democracy.

Aware of the widespread concern that the quality of public education had declined, Bush asserted during the 1988 presidential campaign that he wanted to become known as "the education president." Because the federal deficit, in excess of $200 billion per year, left no room for costly public initiatives, the president shrewdly used symbols to generate popularity. He met with governors to outline a series of worthy goals—complete literacy among teenagers, an increase in the high school graduation rate from 60 percent to 80 percent, better results on tests of competence in science and mathematics—all of which were to be reached in ten years. Both the noble aspirations and the generous timetables mirrored earlier, unsuccessful efforts to improve public education, and as had happened with previous efforts, the issue soon faded. Secretary of Education Lauro Cavazos, the first Mexican-American to serve in the cabinet, proved unable to sustain a consensus for education reform, and Bush fired him in December 1990. The new secretary of education was Lamar Alexander, former governor of Tennessee, who had presided over a revitalization of that state's public education system.

The question of how best to reconcile mass education with high quality defied quick solution. Americans had complained about the low achievement of the bulk of students in the United States ever since high immigration rates had brought children of different backgrounds to the public schools in the nineteenth century. A diverse society, in which the white middle class made up a declining proportion of the entire population, necessarily displayed a wide variation in educational achievement. What made matters worse in the 1980s and 1990s was the shrinking tax base of major cities, which could not afford to provide quality education to poor or immigrant children. Moreover, teaching had once been one of the few occupations open to women, but as women gained the opportunity to enter other professions, low-paying teaching jobs had less and less appeal. With government at all levels unwilling or unable to provide more resources for public education, the problems persisted.

A Renewed Drug War

A similar pattern—initial enthusiasm for a national undertaking, followed by loss of momentum and declining interest—prevailed in the war on illegal drugs. Public opinion polls taken in 1988 and 1989 listed drug abuse and related crime as the issues of most concern to a plurality of Americans. In September 1989 Bush redirected $7.9 billion already scheduled to combat drugs into more resources for prisons, prosecutors, and agents of the Drug Enforcement Agency. Seventy percent of the money was slotted for enforcement and punishment and the remainder for education and prevention. Yet experts who had studied the relationship among poverty, crime, and drugs questioned whether spending over $5 billion to hire agents and build jail cells would do much to solve the problem.

To coordinate federal antidrug policies, Bush appointed William Bennett, formerly Reagan's secretary of education. Bennett promised progress in six months and victory in a year, but spent much of his energy fighting officials in the established federal agencies, denouncing local governments for their slackness, and exchanging insults with members of Congress. In September 1989 he promised to showcase the effort to halt the drug trade in Washington, D.C., where drug-related murders in poor African-American neighborhoods had reached such an alarming rate that the reputation of the nation's capital was badly tarnished. But neither the use of cocaine nor the murder rate declined in Washington, and the mayor of the city was himself brought to trial for cocaine use. Bennett's boosterism for the war on drugs even provoked doubts in the White House about the government's ability to curb the use of narcotics among poor and minority youth. Unable to make genuine progress in this area, Bennett and Bush stressed data showing a decline in casual drug use among the middle class. By late 1990, opinion polls revealed waning concern about the use of drugs; ordinary citizens and public officials alike began to worry more about Iraq and the slowing economy. With the issue attracting less attention than before, Bennett resigned as director of drug policy.

Environmental Concerns

Public fear about the degradation of the environment, muted during the Reagan years by the popular belief that government regulation shackled economic activity, revived during the Bush administration. Bush proclaimed during the 1988 campaign that he wanted to be the

Your cheeseburger box
will be around even longer.

Most things made on this planet last less than
a few centuries. But styrofoam is forever.
It will never decompose. Never disintegrate.
Never go away. And neither will the garbage
problems it creates, unless we find solutions.
Your donation can help. Send your check to The
Environmental Challenge Fund, Radio City Station,
Box 1138, New York, NY 10101-1138, and help build
scholarships for environmental education.
Or the most enduring monument left on earth
by our civilization may be a mountain of trash.

Created as a public service by Sullivan Higdon & Sink/Wichita

The environmental movement revived in the
late 1980s as Americans once more expressed
concern that pollution, waste, and misuse of
natural resources would make life in the future less enjoyable and healthful than it had
been in the past. *Courtesy of Sullivan, Higdon
& Sink, Wichita, Kansas.*

environmental president as well as the education president. His media consultants designed a series of television ads showing fouled
beaches along the East Coast and raw sewage in Boston Harbor. The
latter further weakened Dukakis's reputation as a competent manager, despite his accurate riposte that Washington had reneged on a
promise to pay for a water treatment plant. Critics disparaged Bush's
political opportunism and doubted the depth of his commitment to
the environment. Still, Bush achieved better relations with environmentalists than Reagan had, because Bush acknowledged the problem and believed that government had a role in the solution.

After a tanker owned by Exxon ran aground in Alaska's Prince William Sound, causing the largest oil spill in American history, the
Coast Guard demanded that the oil company spend $2 billion to wash
the crude oil from beaches and try to clean the feathers and fur of
thousands of marine animals befouled by the spill. The Justice Department prosecuted the captain of the tanker for operating it while
under the influence of alcohol. Having an identifiable villain helped

focus public attention on the environment, as did the media-inspired celebration of the twentieth anniversary of the first Earth Day, on April 20, 1990. Across the country people promised to conserve energy, recycle their trash, and patronize businesses that demonstrated concern for the environment.

The record on actual environmental initiatives was mixed. Voters, put off by the price of clean-ups, defeated costly environmental initiatives in California and New York in the 1990 election. Equally fearful of spending money, federal officials responded slowly, even scornfully, to scientific concerns about global warming. Many scientists believed that excessive burning of petroleum had caused the build-up of a thick layer of carbon dioxide gas in the upper atmosphere that might turn the Earth into a giant greenhouse. Some climatologists and meteorologists feared that the Earth's temperature would rise over the next hundred years, melting the polar ice caps, drowning coastal cities, and turning the fertile farmland of the Midwest into deserts. Not all scientists agreed, however, and the administration sided with the skeptics, demanding more studies of the likelihood of global warming. However, officials displayed little inclination to revive the discarded energy policies of the 1970s, which had been designed to reduce gasoline use. When reporters criticized Bush for setting a poor example with his fondness for driving his gasoline-powered boat at top speed, the president testily replied that he believed Americans should be able to "prudently recreate."

Although the Bush administration shied away from a general attack on environmental problems, fearful of costs and of opposition from special interest groups, it did strengthen some environmental laws. Congress approved the first overhaul of the Clean Air Act in thirteen years, setting stricter standards for automobile emissions and requiring municipalities to reduce smog. The measure also addressed for the first time the issue of acid rain: the increasing amount of sulfuric acid in rainfall throughout the Midwest and Northeast, caused by the burning of high-sulfur coal. In addition, Congress increased the liability of shipping companies for oil spills and agreed to preserve large coastal areas from Alaska to New England from further development by oil companies.

The Revival of Discordant Social Issues

Despite the general sense that public policy in the 1990s would prove less contentious than in the previous fifteen years, controversy over individual rights struck a discordant note. Two 1989 Supreme Court decisions reminded people of issues that had recently divided them. The Court briefly revived controversy about the American flag when it affirmed that the First Amendment, through its free speech clause, protected the right of protesters to burn the flag. Expressing shock and hoping to rekindle the emotions of the 1988 election campaign, Bush proposed a constitutional amendment to ban flag burning. Public opinion polls taken in the wake of the Court's decision reflected a 67 percent support for such an amendment, and observers predicted that once more Democrats would find themselves on the defensive in future elections. By the fall, however, the issue had faded, and no amendment emerged from Congress.

A decision regarding abortion produced longer-lasting ramifications. In *Webster* v. *Reproductive Services of Missouri*, the court ruled by a five-to-four margin that states could impose restrictions limiting the availability of abortion. State legislatures could prohibit public hospitals from performing abortions and could ban public employees from participating in or assisting the procedure. Writing for the five-member majority, Chief Justice William Rehnquist asserted that "nothing in the Constitution requires states to enter or remain in the business of performing abortions." Although the decision did not overturn the landmark 1973 ruling in *Roe* v. *Wade* that legalized abortion, it worried the advocates of abortion rights. Harry Blackmun, principal author of *Roe* v. *Wade*, issued a dissenting opinion. "I fear for the future," he said. The right to abortion remained "for today, at least. But the signs are very ominous and a chill wind blows."

In the wake of the *Webster* decision, supporters and opponents of abortion rights mobilized for battles in the state legislatures. Abortion opponents believed they had the upper hand, but in most cases they did not. Relatively few state bills limiting the right of abortion were passed by legislatures, and some of those passed did not survive vetoes by the governors or review by the courts. Louisiana, Pennsylvania, and Utah, both of which enacted highly restrictive statutes, proved to be notable exceptions to this trend.

The future availability of abortion played a role in many elections in 1989 and 1990. Usually, but not always, the issue worked to the benefit of supporters of abortion rights. The partisan divisions predicted in the aftermath of *Webster*, with Democrats affirming the right to choose and Republicans opposing abortion, failed to materialize. Candidates of both parties took positions on each side of the issue, and Republicans understood that most voters preferred the status quo. Fearful of an anti-Republican backlash among young women, Lee Atwater, chairman of the Republican National Committee, reversed his usual emphasis on slashing ideological attacks. He claimed that the party was "a big tent" where people of differing views on abortion could comfortably coexist.

For his part, Bush maintained a low profile on the issue. In 1988 he had asserted that "abortion is murder," but in earlier years he had supported a woman's right to choose. The matter came to a head for

Bush in July 1990, when liberal Supreme Court Justice William Brennan retired. If Bush appointed an ardent opponent of abortion, he would solidify his support among conservatives, who had never trusted his commitment to their cause. Such a choice, however, would have difficulty winning confirmation from the Democratic Senate and would weaken Republican support among pro-choice voters. Bush finessed the issue with the nomination of David Souter, a former judge of the New Hampshire Supreme Court who had served for a few months on the federal bench. Souter, who had never expressed himself publicly on the issue of abortion, kept his views to himself throughout his confirmation hearings. Many supporters of the right to choose gave him the benefit of the doubt, but some feminist and civil rights groups opposed his confirmation. The National Organization for Women, the National Women's Political Caucus, and the Leadership Conference on Civil Rights asserted that the issue of privacy carried such weight that senators should not have to guess about the nominee's opinions. Despite such opposition, Souter easily won confirmation, and most senators felt relieved that they could avoid a controversial stand on the abortion issue. The question of whether the Court would reverse *Roe v. Wade* arose again after Thurgood Marshall, the first African-American Supreme Court justice, announced his retirement in June 1991. To replace him Bush nominated Clarence Thomas, a forty-three-year-old conservative African-American federal appeals court judge. Although a former subordinate accused Thomas of sexually harassing her in the early 1980s, the Senate confirmed him by a narrow margin of 52 to 48.

Controversy also erupted over appropriate limits to public speech. A wave of public insults directed at women, nonwhites, and homosexuals brought the issue to the fore. In an effort to suppress such outrageous speech, feminists and defenders of gays and minorities often parted company with their traditional allies among civil libertarians and found themselves in an uneasy alliance with social conservatives. One prominent instigator of the controversy was Andrew Dice Clay, a white comedian who enjoyed brief notoriety with a popular nightclub act in which he made vicious remarks about women, blacks, Hispanics, and gays. Similarly, 2 Live Crew, a black rap music group, released several albums with violently antifemale remarks. Municipalities banned Clay's performances, and the members of 2 Live Crew were arrested. An increase in verbal harassment of nonwhites and women on college campuses also provoked resentment. Universities drafted codes of conduct that banned abusive speech and insulting laughter. Many civil libertarians, believing that any restrictions on freedom of speech threatened the freedom of all, resisted the efforts to regulate nightclub acts, song lyrics, or campus insults. But many people supported the restrictions, on the ground that coarse

TIMEOUT FOR RELOADING

As the federal budget deficit remained high in the late 1980s and early 1990s, Americans blamed officeholders of both parties for their failure to make the politically painful choices necessary to bring government revenue and spending in line. *Reprinted with special permission of King Features Syndicate, Inc.*

language and angry epithets made life unbearable for the targeted groups.

The Budget Deficit

Worry about the size of the federal budget deficit overshadowed other considerations of public policy in 1989 and 1990. Critics of the borrowing of the 1980s believed that the rising debt would erode capital formation and render American firms unable to compete in world trade. Commentators and politicians unhappy with the federal budget deficit predicted that unless the government made the unpopular decision to raise taxes and cut benefits for the middle class, the American economy would fall behind the economies of Japan and Germany. Now a recession threatened economic growth, but the Federal Reserve Board refused to lower interest rates unless something was done to reduce the federal budget deficit below the $260 billion expected for 1991.

In the spring of 1990, facing widespread fear of impending economic calamity, President Bush finally dropped his premier promise of the 1988 campaign—"no new taxes." He entered into negotiations with a small group of congressional leaders to hammer out a budget agreement that would raise taxes, cut middle-class entitlements, and ultimately slice $500 billion from the deficit over five years. In late

September, the budget negotiators agreed on a package of income and excise tax increases, combined with cuts in such popular programs as Medicare and unemployment insurance. The secretly negotiated agreement nearly came undone, however; its adoption was blocked by an unusual coalition of liberal Democrats, angry at the cuts in social programs, and conservative Republicans, dismayed that Bush had accepted new taxes. Nevertheless, a month later Congress passed a modified version of the tax increases and budget cuts. The law reduced the burden on elderly recipients of Medicare by increasing payroll taxes on workers. It also raised tax rates on the top 2 percent of earners by cutting their deductions, and it boosted taxes on gasoline, alcohol, and big-ticket luxury items. Congress expected these measures to reduce the deficit by $40 billion in the next year and $490 billion over the next five years. From the record of previous plans to lower the deficit, however, such hopes appeared exaggerated. Within a month officials acknowledged the arrival of the long-anticipated recession, which reduced revenue and further strained the government's resources, and the 1991 deficit exceeded $267 billion, the largest in history.

AMERICA AND THE POST–COLD WAR WORLD

The years 1989 and 1990 saw some of the most dramatic changes in world politics since 1945. The world order anticipated by Franklin Roosevelt in 1945 seemed at last to be emerging as the Cold War ended. Communism collapsed in Europe even as the United States and the Soviet Union dropped their rivalry. Former adversaries of the Soviets in Europe and North America agreed to provide billions of dollars worth of aid to slow the disintegration of the Soviet Union's economy and society. As planners had hoped in 1945 Germany was united and free, a democratic Eastern Europe was unoccupied by foreign troops, and a rebuilt, demilitarized Japan was a major player in world politics. The United Nations functioned effectively as an instrument of great power cooperation. These events, however, did not prevent the United States from continuing to assert its power in nonindustrial regions around the globe.

American foreign affairs officials in the Bush administration were experienced and knowledgeable. National Security Adviser Brent Scowcroft had held the same position in the Ford administration. Secretary of Defense Richard Cheney had served as chief of staff to President Ford and gone on to an influential position in the House of Representatives. Secretary of State James Baker III, Bush's closest political friend, had been White House chief of staff and secretary of the treasury in the 1980s. Colin Powell, chairman of the Joint Chiefs of Staff, had served as Ronald Reagan's last national security adviser.

Their slowness to adjust to the end of the Cold War drew criticism in 1989, but the Bush administration eventually made the most of opportunities to create a new relationship with the Soviet Union. The new order generated high hopes at least until the beginning of 1991. Then the United States won a war with Iraq, reversing that country's annexation of Kuwait. The victory proved enormously popular, creating a sense of patriotic pride and national unity not seen in over a generation. Yet the war also left many unanswered questions about the shape of the post–Cold War world.

The Earthquake in the Communist World

Soviet President Mikhail Gorbachev ended his country's control over Eastern Europe in the summer of 1989. With the Soviet Union undergoing its most complete political and economic upheavals since the advent of Communist rule, Moscow no longer had the resources or the desire to impose its will on its western neighbors. In July, shortly after the first democratically elected parliament in over seventy years assembled in Moscow, Gorbachev told the annual meeting of the Warsaw Pact, the military alliance of the Communist states, that Moscow no longer cared how the Eastern European states ran their affairs. Discarding generations of Communist dogma, he declared, "There is no universal road to socialism." By the spring of 1991, all of the Eastern European states had taken the road to capitalism, free markets, and anticommunism (see map, page 588).

Revolutions soon swept aside the Communist governments throughout Eastern Europe. When the Communist regime in East Germany disintegrated, that nation soon disappeared as a separate country. The Berlin Wall fell in circumstances eerily similar to the emigration crisis leading to its construction in 1961. Hundreds of thousands of East Germans fled to the West in the summer of 1989. Many of those who remained demonstrated against their government during the autumn. Instead of confronting their own people with police or soldiers or asking for Soviet help, which would not have been forthcoming anyway, the East German Communists gave up power. They opened the wall on November 9, and wrecking balls began destroying it during the winter. Concrete chunks of the wall became a popular Christmas gift in Europe and America. In parliamentary elections in March 1990, the Christian Democrats swept to power on the promise of unification with wealthy West Germany. On October 2, 1990, the East German Democratic Republic merged with the West German Federal Republic into a single, capitalist German state. Three of the other Warsaw Pact states, Poland, Hungary, and Czechoslovakia, also underwent peaceful democratic revolutions. Elections in each country brought to power governments promising the end of communism, the institution of market economies, and, eventually, a

Democratic Movements in Eastern Europe, 1989–1991

prosperity like that in the West. Only Rumania and Bulgaria experienced bloodshed or major resistance from officials of the old order during the transition from communism.

The ferment spread from Eastern Europe into the Soviet Union itself. The Baltic states of Lithuania, Latvia, and Estonia, annexed by the Soviet Union in 1940, declared their independence in 1990. Moscow refused to recognize their independence; and Gorbachev, lionized in the West, found himself on the defensive at home. Movements to secede from the Soviet Union also arose in the republics of Armenia, Azerbaijan, Georgia, Moldavia, and the Ukraine. The Communist party lost power in local elections, and non-Communists led

From 1961 to 1989 the ugly Berlin Wall stood as a symbol of the repressive Communist regimes of Eastern Europe and the Soviet Union. When the wall was opened in November 1989, jubilant West Berliners climbed on top of it near the Brandenburg Gate to celebrate the apparent end of communism and the imminent reunification of Germany. *UPI/Bettmann Newsphotos.*

the municipal governments in Moscow and Leningrad. In July 1990, Boris Yeltsin, leader of the Russian parliament, resigned from the Soviet Communist party and became a major challenger to Gorbachev. Yeltsin won election as president of the Russian republic in June 1991. Meanwhile, seemingly powerless to arrest the slide of the Soviet economy, Gorbachev vacillated between supporting economic reformers and compromising with hard-liners in the Communist party and the military.

Americans watched the collapse of communism with considerable satisfaction but less intensity than might have been expected. People with family or cultural ties to Eastern Europe had the greatest stake; emigrants from Poland even voted in that country's presidential election. For the majority of Americans, however, the personalities and issues seemed remote from their ordinary concerns. Now that the Soviet Union was no longer considered a threat, Eastern Europe could go its own way without attracting much notice.

The Bush administration stayed on the fringe of events in Eastern Europe in 1989. Bush resisted Gorbachev's request for an early summit. Secretary of Defense Cheney opposed efforts to cut the military budget in 1989, despite signs that the Soviet threat was melting daily. Commentators accused Bush of failing to display leadership by not jetting to Berlin to sing the praises of democracy soon after the Berlin Wall opened. Yet the president sensibly avoided the appearance of gloating over the Soviets' discomfiture. Once it became clear that the Soviets wanted to play by new rules in Europe and elsewhere, Bush and Gorbachev established a political partnership. The two met six times in the nineteen months after December 1989, making friendly encounters between the leaders of the two superpowers almost as routine as Washington's consultations with the leaders of Britain, France, Japan, Canada, or any other major ally. Bush and Gorbachev formally acknowledged the end of the Cold War at a thirty-four-nation meeting of the Conference on Security and Cooperation in Europe in November 1990.

The end of the confrontation between capitalism and communism portended more of an unsteady alignment than a tight alliance between the United States and the Soviet Union. The turmoil within the Soviet Union was too great to make Moscow a completely predictable partner. The erosion of Communist rule set in motion processes Gorbachev could not control, and he often shifted his positions. He alternately favored hard-liners within the Communist party who resisted reforms and radicals who demanded faster progress toward free markets, political pluralism and demilitarization. In January 1991 he sided with the Red Army when it exerted control over the Baltic Republics and fired on a crowd in Vilnius, Lithuania, killing fourteen unarmed demonstrators. The Bush administration protested mildly, not wishing to weaken Soviet support for a United Nations-sponsored coalition against Iraq. Yet East-West relations improved once more in the summer, as Gorbachev and Yeltsin aligned themselves against the hard-liners. In June the Soviet Union and its former Eastern European allies disbanded the Warsaw Pact and COMECON. The next month Bush went to Moscow to sign a Strategic Arms Reduction Treaty, cutting the number of each side's strategic missiles and bombers by about one-third. On August 18 Gorbachev's opponents in the military, the secret police and the Communist party tried to depose him in a coup d'etat; but Yeltsin and hundreds of thousands of ordinary Soviet citizens resisted, restoring Gorbachev within three days. In the immediate aftermath of the failed coup, the Soviet Union underwent the most far-reaching changes since 1917: the Communist party lost its remaining power; several republics declared independence; and the future authority of the central government could not be predicted.

In contrast to events in the Soviet Union and its former satellites, political reform did not flourish in China. In the spring of 1989 Chinese university students staged a series of demonstrations in the country's largest cities. In Beijing thousands occupied Tiananmen Square in front of the mausoleum housing the embalmed body of revolutionary leader Mao Zedong. They constructed a giant statue, the "Goddess of Democracy," a rough, plaster replica of New York's Statue of Liberty, and made speeches demanding freedom of expression and better jobs for college graduates. Scores of students began a hunger strike to force the government to grant their demands. Their every move was followed by hundreds of television reporters, and the media presence magnified the significance of the protest movement for Americans, who could hardly resist the flattery of seeing their society serve as the model for the Chinese. Yet the authoritarian government would not budge. Deng Xiaoping, China's leader since the late 1970s, ordered the army to crush the uprising in June.

The brutal repression of the democracy movement in China stunned Americans, who watched events unfold on television. Some people took out their disappointment on the Bush administration, which showed minimal sympathy for a movement that had briefly captured America's heart. Bush, who had served as United States representative to China in 1974 and 1975, believed it important to maintain cordial relations with Beijing at almost any cost and resisted efforts to punish China. By late 1990 the democracy movement had faded into a sad memory, and the political partnership between the governments in Washington and Beijing resumed. Had it not been for the presence of the TV cameras, itself a product of the erosion of Cold War suspicions, the democracy movement would hardly have registered in the West.

The demise of the fledgling democracy movement in China could not overshadow the significance of the successes in Eastern Europe and the Soviet Union. The end of nerve-wracking, deadly, and expensive competition between the Soviet and American superpowers offered the brightest opportunity of the entire postwar period. The fear of nuclear annihilation faded, and anticommunism, once the focal point of political debate in the United States, seemed irrelevant to contemporary concerns. Polling organizations that had tracked attitudes toward the Soviet Union for forty years discovered the lowest index of fear of Moscow's intentions and the most positive opinion of the Soviet leadership ever recorded. The long-term American policy of containment had succeeded, probably beyond the wildest dreams of its sponsors.

The United States now stood alone as a military superpower. Yet the superficial resemblance to the situation in 1945, when the United States had dominated world politics, was misleading. The decades of struggling to maintain military equality or superiority to the Soviet Union had taken their toll on the American economy. Despite its preeminence in military terms, the United States faced a future of serious economic competition from its allies in Europe and Japan.

Exerting American Control in the Third World

One unexpected but in retrospect understandable sequel to the end of the Cold War and the abandonment of the American anti-Communist stance was the persistence of American interventionist behavior abroad. Although the United States no longer used the Soviet threat to justify its foreign policy, officials argued that instability and threats to the new world order required that the United States continue to assert its power in foreign lands. Without fear of Soviet opposition, Washington exercised its dominance in the Western Hemisphere as strongly as ever before. It also continued to intervene in other regions of the globe. Instability and turbulence did not disappear in the Third World with the dissipation of the Cold War. Only rigid anti-Communists, who truly believed that most of the world's problems originated in the Kremlin, expected otherwise.

One early intervention by the Bush administration was in Panama. Relations with Panama had remained turbulent after the 1978 ratification of treaties in which the United States pledged to relinquish sovereignty over the Panama Canal and the Canal Zone. Panamanian strongman Omar Torrijos had died in a plane crash in 1981. His death had caused the Reagan administration few regrets, because Reagan had campaigned against the canal treaties negotiated with Torrijos. Manuel Noriega, a long-time CIA informant in the Panamanian armed forces, established his own dictatorship in 1983, believing he retained the backing of the American government. For the next several years Noriega continued to make himself available to the CIA while simultaneously acting as a go-between for such diverse personalities and movements as a Colombian drug cartel, Fidel Castro, and the contra rebels opposed to the leftist government of Nicaragua. By 1988 Noriega's involvement in the drug trade had become an open secret and hence an embarrassment in Washington. A federal prosecutor in Miami tried to indict him for drug trafficking. Democratic presidential candidates complained that Bush's connections to Noriega, dating back to Bush's directorship of the CIA in 1976, undermined the administration's antidrug effort.

By 1989 Washington considered Noriega an adversary, and his rule of Panama became more abusive and arbitrary. Noriega called for national elections in May, hoping that soldiers of his loyal National Guard would stuff the ballot boxes with votes for his hand-picked candidate for president. Much to his shock, most Panamanians, including members of the guard, voted for opposition candidate Guillermo Endara. A group of international observers led by former president Jimmy Carter verified massive vote fraud, and Noriega voided the elections. He encouraged mobs known as Dignity Battalions to beat up supporters of his opponents. Conditions deteriorated in Panama throughout the remainder of 1989. Noriega's support evaporated, and Washington turned to a well-established method of ousting dictators—a CIA-sponsored military uprising. The coup d'état failed in October when Noriega refused to surrender to rebel officers and instead shot one of them personally.

For the next two months, critics of the Bush administration in the United States charged that Bush had not been serious in his efforts to oust Noriega. Stung by the renewal of charges that he lacked courage, and certain that a military attack would be cheap, easy, and widely popular among Panamanians, Bush ordered an invasion. At 1 A.M. on December 20, United States paratroopers dropped into Panama, beginning a seventy-two-hour conquest of the country. Fifty-five Panamanian National Guard troops and twenty-three United States soldiers lost their lives in the assault. Civilian casualties were much higher, with estimates ranging from two hundred to four thousand. When Noriega took refuge in the Vatican embassy, American troops surrounded his sanctuary and assaulted him with rock music, which Noriega was known to hate. Exhausted and fearful of capture by angry Panamanians, the dictator surrendered to the Americans on January 3, 1990. The authorities then extradited him to Miami for trial on drug trafficking charges. The case was stalled for over 18 months by Noriega's efforts to implicate U.S. officials in his activities.

The invasion of Panama proved extraordinarily popular in the United States and Panama. Polls revealed that close to 90 percent of Americans surveyed approved of it, and even more Panamanians were relieved to be rid of Noriega. Only a few voices complained that the United States had violated treaties, international law, and its own stand against intervention by evicting the government of Panama. Panamanians expected hundreds of millions of dollars in aid from Washington to rebuild their ruined land, but the United States did not quickly make good on its promises. A year after the invasion, a few poor Panamanians who had welcomed the Yankees now cursed them with chants of support for Saddam Hussein, dictator of Iraq, who had become the latest of Washington's enemies.

War with Iraq

Americans' views of world politics and the use of force faced a new challenge in the months after Iraq invaded and annexed its neighbor Kuwait on August 2, 1990. Iraq moved into Kuwait to seize that nation's vast oil reserves and erase the billions in loans provided by Kuwait during the eight-year war Iraq had waged with Iran. Iraq could hardly have expected the angry reaction its annexation of Kuwait provoked among other Arab nations and the rest of the world. Within hours President Bush, asserting that "this will not stand," began organizing a coalition to force Iraq out of Kuwait. The United Nations imposed an embargo on Iraq—the tightest economic sanctions it had ever enacted—and adopted twelve resolutions calling for Iraqi withdrawal. Under United Nations auspices, Bush assembled a multinational force of more than 700,000 troops from twenty-eight countries; the force was stationed in the Saudi Arabian desert and in the waters near Kuwait. Originally this huge army, navy, and air force assemblage was intended to protect the oil fields of Saudi Arabia from Iraq. In November, however, Bush doubled the size of the United States contingent to over 500,000 in order to provide an "offensive capability" to expel Iraq from Kuwait. The twelfth of the United Nations Security Council's resolutions called on Iraq to leave Kuwait by January 15, 1991, or face attack.

The angry American reaction, the unity within the United Nations—where the Soviet Union, an old ally of Iraq, sided with the United States—and the size of the multinational force arrayed against Baghdad surprised Iraq's leader, Saddam Hussein. He had expected that the world would consider his quarrel with Kuwait a matter for the Arabs to resolve among themselves. Hussein was especially perplexed by the American response in light of earlier American efforts to maintain good relations with his government. Before the invasion, the administration had opposed congressional efforts to stop agricultural credits to Iraq. Moreover, the American ambassador had apologized for Voice of America broadcasts critical of the dreadful human rights record of Hussein's government, and she had told the Iraqi president that the United States "does not intervene in inter-Arab border disputes."

Washington resisted Iraq as strenuously as it did for a variety of reasons. Regret that American diplomacy had encouraged Saddam Hussein's aggression played a role in the United States response, albeit a small one. The Iraqi annexation of Kuwait, which in effect wiped out a member of the United Nations, also violated principles of international law. Yet the United States and other nations had accepted many acts of aggression elsewhere in the previous forty-five years, and Washington's own record in observing international law had been uninspiring. Of greater significance was Washington's fear of Iraq's war-making potential. Baghdad had purchased some of the most sophisticated weapons in the world, had an army of more than 1 million soldiers, and had used poison gas on its own citizens, killing thousands. After the invasion of Kuwait, Washington feared that an unchecked Saddam Hussein could intimidate the remainder of the petroleum-producing states into setting the price of oil at any level he wanted. The effects on the economies of the industrial world could be devastating.

The conflict with Iraq absorbed the public for months, sapping much of Americans' optimism. At first, large majorities supported the embargo of Iraq and the dispatch of troops to defend Saudi Arabia if Iraqi forces crossed into that country. Consensus disappeared, however, in the late fall, after the United States doubled the size of its force and prepared for offensive military action. Opinion polls revealed that most people wanted Iraq to leave Kuwait, and a slender majority would contemplate the use of force to free that country, but a large minority opposed military measures.

Diplomatic efforts to resolve the crisis before the expiration of the deadline on January 15 failed. Iraq refused to discuss withdrawal from Kuwait unless the United States agreed to force Israel into yielding the West Bank of the Jordan and the Gaza Strip to the Palestinians. Saddam Hussein believed that Bush was bluffing and that the United States would not risk a prolonged war with potentially thousands of casualties. Bush's assertion that war with Iraq would not be another inconclusive, Vietnam-style engagement did not persuade Baghdad that the United States seriously contemplated a full-scale attack. Iraq also concluded that the substantial reservations about going to war expressed by many congressional Democrats demonstrated that the American public would not support a war. For his part, Bush rebuffed suggestions that Iraq be given a face-saving way to back down. He rejected "linkage" of the invasion of Kuwait to the Palestinian issue, believing that any deal on such matters would represent appeasement of a dictator he compared to Adolf Hitler.

When Bush concluded in late December 1990 that Iraq would not leave Kuwait peacefully, he decided on war. Mindful of charges that Lyndon Johnson had wrecked his presidency by waging the war in Vietnam without full congressional approval, Bush asked lawmakers for authority to go to war in accordance with the United Nations Security Council's resolutions. Members of Congress conducted one of the most thoughtful foreign policy debates of the post–Second World War era. On January 12 they rejected a plan sponsored by the Democratic leadership to forswear armed force and give economic sanctions more time to work. Both houses of Congress then voted to authorize Bush to use the armed forces to expel Iraq from Kuwait. Nearly all Republicans supported the use of force; two-thirds of the Democrats in the House opposed it, along with forty-five of fifty-six Senate Democrats. Those Democrats who supported the resolution authorizing force provided the margin of victory in each house.

On January 16, 1991, eighteen hours after the expiration of the United Nations deadline for Iraq to withdraw from Kuwait, war began. Planes from the United States, Britain, Italy, France, Saudi Arabia, and the exiled Kuwaiti government began a massive bombardment of Iraq and Kuwait (see map, page 596). Coalition aircraft flew round-the-clock bombing raids against Iraq's military facilities, power supplies, water systems, nuclear installations, and chemical warfare plants. The planes also inflicted ferocious punishment on Iraq's ground soldiers in Kuwait and eastern Iraq. American military briefers refused to speculate on the number of Iraqis killed or injured

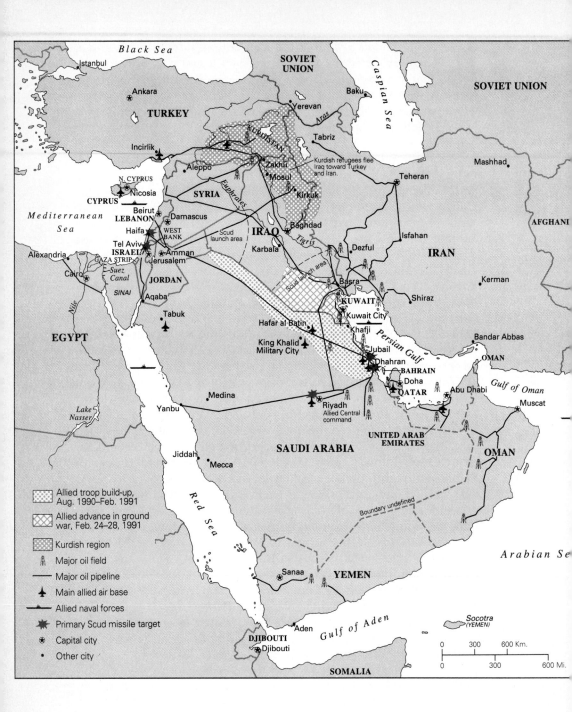

Black Sea

SOVIET
UNION

SOVIET UNION

Istanbul

Ankara

Baku

Caspian Sea

Mashhad

TURKEY

Yerevan

Tabriz

Teheran

AFGHANI

Incirlik

Aleppo

Zakhu

KURDISTAN

Kurdish refugees flee
Iraq toward Turkey
and Iran.

Mosul

N. CYPRUS

Nicosia

SYRIA

Kirkuk

CYPRUS

Mediterranean
Sea

LEBANON

Beirut

Damascus

Euphrates

Baghdad

Isfahan

IRAN

Haifa

Tel Aviv

WEST
BANK

Scud
launch area

IRAQ

Tigris

Dezful

ISRAEL

Karbala

Basra

Kerman

Alexandria

GAZA STRIP

Amman

Scud launch area

Kuwait City

Shiraz

Cairo

Jerusalem

JORDAN

KUWAIT

Khafji

Bandar Abbas

Suez
Canal

Aqaba

Hafar al Batin

Kuwait City

Persian Gulf

OMAN

SINAI

Tabuk

King Khalid
Military City

Jubail

Dhahran

Gulf of Oman

EGYPT

Medina

Yanbu

Riyadh
Allied Central
command

BAHRAIN

Doha

QATAR

Abu Dhabi

Muscat

Lake
Nasser

Red Sea

UNITED ARAB
EMIRATES

OMAN

Jiddah

Mecca

SAUDI ARABIA

Boundary undefined

Arabian Se

Allied troop build-up,
Aug. 1990–Feb. 1991

Allied advance in ground
war, Feb. 24–28, 1991

Kurdish region

Major oil field

Major oil pipeline

Main allied air base

Allied naval forces

Primary Scud missile target

Capital city

Other city

Sanaa

YEMEN

Socotra
(YEMEN)

0   300   600 Km.

0   300   600 Mi.

Aden

Gulf of Aden

DJIBOUTI

Djibouti

SOMALIA

by the bombing, but estimates after the war indicated that the losses were terrible. Between 25,000 and 130,000 Iraqi soldiers and civilians lost their lives.

As soon as the war began, public opinion, which had been so divided days before, united in wide support for the war and President Bush. Americans saw the war unfold on television. Advanced satellite technology enabled people to see the bombing of Baghdad as it occurred, along with Iraqi missile attacks on Saudi Arabia and Israel. With the exception of occasional pictures of an apartment building destroyed in Tel Aviv or a bunker housing hundreds of civilians that was bombed in Baghdad, the pictures did not show death and destruction. Instead, Americans thrilled to pictures of Patriot missiles, manned by United States Army crews, shooting down Iraqi missiles aimed at cities in Israel or Saudi Arabia. Faith in American technology soared with the Patriots. Military briefers strictly controlled the access of journalists to the battlefield and to the soldiers, but they released video pictures of so-called smart bombs finding their targets with breathtaking accuracy.

As the air war went forward for five and one-half weeks, people in the United States contemplated the nature of the 540,000-person American contingent preparing for a ground war. The massive force had executed the most rapid deployment since the Second World War. The all-volunteer armed forces differed sharply from the conscript army assembled twenty-five years earlier to fight the war in Vietnam. Eighty percent were high school graduates, compared to only 60 percent of the Vietnam-era force. More than one-third of the troops who fought in the Persian Gulf war were members of racial minority groups; approximately 20 percent had come from nonwhite backgrounds during the Vietnam era. Unlike the situation in Vietnam, however, racial tension was negligible. Alcohol and drug use also remained low as American authorities, not wishing to offend the religious sensibilities of the Saudi Arabians, established a strict prohibition. In a short war with a volunteer force, morale was high.

Perhaps the greatest difference from the Vietnam conflict was the large number of women—30,000—deployed to the Persian Gulf. Women held all jobs with the exception of combat fighter, but the distinction between combatants and noncombatants was difficult to see. Women flew helicopters, operated Patriot missiles, and were among the first soldiers to enter Iraq and Kuwait when the ground war commenced. Two women were among the twenty-one Americans taken prisoner during the war. The large number of women involved in the fighting presented another unprecedented aspect of the

◀ **The War in the Persian Gulf**

American tanks prepare for the ground war against Iraq in early 1991. *Wide World Photos.*

war. Many had children, left behind with their husbands. Others were married to soldiers, who themselves were participating in the war, so that hundreds of children were left in the hands of grandparents or other caretakers.

After five weeks of nonstop bombing, General H. Norman Schwarzkopf, the American commander, announced that the Iraqi army was on the verge of collapse. Accordingly, hundreds of thousands of United States–led coalition forces began the final attack on Kuwait and eastern Iraq on the night of February 23. Saddam Hussein had boasted that the ground war would be the "mother of all battles," with the Americans and their allies suffering tens of thousands of casualties. But the bombing campaign had so devastated Iraq, disrupted communications, and killed so many soldiers that those who remained put up virtually no resistance. The ground war ended in a rout. The Iraqis fled from Kuwait City, and tens of thousands surrendered to the advancing forces. On the night of February 27, exactly 100 hours after the ground war began and six weeks after the start of the bombing, Bush declared Kuwait liberated and the war over.

The costs of the war for Iraq and Kuwait were extraordinarily high. Apart from the tens of thousands of Iraqis killed in the bombing raids and the brief ground war, Iraq's cities were devastated. Its water treatment plants, electrical grid, communications network, and modern roads and bridges were nearly all destroyed. In the immediate aftermath a civil war broke out between supporters and opponents of Saddam Hussein. Among the rebels were ethnic Kurds who had long resisted Hussein. When the Kurdish rebellion was suppressed, two million Kurds fled their homes in northern Iraq, fearing brutal attacks from the remainder of Hussein's forces. Thousands of the refugees died in makeshift mountain camps until United States–led allied forces encouraged them to return to their homes by creating a 100-square-mile security zone inside northern Iraq.

Kuwait, for its part, had suffered seven months of terror: Iraqi forces had looted everything of value from ordinary Kuwaitis, had tortured or killed thousands of people, had eaten or shot the animals in the zoo, had stolen over $1 billion worth of artifacts from the national museum, and had set fire to over six hundred of the nine hundred oil wells in the country. Experts predicted that it would take one to three years to put out the fires and restore Kuwait's oil production. In the meantime, the thick black smoke from the fires threatened the environment for hundreds of miles. Further damage to the environment came from Iraq's release of approximately 10 million barrels of crude oil into the gulf during the war. American losses, on the other hand, were minimal. In contrast to dire predictions that the United States forces might suffer 10,000 to 20,000 dead and wounded, fewer than 150 soldiers lost their lives in battle, and about 200 were wounded.

The memory of Vietnam was prominent in the minds of many Americans during and after the fighting. It became evident that different groups had drawn various lessons from America's longest, most divisive war. Bush repeatedly told the country that the war with Iraq would not be another Vietnam—that is, long and frustratingly unsuccessful. Once the war ended, he exulted that "we've kicked the Vietnam syndrome," the reluctance to use American troops abroad for fear of another failure. The military, for its part, learned from Vietnam that it should use massive power, applied quickly, not gradually, and it followed that strategy against Iraq. Convinced that negative press coverage had undermined public support for the Vietnam War, the military also adjusted its informational strategy, keeping journalists on a tight rein. Ordinary people drew their own lessons from Vietnam; they vowed that regardless of their own opinions of the wisdom of going to war, they would support the soldiers fighting it. Homeowners put up thousands of American flags, banners reading "We support our troops," and yellow ribbons, the symbol since the Iranian hostage crisis of concern for loved ones in danger abroad.

As the war went well and the costs to the United States seemed low, support for the president surged. When the war ended, public opinion polls recorded that about 90 percent of respondents thought he was doing a good job, the highest approval rating for a president since the Second World War. Nevertheless, a small group of people remembered the moral and political costs of Vietnam and did not want them repeated in the Persian Gulf conflict. An antiwar movement, similar to the one that had opposed American involvement in Vietnam, stirred briefly before the war and at its very beginning. Chants of "Hell no, we won't go, we won't fight for Texaco" and "No blood for oil" were widely heard at antiwar rallies. Some instances of harassment of Arab-Americans made front-page news and were taken by critics as a sign that the war against Iraq had produced vicious intolerance at home. Yet the quick, decisive victory and the lack of a draft to galvanize students kept opposition to the conflict from approaching the size or intensity of resistance to the war in Vietnam.

With the end of the Persian Gulf war, the United States promised to use its power and prestige to foster stability in the region and throughout the world. Israel had been on the same side as several of its traditional Arab enemies (Saudi Arabia, Kuwait, and Syria), and the Palestine Liberation Organization had undermined its standing among moderate Arabs by backing Iraq. This new alignment seemed to present an opportunity for the United States to mediate among old rivals, but whether it would lead toward a settlement of differences between Israel and its neighbors or between Israelis and Palestinians remained an open question.

Of even greater importance for the United States was the question of the proper use of American power. It remained to be seen whether Americans would conclude that the two wars of the Bush administration represented the right way for the United States to protect the stability of the new world order. The war had shown an American president carefully orchestrating a grand coalition against an aggressor. Bush had used the United Nations and the easing of tensions with the Soviet Union to project American power in ways not seen since the end of the Second World War. With the United States dominant militarily in 1991, might it become even more assertive in the future? Americans had reacted with regret and soul-searching to the debacle in Vietnam. That war had contributed to the widespread sense of frustration with public institutions and leaders. Would the success against Iraq produce the opposite reaction, leading once more to the arrogant assumptions of American military and moral authority that had characterized the involvement in Vietnam?

A DIVERSE NATION IN THE 1990s

If Americans seemed largely united during the Persian Gulf war, society at home remained diverse and sometimes divided. Regardless of what happened overseas, Americans in the 1990s continued to wrestle with the impact of developments of the last half-century. Economic developments made the future seem bleaker than the prosperous era following the Second World War; indeed, some analysts spoke of an irreversible decline in American wealth and influence as other nations surged to the forefront. If the economic pie was shrinking, the question of how it would be divided took on additional significance. Internally, the United States had become a more pluralistic society than ever before. Many ethnic groups enjoyed greater tolerance, but some old animosities persisted, and racial tensions in particular had lasted well beyond the removal of legal barriers to integration. Meanwhile, immigrants still streamed into the United States, and the center of population continued its drift toward the South and West. The one constant in American society appeared to be change.

Visions of America in Decline

One important issue that briefly surfaced during the 1988 presidential campaign was the crumbling infrastructure of the American economy. Estimates for repair of the nation's decaying highways and bridges ranged from $50 billion to $200 billion. No new airport had been constructed in the United States since 1974; not surprisingly, the air transportation system suffered bottlenecks, delays, and occasional tragic collisions. The nation's expensive and chaotic medical system also prompted concern. Americans paid 12% of their GNP for health care, 50% to 100% more than residents of other industrial nations. Those with full medical insurance, received the best care in the world, but 37 million people, most of whom worked, had little or no insurance coverage. Excluded from the benefits of prohibitively expensive high-tech medicine, the overall health of the uninsured working poor lagged far behind that of more fortunate Americans. Some of the Democratic presidential candidates complained about the national neglect of such issues, but little was done to change matters.

The continuing shift of employment from manufacturing to service industries also caused concern. To be sure, some jobs in the service sector paid well. For example, most lawyers and doctors earned handsome livings, and the boom in such upscale professions meant a rising income for certain segments of society. The number of lawyers in the United States increased by nearly 50 percent in the 1980s; by 1990 the country had 756,000 lawyers, more than the total in the rest of the world. The number of medical doctors also rose from 279,000 in 1970 to 554,000 in 1988. An even greater increase occurred among real estate agents, a group which grew from 100,000 members to 800,000 in the twenty years after 1970.

In percentage terms, the increase in upscale service positions was impressive, but the vast majority of new jobholders did not find work as professionals. Those without a college education earned less in the new service jobs than their parents or elder siblings had in manufacturing. Steady work became even more uncertain, because service

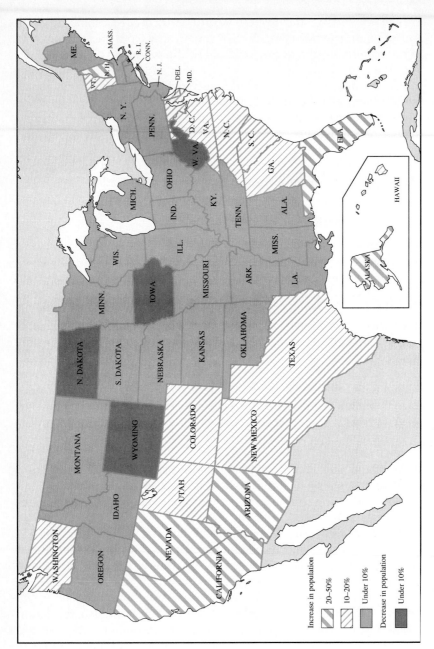

The Continued Shift to the Sunbelt, 1980–1990

Increase in population

20–50%

10–20%

Under 10%

Decrease in population

Under 10%

employers hired in good times and laid off employees in downturns. A so-called K-mart economy developed in many of the booming regions of the Sunbelt, where young, uneducated, and unskilled workers found work paying only $4 to $6 per hour in discount stores, supermarkets, fast-food stores, auto repair shops, hair salons, or banks. Towns that had encouraged chain stores to set up branches, and even those where large manufacturing industries had established small local assembly lines, found themselves longing for home-grown businesses and entrepreneurs to create wealth and economic diversity. A city council member in one fast-growing Florida city lamented, "We've had a lot of growth. But it was just quantity, not quality."

During the 1980s younger workers found it harder to make ends meet. The purchasing power of households in which the principal wage earner was less than twenty-five years old fell 19 percent from the beginning of the decade to the end. Households whose major wage earner was twenty-five to thirty-four years old also saw their purchasing power erode in the 1980s. Conditions for most age groups above thirty-five held steady or improved marginally. Only people over sixty-five, whose Social Security and other pension payments were linked to changes in the cost of living, saw their incomes rise significantly. The sense that the younger generation was losing ground helped revive the fears of the late 1970s. By 1990 public opinion polls once more reflected a widespread belief that the future would be grimmer than the past and that children would have a harder time achieving economic security than did their parents.

In explaining these trends, some analysts quoted Yale University historian Paul Kennedy, one of the most prominent advocates of the school of thought that the United States had entered a period of relative decline. In his best-selling book, *The Rise and Fall of the Great Powers*, Kennedy argued that the United States had entered a period of "imperial overreach," similar to patterns established by Spain in the seventeenth century and Britain in the nineteenth century. The United States could no longer afford to maintain its vast military commitments around the globe. It had paid for them with borrowed money that might have been better invested in improving the American economy. Like the declining empires of old, the United States risked being overtaken economically by other nations, which had been spared the costs of maintaining military bases overseas and of intervention in foreign wars.

Migration and Immigration

The 1990 census revealed the persistence of the demographic, economic, and social trends that had taken shape in the 1960s and 1970s. The entire population stood at slightly under 250 million, a gain of about 23 million in the decade. Americans continued to move to the

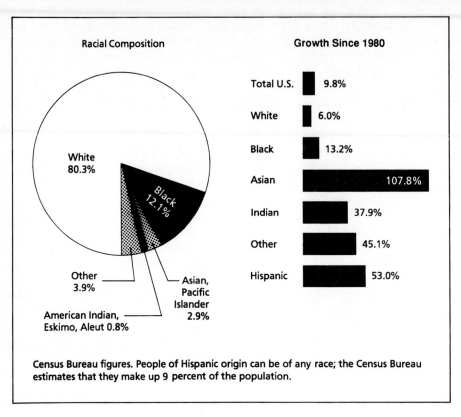

Racial Composition

White 80.3%

Black 12.1%

Other 3.9%

Asian, Pacific Islander 2.9%

American Indian, Eskimo, Aleut 0.8%

Growth Since 1980

Total U.S. 9.8%

White 6.0%

Black 13.2%

Asian 107.8%

Indian 37.9%

Other 45.1%

Hispanic 53.0%

Census Bureau figures. People of Hispanic origin can be of any race; the Census Bureau estimates that they make up 9 percent of the population.

Population Growth, 1980–1990

Sunbelt states in the West and the South (see map); immigration, mostly from the Third World, accounted for one-third of the population growth of the decade; older cities of the Northeast and Midwest lost population; and for the first time, over 50 percent of Americans lived in suburbs.

The shifts in population dramatically altered the sectional balance of power in the House of Representatives. After the 1992 election California would gain seven seats, to fifty-two. No state had had such a large share of the representatives since New York had exercised similar power and influence in the 1880s. For its part, New York continued to lose seats, falling from thirty-four to thirty-one. Texas gained three seats, to a total of thirty, only one less than New York; most observers believed that Texas would soon overtake New York and become the second largest state in the census taken in the year 2000. Other Sunbelt states also gained representation, while areas of the traditionally populous industrial eastern and Midwestern regions saw their share of representation in the House decline.

The shift toward nonwhite minorities was the sharpest of the twentieth century (see figure). Whites in general represented about 80 percent of the total population; whites of European background only about 76 percent. The remainder were primarily African-American, Hispanic, Asians, and Native American. Much of the growth in the nonwhite population came from an additional 7.6 million Hispanics, half of whom were immigrants. Seven million people immigrated legally to the United States during the 1980s, and the vast majority of them were of non-European origin. In California, nonwhites or Latinos contributed a majority of the public schoolchildren and accounted for 42 percent of the entire population of the state. Forty percent of the students in New York's schools were nonwhite. In the telephone book for San Jose, California, there were more people with the surname Nguyen, a common Vietnamese name, than with the surname Jones. Two hundred thousand people of Middle Eastern ancestry lived in the Detroit area. Nearly 1 million people from Southeast Asia or their children lived in cities across the country. The immigration trends, combined with the high birth rates among African-Americans, Hispanics, and Asians, led some experts to predict that by the year 2050 a majority of the American population would trace its roots to non-European cultures.

Class, Race, and Cultural Pluralism

The continued movement to the Sunbelt and the allure of the United States for immigrants demonstrated the robustness of American society. But divisions between races and economic classes led to a bleaker picture: a sizable proportion of the American population was trapped in poverty and assailed by racial or ethnic hatreds. The proportion of Americans living in poverty declined slightly at the end of the eighties to 12.8 percent of all Americans, yet the poverty rate remained higher than at any time in the 1970s (see figure, page 606). Vast differences existed among ethnic groups. Ten percent of whites were considered poor, versus 26 percent of Hispanics and 30 percent of blacks. Deprivation continued to fall most heavily on single mothers and children. Despite gains made since the 1960s, many elderly were also poor. Half of the people classified as poor were less than eighteen years old or over sixty-five. Half of black children under the age of six were poor.

The term *underclass* was in wide use by the end of the 1980s to describe poor people, mostly urban, mostly nonwhite, who depended on welfare, had high rates of unemployment and little education, and contributed greatly to the crime rate. The idea of an underclass suggested a loss of hope for the poorest African-Americans. They lived outside the circle of aspirations of middle-class Americans. Young black men experienced some of the direst consequences of

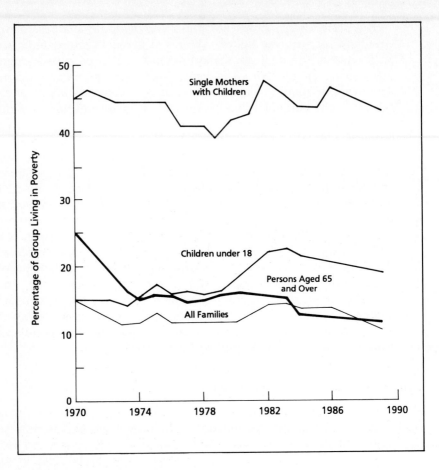

Poverty in America, 1970–1989

generations of poverty and deprivation. Nearly one-fourth of black men between the ages of eighteen and thirty had criminal records, were serving jail terms, or were on probation. The media seized on violent crimes committed by young blacks and Hispanics against middle-class whites. A night of "wilding"—a rampage of rape and mugging through New York's Central Park in which a thirty-one-year-old white woman was sexually assaulted and nearly beaten to death—attracted headlines for a year. News stories that black teenagers assaulted and even killed one another for expensive athletic shoes also contributed to racist stereotypes that young black men were dangerous and unpredictable. At the end of the decade the murder rate for black men under thirty remained the highest of any group, and a young black man had a greater chance of dying from a gunshot wound than from any other cause.

Reports of the dreadful conditions among the poorest of urban African-Americans minimized the revival of a spirit of community crossing class lines. Rather, the picture was so bleak that many middle-class and suburban Americans came to hold inner-city residents responsible for their own misery. Consequently, whites paid less attention to information about the racism that was still directed toward African-Americans. Videotapes made with hidden cameras showed blacks turned away from buying houses in comfortable suburbs. Another tape showed several Los Angeles police officers brutally beating a black man they had arrested for speeding. These events aroused some concern, yet even dramatic evidence of the persistence of racism did not alter the common perception that the problems of the poor could not be solved by the larger society.

The plight of the poorest African-Americans also contrasted sharply with the conditions of other people of color. *Time* magazine, which devoted a cover story to the growing ethnic diversity in the United States, reported uneasiness among blacks about the growing size of other nonwhite ethnic groups. Hispanics stood to surpass African-Americans as the largest nonwhite group early in the twenty-first century. Asians and Hispanics fared better than blacks economically, and African-Americans feared that their needs would increasingly be ignored by the larger society.

People of all ethnic backgrounds struggled to balance claims for recognition and respect for one another. Controversies continued over affirmative action programs designed to redress centuries of racial discrimination. The issue erupted into the political arena in October 1990, when President Bush vetoed a civil rights act that would have permitted nonwhites and women greater leeway to sue businesses for discrimination in employment. The president claimed that the act would lead employers to establish rigid hiring and promotion quotas. But advocates of affirmative action believed that his veto merely pandered to the resentments of white males, who saw their privileged position being eroded in a more pluralistic society.

The issue of ethnic balance caused special strains in colleges and universities, which faced new difficulties in deciding what should be included in the curriculum and what kinds of people should be hired to teach. Trying to recognize the new cultural diversity of the United States, some universities insisted that students learn something about non-European cultures. Moreover, college administrators—sometimes acting on their own initiative, sometimes in response to pressure—demanded that admission and hiring policies be changed so that a greater proportion of the student body and the faculty would be nonwhite and female. These moves to celebrate the pluralism of the United States sometimes produced a backlash. Efforts to broaden the curriculum to include the literature, thought, and art of Asia, Africa, and Latin America provoked complaints from some whites,

The New Immigrants

The decade of the 1980s saw one of the largest influxes of immigrants in American history. Even more important, the changing pattern of national origins became pronounced: about 45 percent of the newcomers came from Asia and the Middle East, and another 45 percent from nations in the Western Hemisphere. No European country was among the top ten places of origin. Countries with extensive cultural, military, or economic contacts with the United States—for example, the Philippines, Korea, and Mexico—provided the lion's share of the immigrants.

The diversity of the newcomers made it difficult to generalize about them. Some of the Asians were highly educated doctors and nurses who joined the staffs of big-city hospitals; some were engineers who pursued careers with

men, and traditionalists who believed the cultural heritage of the West was being unjustly subordinated. Hiring practices that appeared to favor women or minorities led to bitter arguments about the nature of the university and the importance of traditional academic credentials.

AN UNFINISHED AGENDA

As they had since the mid-1960s, American institutions strained to manage continued, rapid change. The strong federal government and the assertive presidency, characteristic of the postwar epoch, remained central features of modern American life. The federal judiciary continued to influence the way people related to one another and their government. But opinions about American government and society were mixed. Some people remained skeptical about the quality

high-technology firms. Other Asians from urban backgrounds pooled their resources to establish small retail businesses. Many Vietnamese, Filipinos, and other Asians from rural backgrounds found low-paying employment in service industries or manufacturing. Immigrants from Mexico and the rest of the Western Hemisphere often came from rural areas and had little education or wealth when they arrived. They settled in urban centers of the West, Southwest, and Midwest, where they worked in unskilled service and manufacturing positions.

Newcomers often experienced "exile shock" in their first years in the United States. Even if they had come to America to escape mistreatment or earn a better living, they sometimes felt unhappy with the unfamiliar surroundings and with the prevailing materialism of American society. As a Hmong man from the highlands of Cambodia lamented, "Everything is money first." Parents who encouraged their children to adapt to American ways often grew dismayed when those same children rejected the family's traditional customs.

As had been the case during earlier periods of immigration, nativists opposed the admission of strangers on the ground that their presence would undermine American cultural values. Especially during economic downturns, immigrants became the targets of people who felt their own status and well-being threatened. Yet most economists and many thoughtful social observers believed that the arrival of the new immigrants enriched the United States. ∎

of national leadership and the ability of institutions to meet people's needs.

Part of the continued anxiety about political, professional, educational, and religious institutions rested on real shortcomings. Leaders were often short-sighted and unwilling to take actions that might offend important groups or individuals. Yet the difficulty of institutions in managing change was magnified and distorted by the mass media, especially television, another feature of the post–Second World War environment. As Americans moved, divorced, changed or lost jobs, and loosened ties to family, religion, and government, they became more dependent on mass media for information and opinions. In many important ways, modern mass media made people more informed about the wider world than ever before. The speed of satellite communications would have astonished Americans in the Second World War. Yet greater information did not always lead to greater understanding or perspective. Because television loved drama and conflict, whether real or imagined, it did not provide a balanced view. As they approached the uncertainties of the future, Americans perhaps believed too much in the world they saw on television—a world that was a threatening place, one that could not be made safe or predictable by rational human action.

For forty-five years after the Second World War the United States was the dominant military and economic power in the world. For nearly all of that time competition between the Soviet Union and the United States was the primary issue of international relations. The Cold War helped create the modern American state, in which the president ruled supreme and military spending sped development of the Sunbelt. The post–Second World War period also brought extraordinary American prosperity. But the end of the Cold War coincided with the rise of a global free market economy, in which the robust economies of Europe and Japan challenged the preeminence of the United States. In some ways this would be a more difficult challenge than any of the Cold War era.

In the 1990s Americans had a vast, unfinished agenda for their country. Most thoughtful people believed in the need for concerted action to increase the productivity of American industries; there was also substantial agreement that such issues as protection of the environment, improvement of education, reforming the health care system, and restoration of the nation's crumbling infrastructure should be given high priority. However, little consensus existed about solutions to any of these important problems, and attempts to achieve consensus were complicated by continuing social conflicts. Lacking a vibrant sense of community, Americans had difficulty coming to terms with wide differences in wealth and power in their diverse society. Racial animosities, differences between ethnic groups, and the ongoing struggle for equality between women and men left a large gap between the social harmony that Americans desired and the reality of continued conflict.

Francis Fukuyama, a State Department official in the 1980s, wrote a provocative analysis of the end of the Cold War in which he argued that the waning of Communist ideology represented "the end of history." He meant that once the values of a mixed economy and representative government were established worldwide, all that would remain was the working out of details. It is already apparent, however, that events have become no simpler in the aftermath of the Cold War. For generations Americans have struggled to make their government, economy, social arrangements, and private lives reflect their personal and national needs. Their efforts have achieved partial success but have also left many people frustrated and uneasy. In the future Americans will continue to make history as they attempt to deal with the many items on their unfinished agenda. ■

FURTHER READING

On politics, see: Jack Germond and Jules Witcover, *Whose Broad Stripes and Bright Stars? The Trivial Pursuit of the Presidency, 1988* (1989); Sidney Blumenthal, *The Last Campaign of the Cold War* (1990); Michael Barone, *Our Country* (1989). On economic and social policy, see: David Halberstam, *The Next Century* (1991); Robert Reich, *The Work of Nations: Preparing Ourselves for Twenty-first Century Capitalism* (1991); William Julius Wilson, *The Truly Disadvantaged: The Inner City, the Underclass, and Public Policy* (1987). On the question of the relative decline of the United States, see: Paul Kennedy, *The Rise and Fall of the Great Powers* (1987); David Calleo, *Beyond American Hegemony* (1987); Joseph Nye, Jr., *Bound to Lead: The Changing Nature of American Power* (1990). On foreign policy, see: Bob Woodward, *The Commanders* (1991); also consult the quarterlies *Foreign Affairs* and *Foreign Policy* and the annual issues of *America and the World* published each winter by *Foreign Affairs*. Until books on recent events appear, consult the major journals of public affairs: *The Atlantic, Dissent, Harper's, The Nation, The New York Review of Books, The New Republic, The National Review, The Public Interest*. Newsweeklies, when used with care, also contain useful information and interpretations. See *Business Week, The Economist* (London), *Newsweek, Time*, and *U.S. News and World Report*.

INDEX

Abbey, Edward, 361
Abernathy, Ralph David, 155–156, 348
Abortion: Bush's position(s) on, 583–584; Carter's position on, 451, 458–459; government funding of, 528; Supreme Court decisions on, 410–411, 583
Abrams, Elliot, 534
Acheson, Dean, 70, 92–93, 99, 101–102, 316–317; and Bay of Pigs, 208; and China, 103–104; and Cuban missile crisis, 221; and Korean War, 109–110; McCarthy on, 106; and NATO, 99; plan for international control of atomic energy, 89; and Portugal, 216; and Vietnam, 104–105
Acid rock, 339
Ackroyd, Dan, 445
ADA. See Americans for Democratic Action
Adams, Sherman, 160; on *Sputnik I*, 187–188
Adelman, Kenneth, 534
Adenauer, Konrad, 97
AEC. See Atomic Energy Commission
Affirmative action programs, 459–460, 607
Affirmative discrimination, 478
The Affluent Society, 135
Afghanistan, Soviet invasion of, 548–549
AFL-CIO, 127; in 1972 election, 419

African-Americans, 148–149. *See also* Civil rights movement; in baseball, 74; and Democratic party, 154; infant mortality rate, 254; migration of, 149–150; music of, 141, 340; political offices held by, in 1960s, 257–259, 359–360; post-World War II, 73; poverty among, 605–607; status of, 75, 157; in Vietnam, 305; voter registration drives, 257, 328; in wartime, 29–32, 40; women, in wartime, 28
Agent Orange, 299
Agnew, Spiro T., 318, 320, 350, 370; resignation from vice presidency, 431–432
Agricultural Adjustment Act (AAA), 5, 11
Aid for Families with Dependent Children (AFDC), 401
AIDS, 528–530; public education campaign about, 529
Aiichiro, Fujiyama, 49
Ailes, Roger, on Nixon, 365
Alabama: and Freedom Riders, 233; Montgomery boycott, 156
Albert, Carl, 432
Alexander, Lamar, 579
Alexander v. *Holmes County Board of Education*, 406
Allen, Richard, 536
Allende Gossens, Salvador, 388–389

Alliance for Progress, 196, 212, 274–275
Alpert, Richard, 342
Altamont Speedway rock festival, 346
American Communist Party, 64, 66
American Federation of Labor, 127
American Federation of State, County and Municipal Employees (AFSCME), 127
American Indian Movement (AIM), 360
American Legion, 56
American Medical Association, 68
Americans for Democratic Action (ADA), 78
Anderson, John, 487; presidential bid, 1980, 489
Anderson, Marian, 9
Andrews, Julie, 422
Andropov, Yuri, 542
Anglo-Iranian Oil Company, 178
Antiballistic missile (ABM) treaty, 381–382
Anti-Communism, 43, 52. *See also* Red Scare
Anti-Communist alliances, forged by Eisenhower administration, 173–175
Anti-Semitism: post-World War II, 82; in wartime, 34–35, 40
Antiwar movement during Vietnam, 307–309; on campuses, in 1960s, 336–337; and Democratic convention in Chicago, 1968, 349–350; and invasion of Cambodia, 371–374; and Nixon administration, 369–370
Antiwar movement and war with Iraq, 599–600
Arevalo, Juan Jose, 179–180
Arkansas, desegregation of schools in, 153–154
Armed Services Committee, Preparedness Subcommittee, 188
Arms control: negotiations, during Reagan administration, 563–568; and Nixon administration, 381–383
Arms race: anxieties about, 539–541; during Reagan administration, 538–544; and space race, 187–190; United States' lead in, 190
Arms sales in Middle East, 390
Arms sales to Iran: by Nixon administration, 382; by Reagan administration, 558. *See also* Iran-contra affair
Armstrong, Neil, 364

Army-McCarthy hearings, 172
Army of the Republic of Vietnam (ARVN), 284–285, 287, 368–369, 373–374
ARVN. *See* Army of the Republic of Vietnam
Ashbrook, John, 387
Asian immigrants, 72, 604–605, 608–609; in 1960s, 261–262
Aspin, Les, 447
Assassination(s): of 1968, 318–319, 348–349; of John Kennedy, 236–239
Atlantic Charter, 19
Atomic age, 90
Atomic bomb. *See* Atomic weapons
Atomic cities, 24
Atomic diplomacy, 50
Atomic Energy Act of 1946, 89–90
Atomic Energy Act of 1954, 123
Atomic Energy Commission (AEC), 89–90, 193
Atomic era, 49
Atomic weapons, 100; American, 100; American use of, against Japan, 48–51; intermediate-range nuclear missiles (IRBMs), 219; as issue in 1964 presidential election, 251; Soviet, 100; Soviet-American relations and, 88–90; testing, 193; use, Eisenhower's ideas on, 167–168; as weapon of choice, 165
Atoms for Peace program, 193
Atwater, Lee, 583
Austin, Hudson, 551
Auto age, 128–129
Automobile industry: in 1940s, 128; in 1970s, 461

Baby Boom, 60–61, 124–125
Baez, Joan, 236, 339
Baker, Bobby, 246
Baker, Ella, 157, 329
Baker, Howard, 429, 566
Baker, James A. III, 501–502, 506, 586, 590; as White House chief of staff, 498
Baker v. *Carr*, 267–268
Bakke, Allan, 459
Bakker, Jim and Tammy Faye, 477, 526–527
Balaguer, Joaquin, 276
Balance of payments deficit, 414
Ball, George, 292, 294–295

Bush administration: domestic policies, 577–586; economic policy, 584–586; foreign policy, 586–600

Busing, 408–409; Carter's position on, 451; and Nixon administration, 404–406

Butler, John M., 108

Butler, Pierce, 11

Butterfield, Alexander, 430–431, 438

Byrd, Harry F., 152

Byrnes, James F., 24, 30, 38–39, 45, 50, 87

C. Turner Joy, 289

Caddell, Patrick, 467; on presidential election of 1980, 489

Califano, Joseph, 458–459

California Supreme Court, and unmarried couples, 471–472

Calley, William, 370

Cambodia, invasion of, 1970, 352, 368, 370–374

Camp David, 192; spirit of, 193

Camp David peace process, 479–480

Campus activism: and invasion of Cambodia, 371–374; of 1960s, 333–337, 351

Capehart, Homer, 106

CAPs. *See* Community Action Programs

Carlucci, Frank, 536, 566

Carmichael, Stokely, 329, 331–332, 348, 357

Carnegie Endowment for International Peace, 69

Carson, Rachel, 229–231; *Silent Spring,* 361

Carswell, G. Harrold, 371, 407

Carter, Billy, 453

Carter, James Earl "Jimmy," 592; cancellation of water projects, 457; debates with Ford, 453–454; debates with Reagan, 487–488; and decline of presidential authority, 455–468; election as president, 454–455; energy policy, 463–465; and federal income tax, 467; foreign policy, 478–487; and human rights abroad, 480–481; and Iranian hostage crisis, 484–487; and Middle East, 479–480; and Tip O'Neill, 456; pardon of Vietnam draft resisters, 304, 451, 456; as president, 441–442, 455–468; presidential bid, 1976, 450–455;

presidential bid, 1980, 487–489; pussyfooting approach, 464; Rose Garden strategy, 485; and SALT-II, 484

Carter, "Miz" Lillian, 453

Carter administration: and abortion, 458–459; and affirmative action, 459–460; and China, 396; energy policy, 463–465; eptitude question, 466; foreign policy, 478–487; and human rights, immigrants, and refugees, 480–481; and Middle East, 396, 479–480; and national malaise, 465–468; and Panama, 479

Casals, Pablo, 205

Case, Clifford, 466

Casey, William, 536–537; and contras, 555–556, 560–561

Castillo Armas, Carlos, 180

Castro, Fidel, 195–196; and Bay of Pigs, 208–209

Castro, Raul, 219

Cavazos, Lauro, 579

CCC. *See* Civilian Conservation Corps

Central America, Reagan administration's policy toward, 549–553

Central Intelligence Agency (CIA), 95–96. *See also* Iran-contra affair; and Afghanistan, 548; and antiwar movement, 308, 334; assistance to Contras, 555; and Bay of Pigs, 208–209; and Belgian Congo (Zaire), 215; and Chile, 388–390; in drug trade, 306; during Eisenhower administration, 170–171, 208; LSD (lysergic acid diethylamide) project, 170–171; Operation Chaos, 308–309; Operation Mongoose, 209–212, 222; during Reagan administration, 536–537; in Vietnam, 285; and Watergate scandal, 425

Central Treaty Organization (CENTO), 173

CETA. *See* Comprehensive Employment and Training Act

Chamberlain, Neville, 13

Chambers, Whittaker, 69–70

Chamoun, Camille, 185

Chaney, James, 328–329

Channel, Carl "Spitz," 556, 562

Chase, Chevy, 442, 445

Chastity clinics, 528

Chavez, Cesar, 349, 360

Cheney, Richard, 586, 589
Chennault, Anna, 320
Chernenko, Konstantin, 542
Chiang Kai-shek. *See* Jiang Jieshi
Chicago, Democratic convention in, 1968, 349–350
Chicanos. *See* Mexican-Americans
Child abuse, 473
Child-rearing practices, in 1970s, 472
Chile, Nixon administration and, 388–390
China. *See also* People's Republic of China: loss of, 102–104; role at Geneva talks, 177
China Aid Act, 104
China White Paper, 104
Chomsky, Noam, 336
Christian, George, 308
Christianity, as measure of Americanism, 133–134
Chrysler Corporation, 553; in 1970s, 461
Church, Frank, 286, 372, 383, 452, 498
Churchill, Winston: and changing nature of Communism, 170; on Dulles, 165; Iron Curtain speech, 86; and World War II, 17–20, 47–48
CIA. *See* Central Intelligence Agency
CIO. *See* Congress of Industrial Organizations
Citizens' Councils, 152
City of Richmond v. *J. A. Croson Company,* 523
Civil Aeronautics Board, and deregulation, 458
Civilian Conservation Corps (CCC), 6, 38
Civil liberties, Supreme Court and, 158
Civil rights: and conservative justice, 521–523; Eisenhower and, 153–154; and 1948 election, 78–79; Johnson's promotion of, 247; post-World War II, 72–77; Supreme Court decisions on, in 1970s, 408–409
Civil Rights Act of 1957, 154, 232
Civil Rights Act of 1964, 247–249, 269, 279, 404, 408, 410
Civil rights movement, 73, 77, 82, 119; and Black Power, 326–332; community action, 154–157; Freedom Riders, 233–234; lunch counter sit-ins, 157; March on Washington, 235–236; in Mississippi, 234–235; Montgomery boycott, 156; and

Nixon administration, 404–406; in 1950s, 148–158; in 1960s, 231–236, 359; student involvement in, 333; white resistance to, 270, 272–273
Civil Works Administration (CWA), 6
Clancy, Tom, 553
Clark, Jim, 331
Clark, Mark, 352
Clark, Ramsey, 309, 411
Clark, Tom, 55, 65
Clark, William P., 536, 544
Clarke, Arthur C., 225
Clay, Andrew Dice, 584
Clay, Lucius, 95–96
Clean Air Act, 582
Cleaver, Eldridge, 326, 362, 514
Cleveland, Ohio, bankruptcy of, 462
Clifford, Clark, 77–79, 91, 311–312, 315–316
Clifford Report, 91–92
Clubb, O. Edmund, 108
Club of Rome, 465
CMEA. *See* Council for Mutual Economic Assistance
Cohen, Ben, 7
Cohn, Roy, 130
Colby, William, 448
Cold War, 51–52, 84; aftermath of, 608–610; during Carter administration, 478; causes of, 84–85; Cuban missile crisis, 219–223; end of, 566–569, 571; institutionalization of, 95–96; ramifications of, 99–106, 116–117; refugees as reflection of, 187
College sports, in 1970s, 463
Collins, J. Lawton, 284, 286
Colson, Charles, 376
Columbia University, student protests, 1968, 336–337
COMECON. *See* Council for Mutual Economic Assistance
Commission on National Goals, 161
Commission on the Status of Women (CSW), 353
Committee for a Sane Nuclear Policy (SANE), 194, 308
Committee on the Present Danger, 478
Committee to Re-elect the President (CREEP), 416–417, 421–422, 427, 437–438
Commoner, Barry, *Science and Society,* 361
Communes, of 1960s, 346–347

Communications Satellite Corporation (Comsat), 226
Communications satellites, 225
Communism, 568; changing nature of, after Stalin, 169–170; collapse of, in Europe, 587–591; in United States, 64
Communist Democratic Republic of Vietnam. *See* North Vietnam
Community Action Programs (CAPs), 256
Comprehensive Employment and Training Act (CETA), 255, 400
Comsat. *See* Communications Satellite Corporation
Congalez, Virgilio, 424
Congress. *See also* Eightieth Congress: and energy policy, 464; foreign policy role of, 394–395; procurement regulations, 544; public animosity toward, in late 1980s–early 1990s, 578; and Reagan, 502
Congressional election: of 1942, 38; of 1946, 55; of 1958, 159; of 1964, 251–252; of 1966, 272–273; of 1970, 416; of 1974, 440, 445–446; of 1986, 560
Congress of Industrial Organizations (CIO), 5, 30, 127
Congress of Racial Equality (CORE), 73–74, 232–234, 327; Ink for Jack campaign, 233
Connally, John, 237, 413–414
Connor, Eugene "Bull," 235
Conscientious objectors, 303
Conservative movement, in 1970s, 476–478
Constitution, U.S.: First Amendment, 265–266; Fourteenth Amendment, 151; Twenty-fifth Amendment, 432; Twenty-second Amendment, 116, 120; Twenty-sixth Amendment, 420
Consumer price index, rate of increase in, in 1979, 460
Consumer Products Safety Commission (CPSC), 403–404
Consumer protection, 402–404
Consumer spending, during 1950s, 126–127
Containment, 84, 90–99, 119, 310, 568
Continental Illinois bank, 520
Contraception, during 1950s, 131
Contras, 555; diversion of funds to, by Reagan administration, 558–560
Cooper, John Sherman, 372
Coors, Joseph, 541, 556

Corcoran, Thomas, 7
CORE. *See* Congress of Racial Equality
Corporation for Public Broadcasting (CPB), 259–260
Corso, Gregory, 338
Costanza, Midge, 459
Council for Mutual Economic Assistance (CMEA or COMECON), 99, 590
Council of Economic Advisers, 54
Council of Federated Organizations, 328
Counterculture, of 1960s, 338–347, 359
Cousins, Norman, 194
Cox, Archibald, 429, 431, 433
Crack, 524
Cranston, Alan, 520
Creation science, 266
Credibility gap, 309
Credit card business: introduction of, 126–127; rise of, 263
CREEP. *See* Committee to Re-elect the President
Crime, and Nixon administration policy, 411–412
Critics of mass society, during 1950s, 134–135
Cronkite, Walter, 314, 364, 465
Cruise missiles, 538
Cuban missile crisis, 208, 219–223
Cuban refugees, 481
Cuban Revolution, 195–196; refugees from, 187
Cults, in 1970s, 476–477
Culture of dissent, legacies of, 359–361
Culture of protest. *See also* Antiwar movement: and Vietnam war, 282, 334–336
CWA. *See* Civil Works Administration
Czechoslovakia, Soviet invasion of (1968), 279

Daley, Richard J., 318, 350, 418
D'Aubuisson, Robert, 550
Daughters of the American Revolution, 9
Davies, John Paton, 108
Davis, Miles, 338
Davis, Nancy, 494
Davis, Sammy, Jr., 412
The Day After, 540
Days of Rage, 352
Dean, John, 422, 425–426, 428–429, 433

Deaver, Michael, 502–503, 506; and Oliver North, 556; and Star Wars, 542
Declaration of Liberated Europe, 20–21
Declaration of the United Nations, 17
DeConcini, Dennis, 520
Decter, Midge, 534
Deep Throat, 426–427
Defense spending: by 1953, 108, 114; and NSC-68, 102; post-World War II, 22; during Reagan administration, 501, 533
de Gaulle, Charles, 277
Democratic National Committee, 55
Democratic party: in 1968, 317–322; in 1972, 418–419; in 1977, 455–456; and African-Americans, 154; in 1942 election, 38; in 1944 election, 39; in 1952 election, 116–117; in 1956 election, 159; in 1958 election, 159; in 1964 election, 251–252; in 1974 election, 445; in 1976 election, 455; in 1984 election, 504, 506; in 1986 election, 507–508; in 1988 election, 572–574; post-World War II, 55
Democratic party convention: in 1972, 418; 1948, 78–79; Atlantic City, 1964, 329; Chicago, 1968, 349–350
Democratic Republic of Vietnam (North Vietnam), 178
Demographic trends, 1980–1990, 602–605
Deng Xiaoping, 591
Dennis, Eugene, 66
Dennis v. *United States*, 66, 72
Department of Defense. *See also* Defense spending: creation of, 95; Directive 59, 484; procurement regulations, 544
Department of Education, *A Nation at Risk* study of 1983, 525
Department of Energy, 463–464
Department of Health, Education and Welfare, 123
Department of Housing and Urban Development (HUD), 256, 519
Department of Transportation, 256
Deregulation, 458; effects of, 518–520
Desegregation, 73–74, 405–406; in education, 152–154; in professional and college athletics, 140–141
De Soto patrols, 289
Détente, 190–195, 208, 223, 279, 380–384, 448; decline of, 383–384, 483–484

Dewey, John, ideas of progressive education, 146
Dewey, Thomas E., 39; and 1948 election, 69, 79–80
DeWitt, John, 36
Dillon, C. Douglas, 206
Dirksen, Everett, 248–249
Discrimination. *See also* Anti-Semitism: Johnson administration's attack on, 269; post-World War II, 34; in wartime, 29–34
Disney, Roy, 136
Disney, Walter E., 136–137
Displaced persons, 71–72
Displaced Persons Act, 72
Displaced persons camps, 72
Dissent: rise of, with Vietnam war, 306–311; of 1960s, legacies of, 359–361
Divorce: changing attitudes toward, 469; in 1970s, 469–470, 472
Dixiecrats, 79
Dixon, Richard M., 422
D-5 missile, 538
Dobrynin, Anatoly, 366–367, 381
Dodd, Christopher, on Central America, 549
Dohrn, Bernardine, 336
Dole, Robert, 450
Dollar-a-year men, 23–24
Dollar gap, 92
Dominican Republic, U.S. intervention in, in 1965, 276
Domino theory, 284
Doolittle, James, 170
Douglas, Paul, 272–273
Douglas, William O., 31, 66, 86, 158, 265, 267–268, 432
Dow Chemical, 335
Dow Jones Industrial Average, in 1987, 508
DPs. *See* Displaced persons
Draft: peacetime, 14, 95; and Vietnam war, 301–306, 368
Draft resistance, and Vietnam war, 302–304, 335–336
Draft resisters, pardon for, 304, 451, 456
Drugs, war on: in Bush administration, 580; Just Say No campaign, 524–525; during Nixon administration, 411–412
Drug use: among military in Vietnam, 306, 369; by counterculture of 1960s,

Homosexuality, 360; classification of, 475; controversy about, in 1970s, 474–476; during 1950s, 130
Hooker Chemical Company, 464
Hoover, Herbert, 30
Hoover, J. Edgar, 67, 206–207, 368, 370
Hoovervilles, 3
Hopkins, Harry, 6, 8, 30
Horowitz, David, 514
Horton, Willie, 575
Hostages. *See also* Iranian hostage crisis: in Lebanon, 557
Hot line, 278
House Committee on Un-American Activities (HUAC), 12, 64, 67, 69–70, 75
House Judiciary Committee, and Watergate, 433, 437
Housing Industry, post-World War II, 58–59
Howard, Roy, 105
Hruska, Roman, 407
HUAC. *See* House Committee on Un-American Activities
HUD. *See* Department of Housing and Urban Development
Hudson, Rock, death of, 529
Hughes, Charles Evans, 11, 75–76
Human rights, during Carter administration, 480–481
Humphrey, Hubert H., 201, 248, 329, 350, 386–387, 402, 417, 452; on anti-communism, 66; on civil rights, 79; presidential bid, 1968, 319–321; as vice president, 250
Hungary, 1956 uprising, and refugee politics, 185–187
Hunt, E. Howard, 376, 424–426, 428
Hunt, Nelson Bunker, 556
Hunt brothers, 468
Hurst, Fannie, 57
Hussein (King of Jordan), 278, 391
Hussein, Saddam, 547, 594–600
Huxley, Aldous, 342
Hydrogen bomb, 100–102

IBM. *See* International Business Machines Corporation
Icahn, Carl, 512
Ickes, Harold, 6, 30
IMF. *See* International Monetary Fund
Immigrants: resettlement programs for, 481; in 1970s, 482–483; in 1980s, 530

Immigration, 71–72; 1980–1990, 602–605; during Carter administration, 481–483; patterns of, in 1980s, 608–609; during Reagan administration, 530–531; reform, under Johnson's Great Society, 260–262; sources of, in 1960s, 261–262
Immigration and Nationality Act, 72
Income: of average family, 1977–1988, 516; of professional athletes, 463, 512
Income gap, in 1980s, 516
Income tax. *See also* Taxes: bracket creep, 500
Indochina War, 1946–1954, 283–284
Indochinese refugees, 187
Inflation: in Ford years, 446; in late 1960s, 263–264; in Nixon years, 413, 415; post-World War II, 54; in 1960s, 273; in 1970s, 460, 468; in 1980s, 500, 511
INF talks, 541
INF treaty, 566–567
Ink for Jack campaign, 233
Inland Steel Company, 227
Intercontinental ballistic missiles (ICBM), 381
Interest rates, in late 1960s, 264
Intermediate Nuclear Forces. *See* INF
Intermediate-range nuclear missiles (IRBMs), 219
Internal Security Act of 1950, 66–67
International Bank for Reconstruction and Development (World Bank), 19, 87
International Business Machines Corporation (IBM), 24, 127
International Monetary Fund (IMF), 19, 87
Interstate Commerce Commission, 44
Iran: arms sales to, 382, 558; coup of 1953, 178–179; East-West disputes in, 88; Nixon's relations with, 382; oil and politics in, 178–179; Reagan's ties to, 557; U.S. aid and intelligence to, 547; war with Iraq, 548
Iran-contra affair, 508, 554–563
Iran-contra hearings, 561–563
Iranian hostage crisis, 484–487, 557
Iranian revolution, 484–485
Iraq: U.S. aid and intelligence to, 547–548; U.S. war with, 586, 593–600; war with Iran, 548
IRBMs. *See* Intermediate-range nuclear missiles

Iron triangle, 510
IRS, political use of, by Nixon administration, 422
Isolationism, of mid-1930s, 12–13
Israel, 390; and Iran, 548; and war with Iraq, 595, 600; and Lebanon, 544–546; in Six Day War, 277–278; and Suez Canal, 184
Israel–Egypt peace treaty, 396, 479–480

Jackson, Henry, 188, 383, 448, 451
Jackson, Jesse, 359, 504, 573
Jackson State, Mississippi, student demonstrators killed at, 353
Jacobsen, David, 560
Jagger, Mick, 339, 346
Japan, U.S. aid to, 95
Japanese Americans, internment of, in wartime, 35–38, 40
Jarvis, Howard, and Proposition 13, 466
Javits, Jacob, 392, 394
Jaworski, Leon, 433
Jefferson Airplane, 351
Jencks v. *United States*, 158
Jenco, Lawrence, 559
Jew Deal, 8
Jews. *See* Anti-Semitism
Jiang Jieshi (Chiang Kai-shek), 102–103
Jingoism, and national politics, 553–554
Job Corps, 254–256
Johnson, Lady Bird, 260
Johnson, Lyndon B., 67, 101, 123, 148, 161, 188, 190, 201, 238. *See also* Great Society; becomes President, 246–247; and civil rights, 154; and détente, 279; on Diem, 288; economic policy, 262–264; foreign policy, 274–280; and Fortas nomination, 268; Great Society programs, 159; Howard University speech (1965), 269–271; political background of, 244–246; political career of, 243; as politician, 244; presidential election, 1964, 249–252; as social reformer, 243; on space exploration, 364; and space race, 224; travels as vice president, 246; unhappiness as vice president, 245–246; and Vietnam, 287, 306–307, 312, 315–316
Johnson administration. *See also* Great Society; War on Poverty: and Alliance for Progress, 274–275; and Dominican Republic, 276; efforts at social reform, white backlash against, 243, 272, 280; and NATO, 277; Soviet-American relations during, 278–279

Joint Chiefs of Staff, 85, 95; and Korea, 109
Jones, Jim, 476–477
Jones, T. K., 541
Jonestown, 477
Joplin, Janis, 326, 339–342
Jordan, 391; in Six Day War, 277–278
Jordan, Hamilton, 456
Jordan, June, 326
Judd, Walter, 105
Junk bonds, 513
Justice Department, 24; Civil Rights Division, 73
Juvenile crime, fear of, in mid-1950s, 144–145
Juvenile delinquency, in 1950s, 144–145

Kalmbach, Herbert, 423, 426
Kampelman, Max, 534
Kassim, Abdel Karim, 184
Katzenbach, Nicholas deB., 249
Kearns, Doris, 244
Keating, Charles, 520, 578
Keating, Kenneth, 220
Keating Five, 578
Keats, John, 134
Kefauver, Estes, 115, 145, 159
Kemp, Jack, 499, 512
Kemp-Roth economic plan, 499–500
Kendall, Donald, 423
Keniston, Kenneth, *The Uncommitted,* 326
Kennan, George F., 84, 97, 101, 164, 307–308, 568; Long Telegram, 91
Kennedy, Anthony, 522–523
Kennedy, Caroline, 246
Kennedy, Edward, 385, 422; on Carter, 486; and social welfare programs, 467
Kennedy, Jacqueline, 205, 237, 246
Kennedy, John, Jr., 246
Kennedy, John F., 67, 105, 159, 161, 190, 196, 199, 206–207, 247, 353, 365; assassination, 236–239; and Bay of Pigs, 208–209, 211; Berlin policy, 216–219; cabinet, 205–206; and civil rights, 203, 232–236; and Cuban missile crisis, 219–220; and détente, 223; and domestic affairs, 199–200, 225–231; feud with Blough, 226–227;

Laffer curve, 499
Laird, Melvin, 368–369
Lakeland, Peter, 392
Lance, Bert, 458
Lansdale, Edward, 211
Laos, invasion of, in 1971, 373–374
Lardner, Ring, Jr., 68
Lasch, Christopher, 361, 477
Latchkey children, 472
Latin America, Johnson's policy
    toward, 274–276
Latin American immigrants, in 1960s,
    261–262
Latinos, 360
Lawson, John Howard, 68
League of United Latin American
    Citizens (LULAC), 360
Leahy, William, 21, 46
Leary, Timothy, 342
Lebanon, 185, 544–546; American
    Embassy in, 545–546
Lederer, William J., 175
Le Duc Tho, 377–379; Peace Prize, 380
Leisure products, 513
LeMay, Curtis, 320
Lend-Lease program, 14–15, 22
Lennon, John, 339
Lerner, Max, 28
Lesbians. *See* Gay rights
Levitt, William, 59, 61
Levittown(s), 59–61
Lewis, John, 236, 331
Lewis, John L., 26
Libya, and terrorism, 546–547
Liddy, G. Gordon, 376, 412, 422, 424,
    426, 428
Lillienthal, David, plan for
    international control of atomic
    energy, 89
Limited Test Ban Treaty, 223, 279
Lincoln Federal Savings and Loan, 520
Linkletter, Art, 412
Lippmann, Walter, 80; on Eisenhower,
    120
Little Boy, 48
Lockheed Aviation, 188
Lodge, Henry Cabot, and Vietnam,
    286–289
Loeb, William, 417, 449
Long, Russell, 295
Lon Nol, 371
Love Canal, New York, 464–465
Lowell, Robert, 336
Low-income housing, 273

LSD. *See* Lysergic acid diethylamide
Luce, Clair Boothe, 79
Luce, Henry, 2, 22, 51–52, 105
Lumumba, Patrice, 181
Lundberg, Ferdinand, 130
Lysergic acid diethylamide (LSD), 341

MacArthur, Douglas, 49, 120; and
    Korean War, 110–112, 114
MacLeish, Archibald, 39
Maddox, 289
Maddox, Lester, 450
Mafia, 115, 206
Mailer, Norman: *Armies of the Night*,
    336; on Nixon, 365
Major, John, 565
Malcolm X, 270–271, 330
Malenkov, Georgi, 169
Manhattan Project, 14, 45, 48
Mann, Thomas, 274–275
Mann Doctrine, 275
Mansfield, Mike, 295, 310, 385
Manson Family, 346, 449
Manufacturing industry, decline of, in
    1970s and 1980s, 461–462
Manzanar relocation center, 37
Mao Tse-tung. *See* Mao Zedong
Mao Zedong, 102–103, 170, 352, 384,
    386; and Korean War, 112; on
    Soviets, 183
Maples, Marla, 515
Mapp v. Ohio, 266, 408
March on Washington, 235–236, 327–
    328
Marcos, Ferdinand, 537
Marcuse, Herbert, 135, 333
Marijuana, 341–342
Marshall, George C., 78, 93, 99, 112,
    120; in China, 103
Marshall, Thurgood, 76, 149–151,
    265
Marshall Plan, 64, 79, 84, 94; China
    Aid Act, 104; congressional approval
    for, 94–95
Martinez, Eugenio, 424
Marvin, Lee, and Michele Triola
    Marvin, 471–472
Matsu, U.S. showdown with China
    over, 181–183
Matusow, Allen, 257
Max, Peter, 343
Mayaguez incident, 447
McCain, John, 520
McCarran, Pat, 66, 71, 105, 187

McCarran Act of 1950, 66–67; use of, 158

McCarran-Walter Act of 1952, 72, 186–187

McCarthy, Eugene, 317–319; student supporters of, 348

McCarthy, Joseph, 64, 70, 82, 84, 115, 120, 171, 332; approval rating, 172; and Eisenhower, 123; on homosexuality, 130; and Korean War, 113–114; on George C. Marshall, 171; rise of, 106–108; self-destruction of, 172–173

McCarthy, Mary, 430

McCarthyism, 106; ebbing of, 171–173

McCartney, Paul, 339

McCord, James, 424, 428

McCormack, John, 295

McFarlane, Robert, 536, 554–559

McGovern, George, 317, 319, 377–379, 386, 402, 417–421

McKissick, Floyd, 331

McLaurin, George W., 76

McLaurin v. *Oklahoma State Regents* (1950), 76

McLeod, Scott, 171

McNamara, Robert, 206, 208, 274, 287, 289, 294, 301, 311, 375; and Cuban missile crisis, 221

McQueen, Steve, 422

McReynolds, James C., 10

Meany, George, 419

Me Decade, 477

Medicaid, establishment of, 253–254

Medicare, 280, 585–586; establishment of, 253–254

Medina,.Harold, 66

Meese, Edwin, 502, 560–561; confirmation as attorney general, 506–507

Meir, Golda, 391

Melman, Seymour, 308

Men: changing roles of as fathers, 472–473; in 1970s, 468–475; and sex, during 1950s, 132–133

Mendes-France, Pierre, 177

Menominee Tribe, 158

MEOW (moral equivalent of war), 464

Meredith, James, 234–235

Merry Pranksters, 342

Metalious, Grace, 132

Mexican-Americans, in wartime, 32–34, 40

Mexicans: immigration into U.S., 72, 82, 482; as refugees, 187; undocumented, 530–531

Michaels, Lorne, 444

Middle East: and America, during Bush administration, 593–600; Reagan administration, 544–549; and Carter administration, 479–480; conflict in, in 1960s, 277–278. *See also* Six Day War; crisis of 1973, 390–394; and Nixon administration, 390–394; in 1950s, 183–185

Migration, internal, 1980–1990, 602–605

Military budget: from 1975–1989, 538; during Reagan administration, 533, 538

Military spending, during Eisenhower administration, 165

Milk, Harvey, 475–476

Milken, Michael, 512–513

Millett, Kate, 357

Mills, C. Wright, 135, 333

Minimum wage, during Eisenhower administration, 123

Minnow, Newton, 135

Miranda v. *Arizona*, 267, 408

Missiles. *See also* Cuban missile crisis: intermediate-range nuclear missiles (IRBMs), 219

Mississippi: civil rights movement in, 234–235; public education in, 152

Mississippi Freedom Democratic Party (MFDP), 329

Mississippi Freedom Summer Project, 327–329

Missouri compromise, 45

Mitchell, John, 362, 370, 399, 405, 408, 422, 424–425, 428, 430

Miyake, Howard Y., 37

Model Cities program, 255–256

Modern Republicanism, 123

Molotov, V. M., 46, 87, 94

Mondale, Walter, 452, 467; presidential campaign, 504–506

Monetary exchange, in 1970s, 414–416

Montgomery boycott, 156

Moody, Anne, 327, 330

Moon, Sun Myung, 476

Moonies, 476

Moon walk, first, 364

Moore, Sara Jane, 449

Moral Majority, 477–478, 526

Morgan, Robin, 357–358

New Deal, 3–4, 7, 21–22, 30, 80, 244–245, 249; achievements and failures of, 9–12; legislation of, 5–6; programs of, 6–7

New Deal coalition, 77

New Frontier, 201–202, 246; at home, 225–231; outposts on, 198–240; personalities and style on, 204–207

New Journalism, 336, 342, 344

New Left, 347, 359; rise of, 332–337

New Mobilization, 351

New Right, 477; rise of, in 1960s, 249

New York, construction workers' riot, 1970, 373

New York City, debt of, in 1975, 462

New York Times, publication of *Pentagon Papers,* 374–376

New York Times v. *Sullivan,* 265

Ngo Dinh Diem, 177–178, 215, 246, 284, 286–287

Ngo Dinh Nhu, Madame, 286

Nguyen Cao Ky, 300–301

Nguyen Khanh, 288–289

Nguyen Van Thieu, 311, 320, 367, 377–380, 446

Nguyen Vo Giap, 299

Nicaragua. *See* Contras; Iran-Contra affair

Nineties, and beyond, challenges of, 608–610

NIRA. *See* National Industrial Recovery Act

Nitze, Paul, 101–102, 168, 534

Nixon, E. D., 155

Nixon, Pat, 386–387

Nixon, Richard M., 66–67, 69–71, 106, 114, 120, 165, 200; Checkers speech, 121; and détente, 380–384; and Eisenhower, 159; impoundment of federal funds, 403; and Kissinger, 364–367; kitchen debate, 192; and Latin America, 195; pardoned by Ford, 441–446; presidential election, 1968, 319–321, 350; resignation from presidency, 435–436; on Stevenson, 121; Supreme Court appointments, 268–269, 406–408; tax troubles, 434; and Vietnam, 293, 352, 364, 367–380; visit to China, 1972, 386

Nixon administration. *See also* Watergate scandal: abuse of power, 399, 421–424; anticrime policy, 411–412; and antiwar movement, 369–370; and Arab-Israeli conflict, 390–392; and arms control, 381–383; and busing, 404–406; and Chile, 388–390; and China, 384–388; and civil rights, 404–406; consumer protection, 402–404; domestic accomplishments, 436–437; domestic policy, 400–401; drug policy, 411–412; economic policy, 413–416; enemies list, 421–422; environmental protection, 402–404; foreign policy, successes and failures, 395–397; and Great Society, 399–406; and Middle East, 390–394; New Economic Policy, 413–416, 420; political use of IRS, 422; secret cash payments to, 423–424; and welfare reform, 401–402, 437

Nixon Doctrine, 368

NLF. *See* National Front for the Liberation of Vietnam

No-fault divorce laws, 469–470

Noonan, Peggy, 492, 502; on Oliver North, 556

Noriega, Manuel, 592

Norodom Sihanouk, 371

Norris, Chuck, 553

North, Oliver, 555–561

North Atlantic Treaty Organization (NATO): creation of, 97–99; strains during Johnson years, 277; strains during Nixon years, 380–381

North Vietnam, 178, 283; air war against, 292–293

NOW. *See* National Organization for Women

NSC 162/3, 165

Nuclear age, nuclear family in, 130–131

Nuclear arms race, 99–102

Nuclear family, 355; in nuclear age, 130–131; in 1970s, 469, 471–474; in 1980s, 528

Nuclear Freeze Movement, 540

Nuclear power, fears about safety of, 465

Nuclear sufficiency, 382–383

Nuclear test ban, 193–195, 223

Nuclear weapons. *See* Atomic weapons

O'Brien, Lawrence, 424

Obscenity, Supreme Court's definitions of, 265–266

Occidental Petroleum, 464
Occupational Safety and Health
   Administration (OSHA), 403–404,
   518
O'Connor, Sandra Day, 522
OEO. *See* Office of Economic
   Opportunity
Office for Drug Abuse and Law
   Enforcement (ODALE), 412
Office of Civil Rights, in Justice
   Department, 405
Office of Economic Opportunity
   (OEO), 256–257
Office of Price Administration (OPA),
   26, 54
Office of War Information (OWI), 28
Office of War Mobilization (OWM), 24
O'Hare, Madeline Murray, 133
Oil: and politics, in Iran, 178–179; price
   of, in 1970s, 415, 460
Oil embargo, of 1973–1974, 393, 415
Old Left, 332
Olympics, 1984, 553
O'Malley, Walter, 141
O'Neill, Thomas P. "Tip," 392, 427,
   498, 553, 555; and Jimmy Carter, 456;
   on Democratic Party, 455; and
   Hamilton Jordan, 456; and Reagan,
   502
OPA. *See* Office of Price
   Administration
Operation Mongoose, 209–212, 222
Operation Rolling Thunder, 292–293
Operation Solarium, 164–165
Operation Wetback, 187
Oppenheimer, J. Robert, 100–101
Oral contraceptives, use of, 228–229
Organization of American States, 180
Oriental Exclusion Act of 1924, 71
Ortega, Daniel, 556
Osborne, John, 442
OSRD. *See* War Department, Office of
   Scientific Research and Development
Oswald, Lee Harvey, 237–238
The Other America, 230
OWI. *See* Office of War Information
OWM. *See* Office of War Mobilization

Packard, Vance, 134–135
Pahlavi, Mohammed Reza, 178, 382,
   484–485
Palestine Liberation Organization
   (PLO), 544, 546, 600

Palestinians, and Israel, 546, 595, 600
Panama: American intervention in, in
   1989–1990, 592–593; and Carter
   administration, 479; and Johnson
   administration, 275–276
Pandora's Box, 325
Panetta, Leon, 405
Parker, Charlie "Yardbird," 338
Parks, Rosa, 154–156
Pauling, Linus, 193–194
Peace Corps, 213–215
Peace movement, rise of, during
   Vietnam war, 306–311
Peale, Norman Vincent, 133
Pearl Harbor, 15
Peck, Gregory, 422
Pegler, Westbrook, 36
Pell, Claiborne, 383
Pendergast, "Boss" Tom, 44
Penn Square (Oklahoma) bank, 520
Pennsylvania v. *Nelson*, 158
Pentagon, march on, 1967, 335
Pentagon Papers, 374–376
People's capitalism, 127–128
People's Park, 351
People's Republic of China: Cultural
   Revolution, 384; democracy
   movement in, in 1989, 590–591; and
   Korean War, 112–114, 168–169;
   nuclear development program, 183;
   relations during Carter years, 396;
   relations during Nixon years, 384–
   388; Quemoy and Matsu, 181–183;
   relations during Reagan
   administration, 538; in 1950s, 181;
   U.S. recognition of, 104
People's Temple, 476–477
Peress, Irving, 172
Perestroika, 563
Perkins, Frances, 8
Perle, Richard, 534
Perot, H. Ross, 423
Pershing II missile, 539
Persian Gulf, 547–548
Pesticides, use of, 229
Phillips, Kevin, *The Emerging Republic
   Majority*, 405
Phillips v. *Martin Marietta*, 410
Pickens, T. Boone, 512
Pierce, "Silent" Sam, 519
Pinochet, Augusto, 389
Playboy magazine, 132
Pledge of Allegiance, 133

career, 495–497; economic policy,
499–500; elected governor of
California, 273; emergence of, 493–
498; and energy, 464; foreign policy,
533–569; as governor, 496; as The
Great Communicator, 502–503;
gubernatorial bid, 1966, 495–496;
inauguration as governor, 496; and
Iran, 486; and Nicaragua, 554;
nominations to Supreme Court, 521–
522; on opposition to taxes, 466–467;
as president, 531–532; presidential
bid, 1976, 449–450, 497; presidential
bid, 1980, 487–489, 497–498;
presidential bid, 1984, 506, 553; on
Qaddafi, 547; re-election as
president, 503–504; and religion, 526;
on SALT II, 540; and sex and gender,
528; on Soviet Union, 535–536; Star
Wars, 541–542; and televangelism,
526–527

Reagan administration, 498–501, 508–
520; and Afghanistan, 548; arms
build-up during, 538–539; and arms
race, 538–544; arms sales to Iran, 558;
budget slashing, 518–519; and
culture of greed, 512–515; and
defense spending, 501; and deficits,
509–511; and deregulation, 518–520;
economic agenda, 499–500; foreign
economic assistance programs, 537–
538; foreign policy, toward Central
America, 549–553; and Iraq, 548;
policy on terrorism, 557; and SALT
II, 540; economic policy, 512;
economic recovery during, 511–512;
major tax reform of, 507; sleaze
factor, 506

Reagan era. *See* Reagan administration

Reagan revolution. *See* Reagan
administration

The Realist, 347

Rebozo, Charles "Bebe," 422

Recession: of 1937–1938, 11; of 1960,
11; of 1981–1983, 500–501; of 1989–
1990, 585

Reconstruction Finance Corporation, 5

Recording industry, in 1950s, 143

Red Channels, 68

Red China. *See* People's Republic of
China

Red Cross, 32

Red Scare, 43, 52, 63–71, 82, 84, 123;
Chambers-Hiss case, 68–71;

government crusade, 64–67;
Hollywood hearings, 67–68

Redstone rocket, 188

Reed v. *Reed*, 410

Reedy, George, on McCarthy, 108

Refugee Act of 1980, 481

Refugee politics, and Hungarian
uprising of 1952, 185–187

Refugee Relief Act, 187

Refugees. *See* Immigrants

Regan, Donald, 561, 565–566; as chief
of staff, 506

Rehnquist, William, 403, 406, 408, 522,
583

Reid Cabral, Donald, 276

Religion: in American life, during
1950s, 133–134; electronic churches,
477; and public life, in 1980s, 526–
527; revival of, in 1970s, 476–478;
Supreme Court's rulings on, in
1960s, 266

Republican party. *See also* New Right:
in 1942 election, 38; in 1944 election,
39; in 1946 election, 55; in 1952
election, 116, 121–122; in 1964
election, 249–252; in 1966 election,
272–273; in 1980 election, 489, 498; in
mid-1970s, 443; presidential
campaign of 1980s, 466, 489

Republic of Vietnam. *See* South
Vietnam

Resolution Trust Corporation, 520

Reston, James, 406, 422

Resurrection City, 349

Reuther, Walter, 78, 194

Revel, James, 156

Revenue sharing, 400

Rexroth, Kenneth, 145

Rhee, Syngman, 109, 169

Rhodes, James, 353

Rhodes, John, 434

Rhythm and blues (R&B), 141

Rice, Donna, 573

Richards, Ann, 574

Richardson, Elliot, 433

Rickey, Branch, 74–75

Ridgway, Matthew, 114

Riegle, Donald, 520

Riesman, David, 134

Rivercomb, William, 187

Roberts, Oral, 477, 526–527

Roberts, Owen, 11

Robertson, Pat, 477, 526–527

Robeson, Paul, 75

Securities Act of 1933, 5
Securities and Exchange Commission, 5, 7, 518
Segregation: on buses, 154–156; *de facto*, 405; in public schools, 149–152; in schools, 75–77
Segretti, Donald, 417
Selective Service, 368; and Vietnam war, 301–302
Senate Watergate Committee, 428–431, 437
Serial monogamy, 472
Service, John S., 108
Service industries, growth of, 601
Servicemen's Readjustment Act of 1944. *See* GI Bill
700 Club, 526
Seventies: as Me Decade, 477; national malaise in, 465–468
Sex: in 1950s, 131–133; in 1960s, 338–341; in 1980s, 528–530; in 1960s counterculture, 345
Sex discrimination: legislation against, 248, 354; Supreme Court decisions on, 409–411
Sexism, 357
Sexual Behavior in the Human Female, 132
Sexual revolution, 359; and controversy about pornography, 474; in 1980s, 528
Shales, Tom, 445
Sheehan, Neil, 375
Sheen, Fulton J., 133
Shelly v. *Kraemer*, 75
Shepard, Alan, 224
Shriver, Sargent, 256, 419; and Peace Corps, 213
Shultz, George P., 422, 536, 544–545, 558; and Qaddafi, 547; and Reagan, 556
Shuttle diplomacy, 392–394
Shuttlesworth, Fred, 156
Silent Spring, 229, 231
Silverado Savings and Loan, 520
Simpson-Rodino Act of 1986, 531
Sino-Soviet relations, in late 1950s, 183
Sipuel, Ada, 76
Sipuel v. *Board of Regents of the University of Oklahoma*, 76
Sirhan, Sirhan, 319, 349
Sirica, John J., 428, 431, 433, 437

Sit-ins: lunch counter, 157; in 1960s, 232
Six Day War, 277–278
Slater, Philip, *The Pursuit of Loneliness*, 326
Sloan, Hugh W., Jr., 422–423
S&Ls. *See* Savings and loans
Smith, Al, 9
Smith, Howard K., 45
Smith, Howard W., 353–354
Smith Act, use of, 158
Smith v. *Allwright*, 74
SNCC. *See* Student Non-Violent Coordinating Committee
Social commentators, during 1950s, 134–135
Social Security, 7, 52, 81; during Eisenhower administration, 123
Social Security Act of 1935, 5–6
Social Security Administration, 24
Solar Energy Research Institute, 464
Solzhenitsyn, Aleksandr, 448
Somoza, Anastasio, 554
Sorensen, Theodore, 457–458; and Cuban missile crisis, 223
Souter, David, 584
South Carolina, public education in, 152
Southeast Asians, immigration of, 481
Southeast Asia Treaty Organization (SEATO), 173, 177, 284
Southern Christian Leadership Conference (SCLC), 156–157, 327
Southern Manifesto, 152
Southern strategy, 405
South Vietnam, 178, 284; nation building in, 1954–1960, 284; Saigon, population of, 300
Soviet-American relations. *See also* Cold War; East-West disputes: in 1988, 508; and atomic weapons, 88–90; balance of terror, 191–193; Berlin confrontation, 216–219; during Bush administration, 589–590; during Carter administration, 483–484; Clifford Report, 91–92; détente, 190–195, 208, 223, 279; during Johnson administration, 278–279; during Kennedy administration, 216; Long Telegram, 91; during Nixon administration, 366–367; postwar conflict, 46–47. *See also* Cold War;

Pentagon Papers decision, 376; on publication of erotic literature, 132; during Reagan administration, 523; and religion, 266; on right to privacy, 267, 410; during Roosevelt administration, 11, 31; ruling on Nixon's claim to executive privilege, 435; Truman and, 68; on voting rights, 267–268; Warren Court, 264–269, 406

Sutherland, George, 10–11

Swaggart, Jimmy, 526–527

Swann v. *Charlotte-Mecklenburg Board of Education*, 408

Sweatt, Hermann Marion, 76

Sweatt v. *Painter*, 76

Symington, Stuart, 161; on missile gap, 190

Synthetic Fuels Corporation, 464

Syria, in Six Day War, 277–278

Szulc, Tad, 396

Taft, Robert, 55–56, 120, 124, 249; and Eisenhower, 123; and Korean War, 113; and McCarthyism, 107

Taft-Hartley Act of 1947, 56, 78; repeal of, 81

Taiwan, 385–386

Tarr, Curtis, 368

Tate, James, 256

Tate, Sharon, 346

Taxes. *See also* Income tax and Bush administration, 585; opposition to, of 1970s, 466–467; in 1980s, 516

Tax limitations, of 1970s, 466

Taylor, Maxwell, 292–294, 312; and Cuban missile crisis, 221

Teamsters Union, 127

Technology, during 1950s, 127–128

Teheran Conference, 1943, 25

Televangelism, 477, 526–527

Television, 61–63; average hours watched by children, 472; effect on campaigns, 201–202, 577; Great Society provisions for, 259; influence on American life, 63; influence on radio, 63; in 1950s, 135–140; sports and, 140–141; and Vietnam war, 309

Teller, Edward, 194, 541

Temporary Commission on Employee Loyalty, 65

Tennessee Valley Authority (TVA), 5, 7

Tennessee Valley Authority v. *Hill* (1978), 457

Terrorism, 546–547; Reagan's policy on, 557

Texas, at 1963 election, 236–237

Thatcher, Margaret, 563–565

Thich Quang Duc, 286

Third World, 173; aid programs for, 175; American intervention in, in 1990s, 591–593; challenges of, America and, 173–185; rise of, 174

Thomas, J. Parnell, 67–68

Thomas, Norman, 308

Thompson, Hunter S., 344

Three Mile Island, 465

Thrifts. *See* Savings and loans

Thurmond, Strom, and 1948 election, 79–80

Time, Man of the Year, 1945, 90

Tinker v. *Des Moines School District,* 265

Tito, Josep, 94

Torrijos, Omar, 592

To Secure These Rights, 73

TOW antitank missiles, sale to Iran, 558–559

Tower, John, 561

Tower Commission report, 561

Treasury bonds, 23

Tripps Festival, 342

Trudeau, Garry, 574

Trujillo, Rafael, 181, 213, 276

Truman, Harry S, 39, 43–52, 68–69, 85, 117, 121, 247; and atomic weapons, 89–90; decision to use atomic bomb, 48–51; and China, 103–104; on civil rights, 73, 78–79; and Communism, 64–65, 67, 70; and 1948 election, 77–82; on hydrogen bomb, 101–102; and immigration, 72; and Korean War, 109–110, 112–115; and labor troubles, 55; and MacArthur, 111–112, 114; Man of the Year, 90; and Marshall Plan, 94–95; relationship with Roosevelt, 45; on Soviet-American relations, 91–92; and Soviet Union, 85–86, 88; and Supreme Court, 68

Truman administration: Committee on Civil Rights, 73, 78; Council of Economic Advisers, 102; foreign policy, 93; reforms of, 95–96; twenty-one-point program, 52; twilight of, 115–116; and Vietnam, 104, 283

Truman Doctrine, 79, 84, 93; impact of, 93–94
Trumbo, Dalton, 68
Trump, Donald, 512, 514–515
Turkey: East-West disputes in, 88; U.S. aid to, 93
TVA. *See* Tennessee Valley Authority
TWA hijacking, 1985, 557
2 Live Crew, 584
Tydings, Millard, 107–108

Ubico, Jorge, 179
Udall, Morris, 451
The Ugly American, 175
Underclass, 605; in 1980s, 517–518
Unemployment rates: in 1929, 10; in 1933, 10; in 1936, 10; in 1938, 11; among blacks, 270; in Johnson years, 262; in Nixon years, 413; post-World War II, 54; in 1970s, 468; in 1980s, 511
Unidentified flying objects, 100
Unification Church, 476
Union Oil of California, 464
Unions, 127
United Arab Republic, 184
United Farm Workers, 349, 360
United Fruit Company, 179–180
United Mine Workers, 26
United Nations, 19–20, 69, 568; in Korean War, 110; and Persian Gulf war, 593–594
United Service Organization (USO), 28
United States Steel Corporation, 226–227
United States v. *Seegar,* 303
University of California Board of Regents v. *Bakke,* 459
University of Mississippi, and civil rights, 234–235
University of Oklahoma, 76; Law School, 76
University of Texas at Austin, Law School, 76
Urban Affairs Council, 400
Urban League, 326
Urban riots: 1968, 318; after King assassination, 348; and Black Power movement, 331–332; Watts, 1965, 331
USO. *See* United Service Organization
U-2 spy plane, 188

Vance, Cyrus, 317, 483; and Iranian hostage crisis, 486–487
Vandenberg, Arthur, 93
Van Devanter, Willis, 10
Van Doren, Charles, 139
Vanguard rocket, 188–189
Vanik, Charles, 383
Vann, John Paul, 286
Varela, Mary, 356
Vaughn, Harry, 115
Veterans Administration (VA), 57, 59
Victory gardens, 27
Vietcong, 284, 297–299
Vietminh, 283–284
Vietnam. *See* North Vietnam; South Vietnam
Vietnam Summer, 307–308, 335
Vietnam syndrome, 533
Vietnam war, 176–178, 243, 272; American casualties, 322; American ground war in, decision for, 293–295; American involvement in, 104–105; 1945–1964, 282–291; Americanization of, 1965, 291–295; battle for Dienbienphu, 176–177, 283; battle for Hue, 313; body count, 297, 305; Communist victory, in 1975, 446–447; course of, 1966–1967, 295–301; and culture of protest, 282, 334–336; economic effects of, 263; effects on Vietnamese society, 299–301; escalation of, 291–295; guerrilla tactics in, 297; and Gulf of Tonkin resolution, 288–291; and Kennedy administration, 1961–1963, 284–288; military service in, 301–306. *See also* Draft; and Nixon administration, 364, 367–380; number of U.S. troops in, 295–296; Operation Rolling Thunder, 292–293; Paris peace agreement, 376–380; Paris peace talks, 320, 373; and rise of dissent, 306–311. *See also* Antiwar movement; strategy of attrition, 297–299, 315; Tet offensive, 312–314, 375; tour of duty in, 304–306; veterans, long-term effects on, 322; Vietnamization of, 366–369
Vietnam War Moratoriums of 1969, 351, 369
Viguerie, Richard, 521
Vincennes, 548
Vincent, John Carter, 108

Vinson, Fred, 66, 151
Virginia, public education in, 152
VISTA (Volunteers in Service to America), 256
Volcker, Paul, 413–414, 467–468, 500
von Braun, Wernher, 87–88, 188
Von Hoffman, Nicholas, 344
Voodoo economics, 497
Voter turnout: in 1972 election, 419–420; in late 1970s, 440
Voting, "one person, one vote" principle, 267–268
Voting rights, Supreme Court on, 267–268
Voting Rights Act of 1965, 249, 257–259, 269, 279; renewal of, 521
V-2 rocket, 188

Wage and price controls, of Nixon administration, 414–415, 437
Wagner Act. *See* National Labor Relations Act
Wallace, Bess, 44
Wallace, George, 350, 405, 417, 451; presidential bid, 1968, 319–321
Wallace, Henry A., 2, 39, 45; and 1948 election, 79–80; on foreign policy, 91–92
Wallach, E. Robert, 506
Wall Street: merger mania in, 512–513; minicrash of 1987, 508
Wall Street wizards, 513
Wanniski, Jude, 512
War Brides Act of 1946, 71
War Department: Office of Scientific Research and Development (OSRD), 24; Operation Paperclip, 87
War Lords of Washington, 23–24
Warner, Jack, 67
War on Poverty, 247, 273–274, 279–280; and Nixon administration, 399–401; programs of, 252–262
War Powers Act, 394–395, 447
War Refugee Board, 34
War Relocation Authority, 36
Warren, Earl, 151–153, 158, 264, 267–268
Warren Commission, 238
Warsaw Pact, 99, 191
Washington buddy system, 457
Washington Post, Watergate coverage, 426–429, 437
Washington v. *Davis,* 408

Watergate scandal, 387, 392–394, 399, 421, 424–435; break-in, 424; cover-up, 424–426; impeachment vote, 432–435; investigation of, 426–429; Saturday Night Massacre, 433; Senate hearings, 429–431
Watt, James, 519
Watts riots, 331
Weapons systems, 538–539; anxieties about, 539–541; costs of, 543–544
Weathermen, 352
Weather Underground, 352
Webster, William, 566
Webster v. *Reproductive Services of Missouri,* 583
Weinberg, Jack, 333–334
Weinberger, Caspar, 403, 501, 536, 566
Weir, Benjamin, 558
Welch, Joseph, 107, 172
Welfare reform, during Nixon administration, 401–402, 437
Wenner, Jann, 344
Westmoreland, William C., 293–294, 297, 300–301, 304, 312, 314–315
Wetbacks, 72
Wheeler, Earle, 294, 368
Wherry, Kenneth, 105
White, Byron, 265
White, Dan, 475–476
White, Theodore, 2, 239, 250
White House Plumbers, 376
Whittaker, Charles E., 158
Whyte, William H., Jr., 134
WIC. *See* Women-Infants-Children program
Wiesband, Edward, 395
Wilkins, Roy, 326
Will, George, on Bush, 574
Williams, Hosea, 156
Wilson, Dagmar, 336
Wilson, Sloan, 134
Wise Men, 312, 316–317
Wolfe, Tom, 342, 344, 477
Women: abuse of, 473–474; education of, 131, 354; post-World War II, 57; employment of, 354; in military, in war with Iraq, 597; post-World War II, 81; in 1950s, 130–133; in 1970s, 468–475; in wartime, 28–29, 40
Women Against Violence in Pornography and Media, 474
Women-Infants-Children (WIC) program, 517

Women's issues, Supreme Court decisions on, 409–411
Women's liberation movement: emergence of, 355–357; and ERA, 473; obstacles to, 357–358
Women's Political Council, 155
Wood, John S., 64
Woodstock Music Festival of August 1969, 345
Woodward, Bob, 424, 426–429, 437
Work Projects Administration, 38
Works Progress Administration (WPA), 6–7, 38
World Bank. *See* International Bank for Reconstruction and Development
World's Fair, New York, 1939, 10
World War II: Axis Alliance, 14; economic effects of, 22–27; Grand Alliance, 15–19, 51; on home front, 21–39; Pearl Harbor, 15; politics during, 38–39; Potsdam Summit, 47–48; transition to peace, 52–63; United States and, 12–21, 40; United States production in, 24–26; Yalta accords, 20, 46–47

WPA. *See* Works Progress Administration
Wright, James, 578
Wright, Richard, *Native Son,* 326
Wyman, Jane, 494

Xuan Thuy, 373

Yalta accords, 20, 46–47
Yarborough, Ralph, 237
Yates v. *United States,* 158
Yeltsin, Boris, 588
Yippies, 347–349
Yom Kippur War, 390–392
Young, Andrew, 156, 359, 451, 480
Young, Whitney, 326
Youth International Party. *See* Yippies
Youth subculture, in 1950s, 144–145
Yuppies, 513–515

Zablocki, Clement, 394
Zahedi, Fazollah, 179
Zhou Enlai, 384–385
Ziegler, Ron, 421, 425, 427, 429

Credits (continued from copyright page)

Biographical profile photo credits

Page 8: Franklin D. Roosevelt Library. *Page 74:* UPI/Bettmann Newsphotos. *Page 100:* Wide World Photos. *Page 136:* Wide World Photos. *Page 166:* Wide World Photos. *Page 230:* Wide World Photos. *Page 270:* UPI/Bettmann Newsphotos. *Page 314:* UPI/Bettmann Newsphotos. *Page 340:* UPI/Bettmann Newsphotos. *Page 374:* UPI/Bettmann Newsphotos. *Page 430:* Wide World Photos. *Page 444:* Photo courtesy of the National Broadcasting Company, Inc. *Page 514:* UPI/Bettmann Newsphotos. *Page 564:* UPI/Bettmann Newsphotos. *Page 608:* UPI/Bettmann Newsphotos.

Map and line art credits

Pages 16 and 18: Carter Findley and John Rothney, *Twentieth Century World*, 2/e. Copyright © 1990 by Houghton Mifflin Company. Used with permission. *Page 23:* From *Nation of Nations: A Narrative History of the American Republic* by Davidson et al., McGraw-Hill, 1990. Reprinted by permission of McGraw-Hill, Inc. *Page 98:* Mary Beth Norton et al., *A People and a Nation*, 3/e. Copyright © 1990 by Houghton Mifflin Company. Used with permission. *Page 111:* From Paterson et al., *American Foreign Policy: A History*, copyright 1988, p. 378. Reprinted by permission of D. C. Heath and Company. *Pages 125 and 126:* Mary Beth Norton et al., *A People and a Nation*, 3/e. Copyright © 1990 by Houghton Mifflin Company. Used with permission. *Page 150:* Reprinted from Figure 4.1 in *Dollars and Dreams: The Changing American Income Distribution*, by Frank Levy, © 1987 Russell Sage Foundation. Used with permission of the Russell Sage Foundation. *Page 174:* Mary Beth Norton et al., *A People and a Nation*, 3/e. Copyright © 1990 by Houghton Mifflin Company. Used with permission. *Page 210:* James Lee Ray, *Global Politics*, 4/e. Copyright © 1990 by Houghton Mifflin Company. Used with permission. *Page 258:* Reprinted by permission of Greenwood Publishing Group, Inc., Westport, CT, from *Voter Mobilization and the Politics of Race: The South and Universal Suffrage, 1952–1984*, by Harold W. Stanley. Copyright © 1987 by Harold W. Stanley and published in 1987 by Praeger Publishers. *Pages 290 and 516:* Mary Beth Norton et al., *A People and a Nation*, 3/e. Copyright © 1990 by Houghton Mifflin Company. Used with permission. *Page 588:* John P. McKay, Bennett D. Hill, and John Buckler, *A History of Western Society*, 4/e. Copyright © 1991 by Houghton Mifflin Company. Used with permission. *Page 604:* The *New York Times*, March 11, 1991. Copyright © 1991 by The New York Times Company. Reprinted by permission.

Text credits

Page 262 (emigration table): Excerpt from David Reimers, *Still the Golden Door* (New York: Columbia University Press, 1985). Reprinted by permission of Columbia University Press. *Page 325* (song lyrics): Excerpt from "For What It's Worth" by Stephen Stills is reprinted courtesy of Warner Chapel Music and FM Management. All rights reserved.